AIRCRAFT CARRIERS

AIRCRAFT CARRIERS

The world's greatest naval vessels and their aircraft

CHRIS BISHOP AND CHRIS CHANT

MBI

This edition published in 2004 by Motorbooks International, an imprint of MBI Publishing Company, Galtier Plaza, Suite 200, 380 Jackson Street, St. Paul, MN 55101-3885 USA

Motorbooks International titles are also available at discounts in bulk quantity for industrial or sales promotional use. For details write to Special Sales Manager at Motorbooks International Wholesalers & Distributors, Galtier Plaza, Suite 200, 380 Jackson Street, St. Paul, MN 55101-3885 USA.

ISBN: 0-7603-2005-5

Produced by:
Amber Books Ltd
Bradley's Close
74–77 White Lion Street
London N1 9PF
www.amberbooks.co.uk

Project Editor: Tom Broder
Design: Colin Hawes

PICTURE CREDITS
Photographs courtesy of U.S. DoD, IWM, US National Archives

Printed in South Korea

Contents

Introduction

When the first experiments were conducted with aircraft at sea, the dreadnought battleship ruled the high seas, and aircraft were seen as a useful tool for spotting the enemy fleet. However the pioneering work of the Royal Navy in World War I, and Billy Mitchell in the United States soon afterwards, showed how deadly aircraft could be to unprotected ships. During the inter-war period the first 'proper' carriers were built and most of today's carrier aviation techniques were developed, including the catapult for launching the aircraft and arrester wires to help stop them on landing.

On the outbreak of war in 1939 many senior naval officers still believed the battleship to be the decisive weapon at sea. Aircraft carriers were seen as important adjuncts to the fleet, and their capabilities had certainly improved dramatically since 1918, but they were not at the forefront of naval strategy. Three events early in the war were to see the carrier elevated to the position of importance in naval warfare it still holds today: the British attack on the Italian fleet at Taranto in 1940; the attack on Pearl Harbor in 1941, itself inspired by events at Taranto; and the sinking of HMS *Repulse* and HMS *Prince of Wales*, two unprotected British battleships, by Japanese aircraft shortly afterwards.

World War II saw the aircraft carrier establish itself as a key strategic asset. Once the Japanese had lost carrier superiority in the Pacific, they were unable to prevent the US Army and Marine amphibious landings from retaking the islands they had lost in 1941–42. After the battle of the Philippine Sea in 1944 and the loss of most of her skilled carrier pilots, the ultimate defeat of Japan was only a matter of time and logistics. Aircraft carriers also played a vital role in the Atlantic and Mediterranean during the war, particularly in the defence of Malta against Axis attack.

The Cold War conflicts of Korea and Vietnam saw US carriers in use as floating airbases, capable of inflicting serious damage on the enemy at little risk to themselves. In the 1970s, however, the Soviet Union began a programme of carrier building using the Yak Forger as a strike aircraft, and at the same time European navies decided to build smaller, cheaper carriers to make use of the Harrier V/STOL technology. Without its two 'pocket' carriers, the United Kingdom's campaign to recapture the Falkland Islands from Argentinian forces in 1982 would have been an impossibility.

As they have done for decades, the modern US carrier fleets dominate the world's oceans, a single carrier carrying more air power than the air forces of most states. The 'Nimitz'-class vessels were used to good effect in the recent operations in Afghanistan and Iraq. However, European navies are now building large carriers again, and both China and India are looking at developing their carrier capability, so US supremacy may soon be challenged.

In this book you will find a detailed directory of the various classes of aircraft carriers that either serve or have served in the world's navies, including the aircraft and helicopters which provide their strike capability. Also covered in these pages is that close relative of the carrier, the assault ship, and the helicopters which are used to transport the troops ashore from them.

The nuclear-powered aircraft carrier USS *Enterprise* (CVN 65) in the Atlantic Ocean during the final stages of loading fresh ordnance on board.

Origins of the aircraft carrier

Air power goes to sea

The aircraft carrier's mobility and flexibility, together with the threat of its mighty armament, provide the front-line forces in the war against terror, and carriers therefore play a vital peace-keeping role in the modern world.

It was these characteristics which enabled the carrier to replace the battleship as the decisive factor in maritime warfare. However, the aircraft carrier's rise to pre-eminence in World War II was far from obvious to naval staffs in the early days of carrier aviation.

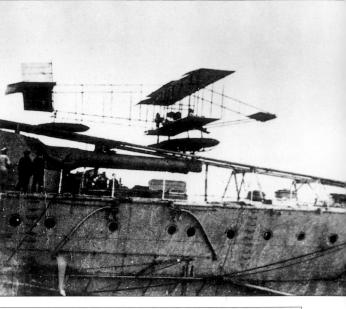

Right: Lieutenant C. R. Samson prepares to make the first flight from a Royal Navy ship, the pre-Dreadnought battleship HMS Africa moored at Sheerness, on 10 January 1912. The aircraft was a Short S.27, and there are claims that a 'secret' take-off was also made in December 1911.

Pioneering service

The US Navy was a pioneer in the race to take aircraft to sea. The service sponsored Eugene Ely and the Curtiss company in 1911, when Ely made the first landing on and take-off from a ship. However, few took the feat as anything more than a barnstorming stunt. One organisation which took things more seriously was the Royal Navy. Within a year of Ely's pioneering efforts, Lieutenant Samson had demonstrated the same capability from the pre-Dreadnought battleships HMS *Africa*, *Hibernia* and *London*. However, the problem of landing on a moving ship presented much greater problems. Flying-off decks were too short for easy landing, and trying to land head-on to a moving ship was almost suicidal.

Seaplanes were much easier to use. They could be launched just like wheeled aircraft, and in 1911 Glenn Curtiss showed how easy it was to land alongside and be hoisted aboard by crane. The Royal Navy used the seaplane-equipped protected

Eugene B. Ely lands a Curtiss pusher on a platform over the stern of the armoured cruiser USS Pennsylvania (CA-4) moored in San Francisco Bay on 18 January 1911. Ely lunched on board the ship and then took off to return to a nearby airfield.

cruiser HMS *Hermes* to great effect in the fleet manoeuvres of 1913.

Reconnaissance was the driving force behind taking aircraft to sea, enabling commanders to 'look beyond the horizon' better than ever before. But even before the outbreak of war, many of the characteristics which would take the aircraft to its present dominant position were present in embryo. In 1912 Samson took a dummy bomb aloft; in 1914 a 1.5-pdr gun

was tested in flight, and the first live airborne torpedo was dropped; and in 1915 the US Navy deployed the first shipboard catapult, powered by compressed air.

Scouting potential

The scouting potential of aircraft saw the adoption by most navies of flying-off platforms on capital ships, the aircraft being used primarily for scouting purposes and to spot for the big guns.

Dedicated seaplane carriers

were in service by 1914, performing much the same mission. However, they were usually converted merchant ships, too slow to keep up with the fleet, and generally served independently, supporting amphibious operations. Aware of the problem, the Royal Navy converted the old Cunard liner *Campania*, which at 21 kts had the speed to keep up with the battle fleet.

In 1915 HMS *Ben-My-Chree* launched a Short Type 184 seaplane to make the world's first successful aerial torpedo attack, sinking a Turkish freighter in the Dardanelles. However, it soon became clear that landplanes

HMS Ben-My-Chree was a fast packet steamer of the Isle of Man Steam Packet Company before being converted as a carrier for four seaplanes. The ship was lost early in 1917 after being hit by Turkish shore artillery.

IJN CARRIERS: EARLY HISTORY

A Gloster Sparrowhawk takes off from the gun turret of the Imperial Japanese navy's *Yamashiro*, a 'Fuso'-class battleship, while underway in Tokyo Bay (right). Sparrowhawks were launched from 10-m (33-ft) launch platforms mounted above the turrets of various major IJN warships. This practice reflected that used in other navies at the time of the aircraft's introduction to shipborne use, and while the Sparrowhawk remained in IJN service until 1928, the service was quick to appreciate the potential of the true aircraft carrier. Thus the Japanese designed the world's first aircraft carrier built as such. This was the 9,500-ton *Hosho*, which was built by Asano at Tsurumi and completed in December 1922 with provision for 21 aircraft. The ship became flush-decked in 1923, when the starboard-side island and tripod mast were removed, and in 1934 the three hinged funnels were fixed in the upright position. The ship was successful but too small, and was followed by the altogether larger half-sisters *Akagi* and *Kaga*.

offered much better performance than floatplanes or flying boats. But taking landplanes to sea called for an entirely new kind of ship, which then began to mature as the aircraft carrier.

The British carried out the first experiments, fitting a flying-off deck onto the bow of the light battlecruiser HMS *Furious*. Landing was perilous: Commander E. H. Dunning proved it was possible, but was killed soon after his first success while attempting to repeat the feat. A landing-on deck was added over the ship's after part, but turbulence from the superstructure made aircraft recovery a chancy business. Even so, seven Sopwith Camels from the *Furious* made the celebrated Tondern raid in July 1918, the world's first carrier strike against land targets. Two Zeppelins were destroyed in the attack on their base.

The first 'flat top'

Never particularly satisfactory, the *Furious* was later completely rebuilt as what was now accepted as a conventional carrier. However, it was followed into service by the world's first true 'flat top', HMS *Argus*, an incomplete merchant ship now completed with a wholly unobstructed flight deck.

An American battle squadron served with the Grand Fleet in the last year of World War I, and its commanders were quick to see the value of the carrier. The US Navy ordered the large collier *Jupiter* to be converted into America's first carrier, the USS *Langley*, which received the designation CV-1. Known to those who served in it as the 'Covered Wagon', the *Langley* was flush-decked, with two hinged funnels on the port side. The former coal holds had been converted to workshops, accommodation and storerooms, while the former upper deck had now become the hangar.

In service the *Langley* could only make 14 kts, which was some 7 kts below the speed of the battle fleet. However in spite of this handicap the vessel served with the fleet.

Test platform

One of the most important contributions made to naval aviation by the *Langley* was to test various systems of arrester gear. When first commissioned *Langley* had a British system of longitudinal wires, which were intended to engage hooks in the aircraft's landing gear and so prevent it from slewing from side to side. To this the US Navy added a back-up system of transverse wires, whose retarding action was achieved by hanging sand-filled shellcases on the ends. Refined into a hydraulic system, this system ultimately proved better, and remains the basis of conventional carrier landings.

Another innovation was the installation of a pair of flush-mounted pneumatic catapults on the flight deck; intended for seaplanes, they later proved that they could accelerate the take-off of conventional aircraft, in the process improving safety and maximising use of the flight deck, and like the arrester gear this procedure is still standard today.

Many lessons were learned with these early carriers, but few of the pioneers of naval aviation could have foreseen the astonishing development of the aircraft carrier over the next decades.

HMS Argus *was converted from an incomplete liner and was commissioned in September 1918 as the world's first true aircraft carrier.* Argus *could reach 20 kts and carried up to 20 aircraft. The ship survived to the end of World War II.*

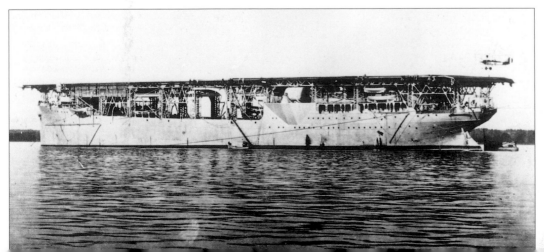

Seen at anchor in 1923 with an Aeromarine biplane landing on the deck, the USS Langley *was the first American aircraft carrier, being commissioned in March 1922 after conversion from a collier.* Langley *carried up to 36 aircraft.*

Pictured before World War II, the USS Yorktown *marked a major evolutionary step in aircraft carrier design with open hangars and a large aircraft complement.*

Inter-war theories
Evolution of the aircraft carrier

The aircraft carrier emerged from World War I as a distinctly limited weapon, but development in the 1920s and 1930s turned it into a large and powerful platform for the projection of massive naval air power.

The scouting potential of the aircraft in World War I persuaded most navies to mount flying-off platforms on their capital ships. Dedicated seaplane carriers were in service by 1916, but it soon became clear that landplanes offered much better performance than floatplanes and flying boats. However, the desire to take landplanes to sea could be satisfied only by the creation of an entirely new kind of ship – the aircraft carrier.

The British carried out the first experiments, fitting a flying-off deck onto the bow of the light battlecruiser HMS *Furious*. Never particularly satisfactory, the *Furious* was then converted into a conventional carrier. The *Furious* was followed into service by the world's first true 'flat top', HMS *Argus*, the converted battleship HMS *Eagle*, and then HMS *Hermes*, designed from the outset as a carrier. Japan followed suit, laying down the carrier *Hosho* soon after the Armistice of November 1918.

A battle squadron of the US Navy served with the Grand Fleet in the last year of World War I, and its commanders were quick to see the value of naval aircraft. At the end of World War I, the US Navy ordered the conversion of the large collier *Jupiter* into the first US carrier, the USS *Langley* (CV-1).

The 1922 Washington Treaty was designed to put a stop to the frantic warship construction that had to a certain extent spurred the outbreak of World War I. The treaty placed few restrictions on the building of carriers, however. In the treaty, aircraft carriers were defined as any warship exceeding 10,000 tons designed for the 'specific and exclusive' purpose of carrying, launching and landing aircraft.

Little limitation

Signatories to the treaty were allowed to build any number of carriers up to an agreed total tonnage, which was 135,000 tons each for the UK and the US, 81,000 for Japan and 60,000 each for France and Italy. No new ship was permitted to exceed 27,000 tons, but the powers were allowed to convert two larger capital ships which would otherwise be scrapped.

To put this in the context of the time, the UK and Japan were only just building their first small carriers designed for the purpose, while the US was still converting the

Above: The two units of the US Navy's 'Lexington' class were based on incomplete battlecruiser hulls and, though very useful warships, had an indifferent ratio between aircraft strength and displacement.

Below: Seen at Kure in October 1945 and one of few large Japanese ships to survive World War II, the Hosho *was Japan's first aircraft carrier, and the world's first carrier built as such from the keel up.*

Above: **Akagi** *was completed with three flight decks, although an island was added and the flight deck revised to a single unit after modernisation in 1938.*

Below: **HMS** Glorious *was one of two conversions of the 1920s from light battlecruiser standard, and was never more than an indifferent aircraft carrier.*

World War I.

The Americans converted the incomplete hulls of two very large battlecruisers. These, completed in 1927 as the USS *Lexington* (CV-2) and USS *Saratoga* (CV-3), were 270-m (890-ft) vessels capable of 34 kts. They represented a massive increase in capability over the 168-m (550-ft) and 15-kt *Langley*, of only five years earlier – an improvement which came with no intermediate evolutionary stages.

Tactical evolution

From 1928 these two big carriers took part in the annual war games of the US Pacific Fleet. The carriers were still considered as auxiliaries – useful scouting platforms, but in no way as important as the battleship. The *Lexington* and *Saratoga* also played their own war games against each other, however, their officers evolving many of the tactical concepts which eventually would be put to use by the fast carrier task forces of World War II.

The British opted for a pair of 22,500-ton vessels, HMS *Glorious* and HMS *Courageous*, which, with only 4.7-in (120-mm) guns, were in no way treaty-limited. As a result of conservative design and 'thinking small', the Royal Navy of 1930 found itself with six carriers carrying far fewer aircraft in total

than the three carriers available to the Americans.

The Japanese followed a similar path with the *Akagi* and *Kaga*, converting incomplete battleship hulls into large fleet carriers.

Still lacking experience in what they really needed, both US and Japanese planners reverted temporarily to smaller ships in the late 1920s and early 1930s. But with ships like the USS *Ranger* (CV-4) and the *Ryujo* they discovered practical limitations which served to underline that bigger was better. The following USS *Yorktown* (CV-5) was a development of the *Ranger*, with an 'open' hangar rather than the 'closed' type used in the *Lexington* and *Saratoga*, to allow up to 80 aircraft to be carried. This arrangement proved highly successful, and formed the basis for the even more successful 'Essex' class.

Japanese concepts

Through the 1920s and 1930s, the Japanese experimented with their carriers, perfecting design and construction methods, and honing the demanding art of blue-water power projection. The *Hiryu*,

the *Soryu* and the 'Shokaku'-class vessels were a match for the US Navy's carriers, and were faster and carried larger air groups than the British ships.

Not until the late 1930s did the British begin to catch up, with the entry into service of HMS *Ark Royal* and the 'Illustrious'-class ships. Designed to operate in European waters, often within reach of land-based bombers, the British carriers featured armoured flight decks. This made them much more capable of withstanding battle damage than the Japanese or American carriers, but imposed severe restrictions on aircraft capacity. It was finally realised that big air wings were more important, and post-war British designs would follow US practice.

By the outbreak of World War II in 1939, all the elements which would allow the carrier to control the seas were in place. Navies were still dominated by the gunnery admirals, however, and few could have foreseen that the aircraft carrier would soon bring to a resounding close five centuries of battleship domination.

Langley. France and Italy had hardly considered the subject. Suddenly, from the leisurely experiments of the first generation of carriers, the signatories found themselves with the parameters defined for the second generation, written to make full use of a plenitude of incomplete capital ship hulls started in

AIRCRAFT AT SEA

Two key developments which appeared on the early aircraft carriers were catapults and arrester gear. Early slow-moving biplanes were able simply to fly off the carrier's deck, but the USS *Langley* was fitted with a pair of flush-mounted pneumatic catapults on its flight deck; intended for seaplanes, they later proved that they could speed up the launching of conventional aircraft. The catapult remains standard to this day. The first arrester gear, developed by the British (an approach to HMS *Ark Royal* is pictured), was a system of longitudinal wires, which were intended to engage hooks in the landing gear of the aircraft and prevent it from slewing from side to side. However, the US Navy added a back-up system of transverse wires, whose retarding action was achieved by hanging sand-filled shell cases on the ends. This system (refined into a proper hydraulic arrester system) proved better, and is the basis of all modern carrier landings.

Escort carriers
Vital defensive/offensive support

The USS Sangamon was an 'Essex'-class carrier which was originally constructed as the civilian tanker Esso Trenton. This ship was also classified as an Auxiliary Aircraft Carrier and Escort Carrier.

From a simple beginning as a British expedient to offer air protection to Atlantic convoys, the escort carrier rapidly matured as a purpose-built warship for a host of vital offensive as well as defensive roles.

World War II saw the emergence of the fleet carrier as the primary offensive weapon of the maritime powers. These began the war as supporters of the battleship, but as the conflict expanded the fleet carrier eclipsed the gun-armed capital ship since its primary weapon, the aeroplane, could strike much farther and with more accuracy than the biggest gun. Carriers were large, expensive and took a relatively long time to build, however, and as a result there were never sufficient numbers to take on the many missions that were demanded. What was needed was clearly a

cheaper and faster means of getting aircraft to sea in numbers, and the result was the escort carrier.

The escort carrier was the product of two separate but almost simultaneous lines of development in the UK and US. The British needed to protect the convoy lifeline which ensured their survival, for as early as 1940 convoys were sustaining serious losses from U-boats and Focke-Wulf Fw 200 long-range aircraft. Air power could counter both. Fw 200s were no match for modern fighters, and U-boats on the surface were vulnerable to air attack. Standard practice in such situations was to

Above: The 20-mm cannons on board HMS Trumpeter are tested. Originally launched as USS Bastian on 15 December 1942, this escort carrier deployed 18-24 aircraft.

dive but, once submerged, the U-boat was far too slow to engage even a slow-moving convoy.

'Atlantic gap'
Land-based aircraft could cover both ends of the Atlantic lifeline, but lacked the range for the 'Atlantic gap' in its centre. There were too few fleet carriers to cover the continuous stream of Atlantic convoys, and losses of merchant ships were high and growing higher.

As a stopgap, the British fielded CAMs (Catapult-Armed Merchantmen), which were standard freighters with a catapult for one

fighter launched from the bow. Although they achieved some success in driving off the Fw 200s, they were one-shot weapons.

In 1940 it was decided to convert the *Hannover*, a captured German ship, into a small carrier, and the ship was commissioned on 20 June 1941. The new carrier was renamed HMS *Audacity* on 30 July 1941, and was a very basic carrier: there was no space for a hangar or a lift, so its eight Grumman Martlet fighters were parked on deck. The carrier escorted its first convoy to Gibraltar in September 1941, one of its

Above: The USS Admiralty Islands was a 'Casablanca'-class escort carrier named after a group of islands in the Pacific which were the scene of fierce fighting in early 1944. It was decommissioned on 24 April 1946 and sold to Zidell Machinery and Supply Company in Portland, Oregon.

Right: The USS Card won a Presidential Unit citation for its extraordinary success in destroying German U-boats during the Battle of the Atlantic. The Card operated with a flotilla of three destroyers and was credited with more U-boat kills than any other combination of ships in history.

Left: HMS Archer was built as an 'Archer'-class Escort carrier in the United States and was acquired by the Royal Navy under the Lend-Lease programme.

Below left: HMS Ruler spent most of its carrier in the Pacific theatre, conducting aircraft and supplies replenishment together with logistic missions.

Below: USS Mindoro was commissioned on 4 December 1945 but, arriving too late to participate in the war, the vessel spent much of its life performing training missions.

aircraft shooting down an Fw 200. It was sunk by *U-571* in December 1941 on its third convoy mission.

The *Audacity*'s short career had shown that the small escort carrier was feasible, and four or five further merchant conversions were completed, together with 18 MACs (Merchant Aircraft Carriers), which were oil or grain bulk carriers with their superstructures removed and flight decks added. They retained their cargo-carrying capability and were manned by mercantile crews, with Fleet Air Arm personnel to maintain and fly the aircraft.

The bulk of the British escort carrier strength was supplied by the US, however. The US Navy originally developed light carriers to ferry aircraft from the US across oceanic distances to theatres of battle all over the world. The first examples were merchant conversions like those completed by the British. The USS *Long Island* was used as a training ship while the *Archer* was supplied to the UK. These were followed by four 'Cimarron'-class fleet oiler conversions.

The US Navy quickly realised these 'jeep' carriers

could play a vital offensive role. The tanker conversions stood in for fleet carriers in the invasion of North Africa, and at the end of 1942 were sent to the Pacific, where US Navy fleet carrier strength had been reduced to two.

Building programme

These early ships paved the way for a major escort carrier building programme. The fleet carrier programme was impressive enough (17 'Essex'-class heavy fleet and nine 'Independence'-class light fleet carriers completed before the end of the war), but between June 1941 and April 1945 the US built 78 escort carriers.

In the Atlantic, the escort carriers were anti-submarine warfare specialists providing continuous cover for convoys. Operating from within the convoy was primarily defen-

sive, however. Later, small task groups sailed independently in positions where they could aid convoys in their general area. Carrier-based aircraft scouted ahead, searching out U-boats before the latter could make contact with a convoy. Out of this technique emerged the successful hunter/killer tactics that finally freed the Allies' North Atlantic shipping.

In the Pacific, 'Jeeps' were faced with a much more varied range of tasks. These included providing air cover for amphibious landings, ferrying planes, resupplying the big carriers and performing tactical air attacks in support of ground forces. Though they were never designed to go toe-to-toe with the Japanese fleet, they performed exceptionally well in that role off Samar during the Battle of Leyte Gulf in October 1944.

'CASABLANCA' CLASS: 50 IN A YEAR

A total of 24 escort carriers was ordered in the US Navy's 1942 building programme, ten of them for delivery to the Royal Navy. While these were under construction, shipbuilder Henry J. Kaiser approached President Franklin D. Roosevelt with a plan to mass-produce escort carriers. The first of these, the USS *Casablanca*, was commissioned on 8 July 1943. In an impressive demonstration of the sheer industrial muscle of the US, the Kaiser yard in Vancouver completed its 50-ship programme exactly one year later on 8 July 1944.

HMS Attacker was originally built as the cargo vessel Steel Artisan until entering service with the US Navy as USS Barnes.

The 'Shokaku'-class fleet carrier Zuikaku, seen in September 1941. The 'Shokakus' were arguably the most successful Japanese carriers of the war and were considerably larger, better armed and more heavily armoured than the 'Soryus' that preceded them.

Japanese carriers
Design and construction

There were three major carrier powers during World War II. However, at the outbreak of fighting, it was the Imperial Japanese navy who in many ways had the world's most advanced carrier arm.

The British were the pioneers in carrier aviation. The Americans developed the concept, its carrier force emerging in 1945 as the decisive factor in combat at sea. But the Imperial Japanese navy's carrier arm was a force which in no small measure was responsible for the Japanese Empire's astonishing run of Pacific victories in the six months following the attack on Pearl Harbor.

During Japan's rapid evolution from a feudal state into a modern industrial power at the end of the 19th Century, the IJN modelled itself on Britain's Royal Navy, and until the end of World War I relations between the two fleets were excellent. It was before and during that war that the British began to champion the use of aircraft at sea, first from seaplane carriers and then from true aircraft carriers.

The Japanese watched early British experiments with great interest, and in 1914 commissioned the *Wakamiya*, a converted cargo vessel which carried four seaplanes. In the autumn of 1914 its aircraft carried out one of the first ship-launched air raids in history, making a surprise attack on the German-held port of Tsingtao.

Like the British, the Japanese became convinced that seaplanes were not entirely effective as strike aircraft, and in 1919 they laid down the their first true aircraft carrier, the *Hosho*. Based on a modified oiler design, the shipbuilders benefited from the presence of a Royal Navy technical mission who already had experience with the carriers *Furious*, *Argus*, *Hermes* and *Eagle*.

Naval planning

Hosho commissioned in December 1922. Reasonably fast but rather small, the *Hosho*'s main contribution to Japanese naval aviation was in developing aircraft carrier techniques and equipment, and in giving Japan's pioneering naval aviators their first true flight deck experiences.

The Washington Treaty of 1922 swept away Japan's ambitious '8-8' plan which had called for the construction of eight large battleships and eight fast battlecruisers. However, the terms of the treaty allowed Japan to convert some of the capital ships on the stocks as aircraft carriers, and like the Americans the Japanese chose to rebuild two fast battlecruisers, the

Above: **Zuiho** *was one of two 'Shoho'-class light carriers that were based on the hulls of submarine depot ships. Although* **Shoho** *was an early war loss at Coral Sea,* **Zuiho** *survived in service until the Leyte Gulf campaign. The smoke plume in the image is from a shadowing vessel.*

Right: *An ex-battlecruiser, as completed,* **Kaga** *was similar in appearance to* **Akagi,** *both ships also sharing a heavy anti-surface battery of 8-in (203-mm) guns.*

A November 1943 photograph of the escort carrier Shinyo, *a conversion of a German passenger liner acquired by the Japanese navy in 1942. The carrier saw little action and survived only until 1944. The ship's main role was as a training carrier.*

Above: The light carrier Ryujo *underway in September 1938.* Ryujo *suffered from stability problems arising from the fact that the double hangar put excessive topweight on a narrow cruiser hull.*

Akagi and the *Amagi*. The *Amagi* was destroyed by an earthquake, however, so the incomplete battleship *Kaga* was used as a replacement.

New carriers

The new carriers reflected the emerging carrier doctrine being formulated by the Imperial navy. Like the Americans, the Imperial navy believed that carriers were best used as strike platforms, able to destroy enemy carrier forces and battle fleets. Japanese carrier air groups consisted of torpedo-bombers and dive-bombers, which would be protected in action by large numbers of escorting fighters. The Japanese were slightly heavier on torpedo-bombers than the Americans, and their dive-bombers were also expected to be able to serve as level bombers.

The need to carry effective air wings meant that Japanese carriers were fitted with double hangars, enabling the *Akagi* and *Kaga* to operate up to 60 aircraft each, increasing to more than 70 after refits in the 1930s. Fleet exercises in the 1930s proved the effectiveness of the task group – several carriers operating together.

The next carrier built after the *Kaga* was the *Ryujo*. Built to use up Washington Treaty tonnage, the *Ryujo* was an experiment in packing as many aircraft as possible onto a cruiser-sized hull. Although it could carry 48 aircraft compared to the dozen or so of a similarly-sized escort carrier, it was extremely top heavy and unstable.

The following designs, *Soryu* and *Hiryu*, were much improved. They were commissioned in 1937 and 1939 respectively. Designed from the keel up as carriers, both had double hangars well integrated into the hull, and both could carry more than 70 aircraft on half the tonnage of the *Akagi* and *Kaga*. Capable of a speed of some 34 kts, they formed the core of the fast carrier task forces used by Japan in the opening months of the Pacific War. They were followed into service by the excellent *Shokaku* and *Zuikaku*. Commissioned in 1941, they were larger, better armed and were better protected than the *Soryu*, and could carry 84 aircraft.

Pacific air power

As tensions with the United States grew through the late 1930s, the Imperial navy knew that any conflict would be fought across the broad expanses of the Pacific, and aircraft carriers would be a vital asset. At the same time as the 'Soryu' class was being built, the Japanese navy began a shadow building programme. This involved building a series of seaplane tenders, oilers, or submarine depot ships which could easily and quickly be converted as aircraft carriers. Slower and less capable than the fleet carriers, they could nevertheless carry between 20 and 30 aircraft, and provided air power to protect Japan's far flung island garrisons.

The defeat at Midway gutted Japan's fleet carrier force. The nation lacked the industrial capacity to match America's massive carrier building programme, and the shadow carriers, together with hurried liner and tanker conversions, had to bear the brunt of increasing US Navy power. Only three more fleet carriers were completed in Japan, the *Unryu* and *Amagi* being repeats of the 'Soryu' design.

The powerful *Taiho* was the first Japanese carrier to be fitted with an armoured flight deck. Displacing over 37,000 tonnes at deep load, it could carry 75 aircraft. However, by the time it appeared in March 1944, Japan was being driven back from her Pacific conquests, and *Taiho* was sunk by an American submarine during the Battle of the Philippine Sea only weeks after finishing its shakedown cruise.

Battleship conversion

The last and greatest Japanese carrier, the *Shinano*, did not even manage that. Converted from the third 'Yamato'-class battleship, the 73,000-tonne leviathan was sunk by the US submarine *Archerfish* while moving to Kure for final fitting out. The massive vessel was not intended to be a combat carrier: the 120 aircraft it was meant to carry would mostly have been used as replacement aircraft for other carriers and for island air bases.

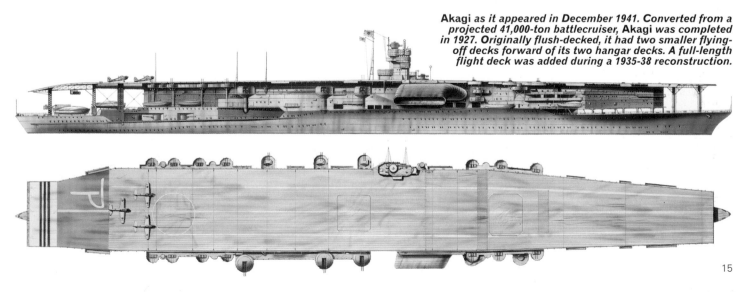

Akagi as it appeared in December 1941. Converted from a projected 41,000-ton battlecruiser, Akagi *was completed in 1927. Originally flush-decked, it had two smaller flying-off decks forward of its two hangar decks. A full-length flight deck was added during a 1935-38 reconstruction.*

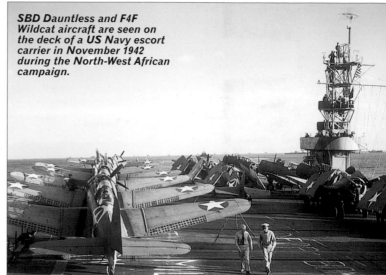

Carrier air wings
World War II naval air power

The aircraft carrier came into existence in the closing stages of World War I. In the early days, as navies tried to develop effective carrier doctrine, most such vessels were intended to operate with the battle fleet. The primary function of the carrier's aircraft was spotting for the battleships' gunfire, though it was quickly realised that carrierborne aircraft could also provide a useful reconnaissance capability.

Planners soon realised that carriers could perform offensive tasks, and the spotting mission was transferred to floatplanes catapult-launched from capital ships and cruisers. The carrier air group began to receive attack aircraft armed with torpedoes or bombs, together with fighters to escort attack missions and defend the carrier.

By the outbreak of World War II, the major carrier navies were those of the UK, US and Japan, which had developed air wings for the offensive carrier mission, but there were significant differences in emphasis.

Allied air groups

The British started World War II with the least capable air groups. This was the result partly of the Fleet Air Arm's inferior aircraft (resulting from RAF control of FAA aircraft procurement) and partly of the Royal Navy's insistence on multi-seat machines for all roles.

At the outbreak of World War II, HMS *Ark Royal* carried an air group of 48 Swordfish torpedo-bombers and 24 Skua fighter/dive-bombers. The lack of a dedicated fighter was not seen as a problem, since Royal Navy doctrine held that the carrier's main defence would be provided by its anti-aircraft guns. Operational experience showed this to be a major error and, as a stopgap, fighters like the Gladiator, Hurricane and Spitfire were navalised. None was particularly satisfactory: the Gladiator was obsolete, the Hurricane lacked folding wings, and the narrow-track landing gear of the Spitfire meant that landing on was always hazardous. The solution was the use of large numbers of much tougher American-built aircraft.

While fleet carriers were still seen primarily as strike platforms, they carried a considerably higher proportion of fighters, and many of these were American. A typical air wing in 1945, that of HMS *Illustrious*, included 36 Corsair fighter/attack aircraft and 16 Avenger torpedo-bombers.

Long-range attack

The US Navy had similar priorities, but placed more emphasis on long-range attack. During the desperate days after Pearl Harbor, the US Navy had to use carriers as its primary offensive weapon, and these proved so effective that when battleships were again available in numbers their primary function became the protection of the carriers.

The Americans had a con-

Above: Flying from MAC ships such as HMS Ancylus, and also escort carriers, elderly aircraft like the Swordfish proved effective in the anti-submarine role. An air attack forced a U-boat to submerge and so lose the speed advantage to catch and attack a convoy.

Below: Mitsubishi A6M2 fighters prepare to leave Shokaku in 1942. Japanese air groups changed little through World War II. More efficient types were built, but by the time they were ready for service US Navy fast carrier task forces had become dominant.

USS Princeton (CV-37) is seen with F4U Corsair, TBF Avenger and SB2C Helldiver aircraft on the flight deck. By this late stage in the war, the availability of carriers in large numbers allowed the US Navy to implement its new doctrine of massed and devastating long-range attacks by fast carrier task forces.

siderable advantage over the British. US Navy aircraft were much better, being designed from the outset for carrier operations. The carriers also embarked much larger air groups: by foregoing the armoured deck, the 'Yorktown' class could be built with a double hangar, allowing a maximum air group of 18 fighters, 36 torpedo-bombers and 36 dive-bombers. As the war progressed the proportion of fighters rose, while pure torpedo-bombers were replaced by multi-role aircraft such as the Avenger.

From 1943 US carriers came off the slipways in increasing numbers. Three or four carriers combined could launch hundreds rather than dozens of aircraft to over-whelm enemy defences. Defence of the carrier also became more efficient. CAPs (combat air patrols) became more effective when added to newly developed radar systems and hugely increased anti-aircraft batteries firing proximity-fused shells. Control was enhanced by specialised CICs (combat information centers), which optimised the varied assets available to the carrier.

By the end of the war, 'Essex'-class carriers were typically carrying over 36 F4U and F6F fighters, 36 SB2C dive-bombers and 24 TBF/TBM torpedo and level bombers. The air group was thus capable of a whole spectrum of missions.

Japanese approach

Japanese forces, designed like US forces to operate over the vast distances of the Pacific, developed similar doctrines in the 1930s. Since carriers were expected to deal with the enemy battle fleet, the Japanese placed more emphasis on torpedo and level bombers than on dive-bombers, but a typical carrier of 1941 operated both types as well as fighters. At the time of Pearl Harbor, the fleet carrier *Shokaku* had an air group of 27 B5N torpedo-bombers, 27 D3A dive-bombers and 18 A6M fighters, with 12 aircraft in reserve. Japanese aircraft were much more lightly built than their American counterparts. This gave them excellent range but was a disadvantage when it came to surviving battle damage, especially from American AA guns and US fighters that were now very well protected and also more heavily armed, and flown in the later stages of the war by pilots who were better trained and more experienced than their adversaries.

Escort carriers

Light and escort carriers were also used in large numbers, primarily for trade protection in the Atlantic and to police the US Navy's long supply lines in the Pacific. In the Atlantic, the main foes were submarines and long-range maritime patrol aircraft. A typical escort carrier of the early period might have an air wing of between 10 and 20 aircraft. Later US Navy escort carriers operating with ASW hunter/killer groups could carry 28 aircraft, split between fighters and torpedo/ASW bombers.

The US Navy's Task Force 38 enters the anchorage at Ulithi Atoll. By this time, in December 1944, the overwhelming might of the Pacific Fleet had obliterated most of the Imperial Japanese Navy.

US Pacific carriers

The Pacific War was the war of the aircraft carrier. From Pearl Harbor to Okinawa, it was the effective use of the carrier aircraft which proved decisive.

When Japanese carrier aircraft struck at the US Pacific Fleet's anchorage on 7 December 1941, a new era in naval warfare was born. Pearl Harbor marked the dawn of carrier warfare across the broad oceans, beyond the wildest imagination of pre-war theorists.

The battleships which many Japanese officers thought would be their main enemy were now sunk or disabled. For at least six months the US Pacific Fleet could only take the offensive with its carriers. As a result, the concept of the fast carrier task force was created, using the carriers' dive-bombers and torpedo-bombers as long-range substitutes for the 16-in (406-mm) gun.

Because the tactics and the aircraft were comparatively primitive, the first attempts by the US Navy to carry the war to Japan were barely effective. There was little that could be done to stop Japan from overrunning Southeast Asia. Nevertheless, a daring raid on Tokyo by North American B-25 Mitchell bombers was flown from the USS *Hornet* in April 1942, and a series of pinprick raids was made on other outposts.

Coral Sea

The first pitched battle, in the Coral Sea, was fought in May 1942 to stop the Japanese from gaining a foothold in New Guinea. The Americans lost one of their largest carriers, the USS *Lexington*, but the Japanese amphibious operation was called off after the small carrier *Shoho* was sunk. It was the first battle in history in which the main units of the opposing fleets never saw one another.

The turning point

Superior American intelligence and improved tactics led to a decisive victory in June 1942. A rash attempt by the IJN to capture Midway resulted in the loss of four front-line carriers in a matter of minutes, along with the world's best naval aircrews. In the months that followed, the Japanese high command squandered the lives of its carrier airmen faster than they could be replaced.

By contrast, the US Navy was soon replacing its lost pilots with thousands of new aircrew, who were flying a new generation of more powerful aircraft.

In June 1944, another great carrier battle in the Philippine Sea destroyed the remnants of the Japanese naval aircrews. The 'Great Marianas Turkey Shoot' saw hundreds of semi-skilled pilots slaughtered. When, four months later, the remains of the Imperial Japanese Navy were flung into the Battle of Leyte Gulf there were hardly any pilots left for the carriers.

Without fuel, the survivors of Japan's once mighty carrier force were sitting targets for the swarms of American aircraft which dominated the skies over Japan.

Right: On 11 May 1945, while supporting the Okinawa invasion, the 'Essex'-class carrier USS Bunker Hill was hit by two kamikazes. Severely damaged, with some 653 men killed, wounded or missing, it could still sail, and managed to return safely to the USA.

Below: USS Wasp (CV-7) was commissioned in November 1943 and replaced the less capable USS Ranger in the Pacific. Sunk on 15 September 1942 during the Battle of Guadalcanal, it was hit by two torpedoes fired from a Japanese submarine and was abandoned an hour later.

US Fleet carriers 1945

Only the enormous industrial capacity of the US could have produced the carrier task forces which broke the IJN. Early losses in the Pacific were more than made up for by new carrier building. For example, USS *Essex* was commissioned on the last day of 1942, and by the end of the war 15 'Essex'-class carriers were in service, with another 11 under construction or ordered.

There were also more than 100 light and escort carriers in service or being built. The small carriers fought in many battles, and were crucial in the anti-submarine war, but it was the fleet carriers recorded here which bore the brunt of the struggle with the Imperial Japanese Navy.

USS Essex *in May 1943. The 15 'Essex'-class fast carriers, commissioned in little more than two years, were a major reason why the course of the Pacific war swung in favour of the United States. The ships were among the most successful carriers ever built, and a number served on into the jet age.*

CARRIER	COMMISSIONED	RECORD
LANGLEY (AV-3)	(CV) 1922	Converted to aircraft transport (AV) pre-war
(EX CV-1)	(AV) 1937	Sunk by bombing off Java 27.2.42
'LEXINGTON' CLASS		
LEXINGTON (CV-2)	14.12.27	Pacific raids 1942. Sunk at Coral Sea 8.5.42
SARATOGA (CV-3)	16.11.27	Torpedoed off Hawaii 11.1.42, Guadalcanal, torpedoed Solomons 31.8.42, E. Solomons, Bougainville, Gilbert Is, Kwajalein, Eniwetok, Pacific raids 1944, operated with British E. Fleet 1944, severe damage (kamikaze) Iwo Jima 21.2.45
'YORKTOWN' CLASS		
YORKTOWN (CV-5)	30.9.37	Pacific raids 1942, damaged at Coral Sea, sunk at Midway 7.6.42
ENTERPRISE (CV-6)	12.5.38	Pearl Harbor (aircraft only), Midway, Guadalcanal landings, Kwajalein, Truk raid, Hollandia, Saipan, Philippine Sea, Palau, Leyte, Iwo Jima, damaged twice (kamikaze) at Okinawa 11.4.45 and 13.4.45
HORNET (CV-8)	20.10 41	Doolittle raid 18.4.42, Midway, sunk at Santa Cruz 27.10.42
'WASP' CLASS		
WASP (CV-7)	25.4.40	Mediterranean service early 1942, Guadalcanal landings, sunk at Battle of E. Solomons, 15.9.42
'ESSEX' CLASS		
ESSEX (CV-9)	31.12.42	Bougainville, Gilbert Is, Kwajalein, Truk raid, Marianas, Palau, Leyte, Iwo Jima, damaged (kamikaze) 25.11.44
YORKTOWN (CV-10)	15.4.43	Gilbert Is, Kwajalein, Truk raid, Hollandia, Marianas, Iwo Jima
INTREPID (CV-11)	16.8.43	Kwajalein, torpedoed Truk raid, Palau, Leyte, severe damage (kamikaze) off Luzon 25.11.44 and also off Okinawa 16.4.45
HORNET (CV-12)	29.11.43	Marianas, Palau, Leyte, Iwo Jima
FRANKLIN (CV-13)	31.1.44	Guam, Palau, Leyte, damaged (kamikaze) Luzon 15.10.44 and 30.10.44, severe damage (bombs) off Kyushu 19.3.45
TICONDEROGA (CV-14)	8.5.44	Palau, Leyte, severe damage (kamikaze) Formosa 21.1.45

CARRIER	COMMISSIONED	RECORD
RANDOLPH (CV-15)	9.10.44	Iwo Jima
LEXINGTON (CV-16)	17.2.43	Gilbert Is, Hollandia, torpedoed off Kwajalein 4.12.43, Marianas, Palau, Leyte, (as flagship), damaged (kamikaze) at Luzon 5.11.44, Iwo Jima
BUNKER HILL (CV-17)	20.5.43	Bougainville, Gilbert Is, Kwajalein, Truk raid, Hollandia, Marianas, Palau, Leyte Iwo Jima, severe damage (kamikaze) Okinawa 11.5.45
WASP (CV-18)	24.11.43	New Guinea, Marianas, Palau, Leyte, Iwo Jima, damaged (bomb) off Kyushu 19.3.45
HANCOCK (CV-19)	15.4.44	Philippines, Iwo Jima, damaged (explosion) 21.1.45 and again (kamikaze) 7.4.45
BENNINGTON (CV-20)	6.8.44	Iwo Jima
BON HOMME RICHARD (CV-31)	26.11.44	Raids on Japan
ANTIETAM (CV-36)	28.1.45	Present at Japanese surrender in Tokyo Bay
SHANGRI-LA (CV-38)	15.9.44	Raids on Japan 1945
'INDEPENDENCE' CLASS		
INDEPENDENCE (CVL-22)	1.1.43	Bougainville, severe damage (torpedo) Gilbert Is 20.11.43, Palau, Leyte
PRINCETON (CVL-23)	25.2.43	Bougainville, Gilbert Is, Kwajalein, Eniwetok, Hollandia, Marianas, Palau sunk at Leyte 25.10.44
BELLEAU WOOD (CVL-24)	31.5.43	Gilbert Is, Kwajalein, Truk raid, New Guinea, Marianas, Palau, severe damage (kamikaze) at Leyte 30.10.44, Iwo Jima
COWPENS (CVL-25)	28.5.43	Gilbert Is, Kwajalein, Truk raid, New Guinea, Marianas, Leyte, Philippines, Iwo Jima
MONTEREY (CVL-26)	17.6.43	Gilbert Is, Kwajalein, Truk raid, New Guinea, Marianas, Palau, Leyte
LANGLEY (CVL-27)	31.8.43	Kwajalein, Eniwetok, Marianas, Palau, Leyte, Philippines, Iwo Jima
CABOT (CVL-28)	24.7.43	Kwajalein, Truk raid, Philippine Sea, Guam, Palau, Leyte, Philippines, Iwo Jima
BATAAN (CVL-29)	17.11.43	Hollandia, Marianas
SAN JACINTO (CVL-30)	15.12.43	Marianas, Palau, Leyte, Philippines, Iwo Jima

The Challenge of the Jet
Carrier operations in the jet age

Increased take-off and landing speeds, as well as heavier weights, were the driving forces behind carrier developments at the dawn of the jet age. The most radical innovation was almost certainly the angled deck.

As World War II ended, the jet age began to dawn for naval aviation. The jets brought some improvements in safety, with their less volatile, kerosene-based fuel proving easier and much safer to store aboard ship, although much more fuel had to be stored. The early jets were no more difficult to land than the last piston-engined fighters, and usually had a better view forward over the nose for the pilot, although their very slow throttle response made flying an accurate approach rather more difficult.

Strategic carriers

One answer was to provide a longer landing run, but the only way of doing this was to increase the size of the carrier itself. The US Navy did, in fact, build bigger aircraft-carriers, but was motivated to do so by the desire to deploy larger Carrier Air Wings and by the wish to embrace new roles. After World War II, the US Navy wanted its carriers to take on a strategic role, including

nuclear strike duties, in order to challenge what was then a USAF monopoly on nuclear weapons. But taking on a nuclear role entailed deploying and embarking bigger, heavier, longer-range aircraft on its carriers.

As an interim measure Lockheed modified 12 Neptunes to P2V-3C configuration, with, among other changes, provision to carry a single 14-kT, 4400-kg (9,700-lb) Mk 1 'Little Boy' atomic bomb. The P2V-3C was intended to take-off from a carrier (using the full deck

USS Saipan embarked the world's first squadron of carrierborne jet fighters in May 1948, after a series of jet compatibility trials. Here one of the aircraft, a McDonnell FH-1 Phantom, launches from one of the ship's two catapults. Note that the strop which attached the Phantom to the catapult shuttle is falling away beneath the fighter.

length and rocket-assisted take-off), but was unable to land back on the ship, having to return to a land airfield or ditch alongside a friendly ship, for recovery. The definitive North American AJ-1 Savage took over the carrier-borne nuclear role from September 1949. This was a large and heavy aircraft, and required strengthened decks, but it could at least land on a

carrier, and could be stowed in the hangar deck. It also featured jet power, in the form of an Allison turbojet, which augmented its two powerful piston engines.

New developments

Arguably the two most important developments in the entire history of the aircraft-carrier were introduced during the 1950s. These were

CARRIER EVOLUTION STRAIGHT DECKS FOR ANGLED DECKS

World War II saw a massive increase in the weight and performance of all combat aircraft, including those deployed aboard aircraft-carriers. These larger, heavier aircraft required higher landing speeds and drove forward a range of improvements and refinements to the aircraft-carrier.

World War II-type carrier

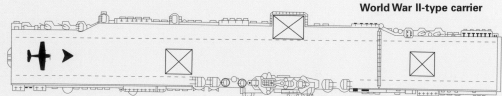

Modern, 'angled-deck'-type carrier

By widening and deepening carriers, naval architects were able to store larger numbers of aircraft on a single vessel. The sheer size of the newer carriers meant that the flight deck was significantly higher than sea level, allowing aircraft to be parked on deck. By widening the carrier and developing the 'angled deck', simultaneous landings and recoveries could be made, considerably speeding up operations.

A pair of USN Demons prepares to take the catapult on a Royal Navy carrier during cross-deck operations. Note that the Skyraiders aft, with their slower take-off speeds, are preparing for a conventional take-off along the length of the deck once the US jets have been launched.

the 'angled deck' and the 'mirror landing aid'. The angled deck derived from British studies into the possibility of using fighters without undercarriages in conjunction with a flexible deck – the elimination of the undercarriage being felt to offer a potentially useful weight saving. An aircraft with no wheels would be hard to manoeuvre on the deck, however, and it was proposed to use the forward end of the deck (pointing straight forward) for take-offs, with an angled deck behind (pointing out away from the ship's centreline) for landings. The flexible deck was abandoned, but the angled deck held out great promise even for conventional carrier aircraft. Trials were undertaken by the Royal Navy, but it was USN interest which led to the angled deck's widespread and near-instantaneous adoption.

Mirror landing aid

Another British invention (subsequently improved and refined by the USN) was the mirror landing aid, a gyro-controlled mirror with angled lights which accurately showed the approaching pilot whether he was on the correct glidepath, or whether he was too high or too low. Together, the angled deck and mirror landing aid slashed the accident rate on aircraft-carriers by 50 per cent, and improved landing accuracy, allowing a reduction in the number of arrester wires provided from a typical 12 to only four. The mirror landing aid was refined and improved (soon

losing the convex mirror!) and the US Navy introduced the concept of using Landing Signals Officers (LSOs) to give the pilot a 'verbal talk-down', using experienced aviators who stood beside the deck assessing the approach from the ship, while the pilot in the landing aircraft concentrated on the now mirror-less landing aid.

Catapult systems

With the increasing weight and take-off speeds of new aircraft, a new means of take-off assistance was required. Air hydraulic catapults were introduced during the war and then, after the war, the RN introduced the even more powerful steam catapult, devised by a serving RNVR commander. The steam catapult provided so much power that some aircraft could even be launched while the carrier was at anchor, with no 'wind over the deck'.

Further upgrades

The massive USS *Forrestal* put all the new improvements into one dramatic package, with an angled deck and four steam catapults, a British-style closed hangar and enclosed hurricane bow. US carriers now maintained Skywarriors and Skyhawks on nuclear alert as a vital part of the Single Integrated Operational Plan (SIOP), their deterrent value enhanced by the carrier's ability to change location unpredictably. During the early 1960s, carriers began to lose their guns, replacing them with defensive SAMs. But the biggest change to the carrier came with the com-

missioning of the US Navy's USS *Enterprise*, which was nuclear-powered. This gave the ship an effectively unlimited range and endurance, provided unlimited steam for the catapults, eliminated the problem of approach turbulence from funnel exhaust gases and allowed a smaller island to be designed, with antennas sited without regard to the chance of funnel smoke corrosion. The increasing cost, value and importance of the aircraft-carrier caused Fleet Air Defence to assume an ever higher priority, and eventually led to the US Navy deploying the world's most sophisticated interceptor (the F-14 Tomcat).

The difficulties inherent in recovering ever-heavier aircraft onto a finite deck space continued to exercise many minds, however, and led to the provision of ever more complex lift augmentation devices on carrier-based aircraft, including double-slotted flaps, flap-blowing and swing wings. But the next major carrier developments were to cope with the arrival of radical VTOL and STOVL aircraft.

A pilot's-eye view of USS Independence *(CVA-62), shows to advantage the ship's angled deck arrangement. Angling the 'landing runway' out from the 'take-off strip' allowed simultaneous launch and recovery operations, and gave the landing pilot a clear deck ahead of him. This meant that if he failed to 'take a wire', he could open up to full throttle and go around again for another attempt.*

F-14 Tomcats formate over the 'Nimitz'-class carrier USS Eisenhower in the Mediterranean in 1988. Displacing over 95,000 tons fully loaded, the 'Nimitz' boats were designed as all-purpose carriers, incorporating the anti-submarine capability of the 'Essex'-class ASW carriers. The first three 'Nimitz' CVNs form a distinct sub-class.

The birth of the supercarrier
From 'Forrestal' to 'Nimitz'

The end of World War II saw the aircraft carrier firmly in place as the most powerful component of the modern navy, and the post-war years saw the United States pursue the most extensive carrier programme.

The landing of the first jet aircraft aboard the British carrier HMS *Ocean* late in 1945 heralded a new era for the aircraft carrier. The rapid advance in jet propulsion was to represent a major threat to that importance, however, and until the carrier could handle the increased size and speed of the new aircraft, naval aviation was to lag behind its land-based counterpart.

The post-war American carrier force was based on the 'Essex'-class carriers of World War II, together with the three large carriers of the 'Midway' class, which had been laid down as fleet carriers for wartime service. Many carriers had been laid up in reserve when the Navy was called to action in Korea.

Initially missions were flown with World War II-era machines like the F4U Corsair. However, the Navy had been experimenting with jets since the late 1940s, and the old propeller-driven aircraft were supplemented by jets like the F9F Panther. Navy aircraft proved highly effective during the war, providing close-support for United Nations troops on the ground.

Angled decks

In order to meet the requirements of jet-propelled aircraft a number of innovations were incorporated into old and new designs in the 1950s and 1960s. By far the most important of these was the angled flight deck. The high landing speeds of jet aircraft entailed comparatively long landing runs, and considerations of safety dictated that such runs be angled away from the longitudinal axis of the flight deck. The resultant change not only removed the possibility of aircraft collisions during a landing but also at a stroke allowed both the opportunity for more attempts to be made and, more importantly, the capability for the carrier to launch aircraft from its bow catapults while landings were being made on the angled deck.

First ordered in 1951, design of the 'Forrestal' class (this is the lead ship, with Skyraiders, Banshees and Furys on deck) was largely based around the Skywarrior bomber and incorporated lessons from the abortive 'United States' project. Forrestal *entered service in 1956.*

The 'Nimitz'-class carriers were built to survive in a nuclear war environment, their air wings well capable of delivering nuclear strikes against well-defended targets in all weathers. Such capability made the carriers prime targets in the Cold War.

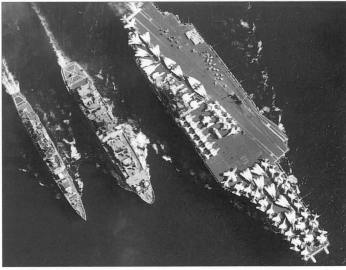

The 'Kitty Hawk'- or 'Improved Forrestal'-class carrier USS **Constellation** *flanked by the replenishment vessel* **Niagara Falls** *and the cruiser* **Leahy** *in the South China Sea in January 1979.*

At the same time that the flight deck revolution occurred, it was realised that something more potent than a hydraulic catapult was needed to launch the jets.

Following trials (again aboard a British carrier, HMS *Perseus*) the solution universally adopted was the steam, or slotted cylinder catapult which drew power from the ship's boilers. It actually took up less space and was much lighter in relation to its power than its hydraulic predecessors. It is the size of the steam catapult and hence its operating capacity in terms of the load that can be accelerated safely, which today influences to a considerable degree the physical parameters and hence the cost of a carrier design.

The F-14 Tomcat weighs in at more than 33 tonnes when fully loaded, and the minimum catapult length required to accelerate such a machine to flying speed is in the order of 90 m (295 ft). To carry sev-

eral examples of such long, powerful catapults requires a very big ship – which is part of the reason that the US Navy's supercarriers are the size that they are.

Deck landing aids

The problems associated with poor landing approaches to the carrier deck were also resolved by supplementing the human deck landing control officer with a mirror landing system – a visual aid that can be seen at a considerable distance by an incoming pilot, who can judge for himself whether or not his approach altitude is correct. However, the landing safety officer still has the final say on whether it is safe for an aircraft to land.

The US Navy wanted to play its part in providing America's post-war nuclear deterrent, in the face of fierce opposition from the USAF and its Strategic Air Command. But the Navy needed much larger carriers

to operate nuclear-capable bombers like the AJ Savage, the A3D Skywarrior and the A2J Vigilante.

Air Force opposition brought the development of the flush-decked USS *United States* to an end, and funds allocated to its construction were transferred to strategic bomber programmes. However, many of its design features were to be used in the USS *Forrestal*, the first new carrier to be designed and laid down for the US Navy after the end of World War II. When it finally entered service, the 'Forrestal' design would introduce the hull form and deck arrangements for all subsequent US Navy carriers.

Commissioned in October 1955, the *Forrestal* was the largest warship built up to that time. Originally intended to be a smaller version of the *United States* design, with a flush deck, it was completely redesigned before construction started and emerged as the first carrier designed and built specifically for jet aircraft operations.

More than 315 m (1,033 ft) long, and with a flight deck over 76 m (250 ft) in width,

the huge new carrier displaced over 75,000 tonnes at full load. *Forrestal* was followed by three sister ships, which were followed in turn by four further conventionally-powered 'Kitty Hawk'-class carriers. Each of these was built to a modified 'Forrestal' design.

Nuclear power

Even as the *Kitty Hawk* was entering service in 1961, however, the future of the American carrier was being heralded by the commissioning of the USS *Enterprise*. The world's first nuclear-powered carrier, the *Enterprise* was built to the same general layout as the 'Forrestals', but enlarged to make room for eight nuclear reactors. These gave the carrier virtually unlimited range.

The lessons learned in the operations of the *Enterprise* were incorporated into the next nuclear-powered carrier, the USS *Nimitz*, which was commissioned in 1975. The 'Nimitz' class has become the standard US Navy carrier design, with another seven ships entering service by the end of the 20th century. The latest examples displace more than 100,000 tonnes.

CVN-75: THE USN'S LATEST CARRIER

March 2003, and the USS *Harry S. Truman* (CVN-75) steams underway in the Eastern Mediterranean. *Harry S. Truman* was deployed in support of Operation Iraqi Freedom, the multi-national coalition effort to eliminate Iraq's weapons of mass destruction, and end the regime of Saddam Hussein. The carrier is the latest 'Nimitz'-class carrier to enter service, and will be followed by a further two vessels, the first of which is named USS *Ronald Reagan*. The later 'Nimitz' vessels displace up to a further 10500 tons compared to their predecessors.

Below: An S-3 Viking prepares for take-off from the USS Enterprise, *the US Navy's first nuclear-powered carrier, with no less than eight reactors. Another notable feature was the island which originally incorporated antennas for electronically scanned main radars.*

Light carriers and V/STOL
Low-cost naval air power

After the conventional aircraft carrier became unacceptably costly and complex during the 1950s and 1960s, some navies acquired smaller ships – dedicated to the carriage of helicopters and/or V/STOL fighter/attack aircraft.

The 1950s and 1960s saw the aircraft-carrier increase in size, cost and complexity, with the US Navy deploying its new nuclear-powered supercarriers, each capable of carrying up to 80 aircraft. However, the size, cost and complexity of these ships meant that few navies could afford to operate them and this led to a requirement for smaller, cheaper carriers carrying helicopters for amphibious assault operations.

Helicopter carriers
The use of aircraft carriers as bases for seaborne assaults was really pioneered by the British during their ill-starred Suez operation. The US Navy had already converted a surplus escort carrier as an experimental helicopter carrier, but Suez provided real combat experience for the concept. At Suez the British used a pair of obsolete light carriers, *Ocean* and *Theseus*, which had been intended to be used as troopships only, pointing the way forward for the development of dedicated helicopter carriers. These emerged as the US Navy 'Iwo Jima' class, which

dispensed with the usual strengthened decks, arrester gear, mirror landing aids, angled deck and steam catapults of the carrier, to concentrate on the carriage of some 24 assault helicopters, able to lift 200 Marines in a single wave.

The success of the assault carrier concept led directly to the development of dedicated ASW carriers, carrying a mix of helicopters and sometimes also some relatively 'easy' and undemanding fixed wing Grumman S-2 Trackers.

Light carriers
The British Hawker Siddeley Harrier was designed as a forward-deployable, land-based fighter bomber. However, trials in 1963 clearly demonstrated that the Harrier could operate from even very small ships (almost any ship that could embark a helicopter) and the US Navy, the Royal Navy and the Soviet navy each began separately examining the concept of a small cheap carrier, embarking STOVL aircraft and helicopters. The US Navy called this type of vessel a 'Sea Control Ship', but eventually cancelled it.

Britain's Royal Navy has operated four 'Harrier Carriers': HMS Ark Royal, Hermes, Illustrious (shown here) and Invincible. Of these, only Hermes was not laid down as a Through-Deck Cruiser, being modified for Sea Harrier operations later in its life.

Budgetary constraints and political considerations forced the RN to officially abandon plans to embark Harriers on its new 'Through Deck Cruisers'. In fact, Britain pressed on with a class of ships that was actually capable of (but not officially intended for)

embarking Harriers, and this ploy paid off when the Sea Harrier was finally ordered in 1975.

In the meantime, however, the delays in Britain had allowed the Soviets to catch up. The original Yak-36 'Freehand' undertook brief trials aboard the

More than any other nation, Britain has proven the concept of the light carrier in modern warfare. HMS Invincible has seen action during the Falklands War and off the Balkans. Its Sea Harriers shot down seven Argentine aircraft in 1982.

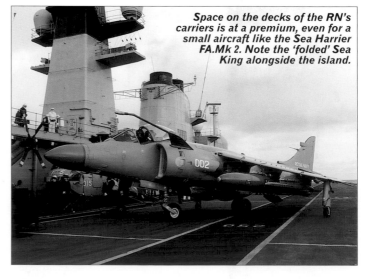

Space on the decks of the RN's carriers is at a premium, even for a small aircraft like the Sea Harrier FA.Mk 2. Note the 'folded' Sea King alongside the island.

CVF: BRITAIN'S NEXT CARRIER

On 30 September 2002, the British Government announced that 150 STOVL F-35B aircraft would be purchased to replace the country's Harrier/Sea Harrier fleet. The aircraft will operate from shore bases and from a new future aircraft carrier known as CVF. A pair of carriers is expected to be bought at a cost of £13 billion with a winning constructor from either BAE Systems (illustrated) or Thales to be announced in February 2003. The carriers will be built in such a way that they may be converted for CTOL operations at some point in the future.

helicopter-carrier *Moskva*, and a new class of 'Aviation Cruisers' was ordered. These were to be equipped with helicopters and a Yak-36-based multi-role fighter bomber. A service trials unit of the all-new Yak-38 'Forger' deployed in December 1975 and the first operational Yak-38 squadron deployed aboard the *Kiev* in July 1976. It was initially cleared for VTOL operations only, with 'rolling take-offs' and short landings cleared from 1979. This led to some misunderstanding, with many believing that the Yak-38's configuration with separate lift jets and propulsion engines, prevented it from making rolling take-offs and landings. The Yak-38 (and the more powerful Yak-38M) remained in service until 1993, with the withdrawal of their carriers.

'Harrier carriers'

The introduction of the Sea Harrier led to another round of alterations to the aircraft-carrier. The Harrier's unique engine configuration makes it easy for it to perform rolling take-offs.

Dedicated 'Harrier Carriers' do not have to be fitted with catapults or arrester gear, making them lighter and cheaper than conventional carrier equivalents. They also feature distinctive 'ski-jump' take-off ramps, although these were initially conceived as a safety device to give con-

In 2002/03, 'Harrier Carriers' were being operated by India, Italy (left), Spain, Thailand and the UK (below). The US Marine Corps operates its Harriers off amphibious assault ships in support of shore operations.

ventional carrierborne aircraft a 'boost' of altitude on launch. British 'experts' did not see the benefit of a ski-jump for conventional take-off and landing (CTOL) aircraft, but realised straightaway that it could increase the payload of a Sea Harrier on launch. It was also realised that much steeper ski-jumps would be useable by STOVL aircraft, and that steeper angles would confer bigger payload/range benefits.

The potential of STOVL aircraft and ski-jumps was convincingly demonstrated in the Falklands, and this led to intensive efforts to market a 'conversion package' which could convert any civilian ship into a temporary 'Harrier Carrier'. Known as SCADS, the package incorporated a ski-jump, runway and containerised hangarage and maintenance facilities.

Although British experts rejected the ski-jump for CTOL applications, the USN felt it had advantages, but that the benefits were outweighed by the cost of rebuilding existing carriers. Nevertheless, the new French carriers are being fitted with a narrow and fairly shallow ramp which will help rotate the noses of the Aéronavale's new Rafales. In the USSR, the ski-jump was embraced with even more enthusiasm on the USSR's new generation of carriers - only one of which – *Tbilisi*, (later *Admiral Kuznetsov*) – entered service. The ski-jump on this Russian ship is almost as steep as that used by the Sea Harrier and is used for STOBAR (Short Take-Off But Arrested Recovery) operations, by aircraft like the Su-27K, without thrust vectoring. By using deck-mounted holdbacks to restrain an aircraft as it runs up to full power, a heavy CTOL fighter like the Su-27K can take-off in a short distance from a relatively small, light ship by using a ski-jump.

Carriers of the future

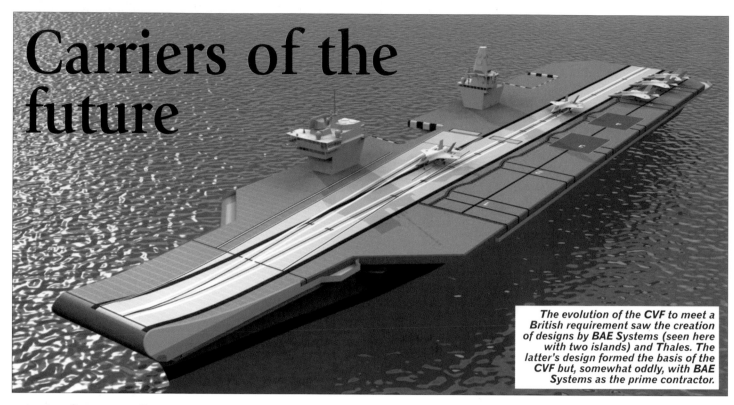

*The evolution of the CVF to meet a British requirement saw the creation of designs by **BAE Systems** (seen here with two islands) and **Thales**. The latter's design formed the basis of the CVF but, somewhat oddly, with **BAE Systems** as the prime contractor.*

Major air power at sea

At a time of changing and uncertain national imperatives, the aircraft carrier is still the most effective platform for long-range power projection, offering huge capabilities and excellent mobility.

The US Navy is committed to the development of an advanced-technology aircraft carrier for service through much of the 21st century. The service's goal is the creation of a sea-based tactical air platform that retains the warfighting relevance of the 'Nimitz' class, while allowing the US Navy to take advantage of maturing technologies to enhance capability at the same time as substantially reducing operating costs. An evolutionary progression of the current 'Nimitz' design, the new CVN-21 will have stealthier features than current carriers, but will not be a completely stealthy vessel.

The first ship is projected to be part of the fleet for at least 50 years through to 2063. In addition to the F/A-18E/F, the CVN-21 design will also integrate two emerging aircraft systems: the Joint Strike Fighter and Unmanned Combat Air Vehicle – Navy (UCAV-N). These three new aircraft systems, coupled with the navy's new Integrated Warfare System (IWS), will provide future joint force commanders with significantly enhanced strategic and operational capabilities.

CVN-21 (formerly known as CVNX-1) will feature a new-design nuclear propulsion plant incorporating the experience of three generations of submarine reactor development. The new propulsion system is necessary to reduce manning, maintenance, acquisition, and life-cycle costs. The new powerplant will be optimised to meet the large-scale electrical demands predicted for 21st century shipboard technology. A new electrical generation distribution system will also be a critical feature of the design.

Key innovative features in the new carrier will include an electromagnetic aircraft launch system that will have reduced manpower and maintenance requirements. This system will also extend aircraft life, as peak loads on the airframe will be reduced. This design utilises technology similar to that used by experimental maglev trains.

The benefits will include freeing the catapults from dependence on ship-generated steam, an increase in available energy, and a major reduction in both weight and volume. CVN-21 will have an advanced armour system to improve combat survivability. Commercial systems will be adapted for use in ship operations, habitability, mooring, and manoeuvring. An advanced weapons information management system will automate the process of inventory control, movement, and deployment of weapons from the magazine directly to the aircraft.

Royal Navy

The UK is also getting back into the 'carrier game'. The Strategic Defence Review announced plans to replace the current 'Invincible'-class carriers from 2012 with two larger and more capable ves-

*Left: An asset as valuable as an aircraft carrier must be very well defended. This **MBDA** image shows the **Charles de Gaulle** firing Aster 15 SAMs from one of the two Sylver A43 octuple launchers of the **SAAM/F** system.*

Below: An artist's concept of a possible CVN-21 configuration. Though based ultimately on the 'Nimitz'-class carrier, the CVN-21 will introduce a number of steadily more radical features.

sels able to operate a more powerful force. Successive operations in the Persian Gulf and off ex-Yugoslavia have demonstrated that aircraft carriers play a key role in force projection, contributing to peace support and, when necessary, military action. In these capacities the carrier offers both a coercive presence that can help contribute to conflict prevention, and also a flexible and rapidly deployable base for operations in which land-based airfields are currently unavailable or facilities ashore are still being established for use.

The three 'Invincible'-class aircraft carriers were designed for Cold War anti-submarine warfare operations in the North Atlantic. While undoubtedly effective in this role, their limited air groups mean they would be unable to fulfil the increasingly challenging demands of the new strategic environment. It was therefore decided to replace these vessels with two larger carri-

A photograph of the PCU (Pre-Commissioning Unit) Ronald Reagan (CVN-76), the US Navy's latest 'Nimitz'-class carrier, reveals the ship testing its countermeasure wash-down system to remove nuclear, biological and chemical agents.

ers that could each operate up to 46 aircraft, of both the fixed- and rotary-wing types.

The Future Aircraft Carrier, or CVF, will be the principal platform for the Royal Navy's and Royal Air Force's JCA (Joint Combat Aircraft), which will replace the two services' Harrier and Sea Harrier warplanes. The JCA will be capable of operating in all weathers, by day and night, to provide air defence for the carrier, as well as flying strike missions and conducting offensive support for ground forces ashore. The carrier air group will also include the Maritime Airborne Surveillance & Control (MASC) system, which will replace the capability provided by Sea King AEW helicopters. MASC will provide sensor coverage against air and surface threats, together with command and control for other air operations. The CVF will also be capable of supporting the operation of helicopters in a wide variety of roles including anti-submarine warfare, attack and support.

The STOVL variant of the F-35 JSF has been selected

Left: The design studies for the UK's planned CVF went though a number of evolutionary forms, this being a BAE Systems study of 2002 for a relatively conventional type with a single island and a 'ski-jump'.

to fulfil the JCA role and, in order to maximise the flexibility that CVF can offer over its potential 50-year service life, the carriers will be built to an innovative adaptable design. The ships will be fitted for but not with catapults and arrester gear, and a 'ski-jump' ramp will be installed in order to facilitate operation of the STOVL F-35 aircraft. If required, post-JSF, the design will be capable of modification to operate aircraft requiring both a catapult launch and arrested recovery.

Other navies

France operates the most modern operational carrier design in the shape of the nuclear-powered *Charles de Gaulle*, a 36,600-ton vessel that entered service in 2000. A second new carrier is scheduled for service in the 2012-15 timeframe, but this will not necessarily be a repeat design. Talks are currently ongoing with the UK about the possibility of combining both nations' distinct carrier requirements.

The Russian navy remains formally committed to air-

craft carrier development on the American model. Indeed, the commander-in-chief of the Russian navy has been quoted as viewing a 'Nimitz'-class CVN as 'ideal', but impractical given today's economic realities. The Russian active carrier fleet now consists only of the *Admiral Kuznetsov*, but maintenance of the vessel is already proving to be problematical. Assembling a trained crew has provided major challenges, and the lack of a carrier training facility on Russian territory is a further impediment to progress.

The only other major carrier project currently under way is in Italy. At 22,000 tons, the new 'Andrea Doria'-class unit will displace twice as much as the current 'Giuseppe Garibaldi' class of light ASW carrier, though it will be less than half the size of future British and French designs, and is a quarter the size of US Navy supercarriers. A multi-role design, the *Andrea Doria* will be able to serve as a landing ship for a force of 450 marines, a helicopter carrier, or an aircraft carrier able to operate eight STOVL fighters such as the F-35 JSF. Work on the ship began in 2001, and the vessel is due for delivery in 2007.

UCAV-N: FUTURE CARRIER AIR VEHICLE

The object of the US Navy's UCAV-N (Unmanned Combat Air Vehicle-Naval) programme is to validate the technical feasibility of creating an affordable naval unmanned combat air system to undertake the SEAD (Suppression of Enemy Air Defences), strike and surveillance roles within the context of the US's 'net-centric' command and control concept. Though optimised for carrierborne operation the UCAV-N is, for cost and interoperability reasons, to possess the maximum possible commonality with the US Air Force's land-based UCAV. The programme is looking at the whole gamut of appropriate technologies to ensure maximum operational capability in concert with low procurement and life-cycle costs, and is assessing the potential for 12 to 16 UCAV-Ns within the 'legacy force' carrier air wing.

USS *Lexington* Aircraft carrier

Under the final terms of the Washington Treaty, the US Navy was allowed to convert two of four incomplete 33,000-ton battlecruisers into aircraft carriers. The ships chosen were the *Lexington* and *Saratoga*, under construction by Fore River at Quincy and New York Shipbuilding at Camden, and the opportunity was sensibly taken to incorporate many ideas from a cancelled aircraft carrier design of 1919.

The **USS *Lexington*** (**CV-2**) was launched in October 1925 and when completed was a remarkable ship with a massive 'island' superstructure on the starboard side, flanked by two twin 8-in (203-mm) gun turrets forward and two aft. Other key features were a hull plated right up to the flight deck but with an opening for the launch and recovery of boats, a two-storied hangar arrangement, two centreline elevators for the movement of aircraft between the flight deck and the hangar decks, and one forward-located catapult. A feature retained from the ship's origins was the turbo-electric propulsion, with four turbo-generators supplying power to eight electric motors coupled two to a shaft.

Escape from Midway

At the time of Pearl Harbor the ship was delivering aircraft to the US Marines holding Midway Island, and so escaped the disaster. *Lexington* was hurriedly refitted, losing its cumbersome 8-in (203-mm) guns and four 5-in (127-mm) guns, although the vessel did receive a few single 20-mm Oerlikon guns to supplement its otherwise very meagre close-range anti-aircraft armament.

The *Lexington*'s first operation was a failed attempt to relieve Wake Island immediately after Pearl Harbor, but at the end of January 1942 the carrier provided cover for a raid on the Marshall Islands and thereafter saw limited action in the South West Pacific. Not until it was joined by the newer aircraft carrier *Yorktown* in March 1942 did the *Lexington* really

begin to flex its muscles.

Counter-strike

After a short refit at Pearl Harbor the *Lexington* returned to the Coral Sea, where the Japanese carriers were supporting an attack on Port Moresby, New Guinea. On 8 May *Lexington*'s SBD Dauntless dive-bombers attacked the Imperial Japanese navy's aircraft carriers *Shokaku* and *Zuikaku*, but without scoring any hits.

Unfortunately while this attack was in progress a Japanese counter-strike hit the *Lexington* with two torpedoes on the port side, and the ship also suffered two bomb hits and several near misses. The 'whip' of the hull from the explosions ruptured the aviation gasoline tanks, so that even after the fires had been extinguished, the lethal vapour continued to seep through the ship. About an hour after the

Above: The USS Lexington *(pictured), together with its sister ship USS* Saratoga, *helped to build the experience upon which the US Navy based its World War II carrier operations. The ships boasted a 137-m (450-ft) long hangar, as well as a 36.6-m (120-ft) hold for knocked-down aircraft. Additional aircraft could be suspended from the hangar roof.*

Left: Lexington's *distinctive funnel provided a useful mounting point for some of the advanced radar equipment that was added during 1941.*

attack a chance spark ignited this vapour, and the ship began to suffer a series of explosions. Six hours after the first hit the order was given to abandon ship, and after escorting destroyers had rescued as many men as possible, the wreck was torpedoed – 216 of 2,951 lives were lost.

In a short war career the *Lexington* failed to inflict severe damage on the enemy, largely as a result of the inexperience of its air group and faulty US Navy tactical doctrine. The loss of a big carrier was a heavy price for the Coral Sea victory.

SPECIFICATION
USS *Lexington* (CV-2) **Displacement:** 36,000 tons standard; 47,700 tons full load **Dimensions:** length 270.66 m (888 ft) overall; beam 39.62 m (130 ft) over flight deck; draught 9.75 m (32 ft) **Propulsion:** four General Electric turbo-generators delivering 156660 kW (210,000 shp) to four shafts **Speed:** 34 kts **Armour:** belt 152 mm (6 in); flight	deck 25 mm (1 in); main deck 51 mm (2 in); lower deck 25-76 mm (1-3 in); turrets 38-76 mm (1.5-3 in); barbettes 152 mm (6 in) **Armament:** (in 1942) eight 5-in (127-mm) AA, 30 20-mm AA and six quadruple 1.1-in (27.9-mm) AA guns **Aircraft:** (1942) 22 fighters, 36 dive-bombers and 12 torpedo-bombers **Complement:** 2,951

To encase the uptakes from 16 boilers, the **Lexington** *and* **Saratoga** *were each given a massive funnel. Both ships had their 8-in (203-mm) guns removed at the outbreak of World War II, and* **Saratoga** *was considerably altered in appearance by 1945.*

USS *Saratoga* Aircraft carrier

Like its sister ship, the USS *Lexington*, which was laid down in January 1921 at Bethlehem (Fore River), launched in October 1925 and commissioned on 14 December 1927, the aircraft carrier **USS *Saratoga* (CV-3)** was launched in April 1925 after conversion from an incomplete battlecruiser hull that had been laid down at New York Shipbuilding, and was commissioned on 16 November 1927. Like its sister ship, the *Saratoga* played a major role in developing the US Navy's important concept of the fast carrier task force, and from 1928 the two ships took part in the annual 'Fleet Problem' wargame of the Pacific Fleet. This organisation was the ideal parent for the two large aircraft carriers, which had the size, range and aircraft strength (by 1936 reduced from 90 aircraft to 18 fighters, 40 bombers and five utility aircraft) to play a decisive part in any future operations in the Pacific Ocean.

As completed, both of the ships has a primary gun armament of eight 8-in (203-mm) guns in four twin turrets grouped ahead and abaft the ships' massive island and funnel combination. The armament had originally been schemed on the basis of 6-in (152-mm) guns, the change to larger-calibre weapons probably being spurred by the probability of encountering 'treaty' cruisers with an armament of 8-in guns.

At the time of Pearl Harbor the 'Sara' was back at San Diego on the US west coast undergoing a short refit, but it sailed shortly after this time and took part with the 'Lex' in an abortive attempt to relieve the garrison of Wake Island. During the ship's refit the four twin 8-in turrets were removed, and in their place *Saratoga* received four twin 5-in (127-mm) L/38 dual-purpose

mountings controlled by two combined high/low-angle director control towers. At the same time the original secondary armament of 12 5-in (127-mm) L/25 low-angle guns was replaced by eight 5-in L/38 dual-purpose guns. The *Lexington*, it should be noted, had been stripped of its 8-in (203-mm) guns but had not been fitted with the 5-in replacement weapons.

The *Saratoga* was torpedoed by a Japanese submarine off Hawaii on 11 January 1942, and needed four months of repairs. At this time the flight deck was enlarged from its original length of 270.66 m (888 ft) to 274.7 m (901 ft 3 in), with width increased to 39.62 m (130 ft). At this time the *Saratoga* was also fitted with a deep port-side bulge to help restore the ship's buoyancy, already degraded from commissioning standard by the addition of extra equipment including a greater number of light AA weapons. The light AA armament was increased by the grouping of 100 40-mm guns in quadruple mountings along the sides of the flight deck and 16 single 20-mm guns at the flight deck's after end. Other changes included the heightening of the bridge, the replacement of the original tripod mast by a pole mast, and the addition of warning and gunnery-control radar.

Guadalcanal action

The 'Sara' was used to ferry fresh aircraft out to the Central Pacific, and so missed the decisive Battle of Midway, but was a welcome reinforcement by 8 June, the day after the sinking of the USS *Yorktown*. *Saratoga*'s fighters and dive-bombers were given the task of softening up the defences of Guadalcanal on 7 August 1942 before the big amphibious landing by the US Marine Corps. The Japanese responded vigorously to this

The USS Saratoga *(CV-3) in March 1932 with a large part of its air group at the forward end of the flight deck. The ship and its sister 'fought' each other in annual manoeuvres.*

The USS Saratoga *in World War II. This aircraft carrier played a major role in the Pacific, but despite its size was slowly relegated to less important tasks as the arrival of modern carriers revealed its limitations.*

challenge, and by 20 August a powerful carrier task force was nearing the Eastern Solomons.

The *Saratoga*, the USS *Enterprise* and the USS *Wasp* were heavily engaged in the Battle of the Eastern Solomons, but the 'Sara' escaped lightly. Not until 31 August did it sustain damage, when it took a torpedo hit from the submarine *I-68* just after dawn. The carrier

was not badly damaged by the hit, in spite of having one boiler room flooded and another partly flooded, but an electrical failure soon put its machinery out of action. Two hours later the carrier got back limited power, and reached Pearl Harbor six days later for six weeks of repairs.

In 1943-44 the *Saratoga* took part in the great 'island-hopping' drive across the Pacific, and in 1944 was detached to the East Indies, where it co-operated with the British and Free French

in attacking Japanese positions in Java and Sumatra. On 21 February 1945 it was hit by a kamikaze while supporting the landings on Iwo Jima. Although repaired, it was restricted to training duties at Pearl Harbor: it is indicative of the *Saratoga*'s battlecruiser origins that though larger than an 'Essex'-class carrier, it carried fewer aircraft.

On 25 July 1946, the *Saratoga*'s stripped hull was finally sunk in Bikini Atoll during the United States's early atomic bomb tests.

'Sara' in September 1944, painted in Camouflage Measure 32/11A. Twin 5-in (127-mm) and light AA guns had by this time replaced the original 8-in (203-mm) guns. Despite its age the ship was still the largest US carrier, if not the most capacious.

SPECIFICATION	
USS *Saratoga* (CV-3)	deck 25 mm (1 in); main deck
Displacement: 36,000 tons standard; 47,700 tons full load	51 mm (2 in); lower deck 25-76 mm (1-3 in); barbettes 152 mm (6 in)
Dimensions: length 270.66 m (888 ft) overall; beam 32.2 m (105 ft 6 in) hull; draught 9.75 m (32 ft)	**Armament:** (in 1945) four twin and eight single 5-in (127-mm) dual-purpose, 24 quadruple 40-mm
Propulsion: four General Electric turbo-generators delivering 156597 kW (210,000 shp) to four shafts	Bofors AA, two twin 40-mm Bofors AA, and 16 20-mm AA guns
Speed: 34 kts	**Aircraft:** (1945) 57 fighters and 18 torpedo-bombers
Armour: belt 152 mm (6 in); flight	**Complement:** (1945) 3,373

USS *Yorktown* Aircraft carrier

The Yorktown (CV-5) and its sister carriers were prototypes for the successful 'Essex' class. Although much smaller than the 'Lexington'-class carriers, they could actually carry more aircraft.

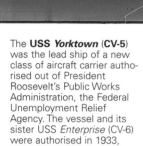

The **USS *Yorktown* (CV-5)** was the lead ship of a new class of aircraft carrier authorised out of President Roosevelt's Public Works Administration, the Federal Unemployment Relief Agency. The vessel and its sister USS *Enterprise* (CV-6) were authorised in 1933, and were followed by the USS *Hornet* (CV-8) five years later.

The design was a development of that of the *Ranger*, with an 'open' hangar rather than the 'closed' type of the *Lexington* and *Saratoga*, to allow up to 80 aircraft to be carried. This arrangement proved highly successful, and formed the basis for the even more successful 'Essex' class.

Battle of Coral Sea

The ship was commissioned in September 1937, and was hurriedly transferred to the Pacific after Pearl Harbor. Under Rear Admiral Frank J. Fletcher, it was sent to the South West Pacific in the spring of 1942, and took part in the Battle of the Coral Sea. Its Air Group 5, comprising 20 Grumman F4F Wildcat fighters, 38 Douglas SBD-5 Dauntless dive-bombers and 13 Douglas TBD Devastator torpedo-bombers, played a major role in the battle, sinking the light carrier *Shoho* in a bril-

liant attack lasting only 10 minutes. On the next day, 8 May, its dive-bombers inflicted damage on the carrier *Zuikaku*, but in return a force of Nakajima B5N 'Kate' torpedo-bombers and Aichi D3A 'Val' dive-bombers penetrated a dense screen of fighters and gunfire to score a devastating hit on the flight deck.

The bomb went through three decks before exploding, and numerous fires were started. The damage control parties brought the fires under control, and the ship was able to return to Pearl Harbor for repairs.

Battle of Midway

Working around the clock, the repair teams were able to get *Yorktown* back in action in only four days, just in time for the Battle of Midway in June 1942. At a crucial point in the battle, *Yorktown*'s dive-bombers took part in the attack on the Japanese carriers, and its aircraft were the only ones able to mount a search for the surviving Japanese carrier *Hiryu*. Even after the *Yorktown* was hit by three 250-kg (551-lb) bombs it was able to operate its aircraft, and it was not until it was hit by two torpedoes that *Yorktown* was fully out of action.

The carrier had already taken considerable punish-

The Yorktown's Curtiss SB2C Helldiver dive-bombers were eventually replaced by Douglas SBD-5 Dauntless dive-bombers, due to the unsatisfactory performance of the former.

ment during the Battle of the Coral Sea, but the *Yorktown* might have survived even this heavy damage, for by first light on 6 June salvage parties had put out the fires and had started to pump out the ship's flooded compartments. However, the Japanese submarine *I-168* put two more torpedoes into it, and early the next morning it capsized and sank.

Four of the eight 5-in (127-mm) anti-aircraft guns can be seen at the front of the USS Yorktown's island. Part of Yorktown's air wing of Curtiss SB2C Helldiver dive-bombers can be seen on the forward portion of the deck.

Above: USS Yorktown sitting in dock, preparing to sail from Pearl Harbor. The vessel would later be lost at the battle of the Coral Sea.

SPECIFICATION

USS *Yorktown* (CV-5)
Displacement: 19,800 tons standard; 27,500 tons with a full combat load
Dimensions: length 246.7 m (809 ft 6 in) overall; beam 25.3 m (83 ft); draught 8.53 m (28 ft)
Machinery: 4-shaft geared steam turbines delivering 89520 kW (120,000 shp)
Speed: 33 kts
Armour: belt 102 mm (4 in); main

deck 76 mm (3 in); lower deck 25-76 mm (1-3 in)
Armament: (1942) eight 5-in (127-mm) AA, four quadruple 1.1-in (27.94-mm) AA and 16 0.5-in (12.7-mm) machine-guns
Aircraft: (1942) 20 fighters, 38 dive-bombers and 13 torpedo-bombers
Complement: 2,919 officers and enlisted men

USS *Enterprise* Aircraft carrier

Attended by tug-boats, the USS Enterprise (CV-6) is seen at harbour in New York. Attempts to preserve the 'Big E' were unsuccessful, but the the impressive ships of the 'Yorktown'-class formed the basis of the subsequent 'Essex'-class aircraft carriers.

Easily the most distinguished carrier of the Pacific War, the 'Big E' played a major role in the US Navy's victory and epitomised the new type of warfare.

The **USS *Enterprise* (CV-6)** was the second of the **'Yorktown' class**, and joined the Pacific Fleet in 1938. Fortunately it and the other two carriers of the Pacific Fleet were away from Pearl Harbor on 7 December 1941 when the Japanese attacked.

Warship Enterprise

When they returned to Oahu they were immediately put into the front line, for the battle fleet no longer existed. Three days afterwards the *Enterprise's* aircraft sank the submarine *I-170*, the first Japanese submarine to be destroyed.

The *Enterprise* escorted its sister *Hornet* on the Tokyo Raid in April 1942, but did not embark B-25 bombers as its aircraft were to be used to sink the Japanese early warning picket line. Neither carrier was back in time for the Battle of the Coral Sea in the following month, but they joined the *Yorktown* in time for Midway in June. Here, the Douglas SBD Dauntlesses from the *Enterprise* sank the carriers *Kaga* and *Akagi*, and *Yorktown's* Dauntlesses flying off *Enterprise's* deck joined the group which sank the *Hiryu*. Two days later the *Enterprise's* dive-bombers sank the heavy cruiser *Mikuma* and damaged the cruiser *Mogami* and two destroyers.

The *Enterprise* covered the Guadalcanal landings in August 1942, and its aircraft shot down 17 Japanese aircraft in two days. During the Battle of the Eastern Solomons on 24 August, the vessel was hit by three bombs, and returned to Pearl Harbor where repairs continued for about two months. In the Battle of Santa Cruz on 26 October, *Enterprise* again took three hits, but was able to operate its aircraft, and as it was now the only US carrier left, it had to remain in the forward area. On 13 November its Grumman TBF Avenger torpedo-bombers finished off the damaged battleship *Hiei*, and next day devastated a troop convoy of 11 ships with no fewer than 26 bomb and six torpedo hits.

'Turkey Shoot'

Enterprise was finally given lengthy repairs in the United States and did not return to the Pacific until mid-1943. On 25 November 1943 one of its Avengers achieved the world's first night 'kill' at sea. It took part in the massive strike on Truk in February 1944, and in the famous 'Marianas Turkey Shoot' during the Battle of the Philippine Sea the following June. It continued in action into 1945, surviving two kamikaze attacks. A third kamikaze strike on 14 May finally brought its career to an end, for it had to return to the United States for major repairs.

At the end of the war, the *Enterprise* had one of the most impressive combat records of any allied ship, having participated and survived several of the major Pacific naval battles. As the holder of 19 Battle Stars, the 'Big E' was a candidate for preservation as a memorial, but efforts to save it came to nothing and in 1958 it was sold for scrap, releasing the name for the first nuclear carrier.

SPECIFICATION	
USS *Enterprise* (CV-6) **Displacement:** 19,800 tons standard; 25,500 tons full load **Dimensions:** length 246.74 m (809 ft 6 in); beam 34.75 m (114 ft) over flight deck; draught 8.84 m (29 ft) **Machinery:** 4-shaft geared steam turbines delivering 89520 kW (120,000 shp) **Speed:** 33 kts **Armour:** belt 102 mm (4 in); main	deck 76 mm (3 in); lower deck 25-76 mm (1-3 in) **Armament:** (1942) eight 127-mm (5-in) AA, four quadruple 1.1-in (27.94-mm) AA and 16 0.5-in (12.7-mm) machine-guns **Aircraft:** (1942) 27 fighters, 37 dive-bombers and 15 torpedo-bombers **Complement:** 2,919 officers and enlisted men

Left: **Enterprise,** *seen with aircraft ranged on the rear of the flightdeck, fought in most of the great Pacific carrier battles, from Midway to the Philippine Sea.*

Below: The much larger hulls of **Enterprise** *and* **Yorktown** *conferred superior seaworthiness than their predecessor* **Ranger,** *and increased speed by 4 kts.*

USS *Ranger* Light fleet aircraft carrier

The first US aircraft carrier designed and built as such, **USS *Ranger* (CV-4)** was the subject of a design exercise undertaken by a service with virtually no experience of aircraft carrier operations. As a result of the Washington Naval Treaty's terms, which had fixed a limit of 69,000 tons on new carrier construction and a maximum of 22,000 tons for any one ship, the new carrier was conceived to a tonnage well below that upper limit so that the US Navy could extract the maximum air fleet out of its allocated tonnage. In the *Ranger*, therefore, basic ship requirements were subordinated to carrier requirements and, by comparison with other navies' carriers, *Ranger* was slower, had inferior gun armament and was less well protected, but on the other hand carried a larger number of aircraft despite its small tonnage.

Construction

The *Ranger* had hangars and a flight deck built up over the hull without side plating, and which therefore made no contribution to the ship's structural strength. *Ranger* was originally designed with a flush deck, but during construction it became clear that an island was needed for several reasons, including the control of flightdeck operations. In combination with other changes, this increased the ship's tonnage well over the planned 13,800 tons. A feature created within the concept of the flush flight deck was the use of six hinged funnels, three on each side, which could be turned to the horizontal position while flight deck operations were in progress. The ship was built with only the most limited

protective armour, including a 25-mm (1-in) flightdeck and 51-mm (2-in) plate along the waterline over the machinery spaces, and this passive protection was complemented by eight 5-in (127-mm) L/25 AA guns in single mountings. The ship's original air group comprised 36 bombers, 36 fighters and four utility aircraft, and aircraft handling features included one elevator between the hangars and the flight deck, a single catapult at the forward end of the flight deck, and three cranes on each side for hoisting seaplanes (and also the ship's boats) in and out. The ship also carried 514210 litres (135,840 US gal) of aviation fuel for supporting aircraft operations.

Performance

Laid down in September 1931 at Newport News and launched in February 1933, *Ranger* recorded a speed of 29.9 kts in its trials at a displacement of 16,169 tons with 40730 kW (54,630 shp). Commissioned in July 1934, the ship was relatively unsuccessful, and in 1939 its captain reported that the ship frequently pitched too much for flight deck operations to be undertaken. *Ranger* was deemed too poorly protected and armed for first-line service. During World War II its operational service, with bolstered armament and another high-angle director control tower supplementing one added earlier in the war, was limited to the North African operation of November 1942 and a carrier raid on Norway in 1943, in company with elements of the Royal Navy's Home Fleet. After this, USS *Ranger* was relegated for use as a training carrier with its 5-in guns

Above: The USS **Ranger** *(CV-4) pictured in 1942. Designed as a flush-deck carrier,* **Ranger** *added a small island during construction.*

Left: Three SB2C Helldivers provide air cover for the **Ranger** *in the Pacific in June 1945. The vessel proved incapable of operating aircraft under heavy weather conditions.*

removed so that new radar equipments could be added.

AEW trials

In 1945, *Ranger* was involved in some of the first trials of AEW (Airborne Early Warning) aircraft, and by that time was armed with only 46 20-mm anti-aircraft cannon. The ship was finally sold for spare parts in January 1947.

SPECIFICATION	
USS *Ranger* (CV-4)	**Armour:** 25 mm (1 in) decks and
Displacement: 14,575 tons standard, 17,577 tons full load	51 mm (2 in) sides and bulkheads
Dimensions: length 234.39 m (769 ft) overall; beam 33.37 m (109 ft 6 in) over flight deck; draught 6.83 m (29 ft)	**Armament:** (1941) eight 5-in (127-mm) AA, 24 1.1-in (27.94-in) AA and 24 0.5-in (12.7-mm) AA; (1943) eight 5-in AA, 24 40-mm AA and 46 20-mm AA
Machinery: 2-shaft steam turbines delivering 39890 kW (39890 shp)	**Aircraft:** 76, 86 as aircraft transport
Speed: 29.25 kts	**Complement:** 1,788 officers and enlisted men (2,000 in war)

USS *Hornet* Fleet aircraft carrier

Although it was the third member of the 'Yorktown' class, the **USS *Hornet* (CV-8)** was authorised some years after its sisters. It commissioned on 20 October 1940, seven weeks before Pearl Harbor. After a shakedown cruise with its air group in the Caribbean in January 1942, the ship embarked the first twin-engine North American B-25 bombers for the famous Doolittle Raid on Tokyo. After two months of intensive trials and training the *Hornet* left for the Pacific on 2 April, carrying 16 B-25 Mitchell bombers.

Surprise raid

The raid on 18 April took the Japanese completely by sur-

prise, and most of the bombers reached China safely. The *Hornet*'s next assignment was the Battle of Midway, on 4-6 June 1942. Although its air group lost all its Douglas TBD Devastator torpedo-bombers and five Grumman TBF Avengers in an unsuccessful strike, and failed to hit the Japanese carrier *Hiryu* in a second strike, on the last day of the battle it made amends by sinking the damaged heavy cruiser *Mikuma* and inflicting severe damage

The new carrier **Hornet** *on trials in 1941. The vessel was commissioned seven weeks before Pearl Harbor and left for the Pacific in March 1942.*

Launched in December 1940, CV-8 was the seventh vessel to receive the name Hornet. The Hornet's role in the Doolittle raid was not revealed until 1943.

on its sister *Mogami*.

The *Hornet* was ferrying US Marine Corps fighters at the time of the Guadalcanal landings in August 1942, but after landing its aircraft it joined the *Wasp* and

Saratoga in the covering force. Although withdrawn to Espiritu Santo to avoid being sunk by submarines, it sortied early in October to attack Japanese targets, and on 25 October met the

Japanese carriers once more, in the Battle of Santa Cruz.

Fatal attack

On 26 October, after the two sides had located one another, the two American carriers launched an air strike (a total of 158 aircraft), while the four Japanese carriers launched most of their 207 aircraft. But while the *Hornet*'s torpedo-bombers and dive-bombers were on their way, 27 Japanese strike aircraft broke through the fighter screen and scored six bomb and two torpedo hits on the *Hornet*. Although heroic efforts were made to extinguish the fires and get the carrier underway, four hours later another Japanese strike scored a torpedo hit and two more

bomb hits. By now the US destroyers screening the *Hornet* were dangerously exposed, with the Japanese searching for them in the darkness. The decision was taken to scuttle the *Hornet*, but to the Americans' dismay, several torpedoes failed to detonate, and a total of 430 5-in (127-mm)

shells fired at the carrier's waterline had no appreciable effect. The waterlogged hulk was abandoned, but the Japanese found it impossible to tow it, and finally two Japanese destroyers gave the *Hornet* its death-blow in the early hours of 27 October.

SPECIFICATION	
USS *Hornet* (CV-8) **Displacement:** 19,000 tons standard, 29,100 tons full load **Dimensions:** length 252.2 m (827 ft 5 in) overall; beam 34.8 m (114 ft 2 in) over flight deck; draught 8.84 m (29 ft) **Machinery:** 4-shaft geared steam turbine's delivering 89520 kW (120,000 shp) **Speed:** 33 kts **Armour:** belt 64-102 mm (2½-4in);	main deck 76 mm (3 in); lower deck 25-76 mm (1-3 in) **Armament:** (1942) eight 5-in (127-mm) AA, four quadruple 1.1-in (27.94-mm) AA, 30 20-mm AA and nine 0.5-in (12.7-mm) machine-guns **Aircraft:** (1942) 36 fighters, 36 dive-bombers and 15 torpedo-bombers **Complement:** 2,919 officers and enlisted men

USS *Wasp* Light fleet aircraft carrier

Under the terms of the Washington Naval Treaty, the US Navy was restricted to 135,000 tons of aircraft-carriers, and so could only build a further 14,700 tons of carriers after the completion of *Lexington, Saratoga Ranger, Yorktown* and *Enterprise*. Thus in 1935 an improved version of the *Ranger* was ordered, also with modest speed and light armour but big aircraft capacity. The opportunity was taken to eradicate the worst faults of the *Ranger*, and the new carrier was given a proper island superstructure and better compartmentation.

The **USS *Wasp* (CV-7)** was commissioned in April 1941, and from the autumn of that year was in the Atlantic on training duties.

Late in March 1942 it went to the Mediterranean to ferry RAF Spitfires to Malta. At the beginning of July it left San Diego for the Pacific and took part in the Guadalcanal landings, where its aircraft flew more than 300 sorties. *Wasp* missed the Battle of the Eastern Solomons as it had been detached to refuel, and it returned to Noumea to take on board a consignment of fighter aircraft for the US Marines on Guadalcanal.

Substantial damage

Early in the afternoon of 15 September 1942 the *Wasp* flew off its fighters, but shortly afterwards was hit by three torpedoes fired by the Japanese submarine *I-19*. Two of the torpedoes

struck it on the port side near the aviation gasoline tanks, while the third struck higher up and damaged the refuelling system, which had already been ruptured.

The ship was very quickly gutted by fire and explosions, which proved impossible to contain as the torpedo detonations had also ruptured the fire mains. In less than an hour the order to abandon ship was given, and *Wasp* continued to burn for another 3½ hours; finally the destroyer USS *Lansdowne* was ordered to sink it, and four torpedoes were fired.

The *Wasp* proved the

The USS Wasp (CV-7) at Pearl Harbor on 8 August 1942, a month before it was sunk. The vessel offered even less underwater protection than the 'Yorktowns'.

least battle-worthy of all American carriers, and its loss provided important lessons for the future. A board of enquiry showed that the majority of the damage was caused by the third torpedo-hit, for the first two hits had left the machinery and auxiliary power undamaged. However, the shock of the

explosions and the 'whip' of the hull had knocked out electrical switchboards and the damage control organisation. Thereafter a series of subsidiary explosions of bombs, torpedoes, ammunition and aircraft fuel tanks wrecked the ship.

A port profile of the Wasp. The tall funnel made the vessel unique among US carriers. A small carrier, Wasp was designed to use up the remaining carrier tonnage allowed under the Washington Treaty.

SPECIFICATION	
USS *Wasp* (CV-7) **Displacement:** 14,700 tons standard, 20,500 tons full load **Dimensions:** length 225.93 m (741 ft 3 in) overall; beam 24.61 m (80 ft 9 in); draught 8.53 m (28 ft) **Machinery:** 2-shaft geared steam turbines delivering 55950 kW (75,000 shp) **Speed:** 29.5 kts **Armour:** belt 102 mm (4 in); main	and lower decks 38 mm (1½ in) **Armament:** (1942) eight 5-in (127-mm) AA, four quadruple 1.1-in (27.94-mm) AA and 30 20-mm AA guns. **Aircraft:** (1942) 29 fighters, 36 dive-bombers and 15 torpedo-bombers **Complement:** 2,367 officers and enlisted men

USS *Essex* Aircraft carrier

Large, sturdy, fast and able to carry large quantities of aircraft fuel and munitions in addition to its own considerable bunkerage, the USS Essex was ideally suited to the fast carrier operations characteristic of the US Navy's carrier operations later in World War II.

Seen in 1943, USS Essex, could handle every type of US Navy carrierborne warplane to enter service in World War II, but before the squadrons started to take-off on a mission, the flight deck could look very crowded.

The units of the 'Essex' class can claim to be the most cost-effective and successful aircraft carriers ever built. The specification, issued in June 1939, was for an improved 'Yorktown' class type but with the displacement increased by 7,000 tons to provide stronger defensive armament, thicker armour, more power and above all, more aviation fuel. With more than 6,300 tons of oil fuel the endurance was 27360 km (17,000 miles) at 20 kts,

while 690 tons of gasoline and 220 tons of ammunition pushed up the number of sorties which could be flown by the carrier's embarked squadrons before these essential supplies had to be replenished. In addition, the same number of aircraft could be carried, although in practice many more could be carried: the nominal strength was 82, but by 1945 a total of 108 latest-generation aircraft could be embarked.

Eleven units of the class

were ordered in 1940 and a further 13 were built during World War II. Building times were extremely short: **USS Essex (CV-9)** was built in 20 months, and the wartime average building time was cut to just 17½ months.

Into battle

The lead ship of its class, the *Essex* reached the Pacific in May 1943, by which time the US Navy's worst problems were over, but the vessel saw considerable and indeed heavy

fighting with the Fast Carrier Task Force, in which it served with the USS *Enterprise* and USS *Saratoga* as well as the light fleet carriers of the 'Independence' class. In the spring of 1944 the *Essex* was withdrawn for a short refit, but returned to join Task Group 12.1 for the raid on the Marcus Islands. Later the *Essex* formed part of the famous Task Group 38.3 within Task Force 38. On 25 November 1944, while supporting the Leyte Gulf landings, the ship was hit on the port side by a kamikaze, suffering 15 dead and 44 wounded, and had to be withdrawn for repairs. The carrier was back in action, however, after only three weeks.

In 1945 the *Essex* returned to TF 38 and took

part in the attacks on Lingayen, Formosa, the Sakishima Gunto, and Okinawa. With TF 58, the *Essex* took part in the final assault on Japan, and was one of the enormous fleet mustered in Tokyo Bay for the Japanese surrender in August 1945. On its return the battered carrier received its first full repairs and was put into reserve.

Capable and rugged

In retrospect, the design of the 'Essex' class proved to be ideal for the US Navy's operations in the Pacific. It was seaworthy and had the endurance needed to cover the enormous distances involved, not only for itself but for its aircraft. Despite its 'open' hangars, the class in general proved surprisingly rugged, and during the first 14 months in action only three units of the class were damaged by enemy action; apart from the USS *Franklin* (CV-13), which reappeared after the war, all returned to active service after sustaining severe battle damage.

Smoke billows from the USS Essex following a kamikaze attack by a Japanese aircraft in the Pacific on 25 November 1944.

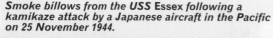

SPECIFICATION	
USS Essex (CV-9)	(127-mm) AA, 11 quadruple 40-mm
Displacement: 27,100 tons standard and 33,000 tons full load	Bofors AA, and 44 20-mm AA guns
Dimensions: length 267.21 m (876 ft 8 in); beam 45 m (147 ft 8 in) over flight deck; draught 8.69 m (28 ft 6 in)	**Armour:** belt 64-102 mm (2.5-4 in); flight deck 38 mm (1.5 in); hangar deck 76 mm (3 in); main deck 38 mm (1.5 in); turrets and barbettes 38 mm (1.5 in)
Propulsion: geared steam turbines delivering 111900 kW (150,000 shp) to four shafts	**Aircraft:** (1943) six fighters, 36 dive-bombers and 18 torpedo-bombers
Speed: 33 kts	**Complement:** 3,240
Armament: (1943) 12 5-in	

USS *Princeton* and 'Independence' class Light carriers

To meet its acute shortage of carriers after Pearl Harbor, the US Navy decided to complete nine 'Cleveland' class light cruisers as carriers. The *Amsterdam* (CL-59), *Tallahassee* (CL-61), *New Haven* (CL-76), *Huntington* (CL-77), *Dayton* (CL-78), *Fargo* (CL-85), *Wilmington* (CL-79), *Buffalo* (CL-99) and *Newark* (CL-100) thus became the ***Independence*** (**CVL-22**), ***Princeton*** (**CVL-23**), ***Belleau Wood*** (**CVL-24**), ***Cowpens*** (**CVL-25**), ***Monterey*** (**CVL-26**), ***Langley*** (**CVL-27**), ***Cabot*** (**CVL-28**), ***Bataan*** (**CVL-29**) and ***San Jacinto*** (**CVL-30**).

'Independence' class

Although it was an ingenious conversion, the results were disappointing, for the small hangar, measuring 65.5 m (215 ft) by 17.7 m (58 ft) could accommodate fewer aircraft than that of the 'Sangamon'-class escort carriers: 33 instead of the 45 planned. However, this **'Independence' class** had the speed to keep up with the fast carriers, and that fact kept its members in the front line.

The *Princeton* was commissioned late in February 1943, just over a month after the lead ship *Independence*, and arrived at Pearl Harbor in August 1943 to begin exercising with the new *Essex* and *Yorktown*. They launched their first strike on 1 September against Marcus Island. Five weeks later the *Princeton* and two other CVLs joined in a successful raid on Wake Island.

Battle of Leyte Gulf

During the Battle of Leyte Gulf the *Princeton* was part of Task Group 38.3, in the main Fast Carrier Group. On the morning of 24 October 1944 a lone D4Y dive-bomber came out of cloud cover and dropped two 250-kg (551-lb) bombs on the flight deck of the *Princeton*. The bombs passed through three decks before exploding, and the blast started fierce fires in the hangar. Six armed Avengers caught fire, and their torpedoes exploded, adding to the carnage. At 10.10 hours, about half an

hour after the attack, other ships were ordered alongside to take off all but essential firefighters and damage-control personnel.

The light cruisers *Birmingham* and *Reno* lay alongside, pumping water and providing power for the carrier's own pumps, and all the while ships and friendly aircraft fought off Japanese air attacks. At 1445 hours it appeared that all fires were out, but at 1523 hours the *Princeton* blew up in a huge explosion. The blast swept

the crowded decks of the *Birmingham*, killing 229 men and wounding 420; the carrier itself had over 100 men killed and 190 injured. Surprisingly the shattered hulk of the *Princeton* was still afloat, but wrecked beyond any hope of salvage. At 1600 hours the carrier was abandoned and the cruiser USS *Reno* was ordered to sink the hulk with two torpedoes after the destroyer USS *Irwin* had missed it with four.

Above: An 'Independence'-class light carrier at sea, the after part of her flight deck crowded with aircraft. Note the four funnels and diminutive bridge island.

Left: An 'Independence'-class carrier rides at anchor. The class made a vital contribution at a time when 'Essex'-class ships were not available in numbers.

Below: As seen from the USS Independence (CVL-22), the USS Langley (CVL-27) pitches in heavy seas en route to attack targets on the Japanese mainland during March 1945. In the background are escorting light cruisers ready to help ward off air attacks.

SPECIFICATION	
USS *Princeton* (CVL-23) **Displacement:** 11,000 tons standard and 14,300 tons full load **Dimensions:** length 189.74 m (622 ft 6 in); beam 33.3 in (109 ft 3 in) over flight deck; draught 7.92 m (26 ft) **Propulsion:** geared steam turbines delivering 74600 kW (100,000 shp) to four shafts **Speed:** 31.5 kts	**Armament:** (1943) two 5-in (127-mm) AA, two quadruple 40-mm Bofors AA, nine twin 40-mm Bofors AA and 12 20-mm AA guns **Armour:** belt 38-127 mm (1.5-5 in); main deck 76 mm (3 in); lower deck 51 mm (2 in) **Aircraft:** (1943) 24 F4F Wildcat fighters and nine TBF Avenger torpedo-bombers **Complement:** 1,569

The **Princeton** *(CVL-23) was converted on the stocks from the hull of the light cruiser Tallahassee. Although cramped, the CVLs were fast and could keep up with the Fast Carrier Groups. Later they operated night fighters.*

The USS Intrepid *trails smoke after a kamikaze hit. In all the vessel was hit three times by kamikazes and was also torpedoed once, but survived.*

USS *Intrepid*

In action

Possessing a maximum speed of 32.7 kts and a range of 27800 km (17,275 miles) at 15 kts, the *Intrepid* was also excellently protected and carried a large air group of advanced aircraft flown by skilled crews. In combination with large quantities of ordnance and aviation fuel, the ship was thus a potent fighting machine well able to take the war to the Japanese across the expanses of the Pacific Ocean. Many times the *Intrepid*'s warplanes devastated Japanese naval and air bases, sank and crippled ships, and supported US amphibious forces. Kamikaze aircraft hit *Intrepid*, making necessary repair visits to the US west coast, but the well-built ship survived to return for more.

The USS Intrepid *launches an attack on targets in the Japanese home islands, an Avenger torpedo-bomber being caught by the camera as it leaves the ship's port catapult, while three Helldivers wait with wings folded. The date was 19 March 1945.*

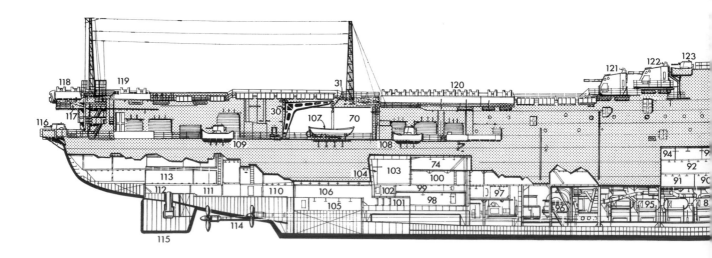

CVS-11: THE 'NEW' *INTREPID*

Decommissioned in 1947, the *Intrepid* was taken in hand for a major upgrade between 1952 and 1954 to re-emerge as the CVA-11 attack carrier with more powerful catapults, a strengthened flight deck and a new island. The ship was then revised with an enclosed bow and angled flight deck before being reclassified in 1962 as the CVS-11 for the anti-submarine role. After service mainly in European waters, the ship was revised for the embarkation of a group of light attack warplanes as a 'special attack carrier' for service off Vietnam, where the vessel is seen in the South China Sea during 1968. The *Intrepid* was finally decommissioned in 1974 and is now a museum.

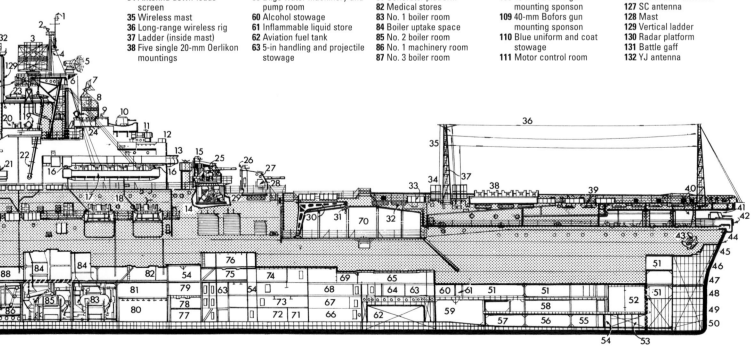

Above: The USS Intrepid *in the Pacific in the spring of 1945. Visible here are two of the four 5-in (127-mm) L/38 DP gun mountings that constituted the heaviest element of the ship's gun armament.*

USS *Intrepid*

1 YE antenna
2 SG surface warning radar antenna
3 SK air warning radar antenna
4 Repair platform
5 SM radar antenna
6 Mast head platform
7 Mk 4 fire control radar antenna
8 Mk 37 director for 5-in guns
9 Target designator, port and starboard
10 40-mm Bofors mounting
11 Mk 51 director
12 Navigating bridge
13 Flag bridge
14 5-in handling room and ready service ammunition
15 5-in L/38 DP twin gun mounting

16 Mk 51 director
17 Six single 20-mm Oerlikon AA gun mountings
18 Three 40-mm Bofors quadruple mountings (three aft)
19 36-in searchlight
20 Single 20-mm Oerlikon AA gun
21 Three single 20-mm Oerlikon AA gun mountings
22 Trash burner smoke pipe
23 Stack hood
24 24-in searchlight
25 Trunnion
26 Mount captain's blast hood
27 Trainer's telescope
28 Side access door
29 Barbette (fixed to ship)
30 Crane jib
31 Main lift hook
32 Life rafts
33 Life net rack
34 Antenna down-leads screen
35 Wireless mast
36 Long-range wireless rig
37 Ladder (inside mast)
38 Five single 20-mm Oerlikon mountings

39 Flight deck
40 Galley deck
41 Forward quadruple 40-mm mounting
42 Forecastle deck
43 30,000-lb stockless bower anchor
44 Main deck
45 Second deck
46 Third deck
47 Fourth deck
48 First platform
49 Second platform
50 Hold
51 Store
52 Chain locker
53 Sump tank
54 Watertight trunk
55 Pump room
56 Incendiary bombs stowage
57 Pyrotechnics stowage
58 Torpedo exercise heads stowage
59 Bilge water machinery and pump room
60 Alcohol stowage
61 Inflammable liquid store
62 Aviation fuel tank
63 5-in handling and projectile stowage

64 Small arms magazine
65 Detention cells
66 Aviation lubricating oil tank pump room
67 40-mm and 20-mm AA ammunition stowage
68 Bomb stowage
69 Bomb vanes stowage
70 Roller curtain openings in hangar sides
71 Aviation lubricating oil
72 40-mm AA ammunition stowage
73 Rocket motor stowage
74 Crew's berthing
75 Damage control HQ
76 Crew's mess
77 CIC (Combat Information Centre)
78 Plotting room
79 Bomb fuse magazine
80 Forward auxiliary machine room
81 Generator platform
82 Medical stores
83 No. 1 boiler room
84 Boiler uptake space
85 No. 2 boiler room
86 No. 1 machinery room
87 No. 3 boiler room

88 Clothes and small stores
89 Fire brick stowage
90 Barber's shop
91 Athletic gear stowage
92 General workshop
93 Crew's toilet
94 Crew's washroom and showers
95 No. 4 boiler room
96 No. 2 machinery room
97 Aft auxiliary machinery room
98 Bomb stowage
99 Rocket motor stowage
100 Aviation stores
101 Plotting room
102 Air flask stowage
103 Torpedo stowage
104 Gas trunk
105 Pump rooms
106 Fruit and vegetable stowage
107 26-ft motor whaleboat
108 40-mm Bofors gun mounting sponson
109 40-mm Bofors gun mounting sponson
110 Blue uniform and coat stowage
111 Motor control room

112 Steering gear room
113 Aviation engine stowage
114 Four-blade propeller and shaft units
115 Rudder
116 Stern 40-mm quadruple mounting
117 Walkway
118 Two single 20-mm Oerlikon AA gun mountings
119 Two single 20-mm Oerlikon AA gun mountings
120 10 single 20-mm Oerlikon AA gun mountings
121 5-in L/38 DP Mk 32 twin mounting
122 5-in L/38 DP Mk 32 twin mounting
123 40-mm Bofors mounting
124 40-mm Bofors mounting
125 Ensign staff
126 Mk 4 radar antenna
127 SC antenna
128 Mast
129 Vertical ladder
130 Radar platform
131 Battle gaff
132 YJ antenna

USS *Intrepid*

The USS *Intrepid* (CV-11) was the third ship of the 'Essex' class, not only the largest class of major warships ever built but also the most effective. The ship and four of its sisters were ordered under Fiscal Year 1940 programmes, while the remaining six of the first group were ordered under FY 1941. A further 15 were laid down during the war, and 17 of them entered service before VJ-Day. The *Intrepid* was floated out of its building dock on 26 April 1943, and such was the speed of wartime construction that it was commissioned on 16 August, less than four months later, and only 20 months after being laid down. The carrier's first task was to finish sea trials and allow the raw crew to 'shake down', and when the ship's organisation was ready the time came to embark the air group. By late 1943 the flying schools had expanded enormously and there was no shortage of well-trained aircrew to make good the losses in battle, but they still needed a period of intense training at sea. Combat experience had shown the need for new tactics, particularly in air defence, and these tactics could only be exercised with an embarked air group.

Air group
The air group of the 'Essex'-class aircraft carrier was a nominal 80 aircraft. In 1943 the air group was somewhat larger, and its 91 aircraft comprised 36 Grumman F4F Wildcat fighters, 37 Douglas SBD Dauntless dive-bombers and 18 Grumman TBF Avenger torpedo-bombers. The capability of these aircraft to undertake sustained operations was ensured by the provision of magazines for a large quantity of ordnance and also tankage for 908500 litres (240,000 US gal) of aviation fuel.

Propulsion
The propulsion arrangement of the 'Essex'-class aircraft carriers was based on an arrangement of four propellers driven by four sets of Westinghouse steam turbines driven by steam from eight Babcock & Wilcox oil-fired boilers. In the early ships, including the *Intrepid*, the turbines were geared, but in the others they were of the direct-drive type. In the ships of the first group as well as the *Hancock* and *Ticonderoga*, the oil bunkerage was 6,161 tons, rising to 6,331 tons in all of the others of the 13-strong second group except the *Randolph*, which carried 6,251 tons of oil.

Flight deck
The *Intrepid* had an overall length of 267 m (876 ft) and a hull beam of 28.35 m (93 ft) although the flight deck was 44.96 m (147 ft 6 in) wide. The design of the 'Essex' class was schemed with three catapults installed as two longitudinal units on the flight deck and one double athwartships unit on the hangar deck. Weight considerations meant that the first ships were completed with only one flight-deck catapult, but the athwartships unit proved effectively useless and was soon discarded, allowing a second catapult to be added on the flight deck.

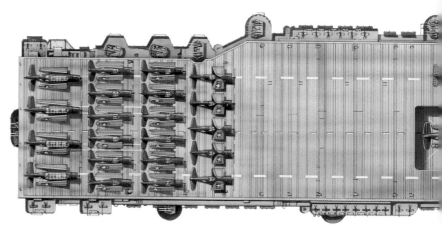

Secondary armament
As completed, the *Intrepid* had a secondary armament of eight quadruple mountings for 40-mm Bofors guns, but the intensity of Japanese air attacks in the war's later stages dictated a radical enhancement of the secondary armament. In the case of the *Intrepid*, this amounted to 17 quadruple Bofors mountings by the end of the war

Tertiary armament
The dictates of high-intensity Japanese air attacks in the Pacific theatre led to the introduction of a steadily enlarged complement of 20-mm Oerlikon cannon in single mountings spotted wherever there was sufficient deck area. By the end of World War II the *Intrepid* carried 52 such cannon, which supplemented the efforts of the 40-mm Bofors guns in putting up a veritable wall of HE projectiles through which Japanese kamikaze aircraft had to penetrate before reaching the ship.

Basic design
Despite the fact that it was designed without any treaty-imposed restrictions and was therefore fully optimised for the US Navy concept of carrier warfare, the design of the 'Essex' class avoided the British concept of the flight deck being built as part of the hull. Thus the hangars and flight deck were built as superstructure, and as such made no real contribution to the strength of the hull.

The vessel is painted in Camouflage Measure 32/A, which it carried from June 1944, when it returned to the Pacific after repairs. During its three months in dock *Intrepid* received three additional quadruple 40-mm Bofors gun mountings below the island, and two more were resited to improve their sky arcs.

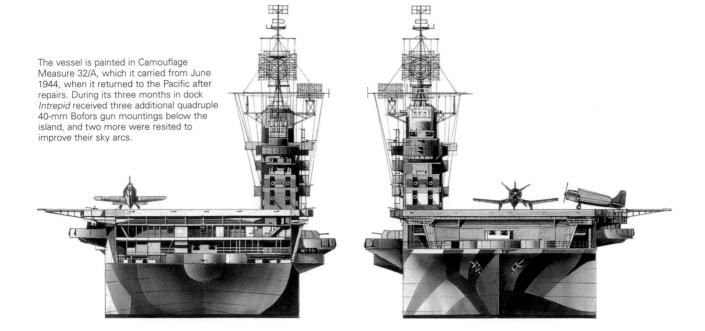

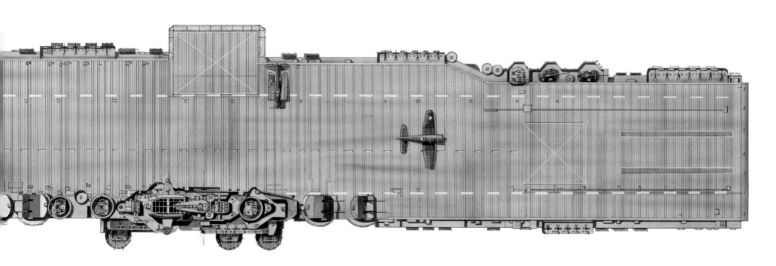

Aircraft elevators

The wooden-planked rather than steel flight deck of the *Intrepid* and the other 'Essex'-class aircraft carriers was connected to the hangar deck by three aircraft elevators. Two of these were in the 'standard' positions in the flight deck fore and aft of the island superstructure, while the third was installed, as had been pioneered in the *Wasp*, on the port side of the flight deck. This last proved so successful that many senior carrierborne aviation officers requested later in the war that the forward elevator be revised to a similar configuration.

Protection

The ships of the 'Essex' class proved themselves to be very well built and excellently protected. Despite heavy damage, none of the ships was lost, and damage was generally repaired quickly. The main belt of armour was 63.5 and 102 mm (2.5 and 4 in) thick along its lower and upper edges respectively, and other thicknesses included 51-76 mm (2-3 in) for the bulkheads, 38 mm (1.5 in) for the flight and main decks as well as the turrets, and 76 mm (3 in) for the hangar deck.

Island

Command and control of the *Intrepid* was exercised from the bridge and other compartments in the island superstructure located, as always on American aircraft carriers, on the starboard side of the flight deck with the stacks from the boiler rooms trunked through its after part. Fore and aft were eight of the ship's 5-in (127-mm) L/38 DP main guns in four twin mountings, the other four being located in single mountings below the port edge of the flight deck. The island carried search radar antennae and two radar-equipped directors for the 5-in gun mountings.

Radio equipment

The arrangement of two lattice masts and horizontal wires, located right forward and off the starboard side of the flight deck was the antenna group for the ship's long-range radio equipment. Also evident is the location, over virtually every other available patch of deck with any type of sky arc, of the ship's secondary and tertiary anti-aircraft guns of 40-mm Bofors and 20-mm Oerlikon cannon.

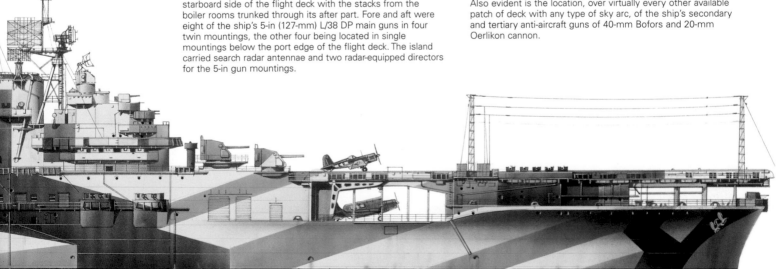

USS *Bogue* Escort carrier

The urgent need for air cover for convoys in the Atlantic was met by converting mercantile hulls into small aircraft carriers. In summer 1941 both the British and the Americans converted merchantmen into the first experimental 'escort carriers' or CVEs, and when these proved their worth orders went out for the first production class of 21 CVEs from US shipyards. Of these, 11 went to the UK as the 'Attacker' class, while the remainder became the US Navy's **'Bogue' class**. Being conversions of partially completed hulls, the 'Bogue' class was a great improvement on the prototypes, and had a full-length hangar, with two centreline lifts. The **USS Bogue (CVE-9)** and its sisters USS *Card* and USS *Core* even had two catapults. They carried 28 aircraft, and the *Bogue* was launched in January 1942. With a good outfit of air-warning radar and

more space than the destroyers and frigates, escort carriers made good flagships for the 'hunter-killer' or anti-submarine support groups, being established in the autumn of 1942. The *Bogue* and its support group sank no fewer than 13 U-boats.

The USS *Bogue* joined the Atlantic Fleet in February 1943 as the Battle of the Atlantic reached crisis point. On the vessel's fourth Atlantic crossing its aircraft sank a first U-boat; two more followed on the next trip. On the seventh cruise, in July 1943, *Bogue*'s aircraft sank one U-boat, and an escorting destroyer sank another.

The worst point of the battle was now over, and the tide had turned against the U-boats. Hunter-killer groups could not take the offensive against U-boats farther out in the Atlantic, and in late 1943 the *Bogue* and its group accounted for three U-boats. After a short break early in

The escort carrier Bogue (CVE-9) with Avenger torpedo-bombers on the wooden flight deck.

1944 to ferry aircraft to the UK *Bogue* returned to submarine-hunting, and in March helped to sink *U-575*. Three more U-boats were sunk by September 1944, when the *Bogue* returned to the US for a period on training duties. *Bogue*'s last hunter-killer mission in April 1945 accounted for the last of 13 U-boats.

In the closing months of

the war *Bogue* was sent to the Pacific, ferrying aircraft and stores to outlying garrisons. With the collapse of

Japan *Bogue* was assigned to 'Magic Carpet' operations, ferrying PoWs and servicemen back to the US.

SPECIFICATION	
USS Bogue (CVE-9)	**Speed:** 18 kts
Displacement: 11,000 tons standard; 15,400 tons full load	**Armour:** none
Dimensions: length 151.1 m (495 ft 8 in) overall; beam 34 m (111 ft 6 in) over flight deck; draught 7.92 m (26 ft)	**Armament:** two 5-in (127-mm) AA, four twin 40-mm Bofors AA and 12 20-mm AA guns
Machinery: 1-shaft geared steam turbine delivering 6340 kW (8,500 shp)	**Aircraft:** (1943) 12 F4F Wildcat fighters and 12 TBF Avenger torpedo-bombers
	Complement: 890 officers and enlisted men

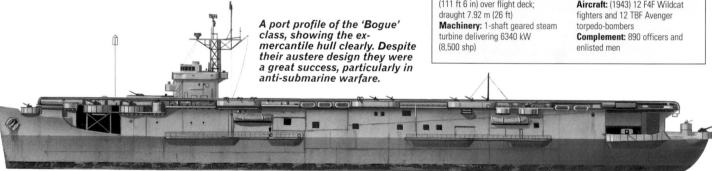

A port profile of the 'Bogue' class, showing the ex-mercantile hull clearly. Despite their austere design they were a great success, particularly in anti-submarine warfare.

'Sangamon' class Escort carrier

The conversion of escort carriers was given top priority in 1942, but the rate at which these useful utility carriers could be brought into service was limited by the number of hulls available. Four newly built US Navy oilers, the *Sangamon* (AO-28), *Santee* (AO-29), *Chenango* (AO-31) and *Suwannee* (AO-33), were taken out of commission in January 1942, reclassified as AVGs (Aircraft Escort Vessels) and were immediately stripped of superstructures and fittings for a conversion lasting six to eight months. Despite being an adaptation, the

The Sangamon's port profile shows its tanker origin, with the original well deck marked by large openings in the sides. Being fast and capacious, they were the most successful of all the CVE conversions.

'Sangamon' class was more successful than the earlier escort carriers, being larger and faster. Designed as tankers, they had their machinery right aft, and thus the small smoke-ducts caused less interference with flying operations. Provision was made for two catapults, although the second unit was not installed until 1944, and a number of large openings in the sides provided good ventilation for the hangar.

The *Santee* (AVG-29, later **CVE-29**) was the first to be commissioned, on 24 August 1942, followed a day later by

the *Sangamon* (CVE-26); the *Suwannee* (CVE-27) was commissioned on 24 September, five days after the *Chenango* (CVE-28). The shortage of carriers in late 1942 and early 1943, combined with their good turn of speed and aircraft capacity meant that these new carriers were used with the main fleet more than other CVEs, and frequently operated together.

All four supported the landings in North Africa in October and November 1942, and then transferred to the Pacific, where they operated with CarDiv 22 in the South Pacific. The *Santee* returned to the Atlantic in March 1943, operating south of the Azores and off the coast of Brazil with a hunter-killer group, but rejoined the other ships of the class in the Pacific in February 1944,

as the great 'island-hopping' drive across the Pacific got underway.

Battle of Leyte Gulf
All four took part in the Battle of Leyte Gulf, forming 'Taffy One' as part of Task Group 77.4. On 25 October the *Santee* was badly damaged by a kamikaze attack, and shortly afterwards by a torpedo hit from the submarine *I-56*, but managed to

survive. Then a kamikaze hit the *Suwannee*, having missed the *Sangamon*. In spite of these hits all three were operational by the spring of 1945. The *Sangamon* was badly damaged by a kamikaze hit off Okinawa on 4 May 1945, and lost 11 dead, 21 seriously wounded and 25 missing, but like its sisters, proved rugged enough to be returned to service.

SPECIFICATION	
USS Sangamon (CVE-26)	**Armament:** two 5-in (127-mm) AA, two quadruple 40-mm Bofors AA, seven twin 40-mm Bofors AA and 21 20-mm AA guns
Displacement: 10,500 tons standard; 23,875 tons full load	
Dimensions: length 168.71 m (553 ft 6 in) overall; beam 34.82 m (114 ft 3 in) over flight deck; draught 9.32 m (30 ft 7 in)	**Aircraft:** (1942) 12 F4F Wildcat fighters, nine SBD Dauntless dive-bombers and nine TBF Avenger torpedo-bombers
Machinery: 2-shaft geared steam turbines delivering 10070 kW (13,500 shp)	**Complement:** 1,100 officers and enlisted men
Speed: 18 kts	
Armour: none	

USS *St Lô* Escort carrier

The success of the converted CVEs led to a fresh design being prepared 'from the keel up', using a mercantile design as a basis but tailoring it to meet CVE needs, rather than adapting a hull on the slipway. These adaptations were more concerned with ease of construction than any radical improvement in operational capability. In all, 50 units of the 'Casablanca' class (CVE-55 to 104) were authorised late in 1942. Although the flight deck was short (152.4 m/500 ft by 32.9 m/ 108 ft), two lifts and a catapult were provided, and as there were two propeller shafts there was greater manoeuvrability than with one shaft. To speed up manufacture, triple-expansion

steam machinery was chosen, but in other respects the 'Casablanca' design took the best of the 'Sangamon', 'Bogue' and 'Prince William' classes, and was a considerable success.

Service entry

The **USS *St Lô*** (**CVE-63**) was laid down as the *Chapin Bay* (**AVG-63**) at Henry Kaiser's Vancouver shipyard in January 1943, but in April the ship was renamed *Midway* in honour of the recent battle, and entered service under that name in October 1943. The name was then allocated to a much bigger carrier, as it was considered too important for such a minor warship, and on 15 September 1944 CVE-63

became the USS *St Lô*. The diminutive carrier had already made two ferry trips out to the Pacific and had supported the amphibious landings in Saipan, Eniwetok, Tinian and Morotai. In October 1944 *St Lô* formed part of 'Taffy Three' (under Rear Admiral Thomas L. Sprague), part of the vast armada which fought the Battle of Leyte Gulf. 'Taffy Three', the most northern group of escort carriers covering the amphibious landing, had already suffered a gruelling bombardment from Japanese surface warships for the best part of three hours during the morning of 25 October 1944. After a lull of about one hour the kamikazes made a low-level attack, five A6M Zeros coming in at low level before climbing rapidly to 1525 m (5,000 ft) and then diving straight onto the flight deck. One of a pair attacking the *Fanshaw Bay* suddenly switched to the *St Lô*, striking the flight deck aft. The two bombs slung underneath the Zero set off gasoline,

bombs and ammunition in the hangar, wrecking the aircraft carrier. The kamikaze hit at 10.53, and five minutes later a huge explosion devastated the carrier. *St Lô* sank about one hour later, with 100 dead and many injured.

The new escort carrier USS Midway (CVE-63) was subsequently renamed St Lô to release the name for a larger and more prestigious carrier. The St Lô was the first US ship lost to a kamikaze attack.

The port profile of the 'Casablanca' class; these ships were an improved version of the 'Bogue' design, tailored for faster construction.

SPECIFICATION	
USS *St Lô* (CVE-63)	**Speed:** 19 kts
Displacement: 7,800 tons standard; 10,400 tons full load	**Armour:** none
	Armament: one 5-in (127-mm) AA, eight twin 40-mm Bofors AA and 20 AA guns
Dimensions: length 156.13 m (512 ft 3 in) overall; beam 39.92 m (108 ft) over flight deck; draught 6.86 m (22 ft 6 in)	**Aircraft:** (October 1944) 17 F4F Wildcat fighters and 12 TBF Avenger torpedo-bombers
Machinery: 2-shaft vertical triple expansion delivering 6715 kW (9,000 shp)	**Complement:** 860 officers and enlisted men

---

USS *Langley* Aircraft transport

The potential of naval aviation was so clearly seen at the end of World War I that the US Navy wanted to press ahead with the construction of aircraft carriers. In order to gain practical experience before building new ships it was essential to carry out experiments, and the quickest and cheapest way was to convert an existing ship.

The large fleet collier *Jupiter* (AC-3) was taken in hand in March 1920. A month later it was renamed **USS Langley** (**CV-1**) and started trials in July 1922. The ship which emerged was flush-decked, with two hinged funnels on the port side. The former coal holds had been converted to workshops, accommodation and storerooms, while the former upper deck was now the hangar. The biggest drawback to the *Langley* was its low speed, for the 5335-kW (7,150-shp) turbo-electric machinery was badly underpowered. In service the *Langley* could only make 14 kts, which was some 7 kts below the speed of the battle fleet. In spite of this handicap *Langley* served with the fleet, and for five years played the role which was to be taken over so successfully by the *Lexington* and *Saratoga* from 1928 onwards.

The old Langley, with the forward part of its flight deck removed, served as a seaplane carrier from 1936. In its short wartime career, the first US carrier acted as an aircraft transport until sunk by Japanese bombers in February 1942.

Although originally designed to operate 24 aircraft, a capacious hangar allowed a maximum of 33 to be accommodated. *Langley* did not stop operating aircraft until 1936, when the vessel was converted to a seaplane carrier and redesignated **AV-3**. After a refit *Langley* reappeared in April 1937 with a short flight deck, as the forward part had been removed.

Trials vessel

One of the most important contributions made to naval aviation by the *Langley* was to test various systems of arrester gear. When first com-

missioned *Langley* had a British system of longitudinal wires, which were intended to engage hooks in the landing gear of the aircraft, and prevent it from slewing from side to side. However, the US Navy added a back-up system of transverse wires, whose retarding action was achieved by hanging sand-filled shellcases on the ends. This system (refined into a proper hydraulic arrester system) ultimately proved better, and is the basis of modern carrier landings. Another innovation was a pair of flush-mounted pneumatic catapults on the flight deck; intended for sea-

planes, they later proved that they could speed up the launching of conventional aircraft, and like the arrester gear, this procedure is still standard today.

The veteran 'Covered Wagon' spent its short war

service as a humble aircraft transport.

On 27 February 1942 a group of Japanese naval bombers operating from Bali caught *Langley* en route for Tjilatjap in Java and the carrier was sunk by five bombs.

SPECIFICATION	
USS *Langley* (CV-1)	(7,150 shp)
Displacement: 11,050 tons standard; 14,700 tons full load	**Speed:** 14 kts
	Armour: none
Dimensions: length 165.3 m (542 ft 4 in) overall; beam 19.96 m (65 ft 6 in); draught 7.32 m (24 ft)	**Armament:** four 5-in (127-mm) guns
Machinery: 1-shaft steam turbo-electric delivering 5335 kW	**Aircraft:** (1923) 30 fighters
	Complement: 410 officers and enlisted men

HMS *Furious* Fleet carrier

The World War II camouflage does not conceal the battlecruiser origins of HMS Furious. The island was not added until 1939.

The several guises of **HMS Furious** represented the transitional stages between what might be termed 'air capable' ships and the true aircraft carrier. As the third of Admiral Fisher's 'tin-clad' light battlecruisers (laid down in 1915), *Furious* was launched in August 1916 but delayed in completion to allow it to ship the navy's largest gun, an 18-in (457-mm) weapon, in single mounts at each end. Although virtually complete in March 1917, *Furious* then had its forward gun removed in favour of a sloping flying-off deck some 69.5 m (228 ft) in length. A hangar beneath this deck accommodated up to 10 aircraft (some seaplanes and some wheeled). Completed thus in July 1917, *Furious* rapidly showed the limitations of carrying aircraft that could not (officially at least) be recovered after a flight. In November 1917, therefore, the after gun mounting made way for a 86.5-m (284-ft) flying-on deck over a second hangar. Much of the superstructure still remained, however, and the high speeds at which *Furious*

steamed to create the necessary wind-over-deck resulted in severe turbulence, causing an unacceptable accident rate among would-be landers-on. Relegated again to flying-off only, the *Furious* still had the distinction of mounting the first real carrier-based air strike when, on 19 July 1918, seven of its Sopwith Camels destroyed two Zeppelins and their sheds at Tondern. A through-deck was obviously required, as on the new *Argus*, and *Furious* was thus modified between 1921-25. Even following this, the ship was still of interim design, having no island. Not until a final pre-war refit did it acquire a vestigial superstructure, topped-off by a diminutive mast that supported a distinctive homing beacon.

Service

Despite its age and infirmities, the *Furious* saw service in Atlantic hunting groups and convoy escorts, the Norwegian campaign, and the North African landings. Its last flying was against the *Tirpitz*, immured in a Norwegian fjord, before going into reserve during

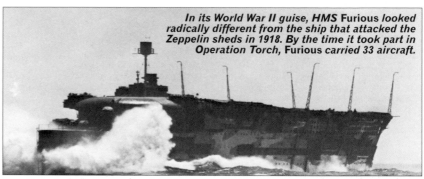

In its World War II guise, HMS Furious looked radically different from the ship that attacked the Zeppelin sheds in 1918. By the time it took part in Operation Torch, Furious carried 33 aircraft.

September 1944. *Furious* was scrapped in 1948.

The first ship to launch an air strike, HMS Furious was originally designed for Admiral Fisher's plan to attack Germany's Baltic coast during World War I.

SPECIFICATION	
HMS Furious	**Speed:** 31.5 kts
Displacement: 22,500 tons standard and 28,500 tons full load	**Armour:** belt 51-76 mm (2-3 in); hangar deck 38 mm (1.5 in)
Dimensions: length 239.5 m (785 ft 9 in); beam 27.4 m (90 ft); draught 7.3 m (24 ft)	**Armament:** six twin 4-in (102-mm) AA, three octuple 2-pdr AA, and several smaller-calibre guns
Propulsion: 4-shaft geared steam turbines delivering 67113 kW (90,000 shp)	**Aircraft:** 33
	Complement: 750 excluding aircrew

Landing on the forward deck of HMS Furious was very dangerous: Squadron Commander E. H. Dunning was killed when his Sopwith Pup overshot and stalled during trials in August 1917. In November 1917 the after 18-in gun was removed in favour of a flying-on deck.

HMS *Eagle* Fleet carrier

HMS Eagle spent the bulk of its service career on the China station, returning to the Mediterranean in spring 1940. When the carrier was finally sunk by a U-boat north of Algiers, it was with the loss of 260 lives.

HMS Eagle flew a total of 31 Spitfire Mk Vs to Malta during three sorties in March 1942 and was sunk in August during Operation Pedestal.

SPECIFICATION	
HMS Eagle	**Armour:** belt 102-178 mm (4-7 in);
Displacement: 22,600 tons	flight deck 25 mm (1 in); hangar
standard and 26,500 tons full load	deck 102 mm (4 in), shields 25 mm
Dimensions: length 203.3 m	(1 in)
(667 ft); beam 32.1 m (105 ft 3 in);	**Armament:** nine 6-in (152-mm),
draught 7.3 m (24 ft)	four 4-in (102-mm) AA, and eight
Propulsion: 4-shaft geared steam	2-pdr AA guns
turbines delivering 37285 kW	**Aircraft:** 21
(50,000 shp)	**Complement:** 750 excluding
Speed: 24 kts	aircrew

Before World War I, Chile ordered two stretched 'Iron Duke'-class battleships from Armstrong's Elswick yard. Only one of these, the *Almirante Latorre*, was well advanced by August 1914; compulsorily purchased by the Admiralty, it was completed in 1915 as HMS *Canada*. Work on an unlaunched sister, the *Almirante Cochrane* (laid down in 1913), ceased with hostilities but the ship was taken in hand, post-Jutland, for completion as an aircraft

carrier. Like the *Hermes* it was far too late for the war, being launched in June 1918 and commissioning for extended trials in 1920. Several versions of the pioneering island superstructure were tried after initial experiments on the *Argus*. This kept the vessel in dockyard hands for a great portion of the period between 1920-23, when the *Hermes* was commissioned. The final version of the island was long and low, topped-off by two funnel

casings with the same thick and thin proportions as the ship's erstwhile sister. The ship's more ample battleship proportions made it considerably slower than the large cruiser conversions, but it had better stability. Despite the fact that it introduced the two-level hangar, the ship still had only modest aircraft capacity.

Inter-war service
Much of the *Eagle*'s pre-World War II service was in the Far East, but the carrier

moved into the Indian Ocean in September 1939, thence to the Mediterranean to replace the *Glorious*. Following air strikes against Italian shipping at Tobruk, *Eagle* was badly shaken by bombing during the action off Calabria, suffering damage that eventually caused it to miss the Taranto raid. Before *Eagle* could refit in the UK, it saw further action

in the Red Sea and the South Atlantic. Arriving back in the Mediterranean early in 1942, *Eagle* was later involved in the famous August convoy (Operation Pedestal) when 41 warships fought through just five out of 14 merchantmen to lift the Malta siege. The *Eagle* was a major casualty, sunk by four torpedoes from *U-73* on 11 August 1942.

HMS *Hermes* Light carrier

The first British carrier actually designed as such (Hosho was actually commissioned a year earlier), HMS Hermes was built along the lines of a light cruiser. The ship carried six 5.5-in (140-mm) guns, as it was not believed that aircraft alone could repel enemy surface attack.

The *Argus* concept was obviously considered sound for early in 1918, before its completion, the keel was laid down for **HMS Hermes**. Although *Hermes* was designed for the job, it was obviously not with the benefit of operational experience. Lacking a precedent, its designers made the ship too small, prompting the Japanese to repeat the error with their pioneer *Hosho*, laid down in the following year. With the end of World War I, construction was leisurely, the ship being launched in September 1919 and with completion delayed until 1923. As a result *Hermes* entered service after the much larger but converted

HMS *Eagle*, which had meanwhile proved the idea of the island superstructure. Like that of the *Eagle*, *Hermes*' island seemed disproportionately large, with a massive battleship-style tripod and fighting top, bearing rangefinders for the unusual armament of six 5.5-in (140-mm) guns: early carriers were expected to be able to repel light surface attack, the potential of their aircraft not having been fully evaluated. A light armour belt was also worked in. An improvement on the *Argus* was a doubling of installed power to give a speed increase of over 4 kts.
A distinctive feature on the after flightdeck was a low hump, designed to deceler-

ate incoming aircraft. This was also copied by the Japanese, but neither fleet found it a success and abandoned it.

Valuable contribution
Though obsolete by World War II, the *Hermes* made an extremely valuable contribution in lower-threat areas. This found the carrier hunting for raiders in the Atlantic, undertaking spotting and reconnaissance missions in operations against the Vichy French in West Africa and the Italians in the Red Sea, giving shore support during the suppression of the Iraqi rebellion of 1941 and escorting Indian ocean convoys. *Hermes* was sunk in April 1942 off Ceylon

Below: HMS Hermes sinks off Ceylon (Sri Lanka) after a Japanese carrier aircraft attack in April 1942. Symptomatic of British handling of the war in the Far East at this time, the carrier had no aircraft aboard and no means of signalling for help if attacked.

during the Japanese carrier raids, but had adequately demonstrated the value of

even a small flightdeck in areas where no other aviation support existed.

SPECIFICATION	
HMS Hermes	**Speed:** 25 kts
Displacement: 10,850 tons	**Armour:** belt 51-76 mm (2-3 in);
standard and 12,950 tons full load	hangar deck 25 mm (1 in); shields
Dimensions: length 182.3 m	25 mm (1 in)
(598 ft); beam 21.4 m (70 ft 3 in);	**Armament:** six 5.5-in (140-mm),
draught 6.9 m (22 ft 7 in)	and three 4-in (102-mm) AA guns
Propulsion: 2-shaft geared steam	**Aircraft:** about 20
turbines delivering 29828 kW	**Complement:** 660 excluding
(40,000 shp)	aircrew

HMS Hermes served in the Far East for most of its career. This photograph clearly shows the unusually large island superstructure. Purpose-built, the vessel carried almost as many aircraft as Eagle, a ship of twice its displacement. Hermes was finally claimed by aircraft from the Soryu, Akagi and Hiryu.

'Courageous' class Fleet carrier

Known, for political reasons, as large light cruisers, Admiral of the Fleet 'Jackie' Fisher's famous trio of light battlecruisers were supposed to be the largest units of a 600-strong, shallow-draught armada that was to be constructed to realise Fisher's strategic vision of landing an army on the Baltic coast of north-eastern Germany, only 130 km (80 miles) from Berlin. The plan died with Fisher's departure from the Admiralty in 1915, but his strange ships were completed as a legacy of this extraordinary but deeply flawed concept.

Both commissioned in January 1917, the first two of these light battlecruisers were **HMS Courageous** and **HMS Glorious** (laid down in March and May 1915, and launched in February and April 1916 respectively), and were found to be virtually unemployable in the active fleet as they were essentially unprotected with a belt only 76 mm (3 in) thick and, with a primary armament of only four 15-in (381-mm) guns in two twin turrets, slow to get on to the target; the secondary armament was 18 4-in (102-mm) guns in six triple mountings. On the only occasion when they saw serious action, against conventional light cruisers of the German High Seas fleet in the Heligoland Bight on 17 November 1917, they suffered more damage than they inflicted.

Though lacking in armament and protection, the two ships were notably fast, achieving 32 kts on the 67104 kW (90,000 shp) delivered to their four shafts by four sets of Parsons geared turbines driven by the steam generated by 18 oil-fired Yarrow small-tube boilers. Under the terms of the Washington Treaty, the two ships were eligible for conversion into aircraft carriers. The process of rebuilding both of the ships started in 1924, the *Courageous* completing in 1928 and the *Glorious* in 1930. The two ships' half-sister *Furious*, which had been completed with two single 18-in (457-mm) rather than four 15-in guns, had been similarly adapted from 1922 to a standard that included

HMS Courageous *and HMS* Glorious, *like HMS* Furious, *were light battlecruisers ('tin-clads') intended for Admiral Fisher's ill-conceived Baltic strategy. This is* Glorious *on its sea trials in 1917. Its speed was an impressive 32 kts, but its lack of armour made it unfit for serious combat.*

HMS Glorious *could be distinguished from HMS* Courageous *by its longer flight deck aft. Its aircraft gave sterling service over Norway in 1940, but it was caught and sunk during the withdrawal by the German battlecruisers KMS* Scharnhorst *and KMS* Gneisenau.

no island and the boiler uptakes led well aft, detracting from its hangar space. The two later conversions had the benefit of developments on HMS *Hermes* and HMS *Eagle*, and their combined funnel and bridge structure had the effect of boosting their air complement considerably.

Twin flight decks

The *Courageous* and *Glorious* had similar forward flight decks, which terminated about 20 per cent of the ship's length back from the bows. The hangar deck was extended forward at forecastle level, allowing smaller and lighter aircraft

(the ships' fighters) to take off from the lower level in favourable circumstances. Both ships were extensively bulged to improve stability. In 1935-36 the short forward flight decks were removed, and the main flight deck, was fitted with two catapults to launch a 3629-kg (8,000-lb) aircraft at 56 kts or a 4536-kg (10,000-lb) aircraft at 52 kts. The ships each had two flight decks 167.64 m (550 ft) long, and the hangars and the flight deck were connected by two centreline elevators each measuring 14.02 by 14.63 m (46 by 48 ft). The aircraft fuel storage comprised a total of 156835 litres (34,500 Imp

gal) in each vessel.

The *Courageous* was the Royal Navy's first major casualty of World War II, being sunk only a fortnight after hostilities had started in September 1939. Its loss brought the *Glorious* back

from the Mediterranean as a replacement and this, too, was lost only nine months later during the evacuation of Norway in June 1940.

SPECIFICATION	
'Courageous' class	**Speed:** 30 kts
Displacement: 22,500 tons standard and 26,500 tons full load	**Armour:** belt 38-76 mm (1.5-3 in); hangar deck 25-76 mm (1-3 in)
Dimensions: length 239.5 m (785 ft 9 in); beam 27.6 m (90 ft 6 in); draught 7.3 m (24 ft)	**Armament:** 16 120-mm (4.7-in) AA guns and four 2-pdr AA
Propulsion: geared steam turbines delivering 67104 kW (90,000 shp) to four shafts	**Aircraft:** about 48
	Complement: 1,215 including aircrew

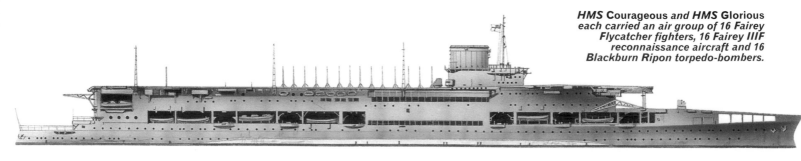

HMS Courageous *and HMS* Glorious *each carried an air group of 16 Fairey Flycatcher fighters, 16 Fairey IIIF reconnaissance aircraft and 16 Blackburn Ripon torpedo-bombers.*

HMS *Ark Royal*
Fleet carrier

Completed in 1938, **HMS Ark Royal** was the Royal Navy's first 'modern' carrier. A combination of meagre naval budgets and the lowly status of the Fleet Air Arm meant that it was the first carrier to join the fleet since the remodelled HMS *Glorious* in 1930. Plenty of time had thus been available to plan the ship, resulting in a thoroughly workmanlike and influential design laid down in 1935 and launched in April 1937. Though similar in size and displacement to the *Glorious*, the new carrier seemed considerably larger, having two levels of hangars with adequate headroom. Three elevators were incorporated, but these were small and, had the ship enjoyed a longer career, would have required replacement to cater for the rapidly increasing size of aircraft. Two catapults (or 'accelerators') were fitted to the vessel from the outset.

The *Ark Royal*'s most innovatory feature was its strength, for the ship introduced armoured flight and hangar decks, with the

HMS Ark Royal, the battlecruiser HMS Renown and the cruiser HMS Sheffield. During the hunt for the Bismarck, Ark Royal's Swordfish aircraft attacked Sheffield by mistake but made up for their error by crippling Bismarck's steering with a daring torpedo attack in appalling weather.

hangar walls an integral part of the main hull girder. Despite this configuration's space-consuming aspects, the ship could stow a far greater number of aircraft than the *Glorious*. Capable of 31 kts, *Ark Royal* was also as fast as the earlier ships.

Though the earlier conversions had 16 medium-calibre guns, these were poorly sited, mainly with a view to defence against surface attack. The *Ark Royal* carried eight twin 4.5-in (114-mm) destroyer-type mountings, with high elevations conferring a true dual-purpose capability. The mountings were sited four on each beam at the flight deck edges

HMS Ark Royal fights off German air attack in the Mediterranean. In the face of heavy bomb and torpedo attacks the ship flew off about 170 Hurricane fighters to reinforce Malta in 1941. It was while returning from one such mission that it was sunk by U-81.

HMS Ark Royal played a major role in the British attacks on the French fleet during 1940. Its aircraft mined Mers-el-Kebir to prevent the French escaping, but at Dakar in Senegal its aircraft were roughly handled by land-based French fighters.

to give good firing arcs. Designers were, at last, alive to the dangers of air attack and a comprehensive fit of smaller automatic weapons was also incorporated. Though aircraft were, indeed, to prove the main hazard to both American and Japanese carriers, the Royal Navy was pitted primarily against fleets without carriers, so suffering most of its carrier casualties to submarine attack: the *Ark Royal* succumbed to a torpedo hit from the *U-81* on 14 November 1941.

SPECIFICATION	
HMS *Ark Royal*	**Armour:** belt 114 mm (4.5 in); deck 64 mm (2.5 in)
Displacement: 22,000 tons standard and 27,720 tons deep load	**Armament:** eight twin 4.5-in (114-mm) AA, four octuple 2-pdr AA, and eight quadruple 0.5-in (12.7-mm) AA guns
Dimensions: length 243.8 m (800 ft); beam 28.9 m (94 ft 9 in); draught 6.9 m (22 ft 8 in)	
Propulsion: geared steam turbines delivering 76051 kW (102,000 shp) to three shafts	**Aircraft:** about 65
Speed: 31 kts	**Complement:** 1,580 including aircrew

Returning to Gibraltar after ferrying aircraft to Malta, Ark Royal was attacked by the German submarine U-81 and hit on the starboard side by a single torpedo.

Below: HMS Ark Royal was as long as dry docking facilities would allow, and was protected by a 114-mm (4.5-in) armour belt. The flight deck had 63-mm (2.5-in) armour and the lifts were offset and rather narrow to maximise deck strength. The positioning of the twin 4.5-in (114-mm) AA guns alongside the flight deck gave them excellent fields of fire.

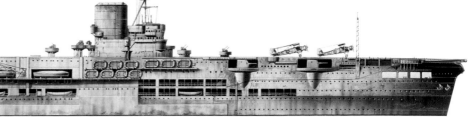

'Illustrious' class Aircraft carrier

HMS *Ark Royal* was very much a prototype, combining speed with increased capacity and new standards of protection. It had hardly been launched when a new **'Illustrious' class** of four aircraft carriers was laid down in 1937 in response to the increasing threat of war. Operational experience was, therefore, not a part of the later concept, which added a 114-mm (4.5-in) hangar wall to the *Ark Royal's* vertical and horizontal protection. Thus the entire vulnerable aircraft accommodation became an armoured box, but so much weight high in the ship limited the protection to only one hangar. So while **HMS *Illustrious*, HMS *Victorious*** and **HMS *Formidable***, all of which were launched in 1939, were not significantly smaller than the *Ark Royal*, they carried far fewer aircraft. There must have been second thoughts on reducing the ships' primary arm so drastically, for **HMS *Indomitable***, launched in 1940 as last of the four, and the two 'Implacable'-class ships that followed, reverted to lighter protection and an extra half-length hangar.

The immense strength of the ships stood them in good stead, for their war turned out to be one of air, rather than submarine, attack. Soon after Taranto, the *Illustrious* survived punishment from dive-bombing that would have sunk any other carrier afloat, a performance echoed by the *Formidable* after Matapan. In the Pacific War most of the ships withstood one or even two kamikaze strikes without having to leave station. But all these immense blows were absorbed mainly by the ships' horizontal protection. It would seem in retrospect that the vertical armour was bought at an excessive price in operational efficiency even though, in the Pacific, the class worked with something like 60 per cent more than its designed aircraft complement. When the Americans copied the armoured deck concept, it was not at the cost of capacity, so carrier sizes began their inevitable escalation. The ships were scrapped in 1956, 1969, 1955 and 1963 respectively.

Above: HMS **Formidable,** *seen here from HMS* **Warspite,** *fought for most of the war in the Mediterranean. An attack by its aircraft on the Italian fleet on 28 March 1941 damaged the battleship* **Vittorio Veneto** *and crippled the cruiser* **Pola,** *which was subsequently sunk.*

Left: Joining the fleet in August 1940, HMS **Illustrious** *steamed to the Mediterranean, where its air group sank two Italian destroyers and raided North Africa.*

Above: Despite having rather lighter protection than its sister ships, HMS **Indomitable** *absorbed a great deal of punishment. It survived two hits from 500-kg (1,102-lb) bombs during Operation Pedestal, a torpedo hit off Sicily in 1943 and several kamikaze attacks in the Far East.*

Below: The 'Illustrious'-class ships were probably the toughest aircraft carriers of World War II, but although their thick armour enabled them to withstand heavy blows, this level of protection was achieved only by a large reduction in aircraft strength.

SPECIFICATION	
'Illustrious' class	**Armour:** belt and hangar wall
Type: fleet aircraft carrier	114 mm (4½ in) except *Indomitable*
Displacement: 23,000 tons	38 mm (1½ in); deck 76 mm (3 in)
standard and 25,500 tons full load	**Armament:** eight twin 4.5-in
Dimensions: length 229.7 m	(114-mm) DP, six octuple 2-pdr AA,
(753 ft 6 in); beam 29.2 m (95 ft	and eight 20-mm AA guns
9 in); draught 7.3 m (24 ft)	**Aircraft:** about 45, except
Propulsion: geared steam turbines	*Indomitable* about 65
delivering 82027 kW (110,000 shp)	**Complement:** 1,400 including
to three shafts	aircrew
Speed: 31 kts	

'Implacable' class Aircraft carrier

Completed some 30 months after the four 'Illustrious' class ships, the two **'Implacable' class** aircraft-carriers were more closely related to the prototype *Ark Royal*, with the hangar walls slimmed down to only 38 mm (1.5 in). This allowed a better weight distribution for the ships' increased displacement, including the all-important lower hangar. The ships were slightly longer but appeared much bulkier than their half-sisters, their larger hull also containing a fourth set of propulsion machinery. This gave them the extra speed that enabled them to pace an American 'Essex'-class unit in the Pacific War, although they were considerably smaller in terms of both size and aircraft capacity.

Delayed completion

Though both were laid down in 1939, **HMS *Implacable*** and **HMS *Indefatigable*** were both launched only in December 1942 and completed in August and May 1944 respectively, their completions having been delayed by altered shipyard priorities. When the ships were most needed, they were still on the stocks, a fact that underlines the truth that the navy fights a war largely with what it has available at the beginning of that conflict.

Once completed, the two ships were active for a comparatively short period. In March 1944, while still a new ship, the *Indefatigable* achieved a 'first' in the first-ever deck landing by a twin-engined aeroplane, a de Havilland Mosquito. Before heading east to join the rapidly expanding British Pacific Fleet, it participated in some of the many carrier strikes against the *Tirpitz*, holed up in Norwegian waters. Though damaging the target sufficiently to keep it almost permanently

HMS Implacable was faster and carried more aircraft than the ships of the 'Illustrious' class. It is seen here as it returns to Sydney, Australia, during 1945.

under repair, the aircraft of the time constituted the ship's weakest operational link until they were replaced by more advanced types. Once they had arrived and become cornerstones of the BPF's offensive capability, the ships were engaged in a war that had in reality already been won, and in which the British participation was not welcomed in all quarters.

After World War II, the ships were employed mainly in the training role before being scrapped in 1955 and 1956 after hardly a decade of service. This was the result of the official decision that it was not worth the vast expense of rebuilding

the ships along the lines of HMS *Victorious*.

Hangarage

The 'Implacable' class aircraft carriers had a flight deck with an effective length of 231.65 m (760 ft) and located some 15.2 m (50 ft) above the deep-load waterline. The deck carried a single catapult capable of launching 7258 kg (16,000 lb) at 66 kts or 9072 kg (20,000 lb) at 56 kts, and was served by two aircraft lifts. Each of these could lift a 9072-kg aircraft, and while the forward lift measured 13.72 by 10.06 m (45 by 33 ft), the after unit measured 13.72 by 6.71 m (45 by 22 ft). There

were two hangars, one above the other, and while the lower unit in the after part of the ship measured 63.4 by 18.9 m (208 by 62 ft) with a height of 4.27 m (14 ft), the upper unit had the same width and height but was considerably longer

at 139.6 m (458 ft). The height was just too little for the ships to embark the powerful Corsair multi-role fighter. Another deficiency was in the aircraft fuel carried: a mere 430280 litres (94,650 Imp gal).

SPECIFICATION	
'Implacable' class	**Speed:** 32.5 kts
Type: fleet aircraft carrier	**Armour:** belt 114 mm (4.5 in);
Displacement: 26,000 tons	hangar wall 38 mm (1.5 in); deck
standard and 31,100 tons full load	76 mm (3 in)
Dimensions: length 233.4 m	**Armament:** eight twin 4.5-in
(765 ft 9 in); beam 29.2 m (95 ft	(114-mm) DP, six octuple 2-pdr AA
9 in); draught 7.9 m (26 ft)	and about 38 20-mm AA guns
Propulsion: geared steam turbines	**Aircraft:** about 70
delivering 82027 kW (110,000 shp)	**Complement:** 1,800 including
to four shafts	aircrew

HMS Implacable is seen while passing though the Suez Canal to join the growing strength of the British Pacific Fleet for the final stages of the war against Japan.

HMS *Argus* Aircraft carrier

Handicapped by lack of speed, HMS Argus was removed from front-line service during the 1930s. It nevertheless had to act as a replacement carrier for Force 'H' after Ark Royal was sunk.

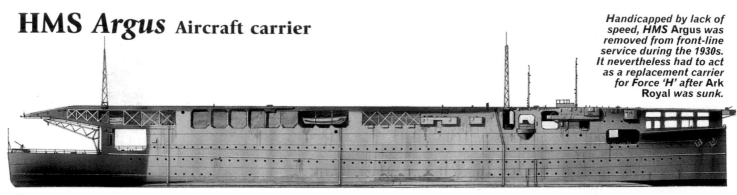

Proposals had been made before World War I for an aircraft-carrier with a straight-through flight deck capable of handling the launch and recovery of wheeled aircraft, but the Royal Navy had to make do with improvised seaplane carriers. It was not until 1916 that the proposer, the Beardmore commercial yard, was given the contract to complete a half-finished Italian liner as a prototype carrier. The ship, the *Conte Rosso*, had been laid down in 1914 and had suitable dimensions plus the high freeboard necessary for the job. No superstructure was planned to interrupt the flight deck which, like those of all pioneering carriers, was pointed at the forward end. A single hangar was provided and the necessary small charthouse retracted into the flightdeck. As full of character as it was devoid of grace, **HMS *Argus***, the world's first 'flat-top', was understandably known as 'The Flatiron'.

Recce duties

The name (in Greek mythology Argus was an all-seeing giant with 100 eyes) suggests that it was seen by planners as being designed for reconnaissance. This was an asset which had been much needed at Jutland, a victory lost for want of good intelligence. *Argus* was commissioned only weeks before the Armistice of November 1918, carrying a squadron of the unpopular Sopwith Cuckoo torpedo aircraft.

In the 1920s *Argus* was bulged to improve stability and to protect against torpedo attack. After the completion of the larger fleet carriers, it acted as a training and target ship, though it was recalled to active service in 1939.

Small and slow by World War II standards, *Argus* gave valuable service ferrying fighter aircraft to Gibraltar, Malta and Takoradi (for onward staged flights to Egypt). Lack of carriers saw it also in operational roles from time to time, notably on an Arctic convoy and at the North African landings. From mid-1943 it was used only for training in home waters, being paid off in 1944. HMS *Argus* was scrapped in 1947.

Above: Argus off the North African coast in November 1942. Argus participated in Operation Torch, but by 1943 had been relegated to the role of training carrier.

As the only true carrier in service anywhere for five years after World War I, HMS Argus was vital in proving the validity of the aircraft carrier concept.

SPECIFICATION

HMS *Argus*
Type: training, aircraft-ferry and second-line aircraft-carrier
Displacement: 14,000 tons standard and 15,750 tons full load
Dimensions: length 172.2 m (565 ft); beam 20.7 m (68 ft); draught 7.3 m (24 ft)
Propulsion: 4-shaft geared steam

turbines delivering 15660 kW (21,000 shp)
Speed: 20.5 kts
Armour: none
Armament: six 102-mm (4-in) AA, and several smaller-calibre guns
Aircraft: about 20
Complement: 370 excluding aircrew

HMS *Audacity* Escort carrier

Though contingency plans existed pre-war to convert merchant ships to auxiliary aircraft carriers, the production of the first such ship seems, in retrospect, to have been leisurely considering the urgency of the situation. The hull selected for conversion was that of the fire-damaged *Hannover*, an almost new Hamburg-Amerika cargo liner seized by the Royal Navy off San Domingo in February 1940. The new carrier was commissioned as **HMS *Audacity*** in June 1941 with the functions of carrying fighters to curb the menace of the long-range German maritime aircraft and, if possible, Fairey Swordfish to provide a measure of anti-submarine protection. Its facilities were basic, a 140-m (460-ft) flight deck being laid from the raised forecastle over a lowered bridge structure to a built-up poop. There were just two arrester wires and a barrier; no elevator was fitted because there was no hangar: the six aircraft were stowed and serviced on deck, flight operations involving much manual rearrangement. Because of a shortage of Hawker Sea Hurricanes, it took Grumman Martlets to sea for the first time in the Royal Navy. Contrasting with the spartan aviation arrangements, *Audacity* retained much of its original accommodation.

Initial journey

September 1941 saw the carrier's first trip, with the UK-Gibraltar convoy OG41. Heavy attacks from both submarine and aircraft sank six ships but greater losses were prevented by the *Audacity*'s aircraft, which caused several U-boats to dive and lose contact. They also shot down a Focke-Wulf Fw 200C and chased off several other intruders. The *Audacity* returned with the next convoy, HG76, in mid-December 1941. During a four-day non-stop battle the enemy lost five submarines for two merchantmen. With radar direction, the carrier had downed two more 'snoopers' and spoiled the attacks of various U-boats. On 21 December she herself fell victim to three submarine torpedoes but had succeeding in proving the value of the escort carrier.

SPECIFICATION

HMS *Audacity*
Type: escort aircraft-carrier
Displacement: 5,540 tons standard
Dimensions: length 144.7 m (474 ft 9 in); beam 17.1 m (56 ft); draught 8.3 m (27 ft 3 in)

Propulsion: diesels delivering 3542 kW (4,750 shp) to two shafts
Speed: 15 kts
Armour: none
Armament: one 102-mm (4-in) and some smaller guns
Aircraft: six

HMS Audacity's handful of fighters meant the difference between life or death for a convoy. Employed in protection duties to and from Gibraltar, Audacity was destroyed off Portugal by torpedoes from U-751 in December 1941.

CAM ships Catapult-Armed Merchantmen

Britain's chronic shortage of aircraft carriers in the early years of the war left the Atlantic convoys very vulnerable to long-range German aircraft. A desperate solution was the CAM ship, a merchantman with a fighter aircraft on a forward catapult.

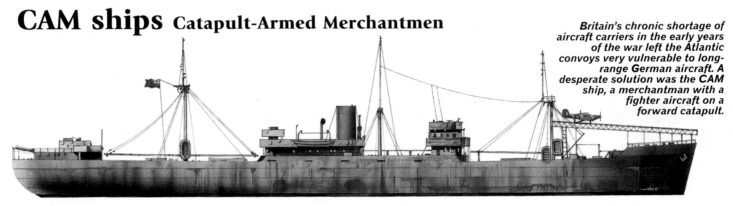

With the European coast from the North Cape to the Spanish border under enemy control by mid-1940, long-range German aircraft began to prove a serious menace to British convoys. The latter, beyond the range of their own air-support and with the escort carrier still in the future, were shadowed relentlessly, the aircraft vectoring in marauding U-boats and, increasingly boldly, attacking stragglers.

In 1940, aircraft alone accounted for 192 Allied ships of 580,000 gross registered tons, a total passed in the first four months of 1941. A somewhat desperate measure to counter these pests was the **Catapult-Armed Merchantman** or **CAM** ship, a series of which were converted while the escort carriers were building. Initially, three merchantmen and the old seaplane carrier **HMS Pegasus** were each fit-ted with a catapult upon which was mounted a Hawker Sea Hurricane Mk IA or Fairey Fulmar fighter. This group, termed **Fighter Catapult Ships**, proved the idea and a 50-ship programme was initiated, using merchantmen of various sizes. All wore the red ensign, carried cargo and had civilian crews but, spanning the forecastle and No. 1 hatch, was the ungainly catapult structure fixed axially and facing forward.

Pilots, drawn from the RAF's Merchant Ship Fighter Unit, would sit for hours, strapped in the cockpit, awaiting the sighting of a 'snooper'. Once launched, they were committed to catching the enemy and returning on a limited amount of fuel. There was no landing-on; if friendly land were close enough (a rare event) the pilot would try to reach it, but, more usually, he had to return to the convoy (often getting shot at) and 'ditch' alongside a likely ship, hoping to be rescued quickly before death arrived from exposure or drowning. It demanded a special sort of bravery.

Easy prey

Once contact was made, the enemy usually fell easily to the high-performance eight-gun fighters. The first recorded kill was by a Hurricane from the **FCS Maplin** early in August 1941, shortly before the CVE HMS *Audacity*'s epic maiden run and, by the end of the year, some six successes had been achieved.

The first CAM ship was the **Empire Rainbow**. The **Empire Lawrence** formed part of the contentious USSR-bound convoy PQ16 in mid-1942. Her aircraft downed one Heinkel He 111 torpedo bomber and dam-aged another, returning to find her ship sunk. During PQ18, the **Empire Morn's** Hurricane, during its brief flight, destroyed one aircraft, broke up the attacks of others and succeeded in making Soviet soil. The CAMs served briefly before being supplemented and then displaced by escort carriers, but their gallant contribution at a desperate time deserves to be fully recognised. No specification is possible for this disparate group of vessels.

Once launched from a CAM ship there was no way of landing; after hopefully destroying the intruder, the pilot of this 'Hurricat' had to bale out over the convoy knowing that unless he was quickly rescued he would die in the icy water. The Hurricane accelerated from the deck with the aid of banks of 3-in (76.2-mm) rockets.

MAC ships Merchant Aircraft Carriers

MAC ships were merchant vessels only partially converted into aircraft carriers; a flight deck was fitted, but the ships could still carry cargo. MAC ships' aircraft protected convoys in the 'Atlantic Gap', the area in mid-Atlantic out of range of Allied shore-based aircraft.

Lead orders for escort carriers (CVEs) were placed in early 1942, but urgent measures were required to close the mid-Atlantic gap during their building. One such was the CAM ship, the other the **MAC (Merchant Aircraft Carrier)**, an ingenious solution later copied by the Japanese. The Ministry of War Transport was, understandably, reluctant to release good-class cargo tonnage for conversion to dedicated CVEs, but the MAC retained the greater part of its cargo capacity while having a flight deck topside.

Breakbulkers required hatches and cargo-handling gear to function, but grain carriers required only small apertures to their holds, through which the hoses for loading and discharging grain could be inserted. This arrangement was fully com-patible with fitting a flight-deck. Like the CAMs, the MACs sailed under the red ensign, only their flight personnel being Royal Navy. Similarly, they were integrated more with the convoy than its escort, though requiring more manoeuvring space.

Appropriately carrying Empire 'Mac' names (particularly so as they came from Scottish yards), the first six were all converted from incomplete ships, with flight-decks measuring 129 by 19 m (423 by 62 ft) and a diminutive hangar aft capable of accommodating four Fairey Swordfish aircraft.

Suitable vessels

From the point of view of cargo requirements and dimensions, tankers were also very suitable candidates for conversion, but the Admiralty had grave doubts about the fire risk. Anglo-Saxon Petroleum (now Shell) resolved the problem on their behalf, resulting in nine of their tankers being converted (though retaining their familiar Shell names) and four more liquid-cargo Empire 'Macs' being launched for the job.

The main difference between the 'wet' and 'dry' ships lay in the lack of a hangar on the tankers, the aircraft remaining topside in all weathers. Despite the urgency of the programme, it was April 1943 before the first MAC entered service. They were exceedingly fortunate ships, all 19 surviving the war to be reconverted.

The dry-cargo class ships were the **Empire Macalpine**, **Empire Macandrew**, **Empire Maccallum**, **Empire Macdermott**, **Empire Mackendrick** and **Empire Macrae**. The equivalent tanker 'Empire Mac' class comprised the **Empire Maccabe**, **Empire Maccoll**, **Empire Mackay** and **Empire Macmahon**. Finally, the units of the 'Shell' class were the **Acavus**, **Adula**, **Alexia**, **Amastra**, **Ancylus**, **Gadila**, **Macoma**, **Miralda** and **Rapana**.

SPECIFICATION	
'Empire Mac' tanker class	**Propulsion:** 1-shaft diesel delivering 2461 kW (3,300 shp)
Type: merchant aircraft-carrier	
Displacement: 8,850 to 9,250 tons	**Speed:** 11.5 kts
Dimensions: length 146.7 to 148 m (481 ft 3 in to 485 ft 6 in); beam 18 to 18.8 m (59 to 61 ft 8 in); draught 8 to 8.4 m (26 ft 3 in to 27 ft 6 in)	**Armament:** one 102-mm (4-in) and some smaller guns
	Aircraft: four
	Complement: 110

SPECIFICATION	
'Shell' class	**Propulsion:** 1-shaft diesel delivering 2796 kW (3,750 shp)
Type: merchant aircraft-carrier	
Displacement: 8,000 gross tons	**Speed:** 13 kts
Dimensions: length 146.5 to 147 m (480 ft 8 in to 482 ft 3 in); beam 18 m (59 ft); draught 8.4 m (27 ft 8 in)	**Armament:** as for 'Empire Mac'
	Aircraft: four
	Complement: 105

British-built escort carriers

Few escort carriers were produced by British yards, which worked on more specialised ships, leaving series production to US yards. There was, understandably, also a reluctance to release good-quality mercantile tonnage for conversion at a time of severe shortage of ships for vital convoys. As a result, only five British-built CVEs saw service, **HMS Vindex** and the roughly similar **HMS Nairana**, the smaller **HMS Activity**, the larger **HMS Campania** and the ex-passenger liner **HMS Pretoria Castle**.

Unlike their American counterparts, which were built from similar hulls, the British escort carriers all differed from each other, and also tended to have longer but narrower flight decks. In addition, the hangar of each ship was served by only one elevator, which made for much manhandling of aircraft. The British-built escort carriers were more solidly built than the American CVEs, however, with steelsided hangars and steel flight decks. On average, the ships each accommodated between 15 and 18 aircraft,

in the approximate ratio of two Swordfish attack aircraft to one fighter (Sea Hurricane, Martlet/Wildcat or Fulmar). The *Activity* stowed fewer aircraft, while the larger *Pretoria Castle*, at a standard displacement of 19,650 tons, spent most of her operational career in the trials and training roles. The four smaller ships were converted from fast cargo liners of the Blue Funnel and Port Lines with a diesel propulsion arrangement and two propellers, and the ships were taken up for wartime naval service with a view to a return them to mercantile use after the end of hostilities.

The *Vindex* and *Nairana* were converted from incomplete fast merchant ship hulls, and were completed in December 1943 as what came nearest to a class of British-built escort carriers. The ships had deep-load displacements in the order of 17,000 tons and a flight deck 150.88 m (495 ft) in effective length. This flight deck was served by a lift measuring 13.72 by 10.36 m (45 by 34 ft), and 18 aircraft were embarked. The other armament was two 4-in (102-mm),

Short of spare merchant tonnage, the UK built few escort carriers, but ships like HMS Vindex seen here in 1944 (and formerly the incomplete cargo hull Port Sydney), proved very successful working with submarine hunting groups.

16 2-pdr 'pom-pom' and 16 20-mm AA guns.

Convoy work

The British CVEs ran extensively with convoys to and from Gibraltar. Working in pairs, they became potent anti-submarine ships. Their Swordfish aircraft were equipped with search radar and they themselves with Asdic (sonar), which allowed co-operation with dedicated hunter-killer groups. Later in the war the ships were used on the Arctic convoy route, the significance of their

efforts on this especially hazardous service being recognised by their wearing the flag of the senior naval officer. However, the British-built escort carriers proved somewhat less successful in

the severe northern conditions, their lack of length making them extremely lively in pitch, which exercised a severe restriction on flight operations for much of the time.

SPECIFICATION	
HMS Pretoria Castle	to two shafts
Displacement: 17,400 tons standard and 23,450 tons deep load	**Speed:** 16 kts
Dimensions: length 180.44 m (592 ft); beam 23.27 m (76 ft 4 in); draught 8.89 m (29 ft 2 in)	**Armament:** two twin 102-mm (4-in) AA, four quadruple 2-pdr AA, and 10 twin 20-mm AA guns
Propulsion: diesel engines delivering 11930 kW (16,000 shp)	**Aircraft:** 15
	Complement: not known

SPECIFICATION	
HMS Activity	delivering 8950 kW (12,000 shp) to two shafts
Displacement: 11,800 tons standard and 14,250 tons full load	**Speed:** 18 kts
Dimensions: length 156.06 m (512 ft); beam 20.24 m (66 ft 5 in); draught 7.65 m (25 ft 1 in)	**Armament:** two 4-in (102-mm) AA and 10 twin 20-mm AA guns
Propulsion: diesel engines	**Aircraft:** 11
	Complement: 700

HMS Nairana is seen here in her 1943 colour scheme as completed. Nairana's wartime service focused on convoy escort duties, embarking No. 835 Sqn's Sea Hurricane Mk IIc aircraft in summer 1944. One of these later claimed a Ju 290. Following the war, the vessel was transferred to the Netherlands to become Karel Doorman.

American-built escort carriers

Like the British, the Americans had pre-war ideas on the conversion of mercantile hulls to auxiliary aircraft carriers. Early in 1941, two C3 hulls were thus earmarked and the first was rebuilt in only three

months, commissioning as the USS *Long Island* (AVG-1) within days of the British *Audacity*. In concept, the American ship was well ahead, having both a hangar and an elevator, although in overall terms the conversion

made poor use of available space. Such early AVGs had a hangar occupying only the after quarter or so of the underdeck space, a similar volume ahead of it being devoted to accommodation, which should have gone

below in the original cargo spaces in the hull proper. Below the forward half of the flight deck the space was open, the overheads being supported on frame structures. What the US-built escort carriers did have was

a catapult (known as an 'accelerator'), and also the popular bunk beds and cafeteria messing.

The *Long Island*'s first sister was not completed until November 1941, and was transferred to the British as **HMS Archer**, being joined later by three more **'Archer'-class** ships. As the American escort carrier construction programme got

HMS Avenger and Biter, pictured here in heavy seas, were both 'Archer'-class escort carriers.

SPECIFICATION	
'Archer' class	(except *Archer* 6711 kW; 9,000 shp) to one shaft
Displacement: 10,366 tons (except *Archer* 10,220 tons) standard and 15,125 tons (except *Archer* 12,860 tons) deep load	**Speed:** 16.5 kts (except *Archer* 17 kts)
Dimensions: length 150 m (492 ft 3 in); beam 20.2 m (66 ft 3 in); draught 7.1 m (23 ft 3 in)	**Armament:** three 4-in (102-mm) AA, and 15 20-mm AA guns
Propulsion: diesel engine delivering 6338 kW (8,500 shp)	**Aircraft:** 15
	Complement: 555

fully into its stride the Royal Navy received eight units of the **'Attacker' class** and 26 units of the very similar **'Ruler' class**. Both had full-length hangars, the later class having improved stowage factors. Following early experience, the British required higher standards of fuel and fire protection than the Americans, promoting a measure of criticism of 'gold-plating'. The earlier ships from American yards were powered by diesel engines, but later units switched to steam plant, which was more easily built and reduced pressure on the manufacturers of diesel engines, a type in growing demand for the US Navy's rapidly expanding submarine arm. Both classes experi-enced a fair share of machinery problems.

With limited capacity for flexibility, CVEs were in general outfitted for a specific role, either in convoy escort or in assault support, their organisation and aircraft complement being tailored to suit. Once available in larger numbers the escort carriers were often integrated directly with anti-submarine groups. They frequently worked in larger groups (five for the Allied landing in Italy at Salerno and nine for the landing in the south of France), but some saw no action, being engaged on aircraft-ferrying rather than operational tasks. All that were still fit were converted to mercantile roles after the war.

The 'Archer' class comprised five ships, namely *Archer*, **Avenger**, **Biter**, **Charger** and **Dasher**, although the *Charger* was retained by the US Navy as CVE-30 for the training of British aircrews in American waters. The 'Attacker' class was larger, and was made up of **Attacker**, **Battler**, **Chaser**, **Fencer**, **Pursuer**, **Stalker**, **Striker** and **Trailer**. Finally there was the 'Ruler' class, which was made up of **Patroller**, **Puncher**, **Ravager**, **Reaper**, **Searcher**, **Slinger**, **Smiter**, **Speaker**, **Tracker**, **Trouncer**, **Trumpeter**, **Ameer**, **Arbiter**, **Atheling**, **Begum**, **Emperor**, **Empress**, **Khedive**, **Nabob**, **Premier**, **Queen**, **Rajah**, **Ranee**, **Ruler**, **Shah** and **Thane**.

SPECIFICATION	
'Attacker' class	(9,350 shp) to one shaft
Displacement: 10,200 tons standard and 14,170 deep load	**Speed:** 17 kts
Dimensions: length 150 m (492 ft 3 in); beam 21.2 m (69 ft 6 in); draught 7.3 m (24 ft)	**Armament:** two 4-in (102-mm) AA, four twin 40-mm AA, and 10 to 35 20-mm AA guns
Propulsion: geared steam turbines delivering 6972 kW	**Aircraft:** 18 to 24
	Complement: 646

SPECIFICATION	
'Ruler' class	one shaft
Displacement: 11,400 tons standard and 15,390 tons deep load	**Speed:** 17 kts
Dimensions: length 150 m (492 ft 3 in); beam 21.2 m (69 ft 6 in); draught 7.7 m (25 ft 3 in)	**Armament:** two 4-in (102-mm) AA, eight twin 40-mm AA, and 27 to 35 20-mm AA guns
Propulsion: geared steam turbines delivering 6972 kW (9,350 shp) to	**Aircraft:** 18 to 24
	Complement: 646

The UK received eight 'Attacker'-class and 26 'Ruler'-class escort carriers from the US. They were used for both convoy escort and anti-submarine warfare, and also provided air support during several of the amphibious assault landings in the Mediterranean.

HMS *Perseus* and HMS *Pioneer* Aircraft maintenance ships

The British quickly found that they had to undertake their naval operations against the Japanese in the Far Eastern campaigns on the basis of long-range sweeps far removed from the support of established bases and maintenance facilities.

These operations were also characterized by high attrition rates in aircraft, for which the best solution was discovered to be 'repair by replacement' as a means of keeping the front-line carrier force fully operational. Experience soon showed that escort carriers were well suited to the task of aircraft ferrying, and these ships were therefore operated extensively in the exchange process.

Lightly damaged aircraft and routine maintenance tasks could be carried out on the fleet carrier itself. Lack of space and time demanded that anything more complex and therefore more lengthy and consumptive of the ship's facilities, in materials and manpower, should be shipped out for repair and, by the very nature of a war fought in a region of the world lacking much in the way of shore establishments, the repair facilities had necessarily to be afloat.

Replacements

With the only specialist maintenance carrier *Unicorn* used permanently in an operational role, two of the new light fleet carriers of the 'Colossus' class were earmarked as replacements. Though lacking the *Unicorn*'s extra hangar, they were marginally faster but looked 'unfinished' with few of the deck-edge fixtures sported by the operational carriers.

HMS *Perseus* and **HMS *Pioneer***, which had been laid down in June and December 1942 by Vickers-Armstrongs on the Tyne and at Barrow for launch in March and May 1944 respectively, were completed in October and February 1945 respectively, and thus only the *Pioneer* succeeded in getting to an operational theatre, arriving with the 11th Aircraft Carrier Squadron in the Far East just in time for the Japanese surrender.

Paradoxically, earlier in the war when they could have been of use, they would (like the *Unicorn*) almost certainly have been pressed into an operational role, leaving CVEs to be used as auxiliaries, while in time of peace too few active flight decks were maintained to warrant their existence. With little post-war application, the *Pioneer*, which was originally to have been named *Mars*, was scrapped as early as 1954. It is worth noting that an earlier intention had been to convert the ships into passenger liners. However, this concept was finally not pursued probably as a result of a combination of cost and a diminishing demand for these ships by a public acquiring a taste for air travel. The *Perseus*, which was originally to have been named *Edgar*, was nearly recommissioned for the Suez affair of 1956, but was then scrapped in 1958.

The other eight 'Colossus'-class light fleet aircraft carriers were the *Colossus*, *Glory*, *Ocean*, *Venerable*, *Vengeance*, *Theseus*, *Triumph* and *Warrior*. These were laid down at seven yards (Harland & Wolff building two units) between June 1942 and January 1943. All of the ships were launched in 1944, but only three of the ships were completed in time for operational service in World War II. The other five were completed after the war, and of the eight ships, four (*Warrior*, *Vengeance*, *Colossus* and *Venerable*) were transferred or sold respectively to Argentina as the *Independencia* in 1958, Brazil as the *Minas Gerais* in 1956, France as the *Arromanches* in 1946 and the Netherlands as the second *Karel Doorman* in 1948. The other four units were kept in British service or loaned to Australia (*Vengeance* between 1952 and 1955) and Canada (*Warrior* between 1946 to 1948), the *Glory*, *Ocean* and *Theseus* being broken up in the early 1960s, and the *Triumph* being converted into a repair ship for further service.

The 'Colossus'-class ships had a flight deck offering an effective size of 210.31 m (690 ft) by 24.38 m (80 ft), one large hangar, one catapult and two lifts together with 37 aircraft.

SPECIFICATION	
HMS *Perseus* and HMS *Pioneer*	two shafts
Displacement: 13,300 tons standard and 18,040 tons deep load	**Speed:** 25 kts
	Armour: minimal
Dimensions: length 211.84 m (695 ft); beam 24.38 m (80 ft); draught 5.59 m (18 ft 4 in)	**Armament:** three quadruple 2-pdr AA and 10 20-mm AA guns
	Aircraft: none
Propulsion: geared steam turbines delivering 31319 kW (42,000 shp) to	**Complement:** not known

HMS Perseus and Pioneer were 'Colossus'-class carriers, completed as maintenance ships unable to operate in a combat role. Too late to serve in the wartime fleet, they were among the first British carriers to be scrapped.

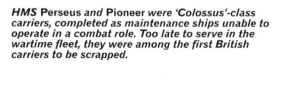

IJN *Hosho*
Light carrier

As with most early Japanese carriers, Hosho spent most of her career as a flush-decked design.

The first carrier built for the Imperial Japanese Navy, like so many others, was a conversion. The naval oiler *Hiryu*, laid down late in 1919, was taken over in 1921 and emerged as the carrier **Hosho** at the end of the following year. The design owed much to a British technical mission, which had broad details of the new British carrier *Hermes* and of the Sopwith Cuckoo torpedo-bomber.

Turbine power

The original triple-expansion steam engines were replaced by destroyer-type turbines to give a speed of 25 kt (46 km/h; 29 mph) and, as in the USS *Langley*, smoke was vented through triple folding funnels, which hinged downwards when flying was in progress. At first the ship had an 'island' navigating bridge, but this proved so unpopular with the pilots that it was removed in 1923.

As with many of the early carriers, the *Hosho* proved very small and lacked suffi-

cient margin of stability to be able to carry her full armament and complement of aircraft. By the outbreak of World War II her air group had shrunk from 21 to 12 aircraft, and all of the original guns had been replaced by light anti-aircraft weapons.

Even so, the *Hosho* provided invaluable experience for the conversion of *Akagi* and *Kaga*, as well as in the design of *Ryujo*, the first Japanese carrier built as such from the keel up. She saw considerable action off the China coast in the 1930s, and ferried aircraft during the Sino-Japanese War, By the late 1930s, however, her operational career was thought to be over, and the *Hosho* was relegated to training duties.

Into combat

Despite her drawbacks the elderly training carrier served with Carrier Division 3 from December 1941, alongside the *Zuiho*, but after four months in the Palau Islands she was

returned to training duties in Japan. She became operational again for the Midway campaign, carrying 11 Nakajima B5N 'Kate' bombers to provide reconnaissance for Admiral Yamamoto's battleships.

Finally withdrawn from the front line in June 1942, the Hosho thereafter led a charmed life. Although damaged by grounding in 1944 and hit twice by American bombs at Kure, she was still afloat when the war ended. She had been finally laid up in April 1945 for lack of aircrew to man her aircraft, and was thus one of the few Japanese carriers still in existence on VJ-Day.

Survivor

She was to have a second lease of life, however, for she was recommissioned as a transport to repatriate Japanese servicemen from all over the Far East, *Hosho* continued in this job until August 1946, but was finally scrapped in 1947 after nearly 25 years of service.

The small size of the Hosho – she could carry less than a dozen aircraft – is evident from this picture taken under the flight deck at the bow.

SPECIFICATION	
Hosho	kW (30,000 shp)
Type: Light carrier	**Speed:** 25 kt (46 km/h; 29 mph)
Displacement: 7,470 tons	**Armour:** not known
standard, 10,000 tons full load	**Armament:** 4 x 140-mm (5.5-in), 2
Dimensions: length 168.1 m	x 80-mm (3.2-in) AA (1941), eight
(551 ft 6 in) overall; beam 18 m	twin 25-mm (0.985-in) AA guns
(59 ft); draught 6.2 m (20 ft 4 in)	**Aircraft:** (1942) 11 'Kate' torpedo
Machinery: two-shaft geared	bombers
steam turbines delivering 22370	**Complement:** 550

IJN *Akagi*
Fleet carrier

The Washington Naval Disarmament Treaty after World War I left the Imperial Japanese Navy with several incomplete capital ships destined for the scrapyard. As the Americans and British had declared their intention of converting similar hulls into carriers, and in the light of successful experience with the *Hosho*, the naval staff decided to press ahead with two similar carrier conversions. Two battlecruisers, to be known as **Akagi** and **Amagi**, were chosen; these were projected as 40,000-ton ships capable of 30 kt (55 km/h; 34 mph).

Earthquake

Work started in 1923 but the hull of the *Amagi* was badly damaged during the great Tokyo earthquake in September, and she was scrapped. The *Akagi* was completed in March 1927. She was a flush-decked ship with two funnels at the starboard edge of the flight deck, a triple flight deck forward, and ten 200-mm (7.9-in) guns, six of them in old-fashioned casemates low down aft.

Ten years later she was completely rebuilt, with a

small island superstructure on the port side, and a full length flight deck. It was hoped that the portside island would simplify operations when operating in company with other carriers (allowing her aircraft to be marshalled separately) but it caused far more landing accidents than a starboard island.

Flagship

With her half-sister *Kaga* she formed Carrier Division 1 as Vice Admiral Nagumo's flagship led the attack on Pearl Harbor. She then led the other carriers on a series of raids through the East Indies and Indian Ocean; the force sinking the British carrier *Hermes*, driving the Allies out of Java and Sumatra and even getting as far as Darwin in northern Australia.

End at Midway

At the Battle of Midway on 4 June 1942, *Akagi's* air group attacked Midway itself and she suffered slight damage when a shore-based torpedo bomber bounced off the deck early in the morning. However, much worse was to come when at 10.22, she was attacked by aircraft from the USS *Enterprise*.

The *Akagi* was hit twice, a 1,000-lb (454-kg) bomb bursting in the hangar and starting a fire among torpedo warheads which spread to aviation fuel spilling from fractured lines. A second bomb (of 500 lb/ 227 kg) also started a fire among aircraft which were parked on the flight deck.

Within 30 minutes the fire was completely out of control. Admiral Nagumo

Akagi was one of the few aircraft carriers ever built to have had her navigating 'island' on the port side. This was to allow her to operate in tandem with the Kaga, which had a starboard island.

had been forced to shift his flag to a light cruiser. The *Akagi* was abandoned but burned for another nine hours or more. After

vain efforts to board her, the order was given to a destroyer to torpedo her, and she sank.

SPECIFICATION	
Akagi	(main deck, beneath double hangar
Type: Fleet carrier	decks)
Displacement: (1941) 36,500 tons	**Armament:** six 200-mm (7.9-in), six
standard, 42,000 tons full load	twin 120-mm (4.7-in) AA; 14 twin
Dimensions: length 260.6 m	25-mm (0.985-in) AA guns added
(855 ft) overall; beam 31.3 m (102 ft	between 1935 and 1938
8 in); draught 8.6 m (28 ft 3 in)	**Aircraft:** (June 1942) 21 Mitsubishi
Machinery: 4-shaft geared steam	A6M Zero fighters, 21 Aichi D3A
turbines delivering 99180 kW	'Val' dive bombers and 21 Nakajima
(133,000 shp)	B5N 'Kate' torpedo bombers
Speed: 31 kt (57 km/h; 36 mph)	**Complement:** 1,340 officers and
Armour: 15-cm (6-in) waterline	men
belt; 7.9-cm (3.1-in) armoured deck	

IJN *Kaga* Fleet carrier

Like her half-sister Akagi, Kaga was completed with a short flight deck and two flying-off decks forwards. This was needlessly complex, and in a mid-1930s refit she acquired a full-length flight deck and a navigation island.

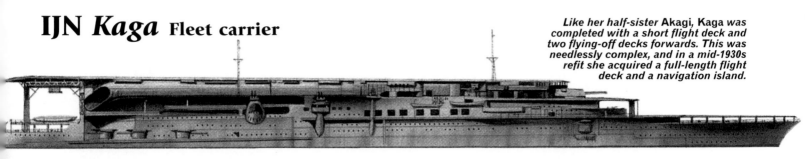

The Japanese battleship **Kaga** was laid down in 1918 and launched in November 1921, but as a result of the Washington Naval Disarmament Treaty of 1922, the incomplete hull was scheduled to be scrapped.

In September 1923, however, a massive and devastating earthquake struck the Tokyo area. Among the effects caused by the quake was severe damage to the docked battlecruiser *Amagi*, which was about to start her conversion to an aircraft-carrier. As a result, the hull of the slightly smaller Kaga was substituted.

The four and a half-year conversion produced a carrier similar to the original *Akagi* conversion, with a flush deck and two short flying-off decks forward.

Unlike *Akagi* however, the *Kaga* had her smoke-ducts trunked on the starboard side.

She was not an unqualified success, and did not become operational until more than two years of trials had been conducted. In 1934, after only four years, she was taken in hand for modernisation.

Upgraded

In her new guise Kaga was considerably improved, with more aircraft (90 instead of 60) and a small 'island' superstructure. However, unlike Western carriers, she still had a large downward-angled funnel below the edge of the flight deck. As displacement had gone up by 9,000 tons (standard), more powerful machinery had to be installed, with

endurance to match, and many of the original faults were eliminated.

The *Kaga* was one of the six carriers which attacked Pearl Harbor on 7 December 1941, when she launched 27 Nakajima B5N 'Kate' torpedo bombers, followed by 18 Mitsubishi A6M Zeros and 26 Aichi D3A 'Val' dive bombers. She and her half-sister *Akagi*, as Carrier Division 1, then took part in the devastating series of strikes in the East Indies, South Pacific and Indian Ocean which destroyed Allied military power in the first half of 1942.

Sunk at Midway

At Midway on 4 June 1942, two hours after successfully beating off American torpedo bomber attacks, *Kaga* was hit by four bombs from

Douglas SBD Dauntless dive bombers from the USS *Enterprise*. Five more bombs were near misses. Blast from the bombs fractured fuel lines, feeding fuel to the fires already started among the aircraft waiting, fully armed and fuelled. Within 30 minutes the 38,000-ton carrier had to be

abandoned, though she continued to burn for another nine hours. At dusk the flames reached a magazine, and she blew up and sank quickly. Over 800 men went down with her, many trapped by the fires and others killed by the blast of the original explosions.

SPECIFICATION	
Kaga	**Armour:** 15.2-cm (6-in) armour belt;
Type: Fleet carrier	3.8-cm (1.5-in) armour deck (main
Displacement: (1941) 38,200 tons	deck, beneath hangars)
standard, 43,650 tons full load	**Armament:** 10 200-mm (7.9-in), 12
Dimensions: length 247.6 m	11.9-cm (4.7-in) AA; AA fit later
(812 ft 4 in) overall; beam 32.5 m	upgraded to 16 127-mm (5-in) DP
(106 ft 7 in) over flight deck;	and 11 twin 25-mm (0.985-in) AA
draught 9.5 m (31 ft 2 in)	guns
Machinery: 4-shaft geared steam	**Aircraft:** 90 fighters, dive-bombers
turbines delivering 95020 kW	and torpedo-bombers
(127,400 shp)	**Complement:** 2,016 officers and
Speed: 28 kt (52 km/h; 32 mph)	men

IJN *Ryujo* Light fleet carrier

Under the Washington Treaty Japan was limited to 80,000 tons of carriers, but as the treaty exempted vessels under 10,000 tons the naval staff decided to build an extra carrier inside the limit.

The initial design was for an 8,000-ton ship carrying 24 aircraft, but the staff added a second hangar to double the aircraft capacity. This pushed the displacement 150 tons over the limit, but nothing was said to Japan's fellow-signatories – the first significant breach of the treaty, and by no means the last.

Even with the illicit extra tonnage, the new carrier, called **Ryujo**, was found to be top-heavy on completion in 1933. She was twice rebuilt, with bulges added, some guns removed and the fore-

castle raised, but by then her true displacement had risen to 12,000 tons.

Bad reputation

As may be imagined, the *Ryujo* was not popular in the fleet. Quite apart from her topweight problems, her flight deck was too small and she carried too few aircraft to be effective; she took longer than other carriers to launch and recover aircraft, because of congestion on the deck. However, the bad experience was put to good use in designing the *Hiryu* and *Shokaku* classes.

The *Ryujo* was not part of the main carrier force which attacked Pearl Harbor. but supported the amphibious landings in the Philippines. In April 1942 she attacked Allied merchant shipping and two

months later she joined in operations against the Aleutian Islands, but her only major (and last) action was the Battle of the Eastern Solomons.

Guadalcanal

Ryujo was chosen to spearhead an operation to reinforce the defenders of Guadalcanal. Escorted by a heavy cruiser and two destroyers, she was used as bait to lure the American carriers away from the main force. It seemed to work well, for at 09.05 on

Ryujo's double hangar looks much too large for the carrier's sleek cruiser hull. Indeed, topweight was always to be a problem for this compromised light carrier design.

24 August 1942 she was spotted from the air – but other search planes also located the *Shokaku* and *Zuikaku*. In the afternoon, Ryujo was heavily attacked by aircraft from the *Enterprise* and *Saratoga*. In a brilliant attack, US Navy dive bombers and torpedo-bombers smothered the carrier, scoring an estimated 10 bomb hits and

two torpedo hits. Japanese records say that only one torpedo hit the carrier, but that was enough to set her on fire from end to end. The doomed ship was unable to steam or steer.

Only 300 survivors left the ship, including Captain Kato, and she sank about four hours later.

SPECIFICATION	
Ryujo	**Speed:** 29 kt (53 km/h; 33 mph)
Type: Light carrier	**Armour:** virtually none
Displacement: 10,600 tons	**Armament:** six twin 127-mm (5-in)
standard, 14,000 tons full load	AA; later modified to four twin
Dimensions: length 180 m (590 ft	127-mm, two twin 25-mm (0.985-in)
6 in) overall; beam 20.8 m (68 ft	and six triple 25-mm mounts
3 in); draught 7.1 m (23 ft 4 in)	**Aircraft:** 24 Mitsubishi A6M Zero
Machinery: two-shaft geared	fighters and 12 Nakajima B5N
steam turbines delivering 48470 kW	'Kate' bombers
(65,000 shp)	**Complement:** 924 officers and men

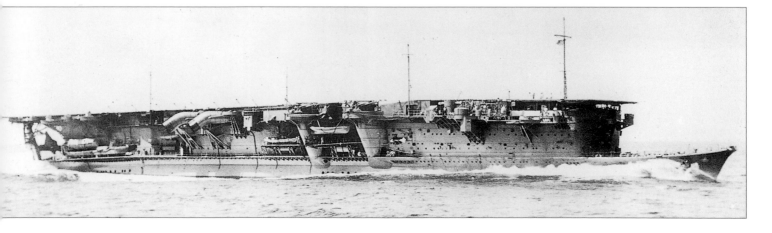

Hiryu Fleet carrier

Hiryu differed from Soryu in having an increased beam to allow more bunkerage (giving an extra 4828 km/3,000 miles in endurance), an increased level of protection and a higher (by one deck) forecastle in the interests of seaworthiness.

Launched in 1941, the **Hiryu** aircraft carrier was built to take account of lessons learnt during the construction of the 10,150-ton light aircraft carrier *Ryujo* and the 18,800-ton carrier *Soryu*. While the ship's machinery remained similar to that of its predecessors, the hull was wider. This permitted additional bunkerage on the vessel, which increased its range by almost 4790 km (3,000 miles).

Hiryu had several interesting design features. These included a port-side island superstructure. This was intended to allow *Hiryu* to operate alongside the larger 34,364-ton carrier *Akagi*. *Hiryu's* aircraft would fly an anti-clockwise circuit, while the *Akagi*, with its traditional starboard island, would operate a clockwise circuit, thus increasing the air cover which could be offered to the rest of the fleet. However, this practice was never used.

Hiryu was relatively light for an aircraft carrier – particularly in relation to Western counterparts – with a standard displacement of 17,300 tons. For example, the USS *Lexington* had a standard displacement of 43,000 tons; while the standard displacement of the USS *Essex* was 30,800 tons.

Airflow disturbance

Hiryu did suffer several disadvantages. The airflow over the flight deck was disturbed by the funnel uptakes which were located on the starboard side of the vessel. This caused the hot exhaust gases from the ship's engines to mix with the air flowing across the flight deck causing dangerous turbulence for the aircraft during landing and take-off from the vessel.

While also facilitating an increase in range, the widened hull accommodated the ship's 1,400-ton ballast which greatly increased the vessel's stability, compared with the earlier *Ryujo* and *Soryu* carriers.

Hiryu was deployed throughout its service life as part of the Second Carrier Division of the 1st Air Fleet. The carrier participated in the attacks on Pearl Harbor, along with the carriers *Kaga*, *Soryu*, *Shokaku* and *Zuikaku*

on 7 December 1941. During the attack, *Hiryu* launched 18 Nakajima B5N 'Kate' torpedo-bombers and nine Mitsubishi A6M Zero fighters during the first wave of attacks at 06.00.

The *Hiryu* continued the onslaught. During the second wave of strikes, the vessel launched 18 Aichi D3A 'Val' dive-bombers and another nine Zeros. Despite deploying 54 aircraft throughout the assault, *Hiryu* only lost five aircraft.

From Pearl Harbor, *Hiryu* steamed towards Wake Island in the central Pacific, and later that month helped to attack the US garrison. The ship then participated in the invasion of Palau in January 1942, and provided air cover for the invasion of the Moluccas Islands, which preceded the conquest of the Dutch East Indies.

In March 1942, *Hiryu* undertook intercepts of Allied shipping around Java, and during an attack on Christmas Island sank the Dutch freighter *Poelau Bras*.

Operation C

During late February 1942 the Japanese conducted a rehearsal for what would be one of the most devastating strikes against the Royal Navy in the Indian Ocean. The carrier aircraft warmed-up with a raid on Darwin and Broome in north-west Australia, when they sank 12 ships and reduced much of the surrounding towns to dust. They lost two aircraft during the attack.

In April 1942, *Hiryu* participated in a dramatic attack against the Royal Navy fleet in the Indian Ocean. Code-named Operation C, the Japanese attacked the Royal Navy base at Colombo in

Ceylon (Sri Lanka). During the attack, aircraft from *Hiryu* helped to sink the heavy cruisers HMS *Cornwall* and *Dorsetshire*.

As they had done during the attack on Pearl Harbor, the Japanese decided to strike on a Sunday morning before breakfast. Shore-based radar tracked the incoming Japanese air armada. RAF aircraft were scrambled, although as the harbour was surrounded by anti-aircraft defences it was not cleared of ships for

Seen on trials off Tateyama in April 1939, Hiryu was an improved Soryu design with increased endurance. The ship had a port-side island, designed to allow simultaneous side-by-side air operations with a conventional carrier. The idea was not a success.

SPECIFICATION	
Hiryu	(152,000 shp)
Displacement: 17,300 tons standard; 21,900 tons full load	**Speed:** 34.4 kts
Dimensions: length 227.4 m (746 ft) overall; beam 22.3 m (73 ft 2 in); draught 7.8 m (25 ft 7 in)	**Armament:** six twin 127-mm (5-in), seven triple 25-mm AA and five twin 25-mm AA guns
Machinery: 4-shaft geared steam turbines delivering 113350 kW	**Aircraft:** 64 aircraft
	Complement: 1,100 officers and men (including air wing).

Last survivor of four Japanese fleet carriers at Midway, Hiryu was struck by SBD Dauntless dive-bombers late on 4 June 1942. Burning fiercely and with its flight deck shattered, the carrier was abandoned and scuttled, sinking some 12 hours later on 5 June.

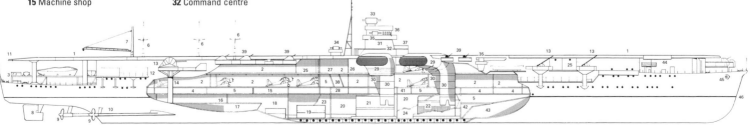

Dawn on 7 December 1941, and a B5N 'Kate' loaded with an 800-kg (1,764-lb) torpedo takes off from the Hiryu. The attack on Pearl Harbor was timed to cause maximum confusion to US forces, with the first waves over target when the Americans were having breakfast.

some time. RAF fighters did intercept the Japanese strike package, although their efforts were largely unsuccessful. For instance, around 40 RAF fighters engaging the Japanese attack were unable to break up the hostile formation, and the RAF force lost around half of its aircraft, whereas the Japanese lost only seven. The attack lasted 30 minutes, but despite the efforts of the Japanese aircraft, the port still functioned.

However, Vice-Admiral Chuichi Nagumo, who was commanding the attack, had another card up his sleeve. He had organised a second strike force, centred around the *Ryujo*, which was too slow to participate in the initial attacks. The follow-up attack force also including the *Hiryu*, which sailed on 1 April from Burma. Burma had been occupied following an invasion by the Japanese in January 1942.

Utter confusion

The second attack was designed to exploit the confusion which had been triggered by the initial strike. One of the biggest successes of the day occurred when the *Hiryu* helped to destroy the Royal Navy aircraft carrier HMS *Hermes*, which had sailed from the harbour during the initial attacks and was particularly vulnerable. *Hermes* carried no fighters, as its air wing had been deployed elsewhere. Furthermore, the

British carrier experienced communication problems when requesting shore-based air support. *Hermes* was devastated by a raid of 85 dive-bombers, which covered the vessel with bombs. The carrier absorbed 40 250-kg (551-lb) munitions, capsized, and sank within minutes. Following the attacks, the force continued its successes, helping to sink over 145,000 tons of merchant shipping.

Hiryu was to meet its fate at the Battle of Midway on 4 June 1942. The carrier was organised into Nagumo's 1st Carrier Striking Force, alongside the *Akagi*, *Soryu* and *Kaga*; plus an additional two battleships and a three cruisers.

The force was scheduled to arrive off the coast of Midway Island on 4 June to begin a heavy bombardment of the American airfield. This would be done to facilitate the arrival of airborne troops

and a transport group by the 6 June.

Hiryu launched 18 'Kate' torpedo-bombers and nine Zeros for the dawn attack. Fortune was on the ship's side, and *Hiryu* managed to avoid the bomb damage suffered by the other three Japanese carriers, which was unleashed by the American counter-attack.

By 10.30, three of the four carriers were suffering major fires. *Hiryu* had lost eight 'Kates' and two Zeros. However, at around midday, waves of *Hiryu*'s aircraft had helped disable the USS *Yorktown* with three direct hits.

Hiryu followed up this attack at 14.45, when a torpedo attack struck a mortal blow against the *Yorktown*. *Hiryu* lost most of its aircraft during this second attack, yet enough aircraft were able to return to the carrier to prepare to conduct a third strike.

Yet the Japanese carrier's

luck was short-lived. While the second wave of attacks against the *Yorktown* was underway the American carrier had launched 10 SBD Dauntless dive-bombers to find and sink the *Hiryu*. Two aircraft, piloted by Lieutenants Samuel Adams and Harlan R. Dickson flying from the USS *Enterprise* located the Japanese carrier. By 16.00, 24 dive-bombers, including 10 refugees from the *Yorktown* were in the air.

They found the *Hiryu* shortly after 17.00, preparing to launch a third strike against the *Yorktown*, with its remaining air wing of four torpedo- and five dive-bombers.

US Marine Corps aircraft dropped four bombs along the centreline of the *Hiryu*'s flight deck, all of which were closely spaced at the forward area of the flight deck. *Hiryu* was then strafed with machine-gun fire by B-17s which had flown from airfields at Midway and Hawaii.

The attacks set fire to the forward part of the ship, yet this did not prevent *Hiryu* from withdrawing to the west. Eventually, the fires spread out of control and for all intents and purposes the vessel was dead in the water.

Japanese destroyers picked up the survivors from the ship and *Hiryu* was torpedoed following an order to scuttle. However, the carrier stubbornly refused to

sink, and remained afloat until 09.00 on 5 June. The vessel was photographed by an aircraft from the carrier *Hosho*, which was accompanying Admiral Yamamoto's force of battleships. The aircraft noted that the carrier still had some survivors aboard, and the destroyer *Tanikaze* was sent to investigate, and if possible rescue the survivors. The ship found nothing. Steaming back to the force following its investigations, *Tanikaze* came under heavy fire from the US Navy, when 50 aircraft attacked the vessel. In a miraculous display of ship-handling, the destroyer escaped.

Hiryu's legacy

Hiryu may have had a curious design, but many of its features were carried over into future designs.

The design for the carrier *Unryu* closely followed that of the *Hiryu*, except the position of the island superstructure was changed to the starboard. However, the design could be produced quickly and cheaply. Of the six carriers which were started by Japan after the Battle of Midway, all were either destroyed outright or severely damaged. The main point of vulnerability proved to be the ease with which bombs could penetrate the flight deck, causing major damage when they exploded in the hangars below.

Hiryu

1 Flight deck
2 Hangar
3 Boat deck
4 Crew quarters, canteens etc
5 Stores
6 Wireless aerials
7 Boat crane
8 Balanced rudder
9 Screws
10 Shaft
11 Safety net
12 Access doors for stores etc
13 Twin 127-mm (5-in) 40-calibre dual-purpose guns
14 Ammunition hoist
15 Machine shop
16 Auxiliary engine room
17 Thin side armour
18 Turbine reduction gear
19 Turbine
20 Boiler room
21 Pair of Kampon boilers (4x2)
22 Water tubes inside boiler
23 Bulkhead dividing engine rooms
24 Bulkhead dividing boiler rooms
25 Ventilating doors to hangar
26 Fire screen
27 Lift
28 Lift machinery
29 Funnel casing
30 Funnel uptake
31 Bridge
32 Command centre
33 Main rangefinder
34 Rangefinder for aft guns
35 AA gun rangefinder
36 Navigating bridge
37 Flight control bridge
38 Aircraft stores
39 25-mm AA guns
40 Main mast
41 Officers' quarters/offices
42 Aviation fuel
43 Fuel
44 Flight deck crew shelters
45 Anchor
46 Waterline
47 Double bottom

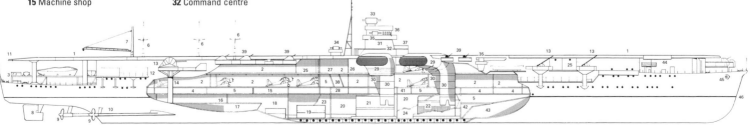

IJN *Soryu* Fleet carrier

Soryu, designed as a carrier, as opposed to being an adaptation, integrated the lower hangar within the hull structure, rather than having it superimposed on top of the hull.

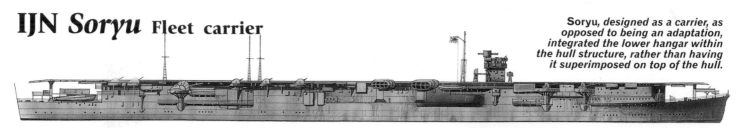

With the experience gained from operating two large carriers and one small, as well as the little *Hosho*, the Imperial Japanese Navy staff felt confident that it could draw up a standard design for future carriers. Under the Second Reinforcement Programme of 1934 the first of this new series, the **Soryu**, was laid down in that year, and she went to sea at the end of 1937. The designers were however still constrained by the Washington international disarmament treaties which limited any particular class of military shipping to a maximum tonnage. After subtracting the overweight *Ryujo* there was only a total of 20,000 tons left. The new carrier was accordingly notified as a 16,000 tonner although displacing some 2,000 tons more; the problem of how to accommodate a second carrier was solved by notifying the other signatories that the Japanese would be withdrawing from all treaty obligations after December 1936.

Long low hull

The *Soryu* was given a starboard island, but as in earlier carriers, smoke was discharged through a pair of downward-curved funnels below the edge of the flight deck. The hull was a very

light structure for a ship of *Soryu's* size. Since powerful, cruiser-type machinery was selected, the carrier proved to be exceptionally fast. Protection was sacrificed in favour of aircraft capacity. However, the excessively long but low hull resulted in very low clearance in the two hangars: 4.60 m (15 ft) in the upper and 4.30 m (14 ft) in the lower hangar. Three centre-line lifts served these hangars, and 63 aircraft could be stowed.

Wake attack

With her half-sister *Hiryu*, the *Soryu* formed Carrier Division 2 and took part in the attack on Pearl Harbor. Thereafter she went with the other fast carriers on their six-month mission to establish Japanese dominance over the Pacific. Her aircraft attacked Wake Island, the Dutch East Indies, Darwin and Ceylon. Then she was assigned to Admiral Yamamoto's Combined Fleet, tasked with the capture of Midway Island early in June 1942.

At 10.26 on 4 June, 17 Douglas SBD Dauntless dive-bombers from the USS *Yorktown* attacked the *Soryu*, scoring three hits down the centre-line of the flight deck. The first 1,000-lb (454-kg) bomb burst in the top hangar and blew out the

forward lift. The second bomb burst among strike aircraft ranged on the flight deck, and the third penetrated to the lower hangar before bursting between the centre and after lifts. The usual deadly combination of ruptured fuel lines and fully bombed-up aircraft produced an inferno, and after only 20 minutes the USS *Soryu* had to be abandoned. The glowing hulk was still afloat for another eight hours after this, but at dusk her magazines blew up and she finally sank.

SPECIFICATION	
IJN *Soryu*	**Speed:** 34.5 kt (64 km/h; 40 mph)
Type: fleet carrier	**Armour:** uncertain
Displacement:: 15,900 tons standard, 19,800 tons full load	**Armament:** six twin 127-mm (5-in) and 14 twin 25-mm AA guns
Dimensions: length 227.50 m (746 ft 6 in) overall; beam 21.30 m (69 ft 11 in); draught 7.60 m (25 ft)	**Aircraft:** 21 Mitsubishi A6M 'Zero' fighters, 21 Aichi D3A 'Val' dive-bombers and 21 Nakajima B5N 'Kate' torpedo bombers
Machinery: 4-shaft geared steam turbines delivering 113350 kW (152,000 shp)	**Complement:** 1,100 officers and men

Soryu served as a model for most succeeding Japanese carrier designs. With an excellent power-to-weight ratio, she was fast and agile and had a large complement of aircraft but, carrying the minimum of armour, she was not built to take punishment.

IJN *Zuikaku* Fleet carrier

Zuikaku, the second ship of the 'Shokaku' class, was laid down in May 1938 and entered service in September 1941. She joined her sister in Carrier Division 5, and for the next three years the two were inseparable. The inexperience of CarDiv 5's aircrews prevented the ships from having anything more than a supporting role during the Pearl Harbor attack, but they were fully worked up by the time CarDiv 5 began its destructive raids on the British in Ceylon. They then left the main carrier force and went to Truk from where they covered the invasion of Port Moresby on 1 May 1942.

Coral Sea

In the ensuing Battle of the Coral Sea CarDiv 5 scored a tactical victory by sinking the *Lexington*, in exchange for the light carrier *Shoho*. The Japanese carriers wasted their efforts on sink-

ing a destroyer and a fleet oiler, which they misidentified as a cruiser and a carrier. A strike by 24 B5N 'Kate' and 36 D3A 'Val' bombers failed to penetrate the US carriers' screen, but on 8 May a similar strike failed to find the *Zuikaku* in a rain squall. Although *Zuikaku* was undamaged her highly trained aircrew had suffered serious attrition. She had to return to Japan with her damaged sister to retrain her air group. As a result CarDiv 5 missed the Battle of Midway, and in the month after Midway it was incorporated into a new CarDiv 1. In the following month it left for the Solomons to challenge American power in Guadalcanal, but so severe was the aircraft shortage that neither carrier had her full complement of warplanes embarked.

In the Battle of the Eastern Solomons, on 24 August 1942, *Zuikaku* damaged *Enterprise* but at

considerable cost. She was seriously mauled at the Battle of the Philippine Sea in June 1944, but her crew managed to overcome the

Wartime modification of the Zuikaku, as with American and British carriers, included an upgrade of her AA defences. In 1943 she was also fitted out with Type 13 air-warning and Type 21 air/surface-warning radar systems.

fires which threatened to engulf the carrier. As a result her petrol bunkers were reinforced with concrete to exclude air from the spaces surrounding them. In October 1944 she formed part of CarDiv 3, assisting in feints to draw the US carriers supporting the Leyte Gulf landings. On 24 October *Zuikaku* launched her last air strike against the enemy. All aircraft in the strike were shot down, and next day the US pilots took their revenge by sinking all four Japanese carriers, in the Battle of Cape Engano. The *Zuikaku* was made the chief target. She was engulfed by two succeeding attack waves of US aircraft. She was hit first by one torpedo and then by a further six and seven bombs. No ship could take such punishment and she soon rolled over and sank.

Zuikaku was lost off Cape Engano during the Battle of Leyte Gulf. As she sank, her crew saluted the naval ensign while it was lowered.

SPECIFICATION

IJN *Zuikaku*
Type: fleet carrier
Displacement: 25,675 tons standard, 32,000 tons full load
Dimensions: length 257.50 m (844 ft 9 in) overall; beam 26 m (85 ft 4 in); draught 8.90 m (29 ft 2 in)
Machinery: 4-shaft geared steam turbines delivering 119310 kW (160,000 shp)

Speed: 34.2 kt (63 km/h; 39 mph)
Armour: 215 mm (8½ in) armour belt; deck 170 mm (6¾ in)
Armament: eight twin 127-mm (5-in) dual-purpose and 12 triple 25-mm (0.99-in) AA guns
Aircraft: 27 fighters, 27 dive-bombers and 18 torpedo-bombers
Complement: 1,600 officers and men

IJN *Shokaku* Fleet carrier

The best carriers extant, at the time of their introduction, the 'Shokakus' had strong AA armament but suffered from a vulnerable fuel system.

Japan's withdrawal from the international treaties limiting warship size of at the end of 1936 enabled her constructors at last to design carriers that suited requirements. Under the 1937 Reinforcement Programme two more carriers were to be built, basically similar to the Hiryu but large enough to accommodate all that was required.

Lessons learned

In the **'Shokaku' class** all the earlier faults were remedied. Two catapults were provided, and a much larger hangar enabled aircraft capacity to be increased from 63 to 75. Even with a considerable increase in power (the most powerful machinery ever fitted in a Japanese warship) the two ships could achieve a range of nearly 16000 km (10,000 miles) as they carried 5,000 tons of fuel. Equally important, they were well armoured and carried a much heavier anti-aircraft armament than their predecessors. In most respects they were the best carriers in the world, being surpassed only by the later 'Essex'-class. Their one principal defect was the light construction of the flight deck, aggravated by totally enclosed yet unprotected double hangars. In addition, like all Japanese carriers, they suffered from vulnerable fuel systems. Not only were the fuel lines to the hangars and flight deck liable to be ruptured by explosions some distance away, but the fuel storage tanks were inadequately protected against shock.

Into action

Shokaku was laid down at the end of 1937 and went to sea in August 1941, just two months before Pearl Harbor. Although she took part in the attack, her aircrews were too inexperienced to do more than bomb the airfields on Oahu. With her sister *Zuikaku* she formed Carrier Division 5, and after their work-up early in 1942 they operated off Ceylon and New Guinea.

During the Battle of the Coral Sea, *Shokaku* was damaged by a strike from the *Yorktown*; although she caught fire she was saved with some difficulty, and had to return to Japan for repairs. The worst casualties were, however, the loss of 86 aircraft and most of their aircrews, so that neither carrier could take part in the Battle of Midway. On 14 July they joined the new Carrier Division 1, with the light carrier *Zuiho*. In the Battle of the Eastern Solomons they damaged the *Enterprise* but again lost precious aircrew and aircraft. On 26 October the *Shokaku* was severely damaged by a dive-bomber strike from the *Hornet*.

During the Battle of the Philippine Sea on 19 June 1944 she was hit by three torpedoes from the submarine USS *Cavalla*, and an explosion from ruptured aviation fuel tanks subsequently sank her.

SPECIFICATION

IJN *Shokaku*
Type: fleet carrier
Displacement: 25,675 tons standard, 32,000 tons full load
Dimensions: length 257.50 m (844 ft 9 in) overall; beam 26 m (85 ft 4 in); draught 8.90 m (29 ft 2 in)
Machinery: 4-shaft geared steam turbines delivering 119310 kW (160,000 shp)

Speed: 34.2 kt (63 km/h; 39 mph)
Armour: belt 215 mm (8½ in); deck 170 mm (6¾ in)
Armament: eight twin 127-mm (5-in) dual-purpose and 12 triple 25-mm (0.99-in) AA guns
Aircraft: 27 fighters, 27 dive-bombers and 18 torpedo-bombers
Complement: 1,600 officers and men

Shokaku during the Battle of the Philippines on 19 June 1944. Her design incorporated the lessons learned from the Hiryu and Soryu. She had much greater armour protection without sacrificing her speed.

Zuiho Light carrier

Originally diesel-powered submarine support ships, Zuiho and its sister Shoho were fitted with steam turbines during conversion. With single hangars, aircraft capacity was 30.

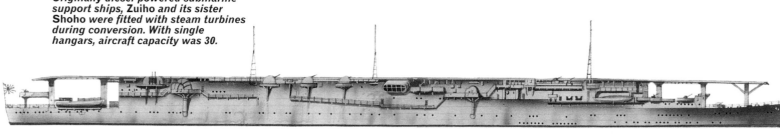

In a desperate attempt to remedy the shortage of aircraft carriers, the Japanese naval staff decided that certain large fleet auxiliaries such as submarine tenders should be designed for rapid conversion to carriers in wartime. One such class was the 'Tsurigizaki' class of high-speed oilers, which were ordered under the 1934 Second Reinforcement Programme; their hulls were specially strengthened. The design was then altered to submarine tenders, and the lead-ship entered service in that role early in 1939. Its sister ship *Takasaki*, however, was not completed, and was laid up in the shipyard for nearly four years. Work on its conversion to a carrier started in January 1940, under the new name **Zuiho**.

Zuiho conversion

Apart from the replacement of the unreliable diesels with geared steam turbines, as much of the original hull was retained as possible. A single hangar was provided, accommodating a maximum of 30 aircraft, with two centreline lifts; there were two catapults but no island superstructure. To retain the high speed and endurance all planned armouring was deleted. The conversion was carried out in a year, and the *Zuiho* joined the Combined Fleet in January 1941. With the old *Hosho* (Carrier Division 3) it was sent to the Palaus in the late autumn of that year and took part in the attack on the Philippines. It then returned to Japan for repairs before taking part in the conquest of the East Indies in the spring.

Surprise attack

Luckily for the carrier, it was with the Support Force at Midway and escaped the destruction of the main carrier force. In the Battle of the Santa Cruz Islands it was part of Admiral Nagumo's Carrier Strike Force. At 07.40 on 25 October 1942 a dive-bomber from the USS *Enterprise* made a surprise attack out of low cloud, dropping its bomb in the centre of the flight deck. With a 15-m (50-ft) crater in its flight deck, the *Zuiho* could no longer operate aircraft, and so after launching its aircraft, the *Zuiho* returned to base.

Decoy

In February 1944 *Zuiho* rejoined Carrier Division 3, and it took part in the Battle of the Philippine Sea, when its aircraft scored a hit on the battleship USS *South Dakota*. In the fighting around Leyte Gulf it was one of the doomed carriers which attempted to decoy the Americans: in the Battle of Cape Engano it was hit

Zuiho off Tateyama a year before Pearl Harbor. Part of the support force at Midway, the carrier escaped destruction and went on to serve in the Solomons and the Philippine Sea before meeting its fate off Cape Engano at Leyte Gulf in 1944.

SPECIFICATION	
Zuiho	(52,000 shp)
Displacement: 11,262 tons standard; 14,200 tons full load	**Speed:** 28.2 kts
	Armour: none
Dimensions: length 204.8 m (672 ft) overall; beam 18.2 m (59 ft 8 in); draught 6.6 m (21 ft 8 in)	**Armament:** four twin 127-mm (5-in) dual-purpose and four twin 25-mm AA guns
Machinery: 2-shaft geared steam turbines delivering 38770 kW	**Aircraft:** 30
	Complement: 785 officers and men

by two bombs on the flight deck and was near-missed six times. In spite of a serious fire and flooding *Zuiho* was under way for another six hours, as the other carriers were picked off. Finally it was *Zuiho*'s turn, and three waves of attackers finally finished the aircraft carrier off.

Shoho Light carrier

The submarine tender *Tsurigizaki* had been serving with the Combined Fleet in 1939-40, but as soon as the conversion of its sister *Takasaki* into a carrier was completed in December 1940 it was taken in hand, re-emerging in January 1942 as the light carrier **Shoho**. *Shoho* did not see any action until the spring of 1942, when it covered the Port Moresby invasion, in the Support Force commanded by Rear-Admiral Aritomo Goto. It was this move by the Japanese which led to the Battle of the Coral Sea, the first carrier versus carrier battle in history.

Bombing attack

The *Shoho* was heading for Port Moresby on 6 May 1942 when at 10.30 it was

Shoho entered service in January 1942, but unlike Zuiho its operational career was extremely brief. Shoho had the unhappy distinction of being Japan's first aircraft carrier loss, sunk by aircraft from USS Yorktown on 7 May 1942 in the Coral Sea.

sighted 100 km (60 miles) south of Bougainville by four B-17 bombers. The four aircraft attempted a high-level bombing attack on the carrier, but caused negligible damage. The two sides were largely ignorant of each other's whereabouts. In a desperate attempt to find the American carriers, *Takagi* flew off reconnaissance planes for a dawn sweep on the next day. At 07.30 they reported a carrier and a cruiser, and the *Shokaku* and *Zuikaku* immediately flew off a large strike. Unfortunately the 'task force' turned out to be the US Navy oiler *Neosho* and its escorting destroyer, the USS *Sims*. It was a fatal error, for while the Japanese were sinking these ships they missed the chance of finding Task Force 17, and left the Americans time to discover the *Shoho*'s carrier group.

Brutal assault

The luckless *Shoho* had been ordered to launch all available aircraft for an attack on the US carriers, and when at 09.50 the *Lexington*'s strike spotted it turning into wind, they encountered no resistance to their attack. The first strike scored no hits, but a near-miss blew five aircraft off its deck. At 10.25 a second strike arrived, from the USS *Yorktown* this time. This strike scored two hits with 1,000-lb (454-kg) bombs on the flight deck, in spite of anti-aircraft fire from the *Shoho*'s escorts. The carrier reeled under the blows, and as it began to lose speed, more bombs and torpedoes found their mark. According to Japanese records as many as 11 more bombs and seven torpedoes hit, and the *Shoho* aircraft carrier burst into flames.

Japanese loss

Approximately six minutes after the last US aircraft had departed the order was given to abandon ship, and at 10.35 the burning carrier rolled over and sank. Only 255 men out of an estimated total of 800 on board were saved. The Japanese had lost their first aircraft carrier.

SPECIFICATION	
Shoho	
Displacement: 11,262 tons standard; 14,200 tons full load	**Speed:** 28.2 kts
	Armour: none
Dimensions: length 204.8 m (672 ft) overall; beam 18.2 m (59 ft 8 in); draught 6.6 m (21 ft 8 in)	**Armament:** four twin 127-mm (5-in) dual-purpose and four twin 25-mm AA guns
Machinery: 2-shaft geared steam turbines delivering 38770 kW (52,000 shp)	**Aircraft:** 30
	Complement: 785 officers and men

'Junyo' class Aircraft carrier conversions

While their capacious liner hulls had room for two hangars, the 'Junyo'-class vessels suffered from a lack of speed, and without catapults aircraft operations were hampered. Both were at the Battle of the Philippine Sea, Junyo being damaged and Hiyo sinking.

Like the trio of 'Taiyo'-class ships that preceded them, the **Junyo** and its sister **Hiyo** of the 'Junyo' class were useful conversions from Nippon Yusen Kaisha liners that had been designed from the outset with this procedure in mind. Where the earlier ships had undergone rebuilding at a late stage, the larger 'Taiyo'-class ships were taken in hand before launching, both being in the water by June 1941, over five months before the Pacific War began, and completed in mid-1942.

Spacious carrier

As they had been designed as passenger liners, they had considerable freeboard and could accommodate two hangars, albeit of restricted headroom. They also had respectably sized flight decks, measuring 210.2 m by 27.3 m (689ft.7in by 89ft 7in), and two centreline elevators, but suffered badly from the combination of their low mercantile speed and lack of catapults.

Additional equipment

The two ships were the first Japanese carriers to incorporate a funnel as part of the island, though it was of strange aspect, canted outward at a sharp angle. Except for the never completed Italian *Aquila*, this pair of carriers were the largest ever converted from mercantile hulls.

Junyo's 53 aircraft could have had a decisive effect at Midway but the ship was engaged in the rather fruitless Aleutians diversion. At Santa Cruz in October 1942 its aircraft damaged the battleship USS *South Dakota* and a cruiser, playing also a significant role in the sinking of the carrier USS *Hornet*. The two sisters operated together as Kakuta's Carrier Division Two but, at the battle of the Philippine Sea, where Ozawa took on the vastly superior force of Mitscher's TF 58, the partnership was broken, the *Junyo* being heavily damaged by bombing and *Hiyo* sunk after blowing up. The *Hiyo* had been struck by two torpedoes and was probably lost from the detonation of a build-up of vapour from leaking Avgas tanks.

Out of service

The *Junyo*, newly repaired, was torpedoed in December 1944 and, though it was not sunk, it never re-entered service, and survived to be one of the very few Japanese naval ships of any size to fall eventually into US hands.

SPECIFICATION	
'Junyo' class	
Displacement: 24,500 tons standard and 26,960 tons full load	to two shafts
	Speed: 25 kts
Dimensions: length 219.2 m (719 ft 2 in); beam 26.7 m (87 ft 7 in); draught 8.2 m (26 ft 11 in)	**Armour:** none
	Armament: 12 127-mm (5-in) DP and 24 25-mm AA guns
Propulsion: geared steam turbines delivering 41760 kW (56,000 shp)	**Aircraft:** 53
	Complement: about 1,220

Seen at Sasebo after the surrender of Japan, Junyo displays the unusual funnel of the class. Converted from passenger liners, the two 'Junyo'-class aircraft carriers were the first in Japanese service to feature a funnel on the island.

Taiho Fleet carrier

Probably the most advanced of all Japanese carriers, Taiho had an armoured flight deck, enclosed bow and the latest in AA defences (including an air warning radar for the first time). Taiho was lost just before the Battle of the Philippine Sea.

In many ways technically the most advanced of the Japanese carriers, the **Taiho** was unique. In 1939 Japanese intelligence learned that the British 'Illustrious'-class carriers would have armoured decks, and so a new type of armoured carrier was planned under the Fourth Reinforcement Programme. The appalling carnage of Midway lent even more emphasis to the need for armoured flight decks, and two more units were ordered in 1942.

The Japanese design differed considerably from the British 'box-hangar' concept, for only the flight deck was protected by 75-mm (3-in) armour, and then only between the lifts. There were two hangars, with the lower hangar being pro-

tected by 35-mm (1-in) armour as well. Waterline armour was also provided but on a more lavish scale, with 150-mm (6-in) of protection abreast of the magazines and 55-mm (2-in) over the machinery,

Weight penalty

All this armour involved a colossal topweight penalty, and to preserve stability the designers were forced to allow one less deck above the waterline, in comparison with the 'Shokaku' class. This meant that the lower hangar deck was just above the waterline, while the bottom of the liftwells were below the waterline.

The opportunity was taken to use the latest defensive guns: a new high velocity 100-mm (3.9-in) Type 98 twin mounting. For the

first time an air warning radar was included. It had been hoped to operate 84 aircraft, but only 75 could be spared by the time the ship was ready. The aircraft were available, but not the sufficiently trained aircrew.

Torpedo strike

The new carrier, to be called *Taiho*, was laid down in July 1941 and went to sea in March 1944. Immediately, it joined Carrier Division 1 (CarDiv 1), and was sent with the *Shokaku* and *Zuikaku* to Singapore. As soon as the air group was trained CarDiv 1 was sent to Tawi Tawi in the southern Philippines to join the First Mobile Fleet. On 19 June, during the Battle of the Philippine Sea, the *Taiho* had just launched its aircraft when the American subma-

rine *Albacore* fired a spread of six 21-in (533-mm) torpedoes, one of which hit. Although its fuel tanks were ruptured, the *Taiho* lost only a little speed, and preparations were made to plank over the jammed forward lift to permit flying operations to continue. However, deadly gasoline vapour was spreading throughout the

ship, and about 5 hours after the torpedo hits, some mischance (probably the switch on an electric pump) sparked off a colossal explosion. The armoured flight deck was split, the sides of the hangar were blown out, and it seems that holes were blown through the keel. About 90 minutes later *Taiho* sank below the waves.

SPECIFICATION	
Taiho	**Armament:** six twin 100-mm
Displacement: 29,300 tons	(3.9-in) AA and 15 triple 25-mm AA
standard; 37,270 tons full load	guns
Dimensions: length 260.5 m	**Aircraft:** 30 Yokosuka D4Y 'Judy'
(854 ft 8 in); beam 27.7 m (90 ft	dive-bombers; 27 Mitsubishi A6M
10 in); draught 9.6 m (31 ft 6 in)	Zero fighters and 18 Nakajima B6N
Machinery: 4-shaft geared steam	'Jill' torpedo-bombers
turbines delivering 134225 kW	**Complement:** 2,150 officers and
(180,000 shp)	men
Speed: 33 kts	
Armour: see text	

'Unryu' class Fleet carrier

The 'Unryu' class were to have been a standard design, produced in quantity. Although 17 were planned, only three of the modified, simplified 'Hiryu' design were built, with only Unryu being completed in time for war service.

Like the Americans, the Japanese recognised that series production of a standard design was the only way of commissioning adequate numbers of good quality carriers in time for the ships to be of any use. To this end the basic 'Hiryu' design was modified and simplified, orders being placed at a variety of shipyards under the 1941-42 War Programme. Seventeen units of this **'Unryu' class** were planned initially but, even though construction of some had started

before the Battle of Midway, the losses incurred convinced the Japanese that shorter term solutions needed to be found in a variety of conver-

sions. These seem to have enjoyed higher priorities because of haste, and the 'Unryu' class programme slowed badly, eventually halting through lack of materials. In the event, only three were ever completed and three more launched.

Production

The three completed were the **Amagi** (August 1944), the **Katsuragi** (October 1944) and **Unryu** (August 1944); the three others launched were the **Aso**, **Ikoma** and **Kasagi**. The main differences between the 'Unryu' and the 'Hiryu' designs was an eleva-

Unryu at sea in 1944. The ship was not destined to serve long, being sunk in December 1944 in the East China Sea. Two torpedoes from the American submarine USS Redfish sent the carrier to the bottom.

tor less and an altered layout of main armament in the former. Though of about the same length, the 'Unryu'-class ships gained stability through a greater beam yet for some unknown reason, had a smaller aircraft capacity. For their size, they were well protected over vitals, and like all larger 'regular' Japanese carriers, the 'Unryu'-class units had a good turn of speed, having the same machinery as later heavy

cruiser classes. With shortages biting, however, two of those launched had to take a couple of sets of destroyer machinery. Despite a one-third reduction in power, the speed penalty was only a couple of knots. The *Amagi* was lost to air attack in Kure during July 1945, the *Katsuragi* survived and was surrendered (for scrapping in 1947) and the *Unryu* was sunk in December 1944 by a US submarine.

SPECIFICATION	
'Unryu' class	to four shafts
Displacement: 17,250 tons	**Speed:** 34 kts for *Unryu* and 32 kts
standard and 22,550 tons full load	for *Aso* and *Katsuragi*
Dimensions: length 227.2 m	**Armour:** belt 25-150 mm (1-5.9 in);
(745 ft 5 in); beam 22 m (72 ft 2 in);	deck 55 mm (2.17 in)
draught 7.8 m (25 ft 7 in)	**Armament:** 12 127-mm (5-in) DP
Machinery: geared steam turbines	and between 51 and 89 25-mm AA
delivering 113345 kW (152,000 shp)	guns
in *Unryu* and 77555 kW	**Aircraft:** 64
(104,000 shp) in *Aso* and *Katsuragi*	**Complement:** 1,450

Shinano Fleet carrier

By far the largest carrier of the war, Shinano was to have been the third 'Yamato'-class battleship. The small aircraft capacity and slow speed pointed to its eventual role as repair and resupply vessel to front-line carriers, a role it was destined never to fulfil.

The catastrophic loss of four carriers at Midway, solely from aircraft from US carriers, convinced the Japanese not only that carriers were more useful than battleships, but also that they needed to urgently increase their numbers.

Most of their ambitious programme of conversions date from this point, none of them more impressive than the **Shinano**. Created from the incomplete third 'Yamato'-class battleship, this giant displaced nearly 72,000 tons full load, a figure not eclipsed until the advent of the US post-war

supercarriers. The hull was already fitted with a 200-mm (7.87-in) armoured deck and vertical protection of the same order, and the ship's great beam (increased further by bulging) allowed for a flight deck of 80-mm (3.15-in) thickness over most of its area.

Despite the ship's size, the flight deck was over 1 m (3 ft 4 in) shorter than that of the *Taiho* of less than half the displacement, although it was far wider. Viewed as probably too slow to act as an attack carrier, *Shinano* was not even fitted with catapults and, although

originally slated to have a small air group of 18 aircraft, it was completed to carry a still-undersized complement of 47. The ship's considerable stowage was looked upon mainly as a repair and re-supply facility for the front-line carriers.

Brief career

Like the *Taiho*, the *Shinano* had an integral funnel and island, but lacked the smaller ship's British-style 'hurricane bow'. *Shinano*'s shortcomings were, in the event, only academic. Not quite complete in time for the Japanese fleet's self-

immolation at Leyte Gulf in October 1944, it transferred from Yokosuka to Kure for a final fitting-out. On the way it was hit by a full spread of six torpedoes from an

American submarine: its watertight subdivision still incomplete, *Shinano* foundered from virtually uncontrolled flooding on 29 November and sank.

SPECIFICATION	
'Shinano' class	to four shafts
Displacement: 64,000 tons standard and 71,900 tons full load	**Speed:** 27 kts
Dimensions: length 265.8 m (872 ft); beam 36.3 m (119 ft); draught 10.3 m (33 ft 10 in); flight deck 255.9 m (839 ft 7 in) by 40.1 m (131 ft 7 in)	**Armour:** belt 205 mm (8.07 in); flight deck 80 mm (3.15 in); hangar deck 200 mm (7.87 in)
	Armament: 16 127-mm (5-in) DP and 145 25-mm AA guns, and 12 28-barrel AA rocket-launchers
Machinery: geared steam turbines delivering 111855 kW (150,000 shp)	**Aircraft:** 18 (later 47)
	Complement: 2,400

'Taiyo' class Escort carrier

The three 'Taiyo'-class vessels were largely used for aircraft transport and training. Their heavy AA armament was to no avail, all three succumbing to submarine attacks from USS Rasher (which sank Taiyo), Barb (Unyo) and Sailfish (Chuyo).

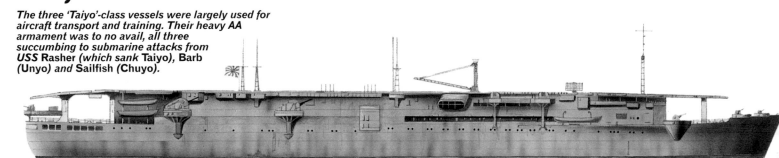

In common with the British and American fleets, Japan's need for escort carriers was met by converting merchant hulls. Kaiyo, seen here in late 1943, was similar to the 'Taiyo'-class conversions.

government subsidised features built into them. The **Taiyo** was the first such example, converted from the *Kasuga Maru* in 1941 as the lead ship of the **'Taiyo' class**, before the outbreak of the Pacific War.

Auxiliary tasks

After a few months of evaluation, the similar *Yawata Maru* and *Nitta Maru* were rebuilt into the **Unyo** and **Chuyo** respectively. Though of a larger size than Western escort carriers, none of them was equipped with arrester gear or catapults which, combined with their low speed, made aircraft launch and recovery difficult. All were lost to submarine torpedo attack within a space of 10 months between December 1943 and September 1944 having spent their lives engaged in auxiliary tasks.

Probably for reasons of weapons availability, the first of the class, the *Taiyo*, was armed with 120-mm (4.7-in) guns. These were probably spare weapons obtained from older destroyers.

SPECIFICATION	
'Taiyo' class	delivering 18790 kW (25,200 shp) to two shafts
Displacement: 17,850 tons standard	**Armour:** none
Dimensions: length 180.1 m (590 ft 11 in); beam 22.5 m (73 ft 10 in); draught 8 m (26 ft 3 in); flight deck 171.9 m (564 ft) by 23.5 m (77 ft 1 in)	**Armament:** eight 127-mm (5-in) DP (except *Taiyo*, see text) and eight (later 22) 25-mm AA guns
	Aircraft: 27
Machinery: geared steam turbines	**Complement:** 800

Carriers were required by the Japanese for other than fleet purposes. Firstly, and with increasing urgency, for the defence of trade. This was a function that had been badly neglected pre-war due to a lack of hard experience and the belief that the war would be short. Secondly, for the training of large numbers of aircrew for carrier operations, a task for

which first-line units could not be spared. Thirdly, for the ferrying of aircraft, a task made essential by the sheer size of the newly-acquired empire, which had airfields thousands of miles from the homeland itself.

Like Western fleets, the Japanese navy rebuilt good-class mercantile tonnage into auxiliary carriers, particularly NYK ships, which had

HMAS *Melbourne* and HMAS *Sydney* Light fleet carriers

Formerly name ship of the British built 'Majestic'-class light fleet carriers, HMAS Melbourne was bought by Australia in 1949. By 1965 the vessel was notable for the tall lattice mast added to carry the newly fitted LW series main search radar.

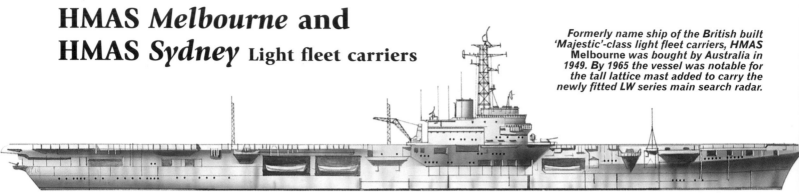

Work on all six of the Royal Navy's **'Majestic'-class** carriers was stopped after the end of World War II. However, because of interest expressed by the Royal Australian and Canadian navies in acquiring carriers, two units were subsequently completed as **HMS Terrible** (bought by Australia as **HMAS Sydney**) and **HMS Magnificent** (loaned to Canada under that name), while work on a third, **HMS Majestic**, was started in 1948 to a greatly modified configuration with 25 40-mm AA guns, a 5.5° angle landing deck, new arrester gear, a mirror landing sight system and a steam catapult. The opportunity to fit a greatly enhanced radar suite was also taken, with no fewer than three Type 277Q height-finding sets, a Type 293 surface search set and a Type 978 navigation set.

Recommissioning as

HMAS Melbourne in October 1955, the carrier embarked an air group of eight Sea Venoms, 12 Gannet ASW aircraft and two Sycamore SAR helicopters. In 1963-67 the *Melbourne* served as the RAN flagship, and its air group was reduced to four Sea Venoms, six Gannets and ten Wessex HAS.Mk 31B helicopters. In late 1967 the ship was taken in hand for strengthening of the decks, lifts, catapult and arrester gear, the fitting of new radar and communications equipment and the reduction of the AA armament numbers. This was to allow for the carriage and operation of A-4G Skyhawks and S-2E Tracker ASW aircraft. The new radars were a mixture of Dutch and American types, together with the old Type 293 and Type 978 sets. The air group now consisted of four Skyhawks, six Trackers and

10 Wessex helicopters, though from 1972 onwards it was again changed to eight Skyhawks, six Trackers and 10 Sea King HAS.Mk 50 ASW helicopters plus two or three Wessex helicopters in the SAR/planeguard role. After a final refit in 1976 it was announced that the *Melbourne* was to serve on until 1985, but as a result of financial constraints it was paid off into reserve during June 1982, and in 1984 was sold for scrap. Although a replacement was scheduled (including at one stage the Royal Navy's *Invincible*), this was a forlorn hope since all navy fixed-wing aircraft were sold or transferred to the Royal Australian Air Force.

HMAS Sydney

HMAS *Sydney* was commissioned into the Australian navy on 16 December 1948, initially carrying a mixed complement of Sea Fury, Firefly

SPECIFICATION

HMS Melbourne
Displacement: 16,000 tons standard and 20,320 tons full load
Dimensions: length 213.82 m (701 ft); beam 24.38 m (80 ft); draught 7.62 m (25 ft); flight deck width 32 m (105 ft)
Propulsion: two-shaft geared steam turbines delivering 31319 kW (42,000 shp)
Speed: 23 kts

Armament: four twin and four single 40-mm AA guns
Aircraft: 27 (see text)
Complement: 1,425 (as flagship)
Electronics: one LW-02 air search radar, one Type 293Q surface search radar, one Type 978 navigation radar, one SPN-35 landing aid radar, one TACAN system and one ECM system

and Sea Otter aircraft. Its complement of 37 aircraft was larger than that of *Melbourne*, despite it being slightly smaller. *Sydney* became the first RAN carrier to serve in combat in October 1951 when it relieved HMS *Glory* during the Korean War. During the conflict the ship performed seven operational patrols and its air wing completed 2,366 sorties. In May 1958 the

ship was paid off into the reserve, but was recommissioned as a troop ship in March 1962. Between 1965-72, the vessel undertook operations in Vietnam deploying four Wessex helicopters for ASW protection duties on 22 voyages to the theatre. *Sydney* was decommissioned in November 1973 and was eventually sold for scrap in 1975.

HMAS Melbourne is seen entering Pearl Harbor in June 1958. The air group at this time comprised 27 aircraft including Sea Venoms and ASW Gannets. The ship was flagship of the Royal Australian Navy, and remained so until its withdrawal from service in 1982.

Independencia 'Colossus'-class light fleet carrier

ARA *Independencia* was launched in May 1944 as the British 'Colossus'-class carrier **HMS Warrior**. *Warrior* was launched from the Harland and Wolff yard in Belfast on 20 May 1944. The ship was lent to the Royal Canadian Navy on completion in 1945 for a period of two years until the

Canadian carrier HMCS *Magnificent* was ready for service. On return from the Canadian service, *Warrior* was used by the Royal Navy for deck landing trials and in 1948-49 was fitted with a flexible landing deck to allow jet fighters with skid-type landing gear to make soft landings. In 1952-53 the ship

was fitted with a new enlarged bridge and a lattice foremast, while in 1955 it was revised together with a 5° angled right deck and stronger arrester gear.

Operation Grapple

Following more deck landing trials work with this new configuration, *Warrior* was

tasked in 1957 to act as the HQ ship for Operation Grapple (the British H-bomb test programme) at Christmas Island in the Pacific Ocean. On its return the ship was offered for sale to Argentina. After subsequent negotiations, a deal was signed in the summer of 1958. The vessel was for-

mally handed over to the Argentine navy on 11 November 1958, and the Argentine ensign was raised for the first time during a ceremony at Portsmouth. The ship sailed under its new name of *Independencia* in December of that year for Argentina, as that nation's first aircraft carrier. As trans-

Originally the British 'Colossus'-class carrier HMS Warrior, the Argentine carrier Independencia had a varied career, serving in Korea as well as being lent to the Canadian navy before being acquired in 1958. Among the aircraft types operated were F4U Corsair fighter/attack aircraft and S-2A Tracker ASW aircraft.

ferred it carried only 12 40-mm AA guns, a number reduced to eight shortly afterwards. However, by May 1962 *Independencia* was spotted with a new battery of one quadruple and nine twin 40-mm guns. In 1963, the carrier was also carrying F4U-5 Corsairs (which formed its most important equipment) and the TF-9J Cougar trainer. Fennec armed trainers were also a common sight aboard the *Independencia*. However, the ship never embarked the F9F Panther on an operational basis, although in theory, it could deploy combat jets. By the end of the ship's career in the late 1960s the embarked air group was made up of six S-2A Trackers (introduced to the carrier in 1962) and 14 Fennecs. In 1970, following the acquisition of ARA *25 de Mayo*, the *Independencia* was placed in reserve. Decommissioned, the vessel was finally sold for scrap in March 1971.

SPECIFICATION	
Independencia	steam turbines delivering
Displacement: 14,000 tons	29828 kW (40,000 shp)
standard and 19,540 tons full load	**Speed:** 24 kts
Dimensions: length 211.84 m	**Armament:** one quadruple and
(695 ft); beam 24.38 m (80 ft);	nine twin 40-mm AA guns (removed
draught 7.16 m (23 ft); flight deck	in 1970)
width 22.86 m (75 ft)	**Aircraft:** 24 (see text)
Propulsion: two-shaft geared	**Complement:** 1,575

Arromanches
'Colossus'-class light fleet carrier

Originally the name ship of the Royal Navy's 'Colossus' class, the Arromanches entered French service in 1946. At the same time as its sisters were in action off Korea, the vessel was involved in the French colonial struggle in Indo-China, making four deployments in eight years.

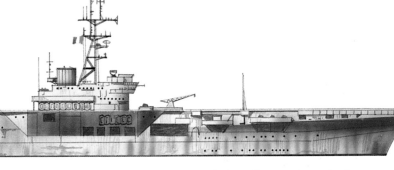

Laid down in June 1942 and launched in September 1943 at the Newcastle yard of Vickers Armstrong Limited as the British 'Colossus'-class carrier **HMS Colossus**, this ship was loaned to the French navy in August 1946 (after 12 months of service in the Far East) for a five-year period. Named **FNS Arromanches** after the beach which was used by the Allies for landing equipment and supplies after D-Day, the ship made two combat deployments to French Indo-China, flying SBD Dauntless and Seafire Mk XV aircraft on the first, and 24 F6F Hellcats and SB2C Helldivers on the second. *Arromanches* was finally purchased outright in 1951 when the loan expired, and was sent on two more Indo-China deployments before the French defeats of 1954. Transferred to the Mediterranean, the *Arromanches* took part in the 1956 Anglo-French Suez landings with F4U Corsairs and TBM Avengers attacking targets around Port Said. The carrier also took part in French military operations in Algeria. In 1957-58 the ship underwent a complete rebuild in which it received a 4° angled flight deck and a mirror landing aid. The AA armament then comprised 43 40-mm guns instead of the original armament of 24 2-pdr and 19 40-mm guns. By the early 1960s all of the 40-mm guns had been removed and the *Arromanches* had been relegated to the training carrier role flying both Alizé ASW aircraft and the Zéphyr jet trainer, to produce personnel for the air groups of the new carriers *Foch* and *Clémenceau*. In 1962 the *Arromanches* also took on the assault role when HSS-1 helicopters from Flotille 33F were embarked. After a further refit in 1968 to carry an air group of 24 helicopters, the carrier was redesignated as a helicopter carrier with ASW, transport, training and intervention missions tasked to it as required. Finally decommissioned in 1974 after 30 continuous years of British and French service, the *Arromanches* was broken up at Toulon in 1978.

SPECIFICATION	
Arromanches	29828 kW (40,000 shp)
Displacement: 14,000 tons	**Speed:** 25 kts
standard and 19,600 tons full load	**Armament:** see text
Dimensions: length 211.84 m	**Aircraft:** 24 (see text)
(695 ft); beam 24.38 m (80 ft);	**Complement:** 1,400
draught 7.16 m (23 ft); flight deck	**Electronics:** one DRBV 22A air
width 36 m (118 ft)	search radar, plus various French,
Propulsion: two-shaft geared	American and British radars and
steam turbines delivering	aircraft landing aids

Arromanches is seen here in the Far East in 1953. On the deck is part of its complement of F6F Hellcat fighters and SB2C dive-bombers. After Dien Bien Phu and French withdrawal from the east, the ship took part in the Suez landings, operating off Port Said.

Vikrant 'Majestic'-class carrier

Formerly the British 'Majestic'-class light fleet carrier **HMS** *Hercules* that had been laid up in an incomplete state since May 1946, the **INL** *Vikrant* (as it was renamed, meaning 'valour') was purchased by India in January 1957, and taken to the Belfast shipyard Harland & Wolff in April 1957 for completion with a single hangar, two electrically-operated aircraft lifts, an angled flight deck and steam catapult. The carrier was also partially fitted with an air conditioning system for tropical service, and commissioned in 1961.

Vikrant missed the 1962 Indo-China War, as it was in dry dock, but its aircraft deployed to Tamil Nadu for combat. *Vikrant* was again undergoing a refit at the time of the 1965 Indo-Pakistan War, although its air units did participate from shore bases.

During the 1971 Indo-Pakistan War, the *Vikrant* operated a mixed air group of 16 Sea Hawk fighter-bombers and four Alizé ASW aircraft off East Pakistan (now called Bangladesh), the elderly Sea Hawks attacking many coastal ports, airfields and small craft in a success-ful operation to prevent the movement of Pakistani men and supplies during Indian army operations to 'liberate' that country.

Major upgrade

Replacement of the Alizé by the Sea King Mk 42 for ASW duties began in 1971, but the last Alizé launch was not until 1987. In January 1979 the *Vikrant* commenced a Service Life Extension Programme (SLEP) at Bombay that ended in January 1982 to enable operations with Sea Harrier FRS.Mk 51 aircraft. Included in the refit was the construc-tion of a 9.75° ski-jump ramp, the fitting of new boilers and engines, the provision of new Dutch radars and the fitting of a new operations control system. The first Sea Harrier ski-jump launch was in March 1990. The new air group consisted of six to eight Sea Harriers, between six and eight Alizés, six Sea King Mk 42 ASW/anti-ship missile and Chetak (Alouette III) utility helicopters.

After a long career, *Vikrant* last went to sea in 1994 and was finally decom-missioned three years later.

SPECIFICATION

Vikrant
Displacement: 15,700 tons standard; 19,500 tons full load
Dimensions: length 213.4 m (700 ft); beam 24.4 m (80 ft); draught 7.3 m (24 ft); flight deck width 39 m (128 ft)
Propulsion: two-shaft geared steam turbines delivering 29,830 kW (40,000 shp)
Speed: 24.5 kts

Aircraft: see text
Armament: nine single 40-mm AA
Electronics: one LW-05 air search radar; one ZW-06 surface search radar; one LW-10 tactical search radar; one LW-11 tactical search radar; one Type 963 carrier controlled approach radar
Complement: 1,075 (including air group) in peace, 1,345 (including air group) in war

Used extensively in the 1971 Indo-Pakistan War, INS Vikrant was the major Indian Navy unit responsible for the blockade of East Pakistan. The air group of Alizé ASW aircraft and Sea Hawk fighter-bombers sank a number of Pakistani naval and merchant craft.

Dédalo 'Independence'-class carrier

The *Dédalo* was an ex-US 'Independence'-class carrier, the **USS** *Cabot*, built during World War II that ended its days in the US Navy as an aviation transport. The vessel was reactivated and mod-ernised as a carrier at the Philadelphia Naval Shipyard before being transferred to Spain on a five-year loan from 30 August 1967, after Madrid had rejected an 'Essex'-class carrier and a conversion of the Italian cruiser *Trieste*. In 1973 the *Dédalo* was purchased out-right and assumed the role of the Spanish navy's fleet flagship. The vessel's flight deck was 166 m (545 ft 6 in) long and 32.9 m (108 ft) wide, and the hangar could accommodate 18 Sea King helicopters with another six on the flight deck. The *Dédalo*'s normal air wing comprised four air groups with at least one with eight AV-8S Matador V/STOL fight-ers, one with four SH-3D/G Sea King ASW helicopters, one with four AB 212ASW anti-submarine and elec-tronic warfare helicopters, and one of four helicopters as required by the mission assigned to the carrier. A maximum of seven four-air-craft groups could be handled aboard. The *Dédalo* was finally decommissioned in August 1989, after having sailed over 804650 km (500,000 miles) and seeing 50,000 landings during its time in the Spanish navy.

Below: The elderly Spanish carrier Dédalo was converted from an ex-US World War II 'Independence'-class carrier. Formerly the flagship of the Spanish fleet, the vessel was replaced by the Principe de Asturias.

Above: As USS Cabot, Dédalo had survived a kamikaze attack during the Battle of Leyte Gulf. Contributing greatly to Spanish carrier aviation doctrine, the vessel survived for 20 years in Spanish fleet service.

SPECIFICATION

Dédalo
Displacement: 13,000 tons standard; 16,.416 tons full load
Dimensions: length 189.9 m (623 ft); beam 21.8 m (71 ft 6 in); draught 7.9 m (25 ft)
Propulsion : four-shaft geared steam turbines delivering 74570 kW (100,000 shp)
Speed: 24 kts
Aircraft: see text

Armament: one quadruple 40-mm AA, and nine twin 40-mm AA
Electronics: one SPS-8 3D radar; one SPS-6 and one SPS-40 air search radar; one SPS-10 surface search/tactical radar; two Mk 29 and two Mk 28 fire-control systems; two navigation radars; one URN-22 TACAN system; one WLR-1 ECM system
Complement: 1,112 minus air group

HMS *Victorious* 'Illustrious'-class carrier

After serving in World War II, **HMS Victorious** was completely rebuilt from the hangar deck up between 1950 and 1957 at Portsmouth Dockyard. During this modernisation the hull was widened, deepened and lengthened while the machinery and boilers were completely renewed. Two steam catapults, new arrester gear and an 8.75° angled flight deck with mirror landing sights (as well as new aircraft lifts and radars) were fitted. A maximum of 35 fixed-wing aircraft were scheduled as the air group, but in the event the *Victorious* never had more than 28 aboard plus eight helicopters. Initial equipment after recommissioning in 1958 comprised Scimitars, Sea Venoms, Skyraiders and Whirlwinds, with Sea Vixens replacing the Sea Venoms in

1960. The carrier was again refitted in 1962 and 1968, but before the latter was finished a minor fire broke out, which was taken by the government of the day as an excuse for scrapping it in the following year as part of the 1966 carrier rundown programme. The final air group composition carried by the ship was eight Buccaneer S.Mk 1s, eight Sea Vixens, two Gannet AEW.Mk 3s and five Wessex helicopters. With these aircraft the vessel conducted air operations during the 1964 Indonesian Confrontation. As one of the fleet's and NATO's

Three of the Royal Navy's four angled deck carriers of the time are seen in this 1960s photograph, only HMS Eagle being absent. Victorious, here seen astern of Hermes and Ark Royal, was a very different vessel from the carrier that attacked the Bismarck.

HMS Victorious was the only wartime fleet carrier to be thoroughly modernised in the 1950s. Seen here just before the start of its protracted refit, the vessel was to emerge after eight years completely rebuilt from the hangar deck up, and able to operate jets of up to 18145 kg (40,000 lb) including the Buccaneer.

strike carrier units, the ship and its Buccaneers were fitted to carry the naval version of the 5/20-kT variable-yield Red Beard tactical nuclear gravity bomb.

SPECIFICATION

HMS Victorious
Displacement: 30,500 tons standard and 35,500 tons full load
Dimensions: length 238 m (781 ft); beam 31.5 m (103 ft 6 in); draught 9.4 m (31 ft); flight dock width 47.8 m (157 ft)
Propulsion: three-shaft geared steam turbines delivering 82027 kW (110,000 shp)

Speed: 31 kts
Aircraft: 35 (see text)
Armament: six twin 3-in (76-mm) Mk 33 AA and one sextuple 40-mm AA gun
Electronics: one Type 984 3D radar; one Type 293Q height-finding radar; one Type 974 surface search radar; one CCA aircraft landing aid
Complement: 2,400

HMCS *Bonaventure*

'Majestic'-class carrier

The British 'Majestic'-class aircraft carrier **HMS Powerful** was laid down in November 1943 and launched in an incomplete state in February 1945. In 1952 the hulk was pur-

chased by the Royal Canadian Navy as **HMCS Bonaventure** and redesigned before its completion to accommodate an 8° angled flight deck, a steam catapult, modern

arrester gear and a stabilised mirror landing sight. *Bonaventure* was also fitted with four twin 3-in (76-mm) AA guns on four sponsons projecting from the hull sides. The island was rebuilt and a tall lattice mast with US radars erected in place of the original tripod model. Entering Canadian fleet service in 1957, the *Bonaventure* had an air group consisting initially of 16 F2H-3 Banshee jet fighters and eight Canadian-built CS2F Tracker ASW aircraft. In 1961 it was changed to an all-ASW force with eight Trackers and 13 HO4S-3 Whirlwind helicopters. The latter were finally replaced by CHSS-2 Sea Kings when they became available. The *Bonaventure*'s mid-life (and last) major refit in 1966-67 saw the fitting of new Dutch radar and the Fresnel landing aid, the

The uncompleted 'Majestic'-class carrier HMS Powerful was sold to Canada and completed as HMCS Bonaventure. Originally equipped with F2H Banshees, by 1961 the carrier had become an ASW-dedicated vessel. By 1968 Bonaventure appeared as shown, with new Dutch radars and with improved sea-keeping.

SPECIFICATION

HMCS Bonaventure
Displacement: 16,000 tons standard and 20,000 tons full load
Dimensions: length 219.5 m (720 ft); beam 24.38 m (80 ft); draught 7.62 m (25 ft); flight deck width 32 m (105 ft)
Propulsion: two-shaft geared steam turbines delivering 29828 kW (40,000 shp)

Speed: 24.5 kts
Armament: four (later two) twin 3-in (76-mm) Mk 33 AA guns
Aircraft: 21-24 (see text)
Complement: 1,370
Electronics: (before 1967-68 refit) one SPS-12 air search radar; one SPS-8 height-finding radar and one SPS-10 surface search radar

The introduction of Bonaventure allowed a new generation of carrierborne aircraft to be operated including the Tracker, used for ASW missions.

removal of the two forward gun sponsons in order to enhance the ship's sea-keeping qualities, and improvements in the accommodation, aircraft handling and anti-fallout protection

facilities. The *Bonaventure* was finally paid off in 1970 for disposal because of the costs of keeping the vessel in service. The carrier was subsequently sold and broken up for scrap.

'Colossus' class Light fleet carrier

HMS Pioneer is seen as completed in 1945 as a maintenance carrier. The carrier was unable to operate aircraft in a combat role, being able to take them aboard only by crane. With its sister ship HMS Perseus, Pioneer continued as a maintenance vessel into the 1950s.

The **'Colossus' class** of light fleet carrier was a World War II design that resembled in many ways a scaled-down 'Illustrious'-class fleet carrier but with a single hangar, no armour and only light self-defence AA guns. The machinery fit was essentially a modified version of that fitted to contemporary cruisers, but with the boilers and engine rooms set one after the other to reduce the effects of a bomb or torpedo hit below decks. Ten units were built and most served with the Royal Navy in the post-war years. **HMS Colossus**, built in 1944, had participated in combat operations during the Pacific War, and was loaned to the French navy as the **Arromanches** in 1946. The vessel was eventually sold to France, while **HMS Pioneer** and **HMS Perseus** were

completed as aircraft maintenance ships, continuing in these roles until scrapped in 1954 and 1958 respectively.

Foreign service

Of the remainder, **HMS Venerable** was sold to the Netherlands as the *Karel Doorman* in 1948 (and discussed separately), while **HMS Warrior** was lent to the Royal Canadian Navy and then recommissioned into the Royal Navy before being sold to Argentina in 1958 as the *Independencia* (discussed elsewhere). **HMS Vengeance** was also lent, in this instance to the Royal Australian Navy between 1952 and 1955, before being placed in reserve and then sold to Brazil in 1957 as the *Minas Gerais*. The other four, namely **HMS Glory**, **HMS Ocean**, **HMS Theseus** and **HMS Triumph**, served com-

Seen at Sasebo in company with the American 'Essex'-class carrier USS Oriskany, the 'Colossus'-class carrier HMS Ocean is preparing to depart for Korea in the spring of 1952. Ocean was one of five 'Colossus'-class carriers to serve in that conflict, although Warrior spent time as an aircraft transport

bat tours off Korea during the war there, with air groups comprising Seafire F.Mk 47s, Sea Fury FB.Mk 11s and Fireflies. The *Ocean* gained an earlier distinction (in December 1945) as the first carrier to receive landings by a jet aircraft, in this case a Vampire. The *Glory, Ocean* and *Theseus* were all scrapped in 1961-62, while the *Triumph* was con-

verted over a seven-year period to become a heavy repair ship. *Triumph* took part in the Beira patrol in the 1960s and was placed in reserve in 1975 and was

scrapped in 1981-82 just before the Falklands War where the heavy focus on sea-air power meant that its services were most needed.

HMS Ocean in company with the cruiser HMS Belfast off Korea. Ocean has a considerable claim to fame: providing the flight deck for the world's first jet carrier landing, when the third prototype de Havilland Vampire landed on in 3 December 1945.

SPECIFICATION	
'Colossus' class	**Speed:** 25 kts
Displacement: 13,190 tons standard and 18,040 tons full load	**Aircraft:** 48
Dimensions: length 211.84 m (695 ft); beam 24.38 m (80 ft); draught 7.16 m (23 ft 6 in); flight deck width 24.38 m (80 ft)	**Armour:** early units 24 2-pdr and 38 to 60 20-mm guns; later units 17 40-mm guns; maintenance ships 16 2-pdr and two 20-mm (later 40-mm)
Propulsion: two-shaft geared steam turbines delivering 29828 kW (40,000 shp)	**Electronics:** Type 281 air search rada; later also fitted with Type 277 height-finding and Type 293 surface search radars

HMS *Centaur* Light fleet carrier

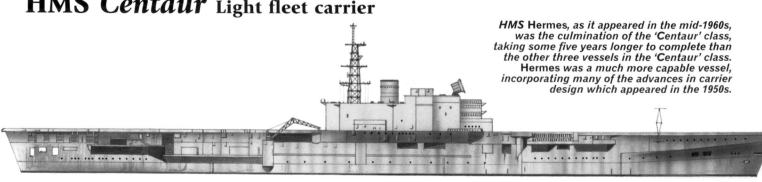

HMS Hermes, as it appeared in the mid-1960s, was the culmination of the 'Centaur' class, taking some five years longer to complete than the other three vessels in the 'Centaur' class. Hermes was a much more capable vessel, incorporating many of the advances in carrier design which appeared in the 1950s.

The history of **HMS Centaur (R06)** rested in the 'Hermes' class of eight carriers that began life on the design boards in 1943 as ships similar to the 'Colossus' class but with significantly

improved capabilities. Following the end of World War II, four of those ships already laid down were retained on the stocks for the new post-war fleet. Three of the ships were

completed to a modified design incorporating as many wartime lessons as possible. These three were the *Centaur, Albion* and *Bulwark*, which were launched in 1947-48 for com-

pletion over the next six years. In fact the *Centaur* was completed to a slightly less capable state than the other two as it had only a 5° line painted along its landing area to simulate an angled

flight deck. The air group was projected as 16 Sea Hawks, 16 Fireflies and four Avenger AEW.Mk 1 aircraft.

In the late 1950s the *Centaur* received a pair of steam catapults, but it soon became apparent that the ship and its near sisters were too small to operate the new generation of aircraft coming into Fleet Air Arm service. During its career *Centaur* served mainly in the Mediterranean and the Far East, including support duties for the Army off the coast of Aden in 1960-64. In January 1964 *Centaur* transported 45 Royal Marine Commando and RAF Belvedere helicopters to quell the rebellion in Tanganyika.

Depot ship

By 1966 *Centaur* had been relegated to the role of a depot ship and was stricken in 1971, the scrapping process starting in the following year. The vessel's final air group comprised 21 fixed-wing aircraft including Sea Vixen all-weather fighters, Scimitar strike fighters and Gannet AEW aircraft. Eight Whirlwind helicopters were also embarked for ASW and SAR duties.

Above: HMS Centaur *as seen in the late 1950s with a good proportion of its air complement topside.* Centaur *had an 5° angled deck painted on to its straight-through flight deck, but was never converted to the fully angled deck of the larger carriers.*

Right: A Sea Vixen FAW.Mk 1 is launched from one of the newly fitted steam catapults aboard HMS Centaur. *Along with* Victorious, *the vessel was used for service trials of the aircraft in November 1958, and its final aircraft complement was to include Sea Vixens alongside Scimitars and Gannet AEW.Mk 3s.*

HMS *Albion* and *Bulwark* Light fleet/Commando carriers

Although sisters of HMS *Centaur*, **HMS *Albion*** (R07) and **HMS *Bulwark*** (R08) were completed with an interim 5.75° angled flight deck and two hydraulic catapults. The new flight deck required the removal of three of the twin 40-mm Bofors mountings from the port side in order to accommodate the overhang. Thus built, the two ships served as part of the British carrier force employed in the 1956 Suez Canal landings. The *Albion* served as a fighter carrier with Sea Hawk and Sea Venom jets plus Skyraider AEW aircraft and Sycamore utility/SAR helicopters, while the *Bulwark* carried Sea Hawks and Avenger ASW/bomber aircraft.

Commando role

However, following the success of the carriers HMS *Ocean* and HMS *Theseus* in the helicopter assault role during this operation, and because of the difficulties for this class in operating the new jet generation, it was decided to convert the *Bulwark* to a Commando carrier. This task was undertaken between January 1959 and January 1960, and resulted in removal of the catapults, arrester gear and

most of the AA guns. Facilities for carrying a 733-man Royal Marine Commando were fitted, as well as the equipment necessary for an air group of up to 16 Whirlwind helicopters and davits for four LCVPs. Although the refit was for the Commando role, the *Bulwark* also retained an ASW capability.

During 1961-62 the *Albion* was similarly converted, but for 900 Commandos and 16 Wessex helicopters. This capability was retrofitted to the *Bulwark* during 1963. The *Albion*'s Commando career was mainly in the Far East, and the vessel was present during the 1966

Indonesian confrontation and the subsequent Aden withdrawal. Immediately following this *Albion* was placed in reserve and was finally stricken from the fleet in 1972 and broken up. In the meantime, the *Bulwark* served in the Mediterranean and the Far East as a Commando carrier, and was also on duty during both the Indonesian and Aden crises.

Interim ASW

Placed in reserve in 1976, *Bulwark* was refitted in 1977 to act as an interim ASW carrier and recommissioned in 1979 to release HMS *Hermes* from the amphibious warfare role. With the

After service in the Far East in the waters off Borneo, Albion *was detached to provide Commando facilities in the withdrawal from Aden. Along with* Bulwark, Albion *was in reserve at the start of the 1970s, but was scrapped in 1972. Needless to say, either vessel could have proved valuable in the Falklands War of 1982.*

advent of HMS *Invincible* in 1980, *Bulwark* was again relegated to the reserve and paid off in 1981 for disposal. The 1982 Falklands War saw the possibility of the carrier recommissioning yet again

for active service, but following a survey the ship was found to be in such a bad state that the idea was quickly dropped and *Bulwark* was eventually sold for scrap and broken up in 1984.

Two Wessex Mk 5 helicopters make an approach to the Commando carrier HMS Albion *after its 1965 refit.* Albion *spent much of its commando career in the Far East, and within months of this photograph the ship was involved with the Indonesian confrontation.*

Royal Marines of 42 Commando double across the flight deck to their *Whirlwind HAS.Mk 7* helicopters in an exercise on board *HMS Bulwark in 1960. The first of the Royal Navy's commando carriers, with fixed-wing aircraft operating equipment removed, the carrier was joined in the role by* **HMS** *Albion. Both vessels saw considerable action during the 1960s, including the 1961 Iraqi crisis, the Indonesian Confrontation and the British withdrawal from Aden.*

Royal Navy carriers
Developments of the 1950s and 1960s

The Korean War proved the value of shipborne tactical air power in the nuclear age, and the Royal Navy maintained an effective force through the 1950s and 1960s. Despite the use of carriers in overseas crises, the government of the day in 1966 axed any likelihood of the UK keeping a fixed-wing carrier into the latter part of the 20th century by cancelling the new carrier programme.

HMS **Eagle** *leads* **Centaur, Albion** *and* **Bulwark** *in a display of carrier power in the mid-1950s. By this stage, all had been modified with a partially angled deck.*

After undertaking major wartime actions, **Victorious** *emerged from a refit for further fleet service after 1950. The carrier received a Type 984 radar in a 'dustbin' fairing, two steam catapults and a full 8° angled deck.*

FLEET AIR ARM STRENGTH

Carrier-assigned units, January 1960

HMS *Albion*

815 Sqn: Whirlwind HAS.Mk 7
849 Sqn 'C' Flight: Gannet AEW.Mk 3
894 Sqn: Sea Venom FAW.Mk 22

HMS *Ark Royal*

800 Sqn: Scimitar F.Mk 1
807 Sqn: Scimitar F.Mk 1
820 Sqn: Whirlwind HAS.Mk 7
824 Sqn: Whirlwind HAS.Mk 7
892 Sqn: Sea Vixen FAW.Mk 1
Ship's Flight: Dragonfly HR.Mk 5

HMS *Bulwark*

848 Sqn: Whirlwind HAS.Mk 7

HMS *Centaur*

801 Sqn: Sea Hawk FGA.Mk 6
810 Sqn: Gannet AS.Mk 4
824 Sqn: Whirlwind HAS.Mk 7
849 Sqn 'D' Flight: Skyraider AEW.Mk 1
Ship's Flight: Dragonfly HR.Mk 5

HMS *Eagle*

806 Sqn: Sea Hawk FGA.Mk 6

HMS *Victorious*

803 Sqn: Scimitar F.Mk 1
831 Sqn 'A' Flight: Gannet ECM.Mk 6, Avenger AS.Mk 6B
831 Sqn 'B' Flight: Sea Venom Mk 21(ECM)
849 Sqn 'B' Flight: Gannet AEW.Mk 3
Ship's Flight: Dragonfly HR.Mk 5

Below: Illustrious, with a Sea Fury and a Seafire Mk 45 on deck, a veteran of numerous successful World War II operations, was converted as a trials and training vessel in 1946, recommissioning in 1948. Between 1949-54 most of the Fleet Air Arm's pilots made their first 'traps' on the ship's deck and it was also used as a troop transport.

Above: In the 1970s the Royal Navy's conventional carrier capability reached its height with the introduction of the Phantom, which provided fleet defence alongside Buccaneer strike aircraft. Both were fully committed to the support of NATO operations in the Atlantic and Mediterranean. Here Ark Royal is seen off the coast of Florida during its final cruise in August 1978, with the Phantom FG.Mk 1s of No. 892 Sqn, the Royal Navy's only operational Phantom unit. As the Royal Navy's last conventional carrier, the 'Ark' was paid off in December 1978.

FAR EAST WORKHORSE: HMS *UNICORN*

Completed in 1943 as an aircraft repair ship for the support of fleet carriers, HMS *Unicorn* was instead initially used in the light fleet carrier role, seeing action at Salerno, before adopting its intended role in the Middle East after October 1943. After a refit in the late 1940s, the vessel returned to the Far East for service during the Korean War. Supporting Commonwealth carrier operations, *Unicorn* shuttled aircraft between shore bases and operational carriers and also provided repair facilities. In addition to aircraft, *Unicorn* also shipped troops and RAF and RAAF Vampires and Meteors to units in the Far East. For brief periods between October 1952 and July 1953 the carrier also launched Sea Fury aircraft (as seen on deck) of No. 802 Sqn for combat missions in conjunction with HMS *Ocean*'s air group. After its Korean War service, *Unicorn* returned to the UK in 1953 and entered the reserve. In June 1959 the carrier was stripped before scrapping in 1960.

HMS *Eagle*

HMS *Eagle* was the logical extension of the wartime 'Implacable' class of carriers, but during its lifetime was to see many of the changes that swept through carrier design in the 1950s. For many years the Royal Navy's spearhead, *Eagle* saw action at Suez and in the Indian Ocean in the 1960s. Although overshadowed in the latter part of its career by its near sister HMS *Ark Royal*, HMS *Eagle* was for many years one of the Royal Navy's primary strike carriers. The *Eagle* is illustrated as it appeared at the time of the Suez Crisis in 1956; during a 1954-55 refit the carrier had received a 5.5° angled deck. In November 1956 *Eagle* lead the Royal Navy's carrier group for Operation Musketeer, the attacks on Egypt during the Suez Crisis. Although reduced to only one catapult, the carrier launched 621 combat sorties by Skyraiders, Sea Venoms (as seen on deck), Sea Hawks and Wyverns.

Eagle *steams with Sea Hawks and Wyverns on deck, sometime in 1956. Note the twin 4.5-in (114-mm) heavy anti-aircraft guns flush mounted with the forward deck and the Sea Hawks ready to depart the forward catapults. The Sea Hawks carry the tern's head insignia of No. 897 Sqn, which flew both FB.Mk 3s and FGA.Mk 6 aircraft. In October 1957, in time for the Suez Crisis, these aircraft were exchanged for the FGA.Mk 6s of No. 895 Sqn.*

Eagle's air wing, late 1960s

Tactically *Eagle*'s Buccaneers were intended to operate below the detection limits of enemy air search radars, approaching the target at high subsonic speeds to deliver their weapon loads either by toss-bombing in the case of the internally carried Red Beard tactical nuclear weapon or by more conventional dive or laydown modes with 500-lb (227-kg) and 1,000-lb (454-kg) HE ballistic bombs, and 2-in (51-mm) or 3-in (76-mm) unguided rockets. Missile attacks could also be performed using wing-mounted radio-guided Martin AGM-12B Bullpups, and photo-reconnaissance missions were possible with a special camera pack mounted in the bomb bay. The two-seater Sea Vixen's main armament comprised two retractable fuselage packs each housing 14 2-in unguided rockets plus various weapons on each of the four inner underwing pylons such as a Firestreak or Red Top IR-guided AAM, a 24-round 2-in rocket pod, a 500-lb HE bomb or a cluster of six 3-in rockets. The two larger outer pylons usually carried a 150-Imp gal (682-litre) fuel tank, though these could be replaced by either a 1,000-lb HE bomb or an AGM-12A Bullpup missile if required.

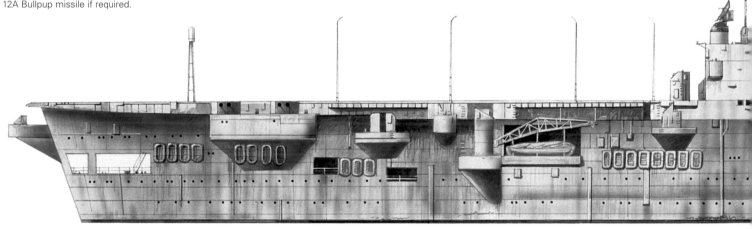

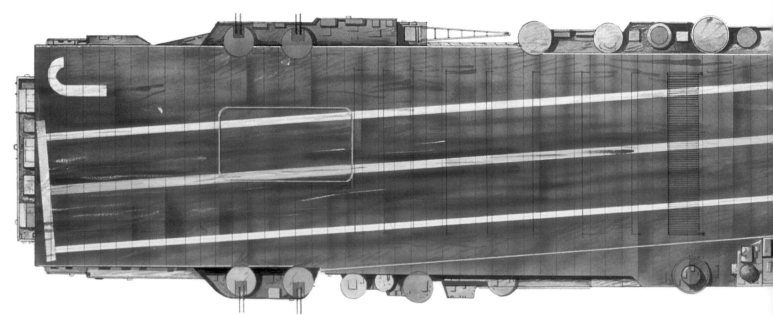

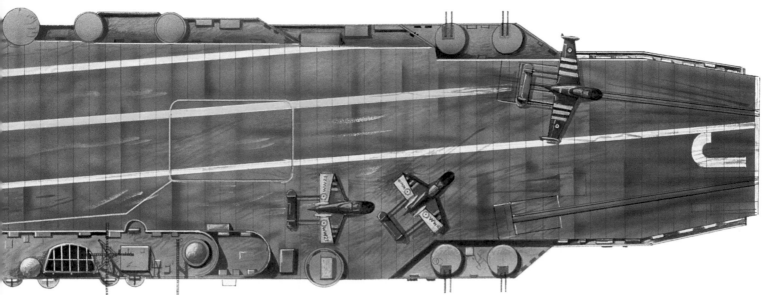

Eagle in action
In the mid-1960s *Eagle* underwent a refit to operate the latest naval strike aircraft, the Buccaneer, and was by the spring of 1966 on station off East Africa enforcing the Rhodesian oil blockade as part of the thankless Beira patrol. In the following year *Eagle* was sent to the waters off Aden during the withdrawal period, there teaming with the other carriers HMS *Hermes* and *Victorious*, the commando carriers *Albion* and *Bulwark*, and the assault ships *Intrepid* and *Fearless* to form the biggest force of major warships the Royal Navy had assembled east of Suez since the Korean war. Apart from the Buccaneers the carrier air group embarked also included a squadron of Sea Vixen FAW.Mk 2s. The early warning element was provided by a flight of Gannet AEW. Mk 3s, while a small number of Scimitar F.Mk 1s in a single flight provided inflight-refuelling facilities with buddy packs. Two helicopters were also embarked for SAR duties.

The Phantom era
After returning from the Far East, *Eagle* was modified to operate the Phantom FG.Mk 1, and undertook extensive trials with the type between March and June 1969. However, it was *Ark Royal* that was in the event fully modified for Phantom operations, despite *Eagle* being more reliable, having a hull in better condition and having a much more advanced sensor fit after its 1964 refit. In addition, the refit in 1968 had installed Phantom equipment including a Phantom-capable waist catapult.

AA armament
At the time of the Suez Crisis, *Eagle* continued to maintain heavy gun armament, much of which was later deleted during a major refit between 1959 and 1964, when a fully angled and sponsoned deck was fitted. After this refit, *Eagle* was armed with six Seacat SAM systems for defensive purposes.

Early service
HMS *Eagle* (originally *Audacious*) was built to an improved 'Implacable' design, and was commissioned into service with an axial flight deck and initially served as a trials deck for the testing of various new prototype aircraft, including the Sea Venom, Gannet and Sea Hawk. The carrier's first air group was embarked in September 1952 and consisted of Firebrands, Fireflies and Attackers, subsequently joined by Sea Hornets and Skyraiders.

One of the four 'Centaur'-class carriers, HMS **Hermes** *is seen in the early 1960s, with Sea Vixens, Gannets and Scimitars and a Whirlwind plane-guard. During its service life,* Hermes *struggled to effectively operate Sea Vixens and Scimitars, its deck and catapults being too short for safety margins.*

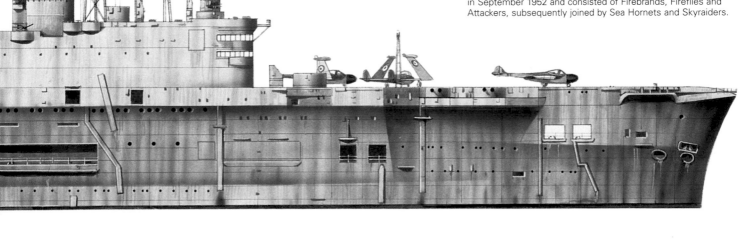

HMS *Ark Royal* Fleet carrier

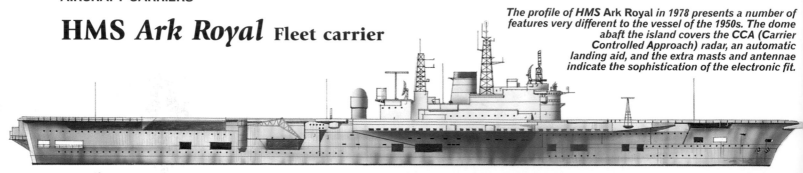

The profile of HMS Ark Royal in 1978 presents a number of features very different to the vessel of the 1950s. The dome abaft the island covers the CCA (Carrier Controlled Approach) radar, an automatic landing aid, and the extra masts and antennae indicate the sophistication of the electronic fit.

Near sister of HMS *Eagle*, **HMS *Ark Royal* (R09)** was completed in 1955 to a more modern configuration with a pair of steam catapults, a 5.5° angled flight deck, a mirror landing sight and a port-side deck-edge lift serving the upper hangar only. The ship's initial air group capacity was 50 aircraft, comprising Sea Hawks, Sea Venoms, Gannet ASW aircraft and Skyraider AEW types plus several utility helicopters. Later in the 1950s, the Wyvern was added to the air group. In 1956 the ship's starboard 4.5-in (114-mm) turrets were removed, and in 1959 the deck-edge lift went.

Returning to sea in 1960, the air wing of the 'Ark' added Scimitars, Sea Vixens and Gannet AEW aircraft. In 1964 the forward pairs of the aft 5-in guns were removed, while the remaining turrets and the last 40-mm Bofors went during the 1967-70 refit. This was to allow for the operation of Phantom fighters. An 8.5° flight deck was fitted, together with new catapults (including a new waist one) and arrester gear. The island was also reconfigured, and the addition of new radars was complemented by the improvement of the older types.

The air group capacity dropped from 48 to 39, a figure which stayed constant for the remainder of the ship's active career. Typically this was 12 Phantom FG.Mk 1s, 14 Buccaneer S.Mk 2s, four Gannet AEW.Mk 3s, six Sea King HAS.Mk 1 (later HAS.Mk 2) ASW helicopters, two Wessex Mk 1 SAR helicopters and Gannet carrier onboard delivery (COD) aircraft. The Buccaneers doubled as tanker aircraft with buddy inflight-refuelling pods and as long-range photo-reconnaissance aircraft with a bomb bay-mounted camera pack, at least one Buccaneer being configured in the latter role at all times.

Retirement

Although suffering throughout its life from mechanical problems, the *Ark Royal* was eventually taken out of service in 1978 as the last of the Royal Navy's conventional carriers. After much public debate as to its future, the vessel was finally towed away from Devonport in 1980 for scrapping. Like its sister ship, the *Ark Royal* had been fitted in the 1960s to carry the Red Beard and later Green Parrot tactical nuclear bombs.

Bearer of an honourable name dating back to the Armada, the Ark Royal ended its career in the 1970s operating Phantoms and Buccaneers, and in spite of mechanical problems was one of the most powerful vessels in the world.

SPECIFICATION

HMS *Ark Royal*
Displacement: 43,060 tons standard and 50,786 tons full load
Dimensions: length 275.6 m (845 ft); beam 34.4 m (112 ft 11 in); draught 11 m (36 ft); flight deck width 50.1 m (164 ft 6 in)
Propulsion: four-shaft geared steam turbines delivering 113346 kW (152,000 shp)
Speed: 31.5 kts

Aircraft: 39 (see text)
Armament: fitted for four quadruple GWS.22 Seacat SAM launchers
Complement: 2,637
Electronics: two Type 965M air search radars, two Type 982 air search radars, two Type 983 height-finding radars, one Type 993 surface search radar, one SPN-35 aircraft landing aid, one Type 974 navigation radar and one ESM system

---

Right: In October 1957 joint operations with the USS Saratoga enabled Ark Royal to play host to F3H Demons of VF-61. The Seahawk is preparing for launch after the Demons, from one of a pair of BS4 steam catapults, and in the background two Skyraider AEW.Mk 1 aircraft are ranged ready for a free take-off.

Left: As completed in 1955, HMS Ark Royal had a heavy gun armament comprising 16 4.5-in (114-mm) and a number of 40-mm Bofors AA guns. The air group of 50 aircraft was to include Sea Hawks, Gannets, Skyraiders and helicopters.

HMS *Eagle* Fleet carrier

Originally to be named **HMS Audacious**, one of a class of four 'Improved Implacable'-class fleet carriers, this hull was fairly advanced at the end of World War II and was therefore chosen to be completed more or less as designed. In January 1946, the name was changed to **Eagle** (**R06**) but the completion of a surviving sistership, HMS *Ark Royal*, was held up to allow the incorporation of numerous improvements. Completed in 1951 the *Eagle* had, in comparison with the original design, a reduced armament of eight twin 4.5-in (114-mm) DP guns, and eight sextuple, two twin and nine single 40-mm Bofors AA guns, more advanced search radars and a grand total of 12 American Mk 37 radar gun directors. An air group of Firebrands, Fireflies and Attackers was initially embarked, later joined by Sea Hornets and Skyraider AEW.Mk 1s. A total of 60 fixed-wing aircraft could be carried, although in 1954 the number was 59 Sea Hawks, Avengers, Skyraider and a Dragonfly SAR helicopter.

From mid-1954 to early 1955 the ship underwent a modernisation refit that resulted in the building of a 5.5° angled flight deck, the fitting of a mirror landing sight and the removal of three single and one sextuple Bofors mounts. In 1956, the ship served as part of the Anglo-French carrier force during the Suez landings, operating a mixed air group of Sea Hawks, Skyraiders, Wyverns and Sea Venoms on strike missions. From mid-1969 to mid-1964, the *Eagle* was taken in hand at Devonport Dockyard for a complete rebuild in which all the forward 4.5-in mounts and all the 40-mm guns were removed, an 8.5° flight deck was fitted, the radar outfit was modernised, and six quadruple Seacat close-

Seen leaving Wellington, New Zealand, in the late 1960s, Eagle *could always be distinguished from* Ark Royal *by the massive Type 984 radar atop the bridge, and the absence of catapult bridles (extensions).*

Right: October 1956, and HMS Eagle, *flagship of Vice Admiral Manley Power, leads HMS Bulwark and HMS Albion on exercise off Malta. Within weeks, they were to be involved in the Suez landing.*

range SAM launchers were fitted. The air group number was reduced to 35 fixed-wing and 10 rotary-wing aircraft, this complement being made up of Sea Vixens, Scimitars, Gannets and Wessex helicopters.

Eagle in action

In 1964 the ship sailed for the Far East and the Indonesian confrontation, which was followed in 1966 by Rhodesia and the Beira patrol to prevent oil reaching the rebel country through Mozambique. In 1967 the carrier moved on to Aden to cover the British withdrawal

from that troubled area. It was during a refit between these operations that the *Eagle* was fitted to carry Buccaneers and had a waist catapult added. Following a further Far Eastern deploy-

ment in 1969 *Eagle* was chosen to perform Phantom trials for the Royal Navy, and in the following year embarked its first ASW helicopter squadron. The ship's career was cut short in the early 1970s by the political decision that it would be too costly to convert *Eagle* to full-time Phantom operations (in fact only minimal changes were required) and the ship became another victim of the

1966 Labour government. *Eagle* paid off in January 1972 and effectively became the floating spares platform for the *Ark Royal*, finally being towed away for scrap in 1978. By the time the carrier was paid off its air group had again been reduced, this time to 30 fixed- and six rotary-wing aircraft, these being Buccaneers, Sea Vixens, Gannet AEW.Mk 3s and Wessex helicopters.

SPECIFICATION	
HMS *Eagle*	**Aircraft:** 36-60 (see text)
Displacement: 44,100 tons standard and 45,100 tons full load	**Armament:** four twin 4.5-in (114-mm) DP guns, and six quadruple GWS.22 Seacat SAM launchers
Dimensions: length 247.4 m (811 ft 8½ in); beam 34.4 m (112 ft 11½ in); draught 11 m (36 ft); flight deck width 52.1 m (171 ft)	**Complement:** 2,750
Propulsion: four-shaft geared steam turbines delivering 113346 kW (152,000 shp)	**Electronics:** one Type 984 3D radar, one Type 965 air search radar, one Type 963 CCA landing aid, one Type 974 navigation radar and one ESM system
Speed: 31.5 kts	

Two Buccaneers overfly HMS Eagle *on deployment in the late 1960s after the addition of a waist catapult. At this late stage of a 20-year career, the carrier's displacement had risen from 45,720 tons in 1951 to a maximum of 54,100 tons.*

HMS *Hermes* Aircraft carrier and Commando carrier

The original post-war **HMS Hermes** was the sixth vessel of the 'Centaur' class, but in October 1945 she was cancelled and the name given to the *Elephant* of the same class. As very little work had been done on this hull the vessel was able to benefit from a complete redesign and was thus commissioned in November 1959 with a 6.5° angled flight deck, a deck-edge aircraft lift as one of the two lifts fitted, and a 3D radar system.

In 1964-6 the new HMS *Hermes* was refitted with two quadruple Seacat SAM systems in place of her original AA armament of five twin 40-mm Bofors mountings, and access to the seaward side of the island was constructed. In 1971, in a further refit, the Type 984 3D radar was replaced by a Type 965 'bedstead' system.

Commando carrier

A comprehensive deck landing light system was fitted after the ship had been paid off for conversion to a commando assault carrier, as she could operate only a 28-aircraft group of Sea Vixen, Buccaneer and Gannet fixed-wing aircraft but not the modern Phantoms.

During this conversion the *Hermes* also lost her arrester wires and catapult, and was converted to carry a complete Marine Commando unit with its associated squadron of Wessex assault helicopters. By 1977 the *Hermes* was again in refit to become an ASW carrier, though she retained the Commando-carrying ability. As such she carried nine Sea King ASW and four Wessex

HU.Mk 5 utility helicopters.

In 1980 the *Hermes* began her third major conversion to change her role yet again, this involving a strengthening of the flight deck and the provision of a 7.5° ski-jump ramp overhanging the bow to allow the operation of five Sea Harriers in place of the Wessex helicopters. In 1982, because of her more extensive communications fit and greater aircraft-carrying ability, the *Hermes* was made the flagship of the task force sent to recover the Falklands.

Falklands air wing

During this operation *Hermes* initially operated an air group of 12 Sea Harriers, nine Sea King HAS.Mk 5s and nine Sea King HC.Mk 4s. However, as the campaign progressed, this

Above: HMS Hermes *with her goalkeeper, a Type 22 frigate, steaming in heavy weather. The Type 22 provided the necessary close-in anti-aircraft and anti-missile defence with the Sea Wolf SAM system that the carrier lacked;* Hermes *was equipped with two Seacat launchers.*

Right: After losing its fixed-wing capability in the early 1970s, Hermes' *role was then altered to that of ASW carrier with a secondary Commando support role. In this incarnation, fixed-wing aircraft returned to the deck, now equipped with a 7.5° ski-jump ramp.*

was modified to 15 Sea Harriers, six Harrier GR.Mk 3s, five ASW Sea Kings and two Lynx helicopters (equipped for Exocet decoy operations). Following its success in the Falklands and after a series of deployments in 1983, *Hermes* underwent a four-month refit beginning in January 1984. After this *Hermes* was used in a training ship capacity in harbour because she was considered too labour-intensive and had not been converted to use the Royal Navy's Dieso fuel type.

Like the 'Invincibles', the Cold War-era *Hermes* carried nuclear depth bombs for her

helicopters, and tactical gravity bombs for the Sea Harriers. Based on comparisons with the American carriers, the number of nuclear weapons carried in these ships was probably around 15, of which approxi-

mately 10 would be for ASW purposes.

In 1986, *Hermes* was purchased by India to become **Viraat**, entering service with that nation's navy in May the following year.

SPECIFICATION	
HMS *Hermes* **Displacement:** 23,900 tons standard; 28,700 tons full load **Dimensions:** length 226.9 m (744 ft 4 in); beam 27.4 m (90 ft); draught 8.7 m (28 ft 6 in); flight deck width 48.8 m (160 ft) **Machinery:** two-shaft geared steam turbine delivering 56675 kW (76,000 shp) **Speed:** 28 kts **Armament:** two quadruple Seacat SAM launchers (approximately 40 missiles carried) **Aircraft:** normally five (later	increased to six) Sea Harriers and nine Sea King ASW helicopters; maximum see text **Electronics:** one Type 965 air-search radar, one Type 993 surface-search radar, one Type 1006 navigation radar, two GWS 22 Seacat guidance systems, one TACAN system, one Type 184 sonar, several passive and active ECM systems, two Corvus chaff launchers **Complement:** 1,350 including air group (plus provision for a complete 750-man Marine Commando unit for which four LCVPs were carried)

The original 6.5° angled flight deck fitted to Hermes *was the largest angle that could be contrived in an aircraft carrier of its size. The subsequent ski-jump ramp added during the ship's 1980 refit was accompanied by a strengthened flight deck to allow operations with the V/STOL Sea Harrier FRS.Mk 1.*

USS *Enterprise* Nuclear-powered aircraft carrier

Initial US studies for a nuclear-powered aircraft carrier go back to 1949, when the 'Forrestal' class of carrier was under construction. A nuclear powerplant was originally earmarked for this class, but was later shelved in favour of conventional engines. The attractions of nuclear powerplants were the promises of longer endurance, enormous range, less time in dock, and cleaner operations.

While the **USS *Enterprise*** (**CVAN-65**) was being developed, a fierce argument was raging in American defence circles over the future role of aircraft carriers in the US Navy. The Kennedy administration was sceptical, and US Defense Secretary McNamara was suspicious of the cost-effectiveness of a ship with a $451,000,000 price tag. As a result, five further vessels in this class were cancelled.

Construction

The keel was laid down for the *Enterprise* in February 1958. She was launched in September 1960 and the ship was completed in November 1961, when she was commissioned. She entered service as the world's second nuclear-powered warship, being eclipsed by the cruiser USS *Long Beach*, which was launched on 14 July 1959. *Enterprise* would later join the *Long Beach* in the *Enterprise* battlegroup, and two years later the carrier was helping to enforce the Cuban blockade.

In 1964, *Enterprise* began her long involvement in the Vietnam War, which would eventually see her completing eight deployments, including assisting the evacuation of Saigon in 1975. In

February 1969, she was badly damaged when a rocket explosion tore through the ship, killing 27 sailors and injuring 344. However, fully repaired, she was to become the first aircraft carrier to deploy F-14 Tomcat fighters in 1974.

Enterprise was the world's first 'supercarrier', and was fitted with a massive nuclear powerplant to give her an impressive top speed of 35 kts. Although the nuclear powerplant was big, it dispensed with the ship's exhaust equipment and fuel oil storage areas, affording valuable extra space, some of which was taken up by enlarged aviation fuel storage areas.

The nuclear powerplant featured eight A2W reactors which drove four geared steam turbines. Power output was rated at 208.88 MW (280,000 shp). Just over two months after launch, on 2 December 1960, her reactors went critical. Over the next 11 months, all eight reactors would come on stream, feeding 32 heat exchangers. This gave the *Enterprise* a range in the region of 400,000 nm (740740 km; 460,230 miles) between refuellings, while operating at a speed of 20 kts. This range allowed her to undertake a round-the-world voyage in 1964, along with the USS *Long Beach* and USS *Bainbridge*, largely to demonstrate the capabilities of nuclear-powered marine propulsion. *Enterprise's* impressive performance gave valuable ammunition to the advocates of marine nuclear propulsion, who noted that the ship's performance would increase yet further as more advanced cores were

An F8U-1 Crusader, flown by Commander George C. Talley, made the first ever deck landing on the Enterprise's flight deck. The high approach speed of the Crusader made landings on the earlier 'Essex'-class carriers a significant problem.

installed in the reactors over time.

However, the supposed self-sufficiency offered by a nuclear powerplant belied the reality that the ship's vast air wing of over 80 aircraft, and huge crew of over 5,500, would require regular replenishment of munitions and food. Nevertheless, it must be emphasised that these replenishments were still less frequent than those required for conventionally powered carriers.

The design of the *Enterprise* flight deck drew heavily on lessons learnt from the 'Forrestal' class, and bore a heavy resemblance to the latter. Three deck lifts were arranged on the starboard side of the hull, with a single lift on the port side. The below-deck hangarage of the carrier was also impressive, and a total of 96 aircraft could be carried

The Enterprise's original box-like island superstructure was designed to accommodate the SPS-32/33 radar system.

by the vessel, although the air wing usually comprised 86 aircraft.

Enterprise also featured a very unusual island superstructure, notable for its box-like appearance, and a dome-shaped top. The island featured several sensors and radar, including the SPS-32/33 flat-panelled phased array radar system, which gave the island its slab

appearance. The only other ship to be fitted with this system was the nuclear-powered cruiser USS *Long Beach*. However, the system was not as successful as was hoped, being difficult to maintain and giving a disappointing performance, and was finally removed from *Enterprise* during a major refit in 1980.

Returning to her home port of San Francisco from deployment in Vietnam, Enterprise's air wing includes RA-5C Vigilantes which were active on reconnaissance flights over Vietnam.

SPECIFICATION

USS *Enterprise* (CVAN-65)
Displacement: 75,700 tonnes; 89,600 tonnes full load
Dimensions: length 342.3 m (1,122 ft 9 in); beam 40.5 m (133 ft); draught 11.9 m (39 ft); flight deck width 76.8 m (252 ft)
Machinery: four shaft, nuclear, Westinghouse A2W reactors, four geared turbines generating 208.88 MW (280,000 shp)
Speed: 20 kts cruising speed; 35 kts top speed.
Armament: three Mk 25 Sea Sparrow octuple launchers

(from 1967)
Aircraft: Up to 85 aircraft; December 1973 air wing included two squadrons each of F-14A and A-7E, one squadron each of A-6A/B, RA-5C, E-2B and EA-6B and one SH-3D detachment
Electronics: SPS-32/33 fixed phased array radar system, including air-search radar, surface-search radar, navigation radar and fire control radar
Complement: 3,325 plus 1,891 air wing

'Essex' class SCB-27A/C and SCB-125 reconstructions
Fleet carriers

Laid down in 1944 but not completed until 1950, the USS Oriskany was the first of the SCB-27A conversions with the modifications to enable the 'Essex' class to operate the upcoming generation of jet aircraft. These aircraft were much heavier than their World War II forebears, so the flight deck had to be strengthened.

At the end of World War II in 1945 the US Navy had a carrier force that was in effect obsolescent as it could not operate the coming generation of jet aircraft. Although a follow-on carrier design was completed in 1946 it was not built, and the US Navy had thus to adopt the policy of reconstructing the carriers of the **'Essex' class** that had been laid up in reserve. The first programme, known as **SCB-27A**, was actually used as the basis to complete the hull of the incomplete **USS Oriskany**. As built, the ship lacked the flight deck guns of its predecessors, but the most powerful hydraulic catapults were fitted and the flight deck itself was considerably strengthened. The island superstructure was rebuilt to improve radar coverage, and a considerable internal rearrangement was made to enhance habitability and survivability. Eight other vessels, the **Essex** (**CV-9**), **Yorktown** (**CV-10**), **Hornet** (**CV-12**), **Randolph** (**CV-15**), **Wasp** (**CV-18**), **Bennington** (**CV-20**), **Kearsarge** (**CV-33**) and **Lake Champlain** (**CV-39**), were then refitted to this standard. Later all but the *Lake Champlain* were given angled flight decks and enclosed bows.

Over the years most of the gun armament was removed and the radar systems changed. As rebuilt, the ships each carried 1,135,620 litres (300,000 US gal) of AVGAS and 725 tons of aircraft ordnance (including 125 tons of nuclear weapons). As more modern carriers entered service, the SCB-27As were switched to ASW operations with S-2 Trackers and helicopters. Many of these ships (CV-9, 10, 12, 15, 18, 20 and 33) underwent the FRAM (Fleet Rehabilitation And Modernization) ASW upgrade during the 1960s in a programme which included the fitting of an SQS-23 bow sonar and a partially automated ASW-orientated Command Information Center. Several of these ASW carriers served tours off Vietnam as screening units to attack units. The air group normally comprised 30 fixed-wing aircraft and 16-18 Sea King ASW helicopters. The *Essex, Kearsarge, Oriskany* and *Lake Champlain* also saw service off Korea during that war in the conventional attack role.

SCB-27A refit
Once the SCB-27A refit programme was under way, it soon became apparent that the advances in carrierborne aircraft technology demanded even more alterations, and thus the **SCB-27C** programme was born. Three ships, namely the **Intrepid** (**CV-11**), **Ticonderoga** (**CV-14**) and **Hancock** (**CV-19**), were so converted in 1951-54 with two steam catapults, revised aircraft lift arrangements and enhanced arrester gear. A further three units to be converted, the **Lexington** (**CV-16**), **Bon Homme Richard** (**CV-31**) and **Shangri-La** (**CV-38**), were then chosen to be refitted to the follow-on **SCB-125** standard, which involved the reconfiguration of the flight deck to an angled landing area and the reshaping of the island superstructure. All three units were out of dock by late 1955 by which time all the SCB-27Cs, except the *Lake Champlain* of the SCB-27As and the *Oriskany*, were undergoing or had undergone similar conversions. Of the SCB-27Cs the *Intrepid* was converted to an ASW carrier and underwent the FRAM modernisation in the mid-1960s, while the *Ticonderoga* went the same

Sikorsky HSS-1 Seabat helicopters aboard the SCB-27A conversion USS Lake Champlain during the late 1950s. The modification entailed tidying up the island and removal of the 5-in (127-mm) flight deck gun mounts.

The USS Intrepid is seen as an ASW carrier in the Atlantic in 1971. The carrier saw action in World War II, suffering many kamikaze attacks. After modernisation Intrepid made three Vietnam tours before decommissioning in 1974. The ship is now preserved as a museum in New York.

way after first serving off Vietnam in the early part of the war as a strike carrier. The *Hancock, Oriskany, Shangri-La* and *Bon Homme Richard* also undertook combat tours off Vietnam flying a variety of fighter and strike aircraft.

Surviving carriers

By the mid-1980s only five of the carriers were extant, the *Lexington* as the sole active ship (the Atlantic Fleet's training carrier in the Gulf of Mexico), and the other four laid up as elements of the Pacific Fleet reserve: the *Bon Homme*

Richard and *Oriskany* as an attack aircraft carrier and aircraft carrier respectively, and the *Hornet* and *Bennington* as ASW support carriers. All of the ships have now gone.

SPECIFICATION	
'Essex SCB-27A' class	**Performance:** speed 30 kts
Displacement: 28,404 tons standard; 40,600 tons full load	**Armament:** eight 5-in (127-mm) and 14 twin 3-in (76.2-mm) guns
Dimensions: length 273.8 m (898 ft 2 in); beam 30.9 m (101 ft 4 in); draught 9.1 m (29 ft 8 in); flight deck width (angled) 59.7 m (196 ft)	**Aircraft:** 45-80 (see text)
	Electronics: SPS-6 (later SPS-12 then SPS-29) air search, SPS-8 (later SPS-30) height-finding and SPS-10 surface search radars, and (FRAM)
Propulsion: geared steam turbines delivering 111855 kW (150,000 shp) to four shafts	SQS-23 bow sonar
	Complement: 2,900

SPECIFICATION	
'Essex SCB-27C' class	**Performance:** speed 29 kts
Displacement: 30,580 tons standard; 43,060 tons full load	**Armament:** four 5-in (127-mm) DP guns
Dimensions: length 272.6 m (894 ft 6 in); beam 31.4 m (103 ft); draught 9.2 m (30 ft 4 in); flight deck width 58.5 m (192 ft)	**Aircraft:** 70-80
	Electronics: one SPS-8 (later SPS-37A and SPS-30) height-finding radar, one SPS-12 surface search radar and one ESM system
Propulsion: geared steam turbines delivering 111855 kW (150,000 shp) to four shafts	**Complement:** 3,545

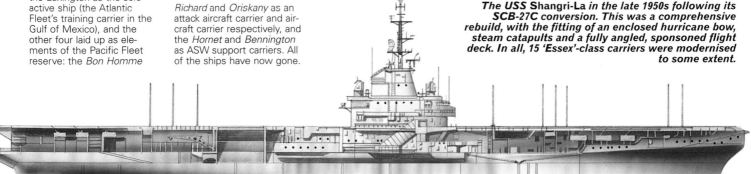

*The USS **Shangri-La** in the late 1950s following its SCB-27C conversion. This was a comprehensive rebuild, with the fitting of an enclosed hurricane bow, steam catapults and a fully angled, sponsoned flight deck. In all, 15 'Essex'-class carriers were modernised to some extent.*

'Hancock' and 'Intrepid' classes
Attack carriers/ASW carriers

Originally units of the 24-strong 'Essex' class, the five ships of these two subclasses were extensively modernised in the 1950s with an enclosed bow, an armoured and angled flight deck, improved aircraft elevators, increased aircraft fuel and new steam catapults. By the mid-1980s the classes were down to a total of three ships, namely the **Lexington** (**CVT-16**), **Bon Homme Richard** (**CVA-31**) and **Oriskany** (**CV-34**) which had been commissioned in February 1943, November 1944 and September 1950 respectively: the **Intrepid**

(**CVS-11**) and **Shangri-La** (**CVS-38**) had been retired. The subclasses had only one unit, the *Lexington*, in active service with the Atlantic Fleet as the US Navy's deck landing training carrier. As such the ship had no aircraft support facilities and the port deck-edge elevator locked as part of the flight deck. The other two ships were in Pacific Fleet reserve and were deleted in the late 1980s, although in 1981 the *Oriskany*, which had suffered a serious hangar fire in October 1966, was the object of a reactivation plan along the lines of the 'New

Jersey'-class battleships. But because of severe limitations in the types of aircraft it could carry (such as the obsolete F-8 Crusader and A-4 Skyhawk), its ordnance load and its fuel stowage, this was vetoed by the US Congress. The *Lexington* ran on to 1999, when it was replaced in the training role by the USS *Forrestal* when that ship was phased out of front-line service. The actual aviation ordnance load is believed to have been in the order of 750 tons, and that of aviation fuel about 1135620 litres (300,000 US gal).

SPECIFICATION	
'Hancock' and 'Intrepid' classes	range 27800 km (17,275 miles) at 15 kts
Displacement: (first two) 29,660 tons standard, 41,900 tons full load; (third) 28,200 tons standard, 40,600 tons full load	**Armament:** two or (CV-34) four 5-in (127-mm) DP guns
Dimensions: length (first) 270.9 m (889 ft) and (other two) 274 m (899 ft); beam (first two) 31.4 m (103 ft) and (third) 32.5 m (106 ft 6 in); draught 9.5 m (31 ft); flight deck width (first) 58.5 m (192 ft), (second) 52.4 m (172 ft) and (third) 59.5 m (195 ft)	**Aircraft:** 60-70 (none in *Lexington*)
	Electronics: one SPS-10 surface search and navigation radar, one SPS-30 or (CVT-16) SPS-12 air search radar, one SPS-43A or (CV-34) SPS-37 air search radar, one SPN-10 and one SPN-43 aircraft landing aids, several Mk 25/35 fire-control radars (none in CVT-16), and one URN-20 TACAN system
Propulsion: geared steam turbines delivering 111855 kW (150,000 shp) to four shafts	
Performance: speed 29.1 kts;	**Complement:** 2,090 plus 1,185 air group or (CVT-16) 1,440

*The USS **Intrepid** served as an ASW carrier during its later years. The last active ship in the class was **USS Lexington**, which remained operational as a training carrier, in the Gulf of Mexico, into the 1990s.*

USS *United States* Attack carrier

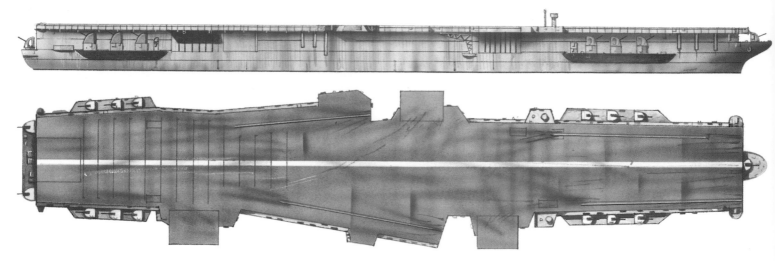

Although cancelled only nine days after its keel had been laid down in April 1949, the **USS United States (CVA-58)** is included here because it was the predecessor of the 'Forrestal' class and its successors, and because by virtue of its advanced design the vessel had a profound effect on future development. *United States* was designed to operate a new generation of US Navy heavy strategic bombers (in the 25/45-ton class) and their attendant escort fighters. Because of the size of the bombers the flight deck had to be large

enough both to park them and to fly them on and off. In the end an armoured and completely flush-deck configuration was chosen with four catapults: two at the bows, and one each to port and starboard in complementing amidships positions and angled outwards to clear the aircraft forward. *United States* would have been the first large US carrier since the *Langley* that would not have had a navigational bridge on the deck. Four deck-edge lifts were also to be fitted (one to port, two to starboard and one at the stern). The aviation fuel

capacity was to be a massive 1892700 litres (500,000 US gal), and the ordance load 2,000 tons. Four **'United States'-class** vessels were to have been built, the later ones nuclear-powered. No major electronics were carried as the escorting warships were expected to take care of this work. The cancellation of the ship was due mainly to its projected role, for the US Air Force objected vigorously to the US Navy duplicating its strategic mission. The funds released were ploughed back to the US Air Force to increase its bomber fleet.

The startling lines of the USS United States design were a result of the fact that early atomic bombs were heavy pieces of equipment, requiring large aircraft, which in turn required large amounts of fuel. To that end, the United States was dedicated solely to the operation of these aircraft and their escorting fighters.

SPECIFICATION	
USS United States	**Speed:** 33 kts
Displacement: 66,850 tons standard and 83,249 tons full load	**Armament:** eight single 5-in (127-mm) DP, eight twin 3-in (76-mm) AA and 20 single 20-mm AA guns
Dimensions: length 331.6 m (1,088 ft); 38.1 m (125 ft); draught 10.5 m (34 ft 6 in); flight deck width 57.9 m (190 ft)	**Aircraft:** 18 bombers and 54 F2H Banshee fighters
Propulsion: four-shaft geared steam turbines delivering 208796 kW (280,000 shp)	**Complement:** 4,127
	Electronics: one SPS-6 air search radar and one SPS-8 height-finding radar

'Forrestal' class Attack carrier

Design of the 'Forrestal' class (this is the lead ship) was dictated by the need to operate the new A3D Skywarrior bomber. As a result, these ships were much bigger than the 'Midways', with hangar decks that were 7.2-m (25-ft) high

The four ships of the **'Forrestal' class** were originally conceived as smaller versions of the ill-fated strategic carrier design, the USS *United States*, with four aircraft catapults and a flush flight deck with no island. However, following a complete redesign they were actually completed as the first carriers designed and built specifically for jet aircraft operations, with a conventional island and an angled flight deck to allow the four catapults to be retained. The ships were the **USS Forrestal**, USS

Saratoga, **USS Ranger** and **USS Independence**, and were commissioned in October 1955, April 1956, August 1957 and April 1959 respectively; their aviation ordnance load was 1,650 tons; and 2.84 million litres (750,000 US gal) of AVGAS aviation fuel, and 2.99 million litres (789,000 US gal) of JP5 aviation fuel were carried for the air wing embarked. The initial total of 90 aircraft carried by each vessel comprised two fighter squadrons with F2Hs or F9Fs, two light attack squadrons with ADs

First of the true 'supercarriers', the 'Forrestals' were able to carry over 80 aircraft. The lead ship is seen in the 1980s, with F-14 Tomcats from VF-11 and VF-31 ready for launch on the bow catapults.

USS **Ranger** *dwarfs the guided missile frigate* **Jacob von Heemskerck** *while refuelling the Dutch ship in the Persian Gulf. The carrier moved into the region in January 1991 to participate in Desert Shield and Desert Storm.*

and A4Ds and supporting reconnaissance, AEW and SAR assets. *Forrestal* and *Ranger* were also equipped for Regulus I missile operations in the 1950s. All four vessels saw action off Vietnam and were redesignated as CVs in the 1970s. After serving on the Cuba blockade in 1962, *Independence* was the first Atlantic Fleet carrier to deploy to Vietnam in June 1965, and supported the A-6 Intruder for its combat debut. *Forrestal* completed just one cruise to the war zone, after suffering a devastating fire in August 1967 which claimed the lives of 134 sailors. During the Grenada landings of November 1983, *Independence* provided the air cover and strike support to the US Marine Corps and US Army Ranger assaults while maintaining ASW cover against any possible incursions by the two Cuban 'Foxtrot' conventional attack submarines. In 1985-86 *Saratoga* was involved in skirmishes with Libya.

SLEP refits

The 'Forrestal' ships had the standard four aircraft elevators to service the flight deck, and three underwent the SLEP refit in the 1980s (in the order *Saratoga*, *Forrestal*, and *Independence*) to extend their service lives into the 1990s. In order to rectify some of the deficiencies encountered in combat operations, the SLEP refits improved the habitability, added Kevlar armour to enclose the vital machinery and electronics spaces, improved the NTDS fitted, added TFCC facility and replaced the catapults. The radar outfit was also

upgraded and the air defence armament strengthened with the addition of the Phalanx CIWS for anti-missile work complementing the Sea Sparrow. As built, the 'Forrestals' had been armed with eight 5-in (127-mm) guns on the sponsons either side of the fore and aft deck. These were removed through the 1960s and 1970s, to be replaced by the Mk 25 (and later Mk 29) Sea Sparrow SAM launchers.

In its later years, Forrestal became the US Navy's Pensacola-based training carrier as **AVT-59**, replacing USS *Lexington*. The remaining three first-line 'Forrestals' were involved in Operations Desert Shield and Desert Storm, *Saratoga* making the fastest transatlantic crossing by a carrier by transiting to the war zone in seven days. Its air wing completed 12,664 operational sorties, but this was to be *Saratoga*'s last action, the carrier retiring in 1994. Prior to decommissioning, *Independence* replaced *Midway* as the carrier permanently forward deployed at Yokosuka, Japan, before itself being relived by *Kitty*

USS **Forrestal** *in the Mediterranean, with F2H-2P Banshee, AD Skyraider, A3D Skywarrior, F9F Cougar, FJ Fury and F3H Demon aircraft embarked. Entering service with the Atlantic Fleet in 1956, Forrestal sailed in the Mediterranean during the Suez Crisis.*

Hawk. The 'Forrestal' class was replaced by new 'Nimitz'-class carriers as these became available, with *Independence* being the last to retire, in September 1998.

SPECIFICATION	
'Forrestal' class	**Speed:** 33 kts (*Forrestal*) or 34 kts
Ships in class (launched):	**Aircraft:** 84, comprising two F-14
Forrestal (1954), *Saratoga* ((1955),	and two F/A-18 squadrons, one of
Ranger (1956) and *Independence*	A-6/KA-6 and E-2, plus EA-6B, S-3
(1958)	and SH-3 support aircraft
Displacement: (first two)	**Armament:** three octuple Mk 29
59,060 tons standard, 75,900 tons	Sea Sparrow SAM launchers, three
full load; (second two) 60,000 tons	20-mm Phalanx CIWS
standard, 79,300 tons full load	**Electronics:** one LN-66 navigation
Dimensions: length (first) 331 m	radar, one SPS-10 surface search
(1,086 ft), (second) 324 m (1,063 ft),	radar, one SPS-48C 3D radar, one
(third) 326.4 m (1,071 ft) and (fourth)	SPS-58 low-level air search (except
326.1 m (1,070 ft); beam 39.5 m	*Ranger*), two SPN-42 and one
(129 ft 6 in); draught 11.3 m (37 ft);	SPN-43A aircraft landing aids, two
flight deck width 76.8 m (252 ft)	Mk 91 fire-control radars (three in
Machinery: four-shaft geared	first two), one URN-20 TACAN
steam turbines delivering	system, one SLQ-29 ESM suite and
193880 kW (260,000 shp) in	three Mk 36 SRBOC chaff launchers
Forrestal and 208795 kW	**Complement:** 2,790 plus 2,150 air
(280,000 shp) in others	group

USS **Saratoga,** *the first of the 'Forrestals' to undergo a SLEP, is seen during the 1980s when with the Atlantic Fleet. These were the first carriers designed with the hangar and flight decks as an integral part of the hull, with gun positions on outboard sponsons. The class was retired as 'Nimitz'-class ships became available.*

'Midway' class

Because of their smaller size, the two 'Midways' had to operate with reduced air groups compared to the US Navy's other carriers. These air groups contained no ASW aircraft or helicopters and used the F-4 Phantom II as their main interceptor in place of the larger and much heavier F-14 Tomcat.

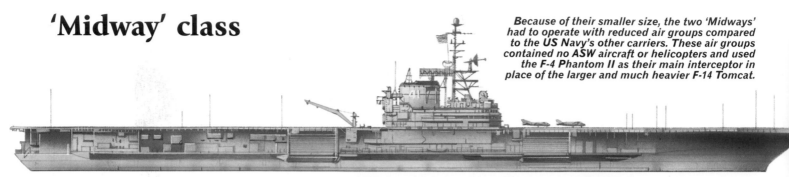

Originally to have numbered six units, the **'Midway' class** suffered the cancellation of three units but entered the post-war years as the only American carriers capable of operating the new generation of heavy attack aircraft without modification. As well as being the only carriers capable, in unmodified form, of operating the post-war generation of heavy nuclear-armed attack aircraft, the 'Midways' were the largest US carriers to be constructed during World War II. However, it was soon found that a refit was needed in the middle to late 1950s to accommodate all recent carrier innovations.

Modifications

All three eventually underwent modernisation programmes which, because they occurred over a long time span, differed considerably in detail. The **USS Midway** (commissioned in September 1945) and **USS Franklin D. Roosevelt** (commissioned in October 1945) were rebuilt under the SCB-110 programme with two steam catapults, the angled flight deck of the SCB-27Cs and a 'hurricane bow', whilst the last unit, the **USS Coral Sea** (commissioned in October 1947), received the SCB-110A modification

which was a somewhat more extensive refit that included the fitting of a third steam catapult in the waist position. By the mid-1960s it was thought necessary for the three vessels to undergo yet another rebuild, and the *Midway* was taken in hand in the latter part of the decade for an SCB-101.66 refit to allow accommodation of the latest generation of carrier aircraft. However, the final cost proved so great that the *Franklin D. Roosevelt* ended with only an austere version of SCB-101.66 in 1968, whilst the *Coral Sea*, having had the SCB-110A improvement, was deemed sufficiently modern to remain in service unaltered.

First retirement

As the vessel in the worst material condition, the *Franklin D. Roosevelt* was stricken in 1977 and broken up. After being struck off, the vessel's name was subsequently assigned to a new 'Nimitz'-class carrier. All three served off Vietnam during the war there. Under the SCB-110/110A refits provision was made for 1,376 tons of ordnance, 134760 litres (35,600 US gal) of AVGAS and 2271240 litres (600,000 US gal) of JP5 aircraft fuel.

Above: A stern view of Midway, considered to be the more capable of the two 'Midway'-class vessels that remained in service into the 1980s.

Left: A US carrier battle group in the Indian Ocean centred on USS Midway, also showing USS Bainbridge, a missile cruiser and the oiler Navasota.

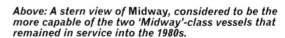

SPECIFICATION

Midway and Coral Sea
Displacement: *Midway* 51,000 tons standard, 64,000 tons full load; *Coral Sea* 52,500 tons standard, 63,800 tons full load
Dimensions: length 298.4 m (979 ft); beam 36.9 m (121 ft); draught 10.8 m (35 ft 4 in); flight deck width 72.5 m (238 ft)
Machinery: four shaft geared steam turbines delivering 158090 kW (212,000 shp)
Speed: 30.6 kts
Aircraft: see text
Armament: two octuple Sea Sparrow SAM launchers (no reloads) in *Midway* only, three 20-mm Phalanx CIWS in both
Electronics: (*Midway*) one LN-66 navigation radar, one SPS-65V air/surface search radar, one SPS-43C

air search radar, one SPS-49 air search radar, one SPS-48C 3D radar; one SPN-035A, two SPN-42 and one SPN-44 aircraft landing aids, two Mk 115 fire-control radars, one URN-29 TACAN system, one SLQ-29 ESM suite, four Mk 36 SRBOC chaff launchers
Electronics: (*Coral Sea*) one LN-66 navigation radar, one SPS-10 surface search and navigation radar, one SPS-43C air search radar, one SPS-30 air search radar, one SPN-43A aircraft landing aid, one URN-20 TACAN system, one SLQ-29 ESM suite, four Mk 36 SRBOC chaff launchers
Complement: *Midway* 2,615 plus 1,800 air group; *Coral Sea* 2,710 plus 1,800 air group

VF-211 F8U-1 Crusaders overfly Midway in the late 1950s. Arranged on the carrier's deck are A3D Skywarriors, a single AD Skyraider, FJ-4 Furys and a HUP Retriever plane guard helicopter on the forward deck landing spot.

During the 1980s, only the *Midway* and *Coral Sea* remained in service, the former was attached to the Pacific Fleet and home-ported in Yokosuka, Japan, and the latter served as a front-line carrier on the strength of the Atlantic Fleet with reduced air groups from carriers that were in refit.

Reduced air wing

Because of their smaller size the 'Midway' class carried the F-4N/S Phantom II in place of the F-14A Tomcat, and did not embark the S-3A Viking. Both carri-

ers were fitted with three deck-edge aircraft elevators, but while the *Midway* had only two steam catapults the *Coral Sea* had three. In their later years, a total of 1,210 tons of aviation ordnance and 4.49 million litres (1.186 million US gal) of JP5 aircraft fuel was carried for the air wing on each ship. The *Midway* was the more capable on account of its extensive refit in 1966, but both ships were phased out by the late 1980s, the *Coral Sea* in 1990 and the *Midway* two years later.

Below: Most thoroughly modernised of the class, USS Midway would have remained a deployable carrier until the turn of the century but was retired in April 1992. In its active life of over 55 years, it may be true to say that Midway experienced a more dramatic enhancement of its capability than any ship in history.

Above: The commissioning of the Franklin D. Roosevelt occurred at a time when a carrier was still expected to fight off air attack by gun power. The 'Midway' class was designed for an air group of some 140 aircraft of World War II type, and this size was to stand them in good stead in the jet age.

Embarking the AJ Savage bomber, USS Coral Sea was the US Navy's first nuclear-capable carrier. The vessel is seen here in the 1980s, the decade which saw its involvement in raids on Libya.

USS *Coral Sea*, 1960s

1 CPO area
2 Balanced rudder
3 Steering compartment
4 Aviation spares/repair shops
5 Screw
6 5-in (127-m) dual-purpose gun
7 Waterline
8 5-in gun fire-control system
9 Aircrew
10 Stores
11 Ammunition
12 Aviation spirit
13 Mk 7 arrester wire system
14 Crew area
15 Engine room
16 Boiler room
17 Ship's service turbo generator
18 Pump room
19 Auxiliary machine room
20 Double bottom
21 Former position of armour belt
22 Frensel deck landing mirror
23 53-ton deck edge lift
24 Aircraft crane
25 Bridge
26 Gallery platform
27 Mast
28 Funnel
29 SPS-43 radar
30 SPS-30 radar
31 Air defence position
32 Navigation bridge
33 Flag bridge
34 Control centre
35 Ventilators
36 Flying deck
37 Hangar
38 Wing compartments
39 Fuel tanks
40 Type C11 catapult
41 Hawser pipe
42 Capstan
43 Anchor
44 Mooring ring
45 Hawser reel
46 Chain locker
47 Forefoot
48 Officer's quarters
49 Walkway
50 Bomb stowage magazine

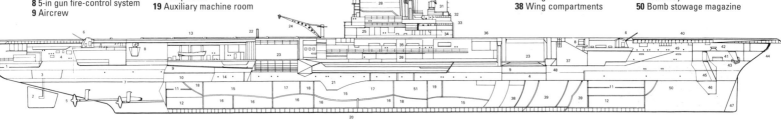

Minas Gerais 'Colossus'-class carrier

A sistership of the Argentinian *25 de Mayo*, the ex-*Vengeance* started life in the Royal Navy in 1945. Three years later the carrier was fitted out for an experimental cruise to the Arctic and was then lent to the Royal Australian Navy in 1953. The vessel was returned to the Royal Navy in 1955 and was purchased by Brazil in December 1956 as the **NAEL *Minas Gerais***. The ship was then transferred to the Netherlands, for a comprehensive refit between 1957-60 with new weapons, a 13365-kg (29,465-lb) capacity steam catapult, an 8.5° angled flight deck, a mirror sight deck landing system, a new island superstructure, new US radars and two centre-line aircraft elevators. The hangar was 135.6 m (445 ft) long by 15.8 m

(52 ft) wide and 5.3 m (17 ft 6 in) high. In 1976-81 the carrier underwent another refit to allow operations through to the 1990s. A datalink system was installed so that the carrier could co-operate with the 'Niteroi' class of frigates in service with the Brazilian navy, and the obsolete American SPS-12 radar was replaced with a modern SPS-40B two dimensional air search system. The role of the *Minas Gerais* throughout its service with the Brazilian navy was anti-submarine warfare with an air group (since the late 1970s) of eight S-2 (P-16) Trackers of the Brazilian air force (the Brazilian navy was not allowed to operate fixed-wing aicraft) plus four navy SH-3/ASH-3 Sea King ASW helicopters, two UH-12/

UH-13 Esquilo and two Bell 206B utility helicopters. The *Minas Gerais* was retired in 2001.

Above: **Minas Gerais** *operated with a combined* **Força Aérea Brasileira** *and navy air group, which until their retirement in 1996 included FAB P-16 Tracker ASW aircraft.*

The **Minas Gerais** *completed its final cruise in February 2001, shortly after having conducted operations with the newly acquired A-4KU Skyhawk (known locally as AF-1) aircraft, which now serve aboard the new 'Clémenceau'-class carrier* São Paulo.

SPECIFICATION

Minas Gerais
Displacement: 15,890 tons standard; 19,890 tons full load
Dimensions: length 211.8 m (695 ft); beam 24.4 m (80 ft); draught 7.5 m (24 ft 6 in); flight deck width 37 m (121 ft)
Machinery: two-shaft geared steam turbines delivering 29830 kW (40,000 shp)
Speed: 25.3 kts

Armament: two quadruple 40-mm AA, and one twin 40-mm AA
Aircraft: see text
Electronics: one SPS-40B air search radar, one SPS-4 surface search radar, one SPS-8B fighter-direction radar, one SPS-8A air control radar, one Raytheon 1402 navigation radar and two SPG-34 fire-control radars
Complement: 1,300 with air group

'Clémenceau' class Aircraft carrier

The **Clémenceau** was the first carrier designed as such to be completed in France. Built in the late 1950s and commissioned in November 1961, it incorporated all the advances made in carrier design during the early 1950s, namely a fully angled flight deck, mirror landing sight and a fully comprehensive set of air search, tracking and air control radars. The flight deck was 165.5 m (543 ft) in length and 29.5 m (96 ft 9 in) in width, and was angled at 8° to the ship's centreline. Two aircraft lifts, each rated at 2036 kg (44,895 lb) were provided, one abaft the island on the deck edge and the other offset to starboard and just forward of the island.

Two steam catapults were fitted, one on the port side of the bow and the other on the angled flight deck. The hangar had a usable area of 152 m (499 ft) by 24 m (78 ft 9 in) by 7 m (23 ft). The fuel capacity of the *Clémenceau* was 1200 m³ of JP5 aircraft fuel and 400 m³ of AVGAS while its sistership, the **Foch** (commissioned in July 1963), carried 1800 m³ and 109 m³ respectively. During the period September 1977 to November 1978 the *Clémenceau* underwent a major refit, with the *Foch* following between July 1980-81. During these refits both ships were converted to operate the Super Etendard strike fighter, for which they carried AN52

Right: The second unit of the 'Clémenceau' class, **Foch** *was laid down in 1957, launched in 1960 and commissioned in 1963. The vessel is seen here after its commissioning into Brazilian navy service as the* São Paulo.

Left: The São Paulo *arrived in Brazil in February 2001, immediately replacing the* Minas Gerais. *The introduction of ex-Kuwaiti Sykhawks signalled a new era for the Brazilian navy, their primary mission being task force CAPs armed with AIM-9 Sidewinders.*

After modification, the two 'Clémenceau'-class carriers served on until the 1990s with the French navy. Clémenceau *paid off in March 1998, with* Foch *following in November 2000.* Clémenceau *occasionally acted as a helicopter carrier for amphibious operations, with SA 330 Pumas, AS 532 Cougars and SA 342 Gazelles of the Aviation Légère de l'Armée de Terre (ALAT) embarked. During Operation Salamandre, the French deployment to the Gulf in 1990,* Clémenceau *ferried 30 Gazelles and 12 Pumas to Saudi Arabia.*

Seen entering Nice in the early 1980s with Super Etendard, Etendard IVP, F-8E(FN) Crusader, Alizé, Lynx and Super Frelon aircraft embarked, **Foch,** *together with* **Clemenceau,** *provided air support to the French contingent in Lebanon in 1983.*

15-kt tactical nuclear gravity bombs in their magazines. They also received SENIT 2 automated tactical information processing systems as part of their C³ suites. Following the refits the two carriers' air groups comprised 16 Super Etendard, three Etendard IVP reconnaissance aircraft, 10 Crusader interceptors and seven Alizé ASW aircraft, plus two Super Frelon ASW and two Alouette III utility helicopters. The carriers could also act, if required, as helicopter carriers with an air group of 30-40 helicopters depending upon the types embarked. During the Lebanon crisis of 1983 France used one of the carriers in support of its peace-keeping force, Super Etendards being used to attack several gun positions that had engaged French troops. The *Foch* and *Clémenceau* were refitted again in 1985-88, receiving Crotale missile launchers in place of two 100-mm guns and storing ASMP nuclear missiles in the magazines. In 1992-93, a removable 1.5° mini-ski jump was fitted on the forward catapult of *Foch* for the deck landing trials of the Rafale M in 1993-94 and in 1995-97 *Foch* was further modified to operate the Rafale M as well as two sextuple Sadral launchers for Mistral SAMs.

Refitted by DCN, *Foch* was commissioned into the Brazilian navy as the **NAE São Paulo**. The carrier has an airgroup built around some of the A-4 Skyhawks acquired from Kuwait in 1998 and replaced the *Minas Gerais*. The *São Paulo* has had all gun and missile armament removed except for a few machine-guns; there are at present no defensive systems to protect the ship. However, with the end of the *25 de Mayo*, the *São Paulo* gives Brazil the only operational aircraft carrier in South America. The national prestige value of a major warship remains as potent in that continent as it was at the beginning of the 20th century when Brazil, Chile and Argentina bought dreadnought battleships from European yards in a similar display of conspicuous expenditure, regardless of practical defence strategy.

25 de Mayo 'Colossus'-class carrier

The **ARA *25 de Mayo*** was originally a 'Colossus'-class carrier purchased from the UK by the Dutch and commissioned into the Royal Netherlands navy on 28 May 1948. In April 1968 the ship suffered a serious boiler room fire, and was subsequently judged to be uneconomical to repair. In the following October Argentina bought the vessel, which was refitted and commissioned into the Argentinian navy in the Netherlands. The vessel sailed for Argentina on 1 September 1969.

The vessel was fitted with a modified Ferranti CAAIS data-processing system and Plessey Super CAAIS console displays. This system allowed the ship to control its carrier-based aircraft and to communicate via datalinks with the two Type 42 destroyers of the Argentinian navy and their ASAWS 4 action information systems. The carrier's modified superstructure differed considerably from those of other ex-British carriers in service with other navies. In 1980-81, the ship underwent a further refit to increase the strength of the flight deck and add extra deck space to allow two extra aircraft to be parked in readiness for the Super Etendards that Argentina was acquiring.

Falklands War

Luckily for the UK none of these strike aircraft had qualified to land on the carrier by the time of the Falklands War, and the carrier's air group consisted of eight A-4Q Skyhawks, six S-2E Trackers and four SH-3D Sea Kings. The *25 de Mayo* played a major part in the initial landings on the Falklands and was ready to launch a strike against the British task force on 2 May 1982 when fate intervened in the form of poor flying conditions. The subsequent sinking of the *Belgrano* then forced the Argentine carrier to retire to the relative safety of Argentina's coastal waters, where it played no further part in the proceedings and landed its air group for land-based operations. After the Argentine loss of the Falklands the remaining Super Etendards were delivered. These were rapidly deck-qualified and the new make-up of the air group was 20 fixed-wing and four rotary-wing aircraft: eight Super Etendards, six A-4Q Skyhawks, six S-2E Trackers and four Agusta-built AS-61D Sea Kings. The vessel was inactive for most of the 1990s, and was officially retired in 1997.

Left: The deck of the **25 de Mayo** *in the mid-1980s supported A-4Q Skyhawk and Super Etendard aircraft. Note the steam from the catapult, indicating that an aircraft has just left the flight deck.*

The main target for the British SSN force during the Falklands conflict was **25 de Mayo,** *the flagship of the original task force that invaded the islands.*

'Charles de Gaulle' class Nuclear-powered carrier

In September 1980, the French government approved the construction of two nuclear-powered aircraft carriers to replace its two conventionally powered 'Clemenceau'-class carriers that date back to the 1950s. However, the French CVN programme has been bedevilled by political opposition and technical problems, both with the vessel and the aircraft. The first ship of the class, **FS *Charles de Gaulle*** was laid down in April 1989 and launched in May 1994 but not commissioned until May 2001. Repeated budget cuts delayed work but so did a number of errors in its construction. Thus, even in 2003 the *Charles de Gaulle* is non-operational and still lacks a proper air group. The navalised Rafale remains delayed, leaving the carrier to operate an air group comprising 20 Super Etendards. As

completed the *Charles de Gaulle* was unable to operate E-2C Hawkeye aircraft as critical dimensions were wrongly measured. Between 1999-2000, the angled flight deck was lengthened accordingly, and additional radiation

shielding was also added. Prospects for a second (perhaps conventionally-powered) ship of the 'Charles de Gaulle' class remain poor; although the navy has pressed for one (to be called ***Richelieu*** or, possibly,

Clémenceau), political and popular support for such an expensive investment may never be forthcoming.

The *Charles de Gaulle* is equipped with a hangar for 20-25 aircraft (around half the air group) and carries the

same reactor units as the 'Le Triomphant'-class SSBN: this permits five years of continuous steaming at 25 kts before refuelling. Seakeeping behaviour is improved through the fitting of four pairs of fin stabilisers.

Charles de Gaulle has a pair of 75-m (246-ft) US Type C13F catapults which can launch 23-tonne aircraft. Enhanced weight capability allows the flight deck to allow AEW aircraft operations

SPECIFICATION

Charles de Gaulle
Displacement: 40,600 tons full load
Dimensions: length 261.42 m (857 ft 8 in); beam 64.4 m (211 ft 4 in); draught 8.5 m (27 ft 10 in)
Machinery: two Type K15 reactors delivering 300 MW (402,145 shp) and two turbines delivering 56845.2 kW (76,000 shp) to two shafts
Speed: 28 kts (limited to 25 kts)
Aircraft: up to 40 aircraft, including 24 Super Etendard, two E-2C Hawkeye, 10 Rafale M, and two SA 365F Dauphin (plane-guard) or AS 322 Cougar (CSAR)

Armament: four Sylver octuple VLS launchers for Aster 15 anti-missile missiles, two Sadral PDMS sextuple launchers for Mistral SAMs, eight Giat 20-mm guns
Countermeasures: four Sagaie 10-barrel decoy launchers, LAD offboard decoys, SLAT torpedo decoys (to be fitted)
Electronics: DRBJ 11B air search radar, DRBV 26D Jupiter air search radar, DRBV 15D air/surface search radar, two DRBN 34A navigation radars, Arabel 3D fire-control radar
Complement: 1,150 plus 550 aircrew and 50 flag staff; can accommodate 800 marines

*The island of the **Charles de Gaulle** is located well forward in order to provide protection from the weather for the two 36-ton capacity aircraft lifts.*

Viraat 'Hermes'-class carrier

Flagship of the Indian fleet, Viraat has undergone a number of modifications since it was commissioned into Indian service in 1986. These include new safety features and defences, the latter including the Israeli Barak close-in missile defence system with anti-missile capability. The vessel is due to be replaced by a new 'Vikrant'-class CTOL carrier.

SPECIFICATION

Viraat
Displacement: 28,700 tons full load
Dimensions: length 208.8 m (685 ft); beam 27.4 m (90 ft); draught 8.7 m (28 ft 6 in)
Machinery: four boilers generating 56673 kW (76,000 shp) to two shafts
Speed: 28 kts
Range: 6,500 miles (10460 km) at 14 kts
Aircraft: (normal) 12-18 Sea Harrier FRS.Mk 51/60, up to seven Sea King Mk 42 or Ka-28 'Helix-A'; three Ka-31 on order

Armament: two octuple VLS launchers for Barak missiles, four Oerlikon 20-mm guns, two 40-mm Bofors guns, and four AK-230 30-mm guns
Countermeasures: two Corvus chaff launchers
Electronics: Bharat RAWL-02 Mk II air search radar, Bharat RAWS air/surface search radar, Bharat Rashmi navigation radar, Graseby Type 184M hull-mounted active search/attack sonar
Complement: 1,350 including 143 officers with the air group

Viraat is fitted with a 12° ski jump and a reinforced flight deck with armour over the magazines and machinery spaces. Capacity is provided for 30 Harriers.

HMS *Hermes* was commissioned into the Royal Navy in November 1959, having been built at Barrow-in-Furness between 1944-53. Four years after playing a crucial role in the liberation of the Falklands, *Hermes* was sold to India. Refitted, the ship was commissioned into the Indian Navy as the **INS *Viraat*** in May 1987. Refitted again from July 1999 to December 2000, *Viraat* returned to the fleet in June 2001 and is planned to remain in service until 2010, by which time a 32,000-ton CTOL carrier (which has been approved for construction) is scheduled to enter service.

Modifications since its Falklands days include the substitution of Russian AK-230 six-barrel 30-mm guns for the old Sea Cat SAM system (these may in turn be replaced by Kashtan CIWS); new fire control, search and navigation radars; new deck-landing aids; improved NBC protection; conversion of boilers to use distillate fuel; and after 2001, the IAI/Rafael Barak SAM. Like *Hermes*, *Viraat* is fitted to carry up to 750 troops and four LCVPs are carried for amphibious landings, and in addition up to 80 lightweight torpedoes can be carried in the magazine. However, *Viraat* may be retired early now that India has finally completed a deal with Russia to buy the 'Kiev'-class carrier *Admiral Gorshkov* and with it, a number of MiG-29K fighters – a $700 million refit and through-deck conversion for the *Gorshkov* is supposed to be completed by 2008. The Sea Harriers carried by the *Viraat* are scheduled for modernisation too but this may be shelved with the advent of the MiG-29Ks.

Giuseppe Garibaldi ASW carrier

Designed as a gas turbine-powered helicopter carrier, the **ITS *Giuseppe Garibaldi*** incorporates features suiting it for the carriage and operation of V/STOL fighters. The flight deck is 173.8 m (570 ft 2 in) long and 21 m (68 ft 11 in) wide, and is fitted with a 6.5° ski-jump ramp. The hangar is 110 m (360 ft 11 in) long, 15 m (49 ft 3 in) wide and 6 m (19 ft 8 in) high, and is built to accommodate 12 SH-3D or EH 101 ASW helicopters, or 10 AV-8B aircraft and one SH-3D, although the available height permits the embarkation of CH-47C helicopters if required. A maximum air wing comprising 18 helicopters (six on deck) or 16 AV-8Bs can be embarked. Two aircraft lifts are fitted (one forward and one abaft the island), and there are six marked flight deck spaces for helicopter operations.

ASW role

The *Garibaldi* was designed specifically to provide ASW support for naval task forces and merchant convoys, and as such is fitted with full flagship facilities plus command, control and communication systems for both naval and air force operations. In emergencies it can also carry up to 600 troops for short periods. The extensive weaponry fitted also allows it to operate as an independent surface unit. The carrier carries a bow-mounted active search sonar. To permit helicopter operations in heavy weather the vessel has been fitted out with two pairs of fin stabilisers, and the aircraft maintenance facilities are sufficient not only to service the ship's own air group but also the light ASW helicopters of any escorting warships.

Commissioned in September 1985, the *Garibaldi* originally operated solely as an assault carrier with SH-3s and AB 212s embarked. After the Italian navy was given political clearance to operate fixed-winged types, AV-8Bs were acquired, although these have only been routinely embarked since December 1994. Under modernisation, the Teseo Mk 2 SSM launchers are to be removed and replaced with SATCOM domes, and Aster 15 missiles will eventually replace Aspide.

Flagship of the Italian navy, the Giuseppe Garibaldi *and its air group are one of the more powerful naval forces in the Mediterranean. As well as regular air group operations, the ship can act as an assault carrier, and has operated army CH-47Cs, AB 205s and A 129s.*

SPECIFICATION

Giuseppe Garibaldi
Displacement: 10,100 tons standard; 13,139 full load
Dimensions: length 179 m (587 ft 3 in); beam 30.4 m (99 ft 9 in); draught 6.7 m (22 ft)
Machinery: two-shaft gas turbine (four Fiat/GE LM2 500) delivering 59655 kW (80,000 shp)
Speed: 30 kts
Aircraft: 12-18 helicopters or 16 AV-8B Harrier II or combination
Armament: eight OTO Melara Teseo Mk 2 SSM launchers, two octuple Albatros launchers for Aspide SAMs (48 missiles), three twin 40-mm Breda guns, two triple 324-mm (12.75-in) B-515 torpedo tubes for Mk 46 ASW

torpedoes
Countermeasures: various passive ESM systems, two SCLAR chaff launchers and one DE 1160 sonar
Electronics: one SPS-52C long-range 3D air search radar, one SPS-768 D-band air search radar, one SPN-728 I-band air search radar, one SPS-774 air/surface search radar, one SPS-702 surface search/target indication radar, three SPG-74 gun fire-control radars, three SPG-75 SAM fire-control radars, one SPN-749(V)2 navigation radar, one SRN-15A TACAN system, one IPN-20 combat data system
Complement: 550 normal, 825 maximum including air group

Garibaldi is well defended for a Western carrier, with eight Teseo Mk 2 anti-ship missile launchers and two octuple Albatros launchers for 48 Aspide SAMs.

'Kuznetsov' class Heavy aviation cruiser

The 'Kiev' class could never be considered true aircraft carriers. From the 1960s onwards, the rapidly expanding Soviet Navy began to see its lack of such a vessel to be a handicap, especially to a navy looking to spread its influence around the world.

Several abortive projects were started, including the 1973 design for a nuclear-powered aircraft carrier of 85,000 tons which would be capable of accommodating 60 to 70 aircraft. In the early 1980s, two less ambitious projects began to make serious progress, the **Project 1143.5** which was to become the **Kuznetsov** and the 75,000-ton **Project 1143.7** which, had it been built, would have been the **Ulyanovsk**. This nuclear-powered ship with twin catapults was proposed to carry the upgraded Su-27KM and Yak-44 AEW/ASW fixed-wing aircraft within its complement of 60-70 aircraft.

Propulsion

Initially, Western analysts anticipated that the ships would have a combined nuclear and steam (CONAS) propulsion plant similar to the *Kirov* battle cruiser and the *SSV-33* support/command ship. However the class was in fact conventionally propelled with oil-fired boilers.

Although superficially similar to American carriers, the 60,000-ton Soviet aircraft car-

Two starboard lifts carry the aircraft from the hangar to the flight deck. The ship was designed to operate Su-27K, MiG-29K, Yak-41 (and later the heavier and more capable Yak-43) supersonic STOVL fighters, but the only fixed wing aircraft regularly taken to sea have been the Su-27K (Su-33) and Su-25UTG, the latter being used as an unarmed trainer.

The first unit was originally named **Riga**. The name was changed to **Leonid Brezhnev**

Vastly more capable than the preceding vessels of the 'Kiev' class, the Kuznetsov is also vastly more expensive. The cash-strapped Russian navy can ill afford such a vessel, and no more are to be built in the foreseeable future.

and handed the hulk over to Ukraine. In 1998, the sale of the *Varyag* was announced – to a Macau-based entertainment company. The

The huge expanse of the Kuznetsov's flight deck is as large as that of a US Navy supercarrier, though it operates with a much smaller air wing.

rier was always intended to be subordinate to missile submarines operating in their 'bastions' in the Arctic. It is capable of engaging surface, subsurface and airborne targets. The lack of catapults precludes launching aircraft with heavy strike loads, and the air superiority orientation of the air wing is apparent.

The flight deck area is 14700 m² (158,235 sq ft) and aircraft take-off is assisted by a bow ski-jump angled at 12 degrees in lieu of steam catapults. The flight deck is equipped with arrester wires.

and then to **Tbilisi** before settling in October 1990 on **Admiral Flota Sovetskogo Soyuza Kuznetsov**, normally being shortened to **Admiral Kuznetsov**.

Abortive construction

Construction of a sister ship (**Project 1143.6**), initially named **Riga** and later **Varyag**, the second of the class, started in December 1985 at Nikolayev, and the ship was launched in November 1988. Late in 1991 the Russian Defence Ministry stopped financing the carrier,

unfinished hull was towed to the Far East where it was converted into an entertainment complex and casino – though Russian media reports claim the company is a front for the Chinese navy.

Like its predecessors, the Kuznetsov is primarily an ASW platform, and as such is armed mainly with helicopters. However, the Su-27K 'Flanker' interceptor gives it a considerable counter-air capability.

SPECIFICATION

'Kuznetsov' class
Type: Heavy Aviation Cruiser (Aircraft Carrier)
Displacement: 46,600 tons standard; 59,400 tons full load
Dimensions: length 304.5 m (999 ft); beam 67 m (219 ft 10 in); hangar deck length 183 m (600 ft); draught 11 m (36 ft 1 in)
Propulsion: 8 boilers powering four turbines delivering 149 MW (200,000 shp) to four shafts
Speed: 29 kts
Aircraft: Designed to carry the cancelled Yak-41 STOVL fighter and MiG-29K; typical complement of twelve Sukhoi Su-27K/33 plus 24 Kamov Ka-27/31 Helix for utility, ASW, AEW and missile targetting; in future will carry Su-27KUB combat trainer and possibly the Su-33UB multirole fighter
Armament: Twelve-cell VLS for P-700 Granit (SS-N-19 'Shipwreck') SSMs, 24 eight-round Kinshal (SA-N-9 'Gauntlet') vertical SAM

launchers with 192 missiles, eight combined gun/missile close air defence systems with eight twin 30-mm Gatling guns and Klinok (SA-N-11 'Grison') missiles, two RPK-5 (UDAV-1) ASW rocket systems with 60 rockets
Electronics: One 'Top Plate' (MR-710 Fregat-MA) 3D air/surface search radar, two 'Strut Pair' (MR-320M Topaz) 2D search radars, three 'Palm Frond' navigation radars, four 'Cross Sword' (MR-360 Podkat) SA-N-9 fire control radars, eight 'Hot Flash' (3P37) SA-N-11 fire control radars, one 'Fly Trap B' aircraft control system, one Zvezda-2 sonar suite including an 'Ox Yoke' (MGK-345 Bronza) hull mounted system, one Sozbezie-BR ESM/ECM suite, two PK-2 and ten PK-10 chaff and decoy launchers
Complement: 2,626 including 626 air personnel and 40 flag staff.

'Kiev' class Aviation cruiser

The impetus behind the development of an aviation capability by the Soviet Navy was provided by the entry into service of the US navy's Polaris missile submarines. The two 'Moskva'-class helicopter carriers were completed in the late 1960s, but they were fairly limited and notoriously unreliable. Work on an improved helicopter carrier began in 1967. The **Project 1143** vessels, which were known in the USSR as the 'Krechyet' class, were much larger than the 'Moskva'-class.

Into service

The new carriers were built at the Chernomorsky yard at Nikolayev on the Black Sea. The 42,000 ton **Kiev** was the first of the class. It passed through the Bosphorous on 18 July 1976, to international protests about possible infractions of the Montreaux Convention. Three more ships were later built in this class; **Minsk**, **Novorossiysk** and **Baku** (later renamed **Admiral Gorshkov**). Because of improvements which included a phased array radar, extensive electronic warfare installations, and an enlarged command and control suite, the *Baku* was sometimes considered a separate class. A fifth unit was approved in 1979, but not built.

Aviation cruisers

Classified as PKRs (Provtivolodochny Kreyser, or aviation cruiser), they were much closer to conventional

aircraft carriers than the 'Moskva' class. They had a large island superstructure to starboard, with an angled flight deck to port. However, unlike American carriers, the bow of the ships carried a very heavy armament fit, including the long-range, nuclear-capable P-500 Bazalt anti-ship missile, known to NATO as the SS-N-12 'Sandbox'. The air wing consisted of up to 22 Yakovlev

Lacking catapults and arrester gear, the 'Kiev'-class carriers were much less capable aviation platforms than the US Navy's supercarriers.

SPECIFICATION

'Kiev' class

Type: Anti-submarine/aviation cruiser

Displacement: 36,000 tons (38,000 tons *Gorshkov*) standard; 43,500 tons (45,500 tons *Gorshkov*) full load

Dimensions: length 274 m (899 ft); beam 32.7 m (107 ft 4 in); flight deck 53 m (173 ft 10 in); max draught 12 m (39 ft 4 in)

Propulsion: eight turbo-pressurised boilers powering four steam turbines delivering 149 MW (200,000 shp) to four shafts

Speed: 32 kts

Aircraft: 12 Yakovlev Yak-38 'Forger' VTOL fighters plus up to 17 Kamov Ka-25 'Hormone' or Ka-27 'Helix' ASW helicopters

Armament: Two Shtorm (SA-N-3 'Goblet') twin SAM launchers with 72 missiles, two Osa-M (SA-N-4 'Gecko') twin SAM launchers with 40 missiles, four Kinshal (SA-N-9 'Gauntlet') eight-cell vertical

launchers with 96 missiles (*Novorossisk* only) or 192 missiles (*Gorshkov* only), eight P-500 Bazalt (SS-N-12 'Sandbox') anti-ship missile tubes for 16 missiles, four 76-mm (3-inch) guns in two twin DP mounts (two single 100-mm/3.9-inch in *Gorshkov*), eight AK 630 six-barrel 30-mm CIWS, two RBU 6000 ASW rocket launchers, ten 533-mm (21-in) torpedo tubes

Electronics: 'Plate Steer' air search radar, 'Sky Watch 4' phased array radar (on *Gorshkov*), two 'Strut Pair' surface search radars, three 'Palm Frond' navigation radars, one 'Trap Door', one 'Kite Screech', four 'Bass Tilt' and four 'Cross Sword' fire control radars, one 'Fly Trap' and one 'Cake Stand' aircraft control and landing system, 'Horse Jaw', 'Horse Tail' and variable depth sonars, two twin chaff launchers plus full ECM/ESM and IFF suite

Complement: 1,600

First seen in the Mediterranean in 1976, the 44,000 ton 'Kiev'-class V/STOL carriers of the Soviet Navy were impressive vessels.

Yak-38 'Forger' VTOL fighters and 16 Kamov Ka-25 'Hormone' or Ka-27 'Helix' helicopters. Ten of the helicopters were ASW machines, with two utility/SAR machines and four missile-guidance aircraft. None of the vessels are in service today – *Kiev*, *Minsk* and *Novorossiysk* were decommissioned in 1993 and were later sold for scrap. The *Admiral Gorshkov*, inactive since 1991, is to due to be transferred to the Indian navy, following the addition of a redesigned 'Kuznetsov'-style flight deck incorporating a 'ski-jump' built into a newly raised bow.

The 'Kievs' were hybrid carrier/cruisers, carrying a very heavy missile armament capable of engaging submarine, surface ship and airborne targets.

Principe de Asturias Light aircraft carrier

To replace the *Dédalo* (ex-'Independence'-class light aircraft carrier USS *Cabot*) from 1986, the Spanish navy placed a 29 June 1977 contract for a vessel with gas turbine propulsion. The design of the new Spanish ship, prepared by Gibbs and Cox of New York, was based on the Enal design variant of the US Navy's abortive Sea Control Ship. Originally to have been named the **SPS Almirante Carrero Blanco** but then renamed as the **Principe de Asturias** before being launched, the new ship is analogous in many respects to the three British light aircraft carriers of the 'Invincible' class.

Slow completion

The *Principe de Asturias* was laid down on 8 October 1979 at the Ferrol yard of the Bazán company, was launched on 22 May 1982, and commissioned on 30 May 1988. The long

period between the launch and the commissioning was attributable to the need for changes to the command and control system, and also to the addition of a flag bridge to facilitate the ship's use in the command role.

The *Principe de Asturias* has a flight deck measuring 175.3 m (575 ft 2 in) in length and 29 m (95 ft 2 in) in width, and this is fitted with a 12° 'ski-jump' ramp blended into the bow. Two aircraft lifts are fitted, one of them at the extreme stern, and these are used to move aircraft (both fixed- and rotary-wing) from the hangar, which has an area of 2300 m² (24,760 sq ft).

For the *Principe de Asturias*' air wing, Spain ordered the EAV-8B (VA.2) Harrier II V/STOL multi-role warplane (from early 1996, radar-equipped Harrier II Plus were delivered) and the SH-60B Seahawk ASW helicopter. The standard aircraft

complement is 24, although this can be increased to 37 in times of crisis with the aid of flight-deck parking. The standard aircraft mix is six to 12 AV-8Bs, two SH-60Bs, two to four AB 212ASW helicopters, and six to 10 SH-3H Sea King helicopters including three fitted with Searchwater radar to operate in the AEW role.

Advanced electronics

The fully digital Tritan command and control system is fitted with the Link 11 and Link 14 data transmission/reception terminals of the Naval Tactical Display System, and there is also the standard complex of air- and surface surveillance radars, aircraft and gun control radars, and countermeasures both electronic and physical. The ship also carries two LCVPs, and two pairs of stabilisers are fitted for stability in heavier seas.

Above: The Principe de Asturias *has a straight flight deck and a substantial 'ski jump' rise at the bow for the launch of heavily laden Harrier II aircraft.*

SPECIFICATION	
Principe de Asturias	**Armament:** four 12-barrel Meroka
Displacement: 16,700 tons full load	20-mm CIWS
Dimensions: length 195.9 m (642 ft 9 in); beam 24.3 m (79 ft 9 in); draught 9.4 m (30 ft 10 in)	**Electronics:** one SPS-55 surface search radar, one SPS-52 3D radar, four Meroka fire-control radars, one SPN-3SA air control radar, one
Machinery: two General Electric LM 2500 gas turbines delivering 34300 kW (46,000 shp) to one shaft	URN-22 TACAN system, one SLQ-25 Nixie towed decoy and four Mk 36 SRBOC chaff launchers
Speed: 26 kts	**Complement:** 555 plus a flag staff
Aircraft: see text	and air group of 208

The hangar of the Principe de Asturias *opens at its after end onto one of the two aircraft lifts. Spotted round the ship's two sides and the stern are the four Meroka defensive guns, each with 12 20-mm barrels.*

Chakri Naruebet Light aircraft carrier

The **HTMS *Chakri Naruebet*** ('The Great of the Chakri Dynasty') is the newest and most powerful warship of the Royal Thai navy, which otherwise comprises a dozen frigates and a similar number of corvettes and fast attack craft plus amphibious forces. The ship is the first aircraft carrier to be operated by a country in Southeast Asia. Built at Ferrol in Spain by the Bazán company, the vessel was laid down on 12 July 1994 and launched on 20 January 1996. Sea trials began in October 1996 and the ship spent the first months of 1997 working up with the Spanish fleet. (*Chakri Naruebet* is very similar to the Spanish *Principe de Asturias*.)

Arriving in Thailand in

August 1997 the vessel is in active service with the Third Naval Area Command and its home port is Rayong. However, the planned primary anti-aircraft armament (a Mk 41 LCHR 8-cell VLS launcher for Sea Sparrow missiles and four Vulcan Phalanx CIWS mountings) has not been installed, leaving the vessel protected by just Mistral infra-red homing missiles with a maximum range of 4000 m (4,375 yards). The *Chakri Naruebet* makes few operational sorties, and when it does put to sea it is usually to carry members of the Thai Royal family. The vessel is therefore to be regarded less as a V/STOL amphibious warfare capable carrier and more as the most expensive royal yacht afloat.

The Chakri Naruebet *was ordered to give the Thai navy the means to support the country's amphibious forces, but the country's financial problems then prevented the addition of the defensive weapons vital to survival in contested waters.*

SPECIFICATION	
Chakri Naruebet	SAM launchers
Displacement: 10,000 tons standard; 11,485 tons full load	**Aircraft:** up to six AV-8S Matador fixed-wing aircraft and six S-70B Seahawk; alternatively Sea King, S-76 or Chinook helicopters
Dimensions: length 182.6 m (599 ft 1 in); beam 21.9 m (73 ft 10 in); draught 6.21 m (20 ft 4in)	
Propulsion: two gas turbines and two diesels delivering 32985 and 8785 kW (44,240 and 11,780 shp) respectively to two shafts	**Electronics:** SPS-32C air-search and SPS-64 surface-search radars, MX1105 navigation radar, hull-mounted sonar, four SRBOC decoy launchers, and SLQ-32 towed decoy
Speed: 26 kts	
Armament: two 0.5-in (12.7-mm) machine guns and two Mistral	**Complement:** 455 plus 146 aircrew and 175 marines

A side view of the **Chakri Naruebet** *reveals the considerable similarity between this major element of the Royal Thai navy and the* **Principe de Asturias** *of the Spanish navy, which was built by the same yard.*

'Invincible' class Light aircraft carrier

The demise of the British fixed-wing aircraft carrier, with the cancellation of the CVA-01 fleet carrier programme in 1966, led in 1967 to a Staff Requirement for a 12,500-ton command cruiser equipped with six Sea King ASW helicopters. A redesign of this basic concept to give more deck space showed that a nine-helicopter air group was much more effective. A new specification resulted in a design that became known as the 19,500-ton 'through deck cruiser' (TDC), a term used for what was essentially a light carrier design because of the political sensitivity with which politicians viewed the possibility of a carrier

resurrection at the time. Despite this, the designers showed initiative in allowing sufficient space and facilities to be incorporated from the outset for a naval version of the RAF's Harrier V/STOL warplane. The designers were duly awarded for such foresight in May 1975 when it was announced officially that the TDC would carry the Sea Harrier. The first of the **'Invincible' class**, HMS **Invincible**, which had been laid down in July 1973 at the Vickers shipyard at Barrow-in-Furness, was not delayed during building. In May 1976 the second ship, HMS **Illustrious**, was ordered, and in December 1978 the third, HMS **Indomitable**, was con-

tracted. However as a result of public disquiet, the Admiralty in placatory mood renamed the ship HMS **Ark Royal**. The ships were commissioned in July 1980, July 1982 and November 1985.

Gas turbines

The ships of the class are the largest gas turbine-powered warships in the world, with virtually every piece of below-deck equipment, including engine modules, suitable for maintenance by exchange. During building both the *Invincible* and the *Illustrious* were fitted with 7° 'ski-jump' ramps, while the *Ark Royal* has a 15° ramp. In 1982 it was announced that the *Invincible* was to be sold to Australia as a helicopter

carrier to replace HMAS *Melbourne*, leaving only two carriers in British service. However, the deal was cancelled after the Falklands campaign as it was realised by the government that three carriers ought to be available to ensure two in service at any one time. During Operation Corporate the *Invincible* started with an air group of eight Sea Harriers and nine Sea King ASW helicopters. However, as a result of losses and replacements this was modified to a group of 11 Sea Harriers, eight ASW Sea Kings and two Lynx helicopters configured to decoy Exocet missiles. One of the problems was that most of the extra aircraft had to be

accommodated on the deck as there was insufficient room for them in the hangar. The *Illustrious* was hurried through to completion in time to relieve the *Invincible* after the war, and went south with 10 Sea Harriers, nine ASW Sea Kings and two Sea King AEW conversions. The vessels were also fitted with two 20-mm Phalanx CIWS mountings for anti-missile defence and two single 20-mm AA guns to improve on the previous non-existent close-in air defences. The normal air group consisted of five Sea Harriers and 10 Sea Kings (eight ASW and two AEW).

TDCs in service

Since the 1980s the Royal Navy has run two ships with the third undergoing a refit. The *Invincible* was brought to the standard of the *Ark Royal*, then *Illustrious* followed. The *Ark Royal* started a two-year refit in 1999.

In recent years six RAF GR.Mk 7 Harriers have been regularly embarked for ground-attack missions under Joint Force Harrier. *Illustrious* has had its Sea Dart missile launcher removed to allow space for a flight extension and a new ordnance magazine. The *Invincible* was on station off the Adriatic in 1994 when Sea Harrier F/A.Mk 2s were first operationally deployed.

Above: The primary long-range air defence weapon installed on the carriers of the 'Invincible' class was the Sea Dart surface-to-air missile fired from a twin-arm launcher beside the forward edge of the flight deck.

Left: The 'Invincible'-class carriers carry fixed- and rotary-wing aircraft, the former comprising various Harrier and Sea Harrier V/STOL multi-role warplane marks in blends suiting the task in question.

SPECIFICATION	
'Invincible' class	**Aircraft:** see text
Displacement: 16,000 tons standard and 19,500 tons full load	**Electronics:** one Type 1022 air search radar, one Type 992R air search radar, two Type 909 Sea Dart guidance radars, two Type 1006 navigation/helicopter direction radars, one Type 184 or Type 2016 bow sonar, one Type 762 echo sounder, one Type 2008 underwater telephone, one ADAWS 5 action information data processing system, one UAA-1 Abbey Hill ESM suite, and two Corvus chaff launchers
Dimensions: length 206.6 m (677 ft); beam 27.5 m (90 ft); draught 7.3 m (24 ft)	
Propulsion: four Rolls-Royce Olympus TN1313 gas turbines delivering 83520 kW (112,000 shp) to four shafts	
Speed: 28 kts	
Armament: one twin Sea Dart SAM launcher with 22 missiles, two 20-mm Phalanx (replaced by Goalkeeper on *Illustrious*) CIWS, and two single 20-mm AA	
	Complement: 1,000 plus 320 air group (provision for emergency Marine Commando)

V/STOL carriers

The 'Harrier carriers'

Considered by the US Navy too small to have an adequate air wing, and not flexible enough to project the power that the Pentagon's naval strategy calls for, the modern light carrier has a number of advantages that the big-deck advocates ignore. The absence of catapults and arrester gear, which largely dictate the size of a carrier and the size of the aircraft it carries, and the much simpler launching and recovery arrangements mean that a V/STOL carrier is much cheaper to build and less challenging to operate than a conventional carrier.

Although now due for an early retirement, the Royal Navy's Sea Harrier FA.Mk 2 remains a capable multirole aircraft, and is capable of carrying up to four AIM-120s in conjunction with its powerful Blue Vixen radar. Fixed-wing equipment for the successors to the 'Invincible' class commissioning in 2012-15 will be an F-35 version.

Above: Marina Militare Italiana TAV-8B trainers on the forward flight deck of Giuseppe Garibaldi. The carrier can carry up to 16 Harriers or a maximum of 18 SH-3 helicopters, although a combination is most common.

The US Marine Corps ultimately accepted 286 AV-8B Harrier IIs into service between 1982 and 1992. The arrival of the AV-8B Harrier II Plus in 1995 brought with it an even greater transformation than that from AV-8A to AV-8B, the addition of the APG-65 multi-mode radar opening up a whole new range of weapons options carried on a new eight-hardpoint wing, and including the AIM-120 AMRAAM. A Harrier II Plus from the USMC's VMA-542 'Flying Tigers' is illustrated.

AGM-65 Maverick

Although integration of modern weapons with the Harrier II Plus has proceeded slowly, the Maverick remains an important and capable weapon. The USMC is unique in using the AGM-65E variant with a laser seeker head. Previous variants relied on TV or imaging infra-red guidance.

SPECIFICATION	
HMS *Ark Royal*	**'Wasp' class**
Displacement:	**Displacement:**
Standard: 16,000 tons **Full load:** 19,500 tons	**Light:** 28,233 tons **Full load:** 40,532 tons
Dimensions:	**Dimensions:**
Length: 206.6 m (677 ft) **Beam:** 27.5 m (90 ft) **Draught:** 7.3 m (24 ft)	**Length:** 253.2 m (844 ft) **Beam:** 31.8 m (106 ft) **Draught:** 8.1 m (32 ft)
Propulsion:	**Propulsion:**
Four gas turbines delivering 83529 kW (112,00 shp) to four shafts	Two geared steam turbines delivering 33849 kW (70,000 shp) to two shafts
Performance:	**Performance:**
Speed: 28 kts **Range:** 11,265 km (7,000 miles) at 19 kts	**Speed:** 22 kts **Range:** 17594 km (10,933 miles) at 18 kts
Armament:	**Armament:**
Three Mk 15 Phalanx CIWS, and two 20-mm Oerlikon guns	Two Mk 29 Sea Sparrow SAM launchers, two Mk 49 RAM launchers, two/three Mk 15 Phalanx CIWS, four 25-mm Mk 38 guns
Aircraft:	**Aircraft:**
(Typical force projection air wing) eight Sea Harrier FA.Mk 2, eight Harrier GR.Mk 7, four Sea King AEW.Mk 1, two Sea King HAS.Mk 6	(Sea control role) 20 AV-8B and six SH-60 or (assault) six AV-8B plus helicopters (maximum of 42 CH-46)

Derived from the 'Tarawa' LHAs, the seven vessels of the 'Wasp' class are larger and capable of operating three LCACs in addition to helicopters, AV-8Bs and traditional landing craft. The long flight deck allows heavily laden helicopters and aircraft to employ a rolling take-off. The MV-22B seen on the deck of USS Essex, is replacing the CH-46 and the CH-53D in troop assault and transport roles.

SEA KING: ROYAL NAVY WORKHORSE

Although the Royal Navy's 'Invincible'-class carriers are most closely associated with the Harrier, for much of the Cold War it was the Sea King helicopter, armed with nuclear depth charges, that provided the principal tool for the vessels' primary role of ASW in the Atlantic. V/STOL fighters were embarked to provide air defence primarily against Soviet MP aircraft. During Operation Corporate, the Sea Kings were tasked with protecting the Task Force from Argentine submarines, and the lack of AEW coverage during this conflict prompted the development of a dedicated AEW Sea King variant. The resultant AEW.Mk 2 was the first helicopter-based AEW platform to be deployed. Today the Sea King complement on the 'Invincibles' is dominated by upgraded AEW versions of No. 849 Sqn, with a smaller number of HAS.Mk 6s for ASW and plane-guard duties. For the assault and troop transport roles, the 'Invincibles' accommodate the Sea King HC.Mk 4 version (pictured with *Invincible*), normally assigned to HMS *Ocean* and the 'Intrepid' LPDs.

YAK-38 'FORGER': SOVIET V/STOL PIONEER

Often considered as a Soviet counterpart to the Royal Navy's first generation Harrier, the Yak-38 'Forger' was a very different aircraft, being used only as a light attack aircraft, whereas the Harrier FRS.Mk 1 was principally used for air defence duties. Unlike the Harrier the Yak-38 carried no radar, and was equipped with four underwing pylons for the carriage of Kh-23 (AS-7 'Kerry') radio command-guided ASMs, unguided bombs and rockets and R-60 (AA-8 'Aphid') AAMs (pictured). The Yak-38 provided the Soviet navy with much experience in fixed-wing carrier operations, the type being operated from civil ships, and in the land-based role over Afghanistan, as well as from the 'Kiev'-class carriers. A typical 'Kiev' class air group included 20 Yak-38s or Ka-25/27 ASW helicopters in *Kiev* and *Minsk*; *Novorossiysk* and *Baku* could carry 28 'Forgers' or ASW helicopters. After gaining experience on the Yak-38, the Soviet navy was due to receive the supersonic Yak-41M 'Freestyle' STOVL fighter, but this promising project was cancelled in 1992.

HMS *Ark Royal*

The name *Ark Royal*, originally carried by an English galleon fighting the Spanish Armada in 1588, has been associated with Royal Navy aircraft carriers since World War I. It was the name of Britain's largest carrier in the years before World War II, and its successor was the last conventional carrier to serve in the British fleet. The current *Ark Royal* is the third ship in the 'Invincible' class. In March 2003, the carrier was operational in the Persian Gulf with the Royal Navy Task Force and conducting operations in support of Operation Iraqi Freedom.

Command and control

Ark Royal is fitted with the ADAWS 10 Action Data Automation Weapon System. This sophisticated electronic, computerised network controls deployment of the ship's weapons and aircraft, and by means of data-links it can command and control escorting and co-operating forces.

'*Ark*' in the Gulf

'Invincible'-class carriers have supported the UN monitoring of Iraq as part of Operation Southern Watch. Most missions have been for air defence, with the Sea Harrier FA.Mk 2. On 1 February 2003, the USS *Montpelier*, a nuclear submarine, along with a British flotilla consisting of *Ark Royal*, helicopter carrier HMS *Ocean*, and three destroyers and seven supply ships, all transited the Suez Canal as they made their way to the Persian Gulf in preparation for war. These vessels of the Royal Navy Task Force joined the other 10 Royal Navy vessels already in the region to take part in Operation Iraqi Freedom.

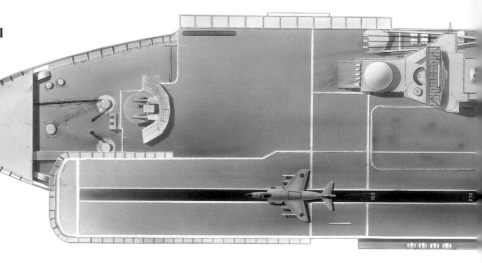

Close-in weapon systems

Ark Royal was completed with three American-built Mk 15 Phalanx close-in weapon systems. Phalanx is based on the Vulcan aircraft cannon, and its six rotating barrels can fire at a rate of up to 3,000 20-mm cannon shells per minute. Located at the bow, and on sponsons at the stern and on the starboard side of the superstructure, the Phalanx systems are designed to provide last-ditch defence against sea-skimming missiles. Under an upgrade on Invincible and *Illustrious*, these have been replaced by three examples of the even harder-hitting Dutch Goalkeeper system. This a seven-barrel 30-mm Gatling gun, with a similar range to the Phalanx, but a rate of fire increased to 4,200 rounds per minute. Single 20-mm Oerlikon guns are also carried on the starboard side of the island superstructure.

Joining the fleet in 1985, **Ark Royal,** *the third 'Invincible'-class vessel, allows the Royal Navy to always have two carriers on call, and one usually in reserve or undergoing refit. Note the forward Phalanx* **CIWS.**

'Ski-jump'

The 12° 'ski-jump' ramp at the forward end of the *Ark Royal*'s flight deck is a British innovation that enables Sea Harriers to be launched fully laden after a short take-off roll, where a vertical take-off can be managed only with a reduced payload. The earlier *Invincible* and *Illustrious* were completed with 7° ramps. Entering service in 1985, *Ark Royal* was able to incorporate lessons learned from the Falklands War into its design. The most obvious of these is the longer and steeper 'ski-jump' ramp, but accommodation was also increased and the Flag command and control facilities were improved.

Flight deck

Because light carriers operate short take-off/vertical landing (STOVL) fighters, there is no need for the catapults and arrester gear that dictate the size of modern supercarriers. *Ark Royal*'s deck is 167 m (548 ft) long and 35 m (125 ft) wide, and is arranged with a Harrier take-off run at the bow and nine numbered helicopter and Harrier landing spots along the length of the vessel.

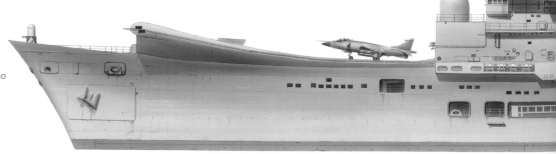

Communication

Ark Royal is equipped with a pair of SCOT 2D satellite communication antennae, situated abaft the second funnel. SCOT allows messages to be sent over Britain's Skynet military satellites as well as NATO networks and the American Defense Satellite Communications System.

Missile fire control

The Sea Dart missiles were controlled by two Type 909 fire-control radars (since removed). The Type 909 tracks the target, and points the launcher automatically. The Sea Dart missile homes in on the radar reflection. The system is also reported to be able to direct guns and missiles against surface targets. Gun fire-control is provided by a Rademec optronic director.

Helicopters

Although normally equipped with Sea King ASW helicopters, *Ark Royal* is capable of operating the larger Merlin helicopter. A typical Cold War era ASW air wing comprised a full squadron of Sea King HAS.Mk 6s (nine helicopters) supported by three Sea King AEWs. Another potential role is assault, for which the *Ark Royal* carries Sea King HC.Mk 4s or even RAF Chinooks displacing some of the typical air wing. The current deployed Sea King versions are the HAS.Mk 6 (ASW/SAR/utility helicopter) and AEW.Mk 7 (AEW variant). For commando operations the carrier can also ship the Gazelles and Lynx helicopters of the Royal Marine support unit.

Sea Dart

The 'Invincible'-class light fleet carriers were originally equipped with Sea Dart area-defence surface-to-air missiles. The GWS 30 twin launcher was located next to the 'ski-jump' on the starboard side, and connected with a magazine containing 22 missiles. Sea Dart has an effective range of more than 65 km (40 miles), and can engage targets flying at altitudes between 30 and 18000 metres (100 to 60,000 ft).

'Ark' in action

Although the 'Invincibles' saw no direct action in the 1991 Gulf War, *Ark Royal* deployed to the eastern Mediterranean to secure the area against Iraqi attack during Operation Desert Storm. The carrier was in the Adriatic in 1993 for Operation Grapple, the UK's contribution to the UN Deny Flight 'no-fly' operations over Bosnia. Remaining in this theatre through the escalating Balkan wars, *Ark Royal* lost a Sea Harrier FRS.Mk 1 to an SA-7 'Grail' missile in April 1994. In September 1995, Sea Harriers took part in Operation Deliberate Force, attacking Serb targets in Bosnia.

Propulsion

Ark Royal is powered by four Rolls-Royce Olympus gas turbines. The advantage of using such engines is that they are smaller, lighter, and much quicker to run up to full power than conventional steam turbines. Vessels so propelled have much improved acceleration, which is vital when your main task is the hunting of high-speed nuclear-powered submarines.

Aircraft complement

The 'Invincible' class was designed to ship five Sea Harriers, but since the Falklands, the normal complement has risen to eight. The latest FA.Mk 2 variant (FRS.MK 1 is illustrated) can carry a wide variety of air-to-surface and air-to-air weaponry, and its Blue Vixen radar gives the fighter a look-down, shoot-down capability. A typical post-Cold War air group now consists of eight FA.Mk 2s, a similar number of RAF Harrier GR.Mk 7s, four Sea King AEWs and just two Sea King HAS.Mk 6s to provide SAR cover and limited ASW protection.

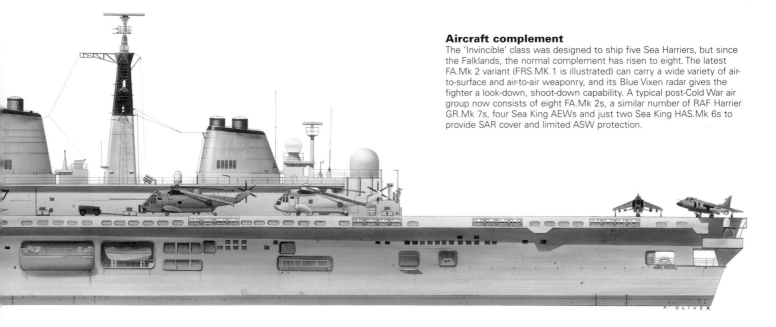

'Improved Forrestal' class *America, Constellation, JFK & Kitty Hawk*

USS America (CVA 66), commissioned in January 1965, first entered service with the Atlantic Fleet and made three combat deployments to Southeast Asia during 1968-73. In 1975 the vessel was modified to handle F-14 and S-3 aircraft, and in 1980 became the first carrier to receive the Phalanx CIWS. America was involved in action against Libya in 1986 and Iraq in 1991.

Built to an **'Improved Forrestal'-class** design, these four carriers in reality constitute three sub-classes that are easily distinguished from their predecessors by the fact that their island superstructures are set farther aft. In addition, two of their four aircraft elevators are forward of the island, the 'Forrestals' having only one in this location. A lattice radar mast is also carried abaft of the island.

USS *America*

The **USS *America*** (commissioned in January 1965) was very similar to the first two ships (**USS *Kitty Hawk*** and **USS *Constellation***, commissioned in June 1961 and January 1962), and was built in preference to an austere-version nuclear-powered carrier. It was, however, the only US carrier of post-war construction to be fitted with a sonar system. The last unit,

the **USS *John F. Kennedy***, was built to a revised design incorporating an underwater protection system developed originally for the nuclear carrier programme, and was commissioned in September 1968. All four were built with steam catapults and carried some 2,150 tons of aviation ordnance plus about 7.38 million litres (1.95 million US gal) of aviation fuel for their air groups. These are again similar in size and composition to those of the 'Nimitz' class. The tactical reconnaissance element in each of the air wings is usually provided by a handful of Grumman F-14 Tomcats equipped with a digital TARPS (tactical airborne reconnaissance system) pod. Replacement of the Tomcat in all its roles by the Boeing F/A-18E/F Super Hornet multi-role fighter and strike aircraft is under way, although this aircraft has initially deployed on units of the 'Nimitz' class.

The ships were all fitted with full Anti-Submarine Classification and Analysis Center (ASCAC), Navigational Tactical Direction System (NTDS) and Tactical Flag Command Center (TFCC) facilities, *America* being the first carrier to be fitted with the NTDS. The ships all had the OE-82 satellite communications system, and were the first carriers able simultaneously to launch and recover aircraft easily; on previous carriers this was considered a tricky operation. Three of the ships passed through a SLEP (service life extension programme), but *America* was retired in the early 1990s without SLEPing. *Constellation* was retired in 2003 and *Kitty Hawk* is due to remain with the Pacific Fleet until 2008. *JFK* is scheduled to remain on Atlantic Fleet strength until at least 2018.

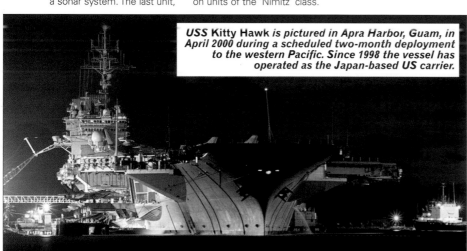

USS Kitty Hawk *is pictured in Apra Harbor, Guam, in April 2000 during a scheduled two-month deployment to the western Pacific. Since 1998 the vessel has operated as the Japan-based US carrier.*

Above: Kitty Hawk *refuels the 'Sumner'-class destroyers* McKean *and* Harry E. Hubbard *in 1962, a year after entering service with the US Pacific Fleet.*

Below left: USS Constellation *(foreground) and* Kitty Hawk *conduct joint carrier operations in the western Pacific Ocean in August 1999.* Constellation *was retired in favour of USS* Ronald Reagan *in 2003, whilst* Kitty Hawk *will be replaced by CVN 77 in 2008.*

SPECIFICATION

USS *John F. Kennedy*
Displacement: 81,430 tons full load
Dimensions: length 320.6 m (1,052 ft); beam 39.60 m (130 ft); draught 11.40 m (37 ft 5 in); flightdeck width 76.80 m (252 ft)
Machinery: four-shaft geared steam turbines delivering 209 MW (280,000 shp)
Speed: 32 kt (59 km/h; 37 mph)
Aircraft: air wing depends on mission; includes up to 20 F-14 Tomcat, 36 F/A-18 Hornet, four EA-6B Prowler, four E-2C Hawkeye, six S-3B Viking, two ES-3A Shadow (until 1999), four SH-60F Ocean Hawk and two HH-60H Rescue Hawk
Armament: three octuple Mk 29 Sea Sparrow SAM launchers (no reloads), three 20-mm Vulcan Phalanx close-in weapons systems (CIWSs); two Phalanx mountings

scheduled to be replaced by Sea RAM (Rolling Airframe Missile) CIWS
Electronics: one SPN-64(V)9 navigation radar, one SPS-49(V)5 air search radar, one SPS-48E 3D radar, one Mk 23 TAS (Target Acquisition System), one SPS-67 surface search radar, six Mk 95 fire control radars, three Mk 91 MFCS (Missile Fire Control System) directors; one SPN-41, one SPN-43A and two SPN-46 CCA (Carrier-Controlled Approach) radars, one URN-25 TACAN system, one SLQ-36 Nixie towed torpedo decoy, SLQ-32(V)4/SLY-2 ESM/ECM suite, SSTDS (Surface Ship Torpedo Defence System), four SRBOC Mk 36 chaff/flare launchers
Complement: 2,930 (155 officers) plus 2,480 air group (320 officers)

USS *Enterprise* (Post-refit) Nuclear-powered carrier

The use of nuclear power as the propulsion plant allows USS Enterprise to carry sufficient aircraft fuel and ordnance for 12 days of sustained air operations before having to undergo replenishment.

The world's first nuclear-powered aircraft-carrier, the **Enterprise** was laid down in 1958 and commissioned in November 1961, as what was then the largest warship ever built. Since exceeded in size by the 'Nimitz'-class ships, the *Enterprise* was built to a modified 'Forrestal'-class design, with its larger dimensions dictated by the powerplant of eight A2W pressurised water enriched-uranium fuelled nuclear reactors. The high cost of its construction prevented five other vessels in the naval building programme from being built.

Major refit

From January 1979 to March 1982 *Enterprise* underwent an extensive refit which included the rebuilding of its island superstructure and the fitting of new radar systems and a mast to replace the characteristic ECM dome and billboard radar antenna that had been used since it was built. *Enterprise* is equipped with four steam catapults, four deck-edge aircraft elevators and carries 2,520 tons of aviation ordnance plus 10.3 million litres (2.72 million US gal) of aircraft fuel. Like that of other US carriers the *Enterprise*'s ordnance has included 10-kT B61, 20-kT

USS Enterprise, the US Navy's oldest active nuclear-powered carrier and a veteran of the Cuban Missile Crisis, steams in the Arabian Gulf in support of Operation Southern Watch in September 2001.

B57, 60-kT B43, 100-kT B61, 200-kT B43, 330-kT B61, 400-kT B43, 600-kT B43 and 900-kT B61 tactical nuclear gravity bombs, 100-kT Walleye air-to-surface missiles and 10-kT B57 depth bombs, while 1.4-MT B43 and 1.2-MT B28 strategic bombs could be carried as and when required. The air group is similar in size and configuration to that carried by the 'Nimitz'-class carriers, and the *Enterprise* is fitted with the same ASCAC, NTDS and Tactical

Flag Command Center (TFCC) facilities. In addition to its OE-82 satellite system it also carries two British SCOT satellite communications antenna units for use with British fleet units and NATO. These two systems were fitted in 1976.

Enterprise is currently deployed with the Atlantic Fleet and was SLEPed between 1991 and 1994. It is estimated that it will be eventually paid off in about 2014.

Above: Air traffic controllers on board USS Enterprise assist in guiding strike aircraft in and out of Iraq during Operation Desert Fox in December 1998.

USS Enterprise (top) and USS George Washington, the fast combat support ship USS Supply (centre) and the ammunition ship USS Mount Baker (bottom) steam in formation in the western Mediterranean during turnover operations in 1996.

SPECIFICATION

USS Enterprise
Displacement: 75,700 tons standard, 93,970 tons full load
Dimensions: length 342.30 m (1,123 ft); beam 40.50 m (133 ft); draught 10.90 m (39 ft); flightdeck width 76.80 m (252 ft)
Machinery: four-shaft geared steam turbines (eight A2W nuclear reactors) delivering 209 MW (280,000 shp)
Speed: 33 kt (60 km/h; 38 mph)
Aircraft: see 'Improved Forrestal' class
Armament: three octuple Mk 29 Sea Sparrow launchers (no reloads), three 20-mm Vulcan

Phalanx CIWS (may be replaced by Sea RAM)
Electronics: one SPN-64(V)9 navigation radar, one SPS-49(V)5 air search radar, one SPS-48E 3D radar, one Mk 23 TAS, one SPS-67 surface search radar, six Mk 95 fire control radars, three Mk 91 MFCS directors; one SPN-41, one SPN-43A and two SPN-46 CCA radars, one URN-25 TACAN system, one SLQ-36 Nixie towed torpedo decoy, SLQ-32(V)4/SLY-2 ESM/ECM suite, SSTDS, four SRBOC Mk 36 chaff/flare launchers
Complement: 3,215 (171 officers) plus 2,480 air group (358 officers)

'Nimitz' class
Nuclear-powered aircraft carrier

The first three **'Nimitz'-class** carriers were originally designed as replacements for the elderly 'Midway' class. The largest and most powerful warships ever built, they differ from the earlier nuclear-powered USS *Enterprise* in having two reactors rather than eight, with ordnance magazines between and forward of them. This increases the internal space available to allow some 2,570 tons of aviation weapons and 10.6 million litres (2.8 million US gal) of aircraft fuel to be carried. These totals are sufficient for 16 days of continuous flight operations before stocks have to be replenished. The class is also fitted with the same torpedo protection arrangement as carried by the USS *John F. Kennedy*, and is laid out with the same general arrangement and electronic fit as the JFK.

Flight deck
Four deck-edge aircraft elevators are available: two forward and one aft of the island on the starboard side and one aft on the port side. The hangar is 7.80 m (25 ft 7 in) high, and like those of other US carriers can accommodate, at most, only half of the aircraft embarked at any one time; the remainder is spotted on the flight deck in aircraft parks. The flight deck measures 333 x 77 m (1,093 x 253 ft), the angled section being 237.70 m (780 ft) long. It is fitted with four arrester wires and an arrester net for recovering aircraft. Four steam catapults are carried, two on the bow launch position and two on the angled flight-deck. With four catapults

the carrier can launch one aircraft every 20 seconds.

Air Wing
The standard US Navy air wing at the beginning of the 21st Century includes 20 F-14D 'Bomcats' (Tomcats with a strike role), 36 F/A-18 Hornets, eight S-3A/B Vikings, four E-2C Hawkeyes, four EA-6B Prowlers, four SH-60F and two HH-60H Seahawks. Air wings can be varied according to the nature of the operation: for example, in 1994, 50 army helicopters replaced the usual air wing on the Eisenhower during peacekeeping operations off Haiti. There are also facilities for a Grumman C-2A Greyhound carrier on-board delivery aircraft.

A million miles
The core life of the A4W reactors fitted is, under normal usage, expected to provide a cruising distance of some 1287440 to 1609300 km (800,000 to 1,000,000 miles) and last for 13 or so years before the cores have to be replaced. Although the class is relatively new, it is planned for the 'Nimitz'-class to undergo Service Life Extension Program (SLEP) refits by 2010 in order to extend their service life by 15 years.

As the primary means of American power projection, the ships of the 'Nimitz' class have seen a considerable amount of use around the hotspots of the world. The USS Nimitz (CVN-68), commissioned in May 1975, was the base for the abortive Iranian hostage rescue mission in 1980. In 1981 her fighters were in action against Libya. Transferring from the

Atlantic to the Pacific in 1987, Nimitz deployed to the Persian Gulf and Asian waters on numerous occasions over the next decade. In 1998 the carrier returned to Norfolk for a two-year refuelling refit.

Eisenhower
Commissioned in October 1977, USS *Dwight D. Eisenhower* (CVN-69) serves with the Atlantic Fleet. The carrier has made eight Mediterranean deployments, and was the first US carrier to respond to the Iraqi invasion of Kuwait. In 1994, 'Ike' supported peacekeeping operations off Haiti, and in succeeding deployments supported US policy in the Persian Gulf.

Assigned to the Pacific fleet in 1982, the USS Carl Vinson (CVN-70) has conducted numerous deployments in the Pacific and Indian Oceans, as well as the Arabian Sea. Most

recently, the Vinson has played a major part in the war in Afghanistan.

USS Eisenhower steams in company with the guided missile cruiser California in the early 1980s. For a quarter of a century, the 'Nimitz' class carriers have been the world's most powerful warships.

SPECIFICATION

'Nimitz' class
Displacement: 81,600 tons standard, 91,487 tons full load
Hull dimensions: length 317 m (1,040 ft); beam 40.80 m (134 ft); draught 11.30 m (37 ft);
Flightdeck dimensions: length 332.90 m (1,092 ft); width 76.80 m (252 ft)
Machinery: two A4W/A1 G nuclear reactors powering four geared steam turbines delivering 208795 kW (280,000 shp) to four shafts
Speed: over 35 kt (65 km/h; 40 mph)
Aircraft: capacity for up to 90, but current USN air wings usually comprise 78-80 aircraft
Armament: three octuple Sea Sparrow SAM launchers (no

reloads); four 20-mm Phalanx close-in weapon systems (CIWS); two triple 32-cm (12.6-in) torpedo tubes
Electronics: (first three) one SPS48E 3D air-search, one SPS-49(V)5 air-search; one SPS-67V surface-search; one SPS-67(V)9 navigation; five aircraft landing aids (SPN-41, SPN-43B, SPN-44 and two SPN-46); one URN-20 TACAN system; six Mk 95 fire-control radars; one SLQ-32(V)4 ESM suite; four Mk 36 Super RBOC chaff launchers; SSTDS torpedo defensive system; SLQ-36 Nixie sonar defence system; ACDS combat data system; JMCIS combat data system; four UHF and one SHF SATCOM systems
Complement: 3,300 plus 3,000 air group

The USS Carl Vinson displays about a third of a standard air wing on deck. Most of the strike aircraft can fight both air-to-air and air-to-ground.

Improved 'Nimitz' class   Nuclear-powered aircraft carrier

In 1981 the first of at least six **Improved 'Nimitz'-class** carriers was ordered after much discussion both within the Congress and the Pentagon. These vessels were completed with Kevlar armour over their vital areas and have improved hull protection arrangements. The Kevlar armour has been retrofitted to the earlier carriers, as have many of the advanced systems built into the newer ships.

Enlarged

Broader in the beam by about two metres, the newer carriers have a full-load displacement in excess of 102,000 tons (and may exceed 106,000 tons in some circumstances). The ship's complement of 3,184 personnel (203 officers) does not include the air wing of 2,800 aircrew (with 366 officers); and 70 flag staff (with 25 officers).

The combat data systems fitted to the improved carriers are based around the Naval Tactical and Advanced Combat Direction System (ACDS), with Links 4A, 11, 14, and 16 communication and data links. Weapons control is managed by three Mk 91 Mod 1 MFCS directors for the Sea sparrow missile. USS *Nimitz* is being fitted with the SSDS Mk2 Mod 0 ship self-defense system, developed by Raytheon. The SSDS will provide automated self-defence against anti-ship cruise missiles (ASCMs) by integrating and co-ordinating the ship's weapon and electronic warfare systems.

Electronic war

The Raytheon AN/SLQ-32(V) electronic warfare system detects hostile radar emissions by two sets of antennae and the system analyses the pulse repetition rate, the scan mode, the scan period, and the frequency.

The massive flight deck of the USS Harry S. Truman is as large as three football fields, and provides the base for an air wing stronger than most of the world's smaller air forces. The aircraft carrier is a powerful element of US foreign policy. Bill Clinton once said that the first thing any President asked when being presented with a new crisis anywhere in the world was, 'Where are the nearest carriers?'

The system identifies the threat and direction, provides a warning signal and interfaces to the ship's countermeasures systems.

The first improved 'Nimitz' was the USS *Theodore Roosevelt* (CVN-71), which commissioned in October 1986. Roosevelt saw extensive action in the Gulf War. USS *Abraham Lincoln* (CVN-72) was commissioned in November 1989 and her first major operation was the evacuation of American forces from the Philippines after the eruption of Mount Pinatubo. USS *George Washington* (CVN-73) was commissioned in July 1992, followed by USS *John C. Stennis* (CVN-74) in December 1995 and USS *Harry S. Truman* (CVN-75) in 1998. USS *Ronald Reagan* (CVN-76) was christened by Mrs Nancy Reagan in 2001.

The 10th and last of the class, CVN-77, will enter service in 2008. This will be a transitional design, incorporating new technology that will significantly reduce the crew requirement. It will test systems intended for a new class of carriers (CVNX) due in the following decade.

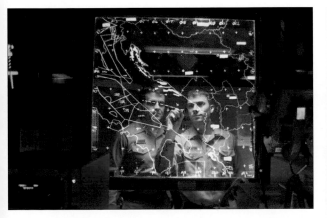

Above: Sailors man the status board in the control centre of the USS Theodore Roosevelt (CVN-71).

Right: Over the last 20 years, US carriers have maintained a near-continuous presence in the Indian Ocean. Here, USS George Washington (CVN-73) takes over the watch from the USS Enterprise (CVN-65).

US Carrier Battle Group

Air power at sea

Representing the ultimate manifestation of US military might and global power, the US Navy's supercarriers form the cores of powerful battle groups. Each carrier acts as the operations centre of its battle group, while its accompanying ships provide it the protection it needs to launch and recover sustained air operations over ranges of several hundred miles.

Above: Launching aircraft such as this JDAM-armed F/A-18E, allows US carriers to strike with an accuracy of 13 m (43 ft) across ranges of several hundred miles. This VFA-115 'Eagles' Super Hornet is performing a 'touch-and-go' on **Abraham Lincoln***.*

Below: Like the aircraft above, this F-14D, hailing from VF-31, was photographed during operation Enduring Freedom. It has just launched from **Abraham Lincoln***'s No. 3 catapult.*

Above: Time is limited for both the F/A-18C and the USS **Kitty Hawk** *from which this example is flying. The Hornet is likely to remain in service well beyond* **Kitty Hawk***'s 2008 retirement date, however. The carrier is the US Navy's only permanently forward-deployed carrier and is based at Yokosuka, Japan.*

Below: The US Navy and Marine Corps have responsibility for US jamming needs. This VAQ-137 'Rooks' EA-6B Prowler jamming aircraft, was photographed over the Arabian Sea, during Enduring Freedom operations from USS **Theodore Roosevelt***.*

Right: Although the S-3 has given up much of its original ASW role, the aircraft remains a useful force multiplier. USS **George Washington** *is home to this VS-30 'Diamond Cutters' S-3B.*

Below: Although they are not permanently carrier based, the C-2A Greyhound carrier onboard delivery (COD) aircraft, such as this VCR-40 'Rawhides' machine, provide a vital supply and mail service.

Below: Transferring supplies from the Military Sealift Command ship USS **Supply** *to USS* **George Washington** *during Enduring Freedom, this CH-46 belongs to HC-8 'Dragon Whales'. Even in its latest CH-46E form, the Sea Knight is well overdue for retirement. Recent operations have also seen USMC CH-53s operate from carrier decks.*

*With major upgrades planned, the **E-2C H**awkeye will remain the **US** Navy's primary **AWACS** asset well into the 21st century. The VAW-115 'Liberty Bells' aircraft, shown above aboard **Kitty Hawk** in the **South China Sea**, shows the type's compact size. The VAW-125 E-2C crewman 'in the office' at left, is monitoring the air defence of New York off the US east coast as part of operation Noble Eagle.*

FLIGHT DECK PERSONNEL: CARRIER COLOURS

The crew involved in carrier flight operations have specific, clearly defined roles and are recognised by the colour of their jerseys, helmets ('cranials') and life vests ('float coats').

Brown: Air wing plane captains and air wing line leading leading petty offiers.

Green: The 'frogs' include catapult and arresting gear crews, air wing maintenance personnel, cargo handlers, ground support equipment troubleshooters, helicopter landing signal personnel and hook runners.

Blue: Plane handlers (pictured, monitoring hangar movements), elevator operators, tractor drivers, mesengers and phone talkers.

Yellow: Aircraft handling officers, catapult and arresing gear officers and plane directors (pictured).

Red: Ordnancemen (pictured, removing AIM-9 from aircraft), crash and salvage crews and explosive ordnance disposal.

Purple: The 'grapes' are crew concerned with aviation fuels. Pictured is an airman taking aircraft fuel samples.

White: A broad category including air wing quality control personnel, squadron plane inspectors, landing signal officers, air transfer officers, liquid oxygen crews, safety observers (pictured) and medical personnel.

Sikorsky's **SH-60B** Seahawk naval helicopter has spawned a number of significant variants. These include the **HH-60H** Rescue Hawk (above) which is specially equipped for *SAR* and special forces infil/exfil missions. The **MH-60S** Knighthawk (above right) is a utility transport and SAR helicopter, originally designated **CH-60S**, and represented here by an *HS-5* 'Nightdippers' aircraft. The operation in progress is a typical one for the MH-60S, since it is replacing the utility-tasked CH-46s: ammunition is being offloaded aboard ship. In **SH-60F** Ocean Hawk form, the H-60 performs a multi-role tasking, which includes plane guard, as shown by this *HS-8* machine working around **John C. Stennis**, *during Enduring Freedom.*

AIRCRAFT CARRIER ARMAMENT: SELF DEFENCE

Generally, aircraft carriers rely on their air wing and the ships of their accompanying battle group for air defence. However, a carrier represents such a large and tempting target that a determined enemy is bound to get some forces through the ship's defensive screen. These forces could range from low-flying aircraft or missiles, to patrol craft or inflatable boats. The carrier must therefore be equipped with a range of self-defence weapons, and these typically include RIM-7 Sea Sparrow (right) as a primary system, housed in Mk 29 octuple launchers. *Harry S. Truman*, one of whose RIM-7 batteries is illustrated, has two NATO Sea Sparrow batteries of eight missiles each. Combining elements of both the Sidewinder and Stinger AAMs, the RIM-116 Rolling Airframe Missile (RAM) is a specialist anti-cruise missile weapon. Here (below right) a RIM-116 launcher is loaded aboard *Kitty Hawk*. The Mk 15 Phalanx 20-mm six-barrelled CIWS system (below middle), seen here on *John C. Stennis*, is an autonomous weapon and very much a last ditch defence against missiles and aircraft. Finally, the best way to deal with close-in surface threats is undoubtedly the 0.50-in (12.7-mm) machine-gun, as seen below, mounted in *Abraham Lincoln*'s hangar bay.

Above: Nimitz has seen a great deal of combat service. Here the 'Air Boss' and his assistant ('Mini-Boss') control flight operations in the Persian Gulf during the 1990s, in support of operation Southern Watch.

Above: This October 1997 shot shows both Nimitz's pennant number (CVN 68) and the increasing numerical superiority of the Hornet in a typical carrier air wing to advantage.

Below: Home ported at San Diego, the 'Ticonderoga'-class guided missile cruiser USS Princeton (CG 59) is seen here from the flight deck of USS Nimitz, during September 2002. Note the Hawkeye and Viking aircraft on deck.

Above: A carrier battle group typically consists of four to six ships supporting the carrier. Here Nimitz steams with part of its battle group, including the Aegis guided missile cruiser Port Royal (CG 73), and the nuclear attack submarine Annapolis (SSN 760).

Below: In 2001/2002, Nimitz re-emerged after an extensive refit and with its reactors refuelled. It returned to operations during 2002 part of its first post-refit air wing is VFA-14 'Tophatters' and its F/A-18E Super Hornets. Carrier aircraft usually carry their parent ship's name above the Navy titling on their rear fuselage.

USS *Nimitz*

Commissioned in May 1975, USS *Nimitz* is more than likely to remain in service until at least 2025, modern aircraft carriers being reckoned to have a useful operational life of around 50 years. The ship is one of ten vessels in the 'Nimitz' class, the remainder being *Dwight D. Eisenhower* (commissioned in October 1977), *Carl Vinson* (March 1982), *Theodore Roosevelt* (October 1986), *Abraham Lincoln* (November 1989), *George Washington* (July 1992), *John C. Stennis* (December 1995), *Harry S. Truman* (July 1998), *Ronald Reagan* (due for completion in 2002) and the as yet un-named CVN-77, which will be commissioned in 2008. *Nimitz* is home ported at Norfolk, Virginia, just a stone's throw away from the Newport News shipyards where all of the 'Nimitz'-class have been, or are still being built.

Machinery

A pair of reactors, widely spaced amidships, provide the energy to drive the eight steam turbine generators which propel *Nimitz* and provide electrical power for its on board services. Thanks to its nuclear power, the ship has almost unlimited range and a 30-kt (56 km/h; 35 mph) top speed.

Elevators and hangars

In layout, the 'Nimitz'-class flight deck is similar to that of *John F. Kennedy* and is similarly served by four deck-edge aircraft elevators. The larger size of the 'Nimitz' ships has allowed an increase in hangar head room, however, which is up to 7.77 m (25 ft 6 in). In addition, greater tankage for aviation fuel is provided (1,059,912 litres; 280,000 US gal) and the magazines are larger. The later are able to accommodate up to 2,600 tons of aircraft ordnance, allowing sustained operations, especially with modern PGMs.

Flight deck

With an area of around 1.8 ha (4.5 acres), the flight deck has four catapults. At the stern, four arrestor wires trap recovering aircraft, with pilots generally aiming to take the third 'wire' as a matter of professional pride. Below deck, hangars run almost the full length of the ship, providing cover for relatively deep aircraft maintenance work, as well as for those aircraft not required for any one cycle. About half the ship's complement is dedicated to the operation of its air wing. In 2002, a typical air wing might consist of E-2C Hawkeyes, EA-6B Prowlers, F-14A/B/D Tomcats, F/A-18C/D Hornets, F/A-18E/F Super Hornets, H-60 helicopters and S-2B Vikings.

Phalanx

Platforms to either side of the forward flight deck mount Phalanx CIWS (spoken as 'sea-whizz') units. Phalanx works independently of other ship systems, providing close-in defence even if other key systems are down due to battle damage or crew incapacity. An RIM-116 RAM launcher is also located on the starboard side of the forward flight deck.

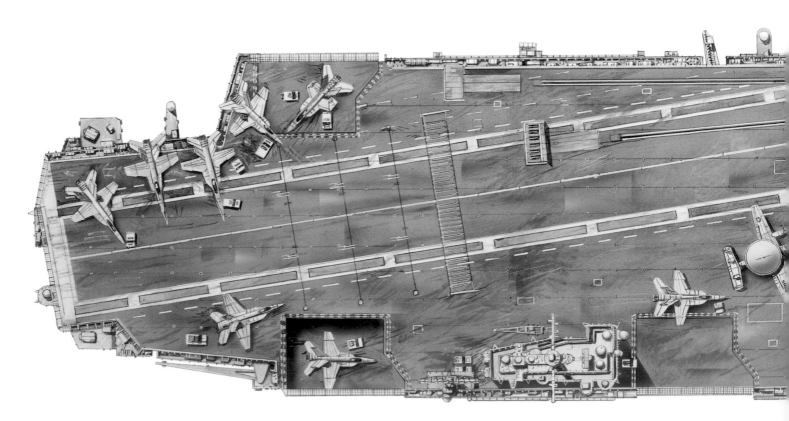

Complement

Typically, *Nimitz* is crewed by around 6,000 personnel. A maximum of 70-day's worth of food can be carried, while fresh water in produced by four distilling units. These can desalinate and purify in excess of 1,514,160 litres (400,000 US gal) of sea water per day to service the needs of the crew and its powerplant. The dental and medical needs of the crew are handled by five dentists and six doctors. One of the doctors is a general surgeon and the ship boasts a 53-bed hospital, allowing it to function as a hospital ship for its battle group.

Catapults

Known informally as 'fat cats', each of the four steam catapults aboard *Nimitz* can launch a 37,700-kg (83,000-lb) aircraft at flying speed in a distance of around 91 m (300 ft). The thrust provided by the catapults is carefully adjusted according to the weight of the aircraft being launched. Such is the efficiency of the ship's flight deck, that up to four aircraft can be launched in 60 seconds.

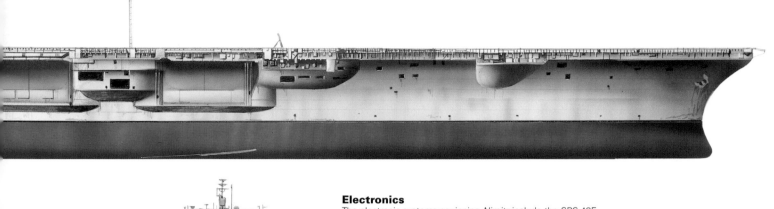

Electronics

The electronic systems equipping *Nimitz* include the SPS-48E three-dimensional air search radar, SPS-49(V)5 two-dimensional air search radar and three Mk 91 Mod 1 missile fire control systems (MFCS) directors. The ship also has an SLQ-32(V)4 jamming system and a WLR-1H ESM set.

Future air wing

Radical changes are in store for the US Navy air wings. In 15 years, it is likely that the typical air wing will include E-2 Hawkeyes, F/A-18E/F Super Hornets, F-35s, and H-60 helicopters. The EA-6B may soldier on but seems likely to be replaced by the EA-18 Growler, while the F/A-18 Hornet, especially in F/A-18D form may also still remain an important type.

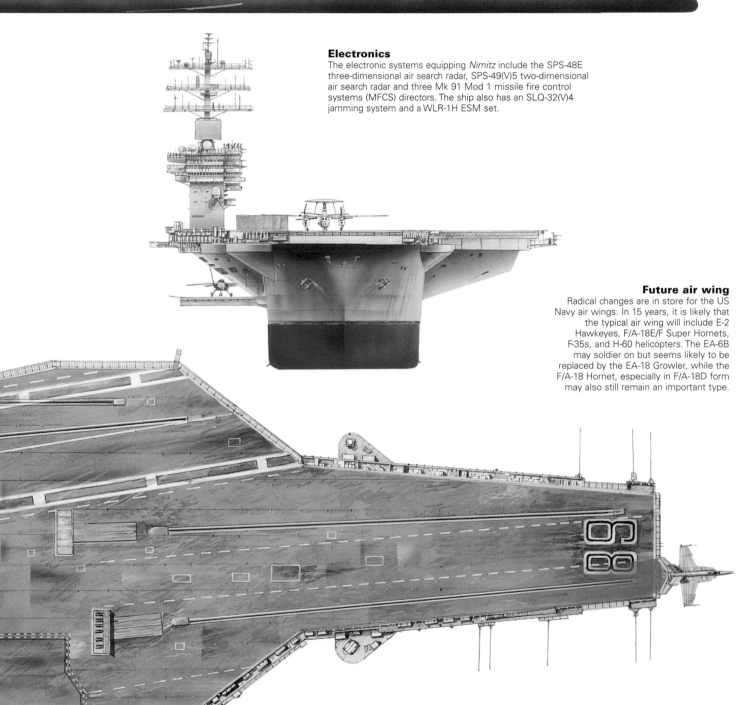

CVNX Aircraft carrier

The **CVNX** programme is the core of the US Navy's determination to procure a new generation of large aircraft carriers that will enable it to maintain its capability for long-range power projection right through the 21st century. The service's long-term goal is the placing in service of up to 10 new aircraft carriers built at the rate of about one every five years and based on a design derived from that of the current 'Nimitz' class but with considerable 'upgradability' built into the design so that new technologies can be incorporated as and when they become available. Within this overall concept there is a desire to ensure a reduction in ownership cost while keeping the Navy's core capabilities for the delivery of high-volume firepower and at the same time enhancing survivability, sustainability and mobility.

Newport News

To be built by Northrop Grumman Newport News, in accordance with a decision of July 2003, the **CVNX 1** (now redesignated as the **CVN 21**) is to follow the last of the current series of 'Nimitz'-class carriers, and is to be ordered in the 2007 fiscal year to attain initial operational capability in 2014, when the new carrier

will replace the USS *Enterprise*, commissioned in 1961.

The CVN 21 will feature a new nuclear propulsion plant developed via three generations of submarine reactor technology. The use of a new powerplant arrangement indicates the need for reductions in acquisition, manning, maintenance and life cycle costs, and this powerplant will provide the CVN 21 with all the electrical power that will be required for the operation of 21st century shipboard technology. A new system for generating and distributing electrical power will also be a vital element of the design, and will enhance combat capability in aspects such as survivability, availability and flexibility.

Enhanced survival

For survivability, a redundant grid electrical system will enhance damage control features, electrical auxiliary systems will reduce maintenance and allow the more efficient use of electrical power. Reduced maintenance and greater reliability will allow the CVN 21 to offer greater availability thanks to shorter shipyard maintenance visits. The advanced electrical features of this new powerplant will open the way for the CVN

The CVNX is based on the hull of the 'Nimitz'-class carrier, but will be built in a new steel for lighter weight and greater strength. This artist's impression conveys one of several options for the layout of the new ships.

21 to make maximum use of advanced technologies as they become available. It is also intended that the CVN 21 will also trim operating costs and crewing requirements.

Interim standard

The transitional CVN 21 is to be followed by the **CVNX 2** (presumably to be redesignated as the **CVN 22**), which will mark the culmination of the evolution of the aircraft carrier in the programme inaugurated with the CVN 76. The most important features of CVNX 2 will be an electromagnetic aircraft launching system for further reduced crewing and maintenance needs, as well as lower wind-over-deck requirements for the launch and recovery of aircraft, and extended airframe life as peak loads will be reduced.

Based on technology similar to that used by 'maglev' trains, the system will liberate catapults from reliance on ship-generated steam, and at the same time increase the available energy and markedly reduce weight and volume.

The CVNX 2 will have systems reconfigurable to enhance operational flexibility, an advanced protective system to boost survivability in combat and, wherever possible, adaptations of commercial systems for tasks such as ship operations, habitability, mooring, and manoeuvring. An advanced information management system will automate weapons' inventory control, movement and deployment from the magazines to the aircraft. Long-term objectives for the CVNX 2 are further major

reductions in total operating costs and crew requirements.

Power projection

Thus the US Navy is firmly committed to the aircraft carrier in the 21st century on the basis of the use and retrofit of advanced technological applications, the service's object being the operation of a sea-based tactical air platform retaining the full operational capabilities of the 'Nimitz' class in conjunction with an architecture optimised for the introduction of changes. This will permit the service to exploit cost-cutting and capability-enhancing technologies as they mature.

The CVNX will be 'stealthier' than current carriers, but perhaps unsurprisingly will not be a completely stealth design.

ex-*Admiral Gorshkov* & 'Vikrant' class Aircraft carriers

In accordance with its doctrine of a blue-water navy, India has operated aircraft carriers since 1961, when its navy commissioned the ex-British light aircraft carrier **Hercules** as the 19,500-ton **Vikrant**. It was long appreciated that the ship was too small to operate later-generation naval warplanes, and too elderly to be worth major modification, so pending the advent of more advanced carriers in 1986 India bought another British carrier, the larger 28,700-ton **Hermes**, to be refitted before entry to service in the following year as the **Viraat**. In her refitted form the ship can embark 12 Sea Harrier FRS.Mk 51 STOVL and seven rotary-wing aircraft.

Then in 1999 India accepted the gift of the ex-Soviet carrier **Baku**, already renamed as the **Admiral Gorshkov**, of the 'Modified Kiev' or **Type 1143.3 class**, which had first been commissioned in January 1987 and was then laid up in 1994. The arrangement was that India received the ship essentially free of charge as she was in poor condition and costing the Russians too much even for simple

Due for replacement by a rebuilt ex-Soviet carrier or a new Indian-built carrier, the Viraat is the Indian navy's sole aircraft carrier early in the 21st century. Though moderately useful by local standards, the ship is old and inefficient.

maintenance, on condition that the Indian government paid for the ship's reconditioning and upgrade in a Russian yard. It was only in the later stages of 2003 that the final arrangements were agreed for the three/four-year refurbishment of the ship, which had been gutted of her weapons and most of her operational equipment by the Russians when they laid up the vessel.

The refurbishment and update, which will amount to some 70 per cent of the ship, will include a squadron of MiG-29K warplanes, six Kortik/Kashtan SAM/gun systems for anti-aircraft and anti-missile defence, and a 14° ski-jump at the forward end of the flight deck. The flight deck is of the angled type with a length of 198 m (649 ft 7 in) and three arrester wires, and the two lifts can move 30 and 20

Commissioned into the Indian navy in 1987, the Viraat (ex-Royal Navy Hermes) is at best obsolescent, and though it has the capacity for 30 Sea Harrier FRS.Mk 51 STOVL warplanes, embarks only 12 of these as well as seven helicopters.

tons between the flight deck and the hangar, which measures 130 by 22.5 m (426 ft 6 in by 73 ft 10 in).

In the longer term the Indian navy is to operate two new carriers built in India. The plan was first announced in 1989 with the first ships, to be built by the Kochi Shipyard, scheduled to enter service in 1997 as successor to the original *Vikrant*, which was decommissioned in January 1997. The task of creating the concept of a 28,000-ton design

was entrusted to the Direction des Constructions Navales in France, the object being the creation of a ship capable of exceeding 30 kts and carrying either STOVL or CTOL warplanes. In 1991 the Indian navy was instructed to forget large aircraft carriers and instead base its thinking on smaller ships akin to the Italian 'Garibaldi' class in size and capability, but then in June 1999 the Indian government authorised the funding for a single 'Air Defence Ship'

with a full-load displacement of 32,000 tons, speed of 32 kts, overall length in the order of 250 m (820 ft 3 in), angled flight deck with a ski-jump take-off aid on the non-angled section, ability to operate 36 aircraft (16 fixed-wing of the MiG-29 type and 20 rotary-wing), and armament of SAM launchers and CIWS mountings.

The whole future of aircraft carriers in India, be they Russian or otherwise, is still speculative.

SPECIFICATION	
'Modified Kiev' class	**Electronics:** one 'Plate Steer' air search radar, two 'Strut Pair' surface search radars, one navigation radar, one aircraft control radar, one Lesorub 11434 combat data system, one Bharat EW system, two PK2 chaff launchers, one MG 355 'Horse Jaw' active hull hull sonar, and two towed torpedo decoys
Displacement: 45,400 tons full load	
Dimensions: length 283 m (928 ft 5 in); beam 51 m (167 ft 4 in); draught 10 m (32 ft 10 in)	
Propulsion: four GTZA 674 steam turbines delivering 149200 kW (200,105 shp) to four shafts	
Performance: speed 28 kts; endurance 25500 km (15,845 miles) at 18 kts	**Aircraft:** up to 30 fixed- and rotary-wing (see text)
Armament: six Kortik/Kashtan SAM/gun mountings	**Crew:** 1,200 plus an air group of undetermined size

'Andrea Doria' class Aircraft carrier

In November 2000 the Italian ministry of naval defence contracted with Fincantieri for the construction of the **Andrea Doria**, a NUM (*Nuova Unita Maggiore*, or new major vessel) of the light aircraft carrier type. Work began at the manufacturer's yards in Riva Trigoso (centre and stern) and Muggiano (bow) in July 2001, and the ship will be delivered in 2007.

The vessel is also to have capabilities for the command and amphibious operations roles, these being provided by provision for 145 command staff and 380 marines, the latter rising to 470 for short-endurance operations, plus 24 MBTs, or 60 smaller AFVs or 100 wheeled vehicles, or a mix of these. Vehicles enter and leave the ship via two ro/ro ramps (one stern and one starboard side), and one 7- and two 15-ton cranes are provided for the loading and unloading of logistic and ordnance items.

Aster-15

The ship's most important features will be its great flexibility in tactical terms, and its ability to perform the aircraft carrier role in conjunction with the delivery of men and/or wheeled and tracked vehicles for both the military and humanitarian tasks.

To carry out these tasks, the vessel will have a flight deck (with two lifts) for both fixed- and rotary-wing air-

*Above: Melding two naval power projection concepts (those of assault ship and aircraft carrier) into a single ship, the future **Andrea Doria** will be one of the most versatile ships on the high seas. Moreover, it will offer significant savings to the Italian navy by virtue of its design.*

craft, and a hangar/garage of about 2500 m² (26,910 sq ft). In this way the ship will also have an amphibious capacity through rapid transport via helicopter even at considerable distances from the landing force. Other features will be a hospital with three operating rooms, wards for hospitalised patients, X-ray and CT equipment, dentist's surgery, and laboratory.

The carrier will be armed

with the Aster-15 SAM fired from vertical-launch systems and operated in conjunction with the EMPAR multi-function phased-array radar, which provides simultaneous surveillance, tracking and weapons control. The vessel will also be armed with two Otobreda 76.2-mm (3-in) Super Rapid guns and three 25-mm anti-aircraft guns, and will include advanced radar and EW systems.

SPECIFICATION	
'Andrea Doria' class	**Electronics:** one RAN-40S or S-1850M long-range air search radar one EMPAR air search and missile guidance radar, one SPS-791 surface search radar, one SPN-753G(N) navigation radar, one Vampir optronic director, one SPN-41 aircraft control radar, one 'Horizon'-based combat data system, one EW system, two SCLAR-H chaff/decoy launchers, and one SNA-2000 mine avoidance sonar
Displacement: 26,500 tons full load	
Dimensions: length 234.4 m (769 ft); beam 39 m (128 ft); draught 7.5 m (24 ft 7 in)	
Propulsion: COGAG with four LM 2500 gas turbines delivering 87980 kW (118,000 shp) to two shafts	
Performance: speed 30 kts; endurance 13000 km (8,080 miles) at 16 kts	
Armament: four Sylver 8-cell vertical-launch systems for Aster-15 medium-range SAMs, two 76.2-mm (3-in) Super Rapid DP guns, and three 25-mm cannon	**Aircraft:** eight AV-8B or F-35 fixed-wing aircraft and 12 EH.101 helicopters
	Crew: 456 plus 211 air group

Early carrier aviation
Developing carrier techniques

Britain's World War I carriers revealed both the limitations and the advantages of this type of ship. However, wartime work in the UK, along with post-war trials in the UK and the US laid the foundations of the modern aircraft carrier.

The operation of aircraft from ships at sea goes back to the dawn of aviation itself. On 14 November 1910 – only seven years after the Wright Brothers' historic hop at Kitty Hawk, NC – Eugene Ely flew his Curtiss from a flimsy platform on board the anchored warship, USS *Birmingham*. Just over a year later, on 10 January 1912, the Royal Navy's Commander Charles Samson achieved a similar feat, taking off from HMS *Africa*. On 9 May 1912, Samson went one better, taking off from HMS *Hibernia* while the ship was underway – the first take-off from a moving ship.

Eugene Ely, a professional test pilot for Curtiss, made history on 18 January 1911 by becoming the first person to land an aircraft on a warship. His Curtiss Model D touched down on a large 36-m (119-ft) platform fitted on the stern of the light cruiser USS Pennsylvania.

Since then, the story of the carrier and carrier aircraft development has often been one of British invention or innovation being properly developed and exploited by the US Navy, so that most of the principal features of the modern aircraft carrier are British inventions, yet only the US Navy operates a significant number of carriers, and its carriers are the most capable and advanced ever launched.

Dunning's experiment
During World War I, the Royal Navy's Squadron Commander Dunning made the world's first landing on a moving ship, successfully landing his Pup aboard HMS *Furious*. However, this was experimentation without an immediately obvious application, and actually set back the Royal Navy's carrier programme. It led to the first-generation carriers

In July 1919, the US Congress authorised conversion of the fleet collier Jupiter into the US Navy's first aircraft carrier – USS Langley. In this early 1920s image, a Vought VE-7SF fighter is approaching to land aboard the docked ship.

being modified with completely flush decks, and the two ships (*Argus* and *Furious*) entered full service only after World War I ended. In fact, plans were afoot to launch a raid by 20 torpedo-carrying Sopwith Cuckoos against the German High Seas Fleet, from the *Argus*,

HMS *FURIOUS:* EARLY CARRIER TRIALS

Probably the most advanced British aircraft-carrier to serve in World War I, *Furious* was commissioned in an attempt to overcome the shortcomings inherent in the contemporary seaplane carriers. Early trials led to the fitting of an aft landing-on deck (below) fitted with longitudinal wires to keep skid-equipped aircraft straight as they landed. Arrester wires weighted with sandbags were also used. Among the ship's most advanced features were its electric aircraft lifts, one forward (right) and one aft, which could move aircraft to and from the hangars below decks.

before the Armistice led to the raid's cancellation.

Although proper aircraft-carriers did not see action in World War I, their potential became clear. For example, after making a first take-off from a towed barge on 1 August 1918, Flight Sub Lieutenant Stuart Culley made history on 11 August, taking off from a barge towed by HMS *Redoubt* to intercept and shoot down Zeppelin *LZ100*. The barge had allowed his fighter to be put in the right place at the right time, and pointed the way towards using ship-board fighters in areas inaccessible to land-based machines. Unfortunately, though, landing on the barge was impossible and Culley and the other early pioneers were expected to ditch or struggle back to an airfield.

The first attempts to land on moving ships necessitated using aircraft with very short landing runs and slow landing speeds putting down on the largest flat surface that could be provided on a ship, sometimes with deck crew rushing forward to grab the wing tips as the aircraft landed. For many years (and even into World War II), many aircraft would land on carriers without arrester gear, and sometimes even without brakes. This was quite plainly dangerously impractical and unsatisfactory, however, and the provision of arrester gear to stop an aircraft as it landed was the first real attempt to make aircraft 'carrier-compatible'. Early experiments involved the use of parallel wires running fore-and-aft along the deck, which would be picked up by hooks on an aircraft's skids. Eventually, the solution was found by using transverse wires arranged across the deck, with carrier aircraft having a 'drop down' arrester hook to snag these. Such hooks first started to become common on US naval aircraft during the late 1920s.

DUNNING: LANDING TRIALS ON *FURIOUS*

During the summer of 1917, Squadron Commander Dunning flew a series of landing trials onto the forward flightdeck of HMS *Furious*. At the point of touch down, groundcrew men ran forward to grab at straps on the wing tips of Dunning's Sopwith Pup (above and above right), helping to drag the aircraft onto the deck and stop it. Tragically, on his third attempt Dunning was killed when his Pup cartwheeled over the side and into the sea (right). As a result of this accident, *Furious* was fitted with an aft deck for landing-on and Pups for carrier use were fitted with skids as described above.

A batman brings a Swordfish in to land on HMS Smiter in April 1945. Batmen led a dangerous life on carriers, frequently making use of the back-up net. Their job was made more hazardous by the narrowness of the escort carrier deck.

World War II carrier aircraft

Developments

Even before the outbreak of World War I, early aviation pioneers had experimented with operating aircraft from warships. By the outbreak of World War II, the dedicated aircraft carrier had evolved, becoming the dominant warship of the conflict.

The early carriers were effectively ships with a simple runway perched on top. This meant that the deck had to be empty for an aircraft to land, if it was to be able to 'go around' or otherwise a safety barrier had to be rigged to stop the aircraft before it crashed into any others parked at the front of the deck. Such barriers were introduced during the 1930s, and with them came 'Batsmen' or Deck Landing Control Officers (LSOs in American parlance), who used flags or 'bats' to help the pilot touch down more accurately, and to help ensure that he would engage an arrester wire and avoid going into the barrier.

The next major improvement was to the carriers themselves, with the addition of a superstructure offset to one side of the deck (inevitably to starboard, to allow 'left-hand circuits'), housing the funnel and flight control, and known as the 'island'. *Hermes*, the first carrier built as such from the keel up, was the first to feature an island.

Catapults

Another improvement to the ships themselves which began to appear before the war was the hydraulic catapult or 'accelerator', designed to accelerate the aircraft to flying speed more quickly, and based upon the catapults used by cruisers and battleships to launch their seaplanes. A further change in basic carrier design was introduced with the *Ark Royal*, launched in 1937, which had an armoured steel deck – an innovation which could have saved many US carriers from the ravages of the kamikazes only a few years later.

An early innovation applied to carrier aircraft themselves was the fitting of folding wings, to allow them to use small lifts down into the hangar deck, and so that they took up less deck space when parked. Apart from the provision of radio direction-finding and, later, radar, there were few other technological developments in carriers or in the carrier-specific features of carrier aircraft until late in World

Below: This F6F-5 awaits launch aboard the USS Bennington, poised for more action against Japanese targets. Note that the aircraft is attached to a catapult shot, ready to be hydraulically thrust forwards to flying speed.

GERMAN CARRIER AIRCRAFT: AN AIR WING FOR *GRAF ZEPPELIN*?

German plans for an aircraft carrier saw the creation of a Bf 109B squadron in 1939 to begin training for eventual deployment afloat. The operational equipment was to have been the Bf 109T ('T' for 'Träger' – carrier), a version of the Bf 109E-1 with extended folding wings, revised flaps and overwing spoilers. Ten Bf 109T-0s were built, being extensively tested in anticipation of the Bf 109T-1 operational aircraft. When work on the aircraft carrier *Graf Zeppelin* was halted in May 1940, the 60 Bf 109T-1s under construction were completed as Bf 109T-2s (pictured), stripped of carrier features but retaining the high-lift devices and extended wings for use as land-based fighters. A navalised version of the Ju 87, the Ju 87C, was also designed as a dive/torpedo bomber, while the Ar 197 V2 was a naval biplane fighter.

Left: This Hellcat was photographed as it was being stowed on the deck of the USS Hornet *(CV-12), after a raid on the Marianas. The wings folded back manually, rotating through approximately 90° to lie with their undersurfaces roughly parallel to the fuselage sides.*

Below: The minimal margin for error aboard the small escort carriers was such that if the pilot of a 'tricky' aircraft such as the Hellcat 'took the wire' too late in his landing, a 'floating landing' could result in the aircraft being thrown towards the carrier's island. The 'wire' has already been engaged in this shot.

War II. Wood and fabric gave way to metal, of course, and the biplane gradually gave way to the monoplane (though the biplane's low landing speed and short landing distance made it particularly well suited to shipboard operations).

Carrier impact

In the war in the Pacific, in particular, it can be seen that the aircraft carrier changed the very way in which naval warfare was fought. To judge the carrier's pivotal importance in the Far East, one only has to remember Pearl Harbor, Jimmy Doolittle's B-25 raid on Tokyo, and the battles of Coral Sea, Midway, Santa Cruz, the Philippine Sea, and Leyte Gulf.

Landing speeds

As aircraft improved, landing speeds also increased, while types such as the F4U Corsair proved very difficult to land on a carrier deck. Most of the jet fighters which emerged during the war had

high landing speeds, but gave their pilots a better view forward over the nose and the aircraft, in some respects, proved easier to manage on board ship. On the last of the piston-engined carrierborne aircraft it became increasingly easy to 'miss' or skip over the arrester wires (or even the barrier), and safety became a real concern. This drove forward a collection of further improvements, many of which did not appear until well after the war.

Right: Wing-folding allowed most Seafires, like this Mk III, to be stored below decks on board the smaller of the RN's carriers. A double fold was necessary, such was the restricted space in carrier hangars.

A Seafire F.Mk IIC prepares to make a three-point landing. Its long nose, finely balanced controls, narrow-track undercarriage and an approach speed only slightly above stall speed made the Seafire a handful for pilots. Note the impressively-sized hook.

These SBDs are seen aboard USS Yorktown (CV-10) during the carrier's 'shake down' cruise in the Atlantic during April/May 1943. USS Ranger (CV-4) is in the background.

World War II carrier air groups Carrierborne air power

It is easy to consider the aircraft carrier as a key player only in the Pacific war. In fact, carriers and their aircraft played crucial roles in the Battle of the Atlantic and in the Mediterranean theatre. Undoubtedly, the US emerged as the major producer of carrierborne aircraft, the Royal Navy relying on a navalised Spitfire derivative for much of its fighter work. Japan entered the war as the strongest naval air power, but soon found its aircraft in decline.

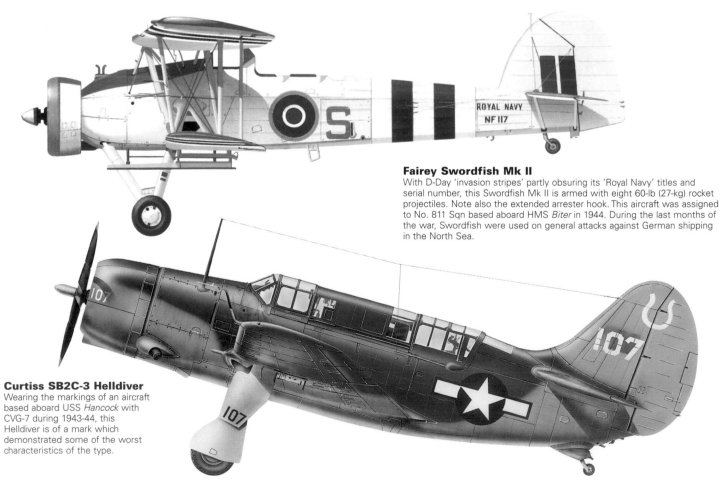

Fairey Swordfish Mk II
With D-Day 'invasion stripes' partly obsuring its 'Royal Navy' titles and serial number, this Swordfish Mk II is armed with eight 60-lb (27-kg) rocket projectiles. Note also the extended arrester hook. This aircraft was assigned to No. 811 Sqn based aboard HMS Biter in 1944. During the last months of the war, Swordfish were used on general attacks against German shipping in the North Sea.

Curtiss SB2C-3 Helldiver
Wearing the markings of an aircraft based aboard USS Hancock with CVG-7 during 1943-44, this Helldiver is of a mark which demonstrated some of the worst characteristics of the type.

Brewster F2A Buffalo

This Brewster F2A-2 Buffalo served with VF-2 'Flying Chiefs' in USS *Lexington*, during March 1941. As the US Navy's first monoplane fighter, the Buffalo was hopelessly outclassed by contemporary Japanese naval fighters.

Grumman F4F-3A

Six Wildcats sent to Ford Island, Hawaii in the immediate aftermath of the Pearl Harbor attack were engaged by US AA gunners, with only this aircraft and another surviving. Viewed in scale with the other aircraft illustrated here, the small size of the Wildcat becomes apparent.

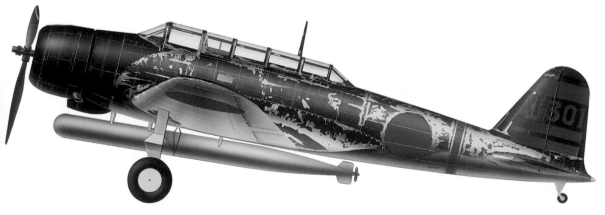

Douglas SBD-5 Dauntless

This machine served with US Marine Corps scout squadron VMS-5 in the Caribbean in 1944. It wears a typical early 1944 Atlantic theatre colour scheme and was actually land based.

Nakajima B5N2 'Kate'

At the outbreak of the Pacific War, the 'Kate' was the most advanced carrierborne torpedo bomber in the world. During the following 12 months, it delivered fatal blows to three separate US Navy aircraft-carriers and supported Japanese amphibious attacks throughout the region. By 1944, technical developments had rendered the aircraft obsolete and it ended its service in second-line units.

Fairey Swordfish Mk I

K5972 was a Swordfish Mk I from the initial Fairey-built production batch. It is seen in the markings of No. 823 Squadron, embarked on HMS *Glorious* in 1936.

Alpha Strikes
US Navy air power over Vietnam

From its low-key entry into the war in 1964 until the final evacuation, the US Navy's carrier force was at the sharp end of the aerial campaign against North Vietnam. While Crusaders and Phantoms tangled with MiGs, many carrier aircraft fought a less glamorous 'dirty war', with bombs and rockets, in support of the ground troops. The carriers also possessed the unique ability to provide a complete package of aircraft, an 'Alpha Strike', capable of attacking the vital and heavily defended targets in the North.

The striking power of US carrier aviation was first tested against North Vietnam on 5 August 1964, when President Lyndon Johnson authorised the Gulf of Tonkin air strikes as retaliation following attacks on US destroyers.

The carriers operating off Vietnam launched strikes against the enemy from one of two positions, Dixie Station for targets in the south and Yankee Station for strikes against the north. The early operations used F-8 Crusaders, A-1 Skyraiders, A-3 Skywarriors, A-4 Skyhawks and E-1 Tracer AEW aircraft. Gradually these machines were phased out of service as new designs reached the war zone, the more modern types including the F-4 Phantom II, A-6 Intruder, E-2 Hawkeye, RA-5C Vigilante and A-7 Corsair II. However, many of the older types continued to serve on the smaller carriers such as *Bon Homme Richard*, *Ranger*, *Hancock*, *Intrepid*, *Oriskany* and *Ticonderoga*, the newer equipment flying from *Constellation*, *Forrestal*, *John F. Kennedy*, *Kitty Hawk* and *Midway*.

Alpha Strikes

Attacks against the North were often flown as massive Alpha Strikes employing up to 70 or 80 aircraft in one huge aerial armada, in an effort to inflict the greatest possible damage on a target. Military planners tended to divide North Vietnam up into Air Force and Navy regions, so that the carrier aircraft were given their own piece of geography to fly against. There were usually two carriers on Yankee Station at any one time, but when the fighting was at its heaviest as many as four were off the enemy coast. Other combat missions included the single-ship 'lone-wolf' missions for which the A-6 Intruder became famous.

The idea of an Alpha Strike should not conjure up images of a massive World War II-style formation thundering towards its target. To the contrary, different components of the mission proceeded at different times, altitudes and headings. Each aircraft was assigned a specific mission such as flak suppression, combat air patrol, or attack. The use of relatively tight formations during the flight into and out of the target area meant that defences would in theory be saturated. Aircrew relied on the mutual

Early in the war A-3 Skywarriors performed bombing missions, even on targets in the heavily defended Hanoi area. As more advanced attack aircraft entered service, the A-3s were converted into tankers. These KA-3Bs provided inflight-refuelling for the returning strike aircraft. Other variants, including the EA-3B, provided Elint.

Vought F-8 Crusaders frequently protected the strike wings. This pair, from VF-211, flew missions from the smaller aircraft-carrier USS Hancock. The Crusader remained in service on these smaller-decked carriers even after the F-4 became available.

GRUMMAN A-6 INTRUDER: THE NAVY'S PREMIER BOMBER

On 1 July 1965, the US Navy's VA-75 'Sunday Punchers' took the formidable Grumman A-6A Intruder into combat for the first time. The unit attacked bridges and other targets at Bac Bang to the south of Hanoi, proving the Intruder's ability to put its bombs on target. In fact, the target finding and hitting capabilities were without comparison. The aircraft could accurately bomb just about any target, at night and in any weather conditions, thanks to its sophisticated nav/attack system. Inevitably there were problems in keeping the system working, but once these had been solved, it took the arrival of PGMs and, in 1968, the F-111A before the USAF could come even close to offering the bombing accuracy that the Navy could guarantee with its Intruders.

Left: In addition to being a fine attack aircraft, the Skyraider proved highly adaptable to other missions. One of the many variants was the EA-1F ECM version. During early missions the EA-1F provided jamming of North Vietnamese defences.

support of the deception and defensive electronic gear, chaff and anti-radiation missiles carried by other aircraft in the strike. It was also a distinct advantage to have other aircrew on the look-out to help spot any incoming MiGs and SAMs.

Air power

Targets would be assigned the night before a planned attack and single- or two-ship Intruder flights would sneak into the target area, to hound and harass. For the other naval aviators involved a fitful night would pass, while the unsung but hard-pressed electricians, mechanics and armourers prepared the aircraft for battle. Aircrew usually did not learn their assignments until morning, when weather, survival, target and threat briefings were held.

At dawn an RF-8A or RF-8G Crusader, escorted by fighters, checked out the weather and flew pre-attack reconnaissance over the target. The first wave of the Alpha Strike then followed, consisting of fighters assigned to drop ordnance, then remain in the area on target combat air patrol (TARCAP) to engage MiGs. With the F-4s deterring the North Vietnamese MiG force, the 'mud-moving' A-7 Corsairs and A-6 Intruders could attack (the A-6s frequently being employed as daylight bombers, despite their all-weather capability). A-4E Skyhawks remained especially effective in the Iron Hand (anti-SAM) role armed with AGM-45 Shrike missiles. Douglas KA-3B Skywarriors provided inflight-refuelling support. Later in the war, the E-2A Hawkeye AEW aircraft added an extra dimension to the Alpha Strike forces' capabilities. Post-attack reconnaissance was the job of the RF-8A/G Crusader or the RA-5C Vigilante.

Combat rescue

Various helicopters were available for the combat rescue mission, most of them based on destroyers sailing alongside the aircraft-carriers in the Gulf of Tonkin. One of the most widely used helicopter types was the Kaman UH-2C Seasprite. One Seasprite pilot won the Medal of Honor when he ventured into Haiphong Harbour, hovered over a moored merchant vessel, and snatched a navy pilot from the shallow waters of the port while being subjected to heavy gunfire.

Ideally, several flights of aircraft attacked with short intervals between them and from different directions. North Vietnam's growing network of SAMs forced carrier aircraft to attack at relatively low altitudes but, despite the very formidable North Vietnamese MiG, missile and AAA defences, aircraft losses remained at an acceptable level.

Despite the awesome destructive capability of the 'Alpha Strikes', the North Vietnamese managed to continue the fight against the South throughout these aerial bombardments. But one thing was clear – the tactical benefits offered by a well-co-ordinated carrier wing flying Alpha Strike would remain an important part of military doctrine for the US Navy in any future war.

At the height of the Cold War, the US Navy deployed 22 front-line Tomcat units, this F-14A hailing from VF-32. The maximum load of six AIM-54s could not be carried operationally from the ship unless rounds were expended on the mission, since it exceeded the F-14A's carrier bring-back weight limitations.

Cold War carrier aviation
Air power at sea

At the end of World War II it was clear to American and British planners that carrier aviation was of vital importance in an unstable world. So the race began to deploy the ultimate air force at sea.

As Winston Churchill's so-called 'Iron Curtain' descended across Europe, the two dominant sea-faring powers to emerge from World War II, Great Britain and the US, were preparing to usher in a new era in carrier aviation. Great changes in aircraft carrier design were just around the corner, but as far as naval aviators were concerned, getting to grips with the new generation of jet-powered carrier fighters was the first

thing on the agenda. The US Navy took its first faltering steps into the jet age with the FH-1 Phantom, while the Royal Navy worked up on the Sea Vampire.

As experience grew and technology improved, a rapid succession of fighter designs came and went, with the result that when the Korean War broke out in 1950, US carriers could boast numbers of F2H Banshee and F9F Panther fighter-bomber and reconnaissance aircraft

Above: Sea Hawk deployment by the FAA peaked around the time of the Suez Crisis in 1956. Seen during 1957-58, the crowded deck of HMS Ark Royal hosts FGA.Mk 6s of No. 804 Sqn (in the foreground) and FB.Mk 5s of No. 802 Sqn. To the right are Sea Venom FAW.Mk 21s of No. 893 Sqn.

Left: At the peak of its Phantom operations in the mid-1970s, the US Navy had around two dozen fighter units equipped with F-4s, split roughly between the Atlantic and Pacific Fleets. Here a VF-92 'Silver Kings' F-4B prepares to trap aboard a carrier some time before 1968, at which time the squadron transitioned from the original naval model to to the improved F-4J.

In 2004, as at any time from the early 1970s on, the Hawkeye is often the first aircraft to launch and the last to recover, co-ordinating other carrier air elements over a dual or even a triple cycle of operations.

Skyraider attack aircraft were the only two piston-engined types to be found at sea in quantity.

By the end of the Vietnam War, a typical carrier air wing might include F-4 Phantoms, F-14 Tomcats, A-6 Intruders, E-2 Hawkeyes and A-7 Corsair IIs, all of which have become classics of Cold War naval aviation. In the UK, the Royal Navy finally standardised its air wings around the Phantom, the Gannet and the stunning Buccaneer, before it abandoned its carriers in 1978. Other nations, including France, maintained a credible carrier capability throughout, with the notable and ironic exception of the USSR.

among their complements. However, heavy attack and bombing missions remained the task of piston-engined types and, indeed, it was not until the Suez Crisis of 1956 that the UK would commit its naval jets to war.

Suez Crisis

During the highly controversial operations off Suez in 1956, Britain flew Sea Hawks and Sea Venoms from its carrier decks, as well as the turboprop-powered Wyvern, alongside the purely piston-engined aircraft of the French navy. Avengers provided AEW cover for the French while the British employed their Skyraider AEW.Mk 1 aircraft in the same role. Later, just prior to the Falklands War of 1982, the Royal Navy forgot just how important AEW cover was for the fleet, retiring the AEW Gannet just in time to

leave the Task Force perilously short of early warning during the forthcoming war.

Jets take over

Spurred on by a Soviet naval threat that never really existed, it was inevitable that the US would become the dominant force in naval air power. By 1957, having dabbled with a carrier-capable Neptune, the US Navy had the world's first all-jet carrier-based nuclear strategic bomber in service in the shape of the A3D-2 Skywarrior. The new bomber

VA-85 'Buckeyes' began converting to the A-6E in December 1971, with TRAM aircraft coming a decade later. This unit's aircraft were involved in the disastrous strikes against Lebanese targets, during which an A-6E was downed, and in action against Libyan targets during Prairie Fire and against Iraqi targets in Desert Storm.

was joined that same year by the superb Crusader fighter and by the time the US was committing carriers to war in Vietnam, the Tracker ASW aircraft and the legendary

A NEW FORM OF CARRIER AIR POWER: HELICOPTERS AT SEA

As well as the jet, post-war developments also brought the helicopter to carrier aviation. Helicopters could obviously fill a number of roles aboard the carrier, some of which had previously been filled by fixed-wing types and others which were new. Of the latter, planeguard is perhaps one of the more important, where a helicopter stands guard around the ship during operations, ready to pick up any crew members unlucky enough to ditch. A level of close-in ASW cover hitherto unavailable to the carrier and its Battle Group could also be supplied, while helicopters soon proved generally useful things to have around for the ship-to-ship transfer of personnel and supplies. Perhaps the classic naval helicopter to emerge during the Cold War period, used in quantity by both the US and the UK, was the SH-3 Sea King. Here, SH-3D ASW helicopters are illustrated.

Along with the F-35C, the F/A-18 Super Hornet (illustrated), is very much the future of US Navy offensive operations. This aircraft was photographed as it approached USS Ronald Reagan, the Navy's newest carrier, during trials in 2003.

Future carrier aviation

21st century carrier aircraft

Maintaining and operating an aircraft-carrier is a phenomenally expensive proposition. It is no surprise, therefore, that the US Navy is the unsurpassed champion of carrierborne aviation. Nevertheless, the aircraft-carrier is increasingly less rare and several nations, including India and the UK, have ambitious carrier programmes in progress for the future.

A nation's ability to move powerful forces to a troublespot in order to enforce its will has long been one of the most desirable military capabilities. In the years following World War II, this capability has been used time and again, primarily by the world's dominant navy (that of the US), but also by the lesser nations of naval aviation, such as France, Italy and the UK.

Continuing trend

Late 20th century conflicts and those of the nascent 21st century have continued the trend for peacekeeping and 'international policing' operations. Such missions

demand great flexibility from a carrier air wing and often call for integrated operations.

For the US Navy, during the first decade of the new millennium the F-14 Tomcat will disappear from service. The Navy is heading for a carrier air wing primarily consisting of F/A-18E/F and F-35C fighters, with Hawkeye 2000 and Advanced Hawkeye AEW&C aircraft, and SH-60R helicop-

Having already swallowed the somewhat bitter pill of having its Sea Harrier force combined with the RAF's Harriers, the Royal Navy is now to lose its Sea Harrier FA.Mk 2 (illustrated) aircraft all together. The new Joint Force Harrier units will fly upgraded Harrier GR.Mk 9 aircraft, based on the GR.Mk 7 and possibly with podded radar for AIM-120 compatibility.

Right: Sikorsky is to deliver the MH-60R (as here) multi-role and MH-60S utility helicopters in some numbers. The former should enter service from 2005; the latter joined the fleet in 2002.

EUROPEAN CARRIERBORNE AIR POWER: Europe's carrier capabilities

Western Europe boasts four carrier-operating nations: France, Italy, Spain and the UK. Of these, France has by far potentially the most capable aircraft/ship combination in the form of the Rafale M and *Charles de Gaulle*. A second ship will also be built, by which time the Super Etendard will most likely have been phased out, leaving Rafale and E-2C (below) as primary equipment. Italy operates AV-8B Harrier II Plus fighters and Sea King helicopters from *Giuseppe Garibaldi* (right, with *Charles de Gaulle* in the background). A second carrier is to be deployed and F-35 is likely to be bought. Spain has a similar capability with *Principe de Asturias*, but has no plans for major changes. Lastly, the UK has three through-deck cruisers, which are due to be replaced by two new, larger, F-35-equipped carriers.

Left: Emphasising the importance of cross-deck operations, this Aéronavale E-2C operated from USS John C. Stennis during Operation Enduring Freedom in March 2002.

ters. In addition, a new type may be developed to replace the S-3B Viking in its many and varied roles.

Outside the US and western Europe, the carrier-operating nations are Brazil, India, Russia and Thailand. Brazil began operating the ex-French carrier *Foch* as the *Sao Paulo* in 2001/02. The ship is equipped with ex-Kuwaiti A-4 Skyhawks and ex-USN S-2 Trackers modified as AEW platforms. Sea Kings are also carried, and there seems little likelihood of major changes or additions in the near future.

India refitted its remaining carrier, INS *Viraat*, for service into the 2010-12 period. The carrier's air wing consists of Sea Harrier FRS.Mk 51 fighters, Sea Kings and probably Ka-31 AEW helicopters. By the time *Viraat* is decommissioned, the country plans to have built an 'air defence ship', as well as having the former *Baku/Admiral Gorshkov* in service with a MiG-29K air wing.

Russia's navy operates a single carrier, *Admiral Kuznetsov*, with an air wing comprised primarily of Su-33 aircraft. Operations have been somewhat limited, but the ship has turned in impressive performances during exercises.

Finally, Thailand continues to struggle to find the funds to put its carrier, *Chakri Naruebat*, to sea. Indeed, similar funding problems have afflicted its AV-8 aircraft, which are rarely flown.

With the introduction of the F/A-18E/F to former Tomcat units, a change in unit designation has been brought about. VFA-41, a fighter and attack unit, was previously VF-41, an all-fighter F-14 squadron. Now, more than ever, the US Navy seems to be returning to the use of bright markings for publicity and morale-boosting purposes. This F/A-18F is marked as VFA-41's CAG bird.

Aichi D3A 'Val'
Carrier dive-bomber

Although considered obsolescent in 1941, the **Aichi D3A** with its fixed spatted landing gear was the first Japanese aircraft to drop bombs on American targets when aircraft of this type took part in the surprise attack on Pearl Harbor on 7 December 1941.

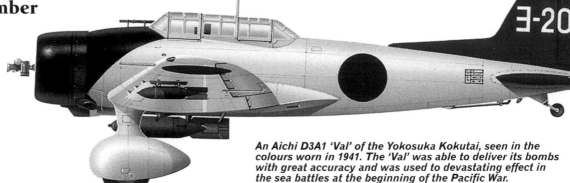

Pinpoint bomber

Designed to a 1936 carrier-based dive-bomber requirement, the prototype was flown in January 1938 with a 529.4-kW (710-hp) Nakajima Hikari 1 radial engine. Production **D3A1** aircraft had slightly smaller wings and were powered by the 745.7-kW (1,000-hp) Mitsubishi Kinsei 43 radial. A dorsal fin extension considerably improved the aircraft's manoeuvrability, but the armament of only two forward firing 7.7-mm (0.303-in) machine guns, with another of the same calibre in the rear cockpit, was undeniably puny.

The D3A1 saw operational service late in 1940 with the Imperial Japanese Navy in support of Japanese forces in China and Indo-China. D3As were flown in all major carrier actions during the first 10 months of the war and sank more Allied naval vessels than any other Axis aircraft. Among British casualties in D3A1 attacks were HMS *Hermes* (the world's first carrier to be

An Aichi D3A1 'Val' of the Yokosuka Kokutai, seen in the colours worn in 1941. The 'Val' was able to deliver its bombs with great accuracy and was used to devastating effect in the sea battles at the beginning of the Pacific War.

sunk by carrier aircraft), and the cruisers *Cornwall* and *Dorsetshire*. Heavy losses among D3A1s during and after the Battle of the Coral Sea in May 1942, however, forced withdrawal by most of the survivors to land bases.

In 1942 the D3A2 was introduced with increased fuel capacity and a more powerful engine, but even

though more were built than of the original model, by 1944 the aircraft was hopelessly outclassed by American fighters and proved horribly vulnerable. Nevertheless, D3As remained in front-line serv-

ice until late 1944, and a small number was even employed in kamikaze attacks.

Production amounted to 476 D3A1s and 1,016 D3A2s. The Allied reporting name was '**Val**'.

The Aichi D3A was Japan's principal carrier-based dive-bomber for the first two years of the Pacific War. Lacking armour plating or self-sealing fuel tanks, the lightly-armed D3A suffered heavy losses to US fighters.

SPECIFICATION	
Aichi D3A2	maximum take-off 3800 kg (8,378 lb)
Type: two-seat carrierborne dive-bomber	**Dimensions:** wing span 14.38 m (47 ft 2 in); length 10.20 m (33 ft 5½ in); height 3.85 m (12 ft 7½ in); wing area 34.90 m² (375.7 sq ft)
Powerplant: one 969.4-kW (1,300-hp) Mitsubishi Kinsei 54 radial piston engine	**Armament:** two forward-firing 7.7-mm (0.303-in) Type 97 machine-guns in the nose and one trainable
Performance: maximum speed 430 km/h (267 mph) at 6200 m (20,341 ft); climb to 3000 m (9,843 ft) in 5.76 minutes; service ceiling 10500 m (34,449 ft); range 1352 km (840 miles)	7.7-mm (0.303-in) Type 92 gun in the rear cockpit, plus one 250-kg (551 lb) bomb under the fuselage and two 60-kg (132-lb) bombs under the wings
Weights: empty 2570 kg (5,666 lb);	

Mitsubishi A6M 'Zeke' Carrier fighter

Without doubt the most famous Japanese single-seat fighter aircraft of World War II, the **Mitsubishi A6M Type 0**, popularly known as the '**Zero**', was the first carrier-borne fighter in the world capable of outperforming any contemporary land-based fighter it was likely to confront. Due to inept Allied intelligence it was able to achieve immediate air superiority over the East Indies and Southeast Asia from the day Japan entered the war.

One of the greatest warplanes of all time, the 'Zero' was in the front line all through the Pacific War. These A6M6c fighters of the Genzan Kokutai are seen on home defence duties in May 1945.

First flight

Designed under the leadership of Jiro Horikoshi in 1937 as a replacement for the neat but obsolescent A5M, the prototype **A6M1** was first flown on 1 April 1939 with a 582-kW (780 hp) Mitsubishi Zuisei 13–cylinder radial engine. Production **A6M2** fighters with two wing-mounted 20 mm cannon and two nose-mounted

Below: A very early Mitsubishi A6M2 of the 12th Combined Kokutai, serving in the Hankow region of China in the winter of 1940-41.

SPECIFICATION

Mitsubishi A6M5b 'Zeke'
Type: single-seat carrierborne fighter
Powerplant: one 820-kW (1,100-hp) Nakajima NK2F Sakae 21 radial piston engine
Performance: maximum speed 565 km/h (351 mph) at 6000 m (19,685 ft); climb to 6000 m (19,685 ft) in 7 minutes; service ceiling 11740 m (38,517 ft); maximum range 1143 km (710 miles)

Weights: empty 1876 kg (4,136 lb); normal loaded 2733 kg (6,025 lb)
Dimensions: wing span 11.00 m (36 ft 1 in); length 9.12 m (29 ft 11 in); height 3.51 m (11 ft 6¼ in); wing area 21.30 m² (229.28 sq ft)
Armament: one 7.7-mm (0.303-in) Type 97 and one 13.2-mm (0.52-in) Type 3 machine-gun in the nose and two wing-mounted 20-mm type 99 cannon, plus underwing provision for two 60- or 250-kg (132- or 551-lb) bombs.

7.7 mm (0.303-in) machine guns were fitted with the 708-kW (950-hp) Nakajima Sakae 12 radial. It was with this version that the Japanese navy escorted the raiding force sent against Pearl Harbor, and gained air superiority over Malaya, the Philippines and Burma.

In the spring of 1942 the **A6M3** with two-stage supercharged Sakae 21 entered service, later aircraft having their folding wing tips removed. The Battle of Midway represented the Zero's combat zenith; thereafter the agile Japanese fighter found itself ever more outclassed by the American F6F Hellcat and P-38 Lightning.

A6M5 variant
To counter the new American fighters the **A6M5** was rushed to front-line units; this version, with Sakae 21 engine and improved exhaust system, possessed a top speed of 565 km/h (351 mph). More of the A6M5 and its sub-variants were produced than any other Japanese aircraft. A notable subvariant was the **A6M5d-S**, a night fighter conversion armed with a 20-mm cannon mounted obliquely in the rear fuselage. It was five A6M5s of the Shikishima kamikaze unit that sank the escort carrier *St Lo* and damaged three others on 25 October 1944.

Further development led in late 1944 to the **A6M6**, with water-methanol boosted Sakae 31 engine and self-sealing fuel tanks. Operational units carried out field conversions of many aircraft to carry a 250-kg (551-lb) bomb, enabling them to be used as fighter-bombers. The final production **A6M7** which entered service in mid-1945 was modified specially for this role. A float version, the **A6M2-N**, was given the Allied reporting name of **'Rufe'**. All other A6Ms were known as **'Zekes'**, though the Japanese nickname of **'Zero-Sen'** became even more widely used. When the production lines finally closed, a total of 10,449 A6Ms had been built by Mitsubishi (3,879) and Nakajima (6,570).

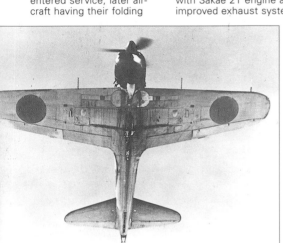

A6M5c Reisen 'Zeke'

The A6M5c (Model 53c) was one of the late-war stop-gap variants of the Zero that were introduced in an attempt to stem the tide of American air superiority. It combined the basic improvements of the standard M5 model with heavier firepower – two extra 13.2-mm (0.52-in) heavy machine-guns in the wings, carried outboard of the 20-mm cannon.

Construction
The A6M5 combined non-folding wings with rounded tips and thicker skins, separate exhaust stacks, and better protection including self-sealing tanks and rear armour for the pilot.

Guns
The A5M's armament comprised a 13.2-mm Type 3 heavy machine gun above engine, two 20-mm Type 99 cannon inboard on wings and two more Type 3s carried outboard.

Production
Only 93 A6M5cs were built.

Warload
The lightly-built Zero could only carry two 60-kg (132-lb) bombs, one under each wing, but for kamikaze suicide missions it could replace the external fuel tank with a single 250-kg (551-lb) bomb.

Engine
The NK1F Sakae 21 radial piston engine delivered a total of 843 kW (1,130 hp).

Performance
The A6M5c could reach a maximum speed of 565 km/h (351 mph), and it had a service ceiling of 11740 m (38,517 ft).

Nakajima B5N 'Kate'
Carrier-based torpedo bomber

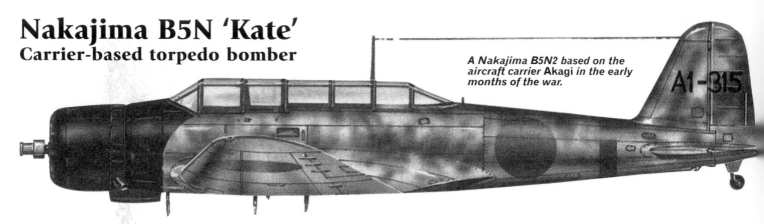

A Nakajima B5N2 based on the aircraft carrier Akagi in the early months of the war.

Designed to a 1935 requirement, and already in service for four years when Japan entered the war, the **Nakajima B5N Navy Type 97 Carrier Attack Bomber** was the best carrierborne torpedo-bomber in the world in 1941. Powered by a Nakajima Hikari radial engine, the low-wing three-crew monoplane first flew in January 1937. Its inwardly-retracting wide-track landing gear made for an exceptionally clean airframe. By 1938, production B5N aircraft were embarking in Japan's carriers, and shore-based units were deployed in China.

In 1939 the improved **B5N2** appeared with a more powerful Sakae 11 engine in a smaller cowling, although armament and bombload were unchanged. This version remained in production until 1943.

When Japan attacked the USA in December 1941, the B5N2 had wholly replaced the B5N1 with operational units, and 144 B5N2s were involved in the fateful attack on Pearl Harbor.

Over the next 12 months aircraft of this type were to sink the American carriers USS *Hornet*, *Lexington* and *Yorktown*. Given the reporting name **'Kate'** by the Allies, the B5N certainly earned the respect of the Americans and in all the major carrier battles of the Pacific War it attracted the undivided attention of defending fighters.

Vulnerable

However, good though it was in 1940, the introduction of new American fighters meant that by 1943 the 'Kate' was vulnerable. With its puny defensive armament of a single machine-gun, and its performance crippled when

laden with a large bomb or torpedo, the B5N began to suffer very heavily. The type was still fully committed during the Solomons campaign in 1942 and 1943, but the survivors were withdrawn after the Philippine battles of 1944.

Thereafter, on account of their excellent range, they were assigned to anti-submarine and maritime reconnaissance duties in areas beyond the range of Allied fighters. Total production of all models of the B5N reached 1,149.

Two late-model B5N2s overfly the mighty battleship Yamato. Carrierborne aircraft were to prove decisive in eliminating the threat of the big-gun warship, which had ruled the oceans for centuries.

The pilot of an early B5N – identifiable from its larger engine cowling – conducts pre-flight checks at an airfield in China some time in the late 1930s.

SPECIFICATION	
Nakajima B5N2 'Kate'	1990 km (1,237 miles)
Type: three-crew carrierborne torpedo-bomber	**Weights:** empty 2279 kg (5,024 lb); maximum take-off 4100 kg (9,039 lb)
Powerplant: one 746-kW (1,000-hp) Nakajima NK 1B Sakae 11 radial piston engine	**Dimensions:** span 15.52 m (50 ft 11 in); length 10.30 m (33 ft 9½ in); height 3.70 m (12 ft ½ in); wing area 37.70 m² (405.8 sq ft)
Performance: maximum speed 378 km/h (235 mph) at 3600 m (11,811 ft); climb to 3000 m (9,843 ft) in 7 minutes 42 seconds; service ceiling 8260 m (27,100 ft); range	**Armament:** one 7.7-mm (0.303-in) Type 92 trainable machine gun in rear cockpit, plus one 800-kg (1,764-lb) torpedo or equivalent bomb weight

Nakajima B6N *Tenzan* 'Jill' Carrier-based torpedo bomber

At a time when the triumphs of the B5N were still almost three years in the future, the Imperial Japanese Navy issued a specification for a replacement, recognizing that only limited overall design improvement of the B5N could be achieved in the B5N2.

Accordingly, design of the **Nakajima B6N** went ahead in 1939 and, despite the navy's preference for the Mitsubishi Kasei radial, a Nakajima Mamoru was selected for the prototype which flew early in 1941.

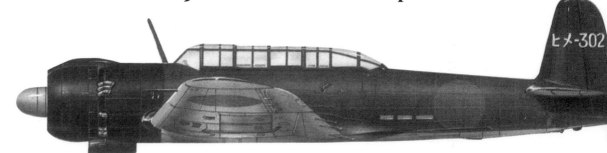

Known as the **Tenzan** or **'Heavenly Mountain'**, the B6N superficially resembled the earlier aircraft, but the much increased power and torque of the big engine and

Above: This Nakajima B6N 'Tenzan' is depicted in the colours worn by Imperial Japanese Navy aircraft in 1944, when many operated from land bases.

four-bladed propeller was found to impose considerable directional stability problems, demanding that the vertical tail surfaces be offset to one side. Flight trials dragged on, and were further delayed by troubles during carrier acceptance tests. Then Nakajima was ordered to stop production of the Mamoru engine, so modifications had to be introduced to suit installation of the Kasei.

In due course B6N1 aircraft, given the Allied code name **'Jill'**, were embarked in the carriers *Shokaku, Taiho, Hiyo, Junyo* and *Zuikaku*, and took part in the catastrophic battle in the Philippine Sea which took place in June 1944. Many were lost when the three first-named carriers were sunk. In that month, production started of the slightly improved **B6N2**, of which 1,133 were produced before the end of the war. Only 133 of the Nakajima-engined B6N had been built.

The heavy losses among Japanese carriers in the American advance on the Philippines resulted in the 'Jill' being largely deployed ashore, particularly after the Battle of Leyte Gulf. After, many B6Ns were consigned to the kamikaze role.

Left: *Nakajima insisted on using its own Mamoru 11 radial engine in the B6N, but production was stopped after only 135 had been fitted. Later aircraft were powered by the Misubishi Kasei.*

Above: *Although most of Japan's pre-war carriers had been lost by the time the Tenzan became operational, new-build vessels meant that the B6N saw extensive seaborne service in the great battles of 1944.*

SPECIFICATION	
Nakajima B6N2 'Jill'	**Weights:** empty 3010 kg (6,636 lb); maximum take-off 5650 kg (12,456 lb)
Type: three-crew carrierborne torpedo bomber	**Dimensions:** span 14.89 m (48 ft 10 in); length 10.87 m (35 ft 8 in); height 3,80 m (12 ft 5½ in); wing area 37.20 m² (400.43 sq ft)
Powerplant: one 1380-kW (1,850-hp) Mitsubishi MK4T Kasei 25 radial piston engine	
Performance: maximum speed 481 km/h (299 mph) at 4900 m (16,076 ft); climb to 5000 m (16,404 ft) in 10 minutes 24 seconds; service ceiling 9040 m (29,659 ft); range 1746 km (1,085 miles)	**Armament:** one trainable 13-mm (0.51-in) Type 2 machine-gun in rear cockpit and one 7.7-mm (0.303-in) Type 97 machine-gun in ventral tunnel position, plus one 800-kg (1,764-lb) torpedo or equivalent bomb weight

Yokosuka D4Y *Suisei* 'Judy'
Carrier-based dive bomber

A Yokosuka D4Y3 of the 601st Kokutai, Imperial Japanese Navy. This model introduced the reliable Mitsubishi Mk8P Kinsei 62 radial engine, which solved many of the problems caused by the earlier Aichi Atsuta engine.

Well-proportioned and purposeful in appearance, the **Yokosuka D4Y** possessed an excellent performance and owed much of its concept to the German He 118, for whose manufacturing rights Japan negotiated in 1938. Designed as a fast carrier-based attack bomber and powered by an imported Daimler-Benz DB 600G engine, the D4Y1 was first flown in December 1941.

D4Y1-C reconnaissance aircraft were ordered into production at Aichi's Nagoya plant, the first of 660 aircraft being completed in the late spring of 1942. The first service aircraft were lost when the *Soryu* was sunk at Midway. Named **Suisei** or **'Comet'** in service, and codenamed **'Judy'** by the Allies, many D4Y1s were completed as dive bombers.

Battle losses
Over 170 Suiseis of the 1st, 2nd and 3rd Koku Sentais were embarked in nine carriers in the Philippine Sea in June 1944. Tasked with stopping the American invasion of the Marianas, they suffered the fate of most of the Japanese aircraft in that battle. Even though the D4Y had fighter-like performance, its lack of protection made it easy meat in combat. The 'Judys' were intercepted by swarms of US Navy carrier fighters, suffering heavy casualties without achieving any success.

A new version with 1044-kW (1,400-hp) Aichi Atsuta 32 engine, based on the German DB 601, appeared in 1944 as the D4Y2 but, in the interests of preserving high performance, armour protection for crew or fuel tanks was again omitted. The sole improvement in gun armament was the inclusion of a 13-mm (0.51-in) trainable gun (replacing the previous 7.92-mm/0.31-in gun) in the rear cockpit. This version suffered heavily in the battle for the Philippines.

Night fighter
By the end of 1944, Japan's home islands were under direct and devastating attack from American heavy bombers. Some D4Y2s were pressed into service as night fighters, fitted with an upward-firing 20-mm cannon.

Although lacking radar, the type's excellent speed and service ceiling meant that it could reach the B-29 Superfortresses, raining destruction upon Japan and the night-fighting Suiseis achieved some small success in the defence of the homeland.

Reliability problems with the Atsuta (DB 601) engine led to adoption of a reliable Kinsei 62 radial in the D4Y3. This engine was retained in the D4Y4 which was developed in 1945 as a single-seat suicide dive-bomber, carrying an 800-kg (1,764-lb) bomb semi-recessed into the fuselage. A total of 2,033 production D4Ys was completed.

SPECIFICATION	
Yokosuka D4Y3 'Judy'	maximum take-off 4657 kg (10,267 lb)
Type: two-seat carrierborne dive bomber	**Dimensions:** span 11.50 m (37 ft 8¾in); length 10.22 m (33 ft 6½ in); height 3.74 m (12 ft 3 in); wing area 23.60 m² (254.04 sq ft)
Powerplant: one 1163-kW (1,560-hp) Mitsubishi MK8P Kinsei 62 radial piston engine	
Performance: maximum speed 575 km/h (357 mph) at 6050 m (19,849 ft); climb to 3000 m (9,843 ft) 4.55 minutes; service ceiling 10500 m (34,449 ft); range 1520 km (944 miles)	**Armament:** two fixed forward-firing 7.7-mm (0.303-in) Type 97 machine guns in nose and one 13-mm (0.51-in) Type 2 trainable gun in rear cockpit, plus a maximum bombload of 560 kg (1,235 lb)
Weights: empty 2501 kg (5,514 lb);	

Curtiss SB2C Helldiver Scout/dive-bomber

This SB2C was among those on strength with VB-8 aboard the USS Bunker Hill in June 1944, around the time that the unit began operations against Saipan.

The last of a long line of Curtiss aircraft to carry the name Helldiver (the earlier aircraft being inter-war biplanes), the **SB2C Helldiver** was first flown as the **XSB2C-1** on 18 December 1940. Production **SB2C-1** aircraft featured an enlarged fin and rudder assembly, increased fuel capacity and four 0.5-in (12.7-mm) guns in the wings. The **SB2C-1C** carried an armament of two 20-mm guns in the wings.

Advanced variants

The **SB2C-3** appeared in 1944 with a more powerful engine, and the **SB2C-4** had provision to carry eight 127-mm (5-in) rockets or 454 kg (1,000 lb) of bombs under the wings (in addition to the 454-kg/1,000-lb internal bombload); the SB2C-4 also carried radar in a small pod under the wing, and the **SB2C-5** had increased fuel. Production amounted to 7,199 of all aircraft, including 300 by Fairchild in Canada, 984 by the Canadian Car and Foundry, and 900 produced for the USAAF as the **A-25A Shrike** (most of which were taken over by the US Marine Corps and redesignated **SB2C-1A**). Helldivers first went into action on 11 November 1943 with a raid by VB-17 on Rabaul, but were never well liked. During 1944 they gradually replaced the Douglas SBD Dauntless, and were in constant action against the Japanese. Some 26 Canadian-built aircraft were supplied to the UK as **Helldiver Mk I** machines.

Although it was built in greater numbers than any other World War II dive-bomber and notched up an impressive combat record, the Helldiver was universally disliked by its crews. It handled badly and the SB2C designation was generally held to mean 'Son of a Bitch, 2nd Class'.

SPECIFICATION

Curtiss SB2C-4 Helldiver
Type: two-seat carrier-based scout/dive bomber
Powerplant: one 1419-kW (1,900-hp) Wright R-2600-20 radial piston engine
Performance: maximum speed 475 km/h (295 mph) at 5090 m (16,700 ft); initial climb rate 549 m (1,800 ft) per minute; service ceiling 8870 m (29,100 ft); range 1875 km (1,165 miles)
Weights: empty 4784 kg (10,547 lb); maximum take-off 7537 kg (16,616 lb)
Dimensions: wing span 15.16 m (49 ft 9 in); length 11.18 m (36 ft 8 in); height 4.01 m (13 ft 2 in); wing area 39.20 m² (422 sq ft)
Armament: two fixed forward-firing 20-mm cannon in the wings and two 0.3-in (7.62-mm) trainable machine-guns in the rear cockpit, plus a bombload of 454 kg (1,000 lb) under the wings and 454 kg (1,000 lb) internally

Vought F4U Corsair Carrier and land-based fighter

With its inverted gull wing, the **Vought F4U Corsair** is often considered the best shipborne fighter of the war, and gained an 11:1 kill:loss ratio in the Pacific. Designed by Rex B. Beisel, the **XF4U-1** prototype was first flown on 29 May 1940, the first production **F4U-1** fighters being delivered to VF-12 in October 1942, although most of the early aircraft went to the US Marine Corps. It was a land-based US Marine squadron, VMF-124, that first flew the Corsair into action, on 13 February 1943 over Bougainville. Additional production lines were set up by Brewster and Goodyear, these companies producing the **F3A-1** and **FG-1** respectively. To improve the pilot's field of view, later aircraft

SPECIFICATION

Vought F4U-1 Corsair
Type: single-seat carrier fighter
Powerplant: one 1491-kW (2,000-hp) Pratt & Whitney R-2800-8 radial piston engine
Performance: maximum speed 671 km/h (417 mph) at 6066 m (19,900 ft); initial climb rate 881 m (2,890 ft) per minute; service ceiling 11247 m (36,900 ft); range 1633 km (1,015 miles)

Weights: empty 4074 kg (8,982 lb); maximum take-off 6350 kg (14,000 lb)
Dimensions: wing span 12.50 m (41 ft); length 10.17 m (33 ft 4¾ in); height 4.90 m (16 ft 1 in); wing area 29.17 m² (314 sq ft)
Armament: six forward-firing 0.5-in (12.7-mm) machine-guns in the wings

introduced a raised cockpit, and the **F4U-1C** had a four 20-mm cannon armament. The **F4U-1D**, **FG-1D** and **F3A-1D** were powered by water-injection boosted R-2800-8W engines, and could carry two 1,000-lb (454-kg) bombs or eight 5-in (127-mm) rockets under the wings. Late in the war a night-fighter version, the **F4U-2**, saw limited service with VFN-75 and VFN-101. Wartime production of the Corsair (which continued

The likely key to Corsair's longevity was the combination of its superior air combat capabilities, a high top speed, the ability to absorb combat damage and a strong wing – all of which helped to produce a world-beating warplane.

until 1952 with later versions) reached 4,120 F4U-1s, 735 F3A-1s and 3,808 FG-1s; of these 2,012 were supplied to the UK's

Above: There were many Corsair aces, among them Lt Ira C. 'Ike' Kepford. Here his VF-17 F4U-1A carries a record of his 16 kills.

Right: This FAA Corsair Mk I demonstrates the heavily-framed 'bird-cage' cockpit canopy that was fitted to early Corsairs. This view also shows the type's gull wing to good effect.

Fleet Air Arm and 370 to New Zealand. Indeed, it was the Royal Navy's **Corsair Mk II** aircraft of No. 1834 Squadron that were the first

Corsairs to operate from a carrier in combat when, on 3 April 1944, they took part in operations against the much-feared *Tirpitz*.

Douglas SBD Dauntless Scout/dive-bomber

Developed directly from the Northrop BT-1 (the Northrop Corporation had become a division of Douglas), the prototype of the **SBD Dauntless** two-seat carrier-borne dive-bomber was in fact a much modified production BT-1. Production orders for 57 **SBD-1** and 87 **SBD-2** aircraft were placed in April 1939, the former

being delivered to US Marine Corps bombing and scout-bombing squadrons, and the latter to US Navy scout and bombing squadrons.

Ready for action

The **SBD-3**, with two additional 0.5-in (12.7-mm) guns in the nose, self-sealing tanks and R-1820-52 engine, appeared in March 1941, and by the time of Pearl Harbor in December that year, 584 SBD-3s had been delivered. Some 780 **SBD-4** aircraft (with 24-volt electrical system, but otherwise as the SBD-3 and produced at El Segundo, California) were built in 1942; photo-recce modifications (the **SBD-1P**, **SBD-2P** and **SBD-3P**) were also produced during 1941-42. A new Douglas plant at Tulsa, Oklahoma, built 2,409 **SBD-5** aircraft with 895-kW (1,200-hp)

These SBD-5s are finished in a typical North Atlantic colour scheme, although they were based in the Caribbean with VMS-3.

R-1820-60 engines, following these with 451 **SBD-6** aircraft with -66 engines.

Army version

The USAAF took delivery of 168 SBD-3A, 170 SBD-4 and 615 SBD-5 aircraft, as the **A-24**, **A-24A** and **A-24B** respectively, bringing the total Douglas production

to 5,936 SBDs. They were unquestionably one of America's most important weapons in the Pacific War, and sank a greater tonnage of Japanese shipping than any other aircraft. They also played a key part in the great battles of Midway, the Coral Sea and the Solomons.

SPECIFICATION

Douglas SBD-5 Dauntless
Type: two-crew carrier-based scout/dive-bomber
Powerplant: one 895-kW (1,200-hp) Wright R-1820-60 radial piston engine
Performance: maximum speed 394 km/h (245 mph) at 4816 m (15,800 ft); initial climb rate 363 m (1,190 ft) per minute; service ceiling 7407 m (24,300 ft); range 1770 km (1,100 miles)
Weights: empty 3028 kg (6,675 lb); maximum take-off 4924 kg

(10,855 lb)
Dimensions: wing span 12.65 m (41 ft 6¼ in); length 10.06 m (33 ft); height 3.94 m (12 ft 11 in); wing area 30.19 m² (325 sq ft)
Armament: two fixed forward-firing 0.5-in (12.7-mm) machine-guns and two trainable 0.3-in (7.62-mm) guns in rear cockpit, plus a bombload of one 1,600-lb (726-kg) bomb under the fuselage and two 325-lb (147-kg) bombs under the wings

As well as its most meritorious service in the Pacific, the Dauntless also served over the Atlantic. This VS-41 SBD-3 took part in Operation Torch, flying from USS Ranger.

Grumman F4F Wildcat Carrier fighter

When first flown on 2 September 1937, the **Grumman XF4F-2** single-seat naval fighter prototype proved to be only 16 km/h (10 mph) faster than the Brewster F2A-1. Only when a two-stage supercharged XR-1830-76 engine was fitted was the true potential of the design recognised, and a speed of 537 km/h (334 mph) was recorded during US Navy trials with the **XF4F-3**.

Into production

Some 54 production **F4F-3** fighters were ordered in August 1939, 22 of which had been delivered by the end of 1940, These aircraft, Grumman's first monoplanes for the US Navy which were later named Wildcat, served with US Navy fighter squadrons VF-4 and VF-7. They were followed by 95 **F4F-3A** aircraft with single-stage supercharged R-1830-90 engines.

The Wildcat was ordered by France in 1939 but the entire batch of 81 aircraft was transferred to the British Royal Navy where they served as the **Martlet**, being first flown in combat during 1940.

US Navy and US Marine Corps F4Fs were heavily

Above: Lt Cdr John Raby flew this F4F-4 with the US Navy's VF-9 from the USS Ranger during Operation Torch in November 1942. Raby scored two confirmed kills against the Vichy French during Torch.

engaged during the early months of the war with Japan. Many were destroyed on the ground, but they also scored a number of outstanding victories.

The **F4F-4**, with manually-folding wings (of which 1,169 were produced), was delivered during 1942, and was heavily involved in the battles of the Coral Sea and Midway.

An unarmed reconnaissance version, the **F4F-7**, had a range of over 5633 km (3,500 miles). The F4F-4 was also built by General Motors as the **FM-1**, and a more powerful version, the **FM-2**, operated from escort carriers. FM-1s and -2s were supplied to the UK as the **Wildcat Mk V** and **Wildcat Mk VI**, the name Martlet having been dropped in January 1944.

Total production of the Wildcat (excluding prototypes) was 7,885, including 5,237 FM-1s and FM-2s constructed by General Motors, and 1,100 for the Fleet Air Arm.

Above: This Wildcat Mk V (FM-1) served with No. 813 Sqn, of the Royal Navy's Fleet Air Arm in February 1945. It was flown from HMS Vindex by Sub-Lt Fleischman-Allen.

Above: Among the most obvious recognition features of the FM-2 when compared to other Wildcat variants was its taller fin and rudder.

Above: Marine Corps Wildcat pilots fought courageously from a number of land bases in the Pacific. This aircraft was photographed as it was being wheeled out of its crushed coral revetment on Palmyra Island in July 1943.

Right: These weathered US Navy FM-2 Wildcats are being launched from the USS Makin Island for the attack on Iwo Jima in March 1945.

SPECIFICATION	
Grumman F4F-4 Wildcat **Type:** single-seat shipboard fighter Powerplant: one 895-kW (1,200-hp) Pratt & Whitney R-1830-86 radial piston engine **Performance:** maximum speed 512 km/h (318 mph) at 5913 m (19,400 ft); initial climb rate 594 m (1,950 ft) per minute; service ceiling 10638 m (34,900 ft); range 1239 km (770 miles)	**Weights:** empty 2624 kg (5,785 lb); maximum take-off 3607 kg (7,952 lb) **Dimensions:** wing span 11.58 m (38 ft); length 8.76 m (28 ft 9 in); height 3.61 m (11 ft 10 in); wing area 24.15 m² (260 sq ft) **Armament:** six forward-firing 12.7-mm (0.5-in) machine guns; FM-2 had four guns and provision to carry two 113-kg (250-lb) bombs or six 127-mm (5-in) rockets

Grumman F6F Hellcat Carrier fighter

This VF-27 F6F-5 carries a full underwing load of six high-velocity aircraft rockets (HVARs) and two 227-kg (500-lb) bombs, as well as an underfuselage drop tank.

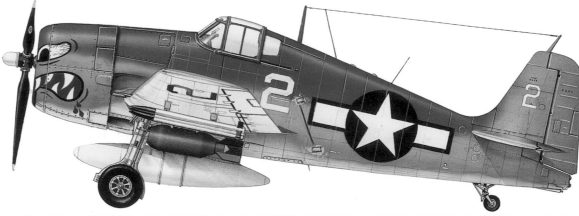

One of America's best wartime shipboard fighters, capably partnering the F4U Corsair, the **Grumman F6F Hellcat** was the logical development of the F4F Wildcat, and was first flown as the **XF6F-3** on 26 June 1942; this was given an uprated engine and flew again five weeks later. Deliveries to VF-9 aboard USS *Essex* started early in 1943; night fighter versions were the **F6F-3E** and **F6F-3N** with radar in a wing pod.

In 1944 the **F6F-5** appeared, with provision for 907 kg (2,000 lb) of bombs. Two 20-mm cannon sometimes replaced the inboard wing 12.7-mm guns. The radar-equipped night-fighter version of this model was the **F6F-5N**; production totalled 6,435 F6F-5Ns, while 252 F6F-3s and 930 F6F-5s served with the British Fleet Air Arm as the **Hellcat Mk I** and **Hellcat Mk II**.

In action

Production of all F6Fs amounted to 12,275, and official figures credited the US Navy and Marine Corps aircraft with the destruction of 5,156 enemy aircraft in air combat, about 75 per cent of all their air combat

The busy flight deck of USS Randolph, CV-15, as Marine Corps F6F-5s of VF-/VBF-12 launch for a strike against Japanese targets in July 1945.

victories in the war. The Hellcat's greatest single triumph came in the largest of all carrier operations, the Battle of the Philippine Sea

in June 1944. Fifteen American carriers embarked 480 F6F fighters (plus 222 dive-bombers and 199 torpedo-bombers); by the end of a week's fighting with Admiral Ozawa's 1st Mobile Fleet, the US Navy's Task Force 58 had destroyed more than 400 Japanese aircraft and sunk three carriers. Hellcats were still serving with the US Navy several years after the war.

SPECIFICATION
Grumman F6F-5 Hellcat

Type: single-seat shipboard fighter
Powerplant: one 1491-kW (2,000-hp) Pratt & Whitney R-2800-10W radial piston engine
Performance: maximum speed 612 km/h (380 mph) at 7132 m (23,400 ft); initial climb rate 908 m (2,980 ft) per minute; service ceiling 11369 m (37,300 ft); range 1521 km (945 miles)
Weights: empty 4190 kg (9,238 lb);

maximum take-off 6991 kg (15,413 lb)
Dimensions: wing span 13.05 m (42 ft 10 in); length 10.24 m (33 ft 7 in); height 3.99 m (13 ft 1 in); wing area 31.03 m (334 sq ft)
Armament: six 12.7-mm (0.5-in) machine-guns in wings, or two 20-mm cannon and four 12.7-mm (0.5-in) guns in wings, plus provision for two 454-kg (1,000-lb) bombs

Above: In service, the Hellcat was a superb fighting machine, having all of the classic Grumman characteristics of toughness and reliability.

Right: As the first operational Hellcat squadron, VF-9 helped in ironing out the type's early problems. These included a tendency to 'weathercock' and to hit the propeller on the deck during a hard landing. These VF-9 aircraft are aboard USS Essex during Operation Galvanic (the Tarawa landings).

A6M Zero versus F4F Wildcat
Pacific adversaries

In the early stages of the Pacific war, the Mitsubishi A6M Zero 'Zeke' established for itself a legendary reputation in air-to-air combat. During Japan's pre-war skirmishes over China the aircraft had proved invincible and the first combats of World War II did little to tarnish the legend. In truth however, the A6M had begun suffering losses almost as soon as it encountered relatively modern Allied types – the F2A, P-40 and Hurricane for example – but it was under the guns of the F4F Wildcat that the aircraft really began to suffer. The F4F could not match the manoeuvrability of the Zero, but it was flown with desperate determination, had heavy firepower and was built to withstand the rigours of combat. Against the F4F and later Allied types of greater performance, the Zero became increasingly obsolete and by the war's end was really suitable for just one mission – that of the kamikaze.

Structural weakness

A primary requirement of the Imperial Japanese Navy was for the Zero to have extremely good range and endurance capabilities. In order to achieve the specified eight-hour range with its design, Mitsubishi had kept the aircraft very light. It used the lightest possible structure, combined with an engine of only moderate power, but had excellent manoeuvrability. Over China against relatively weak opposition, this combination of factors allowed the Zero to put in a fine performance. Against later fighters, especially the Wildcat in the early stages of the war, these qualities became a hindrance. The Zero's light structure could fail under combat stress and little excess power was available. Most seriously, the aircraft was without any form of armour protection for its pilot and systems and was therefore especially vulnerable, since just a handful of hits could prove fatal.

SPECIFICATION	
F4F-4 Wildcat	**Mitsubishi A6M2 Model 21**
Dimensions	**Dimensions**
Length: 8.76 m (28 ft 9 in)	**Length:** 9.06 m (29 ft 8¾ in)
Wing span: 11.58 m (38 ft)	**Wing span:** 12 m (39 ft 4½ in)
Wing area: 24.15 m² (260 sq ft)	**Wing area:** 22.44 m² (241.54 sq ft)
Powerplant	**Powerplant**
One 895-kW (1,200-hp) Pratt & Whitney R-1830-36 Twin Wasp 14-cylinder radial piston engine	One Nakajima NK1C Sakae 12 fourteen-cylinder air-cooled radial, rated at 701 kW (940 hp) for take-off and 708 kW (950 hp) at 4,200 m (13,780 ft)
Weights	**Weights**
Empty: 2612 kg (5,758 lb)	**Empty:** 1680 kg (3,704 lb)
Maximum take-off: 3607 kg (7,952 lb)	**Maximum take-off:** 2796 kg (6,164 lb)
Performance	**Performance**
Maximum speed at 5915 m (19,400 ft): 512 km/h (318 mph)	**Maximum speed at 5915 m (19,400 ft):** 533 km/h (332 mph)
Cruising speed: 249 km/h (155 mph)	**Cruising speed:** 333 km/h (207 mph)
Initial climb rate: 594 m (1,950 ft) per minute	**Initial climb rate:** 6000 m (19,685 ft) in 7 minutes 27 seconds
Service ceiling: 12010 m (39,400 ft)	**Service ceiling:** 10000 m (32,810 ft)
Range: 1239 km (770 miles)	**Normal range:** 1866 km (1,160 miles)
Armament	**Maximum range:** 3105 km (1,930 miles)
Six fixed forward-firing 0.5-in (12.7-mm) Browning machine-guns, plus two 100-lb (45-kg) bombs	**Armament**
	Two 7.7-mm (0.303-in) Type 97 machine-guns in the upper fuselage decking and two wing-mounted 20-mm Type 99 cannon

This A6M2 Type 21 is illustrated as it appeared during the Battle of Midway in June 1942. The aircraft carries the markings of the 2nd Sentai of the 1st Koku Kentai and was based aboard the Hiryu. Midway was something of a turning point for both the Japanese and the Zero, since for the first time the Americans inflicted serious damage on Japanese forces. The Zeros met the Wildcat in force and suffered accordingly, although losses on both sides were heavy and showed parity. The long-term effects of the battles at Midway and in the Coral Sea were more telling however. Japanese industry found it difficult to replace lost equipment and almost impossible to work on improvements. In addition, fully-trained pilots soon proved impossible to replace and the quality of Japanese pilots soon became degraded.

Powerplant improvements

The Zero began the war with an engine of only marginal power. Although this initially proved adequate, both the addition of new equipment to the airframe, as well as the need to respond to improved Allied aircraft, meant that a more powerful engine was soon needed. Unfortunately, engine development did not match the pace of airframe development and Zero was destined to remain short of power throughout its career. Mitsubishi's chief Zero engineer had always wanted to use the 1163-kW (1,560-hp) Mitsubishi Kinsei 62 radial engine in the Zero and this engine was eventually installed in two A6M8 prototypes. In the event however, plans to produce some 6,300 of this much improved aircraft were scuppered by Allied bombing.

Keith Fretwell.

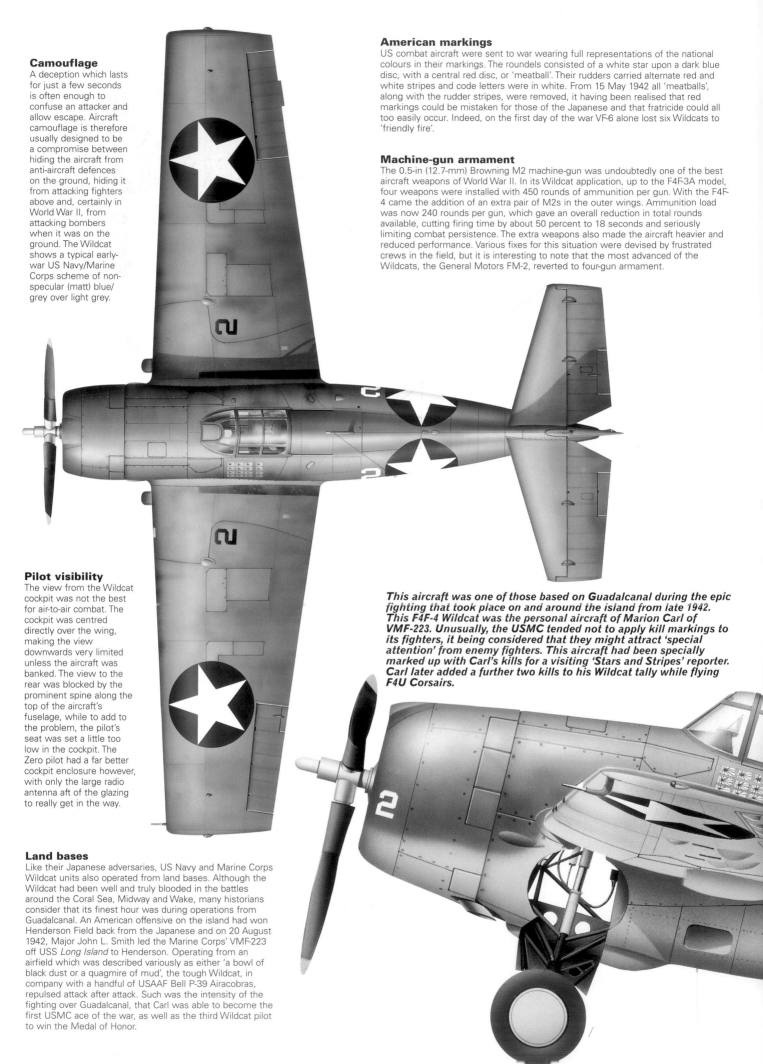

Camouflage

A deception which lasts for just a few seconds is often enough to confuse an attacker and allow escape. Aircraft camouflage is therefore usually designed to be a compromise between hiding the aircraft from anti-aircraft defences on the ground, hiding it from attacking fighters above and, certainly in World War II, from attacking bombers when it was on the ground. The Wildcat shows a typical early-war US Navy/Marine Corps scheme of non-specular (matt) blue/grey over light grey.

American markings

US combat aircraft were sent to war wearing full representations of the national colours in their markings. The roundels consisted of a white star upon a dark blue disc, with a central red disc, or 'meatball'. Their rudders carried alternate red and white stripes and code letters were in white. From 15 May 1942 all 'meatballs', along with the rudder stripes, were removed, it having been realised that red markings could be mistaken for those of the Japanese and that fratricide could all too easily occur. Indeed, on the first day of the war VF-6 alone lost six Wildcats to 'friendly fire'.

Machine-gun armament

The 0.5-in (12.7-mm) Browning M2 machine-gun was undoubtedly one of the best aircraft weapons of World War II. In its Wildcat application, up to the F4F-3A model, four weapons were installed with 450 rounds of ammunition per gun. With the F4F-4 came the addition of an extra pair of M2s in the outer wings. Ammunition load was now 240 rounds per gun, which gave an overall reduction in total rounds available, cutting firing time by about 50 percent to 18 seconds and seriously limiting combat persistence. The extra weapons also made the aircraft heavier and reduced performance. Various fixes for this situation were devised by frustrated crews in the field, but it is interesting to note that the most advanced of the Wildcats, the General Motors FM-2, reverted to four-gun armament.

Pilot visibility

The view from the Wildcat cockpit was not the best for air-to-air combat. The cockpit was centred directly over the wing, making the view downwards very limited unless the aircraft was banked. The view to the rear was blocked by the prominent spine along the top of the aircraft's fuselage, while to add to the problem, the pilot's seat was set a little too low in the cockpit. The Zero pilot had a far better cockpit enclosure however, with only the large radio antenna aft of the glazing to really get in the way.

This aircraft was one of those based on Guadalcanal during the epic fighting that took place on and around the island from late 1942. This F4F-4 Wildcat was the personal aircraft of Marion Carl of VMF-223. Unusually, the USMC tended not to apply kill markings to its fighters, it being considered that they might attract 'special attention' from enemy fighters. This aircraft had been specially marked up with Carl's kills for a visiting 'Stars and Stripes' reporter. Carl later added a further two kills to his Wildcat tally while flying F4U Corsairs.

Land bases

Like their Japanese adversaries, US Navy and Marine Corps Wildcat units also operated from land bases. Although the Wildcat had been well and truly blooded in the battles around the Coral Sea, Midway and Wake, many historians consider that its finest hour was during operations from Guadalcanal. An American offensive on the island had won Henderson Field back from the Japanese and on 20 August 1942, Major John L. Smith led the Marine Corps' VMF-223 off USS *Long Island* to Henderson. Operating from an airfield which was described variously as either 'a bowl of black dust or a quagmire of mud', the tough Wildcat, in company with a handful of USAAF Bell P-39 Airacobras, repulsed attack after attack. Such was the intensity of the fighting over Guadalcanal, that Carl was able to become the first USMC ace of the war, as well as the third Wildcat pilot to win the Medal of Honor.

Pratt & Whitney power

A Pratt & Whitney Twin Wasp radial engine drove the F4F-4's three-bladed propeller. Both the Wildcat and Zero were powered by air-cooled radial engines, a type of powerplant inherently more resistant to combat damage than liquid-cooled powerplants. Often a single hit to the radiator or coolant ducting of a fighter with a liquid-cooled engine was enough to cause a forced landing.

Mitsubishi designed the Zero first and foremost as a carrier-based long-range fighter. As such it featured a very sturdy undercarriage, to withstand the rigours of frequent carrier landings. However, as the war progressed, the Japanese soon found themselves running short of serviceable carriers and the Zeros increasingly operated from land bases. With hindsight, it is clear that the Zero never really mastered the Wildcat, and was never a match for the Allied fighters which reached the Pacific theatre from later in 1942.

Victory tally

It was common practice for Allied pilots to keep a record of their kills in the form of a 'scoreboard' painted on their regular aircraft. In the case of Captain Marion E. Carl, this eventually recorded 16.5 Wildcat victories in the form of Japanese flags. Pilots were awarded a 'whole victory' for any aircraft which they solely shot down, and a fraction of a victory for any aircraft whose destruction they shared. In combat it was often difficult to decide exactly which pilot had downed which machine, especially when leaders and wingmen were both attacking the same target.

AIRCRAFT CARRIERS

This F4F-4 was assigned to Ensign Mortimer C. Kleinmann with VF-5 aboard USS Saratoga. However, on 7 August 1942, the machine was being flown by Lieutenant James Southerland when it downed the first two Japanese aircraft to be destroyed during the Guadalcanal fighting. Unfortunately, Southerland was himself almost immediately shot down, but exacted his revenge in 1945, when he gained ace status by shooting down three more Japanese warplanes.

There was little time for anything other than the most necessary painting maintenance when the Guadalcanal campaign was at its peak, but by September 1942 Major R. E. Galer's groundcrew had managed to find the time to add red markings to his F4F-3. Among Galer's total of 14 kills were seven Zeros, all of them destroyed while Galer was flying Wildcats.

Lt Col Harold Bauer was unusual among Wildcat pilots since he encouraged his fellow flyers to engage in dogfights with Zeros whenever possible. In general, dogfights with the Japanese fighters were studiously avoided by Wildcat pilots and it was generally accepted that an F4F caught alone by a Zero was in dire trouble. Bauer shot down ten aircraft over Guadalcanal with VMF-223 and -224. He flew this F4F-3 from the island with VMF-212 in November 1942, the month in which he was posted missing in action.

Both the Zero and Wildcat remained in front-line service after the initial Pacific skirmishes, although neither would again return to the ranks of the world's top-performing fighters. This F4F-4 flew from USS Santee with VGF-29 during Operation Torch in November 1942. Ensign Bruce Jacques scored a single kill in this machine during the North African landings.

1st Lt Jefferson DeBlanc was the US Marine Corps' 11th highest-scoring F4F ace, with nine kills. Although others had far higher tallies, DeBlanc claimed three of his kills in the same day, while flying this VMF-112 F4F-4 on 31 January 1943. After the combat, DeBlanc found himself doubly handicapped by his low fuel state and damage to his aircraft and was forced to bale out at very low level. Luckily, he was rescued from the sea by friendly forces, under the noses of the Japanese.

Although it wears a late-war Atlantic colour scheme, this FM-2 operated off USS White Plains in the Pacific during November 1944. By this time the Wildcat was very much a secondary fighter compared to the F4U and F6F. The Zero too, was now playing a more minor role, but this VC-4 aircraft, flown by Lt Leo Ferko, was still able to down a pair of Zeros on 24 October 1944.

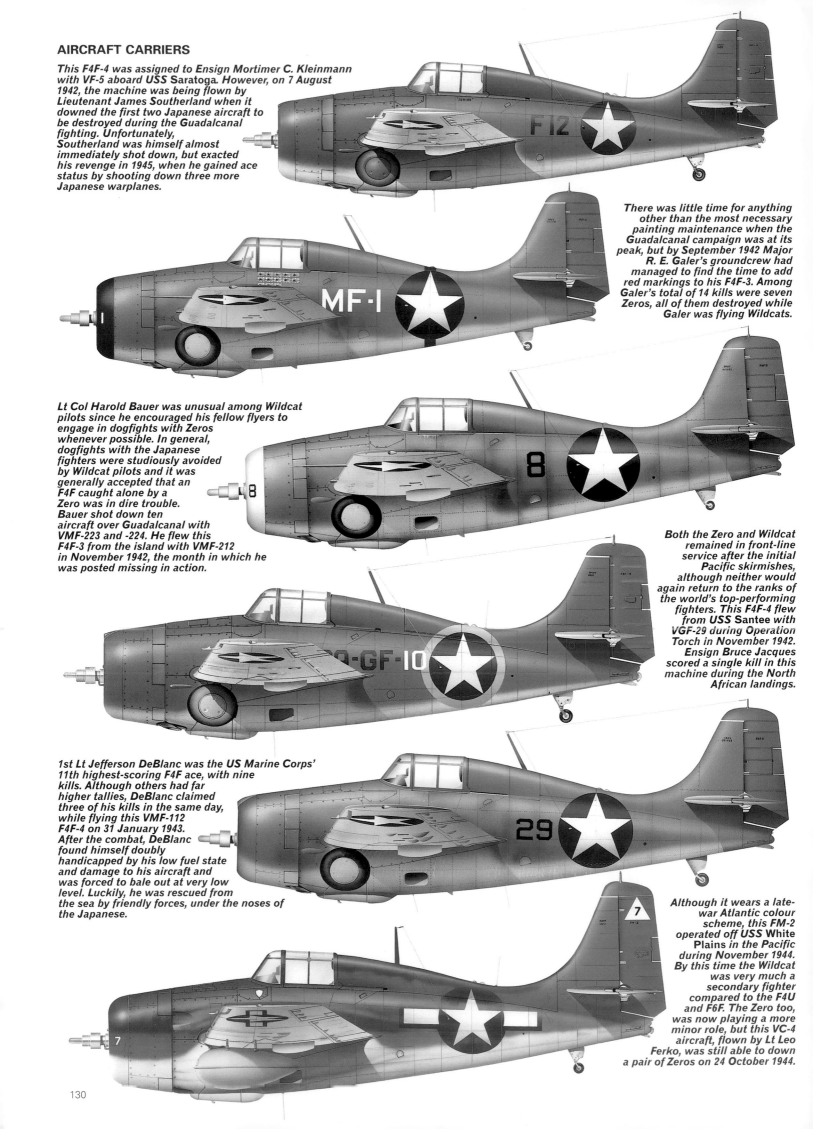

Combat comparison

WEAPONS AND STORES

Standard armament for the A6M2 Type 21 was a hard-hitting combination of two 20-mm cannon and a pair of 7.7-mm (0.303-in) machine-guns. In Europe, the RAF had already discovered that small-calibre machine-guns lacked the punch to penetrate armoured aircraft structures and self-sealing fuel tanks and efforts had been made to get the 20-mm Hispano cannon onto the Hurricane and Spitfire. Conversely, the Japanese, like the Germans, had realised that cannon armament would offer great advantages in combat. The Americans had not considered cannon armament, but usually opted for larger-calibre machine-guns than the British, however, and the early Wildcats carried a pair of 0.5-in (12.7-mm) machine-guns in each wing. The heavier weight of the 0.5-in ammunition compared to the British 0.303-in gave it relatively good penetrating power, while the Zero's lack of armour often meant that just a few hits from the US Navy fighter was enough for a kill.

PERFORMANCE AND MANOEUVRABILITY

In June 1942, the US military carried out exhaustive tests on an A6M2 (above right) that had force-landed in the Aleutians. The tests confirmed that the aircraft did indeed have superb manoeuvrability and in the hands of an experienced pilot was a formidable weapon. It was found to be surprisingly slow in the roll however, and was slow to accelerate in the dive. This last deficiency sent a number of Zeros and their pilots to a fiery grave, as pilots attempted to disengage from enemy fighters by diving and were picked off as their aircraft struggled to gain speed. The Wildcat could not match the manoeuvrability of the Zero and was best used as an air-defence fighter, punching through an attacking force's escort fighters in a diving attack in order to hit the bombers below.

PILOT AND SYSTEMS PROTECTION

Wherever possible, F4F pilots tried to avoid getting into a turning dogfight with Zeros. If combat was joined, the superior hitting power and manoeuvrability of the Zero often told, although the Wildcat was capable of taking far more punishment than the Zero. A concerted effort was usually required to bring down a Wildcat, while the Zero was desperately vulnerable in all areas to the Wildcat's guns. Since the Zero was without armour, enemy rounds had a much greater chance of penetrating its skin to reach vital aircraft structures, and in the case of the fuel tanks this was almost certain to cause major damage. As a further weight-saving measure, in order to achieve long range, it had been decided that self-sealing fuel tanks would not be used. Self-sealing tanks employ a system such that a punctured tank wall is resealed, avoiding fuel spillage and lessening the chances of fire. The lack of self-sealing tanks further added to the Zero's woeful vulnerability. The vulnerability problem was further added to by the later addition of centreline drop tanks (above right). The Zero pilot was also completely unprotected, sitting as he did under a canopy of plain glass and behind

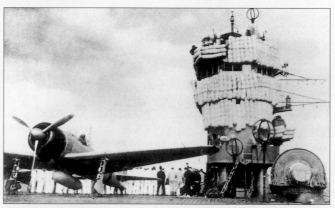

a non-armoured windscreen. There was no protection for the Zero's engine, nor for the fuel tanks. This could be especially worrying for the pilot, since the main fuel tank was located between the engine and cockpit.

F6F Hellcat
Premier US Navy fighter

As undoubtedly the most important US Navy fighter of the war, Grumman's F6F Hellcat played an invaluable role in wresting air supremacy over the Pacific from the Japanese. It also performed sterling work in the ground-attack and close-support roles and although it was not as advanced as the Vought F4U Corsair, it combined everything the Navy fighter pilot needed in a rugged and available airframe.

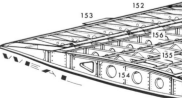

F6F-5 Hellcat
Cutaway key
1 Radio mast
2 Rudder balance
3 Rudder upper hinge
4 Aluminium alloy fin ribs
5 Rudder post
6 Rudder structure
7 Rudder trim tab
8 Rudder middle hinge
9 Diagonal stiffeners
10 Aluminium alloy elevator trim tab
11 Fabric-covered (and taped) elevator surfaces
12 Elevator balance
13 Flush-riveted leading-edge strip
14 Arrester hook (extended)
15 Tailplane ribs
16 Tail navigation (running) light
17 Rudder lower hinge
18 Arrester hook (stowed)
19 Fin main spar lower cut-out
20 Tailplane end rib
21 Fin forward spar
22 Fuselage/finroot fairing
23 Port elevator
24 Aluminium alloy-skinned tailplane
25 Section light
26 Fuselage aft frame
27 Control access
28 Bulkhead
29 Tailwheel hydraulic shock-absorber
30 Tailwheel centring mechanism
31 Tailwheel steel mounting arm
32 Rearward-retracting tailwheel (hard rubber tyre)
33 Fairing

34 Steel plate door fairing
35 Tricing sling support tube
36 Hydraulic actuating cylinder
37 Flanged ring fuselage frames
38 Control cable runs
39 Fuselage longerons
40 Relay box
41 Dorsal rod antenna
42 Dorsal recognition light
43 Radio aerial
44 Radio mast
45 Aerial lead-in
46 Dorsal frame stiffeners
47 Junction box
48 Radio equipment (upper rack)
49 Radio shelf
50 Control cable runs
51 Transverse brace
52 Remote radio compass
53 Ventral recognition lights (three)
54 Ventral rod antenna
55 Destructor device
56 Accumulator
57 Radio equipment (lower rack)
58 Entry hand/footholds
59 Engine water injection tank
60 Canopy track
61 Water filler neck
62 Rear-view window
63 Rearward-sliding cockpit canopy (open)
64 Headrest
65 Pilot's head/shoulder armour
66 Canopy sill (reinforced)
67 Fire extinguisher
68 Oxygen bottle (port fuselage wall)
69 Water tank mounting

70 Underfloor self-sealing

fuel tank (227 litres/ 60 US gal)
71 Armoured bulkhead
72 Starboard console
73 Pilot's seat
74 Hydraulic handpump
75 Fuel filler cap and neck
76 Rudder pedals
77 Central console
78 Control column
79 Chart board (horizontal stowage)
80 Instrument panel
81 Panel coaming
82 Reflector gunsight
83 Rear-view mirror
84 Armoured glass windshield
85 Deflection plate (pilot's forward protection)
86 Main bulkhead (armour-plated upper section with hoisting sling attachments port and starboard)
87 Aluminium alloy aileron trim tab
88 Fabric-covered (and taped) aileron surfaces
89 Flush-riveted outer wing skin
90 Aluminium alloy sheet wing tip (riveted to wing outer rib)
91 Port navigation (running) light
92 Formed leading-edge (approach/landing light and camera gun inboard)
93 Fixed cowling panel
94 Armour plate (oil tank forward protection)
95 Oil tank (72 litres/ 19 US gal)
96 Welded engine mount fittings
97 Fuselage forward bulkhead

98 Aileron control linkage
99 Engine accessories bay
100 Engine mounting frame (hydraulic fluid reservoir attached to port frames)
101 Controllable cooling gills
102 Cowling ring (removable servicing/access panels)
103 Pratt & Whitney R-2800-10W twin-row radial air-cooled engine
104 Nose ring profile
105 Reduction gear housing
106 Three-bladed Hamilton Standard Hydromatic controllable-pitch propeller
107 Propeller hub
108 Engine oil cooler (centre) and supercharger intercooler
109 Oil cooler deflection plate under protection
110 Oil cooler duct
111 Intercooler intake duct
112 Mainwheel fairing
113 Port mainwheel
114 Auxiliary tank support/ attachment arms
115 Cooler outlet and fairing
116 Exhaust cluster
117 Supercharger housing
118 Exhaust outlet scoop
119 Wing front spar web
120 Wing front spar/fuselage attachment bolts

121 Undercarriage mounting/pivot point on front spar
122 Inter-spar self-sealing fuel tanks (port and starboard: 331 litres (87.5 US gal) each)
123 Wing rear spar/fuselage attachment bolts
124 Structural end rib
125 Slotted wing flap profile
126 Wing flap centre-section

127 Wing fold line
128 Starboard wheel well (doubler-plate reinforced edges)
129 Gun bay

SPECIFICATION

F6F-5 Hellcat

Dimensions

Wing span: 13.08 m (42 ft 10 in)
Wing span (wings folded): 4.93 m (16 ft 2 in)
Length: 10.23 m (33 ft 7 in)
Height: 3.99 m (13 ft 1 in)
Wing area: 31.03 m² (334 sq ft)
Wing loading: 410.87 kg/m² (38.17 lb/sq ft)

Powerplant

One 1641-kW (2,200-hp) Pratt & Whitney R-2800-10W Double Wasp 18-cylinder radial piston engine

Weights

Empty: 4152 to 4191 kg (9,153 to 9,239 lb)
Normal take-off: 5670 kg (12,500 lb)
Maximum take-off: 6991 kg (15,413 lb)

Fuel

Internal fuel: 946 litres (250 US gal)

External fuel: 568 litres (150 US gal)

Performance

Maximum speed at medium altitude: 621 km/h (386 mph)
Initial climb rate (clean): 1039 m (3,410 ft) per minute
Service ceiling: 11369 m (37,300 ft)
Cruising speed: 270 km/h (168 mph)
Time to 6096 m (20,000 ft): 7 minutes 30 seconds

Range

Range on internal fuel: 1674 km (1,040 miles)

Armament

Six 0.5-in (12.7-mm) Browning machine-guns each with 400 rounds, plus provision for two or three bombs up to a maximum total of 907 kg (2,000 lb), plus up to six 5-in (127-mm) High Velocity Aircraft Rockets (HVARs)

Above: With the mission over, there was still the challenge of landing back, although the Hellcat's tough construction made it more survivable than some aircraft during the inevitable landing accidents, such as this main landing gear collapse.

Left: VF-12 Hellcats are pictured leaving USS Randolph (CV-15) for a raid on Japan in July 1945. Air Group 12 was something of a 'crack' fighter unit, with its ranks swelled by former VF-9 'Fighting Nine' aces, including Hamilton McWhorter, Armistead M. Smith, Reuben Denoff, John M. Franks and Harold Vita. By the end of the Pacific war, Randolph was carrying the Hellcats of VF-16.

130 Removable diagonal brace strut
131 Three 0.5-in (12.7-mm) Colt Browning machine-guns
132 Auxiliary tank aft support
133 Blast tubes
134 Folding wing joint (upper surface)
135 Machine-gun barrels
136 Fairing
137 Undercarriage actuating strut
138 Mainwheel leg oleo hydraulic shock strut
139 Auxiliary tank sling/brace
140 Long-range auxiliary fuel tank (jettisonable)
141 Mainwheel aluminium alloy fairing
142 Forged steel torque link
143 Low pressure balloon tyre
144 Cast magnesium wheel
145 Underwing 5-in (127-cm) air-to-ground RP
146 Mark V zero-length rocket launcher installation
147 Canted wing front spar
148 Inter-spar ammunition box bay (lower surface access)
149 Wing rear spar (normal to plane of wing)
150 Rear sub spar
151 Wing flap outer-section
152 Frise-type aileron
153 Aileron balance tab
154 Wing outer rib
155 Wing lateral stiffeners
156 Aileron spar
157 Wing outer-section ribs
158 Leading-edge rib cut-outs
159 Starboard navigation (running) light
160 Pitot head
161 Underwing stores pylon (mounted on fixed centre-section inboard of mainwheel leg)
162 Auxiliary fuel tank

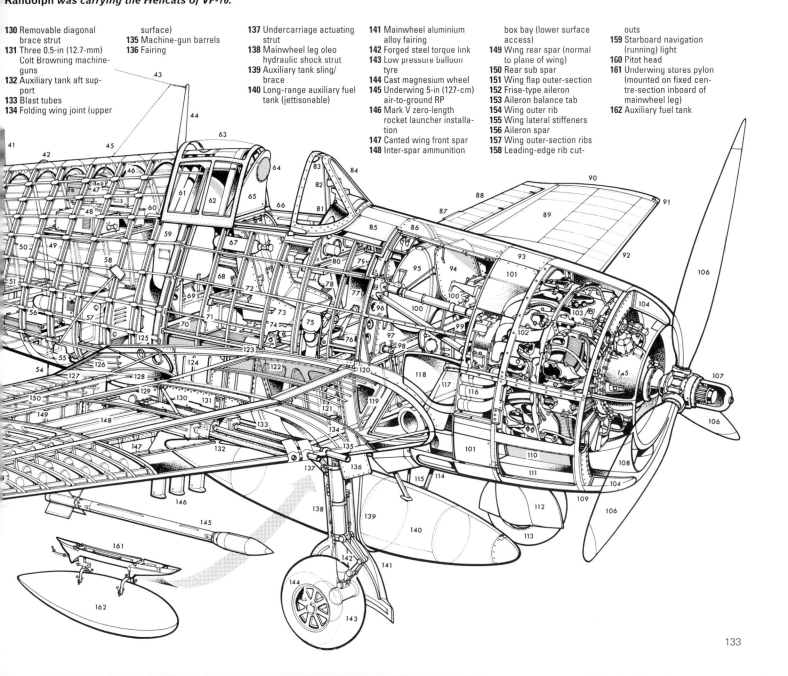

F6F-5 Hellcat

This F6F-5 is shown in a typical late-war Hellcat colour scheme, with no obvious markings to denote its unit or carrier. The aircraft is equipped for an attack mission – ground-attack and close-support operations becoming increasingly important for the type as the war progressed. Note that the light areas on the front view show the position of the folded wings.

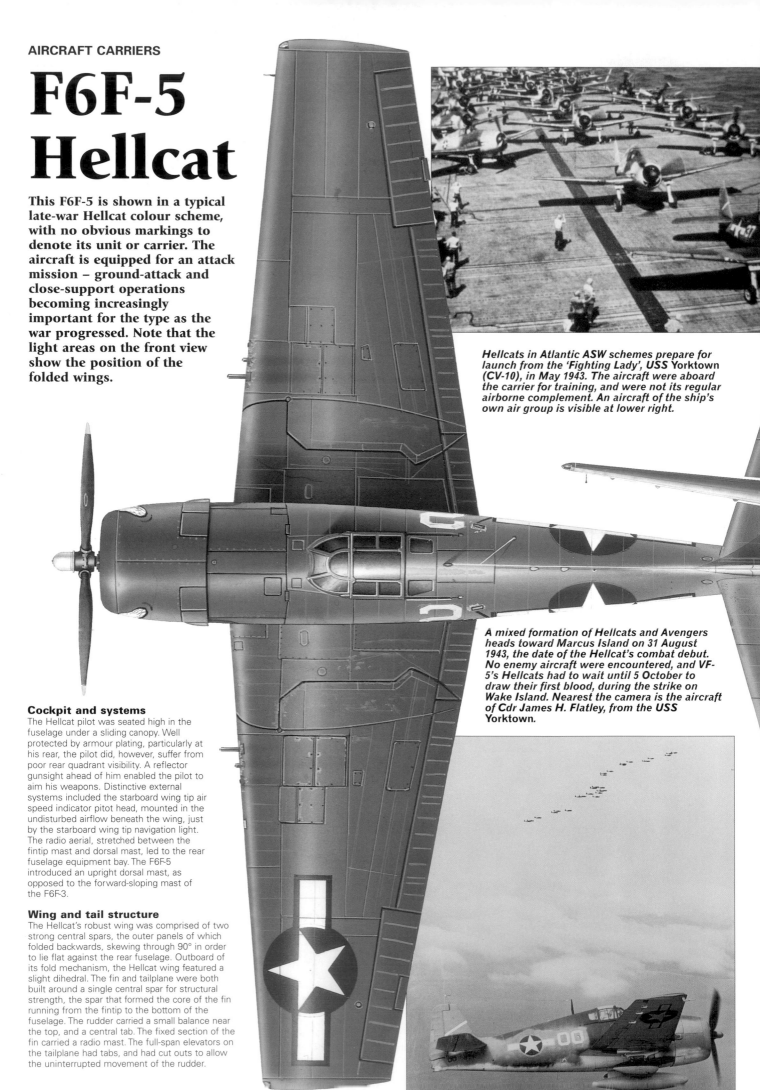

Hellcats in Atlantic ASW schemes prepare for launch from the 'Fighting Lady', USS Yorktown (CV-10), in May 1943. The aircraft were aboard the carrier for training, and were not its regular airborne complement. An aircraft of the ship's own air group is visible at lower right.

A mixed formation of Hellcats and Avengers heads toward Marcus Island on 31 August 1943, the date of the Hellcat's combat debut. No enemy aircraft were encountered, and VF-5's Hellcats had to wait until 5 October to draw their first blood, during the strike on Wake Island. Nearest the camera is the aircraft of Cdr James H. Flatley, from the USS Yorktown.

Cockpit and systems

The Hellcat pilot was seated high in the fuselage under a sliding canopy. Well protected by armour plating, particularly at his rear, the pilot did, however, suffer from poor rear quadrant visibility. A reflector gunsight ahead of him enabled the pilot to aim his weapons. Distinctive external systems included the starboard wing tip air speed indicator pitot head, mounted in the undisturbed airflow beneath the wing, just by the starboard wing tip navigation light. The radio aerial, stretched between the fintip mast and dorsal mast, led to the rear fuselage equipment bay. The F6F-5 introduced an upright dorsal mast, as opposed to the forward-sloping mast of the F6F-3.

Wing and tail structure

The Hellcat's robust wing was comprised of two strong central spars, the outer panels of which folded backwards, skewing through 90° in order to lie flat against the rear fuselage. Outboard of its fold mechanism, the Hellcat wing featured a slight dihedral. The fin and tailplane were both built around a single central spar for structural strength, the spar that formed the core of the fin running from the fintip to the bottom of the fuselage. The rudder carried a small balance near the top, and a central tab. The fixed section of the fin carried a radio mast. The full-span elevators on the tailplane had tabs, and had cut outs to allow the uninterrupted movement of the rudder.

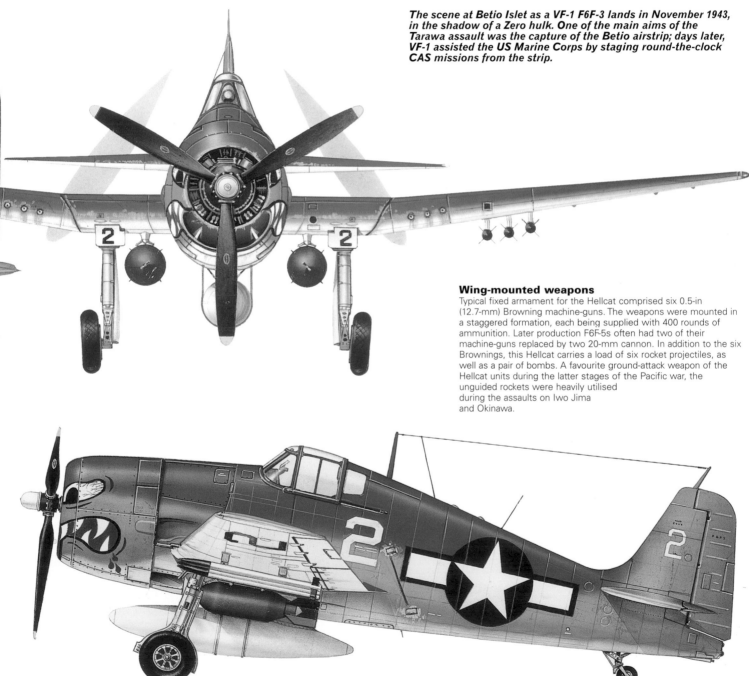

The scene at Betio Islet as a VF-1 F6F-3 lands in November 1943, in the shadow of a Zero hulk. One of the main aims of the Tarawa assault was the capture of the Betio airstrip; days later, VF-1 assisted the US Marine Corps by staging round-the-clock CAS missions from the strip.

Wing-mounted weapons

Typical fixed armament for the Hellcat comprised six 0.5-in (12.7-mm) Browning machine-guns. The weapons were mounted in a staggered formation, each being supplied with 400 rounds of ammunition. Later production F6F-5s often had two of their machine-guns replaced by two 20-mm cannon. In addition to the six Brownings, this Hellcat carries a load of six rocket projectiles, as well as a pair of bombs. A favourite ground-attack weapon of the Hellcat units during the latter stages of the Pacific war, the unguided rockets were heavily utilised during the assaults on Iwo Jima and Okinawa.

Powerplant

The F6F-5 Hellcat was powered by a single Pratt & Whitney R-2800-10W Double Wasp radial engine, with two rows of nine cylinders each. Developing 1641 kW (2,200 hp), the unit was angled down by 3° to allow for the fitting of a zero-incidence wing. The engine drove a three-bladed Hamilton Standard Hydromatic controllable-pitch propeller, mounted ahead of a reduction gear housing. Internal self-sealing fuel tanks under the cockpit and in the inner wing structure carried a total of 889 litres (235 US gal). The tanks were filled through fuselage side and wingroot caps.

Fleet Air Arm operations

The UK's Hellcats logged 52 kills during World War II, from an FAA total of 455. The aircraft quickly came to prominence when providing top cover for strikes against the German battleship *Tirpitz*, and other anti-shipping operations around Scandinavia.

Above: The Fleet Air Arm operated 252 Lend-Lease Hellcats (initially known as Gannet Mk I aircraft), comprising four different variants, and they served with 37 different squadrons. The Hellcat Mk I (shown above) was essentially the same as the USN's F6F-3; the Mk II (later F.Mk II) was the FAA-operated F6F-5; the Mk II(NF)/NF.Mk II was the FAA designation for the F6F-5N night-fighter; and the Hellcat Mk II(PR)/PR.Mk II was based on the camera-equipped FR.Mk II, with all armament removed for high-speed reconnaissance.

Above: Hellcats prepare for Operation Dragoon, the invasion of southern France, in Malta in August 1944. Nearest the camera on the deck of HMS Emperor are JV134 and JV154 of No. 800 Squadron. JV134 was lost in a collision with another Hellcat aboard Emperor on 23 August 1944, and JV154 (previously of No. 804 Squadron until it was absorbed by No. 800 in June 1944) had survived the Operation Tungsten strikes on Tirpitz and other later Norwegian operations.

Above: A snow squall sweeps across the deck of the escort carrier Emperor, prior to the Tirpitz attack of April 1944. Crossing the Arctic circle, Emperor was part of a force of ships from the British Home Fleet that struck Tirpitz in Alten Fjord, leaving it blazing.

Left: HMS Emperor is surrounded by other ships that saw action during the Tirpitz attack, including HMS Furious (nearest), Searcher, Pursuer and Jamaica. No. 804 Squadron claimed Bf 109s and an Fw 190, as well as an He 115 seaplane during May 1944, with Lt-Cdr Stanley G. Orr, its CO, becoming an ace. As well as providing fighter cover for Barracudas and Avengers, FAA Hellcats carried bomb racks following the successful raids on the battleship Tirpitz.

Right: Most famous for their role in the attack on Tirpitz during April 1944, FAA Hellcats were operational in Norwegian waters for a further two months, tasked with escort duties on ASV strikes. Later, HMS Emperor's Hellcats were taken to the Mediterranean for the invasion of southern France in August 1944. No. 800 Sqn was the first FAA Hellcat operator, taking its first deliveries in July 1943.

Left: FAA Hellcats served in the North Atlantic and Mediterranean theatres, and in September 1945 those of No. 800 Squadron sailed to Singapore in order to restore British rule. Hellcats were involved in operations throughout the East Indies, Malaya, Burma, and in the assault on Japan.

Below: A Hellcat F.Mk II of No. 1884 Squadron, JZ935 was lost in a crash-landing after failing to take the correct wire and ending up in the safety barrier aboard HMS Indomitable, in the East Indies on 5 August 1945.

Battle of the Atlantic: The carriers triumph

By the spring of 1943 the Allies were suffering unsustainable losses to Admiral Doenitz's 'wolf packs'. However, by the year's end, improved airborne radar, growing numbers of long-range patrol aircraft and, most importantly, the advent of escort carriers helped to decimate the U-boat force.

This remarkable shift in fortunes, which gave the Allies the initiative in the Battle of the Atlantic, took many months to achieve. The first major triumph took place in May 1943, when an unsurpassed total of U-boats (41) was sunk. RAF and the US Navy maritime aircraft scored several successes during the month, but it was the appearance of escort and light carriers that set the seal on Doenitz's attempts to restore the balance at sea.

Bitter battles

Land-based maritime aircraft began to take such a toll on the U-boats as they transited to their operational areas that on 24 May 1943 Doenitz ordered them south to get away from the troublesome North Atlantic and the Bay of

Biscay. Two days later, the 17-strong U-boat Gruppe lined up from north to south along the 43° West meridian athwart the crowded sea lanes from North America to the Mediterranean. But the US Navy was ready. In addition to USS *Bogue*, USS *Card* went on its first convoy escort mission. The escort pattern provided by the TBF-1s and Wildcats consisted of round-the-clock surveillance up to 400 km (250 miles) ahead and to the sides of the convoys. *Bogue* took up station with a westbound convoy on 1 June, and scored against the Gruppe on 5 June, when *U-217* was located some 101 km (63 miles) north west of the carrier and sunk by a TBF assisted by a Wildcat. One week later, *Bogue* sank *U-118* south west of the Azores. Four more U-boat kills went down in the Bay of Biscay as more and more sea escorts ventured into this area, following Doenitz's withdrawal from the North Atlantic. U-boat crews were now fighting stoutly with their AA guns in actions that were costly to both sides.

American CVE groups continued to operate in the central sector of the Atlantic into October 1943. On 4 October VC-9, based in USS *Card*,

Equipped with Avengers to attack marauding U-Boats and F4F Wildcats (seen here) to counter attacks by Luftwaffe patrol aircraft, US Navy and Royal Navy (illustrated) escort carriers made a major impact in reducing the horrendous losses suffered by Allied shipping in the Atlantic.

sank *U-460* and *U-422* to the north of the Azores. USS *Card* followed up its success with *U-402* on 13 October and *U-584* on the last day of October, while in the meantime, USS *Block Island* despatched *U-220* off Flemish Cap on 28 October. In desperation Doenitz ordered direct transit across the Bay of Biscay in order to avoid the land-based aircraft, but this only served to get the U-boats more speedily into the clutches of the carriers.

After the loss of 19 U-boats in November, bad weather and aggressive Luftwaffe fighter activity brought actions to a reduced state, but by the end of 1943, the sinkings of Allied merchant vessels were down to an average of 30 per month, representing about 130,000 tons. These figures, when compared to the grotesque losses of March 1943 when the Allies lost 120 ships (693,389 tons), give ample indication of the extent of Doenitz's defeat.

*Serving aboard both **US Navy** and **Royal Navy** escort carriers, the Grumman Avenger proved deadly in the anti-U-boat role. This example served with No. 846 Squadron, FAA at Machrihanish.*

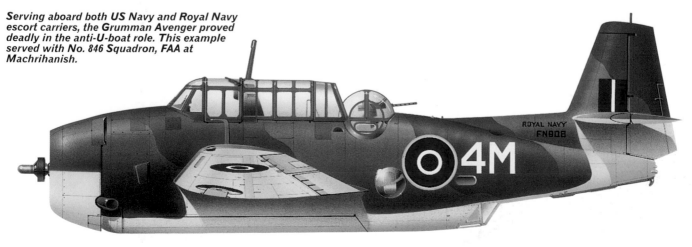

TBM-3 Avenger

A TBM-3 built by Eastern Aircraft, this Avenger served with Torpedo Squadron 4 (VT-4), Air Group 4 (CVG-4), aboard USS *Essex* and is seen as it appeared on 12 January 1945. VT-4 was established on 10 January 1942, on the deck of USS *Ranger* (CV-4) while it was in Bermuda. Operations began with the Douglas TBD-1 Devastator, before transition to the TBF-1 Avenger in August 1942. VT-4's Avengers saw action in October 1943 when *Ranger* was deployed as part of Operation Leader, and VT-4 Avengers attacked German shipping along the Norwegian coast in the first US Navy carrier strike in northern Europe. In July 1944 Air Group 4 (including VT-4) moved to the Pacific, entering combat on 11 November 1944 in support of General MacArthur's return to the Philippines, from the deck of *Bunker Hill* (CV-17). In the ensuing days the squadron's Avengers struck targets at Ormoc Bay, Cavite and Clark Field. In late November 1944 the Avengers of VT-4 transferred to USS *Essex* (CV-9) which was promptly damaged by a kamikaze attack off the Philippines before the Avengers had seen action from their new carrier. In January 1945 the repaired carrier received VT-4's TBM-3 Avengers in time for a series of strikes against Western Pacific and Indochinese targets.

Crew

Three crew manned a typical TBM-3: a pilot, radio operator and bombardier. The pilot was housed in a separate cockpit, while the rear portion of the 'glasshouse' contained the radioman and his Grumman 150SE turret, with a 0.5-in (12.7-mm) machine-gun. The rest of the crew compartment consisted of the so-called 'tunnel' in which the bombardier manned a 0.3-in (7.62-mm) machine-gun in the ventral 'stinger' position. The bombardier's main piece of equipment was a Norden bombsight, fitted to early Avengers in an unusual position, sighted through a transparency aft of the weapons bay. He also had a scope for the aircraft's Air-to-Surface Type B (ASB) radar set, the moveable receivers for which (Yagi antennas) were fitted beneath each wing.

The bombsight was deleted in late-production TBM-3s as horizontal bombing was found to be ineffective against manoeuvring ships and less accurate than glide-bombing when attacking smaller land targets and ships at anchor. The radioman then manned the 'stinger' gun, while a dedicated gunner operated the turret. The pilot was able to use a 0.5-in (12.7-mm) machine-gun in each wing to strafe targets.

Powerplant

Although consideration was given to fitting a 1491-kW (2,000-hp) Pratt & Whitney R-2800 Double Wasp to the TBM-3, Wright's R-2600-20 Cyclone 14, rated at 1417 kW (1,900 hp), was chosen instead, replacing the 1193-kW (1,600-hp) R-2600-8 of the previous production variant, the TBM-1C. A new engine was necessary to counter the marginal performance of the aircraft at normal gross weights, especially when operating from the small decks of escort carriers. The increased cooling requirements of the new variant necessitated some redesign of its cowling: multiple cowl flaps and an oil cooler intake on the lower lip were new features. The R-2600 – a 14-cylinder, twin-bank derivative of Wright's 1920s-vintage nine-cylinder R-1750/-1820 Cyclone – also powered the Curtiss SB2C Helldiver and, as such, is often described as one of America's 'war-winning' powerplant designs. More than 50,000 were built at Wright's Cincinnati plant.

Torpedo

The Mk XIII 'ring-tailed' torpedo was developed by modifying the standard Mk XIII-1A with a 25.4-cm (10-in) steel band welded around the fins. These were first used in August 1944 by VT-13 from aboard USS *Franklin*, west of Iwo Jima. Compared to the unmodified torpedoes, which had to be dropped within a speed range of 185-204 km/h (115-126 mph), and a height of 30.5 m (100 ft), the 'ring tails' could be released from as high as 244 m (800 ft) and as fast as 519 km/h (321 mph). The Mk XIII was designed for aircraft use in about 1938. It had a greater diameter (22.4 in; 569 mm) than the standard 21-in (533-mm) naval torpedo, a steam turbine engine producing 71 kW (95 bhp), a weight of 1383 kg (3,050 lb), and a theoretical maximum speed and range of 85 km/h (53 mph) and 8230 m (27,000 ft), respectively.

No fewer than 19 Fleet Air Arm squadrons received Corsairs, with a total of 1,977 being built for the Royal Navy. This Corsair Mk II's long-range underfuselage fuel tank has burst into flames, having come adrift following a heavy landing.

Engines running, Avengers share the deckspace of USS Yorktown (CV-5) with Grumman Hellcats, preparing for a mass launch. The machines' green hub fairings were a hallmark of Yorktown's air group. One TBF Avenger retains national insignia atop the starboard wing. Yorktown was sunk in June 1942, when deployed to the battle zone at Midway.

12 January 1945

On 12 January 1945, 12 TBM-3s, loaded with torpedoes, roared off *Essex's* flight deck to attack shipping on the Saigon River near Cap St Jacques. Among the pilots was Ensign William H. Cannady, a relatively new pilot to VT-4, flying aircraft number '131' (TBM-3 BuNo. 68417). On this occasion, he shared his aircraft with just one other crew member, Aviation Radioman Third Class (ARM3c) J. C. Gerke. The 'torpeckers' encountered a convoy of merchantmen and their escorts which, along with the shore installations, began filling the sky with intense AA fire. Jinking as they approached the release point at an altitude of 76 m (250 ft), the Avengers dropped their weapons. Cannady's torpedo combined with those of two of his squadron mates to finish off a merchant vessel.

Bombloads

As a glide- or skip-bomber, the Avenger carried a variety of weapons according to mission, but typical stores included one 2,000-lb (907-kg) general-purpose (GP), one 1,600-lb (726-kg) armour-piercing (AP), two 1,000-lb (454-kg) GP, four 500-lb (227-kg) GP, 12 100-lb (45-kg) GP or four 350-lb (159-kg) depth bombs. The latter was the primary anti-submarine weapon used by the Avenger, along with newly developed aircraft rockets. Rockets were introduced in late 1943, initially in 3.5-in (8.8-cm) form and later with 5-in (12.7-cm) calibre warheads. In early 1944, the first 5-in (12.7-cm) High Velocity Aircraft Rockets (HVARs) were used in combat; they were nicknamed 'Holy Moses'.

Grumman TBF/TBM Avenger Torpedo-bomber

This Grumman TBF Avenger is shown in the markings of the USS Randolf Air Group, 1944. The armament in the dorsal turret was one 0.5-calibre machine-gun.

Destined to become one of the best shipborne torpedo-bombers of the war, the **Grumman TBF Avenger** first saw combat during the great Battle of Midway. The **XTBF-1** prototype was first flown on 1 August 1941 after an order for 286 aircraft had already been placed. The first **TBF-1** aircraft appeared in January 1942 and VT-8 ('Torpedo-Eight') received its first aircraft during the following May.

Combat debut

During June, six of VT-8's aircraft were launched at the height of the Battle of Midway, but only one returned – and this with one dead gunner and the other wounded. Despite this inauspicious start, production was accelerating as General Motors undertook production in addition to Grumman, producing the **TBM-1** version. Sub-variants included the **TBF-1C** with two 20-mm cannon in the wings, the **TBF-1B** which was supplied to the UK under Lend-Lease, the **TBF-1D** and **TBF-1E** with ASV radar, and the **TBF-1L** with a searchlight in the bomb bay. Production of the TBF-1 and TBM-1, as well as sub-variants, was 2,290 and 2,882 respectively. General Motors (Eastern Division) went on to produce some 4,664 **TBM-3** aircraft with R-2600-20 engines, and the sub-variants corresponded with those of the TBF-1. The UK received 395 TBF-1Bs and 526 **TBM-3B** aircraft, and New Zealand 43. The **TBM-3P** camera-equipped aircraft and the **TBM-3H** with search radar were the final wartime versions, although the Avenger went on to serve with the US Navy until 1954.

Avengers replaced the hopelessly outclassed Devastator on the torpedo squadrons from 1942 onwards. This Avenger is seen on a practice torpedo run.

Fairey Albacore Biplane torpedo-bomber

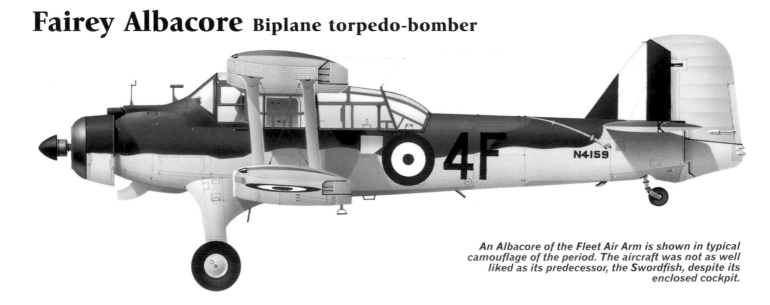

An Albacore of the Fleet Air Arm is shown in typical camouflage of the period. The aircraft was not as well liked as its predecessor, the Swordfish, despite its enclosed cockpit.

Inevitably called the 'Applecore', the Albacore gave good if undistinguished service, especially in North Africa and the Mediterranean. This aircraft is seen dropping a practice 18-in (457-mm) torpedo.

SPECIFICATION	
Fairey Albacore **Type:** three-crew naval torpedo-bomber **Powerplant:** one 794-kW (1,065-hp) Bristol Taurus II radial piston engine **Performance:** maximum speed 259 km/h (161 mph) at 2134 m (7,000 ft); climb to 1829 m (6,000 ft) in 8 minutes; service ceiling 6309 m (20,700 ft); range 1320 km (820 miles) **Weights:** empty 3266 kg	(7,200 lb); maximum take-off 5715 kg (12,600 lb) **Dimensions:** wing span 15.24 m (50 ft); length 12.13 m (39 ft 9½ in); height 4.65 m (15 ft 3 in); wing area 57.88 m² (623 sq ft) **Armament:** one forward-firing 0.303-in (7.7-mm) Vickers machine-gun and two 0.303-in (7.7-mm) Vickers 'K' machine-guns in the rear cockpit, plus one 18-in (457-mm) torpedo or up to 907 kg (2,000 lb) of bombs

Wholly eclipsed by the Swordfish, which it was intended to replace, the **Fairey Albacore** was in essence a cleaned-up version of the celebrated 'Stringbag', with an enclosed cabin to improve the operational efficiency of the crew and a Bristol Taurus radial to provide higher performance despite considerably greater weights. First flown in December 1938, the initial prototype was fitted with a wheeled landing gear, while

the second had twin floats. The Albacore, which was inevitably called the 'Applecore' in service, differed from the Swordfish in being used operationally only on the wheeled type of landing gear.

Into service
The type entered service with the Royal Navy's Fleet Air Arm in 1940, and production amounted to 798 aircraft. The Albacore was first flown in action during

attacks on Boulogne in September 1940. Most Albacores were land-based throughout their careers, but the type's brief moment of glory arrived when the Albacores from the carrier HMS *Formidable* severely damaged the Italian battleship *Vittorio Veneto* during the Battle of Cape Matapan in March 1941. After this time the Albacore was occasionally used for bombing in the Western Desert, usually at night to prevent

the depredations of Axis fighters, and the type played an important part in the operations leading up to the Battle of Alamein in October 1942. In carrier operations the Albacore saw service in the North Atlantic, Arctic, Mediterranean and Indian

oceans; and the type was also used with some success as a support aircraft during seaborne invasions, notably those of Sicily, Italy and northern France, the last aircraft being in the hands of Royal Canadian Air Force squadrons.

Fairey Barracuda Torpedo-bomber and recce aircraft

Complete with anti-submarine radar and underwing depth bombs, this Barracuda Mk II flew with the FAA's No. 785 Sqn on training duties.

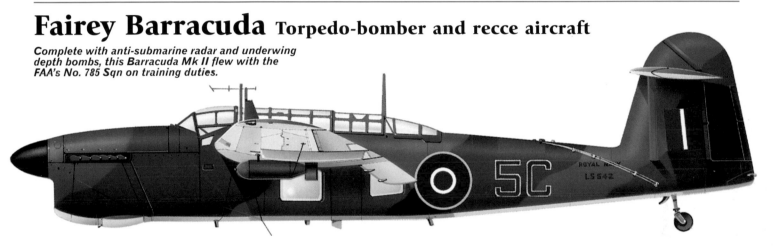

Intended to replace the Albacore, itself a replacement for the Swordfish, the **Fairey Barracuda** was an altogether more advanced aircraft conceptually, and was designed as a high-performance monoplane to meet a 1937 requirement. The intended powerplant was the Rolls-Royce Exe, and the programme was delayed substantially when this engine was abandoned

and the structure had to be revised to accommodate a Merlin engine from the same manufacturer.

Overweight
Thus the Barracuda prototype did not fly until 7 December 1940, and it was immediately apparent that the performance of the heavy Barracuda would be limited by the power available: the 940-kW (1,260-hp)

Merlin XXX in the **Barracuda Mk I** and the 1223-kW (1,640-hp) Merlin 32 for the **Barracuda Mk II** and **Barracuda Mk III**. At a time when production priorities were afforded mostly to the RAF, deliveries of the Barracuda to the Fleet Air Arm were slow to start, and it was January 1943 before Barracuda Is began to enter service with the Fleet Air Arm. The

Barracuda Mk I was little more than a service-test type, only 23 being built. The two main wartime models were thus the Barracuda Mk II with ASV Mk IIN radar (1,635 built by Fairey, Blackburn, Boulton Paul and Westland) and the Barracuda Mk III torpedo-reconnaissance version with ASV Mk X radar (912

built by the parent company). The Barracuda saw limited service in home waters, the high point of its career being a highly successful strike on the German battleship *Tirpitz* in April 1944; but in the Pacific campaigns of 1944 and 1945 the Barracuda was one of the more prominent British aircraft.

SPECIFICATION	
Fairey Barracuda Mk II **Type:** three-crew shipborne torpedo and dive-bomber **Powerplant:** one 1223-kW (1,640-hp) Rolls-Royce Merlin 32 V-12 piston engine **Performance:** maximum speed 367 km/h (228 mph) at 533 m (1,750 ft); climb to 1524 m (5,000 ft) in six minutes; service ceiling 5060 m (16,600 ft); range 1851 km (1,150 miles) **Weights:** empty 4241 kg (9,350 lb);	maximum take-off 6396 kg (14,100 lb) **Dimensions:** wing span 14.99 m (49 ft 2 in); length 12.12 m (39 ft 9 in); height 4.6 m (15 ft 1 in); wing area 34.09 m² (367 sq ft) **Armament:** two 0.303-in (7.7-mm) Vickers 'K' machine-guns in the rear cockpit, plus one 1,620-lb (735-kg) torpedo, or four 450-lb (204-kg) depth charges, or six 250-lb (113-kg) bombs

Altogether more advanced than the Albacore, the Barracuda was delayed by difficulties with engine mounting. When it did reach service in January 1943, the aircraft acquitted itself well, especially during the attacks on Tirpitz.

Fairey Firefly Late-war, two-seat naval fighter

Numbered among the most successful aircraft ever used by the Fleet Air Arm, the **Fairey Firefly** served in its various versions for nearly 15 years, a total of 1,702 being produced before production ceased in 1956. The prototype took to the air on 22 December 1941, and the first production **Firefly F.Mk I** entered service in March 1943. Later production Mk Is were fitted with ASH (air-to-surface H) radar, in which form they became **Firefly FR.Mk I** reconnaissance fighters. Some aircraft were produced as **Firefly NF.Mk I** night fighters equipped with a different radio for night flying, and with shrouded exhausts. Another night-fighter version, the **Firefly NF.MK II**, had AI.Mk X radar whose antennas were housed in radomes on each wing,

while the **Firefly F.Mk IA** was a modification of the Mk I brought up to FR.Mk I standard by the addition of ASH radar. A trial modifica-

tion with a Griffon 61 and a nose radiator was designated **Firefly F.Mk 3**, but this was superseded by the **Firefly FR.Mk 4** reconnais-

sance fighter with a Griffon 74 engine. This went into service in 1946, and was followed by several more post-war Firefly variants.

Wartime service
The Firefly was an immediate success on entering service, participating in

attacks on the German battleship *Tirpitz* as well as taking part in numerous Norwegian raids. It was equally successful in the Pacific, making raids against Japanese occupied islands early in 1945, and against the Japanese mainland shortly before VJ-day.

Above: This aircraft, the seventh Firefly built, but only the third Firefly F.Mk I, was engaged on trials in the summer of 1943. The type entered service in October 1943, with No. 1770 Sqn, FAA.

Left: No. 1770 Sqn took part in the Tirpitz raids in July 1944, before moving to the Far East for operations against Japanese oil refineries in Sumatra. This Firefly F.Mk I was photographed in the latter theatre.

SPECIFICATION	
Fairey Firefly F.Mk I	**Weights:** empty 4423 kg (9,750 lb);
Type: two-seat carrierborne fighter	maximum take-off 6359 kg
Powerplant: one 1294-kW	(14,020 lb)
(1,735-hp) Rolls-Royce Griffon IIB	**Dimensions:** wing span 13.56 m
V-12 piston engine	(44 ft 6 in); length 11.46 m (37 ft
Performance: maximum speed	7 in); height 4.14 m (13 ft 7 in);
509 km/h (316 mph) at 4267 m	wing area 30.47 m² (328 sq ft)
(14,000 ft); service ceiling 8534 m	**Armament:** four 20-mm cannon,
(28,000 ft); range 2092 km	plus eight 60-lb (27.2-kg) rockets or
(1,300 miles)	two 1,000-lb (454-kg) bombs

Fairey Fulmar Early FAA two-seat fighter

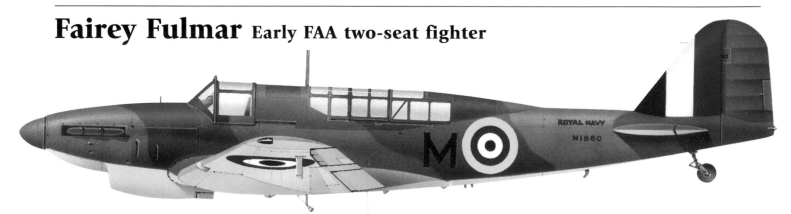

The first true shipborne monoplane fighter for the Fleet Air Arm, the eight-gun **Fairey Fulmar** tends to be overlooked in the part it played in the first three years of the war, until replaced by deck-operating adaptations of the Hurricane and Spitfire, and by the Martlet. Developed from the

Fairey P.4/34 light bomber prototypes which flew in 1937, the Fulmar fleet fighter prototype was first flown on 4 January 1940, with production aircraft being completed soon after. Early trials showed the aircraft to have a disappointing performance, although it was recognised as being a fairly

large aircraft with the same engine as the Hurricane single-seater.

Into production
In 1942, after 127 production **Fulmar Mk I** fighters had been completed, the **Fulmar Mk II** appeared with the Merlin XXX, an engine which raised the fighter's top

This early production Fulmar Mk I was on strength with No. 806 Sqn from June 1940. The type saw its first combat against the Italians, while defending the Malta convoys that year.

speed to 438 km/h (272 mph). Fulmar Mk Is of No. 808 Sqn, FAA were listed in RAF Fighter Command's order of battle during the Battle of Britain,

although they were not engaged in combat. By November 1940, however, Fulmars were in action from HMS *Illustrious* at the time of the Battle of Taranto, and

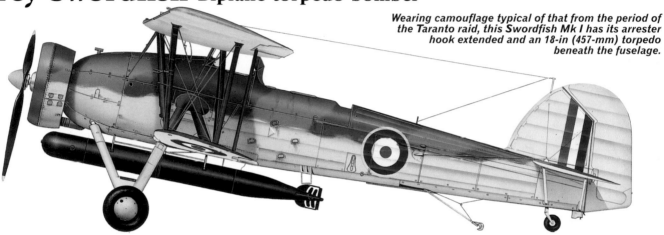

SPECIFICATION

Fairey Fulmar Mk II
Type: two-seat carrierborne fighter
Powerplant: one 940-kW
(1,260-hp) Rolls-Royce Merlin XXX
V-12 piston engine
Performance: maximum speed
438 km/h (272 mph) at 5029 m
(16,500 ft); initial climb rate 402 m
(1,320 ft) per minute; service ceiling
8291 m (27,200 ft); range 1255 km
(780 miles)
Weights: empty 3349 kg (7,384 lb);

maximum take-off 4627 kg
(10,200 lb)
Dimensions: wing span 14.14 m
(46 ft 4½ in); length 12.24 m (40 ft
2 in); height 3.25 m (10 ft 8 in);
wing area 31.77 m² (342 sq ft)
Armament: eight 0.303-in (7.7-mm)
machine-guns in the wings; a few
aircraft also had a single trainable
0.303-in (7.7-mm) machine-gun in
the rear cockpit

soon afterwards from *Ark Royal* defending the vital convoys sailing to Malta. At the Battle of Cape Matapan Fulmars from *Formidable* escorted the Fairey Albacores and Swordfish

which torpedoed the Italian battleship *Vittorio Veneto*. Early in 1942, as Japanese naval forces sailed into the Indian Ocean to threaten Ceylon, two squadrons of Fulmars were based there

as part of Colombo's air defences; when confronted for the first time by the much superior carrier-based Mitsubishi A6M fighters the Fulmars were utterly outclassed and almost all were

A somewhat ungainly and underperforming fighter, the Fulmar suffered from the weight penalty of its second cockpit. The FAA felt that a navigator was required to ensure a safe return to ship, however.

shot down or damaged. A total of 450 Fulmar Mk IIs

was built, and some served as night fighters.

Fairey Swordfish Biplane torpedo bomber

Wearing camouflage typical of that from the period of the Taranto raid, this Swordfish Mk I has its arrester hook extended and an 18-in (457-mm) torpedo beneath the fuselage.

Of all the aircraft regarded as anachronisms the **Fairey Swordfish** torpedo-bomber must be the supreme example, for even back in the 1930s it appeared archaic and cumbersome. Stemming from an earlier design whose prototype had crashed, the first prototype Swordfish (the **T.S.R.II**) first flew on 17 April 1934 and the production **Swordfish Mk I** was prepared to Specification S.38/34 with a slightly swept-back top wing; construction was all-metal with fabric covering. By the outbreak of war in 1939 a total of 689 aircraft had been delivered or were on order, serving with both wheel and float landing gear aboard Royal Navy carriers, battleships, battle-cruisers and cruisers in the

torpedo-spotter reconnais-sance role. Among the memorable events in which the **'Stringbag'** participated was the action at Taranto on 11 November 1940, when Swordfish from HMS *Illustrious* severely damaged three Italian battleships; the crippling of the *Bismarck* in the Atlantic; and the suicidal attack on the German war-ships, *Scharnhorst*, *Gneisenau* and *Prinz Eugen* during their famous escape up the English Channel in February 1942.

Swordfish Mk II
Production of the Swordfish was undertaken largely by Blackburn, the **Swordfish Mk II** being introduced with a strengthened lower wing to allow eight rocket projec-tiles to be mounted, the

Swordfish Mk III with ASV radar between the gear legs, and the **Swordfish Mk IV** conversion of the Mk II with a rudimentary enclosed cabin. Production ended on 18 August 1944, by which time a total of 2,396 Swordfish had been built.

Rocket projectiles added greatly to the armoury of the Swordfish and were especially useful for anti-ship work. Note the type's sturdy undercarriage and extensive rigging.

Those Swordfish with canopies over their rear cockpits were commonly known as Mk IVs, especially in Canada, where they were used for training.

SPECIFICATION

Fairey Swordfish Mk II
Type: three-crew torpedo/anti-submarine aircraft
Powerplant: one 559-kW (750-hp)
Bristol Pegasus XXX radial piston
engine
Performance: maximum speed
222 km/h (138 mph) at sea level;
initial climb rate 372 m (1,220 ft)
per minute; service ceiling 5867 m
(19,250 ft); range 879 km
(546 miles)
Weights: empty 2132 kg (4,700 lb);
maximum take-off 3406 kg

(7,510 lb)
Dimensions: wing span 12.87 m
(45 ft 6 in); length 10.87 m (35 ft
8 in); height 3.76 m (12 ft 4 in);
wing area 56.39 m² (607 sq ft)
Armament: one fixed
forward-firing 0.303-in (7.7-mm)
machine-gun and one trainable
0.303-in (7.7-mm) gun in the rear
cockpit, plus an offensive load of
one 18-in (457-mm) torpedo or
eight 60-lb (27.2-kg) rocket
projectiles

Hawker Sea Hurricane Catapult and carrierborne fighter

This aircraft was part of a batch of Hurricane Mk XA/XIB aircraft built in Canada. While the designations of Canadian-built Sea Hurricanes were a little confused, this machine might best be described as a Sea Hurricane Mk XIB. These aircraft were issued to the FAA and the Royal Canadian Navy, although this aircraft belonged to No. 440 Sqn of the Royal Canadian Air Force!

Based on the RAF's Hurricane, the **Hawker Sea Hurricane** was introduced to provide modern fighter protection for convoys of merchant ships. Over 800 were delivered, the majority of them being conversions of Hurricanes, including many which had already seen operational service. A number were modifications of newly delivered Canadian-built aircraft.

'Huricats' and others

The first version to appear was the **Sea Hurricane Mk IA** fitted with catapult spools so that it could be flown from specially fitted merchant ships in the event of the appearance of an enemy aircraft. These so-called **'Huricats'** were catapulted from CAM-(Catapult-Armed Merchant-) ships, for one-way interception missions against marauding enemy aircraft.

The Mk IA was followed by the **Sea Hurricane Mk IB**, which in addition to the spools, had deck arrester gear to enable it to be used for carrier operations. The **Sea Hurricane Mk IC**, of which only a few were produced, had four wing-mounted 20-mm cannon in place of the machine-guns of the earlier versions and was intended as a bomber destroyer. Converted from the Hurricane Mk IIC, the **Sea Hurricane Mk IIC** combined

the cannon with the Merlin XX engine. Canadian-built aircraft used the foregoing designations, with the exception of a few **Sea Hurricane Mk XIIA** aircraft converted from Hurricane Mk XIIs.

Into combat

Sea Hurricanes first entered operational service in February 1941 with No. 804 Sqn for deployment from

CAM-ships. The first carrier squadron to equip was No. 880 Sqn in March 1941, seeing action in July from HMS *Furious* during a raid on the Arctic port of Petsamo. The following month an aircraft of No. 804 Sqn, catapulted from HMS *Maplin*, accounted for an Fw 200 Condor. The disadvantage of CAM operations was that unless the pilot could reach land he had no

Above: Sea Hurricane operating conditions could be harsh, as shown by this weather-beaten aircraft launching from HMS Vindex for an anti-submarine patrol over the Atlantic.

Right: During CAM-ship launches, the Sea Hurricane Mk IA, or Fulmar, was powered down a short catapult by cordite rockets. A take-off speed of 120 km/h (75 mph) was reached in just 21 m (70 ft).

choice but to ditch his aircraft. The CAM-ship task and aircraft were later passed on to the RAF's Merchant Ship

Some of the Hurricane Mk Is that became Sea Hurricane Mk IBs, had seen combat in the Battle of Britain. They were therefore already somewhat weary.

Fighter Unit at Speke.

When the first escort carriers came into service with the Royal Navy, Sea Hurricanes were attached to several of them, seeing service in the Arctic and the Mediterranean until being replaced in 1943 by Supermarine Seafires and Grumman Wildcats.

SPECIFICATION	
Hawker Sea Hurricane Mk IIC	(750 miles)
Type: carrierborne fighter	**Weights:** empty 2617 kg (5,770 lb);
Powerplant: one 955-kW	maximum take-off 3511 kg
(1,280-hp) Rolls-Royce Merlin XX	(7,740 lb)
V-12 piston engine	**Dimensions:** wing span 12.2 m
Performance: maximum speed	(40 ft); length 9.83 m (32 ft 3 in);
505 km/h (314 mph) at 5944 m	height 3.99 m (13 ft 1 in); wing area
(19,500 ft); service ceiling 10516 m	23.92 m² (257.5 sq ft)
(34,500 ft); range 1207 km	**Armament:** four 20-mm cannon

Supermarine Seafire Carrierborne fighter

This Seafire F.Mk III was active aboard HMS Hunter with No. 807 Sqn, FAA during 1945. The aircraft was used to provide top cover for anti-ship strikes in the Andaman Sea.

SPECIFICATION

Supermarine Seafire F.Mk III
Type: carrierborne fighter
Powerplant: one 1096-kW (1,470-hp) Rolls-Royce Merlin 45, 50 or 55 V-12 piston engine
Performance: maximum speed 566 km/h (352 mph) at 3734 m (12,250 ft); service ceiling 10302 m (33,800 ft); range 748 km (465 miles) on internal fuel
Weights: empty 2449 kg (5,400 lb);

maximum take-off 3175 kg (7,000 lb)
Dimensions: wing span 11.23 m (36 ft 10 in); length 9.12 m (29 ft 11 in); height 3.48 m (11 ft 5 in); wing area 22.48 m (242 sq ft)
Armament: two 20-mm cannon and four 0.303-in (7.7-mm) machine-guns, plus provision for one 500-lb (227-kg) bomb or two 250-lb (113-kg) bombs

Following the success of the Sea Hurricane adaptation, a Spitfire Mk VB was fitted with a 'V' arrester hook and satisfactory trials with the modified aircraft were carried out in HMS *Illustrious* towards the end of 1941. A number of Spitfires with B-type wings were similarly modified and named **Supermarine Seafire F.Mk IB**. In May 1942 the **Seafire F.Mk IIC** began to come off the production line, fitted with the C-type wing with provision for four 20-mm cannon. The Seafire F.Mk IIC also had a reinforced fuselage, catapult spools and rocket-assisted take-off gear (RATOG) provision. A low-altitude version was the **Seafire L.Mk IIC**, a few of which were fitted with cameras for photographic reconnaissance work, being designated Seafire **LR.Mk IIC**. A manually-operated folding wing was introduced on the **Seafire**

F.Mk III, and as with the earlier mark there was a **Seafire L.Mk III** variant for low-altitude work, a few being modified as the **Seafire LR.MK III** for photo-recce duties.

Griffon power
In 1945 the Griffon-engined **Seafire F.Mk XV** appeared, with a sting-type arrester hook, but was too late into service to see wartime action. It was followed by the **Seafire F.Mk XVII**, later **Seafire F.Mk 17**, with a clear-view bubble hood, cutaway rear fuselage and increased fuel capacity. The **Seafire FR.Mk XVII** (**FR.Mk 17**) reconnaissance variant had two cameras.
Based on the Spitfire F.Mk 21, the **Seafire F.Mk 45** had a later Griffon fitted with a five-bladed propeller. The clear-view bubble hood and cutaway rear fuselage, along with a six-bladed contra-rotating propeller, were fitted to the **Seafire**

F.Mk 46, a reconnaissance version being the **Seafire FR.Mk 46**. The final versions, the **Seafire F.Mk 47**, and the **Seafire FR.Mk 47**, had power-folding wings and other changes.

Combat action
The Seafire participated in the North African landings in November 1942, and later at Salerno and in south of France. Its principle failing was highlighted at Salerno, where lack of windspeed over the carrier decks led to numerous collapsed landing gears. Several squadrons were active in the Pacific, and after the war the Griffon-engined versions remained in service until 1954, many with reserve squadrons. The Seafire Mk 47 flew combat missions during the Korean War.

Above: The Seafire F.Mk III featured a double wing fold to allow it to fit in the RN's carrier hangars. A similar wing fold was featured on the Mks XV and 17.

Top: Shown during training aboard Ravager, this Seafire F.Mk IB belonged to No. 760 Sqn FAA. The Seafire's narrow-track main gear made for tricky deck handling characteristics.

Left: With its non-folding wings, the Seafire F.Mk IIC was not ideally suited to carrier use.

de Havilland Sea Hornet Multi-role piston-engined naval twin

Although bearing a strong family resemblance to the highly successful and versatile Mosquito, the **de Havilland Hornet** was in fact a new design and came about as a private-venture response to the need for a long-range, single-seat escort fighter for service in the Pacific. Development began in 1942, the prototype making its maiden flight on 28 July 1944, but like many aircraft which appeared late in World War II, the Hornet suffered heavily through post VJ-Day cancellations. Nevertheless, the Hornet's outstanding performance (it was the fastest twin-engine piston-powered fighter to

serve with any air arm in the world) saved it from total oblivion, the type being employed by the RAF in some numbers between 1946 and 1956.

Naval Hornets
Consideration of the possibility of acquiring a carrier-based variant resulted in the testing of three **Hornet F.Mk 1** aircraft in 1944-45, the third of these being a fully navalised specimen and such was the success of these trials that a production order for 79 **Sea Hornet F.Mk 20** fighters soon followed, deliveries getting underway to No. 801 Sqn in June 1947. Armament

Used as a long-range fighter and strike aircraft, the de Havilland Sea Hornet F.Mk 20 served aboard the Royal Navy's carriers from 1947 to 1951, when it was replaced by the Sea Venom.

was basically similar to that of the RAF Hornet, and this model remained in service until 1951 in a front-line capacity, The next version was the **Sea Hornet NF.Mk 21** night-fighter, whose development began in 1946 although it was not until January 1949 that it attained operational status with the Fleet Air Arm, equipping No. 809 Sqn at Culdrose until 1954, when it finally gave way to jet-powered equipment in the shape of the de Havilland Sea Venom.

Subsequently, the Sea Hornet NF.Mk 21 was reassigned to the training of night-fighter radar operators, a task it performed until 1956 when the handful of remaining aircraft were scrapped.

Production of the Sea Hornet was completed with the **Sea Hornet PR.Mk 22** for photographic reconnais-

sance, about two dozen examples being completed, all of which employed a pair of F52 cameras for use by day and a single K19B camera for night work. In order to undertake the reconnaissance mission, the cannon armament was deleted, its place being filled by the camera installations.

SPECIFICATION	
de Havilland Sea Hornet F.Mk 20	(1,500 miles) with auxiliary fuel
Type: carrierborne escort and strike fighter	**Weights:** empty 6033 kg (13,300 lb); maximum take-off 8405 kg (18,530 lb)
Powerplant: two 1514-kW (2,030-hp) Rolls-Royce Merlin 133/134 inline piston engines	**Dimensions:** wing span 13.72 m (45 ft); length 11.18 m (36 ft 8 in); height 4.32 m (14 ft 2 in); wing area 33.54 m² (361 sq ft)
Performance: maximum speed 748 km/h (465 mph) at 6705 m (22,000 ft); service ceiling 10670 m (35,000 ft); range 2414 km	**Armament:** four 20-mm cannon, plus eight 60-lb (27-kg) rockets or two 1,000-lb (454-kg) bombs

No. 809 Sqn was the only front-line user of the Sea Hornet NF.Mk 21, which it flew between 1949 and 1954. In addition to night-fighting, the NF.Mk 21 could act as a navigation leader for other fighters.

Above: The addition of ASH radar in a nose thimble and the cramming of a radar operator (called an observer in Navy parlance) into the rear fuselage of the Sea Hornet NF.Mk 21, ruined the fine lines of de Havilland's aircraft.

de Havilland Sea Venom Early naval jet fighter

Following the evaluation of a standard RAF Venom NF.Mk 2 night-fighter during the course of 1950, the Royal Navy ordered three fully navalised prototype aircraft as the **de Havilland Sea Venom NF.Mk 20**, the first of which made its maiden flight on 19 April 1951. Subsequent carrier compatibility trials conducted aboard HMS *Illustrious* showed that the type possessed considerable promise, and an initial batch of 50 production Sea Venom NF.Mk 20s was contracted, deliveries getting under way during the mid-1950s.

Attaining operational status with No. 890 Sqn aboard HMS *Albion* in July 1955, the Sea Venom NF.Mk 20 was quickly followed by the **Sea Venom FAW.Mk 21**, which used the more powerful Ghost 104 turbojet engine and which was also

fitted with American APS-57 airborne interception radar. Deliveries of the Sea Venom FAW.Mk 21 began before the Sea Venom NF.Mk 20 became operational, the delivery beginning in May 1955 of what eventually became the most widely

Fastest of all the naval Venoms was the French Sud-Est Aquilon 203. This example served with Aéronavale Flottille 16F and was later armed with the Nord 5103 command-guidance air-to-air missile.

used version, a total of 167 being built for service with the Fleet Air Arm. Production of the Sea

Venom was completed with 39 examples of the **Sea Venom FAW.Mk 22**, which differed mainly by virtue of being powered by the Ghost 105 turbojet.

Like other Fleet Air Arm aircraft of this era, the Sea Venom was in action in the Suez Crisis, being employed against targets in the Canal Zone. However, its combat swansong came in 1960 when No. 891 Squadron's de Havilland Sea Venom FAW.Mk 22s flew a number of missions against Yemeni rebels in Aden.

Second-line duties

Shortly afterwards the Sea Venom was retired from the front-line inventory, although some continued to fly with second-line elements until as late as 1970.

In addition to service with the Fleet Air Arm, 39 **Sea**

SPECIFICATION

de Havilland Sea Venom FAW.Mk 21
Type: carrierborne all-weather fighter
Powerplant: one 22.01-kN (4,950-lb) thrust de Havilland Ghost 104 turbojet
Performance: maximum speed 1014 km/h (630 mph) at sea level; service ceiling 14995 m (49,200 ft); range 1609 km (1,000 miles)

Weights: maximum take-off 7212 kg (15,900 lb)
Dimensions: wing span 13.08 m (42 ft 11 in); length 11.15 m (36 ft 7 in); height 2.59 m (8 ft 6 in); wing area 25.99 m² (279.75 sq ft)
Armament: four 20-mm cannon, plus up to 907 kg (2,000 lb) of external ordnance including bombs and rockets

Venom FAW.Mk 53 aircraft were exported to Australia in 1955, while about 80 aircraft were built under licence by Sud-Est in France, where the type was known as the **Aquilon**. Based on the Sea Venom NF.Mk 20, the Aquilon served with the

Aéronavale from 1955 to 1965, some aircraft being configured to carry the Nord 5103 air-to-air missile. Following delivery of the Vought F-8E(FN) Crusader, the surviving Sud-Est Aquilons were relegated to secondary duties.

De Havilland's Sea Venom was widely employed by the Royal Navy for six or seven years. Its most important combat was during the Suez crisis, when this FAW.Mk 21 was pictured after a wheels-up landing. The fairing over the hook is clearly visible.

Fairey Firefly Multi-role, single-engined naval warplane

SPECIFICATION

Fairey Firefly FR.Mk 4
Type: carrierborne reconnaissance fighter
Powerplant: one 1674-kW (2,245-hp) Rolls-Royce Griffon 74 inline piston engine
Performance: maximum speed 591 km/h (367 mph) at 4265 m (14,000 ft); service ceiling 9725 m (31,900 ft); range 2148 km (1,335 miles)

Weights: empty 4388 kg (9,674 lb); maximum take-off 7083 kg (15,615 lb)
Dimensions: wing span 12.55 m (41 ft 2 in); length 11.58 m (38 ft); height 4.24 m (13 ft 11 in); wing area 30.66 m² (330 sq ft)
Armament: four 20-mm cannon, plus 16 60-lb (27-kg) rockets or two 1,000-lb (454-kg) bombs

One of the most successful World War II designs to originate in the UK, the **Fairey Firefly** initially entered service in 1943 and racked up an impressive combat record in World War II. Notable highlights included the attack on the German battleship *Tirpitz* and a series of strikes on mainland Japan shortly before VJ-Day brought hostilities to a conclusion. In the post-war era, the Firefly demonstrated a considerable degree of versatility, turning its hand to other

duties such as target towing and anti-submarine warfare as well as continuing in its primary function of fighter-bomber. By the time production ceased 1,702 had been built, some remaining active with the Fleet Air Arm until as late as 1957 while others served with Australia, Canada, Denmark, Ethiopia, India, the Netherlands. Sweden and Thailand.

Post-war production initially involved the **Firefly FR.Mk 4** reconnaissance fighter, which flew for the

first time on 25 May 1945. Incorporating a number of new features such as clipped wing tips and redesigned tail surfaces, 160

After serving with distinction in the closing months of World War II, the Fairey Firefly continued to give valuable service for several years. These Firefly FR.Mk 4s are seen in company with a trio of Sea Furies.

were completed by early 1948, and these saw service with several Fleet Air Arm squadrons, some later being modified to **Firefly TT.Mk 4** standard for target-towing duty. The next basic model to appear was the **Mk 5**, variants including the Firefly **NF.Mk 5** night-fighter, the **Firefly FR.Mk 5** day reconnaissance fighter and the **Firefly AS.Mk 5** ASW patrol aircraft; the last eventually became the most numerous

Left: This RAN Firefly AS.Mk 6 was photographed launching from HMAS Sydney in 1955. The Australian Fireflies ceased front-line operations in 1956.

post-war version, over 300 being produced between 1947 and 1950.

Last variants

Production then switched to the three-seat **Firefly AS.Mk 6**, which entered service in 1951, the 149 aircraft built eventually equipping six front-line and six reserve squadrons, and these were followed in 1952 by the **Firefly AS.Mk 7**. Only 36 were completed to this standard, the remaining 160 Mk 7s all being **Firefly T.Mk 7** trainers. Firefly production eventually terminated in March 1956 with the delivery of the last of 24 new-build **Firefly U.Mk 8** target drones, but 54 Mk 5s were also converted as target drones, these being known as **Firefly U.Mk 9** aircraft.

Operationally, British Fireflies of various marks saw considerable post-war action, taking part in the Malayan confrontation as well as the Korean War, while the Dutch Firefly FR.Mk 1s saw combat duty against rebel forces in the Dutch East Indies.

Below: Although a handful of Firefly AS.Mk 7 aircraft was completed for the ASW role, the type was never used on such duties. Instead, all were used as T.Mk 7 trainers and tasked with the instruction of ASW, observer, pilot and RN Volunteer Reserve students. This machine flew with No. 796 Sqn.

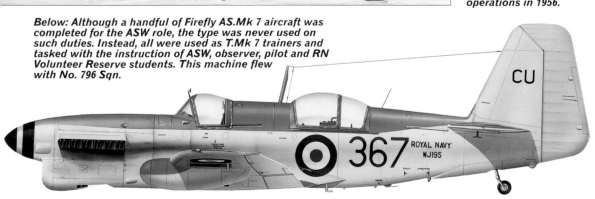

Hawker Sea Fury Carrierborne and land-based fighter bomber

SPECIFICATION

Hawker Sea Fury FB.Mk 11
Type: carrierborne fighter-bomber
Powerplant: one 1849-kW (2,480-hp) Bristol Centaurus 18 radial piston engine
Performance: maximum speed 740 km/h (460 mph) at 5485 m (18,000 ft); service ceiling 10910 m (35,800 ft); range 1127 km (700 miles) on internal fuel
Weights: empty 4191 kg (9,240 lb);

maximum take-off 5670 kg (12,500 lb)
Dimensions: wing span 11.7 m (38 ft 4¾ in); length 10.57 m (34 ft 8 in); height 4.84 m (15 ft 10½ in); wing area 26 m² (280 sq ft)
Armament: four 20-mm cannon, plus up to 907 kg (2,000 lb) of external ordnance including bombs, rockets and mines

With catapult strap attached and engine at full power, a Sea Fury FB.Mk 11 awaits the signal to launch during operations off Korea.

First conceived as a long-range fighter for use by the Royal Air Force in the Pacific against the Japanese, Hawker's initial design was known originally as the **Tempest Light Fighter**. It very quickly generated considerable Royal Navy interest which led to the issue of a formal specification in February 1943, this being followed in April 1944 by an order for 400 aircraft to be shared equally by the RAF and the Fleet Air Arm.

Fury first

The first example of the new fighter to fly was the RAF's **Fury Mk I** on 1 September 1944, while the **Hawker Sea Fury** prototype took to the air for its maiden flight on 21 February 1945. However, the return of peace led to large-scale defence cutbacks, Hawker's newest fighter suffering badly with all the RAF examples and half of the Royal Navy aircraft being cancelled, although the manufacturer did ultimately achieve some modest export sales of the land-based Fury fighter, customers including Egypt, Iraq and Pakistan.

FAA Sea Furies

As far as the Royal Navy's aircraft was concerned, this first flew in production form as the **Sea Fury F.Mk X** on 7 September 1946, duly entering service with No. 807 Squadron in July

1947. Manufacture of the Sea Fury as a pure fighter was, however, destined to be short-lived and only 50 were completed, production thereafter switching to the **Sea Fury FB.Mk 11** fighter-bomber derivative which could carry up to 907 kg (2,000 lb) of external ordnance and which also featured a lengthened arrester hook plus provision for rocket-assisted take-off gear. This variant became the definitive Sea Fury, deliveries beginning in May 1948, and by the time the line closed in the early 1950s some 515 had been completed, as well as 60 examples of the **Sea Fury T.Mk 20** two-seat trainer. By then the Sea Fury had also been engaged in combat in Korea, where it proved to be an excellent ground-attack platform as well as no mean performer in air-to-air combat, emerging victorious over the jet-powered Mikoyan-Gurevich MiG-15 'Fagot' on at least two occasions.

By the mid-1950s the Sea Fury had been supplanted by more modern types with

the Fleet Air Arm, but some export Sea Furies continued to fly with the air arms of Australia, Burma, Canada, Cuba and the Netherlands for a few more years.

Right: Rocket-assisted take-off bottles could be attached behind the Sea Fury's wing trailing edge, as illustrated by this Sea Fury FB.Mk 11.

Below: Wearing the 'O' tail marking of HMS Ocean, from which it flew extensively during the Korean War, this Sea Fury FB.Mk 11 has the black and white identification stripes associated with the conflict on its wings and fuselage. Note the in steps for use by the pilot in reaching the cockpit.

Above: The first Dutch Sea Furies were 10 Mk 50s ordered in October 1946 for use aboard the ex-Royal Navy carrier Nairana. These were joined by another 12 fighter-bomber aircraft from 1950 and licence production by Fokker accounted for a further 26 examples. The type was retired in 1959.

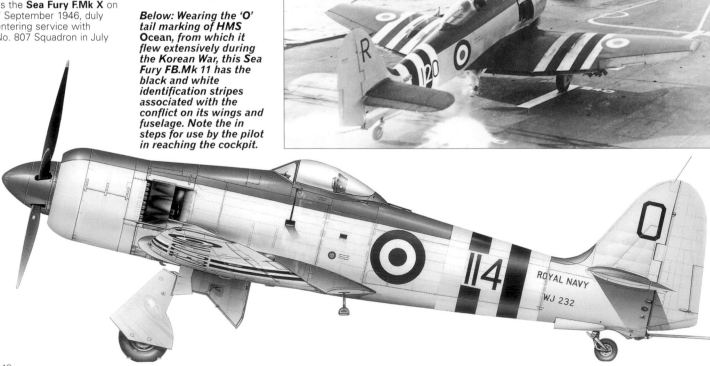

Hawker Sea Hawk Carrierborne jet fighter-bomber

No. 804 Sqn flew this Sea Hawk FGA.Mk 6 from HMS Bulwark *during the Suez Crisis. The black and yellow stripes were a recognition feature applied for the conflict.*

Arising from the P.1040 single-seat land-based interceptor prototype, the **Sea Hawk** first flew in prototype form on 2 September 1947. It was subsequently ordered into production as the **Sea Hawk F.Mk 1**, this being a pure fighter variant powered by a single Nene 101 turbojet engine rated at 22.24 kN (5,000 lb) thrust. Early development of the Sea Hawk was a protracted process, and it was not until 1953 that it began to enter service with the FAA, ultimately equipping most

front-line units and providing the backbone of British naval air power for much of the remainder of the 1950s.

Second fiddle

In the event, Hawker's other main project (the Hunter) rather overshadowed the Sea Hawk, and indeed was responsible for Sea Hawk production being entrusted to Armstrong Whitworth from the **Sea Hawk F.Mk 2** version onwards.
Progressive development of the basic design led to the appearance of rather more

versatile variants, the first of these being the **Sea Hawk FB.Mk 3**, which featured a strengthened wing structure, enabling it to carry bombs, rockets or auxiliary fuel tanks. This was soon followed by the **Sea Hawk FGA.Mk 4** optimised for use in the demanding ground-attack role. Adoption of the more powerful Nene 103 turbojet in 1956 led to the **Sea Hawk FB.Mk 5** and **Sea Hawk FGA.Mk 6** derivatives, these basically being re-engined FB.Mk 3s and FGA.Mk 4s, although some FGA.Mk 6s were built as

The Sea Hawk enjoyed some export success – beginning in 1958, Germany took delivery of 68 Mk 100s and radar-equipped Mk 101s. VA-229 was an example of the anti-ship Mk 100.

such. In addition to production for the FAA, the Sea Hawk also found favour with the naval air arms of India, the Netherlands and West Germany, some of the Indian machines flying into the 1980s.
As far as operational service with the Royal Navy is concerned, the highlight must surely have been the Suez Canal crisis of 1956 when six squadrons flying

from the carriers HMS *Albion,* HMS *Bulwark* and HMS *Eagle* mounted numerous raids on Egyptian airfields, causing substantial damage for the loss of only two aircraft in a week of quite intense activity. By 1960, however, the availability of newer and more sophisticated types such as the Scimitar and Sea Vixen resulted in retirement of the Sea Hawk by the FAA.

SPECIFICATION

Hawker Sea Hawk FGA.Mk 6
Type: carrierborne fighter-bomber
Powerplant: one 23.13-kN (5,200-lb) thrust Rolls-Royce Nene 103 turbojet
Performance: maximum speed 945 km/h (587 mph) at 6095 m (20,000 ft); service ceiling 13565 m (44,500 ft); range 1287 km (800 miles) with auxiliary fuel

Weights: empty 4672 kg (10,300 lb); maximum take-off 6895 kg (15,200 lb)
Dimensions: wing span 11.89 m (39 ft); length 12.09 m (39 ft 8 in); height 2.64 m (8 ft 8 in); wing area 25.83 m² (278 sq ft)
Armament: four 20-mm cannon, plus two 500-lb (227-kg) bombs or 20 3-in (76-mm) rockets

Supermarine Attacker Early carrierborne jet fighter-bomber

After World War II, the UK's hectic pace of aircraft development slowed almost to a halt, as the government invoked a 'ten-year rule' which stated there would be a 10-year warning of any emergency, so new equipment was not urgent. This philosophy was dented by the Berlin Airlift and shattered

by Korea in June 1950, and by this time the Fleet Air Arm's first jet fighter had been in the air two months. The **Supermarine Attacker** prototype had been built to a 1944 specification, using a new Nene-engined fuselage mounted on the wings of the Spiteful with radiators removed. The result was the

Attacker F.Mk 1, a mediocre fighter whose main advantages were cheapness and easy handling at low level.

Ground attack

The type's low-level handling was put to use by adding bombs in the **Attacker FB.Mk 1** version, and the **Attacker FB.Mk 2** had powered ailerons and a stronger metal-framed canopy. The last of 145 of the three marks was delivered in 1953, and these served with No. 736 training and Nos 800, 803 and 890 first-line Squadrons from late 1951 until 1955, thereafter continuing with the RNVR until that force was disbanded in 1957.

Britain's first naval jet to reach a squadron, the Attacker was also exported to Pakistan. Its wing was developed from the Spiteful's, which had in turn been developed from the Spitfire's. FB.Mk 1s are shown.

SPECIFICATION

Supermarine Attacker FB.Mk 2
Type: single-seat carrier-based fighter-bomber
Powerplant: one 22.68-kN (5,100-lb) thrust Rolls-Royce Nene Mk 102 turbojet
Performance: maximum speed 950 km/h (590 mph) at sea level; initial climb (light weight 5216 kg/ 11,500 lb) 1935 m (6,350 ft) per minute; service ceiling (maximum weight) 11890 m (39,000 ft); range (with 1137-litre/250-Imp gal belly

tank) 1700 km (1,060 miles)
Weights: empty 4495 kg (9,910 lb); maximum take-off 7938 kg (17,500 lb)
Dimensions: wing span 11.26 m (36 ft 11 in); length 11.43 m (37 ft 6 in); height 3.03 m (9 ft 11 in); wing area 21 m² (226 sq ft)
Armament: four 20-mm Hispano Mk 5 cannon, plus provision for two 1,000-lb (454-kg) bombs or eight rockets

No. 1831 Squadron became the first Royal Navy Volunteer Reserve (RNVR) unit to be equipped with jets when it received the Attacker FB.Mk 2 in May 1955. The squadron was based at Stretton as part of the Northern Air Division.

Douglas AD/A-1 Skyraider Carrierborne attack aircraft

No survey of carrier aircraft of the 1950s would be complete without some reference to the **Douglas AD Skyraider**, a type which was conceived during World War II. Arriving on the scene too late to participate in that conflict, the Skyraider underwent its combat baptism of fire over Korea and was still very much a part of the US Navy's front-line inventory more than 10 years later when the Vietnam War began, surpassing earlier achievements by being responsible for the destruction of two MiGs in air-to-air combat, as well as amassing an incredible combat record.

SBD replacement

Originally conceived in 1944 as a replacement for the tried and tested Douglas SBD Dauntless dive-bomber, the Skyraider entered service with Attack Squadron VA-19A late in 1946, this marking the start of a career spanning some 26 years during which it demonstrated an as-yet unparalleled versatility. Equally adept at airborne early warning, electronic countermeasures, bombing, close air support, target towing, troop carrying and even VIP transport, no less than 3,180 Skyraiders were completed between 1945 and February 1957, when the assembly line finally closed. These aircraft saw service with the US Air Force, the US Navy and the US Marine Corps as well as overseas air arms including those of France, South Vietnam and the UK.

Flown for the first time in prototype form as the **XBT2D-1** on 18 March 1945,

BuNo. 134589 was a straightforward AD-6. Like all other US Navy aircraft it was redesignated in 1962, in this case as an A-1H. It served until 1965 with VA-145, flying from USS Constellation off the coast of Vietnam.

the type was ordered into production just one month later but soon suffered from VJ-Day cutbacks which at one time seemed likely to threaten the future of the whole project. Fortunately, it survived early vicissitudes and by the end of the Korean War had, in the words of Rear Admiral John Hoskins, commanding Task Force 77 off Korea, become "the best and most effective close support aircraft in the world".

Space does not permit close examination of individual variants (there were at least 28) but in addition to single-seat attack aircraft such as the **AD-1**, **AD-6** and **AD-7**, there was also the multi-place **AD-5** which was perhaps the most interesting Skyraider of all in that it could by means of packaged conversion kits be reconfigured for different missions within just a matter of hours. Flown for the first time in August 1951, variants of the AD-5 subsequently performed AEW (**AD-5W**), ECM (**AD-5Q**), day attack (AD-5) and night attack (**AD-5N**) missions among other tasks, making it easily the most versatile model of this remarkable warplane. In 1962 the type was redesignated as the **A-1 Skyraider** in US service.

Above: The sting is in the tail: the distinctive 'Bumblebee' squadron insignia of VA-176 is seen on this A-1H. A Skyraider from this US Navy unit accomplished the remarkable feat of downing an NVAF MiG-17 'Fresco' in October 1966.

SPECIFICATION	
Douglas AD-7 Skyraider	**Weights:** empty 5486 kg
Type: carrierborne attack aircraft	(12,094 lb); maximum take-off
Powerplant: one 2274-kW	11340 kg (25,000 lb)
(3,050-hp) Wright R-3350-26WB	**Dimensions:** wing span 15.25 m
radial piston engine	(50 ft ¼ in); length 11.84 m (38 ft
Performance: maximum speed	10 in); height 4.78 m (15 ft 8¼ in);
552 km/h (343 mph) at 6095 m	wing area 37.2 m² (400.33 sq ft)
(20,000 ft); service ceiling 7740 m	**Armament:** four 20-mm cannon,
(25,400 ft); range 2092 km	plus up to 3629 kg (8,000 lb) of
(1,300 miles)	external ordnance on 15 hardpoints

Left: The Douglas AD was the main US Navy attack aircraft during the 1950s and 1960s. This example is an AD-7 (A-1J).

Douglas F3D Skyknight Carrierborne jet night fighter

Although produced in only fairly limited numbers, the **Douglas F3D Skyknight** enjoyed a lengthy career by the standards of the day, remaining in front-line service with the US Marine Corps as an electronic countermeasures platform until 1969. During the course of its 18-year career the Skyknight also undertook combat duty in both the Korean and Vietnamese conflicts, and it is probably not widely known that the Skyknight secured a permanent niche in aviation history when, on the night of 2 November 1952, it succeeded in downing a North Korean Yakovlev Yak-15, this marking the first recorded kill in a jet-versus-jet combat at night. Even more remark-

The most successful naval type in air-to-air combat over Korea, the Douglas F3D Skyknight was flown by both the Marines and Navy. This example is a Marine Corps F3D-2. These continued in service until 1969 in the electronic countermeasures role.

able is the fact that the F3D ended the Korean War as the most successful naval fighter type in terms of aircraft destroyed in air combat. Despite their age, two examples of the Skyknight provided valuable service to the US armed forces into the 1980s, being used by the US Army in support of air defence missile testing in New Mexico.

Jet night fighter

Unique in being the US Navy's first jet-powered night fighter, the Skyknight began development in 1945, Douglas being awarded a contract for three **XF3D-1** prototypes in April 1946, and the first of these made its maiden flight from Muroc (now Edwards AFB) on 23 March 1948, this event being followed in June by an order for 28 production **F3D-1** (redesignated **F-10A**

from 1962) fighters. Service acceptance trials were conducted by VC-3 at Moffett Field from December 1950, the type then being handed over to Marine Night Fighter Squadron VMF(N)-542. In the event, the F3D-1 did not see action, being quickly supplanted by the up-engined **F3D-2** (**F-10B**), 237 of which were completed in the early 1950s. It was this model which made the Skyknight's combat debut with VMF(N)-513 in June 1952.

New duties

In US Navy service, the F3D enjoyed only a brief front-line career, being quickly relegated to radar intercept training duties as the **F3D-2T** and **F3D-2T2** (**TF-10B**), the last example being retired in the early 1960s. US Marine Corps composite squadrons contin-

ued to use the **F3D-2Q** (**EF-10B**) on ECM duties, however, and the type again saw action in Vietnam with VMCJ-1 until 1969 when it was finally replaced by the Grumman EA-6A Intruder.

A proposed swept-wing version known as the **F3D-3** was cancelled in 1952, but other service variants were the Sparrow missile-armed **F3D-1M** and **F3D-2M** (**MF-10B**) fighters.

SPECIFICATION	
Douglas F3D-2 Skyknight **Type:** carrierborne night and all-weather fighter **Powerplant:** two 15.12-kN (3,400-lb) thrust Westinghouse J34-WE-36 turbojets **Performance:** maximum speed 909 km/h (565 mph) at 6095 m (20,000 ft); service ceiling 11645 m (38,200 ft); range 2478 km (1,540 miles)	**Weights:** empty 8237 kg (18,160 lb); maximum take-off 12556 kg (27,681 lb) **Dimensions:** wing span 15.24 m (50 ft); length 13.84 m (45 ft 5 in); height 4.9 m (16 ft 1 in); wing area 37.16 m² (400 sq ft) **Armament:** four 20-mm cannon, plus provision for two 2,000-lb (907-kg) bombs

Grumman AF-2 Guardian Submarine hunter/killer aircraft

In 1944 Grumman set out to produce a successor to the war-winning TBF/TBM Avenger torpedo bomber, and the first result was the **XTBF-1**, first flown on 19 December 1945. Looking like a slimmer and neater TBF/TBM, this machine had a Westinghouse X19B-2B (later the Allis-Chalmers J36, otherwise de Havilland Goblin, and Westinghouse J34 turbojets were tested) turbojet in the tail for high-speed boost propulsion. This was later omitted, and at last the first **Grumman AF-2 Guardian** flew in November 1949.

Guardian production

The AF-2 Guardian was put into production in two versions, which operated from US Navy carriers in the ASW (anti-submarine warfare) role in pairs, known as hunter/killers. The hunter was the **AF-2W**, distinguished by its big 'guppy' radome for

AN/APS-20 search radar, the displays and controls for which were in a two-seat rear compartment as in radar-equipped Skyraiders. The killer was the **AF-2S**, which took over when its companion had obtained a

sure 'contact'. First it used its smaller APS-30 radar under the right outer wing to pinpoint its target, using a searchlight in an identical pod under the left wing to illuminate it if necessary. Then it would attack using any of the assortment of weapons carried in an internal bay or on hardpoints beneath the wings.

For its submarine detection role, the AF-2W employed the AN/APS-20 radar set, with its antenna housed in a bulbous ventral radome.

Devoid of the massive underfuselage radome that characterised the AF-2W, the AF-2S was the strike component of the Guardian hunter/killer team.

The Guardians were among the largest single-engined military aircraft, being heavier than a Douglas DC-3, and with a roomy side-by-side cockpit, the AF-2S having a third rear compartment seat for the single radar operator. Grumman delivered 193 of

the AF-2S attack version and 153 of its companion AF-2W model in 1950-53. The company then followed with 40 ASW **AF-3S** machines, which were the first aircraft in service with MAD (magnetic-anomaly detection) gear in a retractable tail-boom mounting.

SPECIFICATION	
Grumman AF-2S Guardian **Type:** three-seat carrier-based ASW and attack aircraft **Powerplant:** one 1790-kW (2,400-hp) Pratt & Whitney R-2800-48W 18-cylinder radial piston engine **Performance:** maximum speed 510 km/h (317 mph) at medium/high altitude; service ceiling 9910 m (32,500 ft); range 2415 km (1,500 miles)	**Weights:** empty 6632 kg (14,620 lb); maximum take-off 11567 kg (25,500 lb) **Dimensions:** wing span 18.49 m (60 ft 8 in); length 13.21 m (43 ft 4 in); height 4.93 m (16 ft 2 in); wing area 52 m² (560 sq ft) **Armament:** internal bay for 1814 kg (4,000 lb) of torpedoes, bombs, depth charges, mines or other stores, with additional wing racks for similar weapons

Grumman F7F Tigercat Twin-engined fighter

VMF(N)-513 'Flying Nightmares' flew this F7F-3N during the Korean war.

Aesthetically perhaps the most pleasing of Grumman's World War II designs, the **F7F Tigercat** was intended primarily for service aboard the 45,000-ton 'Midway'-class aircraft carriers, although in the event it was mainly employed by the US

Marine Corps as a land-based fighter largely as a result of its weight and size. Unique in being the first fighter with tricycle landing gear to be accepted for US Navy service, the Tigercat suffered badly from post VJ-Day cancellations, pro-

duction terminating with the delivery of the 364th aircraft.

Wartime testing
Based on experience gained with the earlier and unsuccessful XF5F Skyrocket design, the initial contract awarded to Grumman in June 1941 covered the construction of two **XF7F-1** prototypes, both of which flew from Bethpage, Long Island, during November 1943. Subsequent testing revealed considerable prom-

ise and the type was ordered into production as the **F7F-1**, deliveries to the US Marine Corps getting under way during April 1944 when VMF-911 became the first squadron to receive Tigercat warplanes.
By this time it had been decided to use the type mainly as a night-fighter, and this policy decision quickly led to the appearance of the **F7F-2N**, a fuel tank being removed to provide room for a radar operator. In addition, the four nose-mounted machine-guns were also deleted in favour of radar but the F7F-2N was still heavily armed, possessing four 20-mm cannon in the wing leading edges. A total of 45

F7F-2Ns was built.
The next version to appear was the **F7F-3**, and this was without a doubt the best-performing Tigercat. Some 189 were built, a few being fitted with reconnaissance cameras as the **F7F-3P**, while 60 two-seat **F7F-3N** night-fighters were also completed before production came to a close in November 1946 with 13 **F7F-4N** aircraft featuring an enlarged vertical tail, improved radar and other refinements
The Tigercat saw action in Korea, US Marine Corps' F7F-3Ns entering combat in October 1950 and performing well by both day and night in the interdiction task.

Grumman's Tigercat only ever saw action with the Marine Corps, despite being designed as a carrier fighter. Several aircraft were handed over to the Navy and converted into drone directors as F7F-2Ds with an extra cockpit for the drone pilot. The drones were mostly F6F-3K and F6F-5K Hellcats.

SPECIFICATION	
Grumman F7F-3 Tigercat	**Weights:** empty 7380 kg
Type: carrierborne fighter	(16,270 lb); maximum take-off
Powerplant: two 2,100-hp	11667 kg (25,720 lb)
(1566-kW) Pratt & Whitney	**Dimensions:** wing span 15.7 m
R-2800-34W radial piston engines	(51 ft 6 in); length 13.83 m (45 ft
Performance: maximum speed	4½ in); height 5.05 m (16 ft 7 in);
700 km/h (435 mph) at 6705 m	wing area 42.27 m² (455 sq ft)
(22,000 ft); service ceiling 12405 m	**Armament:** four 0.5-in (12.7-mm)
(40,700 ft); range 1931 km	machine-guns and four 20-mm
(1,200 miles)	cannon

Grumman F8F Bearcat High-performance piston fighter

Conceived as a replacement for the earlier Grumman F6F Hellcat, the **Grumman F8F Bearcat** was also intended to surpass the Japanese Mitsubishi A6M 'Zeke' (itself no mean performer), and later fighters. Although deliveries began before VJ-Day the Bearcat played no part in World War II, most of the 8,000 or so examples on order being cancelled following the return of peace. Despite being overtaken by events, the Bearcat did see

service with the US Navy in substantial numbers, a total of 1,263 eventually being completed for this service, and many of these were later passed on to the air arms of France, Thailand and South Vietnam.

Bearcat design
Optimised for interception tasks, which dictated a lightweight airframe possessing a good rate of climb, the Bearcat was probably Grumman's finest

In 1946 F8F-1 Bearcats began replacing the F6F Hellcat as the US Navy's main fighter. Here aircraft from VF-15A and VF-16A prepare for launch from USS Tarawa during 1948-49.

SPECIFICATION	
Grumman F8F-1 Bearcat	(1,105 miles)
Type: carrierborne interceptor	**Weights:** empty 3207 kg (7,070 lb);
fighter	maximum take-off 5873 kg
Powerplant: one 2,100-hp	(12,946 lb)
(1566-kW) Pratt & Whitney	**Dimensions:** wing span 10.92 m
R-2800-34W radial piston engine	(35 ft 10 in); length 8.61 m (28 ft
Performance: maximum speed	3 in); height 4.22 m (13 ft 10 in);
678 km/h (421 mph) at 6005 m	wing area 22.67 m² (244 sq ft)
(19,700 ft); service ceiling 11795 m	**Armament:** four 0.5-in (12.7-mm)
(38,700 ft); range 1778 km	machine-guns

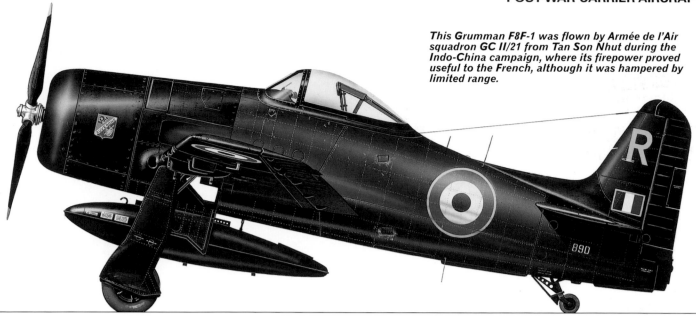

This Grumman F8F-1 was flown by Armée de l'Air squadron GC II/21 from Tan Son Nhut during the Indo-China campaign, where its firepower proved useful to the French, although it was hampered by limited range.

propeller-driven fighter, and had the war continued there is little doubt that it would have given a good account of itself. Standard production machines were capable of speeds well in excess of 644 km/h (400 mph), while the specially modified aircraft flown by stunt pilot Al

Williams actually achieved a speed of 805 km/h (500 mph) at 5790 m (19,000 ft). Even more startling, however, was the Bearcat's rate of climb, one **F8F-1** reaching 3050 m (10,000 ft) in just 94 seconds from brakes-off during November 1946 and managing to set a national record in the process.

Initial production involved the F8F-1 variant, 770 of which were built, and these were followed by 126 **F8F-1B** fighters which had four 20-mm cannon in place of the more usual quartet of 0.5-in (12.7-mm)

machine-guns. Refinement of the basic design resulted in the **F8F-2** which had taller vertical tail surfaces and a revised engine cowling, some 365 being completed in the early post-war years before the jet era arrived and revolutionised carrierborne aviation.

In addition to these new-build aircraft, close to 50 Bearcats were later retrofitted with APS-19 radar as **F8F-1N** and **F8F-2N** night-fighters, while 60 more became **F8F-2P** photographic reconnaissance aircraft, these having only two cannon installed.

Grumman F9F Panther Carrierborne jet fighter

The first jet-powered 'cat' to be produced by the company, the **Grumman F9F Panther** seems to have lacked the charisma of the earlier F8F Bearcat but nevertheless acquired a well-deserved reputation as a rugged and reliable machine. Historically significant by virtue of the fact that it was the first carrierborne jet to get into battle, the Panther performed well in Korea where it constituted the backbone of US Navy

and US Marine Corps air power, and by the time production ceased in late 1952 close to 1,400 had been built.

Night-fighter?
The initial F9F proposal was for a four-engine, two-seat night-fighter, but this was subsequently abandoned before design work was complete, Grumman then turning its attentions to a single-seat, single-engine jet day fighter, two prototypes

duly being ordered with the designation **XF9F-2**. Powered by an imported Rolls-Royce Nene engine, the first of these made its maiden flight on 24 November 1947 and such was the promise shown that substantial orders were soon forthcoming for production-configured **F9F-2** aircraft fitted with the licence-built Pratt & Whitney J42 copy of the Nene.

Although the F9F-2 was the initial production model, the honour of being the first variant to enter service fell to the **F9F-3**, which used the slightly less powerful Allison J33 engine. This joined US Navy Fighter Squadron VF-51 during May 1949 but in the event only 54 F9F-3s were completed, most being modified later to F9F-2 standard. The next version to appear was the **F9F-4** with the Allison J33-A-16, deliveries of this variant beginning in November 1949, about a

VMF-311 first took its F9F-2B Panthers to Korea in December 1950. The unit was the first jet-equipped USMC squadron in the theatre and was joined by VMF-115 from February 1951.

month before the maiden flight of what became the most prolific and, incidentally, the last member of the Panther family. This was the **F9F-5** which was powered by the Pratt & Whitney J48, a licence-built Rolls-Royce Tay, and over 600 were completed by the time production ceased at the end of 1952, this total including a few

photo-recce **F9F-5P** aircraft.

The F9F-5 Panther was the last version to see squadron service and was finally retired by VAH-7 in October 1958, although many Panthers continued to fly after that date with training units, and as **F9F-5KD** (from 1962 **DF-9E**) drone targets and controllers for missile trials.

Seen over Korea, this F9F-2 Panther of VF-721 is typical of the Panthers serving in the Korean War. Internal fuel tankage was almost double that of the similarly powered Hawker Sea Hawk.

SPECIFICATION	
Grumman F9F-5 Panther	**Weights:** empty 4603 kg
Type: carrierborne day fighter	(10,147 lb); maximum take-off
Powerplant: one 31.13-kN	8492 kg (18,721 lb)
(7,000-lb st) thrust Pratt & Whitney	**Dimensions:** wing span 11.58 m
J48-P-6 turbojet	(38 ft); length 11.58 m (38 ft);
Performance: maximum speed	height 3.73 m (12 ft 3 in); wing area
932 km/h (579 mph) at 1525 m	23.23 m² (250 sq ft)
(5,000 ft); service ceiling 13380 m	**Armament:** four 20-mm cannon,
(43,900 ft); range 2092 km	plus up to 1361 kg (3,000 lb) of
(1,300 miles)	external ordnance

Grumman F9F Cougar Swept-wing naval fighter family

First flown in prototype form as the **XF9F-6** on 20 September 1951, the **Grumman F9F Cougar** evolved from the earlier F9F Panther series of fighters. It differed mainly from its predecessors by virtue of possessing swept wings and a swept tailplane, thus earning the distinction of being the first swept-wing carrierborne type to enter service. Apart from this, changes were kept to a minimum to facilitate rapid production. Indeed, the new Cougar entered service just 14 months after its maiden flight took place, initial examples of the Pratt & Whitney J48-engined **F9F-6** (later designated **F-9F**) joining VF-32 of the Atlantic Fleet during November 1951. Shortly after this deliveries to Pacific Fleet units got under way.

Further variants

Production of the F9F-6 totalled 706 aircraft, 60 of which were completed as **F9F-6P** machines for reconnaissance duties, and these were followed by the **F9F-7** (**F-9H**) which was powered by an Allison J33 turbojet. This proved to be only a

temporary change, and after completing 168 F9F-7s Grumman reverted to the Pratt & Whitney J48 engine for the **F9F-8** (**F-9J**), which became the definitive Cougar, well over 1,000 being completed in three basic variants. First to appear was the F9F-8 (601 built) which possessed increased fuel capacity and also introduced a modified 'saw-tooth' leading edge to the wing; and large numbers were later modified to **F9F-8B** (**AF-9J**) standard with provision for air-to-surface guided missiles.

Some 110 specimens of a photo-reconnaissance version designated **F9F-8P** (**RF-9J**) appeared, while the Cougar also lent itself to the training of future naval aviators; a prototype two-seat

YF9F-8T was followed by no less than 400 **F9F-8T** (**TF-9J**) production examples, some of which remained in use with Naval Air Training Command until well into the 1970s.

Cougar phase-out

As far as front-line units were concerned, the Cougar disappeared from the scene early in 1960, the last operational version being the F9F-8P, but many continued to fly long after that date with the Reserve Force and with Air Training Command.

Surplus aircraft became **F9F-6K** (**QF-9F**) and **F9F-6K2** (**QF-9G**) target drones or **F9F-6D** (**DF-9F**) drone directors.

Grumman's F9F-8 Cougar was distinguished from other marks by its large nose blister and redesigned wing. This example served with VF-61.

SPECIFICATION	
Grumman F9F-8 Cougar	(11,866 lb); maximum take-off
Type: carrierborne fighter and	11232 kg (24,763 lb)
attack aircraft	**Dimensions:** wing span 10.52 m
Powerplant: one 32.25-kN	(34 ft 6 in); length 12.85 m (42 ft
(7,250-lb) thrust Pratt & Whitney	2 in); height 3.72 m (12 ft 2½ in);
J48-P-8A turbojet	wing area 31.31 m² (337 sq ft)
Performance: maximum speed	**Armament:** four 20-mm cannon,
1033 km/h (642 mph) at sea level;	plus up to 1814 kg (4,000 lb) of
service ceiling 12800 m (42,000 ft);	external ordnance including bombs,
range 1931 km (1,200 miles)	rockets and napalm tanks
Weights: empty 5382 kg	

The last of the F9F-8s were delivered to the USN in March 1957. This late example has many of the improvements introduced during the course of production of this variant, including an inflight refuelling probe, undernose UHF homing antenna and the AAM-N-7 Sidewinder capability.

Above: This VF-91 F9F-6 was photographed on USS Hornet in the Far East.

Above: Illustrating the broad, stubby wings of the F9F-8, this Cougar carries four of the new Sidewinder air-to-air missiles and two fuel tanks on its underwing pylons. The F9F-8 was also built in a reconnaissance version as the F9F-8P.

Right: Four USMC TF-9J Cougars were the last of the type to see active combat service. During 1966-67, they were flown by H&MS-13 in a Tactical Air Control (Airborne) role, directing attack aircraft against targets in South Vietnam.

Seen here in the markings of Advanced Training Unit 206, this F9F-8T shows how the basic fuselage was lengthened by 86.36 cm (34 in) to accommodate the second cockpit.

North American FJ Fury Naval fighter family

This VF-142 North American FJ-3M Fury displays the type's obvious descent from the F-86 Sabre. The FJ-3M was Sidewinder-capable, and earlier machines were upgraded to this standard.

A navalised variant of the remarkably successful North American F-86 Sabre, the swept-wing **North American FJ-2 Fury** brought the clock full circle, for the Sabre itself evolved from the original straight-wing **FJ-1 Fury**, this being the first US jet fighter to operate from an aircraft-carrier in squadron strength, an event which took place in early 1948, with VF-5A as the unit concerned.

The FJ-1's operational career was very short (it very quickly gave way to the rather more advanced Grumman Panther), and it was not until 1951 that the name Fury reappeared, when the US Navy requested North American to convert a pair of F-86Es for carrier trials. The first of these, designated **XFJ-2**, took to the air for its maiden flight on 19 February 1952, and with the successful conclusion of initial carrier qualification trials aboard the USS *Midway* in that summer, this type was ordered into quantity production.

Fury deliveries

Deliveries to fleet units got under way in January 1954 when Marine Fighter Squadron VMF-122 at Cherry Point began to convert from the F9F-5 Panther, but only 200 General Electric J47-powered FJ-2s had been completed by the spring of 1954 when production switched to the J65-powered **FJ-3**, which eventually became the most widely used version, no less than 538 rolling from the assembly line. By far the majority (458 in all) were completed as FJ-3s, but the advent of efficient missiles resulted in the final 80 appearing as **FJ-3M** fighters with provision for two heat-seeking Sidewinders; a substantial number of early production FJ-3s was subsequently upgraded to this configuration.

Attack Fury

The penultimate variant, the **FJ-4**, was in many ways virtually a new aircraft, featuring a much deeper fuselage and revised wing planform, and this was first flown in prototype form during October 1954, 150 production machines being followed by 222 examples of the more capable **FJ-4B**. This was optimised for close support tasks and incorporated a strengthened airframe, additional underwing hardpoints and a low-altitude bombing system. Introduced to service in 1957, the FJ-4B was finally retired from the front-line inventory in late 1962 although it continued to fly with second line squadrons and Reserve units for several more years, the post-1962 designations being **F-1C** (FJ-3), **MF-1C** (FJ-3M), **F-1E** (FJ-4) and **AF-1E** (FJ-4B). Lesser-used variants were the **FJ-3D** and **FJ-3D2** (**DF-1C** and **DF-1D**) drone director conversions.

This Gull Gray and White VMF-451 FJ-4 is having its arrester hook untangled from USS Lexington's arrester cable. The aircraft has brought back a pair of early Sidewinders, having flown a fighter training mission.

Left: With its axial-flow J35 turbojet, the FJ-1 employed a simple 'straight through' approach to its intake, engine, exhaust configuration. After a short period of service with VF-5A, the FJ-1 became the first Naval Reserve jet.

Below: An FJ-3 Fury from a test squadron completes a trap with the aid of arrester gear and the aircraft's air brakes, which were mounted on the rear fuselage.

North American AJ/A-2 Savage

Carrierborne strategic bomber

Of mixed propulsion, the North American AJ Savage was designed for the delivery of nuclear weapons from a carrier. Although replaced quickly in this role by the Skywarrior, Savages continued in the role of tanker.

The first heavy attack type to see service from aircraft-carriers of the US Navy, the **North American AJ Savage** used a novel method of propulsion, two Pratt & Whitney radial engines being augmented by a tail-mounted Allison J33 turbojet. In practice the type saw only limited use in the strategic bombing role for which it had been designed, being replaced from the mid-1950s onwards by the **Douglas A3D Skywarrior**, but several were subsequently modified to serve as inflight-refuelling tankers with a hose-and-reel unit in place of the turbojet.

Development began soon after World War II came to an end. An initial contract for three prototype **XAJ-1** aircraft was awarded to North American in late June 1946, and construction of these got under way almost immediately, although more than two years were to elapse before the Savage took to the air for the first time on 3 July 1948. In its original guise the Savage was manned by a crew of three and was intended to carry a 4536-kg (10,000-lb) weapon load in an internal bomb bay in its belly.

Production standard

Production-configured aircraft began to enter service with Composite Squadron VC-5 in mid-September 1949, but it was not until the end of August 1950 that this unit was considered operationally ready, this marking the climax of several months of seaborne trials aboard the USS *Coral Sea*. The first variant in service was the **AJ-1**, of which 40 were built, and these were followed by 70 examples of the **AJ-2** which featured slightly more powerful radial engines as well as increased fuel capacity, a slightly longer fuselage and a taller fin and rudder to improve handling qualities.

Final version

The final new-build version was the **AJ-2P**, which was intended for photographic reconnaissance and thus incorporated nose radar and a battery of no less than 18 cameras for use by day and night. A total of 30 AJ-2Ps was built, this being the last model to see squadron service, not being retired from the active inventory until the beginning of 1960. In 1962 all of the surviving AJ-1 and AJ-2 aircraft were subsequently redesignated **A-2A** and **A-2B** respectively.

SPECIFICATION	
North American AJ-2 Savage **Type:** carrierborne nuclear strike aircraft **Powerplant:** two 1864-kW (2,500-hp) Pratt & Whitney R-2800-48 radial piston engines and one 20.46-kN (4,600-lb) thrust Allison J33-A-10 turbojet **Performance:** maximum speed 628 km/h (390 mph); service ceiling 12190 m (40,000 ft); range 3540 km	(2,200 miles) **Weights:** empty 12247 lb (27,000 lb); maximum take-off 23396 kg (51,580 lb) **Dimensions:** wing span 21.77 m (71 ft 5 in); length 19.23 m (63 ft 1 in); height 6.22 m (20 ft 5 in); wing area 77.62 m² (835.5 sq ft) **Armament:** up to 4536 kg (10,000 lb) of bombs carried internally

McDonnell FH-1/FD-1 Phantom Early carrier jet fighter

The first production aircraft designed by the company, the **McDonnell FH-1 Phantom** was notable in also being the first jet designed to operate from an aircraft-carrier. The US Navy placed the original letter of intent on 30 August 1943, and the first prototype made its initial flight from St Louis airport, Lambert Field, on 26 January 1945. The type was certainly not over-powered, because the final propulsion system, adopted after many studies of alternatives, was two slim Westinghouse 19B engines buried in the wing roots. Later produced in small numbers as the J30, these were hardly enough for adequate performance. The first flight is thus all the more remarkable in that, at that

Possessing only marginal performance, the McDonnell FH (FD) Phantom was quickly replaced by more sophisticated jets. However, it was the US Navy's first jet fighter.

time, Westinghouse had been able to deliver only one engine, and one of the wing-root engine bays was empty. At that time McDonnell's US Navy designator letter was D, the prototype being the **XFD-1**,

The Phantom did little but introduce jets to the US Navy, its lack of power making it largely unsuited to carrier operations.

Phantoms were designated FH-1. They were gentle and easy to fly, and on 21 July 1946 a prototype landed on – and took off from – USS *Franklin D. Roosevelt* (a British de Havilland Sea Vampire had made carrier trials the previous year). The production aircraft, deliv-

ered from December 1946, served mainly with US Marine fighter squadron VMF-122. Their fault was lack of performance and lack of firepower, and the next-generation F2H Banshee was a vast improvement on both counts.

but because of confusion with Douglas (which also used letter D) McDonnell was assigned letter H, so that the 60 production

McDonnell F2H/F-2 Banshee

Multi-role naval fighter family

Below: Flying for the first time as the F2D, the McDonnell Banshee was soon redesignated F2H and was first delivered to a squadron in March 1949. This example is an F2H-2 which featured more powerful engines and a longer fuselage than the initial model.

Below: Having flown for the first time on 12 October 1950, the F2H-2P photo-recce variant of the Banshee went on to be produced in some numbers. An aircraft of the US Marine Corps' VMJ-1 is illustrated.

Another early jet-powered type to see service with the US Navy, the **McDonnell F2H Banshee** began life even before the end of World War II when the US Navy requested an improved version of the FH-1 Phantom. Bearing a strong resemblance to the earlier type, the Banshee was rather larger and more powerful, flying in prototype form for the first time as the **XF2D-1** from St Louis, Missouri, on 11 January 1947. Initial trials were successfully accomplished,

McDonnell being rewarded in May 1947 by a contract for 56 production **F2H-1** fighters, which began to enter service with VF-171 of the Atlantic Fleet during March 1949.

Banshee versatility
Like the later Phantom II, the Banshee proved to be a most versatile machine, satisfactorily undertaking day- and night-fighter tasks, all-weather interception, close air support and photographic reconnaissance, with seemingly equal facility in the

course of the next 10 years. Following on from the original F2H-1 came the **F2H-2**, which had slightly more powerful engines and a longer fuselage. Production of the basic F2H-2 totalled 364, some of which were later modified to **F2H-2B** standard for close-support tasks, while 14 examples of the **F2H-2N** specialised night-fighter derivative were also completed, these incorporating airborne interception radar. For reconnaissance, 58 **F2H-2P** aircraft were completed as new, these

being unarmed and featuring a battery of cameras in an elongated nose section.

All-weather Banshee
Production then switched to the **F2H-3** (in 1962 redesignated **F-2C**), which was optimised for all-weather fighter duties, the first of 250 entering service during April 1952 and being easily recognisable by virtue of a fuselage-mounted (rather than fin-mounted) tailplane, but plans to acquire the **F2H-3P** for reconnaissance were abandoned. The final

production model was the **F2H-4** (**F-2D**), which introduced improved APG-41 radar and more powerful engines. The 150th and last bringing production of the trusty 'Banjo' to a close in August 1953.

Apart from serving with the US Navy and US Marine Corps, 39 F2H-3s were supplied to Canada in 1955, these operating from the aircraft carrier HMCS *Bonaventure* until September 1962, when the last examples were retired from service.

This F2H-3 Banshee is about to make a text-book trap (arrested landing). The type saw much service in Korea, where both the Navy and the Marine Corps used it for air combat and ground attack. In its F2H-2P version, the Banshee was one of the most important reconnaissance aircraft of the war.

Dassault Etendard Attack, reconnaissance and tanker aircraft

The original **Dassault Etendard** was the French company's entry in a NATO competition held in 1955 for a light strike fighter, able to operate from unpaved strips. Dassault developed subsequent versions, but these were deemed to be underpowered.

As a private venture, Dassault installed the much more powerful SNECMA Atar 08 turbojet and this version, which first flew on 24 July 1956, was designated **Etendard IV**. After rejection by the NATO nations in favour of the Fiat G.91, the Etendard underwent a protracted modification programme to meet an Aéronavale requirement for a carrier-based attack and reconnaissance aircraft and two versions were developed to fulfil these primary roles.

Both Etendard IV variants were equipped with a long-stroke undercarriage, arrester hook, catapult attachments and associated strengthening, folding wing

tips and a high-lift system which combined leading-edge and trailing-edge flaps, as well as two perforated belly airbrakes.

Etendard IVM

The first version was designated **Etendard IVM**. The prototype of this variant flew for the first time on 21 May 1958, and was followed by six pre-production aircraft.

With its launch bridle falling away, this Etendard IVM launches for another mission. The IVM was a formidable attack aircraft, whose primary role for much of its career was tactical nuclear strike.

The first of 69 production Etendard IVMs was delivered on 18 January 1962, and production was completed in 1964. The Etendard IVM was equipped with Aïda all-weather fire-control radar and a Saab toss-bombing computer. A unique nose-mounted underfin blade fairing contained the guidance aerial for the AS20 radio-command missile. The Etendard IVM was withdrawn from service in July 1991 and has been replaced by the Dassault Super Etendard.

France's naval air arm, the Aéronavale, received 69 production Etendard IVM attack fighters from 1962 onwards, the aircraft being joined in service by 21 Etendard IVPs like that illustrated.

The seventh Etendard was the prototype of the **Etendard IVP**, a recce/tanker version, of which 21 were ordered. The first flight was made on 19 November 1960. The primary design changes included nose and ventral stations for cameras (replacing attack avionics and guns respectively), an independent navigation system, a fixed nose probe for

inflight refuelling, and a 'buddy-pack' hose-reel unit designed by Douglas to allow Etendard-to-Etendard refuelling. Between 1989 and 1994, the surviving Etendard IVPs were upgraded to **Etendard IVPM** standard, before being retired in September 2000, after having seen action over Bosnia and during the Allied Force offensive.

SPECIFICATION	
Dassault Etendard IVP **Type:** single-seat, carrier-based reconnaissance aircraft **Powerplant:** one SNECMA Atar 8B turbojet rated at 43.16 kN (9,700 lb) thrust **Performance:** maximum level speed 'clean' at optimum altitude Mach 1.08; maximum level speed 'clean' at sea level 1099 km/h (683 mph); maximum rate of climb at sea level 6000 m (19,685 ft) per minute; service ceiling 15500 m	(50,850 ft) **Weights:** empty 5900 kg (13,000 lb); maximum take-off 10200 kg (22,485 lb) **Dimensions:** wing span 9.6 m (31 ft 6 in); length 14.4 m (47 ft 3 in); height 14.3 m (14 ft 1 in); wing area 29 m² (312 sq ft) **Armament:** two 600-litre (132-Imp gal) underwing tanks plus bombs or rockets for a maximum external ordnance load of 1360 kg (3,000 lb)

Breguet Br.1050 Alizé ASW carrierborne turboprop

At a comparatively early stage of turbine engine development, a mixed powerplant concept was selected by a number of designers of military aircraft. Such a system offered economical operation by the turboprop for long-range cruise, with the availability of

a supplementary turbojet for take-off with heavy weapon loads or for high speed in combat. Breguet had chosen such a powerplant for the **Br.960 Vultur** naval strike aircraft.

However, experience with the Vultur, first flown on 3 August 1951, led the

French navy to abandon the idea of such a powerplant for a strike aircraft. Instead, Breguet was contracted to develop a three-seat carrier-based ASW aircraft from the Vultur. The second prototype was duly modified to serve as an aerodynamic test vehicle for the new design, the

Vultur's Mamba turboprop being replaced by an uprated 1230-kW (1,650-shp) Mamba, the turbojet engine in the rear fuselage being removed to make room for a large retractable 'dustbin' radome, and dummy streamlined nacelles being mounted beneath the wings.

In a production version these nacelles would serve to house the main landing gear units and sonobuoy equipment. By the time this aircraft had been flown and tested, Breguet had received an order for two full prototypes and three pre-production aircraft, these

Seen in the mid-grey upper and white lower colour scheme worn in the 1970s and early 1980s, this production Alizé served with 4 Flottille. This unit became the first to become operational with the E-2C Hawkeye, in March 2000.

India employed the Alizé for some 25 years, before retiring the type in 1987. The vacant ship-board ASW role was taken over by the Sea King Mk 42 helicopter, one of which is seen here alongside this 'folded' Alizé aboard the carrier Vikrant.

<table>
<tr><td colspan="2">SPECIFICATION</td></tr>
</table>

Breguet Br.1050 Alizé
Type: three-seat, carrierborne ASW aircraft
Powerplant: one Rolls-Royce Dart RDa.7 Mk 21 turboprop rated at 1473 ekW (1,975 ehp)
Performance: maximum level speed 'clean' at 3000 m (9,845 ft) 520 km/h (323 mph); maximum rate of climb at sea level 420 m (1,380 ft) per minute; service ceiling more than 6250 m (20,505 ft); range 2500 km (1,553 miles) with standard fuel
Weights: empty 5700 kg

(12,566 lb); maximum take-off 8200 kg (18,078 lb)
Dimensions: wing span 15.6 m (51 ft 2 in); length 13.86 m (45 ft 6 in); height 5 m (16 ft 4¾ in); wing area 387.51 sq ft (36 m²)
Armament: underfuselage weapons bay accommodating one torpedo or three 160-kg (353-lb) depth charges; racks under inner wings for two 160-kg (353-lb) or 175-kg (386-lb) depth charges; racks beneath outer wings for six 127-mm (5-in) rockets or two AS12 ASMs

being designated **Br.1050** and named **Alizé** (trade wind). The first prototype made its maiden flight on 6 October 1956.

Alizé into service

As finalised, the Br.1050 had hydraulically-folding outer wing panels, retractable tricycle undercarriage, arrester gear and power provided by a Dart turboprop. Production totalled 75 for the French navy, the type initially equip-

ping Flottilles 6F, 4F and 9F and replacing the Avenger.

The Alizé was finally retired by the Aéronavale on 15 September 2000. The type's service use in France had gradually been reduced to just one flottile, 6F, for use in the ASW role from the aircraft carrier *Foch*. An upgrade programme initiated in 1980 introduced Thomson-CSF Iguane radar in the ventral radome, Omega Equinox navigation system,

new communications equipment and ESM in the noses of the underwing stores panniers. This added 15 years to the expected service life, but a further modification programme for 24 surviving aircraft began in 1990 to introduce datalink, better decoy capability and other improvements to give a further service life exten-

sion. A the very end of its career, the Alizé was being employed solely as a surveillance type, having lost its ASW role to helicopters. A few Alizés were flown by Escadrille 59E at Hyères for training and SAR, and with 10S at St Raphael on miscellaneous test tasks.

With the Indian navy, an original 12 Alizés (supple-

mented by later purchase of about a dozen ex-Aéronavale aircraft) served with INAS 310 'Cobras' squadron from the *Vikrant*. The addition of ski-ramps to that carrier forced the remaining five Alizés ashore in 1987; a dwindling number continued in service until late 1992 from Dabolin, when the last example was withdrawn.

Yakovlev Yak-38 'Forger' Multi-role V/STOL fighter

Development of a V/STOL fighter for the Soviet navy's new 'Kiev'-class aircraft carriers began in 1962. Intensive studies bore fruit in the shape of a number of Yak-36 'Freehand' research aircraft, with a Yak-50-style bicycle undercarriage under the fuselage augmented by wing tip outriggers. The aircraft was powered by a pair of 36.78-kN (8,267-lb) R-11V engines, each with a rotating nozzle.

Despite carrying guns and rocket pods, the Yak-36 was never operational, but it did lead directly to the **Yak-38**. The Yak-38 first flew on 28 May 1970 (as the **Yak-36M**), and conducted trials in prototype form aboard *Moskva* in 1972. Further trails were carried out in Kiev from 1974, followed in 1976 by a summer cruise of a test squadron in the Mediterranean.

'Forger-A'

Known in AV-MF service as the Yak-38, the type received the reporting name **'Forger-A'**. Powered by a single 65.59-kN (14,770-lb st) R-27V-300 turbojet with twin

The Yak-38 proved to be only suitable for the light attack role. Its poor handling characteristics and marginal performance were real causes for concern among its crews.

rotating nozzles, the Yak-38 also had a pair of 23.04-kN (5,180-lb st) Koliesov/Rybinsk RD-36-35 single-shaft lift turbojets mounted in tandem immediately aft of the cockpit.

Up to four pylons could be fitted under the inboard sections of the wing. Auxiliary fuel tanks could be carried by some modernised and late production aircraft, which bore the designation **Yak-38M**. The Yak-38M also introduced increased thrust (allowing the carriage of additional fuel), through the introduction of modestly uprated engines.

Two-seat trainer

The Yak-38's unique operating and handling characteristics made the construction of a two-seat trainer essential. The resulting unarmed **Yak-38U**

'Forger-B' (**Yak-36U**) had tandem cockpits under separate sideways-hingeing canopies, with its longer nose having a pronounced 'droop'. A constant-section plug in the rear fuselage compensated for the longer nose but fin area was not increased. The Yak-38U lacked underwing pylons, IR sensor and ranging radar, and thus had no combat capability whatsoever.

Improvements during service included the provision of auxiliary blow-in doors in the sides of the main intakes, and fore-and-aft fences on each side of the upper fuselage intake for the lift jets.

During 1980/81 a handful of Yak-38s were deployed to Afghanistan for air force operational trials and evaluation against the Su-25. The Yak's limited payload and high accident rate made the result a foregone conclusion.

<table>
<tr><td colspan="2">SPECIFICATION</td></tr>
</table>

Yakovlev Yak-38 'Forger-A'
Type: multi-role V/STOL carrier fighter
Powerplant: (Yak-38M) one MNPK 'Soyuz' (Tumanskii) R-27VM-300 turbojet rated at 68.04 kN (15,300 lb st) and two RKBM (Koliesov) RD-36-35FVR turbojets each rated at 29.90 kN (6,725 lb st)
Performance: maximum level speed at sea level 978 km/h (608 mph); maximum rate of climb at sea level 4500 m (14,764 ft) per

minute; service ceiling 12000 m (39,370 ft); combat radius 200 km (124 miles); (Yak-38M) 390 km (242 miles)
Weights: operating empty 7370 kg (16,240 lb) including pilot; maximum take-off 11700 kg (25,794 lb) for STO
Dimensions: wing span 7.02 m (23 ft ½ in); length 15.43 m (50 ft 8 in); wing area 18.69 m² (201 sq ft)
Armament: maximum ordnance 2000 kg (4,409 lb) on four pylons

A Yak-38U shows the type's elongated lines. The door behind the cockpit feeds air to the forward-mounted lift jets.

Blackburn Buccaneer Low-level strike aircraft

The **Blackburn B-103 Buccaneer** proved by its long and distinguished service that it was a far better machine than many would have initially believed. Developed to the Royal Navy's **NA.39** requirement of the early 1950s, the B-103 was the world's first two-seat carrierborne low-level strike warplane to be built for high-speed under-the-radar means of penetration of enemy airspace. In its basic design the airframe incorporated a number of advanced features including a full wing and tail boundary layer control system to give maximum lift, area-ruling of the bulky fuselage, a tailcone split vertically and hinged so that the two halves could be deployed as airbrakes, and a rotary bomb door carrying on

its inner surface conventional or nuclear weapons. The door was rotated to expose the weapons for delivery, avoiding the drag penalty of conventional bomb doors that open into a high-speed airstream.

Design requirements

The B-103 design was chosen in 1955 to meet the NA.39 requirement, an order being placed in July of that year for an evaluation batch of 20 aircraft. Powerplant of the pre-production models, of which the first made its maiden flight on 30 April 1958, comprised two de Havilland Gyron Junior DGJ.1 turbojets each rated at 31.14 kN (7,000 lb st). The full naval 'kit' of folding wings and nose, arrester hook and catapult points was intro-

Steam rises from the deck miliseconds before the catapult stokes this No. 809 Sqn Buccaneer S.Mk 2 into the air. In order to achieve sufficient wing incidence for launch from the short catapult, the Buccaneer was positioned in a nose-up attitude by the use of a hold-back.

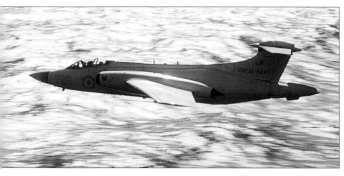

Left: The longest-lived Navy Buccaneer unit, No. 809 Sqn formed as the S.Mk 1 training unit, train aircrew in all facets of flying, including low-level overwater.

duced on the fourth example, which carried out the first carrier compatibility trials. An order for 40 examples of the **Buccaneer S.Mk 1** was placed in October 1959, these machines being powered by the Gyron Junior 101. The first of these aircraft made its maiden flight on 23 January 1962, and on 17 July that year, No. 801 Squadron of the FAA was commissioned as the first operational Buccaneer

squadron, embarking in HMS *Ark Royal* during the following January.

The Buccaneer S.Mk 1 was decidedly underpowered, and the Rolls-Royce Spey turbofan was selected as powerplant for the major production variant, the **Buccaneer S.Mk 2**, the first of 84 production examples making its initial flight on 5 June 1964. The Buccaneer S.Mk 2 had a much greater range than the Buccaneer S.Mk 1, for although the Spey engines provided some 30 per cent more power, they also had a lower fuel consumption rate, and the S.Mk 2 was also equipped for inflight-refuelling. The variant entered FAA service in

October 1965 and the last was retired in 1978.

The RN's Buccaneer S.Mk 2s were not retired when the progressive run-down of the UK's carrier force brought their withdrawal from FAA service, and from 1969 they were transferred to the RAF, with No. 12 Squadron the first to become operational on the Buccaneer S.Mk 2 in July 1970.

Before their retirement the remaining RN Buccaneers had undergone modifications comparable to those of the RAF's Buccaneer S.Mk 2B, receiving the designations **Buccaneer S.Mk 2C** and **S.Mk 2D** without and with Martel capability respectively.

SPECIFICATION

Blackburn Buccaneer S.Mk 1
Type: two-seat strike aircraft
Powerplant: two 31.58-kN (7,100-lb) thrust de Havilland Gyron Junior 101 turbojets
Performance: maximum speed, 'clean' at 61 m (200 ft) 1038 km/h (645 mph); tactical radius 805-966 km (500-600 miles); range 2784 km (1,730 miles)
Weights: empty 13599 kg (29,980 lb); loaded 20412 kg

(45,000 lb)
Dimensions: span 12.90 m (42 ft 4 in); length 19.33 m (63 ft 5 in); height 4.95 m (16 ft 3 in); wing area 47.82 m² (514.7 sq ft)
Armament: maximum bombload of 1814 kg (4,000 lb) in internal bay plus 1814 kg (4,000 lb) on four wing pylons; loads included Red Beard tactical nuclear bomb, AGM-12 Bullpup ASM, 1,000-lb (454-kg) bombs and rocket pods

---

de Havilland Sea Vixen All-weather interceptor

This impressive two-seat all-weather interceptor began life in 1946 and might have been in service in 1951, but thanks to a succession of indecisions and a horrific crash of a prototype, the **de Havilland Sea Vixen** languished until the Royal Navy

renewed interest in 1954. Eventually a fully navalised prototype flew in 1957 and following trials aboard HMS *Victorious* and *Centaur* by 'Y' Flight of No. 700 Squadron, the first **Sea Vixen FAW.Mk 1** unit, No. 892 Sqn, was commissioned on 2 July

SPECIFICATION

de Havilland Sea Vixen FAW.Mk 2
Type: two-seat carrier-based all-weather fighter
Powerplant: two 49.95-kN (11,230-lb) thrust Rolls-Royce Avon 208 turbojets
Performance: maximum speed 'clean' at sea level 1110 km/h (690 mph); range at high altitude on internal fuel 1931 km (1,200 miles); service ceiling 14630 m (48,000 ft)
Weights: empty 11793 kg

(26,000 lb); maximum take-off 18858 kg (41,575 lb)
Dimensions: span 15.54 m (51 ft); length 16.94 m (55 ft 7 in); height 3.28 m (10 ft 9 in); wing area 60.20 m² (648 sq ft)
Armament: four Red Top AAMs and 28 Microcell 2-in (51-mm) rockets, plus provision for offensive loads up to 1361 kg (3,000 lb) on four or six wing pylons, including rocket pods or bombs of up to 1,000 lb (454-kg)

Part of the Sea Vixen's repertoire was buddy-buddy refuelling, here demonstrated by two FAW.Mk 1s from No. 899 Sqn. The weapons carried are de Havilland Firestreak infra-red homing AAMs. The FAW.Mk 2 featured enlarged tail booms which extended forward of the leading edge, and was equipped to fire the more advanced Red Top missile.

1959. The squadron went to sea operationally in HMS *Ark Royal* in March 1960.

Retaining the company's twin-boom layout, the Vixen was unique in seating the pilot high on the left. The radar observer was inside what was called 'the coal hole' low down on the right, with a roof hatch and small window. Immediately beside were the inlet ducts from the wing roots leading to the two turbojets in the rear of the nacelle. The nose was filled by the big GEC AI.Mk 18 radar. No guns were fitted, their place being occupied by two hinged packs, each housing a battery of 14 air-to-air rockets. Wing pylons carried up to four Firestreak IR-homing AAMs, and the Vixen was also cleared to operate in the attack role with a wide range of bombs and air-to-surface missiles such as Bullpup. In practice these aircraft were

No. 892 Sqn was formed out of No. 700Y Sqn in July 1959 as the first operational FAW.Mk 1 unit. FAW.Mk 2s (pictured) were received from December 1965, and the squadron deployed on Hermes *in 1967 before disbanding the following year.*

used mainly as interceptors.

The 92nd aircraft was modified on the production line as the first **Sea Vixen FAW.Mk 2**, with swollen tail booms housing more fuel, and with a modified fire-control system compatible with the much more capable Red Top AAM. As on the Mk 1 aircraft, an inflight-refuelling probe could be attached in the wing leading edge outboard of the left boom, and there were additional avionic items. Total

production of both marks was 148, many Mk 1s being converted after delivery to Mk 2 standard. After replacement by McDonnell Douglas Phantoms from 1970, many Sea Vixens were rebuilt as **Sea Vixen D.Mk 3** pilotless RPV targets.

Royal Navy operators

Fleet Air Arm operators comprised four front-line units. No. 890 Sqn received the FAW.Mk 1 in February 1960

and first deployed on *Hermes* in July. On *Ark Royal* the squadron saw active duty during the Beira Patrol. After 1967 No. 890 Sqn served as an operational trials and training unit with the FAW.Mk 2. No. 892 Sqn operated the Sea Vixen Mk 1 and 2 between 1959-68, conducting Firestreak trials and deploying aboard *Ark Royal*, *Victorious*, *Hermes* and *Centaur*.

No. 893 Sqn became oper-

ational with the Mk 1 in September 1960, and saw active duty during the Kuwait crisis before reforming on the Mk 2 in November 1965 and disbanding in 1970. No. 899 Sqn was also involved in the Beira Patrol, and as the Sea Vixen Headquarters squadron and Intensive Flying Trials Unit, operated both variants between February 1961 and January 1972.

Fairey Gannet ASW and AEW aircraft

Unique in many ways, this distinctive machine began life as the **Fairey GR.17** (from the specification. GR.17/45), the first prototype flying on 19 September

1949. It was designed as an ASW (anti-submarine warfare) hunter-killer able to operate from small carriers yet carry radar and sonobuoys to detect sub-

marines, as well as weapons in an internal bay to kill such submarines as they were found. Delay was caused by a sudden decision to add a third crew member, but eventually the **Gannet AS.Mk 1** entered service with No. 826 Squadron in January 1955.

Propulsion was provided by a turboprop with two independent power sections each driving one half of a double co-axial propeller. Thus, without affecting the handling, either half-engine and its propeller could be shut down in flight to extend mission

Left: Providing the Fleet Air Arm's airborne early warning throughout the 1960s was the Gannet AEW.Mk 3, which replaced the Skyraider AEW.Mk 1 in this role. This aircraft served on board HMS Ark Royal *with No. 849 Sqn.*

endurance. Another advantage was that the engine could operate on ship's diesel oil. The large wing folded in four places to reduce span and height without interfering with access to the rear cockpits or the twin jetpipes, and other features included steerable twin-wheel nose gears, a very large weapons bay and a radar extended from below the rear fuselage. Gannet AS.Mk 1, **Gannet AS.Mk 4** (with uprated engines) and **Gannet AS.Mk 6** (EW variant) aircraft served with the Royal Navy and some other navies, surviving

into the early 1960s in West Germany, Australia and Indonesia. The **Gannet T.Mk 2** and **Gannet T.Mk 5** were trainers.

AEW derivative

Most important in the 1960s was the **Gannet AEW.Mk 3**, the airborne early-warning version built to replace the Skyraider in the Royal Navy's No. 849 Squadron. Powered by an uprated engine, this had a new fuselage with no weapons bay, a single pilot cockpit at the front and a cabin for two radar observers aft of the wing. The tail was also enlarged to balance the big radome of the APS-20A radar, and the landing gear was lengthened. The last was delivered in 1961, and when the RN fixed-wing force was run down and 'B' Flight of No. 849 Squadron left HMS *Ark Royal* in 1978, the UK had no seaborne airborne early-warning capability, something bitterly regretted just four years later in the South Atlantic.

SPECIFICATION	
Fairey Gannet AEW.Mk 3 **Type:** three-seat carrier-based AEW aircraft **Powerplant:** one 2890-kW (3,875-hp) Bristol Siddeley (previously Armstrong Siddeley, later Rolls-Royce) Double Mamba 102 coupled turboprop **Performance:** maximum speed 417 km/h (259 mph); range	1127 km (700 miles); patrol height 7770 m (25,500 ft) **Weights:** empty 7421 kg (16,360 lb); maximum take-off 11340 kg (25,000 lb) **Dimensions:** span 16.61 m (54 ft 6 in); length 13.41 m (44 ft); height 5.13 m (16 ft 10 in); wing area 44.9 m² (483 sq ft)

In the anti-submarine role, the Gannet had a relatively short career before being replaced by the Whirlwind from 1958. These aircraft are from the first batch of AS.Mk 1s and carry the markings of No. 812 Sqn while aboard HMS Eagle *during 1956. A total of seven FAA units operated the AS.Mk 1 variant.*

Supermarine Scimitar Carrierborne strike/attack aircraft

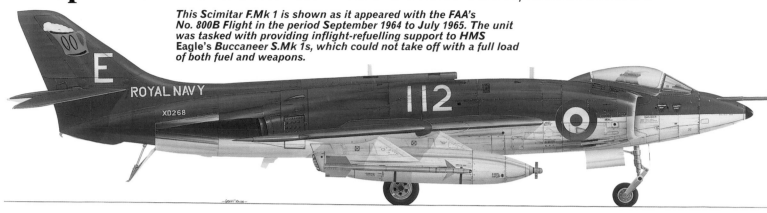

This Scimitar F.Mk 1 is shown as it appeared with the FAA's No. 800B Flight in the period September 1964 to July 1965. The unit was tasked with providing inflight-refuelling support to HMS Eagle's Buccaneer S.Mk 1s, which could not take off with a full load of both fuel and weapons.

In the UK the process of introducing transonic swept-wing fighters into the Fleet Air Arm was painfully slow. Virtually nothing was done in the first five years after World War II; then, apparently unexpectedly, carrier trials of the swept-wing Supermarine Type 510 in November 1950 showed that there need be no problem. Nevertheless, it was almost another 10 years before an aircraft reached the squadrons. Via the butterfly-tailed Type 508 and Type 529 and all-swept Type 525, the halting progress led to the **Type 544**, or **N.113D**, of January 1956. This was fitted with 200-series Avons, large flaps intended to be blown from the engines, folding wings, perforated airbrakes on the rear fuselage and a slab tailplane. It led directly to the first of the 76 **Scimitar F.Mk 1** aircraft that were built in 1957-60.

Scimitar service

A big and tough machine, the Scimitar had been planned as a carrier-based interceptor. By the mid-1950s it seemed that the need was for a low-level bomber and in service the Scimitar spent most of its brief life in attack roles. As these attack roles developed, the Scimitar's nuclear capability was announced, the aircraft being cleared to use the Red Beard device.

After trials, the command-guidance Bullpup missile was integrated but the Scimitar was never really properly equipped with air-to-surface weapon-aiming systems. Service aircraft had nose-mounted inflight- refuelling probes as standard, and the Scimitar's last combat role was carrying a buddy pack for refuelling Hawker Siddeley Buccaneers of No. 800 Squadron in 1965-66. With more advanced avionics, the Scimitar might have had a longer career.

Seen alongside AEW Skyraiders and Sea Venoms, this Scimitar F.Mk 1 is being prepared for a mission. The Scimitar was never successful as an interceptor, but served as an attack aircraft with an impressive turn of speed at low level.

SPECIFICATION

Supermarine Scimitar F.Mk 1
Type: single-seat attack fighter
Powerplant: two 50.03-kN (11,250-lb) thrust Rolls-Royce Avon 202 turbojets
Performance: maximum speed, clean at sea level 1143 km/h (710 mph); combat radius on a hi-lo-hi mission with internal fuel 579 km (360 miles); ferry range 3380 km (2,100 miles); service ceiling 14020 m (46,000 ft)
Weights: empty 11295 kg

(24,900 lb); maximum take-off 18144 kg (40,000 lb)
Dimensions: wing span 11.33 m (37 ft 2 in); length (excluding probe) 16.87 m (55 ft 4 in); height 4.65 m (15 ft 3 in); wing area 45 m² (484.9 sq ft)
Armament: four 30-mm Aden cannon each with 100 rounds, plus four wing pylons each rated at 907 kg (2,000 lb) for AIM-9s, bombs, rocket pods, buddy packs or 200-Imp gal (909-litre) drop tanks

McDonnell Douglas (Hawker Siddeley) AV-8A Harrier STOVL attack, close-support and air-combat aircraft

The US Marine Corps designated its Hawker Siddeley Harriers as the **McDonnell Douglas AV-8A Harrier** (single-seat) and **TAV-8A Harrier** (two-seat) respectively (credit for their origin going to McDonnell Douglas for political reasons). The aircraft had the Pegasus Mk 103 engine but lacked several of the nav/attack systems incorporated in the RAF's Harrier GR.Mk 3. Instead they carried AIM-9 Sidewinders for air-to-air combat, in which role the USMC pilots added a

VMA-231 'Aces' was the third and final operational Marine Corps AV-8A squadron. It came closest to seeing actual combat when deployed aboard the USS Tarawa in 1983 for peacekeeping operations over Lebanon.

remarkable new trick to the Harrier's repertoire. Known as 'VIFFing' (Vectoring In Forward Flight), this makes use of the thrust-vectoring facility in dogfighting situations, where it gave the aircraft an unprecedented manoeuvrability that no other warplane could match. The USMC had one training and three operational squadrons equipped with the AV-8, and in-service AV-8As were later upgraded to **AV-8C** standard with a host of modifications to the airframe and systems.

Other operators
The only other operators of the standard Harrier, equivalent to the USMC versions, have been the Spanish and Thai navies. In Spanish service the type was named as the **Matador**, and nine **AV-8S** single-seat and two **TAV-8S** twin-seat aircraft,

This USMC AV-8A was flown by VMA-231. The aircraft was primarily operated from assault carriers for support of ground forces.

known by the local designations **VA.1** and **VAE.1** respectively, equipped one Spanish squadron based on the light carrier *Dédalo*. With the Spanish navy's purchase of the more advanced McDonnell Douglas/BAe AV-8B Harrier II, the surviving aircraft were available for export, resulting in the purchase during 1997 of seven single- and two twin-seat aircraft by the Thai naval air service. The aircraft were used to help the naval air

service to acquire experience in the operation of STOVL warplanes on the light carrier *Chakri Naruebet* pending delivery of AV-8Bs. However, in the event the Thai navy has suffered funding problems which have prevented *Chakri Naruebet* going to sea for much of the time. In addition, the Harriers are likely to be in poor condition, the lack of funds affecting the supply of spares as well as making the AV-8B purchase unlikely.

SPECIFICATION

McDonnell Douglas (HS) AV-8C Harrier
Type: single-seat ship- or land-based STOVL light attack fighter
Powerplant: one 95.61-kN (21,500-lb) thrust Rolls-Royce Pegasus Mk 103 vectoring-thrust turbofan
Performance: maximum speed over 1186 km/h (737 mph) at low altitude; climb to 12190 m (40,000 ft) in 2 minutes 22 seconds; service ceiling more than 15240 m

(50,000 ft); combat radius with 1367-lb (3,000-lb) external stores load 95 km (59 miles) after VTO
Weights: empty 5529 kg (12,190 lb); maximum take-off 7734 kg (17,050 lb) for VTO or 10115 kg (22,300 lb) for STO
Dimensions: wing span 7.7 m (25 ft 3 in); length 13.87 m (45 ft 6 in); height 3.45 m (11 ft 4 in); wing area 18.68 m² (201.1 sq ft)
Armament: two 30-mm cannon, plus up to 2404 kg (5,300 lb) of disposable ordnance

Douglas F4D/F-6 Skyray Interceptor and attack aircraft

Yet another of Ed Heinemann's designs for the US Navy, the prototype **Douglas XF4D-1 Skyray** flew on 23 January 1951. Inspired by the German Lippisch designs, it was almost a tailless delta, the wing actually being a curved swept wing of low aspect ratio with remarkable drooping slats and with elevons and outboard ailerons on the trailing edge. Another unusual feature was that the skin was composed of inner and outer layers of thin aluminium joined at a series of dimples on the inner skin to give stability. Yet another unusual choice was that the flight controls were fully powered, almost for the first time on a fighter, but in the event of failure the pilot could extend his telescopic control column to give increased leverage in the manual mode.

Optimised interceptor
Designed to climb fast and steeply to intercept bombers attacking the fleet, the **F4D-1** (from its designation popularly nicknamed **'Ford'**) was another US Navy type that began life with the Westinghouse J40 engine. The type succeeded in set-

This F4D-1 was delivered to the US Navy on 22 December 1958 and is shown here as it appeared with VF-162, based at NAS Cecil Field from mid-1960 to late-1961.

ting a world speed record at 1211.5 km/h (752.8 mph) in 1953 but was actually a failure, and the J57 was fitted to the 419 production 'Fords' delivered in 1956-58. Thanks to its early inception the Skyray did not dispense with guns, and in service with US Navy and US Marine Corps squadrons it quickly established itself as a highly agile and popular aircraft. It was one of the first single-seaters to be equipped with a large all-weather interception radar and fire-control system, the Westinghouse APQ-50A and Aero 13. In two successive years the Skyray won the premier tro-

phy awarded to the best of all fighter squadrons based in the US, despite the fact that it equipped the only non-USAF unit to compete.
In 1962 the Skyray was redesignated **F-6A**. By this time it was being replaced in first-line service by the F-4 and F-8, but the type survived with the US Marine Corps' VMF(AW)-115 until 29 February 1964. The last of all the operational Skyrays were a pair of aircraft which served with the Naval Air Test Center's Test Pilot's School to December 1969.
Douglas also developed the **F4D-2N**, later **F5D-1 Skylancer**, as an F4D-1 derivative with advanced all-weather avionics and more fuel. With the F8U-1 about to enter service, only four Skylancers were built.

Douglas F4Ds of Marine squadron VMF-531 formate for the camera, showing the distinctive lines of the aircraft. Bestowed with astonishing vertical climb, the Skyray served with the Marines until 1964 in both interceptor and ground-attack roles.

The Skyray could carry bombs or unguided rockets (illustrated) in the ground attack role, as well as its four wing-mounted 20-mm cannon. For interception duties, AIM-9 Sidewinders were usually carried. This example is from VFAW-3.

SPECIFICATION

Douglas F-6A Skyray
Type: single-seat carrier-based interceptor
Powerplant: one 66.71-kN (15,000-lb) afterburning thrust Pratt & Whitney J57-8 turbojet
Performance: maximum speed 1162 km/h (722 mph) at sea level; range on internal fuel 1931 km (1,200 miles); service ceiling 16765 m (55,000 ft)
Weights: empty 7268 kg

(16,024 lb); maximum take-off 12701 kg (28,000 lb)
Dimensions: wing span 10.21 m (33 ft 6 in); length 13.79 m (45 ft 3 in); height 3.96 m (13 ft); wing area 51.75 m² (557 sq ft)
Armament: four 20-mm Mk 12 cannon each with 70 rounds, plus seven external pylons for 1814 kg (4,000 lb) of bombs, rocket pods or four Sidewinder AAMs

Douglas A3D/A-3 Skywarrior Multi-role warplane

Unquestionably one of the most bizarre of A-3 camouflage patterns was that seen on several VAP-61 aircraft. Night photo-reconnaissance along the Ho Chi Minh Trail, which necessitated flying at low altitude using electronic flash, proved to be hazardous, and VAP-61 lost four aircraft to enemy action. In an attempt to minimise the RA-3B's visual signature, the unit adopted this wrap-around three-colour grey camouflage, which proved quite effective.

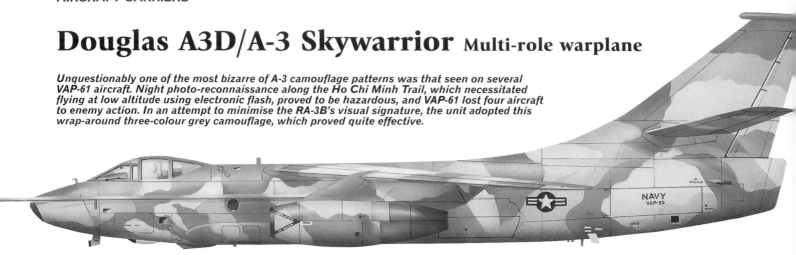

The largest and heaviest aircraft designed for operation from an aircraft carrier when Douglas completed the project design in 1949, the **A3D Skywarrior** originated from a US Navy requirement of 1947 for an attack bomber with strategic strike capability. The type was tailored to deployment on board the giant new aircraft-carriers that were ultimately to materialise as the four aircraft carriers of the 'Forrestal' class.

The Douglas design was a high-wing cantilever monoplane with retractable tricycle landing gear, two podded turbojet engines beneath the wing, and a large internal weapons bay. The high aspect ratio wing was swept back at 36°, providing maximum cruise efficiency and therefore long range. All the tail surfaces were swept, and the outer wing panels and vertical tail surface folded to facilitate flight and hangar deck accommodation.

Prototypes

The first of two **XA3D-1** prototypes made its maiden flight on 28 October 1952, powered by two 31.13-kN (7,000-lb st) Westinghouse XJ40-WE-3 engines. The failure of the J40 meant that the 43.18-kN (9,700-lb st) Pratt & Whitney J57-P-6 was used to power the sole **YA3D-1** production prototype and **A3D-1** initial production model. The first of the 49 A3D-1s flew on 16 September 1953, and deliveries to the US Navy's VAH-1 attack squadron began on 31 March 1956. In 1962 the core designation was changed from A3D to **A-3**, the initial three-seat production version becoming the **A-3A**. Six of these aircraft were later modified for the ECM role with seven-seat accommodation and a mass of specialised equipment under the revised designation **EA-3A**.

The **A3D-2** (from 1962 **A-3B**) entered service in

Eight RA-3Bs were converted to ERA-3B standard and served as electronic surveillance platforms and communications jammers. Split between US Navy electronic warfare squadrons VAQ-33 and VAQ-34, they were finally retired from active military service in 1991.

1957 with the uprated powerplant of two J57-P-10 engines and an inflight-refuelling probe. Surviving examples of these 164 aircraft were later modified, the radar-controlled tail turret (two 20-mm cannon) being replaced by ECM equipment including a chaff dispenser, the nose radome being modified for accommodation of an improved nav/attack radar, and the structure being strengthened to allow use of the LABS (Low-Altitude Bombing System). A reconnaissance variant with cameras in the weapons bay was designated **A3D-2P** (from 1962 **RA-3B**), and these 30 aircraft had the erstwhile weapons bay adapted for the carriage of two operators, 12 vertical and oblique cameras, and

photoflash bombs. Later, eight A-3s were modified for use in the electronic aggressor role, as the **ERA-3B**.

Special roles

The designation **A3D-2Q** (from 1962 **EA-3B**) identified 25 aircraft built specifically for the ECM role, with the weapons bay turned into a pressurised compartment accommodating four operators and their specialist equipment; the type also had forward- and side-looking radar, and a number of IR sensors. The only other new-build model was the **A3D-2T**, a designation used for 12 aircraft that received the revised designation **TA-3B** in 1962 and were operated as eight-seat navigator/bombardier trainers, with the weapons bay revised for an instructor and up to six pupils.

The A3B/A-3 series was also the basis of a number of conversions. The designation **A3D-2Z** was employed for two A-3B conversions that received the revised designation **VA-3B** in 1962 and were operated in the staff transport role with a well-appointed fuselage compartment for two officers. The final variants in US Navy service were the **KA-3B** inflight-refuelling tankers and at least 30 **EKA-3B** tanker and countermeasures aircraft. The EKA-3B remained a standard US Navy Reserve aircraft into the early 1990s.

SPECIFICATION

Douglas A-3B Skywarrior
Type: three-seat carrier-based bomber
Powerplant: two Pratt & Whitney J57-P-10 turbojet engines each rated at 46.71 kN (10,500 lb st)
Performance: maximum speed 982 km/h (610 mph) at 3050 m (10,000 ft); range on standard internal fuel 4667 km (2,900 miles); service ceiling 12500 m (41,000 ft)
Weights: empty 17876 kg

(39,409 lb); maximum take-off 37195 kg (82,000 lb)
Dimensions: wing span 22.1 m (72 ft 6 in); length (excluding probe) 23.27 m (76 ft 4 in); height 6.95 m (22 ft 9½ in); wing area 75.43 m² (812 sq ft)
Armament: typically 5443 kg (12,000 lb) of bombs, including nuclear, plus two 20-mm cannon in radar-directed tail turret

---

This neat four-ship of A3Ds from VAH-5 'Savage Sons', was photographed on exercise over the Mediterranean.

Douglas A4D/A-4 Skyhawk Carrierborne attack aircraft

One of the most successful post-World War II aircraft to serve with the US Navy, the **A-4 Skyhawk** originated as a private-venture design under a team headed by Ed Heinemann.

Thus, when the US Navy began the search for a turbine-powered successor to the Skyraider, Douglas was able to propose a new attack aircraft with a gross weight of about half that of the official specification and one which was considerably faster. Ordered during the Korean War, the prototype was first flown on 22 June 1954 and the first pre-production aircraft on 14 August 1954, with initial deliveries to US Navy Attack Squadron VA-72 beginning on 26 October 1956. Three months later, in January 1957, VMA-224 became the first US Marine Corps squadron to receive Skyhawks.

Vietnam

It was a fortunate period in which to introduce this sparkling new attack aircraft, for by the time the US Navy and US Marines became involved in operations in Vietnam, both of these services were able to deploy the Skyhawk with the greatest confidence in its capability; indeed, such was its effectiveness that steadily improving A-4s remained in production until February 1979. The type was built to a total of 2,960 aircraft including trainers, and exported to the armed forces of several nations. In 2003, Skyhawks remained in service in a variety of original and upgraded forms with Argentina, Brazil, Indonesia, Israel and Singapore. Indeed, Argentina's A-4 fleet has been augmented by 32 radically updated ex-USMC A-4Ms under the designation **A-4AR Fightinghawk**, along with four OA-4M-based **TA-4R** machines. Features of these Lockheed

Wearing the markings of VA-72 'Blue Hawks', this Skyhawk was aboard the carrier USS Independence in the South China Sea during May 1965.

Martin-produced conversions include AN/APG-66 radar and HOTAS controls.

Multiple variants

The Skyhawk was built in a vast number of models, those specifically built for naval use including the first generation **XA4D-1** prototype, powered by a 32.02-kN (7,200-lb) thrust Wright J65-W-2 turbojet; the 19 **YA4D-1** (later **YA-4A** and then **A-4A**) pre-production aircraft; the **A4D-1** (later A-4A) first production aircraft; the **A4D-2** (later **A-4B**) with strengthened rear fuselage, inflight-refuelling equipment, and more power; the **A4D-2N** (later **A-4C**) with terrain-following radar, autopilot, increased power and a number of other improvements; the **A4D-5** (later **A-4E**) improved production version, introducing the 37.8-kN (8,500-lb) thrust Pratt & Whitney J52-P-6A turbojet and two additional underwing hardpoints to allow a maximum weapon load of 3719 kg (8,200 lb); the lengthened, tandem two-seat **TA-4F** production trainer; the **A-4F** final attack production version for the US Navy with the J52-P-8A engine and additional avionics in a hump-back fairing on the rear fuselage; the **EA-4F** conversions of four TA-4Fs to carry stores simulating

Two-seat Skyhawks provided carrier-capable training facilities for USN/USMC aircrew from 1966 until 1999, when the last training examples were replaced by T-45A Goshawks.

Soviet missile and aircraft signatures for dissimilar air combat training; the **A-4G**, similar to the A-4F but with the avionics hump removed and built for the Royal Australian Navy; two **TA-4G** trainers for the RAN; the **TA-4J** trainer for the USN; and the **A-4L** conversion of

A-4Cs after withdrawal from first-line use and upgrading for use by reserve squadrons; all with J65-W-16C engines. So-called second-generation variants and later conversions included the **A-4M Skyhawk II** production version for the USMC,

introducing a number of improvements and the more powerful J52-P-408A engine; the **OA-4M** conversion of the TA-4F for the USMC fast FAC role and the **A-4Q** refurbished ex-USN A-4Bs for service with Argentina's naval air arm.

Right: A late-model A-4M of Marine squadron VMA-324 fires a Zuni air-to-ground unguided rocket at a range in California.

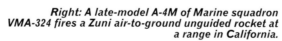

Seen here aboard Argentina's aircraft carrier Veinticinco de Mayo, is one of the Escuadrilla's A-4Qs which were retired in February 1988. The Argentinian navy lost three Skyhawks during the Falklands conflict, all from shore bases, carrier operations being too vulnerable to submarine attack.

SPECIFICATION	
Douglas A-4M Skyhawk II **Type:** single-seat carrier-based attack aircraft **Powerplant:** one Pratt & Whitney J52-P-408A turbojet rated at 49.8 kN (11,200 lb st) **Performance:** maximum speed, 'clean' at sea level 1078 km/h (670 mph); combat radius with external weapons on a hi-lo-hi mission 620 km (385 miles); service ceiling 12880 m (42,250 ft)	**Weights:** empty 4899 kg (10,800 lb); maximum take-off 11113 kg (24,500 lb) **Dimensions:** wing span 8.38 m (27 ft 6 in); length 12.29 m (40 ft 4 in); height 4.57 m (15 ft); wing area 24.15 m² (260 sq ft) **Armament:** two 20-mm cannon, plus up to 4153 kg (9,155 lb) of weapons on five external hardpoints

Grumman A-6 Intruder All-weather attack aircraft

VA-165 'Boomers' transitioned
from the A-1H Skyraider to the
A-6A (illustrated) in 1967.

Korean War experience showed the need for a specially designed jet-powered, carrier-capable attack aircraft that could operate effectively in the worst weather. Accordingly, in 1957 eight companies submitted 11 designs in a US Navy competition for a new long-range, low-level tactical attack and strike aircraft. The **Grumman G-128 Intruder** was selected as the winning design on the last day of the year, and was to fulfil that requirement admirably, becoming a major combat type in the later war in Southeast Asia, and leading to a family of later versions which saw their final combat in 1991.

Intruder development

Eight development aircraft were ordered in March 1959 with the designation **YA2F-1** that was later changed to **YA-6A**. The first of these aircraft flew on 19 April 1960 with the powerplant of two 37.81-kN (8,500-lb st) J52-P-6 turbojet engines: the jetpipes of these engines were designed to swivel slightly downward to provide an additional component of lift during take-off, but this feature was incorporated in only the first four development aircraft. All others had jetpipes with a permanent slight downward deflection.

The first production **A-6A** (originally **A2F-1**) aircraft were delivered to VA-42 in February 1963, and the first

The Intruder's ability to carry a huge number of bombs (30 500-lb/227-kg bombs are present on this A-6A) and to drop them accurately on a target in any weather gave the US Navy and Marine Corps attack communities an enormous leap forward in capability.

unit to fly on combat duties in Vietnam was VA-75, whose A-6As began operating from USS *Independence* in March 1965. The Intruder's DIANE (Digital Integrated Attack Navigation Equipment) gave them a first-class operating ability and efficiency in the worst of the humid, stormy weather offered by the local climate, and with a maximum ordnance load of more than 7711 kg (17,000 lb) the aircraft were a potent addition to the US arsenal in Southeast Asia. Production of the basic A-6A ran until December 1969 and totalled 482 aircraft, plus another 21 built as EA-6A variants,

retaining a partial strike capability but developed primarily to provide ECM support for the A-6A in Vietnam and to act as Elint gatherers. The first EA-6A flew in 1963, and three

YA-6A and three A-6A aircraft were also converted to EA-6A configuration.

The next three variants of the Intruder were also produced by the conversion of existing A-6As. The first of

The inclusion of the dedicated KA-6D tanker in air wings allowed US Navy carriers to undertake wide-ranging autonomous operations, without the need to divert other aircraft from their primary missions to carry out refuelling duties.

Grumman A-6E/TRAM Intruder
Type: two-seat carrierborne and land-based all-weather strike and attack aircraft
Powerplant: two Pratt & Whitney J52-P-8B turbojet engines each rated at 41.37 kN (9,300 lb st)
Performance: maximum speed 1036 km/h (644 mph) at sea level; cruising speed 763 km/h (474 mph) at optimum altitude; initial climb rate 2323 m (7,620 ft) per minute; service ceiling 12,925 m (42,400 ft); range 1627 km (1,011 miles) with maximum warload
Weights: empty 12093 kg (26,660 lb); maximum take-off 26581 kg (58,600 lb) for a catapult launch or 27397 kg (60,400 lb) for a

land take-off
Dimensions: wing span 16.15 m (53 ft); length 16.69 m (54 ft 9 in); height 4.93 m (16 ft 2 in); wing area 49.13 m² (528.90 sq ft)
Armament: up to 8165 kg (18,000 lb) of disposable stores; typical loads might have included up to three B28, B43, B57 or B61 thermonuclear free-fall bombs, or five 2,000-lb (907-kg) Mk 84 or 10 1,000-lb (454-kg) Mk 83 bombs, or 22 500-lb (227-kg) Mk 82 bombs, or four AGM-45 Shrike or AGM-88 HARM anti-radar missiles, or two AGM-84 Harpoon anti-ship missiles, or two AGM-84E SLAM ASMs, or four AGM-65 Maverick ASMs, or four Paveway series LGBs

*Above: With the **TRAM** turret prominent beneath their nose radomes, these A-6Es demonstrate the colours in which the type finished its active service. Note the characteristic offset refuelling probe.*

these was the **A-6B** (19 aircraft), issued to one USN squadron and differing from the initial model primarily in its ability to carry the AGM-78 Standard ARM instead of the AGM-12B Bullpup ASM. For identifying and acquiring targets not discernible by the Intruder's standard radar, Grumman then modified 12 other A-6As to **A-6C** standard with an improved capability for night attack provided by FLIR and low-light-level TV sensors in a turret under the fuselage.

KA-6D tanker

A prototype conversion of an A-6A to **KA-6D** inflight-refuelling tanker standard flew on 23 May 1966, and production contracts for the tanker version were placed. These were subsequently cancelled, but 62 A-6As were converted to KA-6D configuration, equipped with

TACAN instrumentation and carrying a hose-reel unit in the rear fuselage to refuel other carrierborne aircraft. The KA-6D could also operate as a day bomber or as an air/sea rescue control machine, and after withdrawal of the EKA-3B Skywarrior from sea-going duty became the Navy's standard carrierborne tanker.

Definitive Intruder

On 27 February 1970 Grumman flew the first example of the **A-6E** as an advanced and upgraded development of the A-6A. The A-6E followed the A-6A in production, and manufacture eventually encompassed 240 aircraft complemented by 205 A-6A/B/C conversions.

The basis of the A-6E, which retained upgraded forms of the airframe and powerplant of the earlier models, was a new avionics

fit founded on the addition of a Norden APQ-148 multi-mode navigation radar, an IBM/Fairchild ASQ-133 computerised nav/attack system, Conrac armament control unit, and an RCA video-tape recorder for assessing the damage caused during a strike mission. Following the first flight of a test aircraft on 22 March 1974, all USN and US Marine Corps Intruders were progressively updated still further under a

The A-6E had good carrier landing qualities, with sufficient agility and power to cope with most situations. An automatic landing system made life easier for the pilot.

programme known as **TRAM (Target Recognition Attack Multi-sensor)**. This added to the standard A-6E a Hughes turreted optronic package of FLIR and laser detection equipment, integrated with the Norden radar; CAINS (Carrier Airborne Inertial Navigation System) to provide the capability for automatic landings on carrier decks; and provision for autonomous and laser-guided air-to-surface

weapons. The first US Navy squadron to be equipped with this **A-6E/TRAM** version was VA-165, which was deployed aboard USS *Constellation* in 1977. In addition, a separate programme equipped 50 A-6Es each able to carry four Harpoon anti-ship missiles, and a Harpoon capability was later retrofitted to all aircraft, which also received the SWIP upgrade allowing them to carry other guided weapons including the AGM-65 Maverick, AGM-84E SLAM and AGM-88 HARM missiles.

The last Intruders were retired from USN service in 1997, after seeing final combat in 1991, their role being assumed by the Boeing F/A-18 Hornet.

*USS **Theodore Roosevelt** went to war in Desert Storm with two Intruder squadrons. One of them, VA-65, tested some aircraft in desert-style camouflage schemes during combat operations.*

Grumman S2F/S-2 Tracker and TF-1/C-1 Trader
ASW and COD aircraft

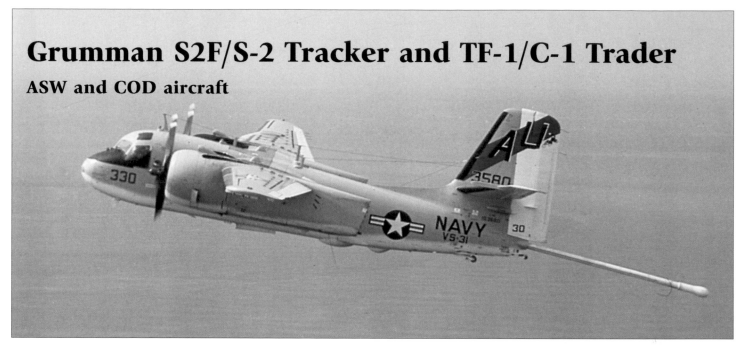

First flown on 4 December 1952, the **Grumman XSW-1** prototype had its genesis in a US Navy specification of two years earlier demanding the previously unattainable quality of being able to operate from a small (i.e. not a giant 'Forrestal'-class) carrier while carrying both ASW sensors and weapons to effect the kill. Previously the task had demanded two aircraft operating in a hunter/killer team. Grumman's **G-89** design was basically a conventional aircraft with a high wing of long span, two piston engines and a cabin ahead of the wing for two pilots and two radar and sensor operators.

ASW equipment
It was no easy job to package all the required items into a compact airframe. The APS-38 radar was put in the rear fuselage, the radome being winched down for use.

A searchlight was installed on the outer right wing, and the MAD (magnetic anomaly detector) was mounted on a tube which could be extended from the rear fuselage well aft of the tail. Sonobuoys could be ejected from the rear of the engine nacelles, and weapons were carried in an internal bay and also on six wing pylons.

Into production
From the start of operational service in February 1954 the **S2F-1**, named **Tracker**, did all that was asked. Production continued until after 1960 and there were many conversions and rebuilds, the later models having APS-88 radar and twice as many sonobuoys (some 32).

Many S-2 Tracker ASW aircraft were later converted into **US-2C** aircraft and various other utility versions used as hacks and for gen-

eral trucking duties. In addition, Grumman was contracted to supply the US Navy with a specially designed transport for COD (carrier on-board delivery) missions. These involve supplying a carrier at sea with personnel, mail and all urgently needed stores.

COD Trader
The requirement dated from 1950, but pressure of other work delayed the **G-96**, which appeared in 1955 as the **Grumman TF-1 Trader**, the designation actually indicating that the aircraft was a trainer (a secondary role). In the rationalised USAF/US Navy designation scheme of 1962, the Trader was redesignated **C-1**. Using the wing, engines and many other parts of the S-2 Tracker, its tail being of the enlarged type introduced with the **S-2D**, the **C-1A** was given a new fuselage with increased

This VS-31 S-2 Tracker displays the sensor used by the aircraft for detecting submarines, a magnetic anomaly detector. This retracts back into the fuselage when not in use. The idea of the extendible sting is to take the detector gear as far away from the metal aircraft as possible.

volume, providing sufficient room for nine, strong, 9-*g* aft-facing passenger seats, or a cargo load of 1587 kg (3,500 lb). All loads entered the aircraft via side doors, large items and small vehicles not being compatible. Of course full carrier compatibility was retained, the fully loaded aircraft making arrested landings and catapult take-offs.

Grumman delivered 87 production C-1A Traders, as well as four of the **G-125** version which entered Navy

service in 1957 as the **TF-1Q** specialised ECM platform with the main cabin taken over by high-power receivers and jamming systems. In 1962 these little-publicised machines were redesignated as **EC-1A** aircraft.

Eventually, from 1965, the Trader began to be replaced by the much more powerful Grumman C-2A Greyhound version of the E-2, but a few continued in second-line service until the end of the decade.

These two Grumman C-1 Traders were photographed on a regular supply mission to a US Navy carrier. The Trader could carry up to nine passengers as well as cargo in its fully-equipped hold.

SPECIFICATION	
Grumman S-2E Tracker **Type:** four-seat carrier-based ASW aircraft **Powerplant:** two 1137-kW (1,525-hp) Wright R-1820-82WA Cyclone piston engines **Performance:** maximum speed 426 km/h (265 mph) at sea level; patrol speed 240 km/h (149 mph); range 1850 km (1,150 miles); endurance 9 hours **Weights:** empty 8633 kg	(19,033 lb); maximum take-off 12187 kg (26,867 lb) **Dimensions:** wing span 22.12 m (72 ft 7 in); length 13.26 m (43 ft 6 in); height 5.05 m (16 ft 7 in); wing area 46.08 m² (496 sq ft) **Armament:** internal bay and six pylons for total load up to 2182 kg (4,810 lb) including ASW torpedoes, depth bombs and rockets

Grumman WF-2/E-1 Tracer Carrierborne AEW&C aircraft

In 1954 the success of Lockheed Super Constellations and other US Navy aircraft tested in the high-flying AEW role, which then was called radar picket duty, caused Grumman to receive a contract for a development of the S2F-1 Tracker specially configured to carry a large surveillance radar. This aircraft, the **WF-1**, never flew; instead the com-

pany type number **G-117** was carried over to a radar-carrying development of the more capacious TF-1A Trader, the **Grumman WF-2**, with the bigger wing and tail. A TF-1 was fitted with a mock-up of the proposed radome and tail to serve as the aerodynamic prototype. This flew on 1 March 1957 and the first of 88 production machines, named **Tracer** and

after 1962 redesignated as **E-1B**, flew on 2 February 1958. (The new designation arrived too late to prevent the widely used unofficial name, from the WF designation, becoming **'Willy Fudd'**.)

'Willy Fudd's' radar
The radar used in the Tracer was the AN/APS-82, with the main racking filling the

SPECIFICATION	
Grumman E-1B Tracer **Type:** four-seat AEW and control aircraft **Powerplant:** two 1137 kW (1,525-hp) Wright Cyclone R-1820-82WA piston engines **Performance:** maximum speed 365 km/h (227 mph) at 1219 m (4,000 ft); initial climb rate 341 m (1,020 ft) per minute; service ceiling	4816 m (15,800 ft); maximum endurance 8 hours **Weights:** empty 9536 kg (21,024 lb); maximum take-off 12232 kg (26,966 lb) **Dimensions:** wing span 22.12 m (72 ft 7 in); length 13.82 m (45 ft 4 in); height 5.13 m (16 ft 10 in); wing area 46.36 m² (499 sq ft)

centre and rear fuselage and the rotating aerial (antenna) housed inside an unusual aerofoil-profile radome like a vast teardrop saucer carried on struts above the fuselage. The front of this fixed radome had a de-icer boot larger than any previously made, while at the rear it was extended to join the centre fin of the completely redesigned three-fin tail. The two operators amidships worked at identical consoles but with different duties, managing not only the main

radar but also extensive IFF and communications systems, the two pilots

handling navigation. In service as detachments of VAW-11 and VAW-12 the

Tracer pioneered shipboard early-warning and fighter direction, being replaced by

the much more capable and larger Grumman E-2A Hawkeye from 1964.

Thanks to its S2F designation, the Tracker was nicknamed 'Stoof' in service. The Tracer was commonly called 'Willy Fudd', but was also known as the 'Stoof with a roof'.

McDonnell F3H/F-3 Demon Naval fighter

This McDonnell F3H-2 Demon served with VF-131, based on the USS Constellation, in the early 1960s.

Like the contemporary Supermarine Swift in the UK, the **McDonnell F3H Demon** was sustaining a big production programme when it was belatedly recognised that the aircraft pouring off the line were unacceptable; an outcry ensued as dozens of aircraft were scrapped or put aside for later rework. McDonnell knew the fault lay solely with the J40 engine, and after years of trauma got a redesigned F3H into US Navy service where it proved a fine aircraft.

Production problems
When the **XF3H-1** prototype flew on 7 August 1951, it was structurally and aerodynamically the most advanced navy aircraft in the world. All wing and tail surfaces were acutely swept, the wing having fully variable camber and the tailplane being a slab. During flight testing the US Navy demanded extra fuel and all-weather radar, and the J40 engine proved totally unable to cope with the increased weight. McDonnell eventually, in 1954, redesigned the aircraft with the J71 engine, with still more fuel and a bigger wing. Production at

last went ahead with 519 in three main models. The **F3H-2** (**F-3B** after 1962) was the basic strike fighter, 239 being delivered. These had the new airframe and engine but retained the original Hughes APG-51 radar matched with gun armament, four wing pylons being added for attack loads. McDonnell delivered 80 **F3H-2M** (later designated **MF-3B**) aircraft which had augmented avionics for all-weather interception and a CW (continuous-wave) target illuminator for use with the primary air-to-air armament of four AIM-7C

Sparrow III missiles, the first time these had entered service. The **F3H-2N** (**F-3C**), of which 144 were delivered, was a limited all-weather fighter with basic APG-51 radar and four Sidewinder AAMs of the radar-guided AIM-9C variety.

Demons had a fairly active career, flying missions around Quemoy and off the Lebanon in 1958. Last deliveries took place in 1959 and replacement by the McDonnell F-4 Phantom II was complete by August 1964 (on first line squadrons) and February 1965 (reserve).

SPECIFICATION	
McDonnell F-3C Demon **Type:** single-seat carrier-based fighter **Powerplant:** one 62.26-kN (14,000-lb) afterburning thrust Allison J71-2 or -2E turbojet **Performance:** maximum speed, clean at sea level 1170 km/h (727 mph); range 2205 km (1,370 miles); service ceiling 13000 m (42,650 ft) **Weights:** empty 9656 kg	(21,287 lb); maximum take-off 15161 kg (33,424 lb) **Dimensions:** wing span 10.77 m (35 ft 4 in); length 17.98 m (59 ft); height 4.44 m (14 ft 7 in); wing area 48.22 m² (519 sq ft) **Armament:** four 20-mm Mk 12 cannon, plus four wing pylons for AIM-9C Sidewinder AAMs or up to 2722 kg (6,000 lb) of various attack weapons

A Demon of VF-61 'Jolly Rogers' launches. The severe delay in its development meant that the F3H-2 had to compete with the F8U Crusader, but the Sparrow III did much to redress the balance.

McDonnell Douglas F-4 Phantom II Multi-role fighter

Resplendent in the colours of VF-142'Ghostriders' aboard USS Constellation, this F-4B Phantom II is configured for the MiGCAP role with four AIM-7 Sparrow missiles carried in wells under the fuselage and four AIM-9 Sidewinders on spreader bars on the inboard pylons. Phantoms dominated the air-to-air fighting over Vietnam (although the Crusader returned a much better kill:loss ratio). The lack of internal cannon and sooty exhaust were the main problems with the otherwise excellent F-4.

Produced as a private company venture in the mid-1950s, the **McDonnell Phantom II** was first ordered as the **AH-1** attack aircraft but then became the **F4H** interceptor with only a single centreline pylon for a giant drop tank. Guns were deleted, four Sparrow III AAMs were recessed under the broad flat belly, a powerful Westinghouse AN/APQ-50 Mod radar was added along with a radar operator in the back seat, and the first of 23 test aircraft flew on 27 May 1958. Though large aircraft, their splendid propulsion system, installed between fully variable inlets and nozzles with carefully arranged secondary flow, gave all-round flight performance never previously attained by any fighter. Early **F4H-1** (**F-4A**) aircraft captured almost every world record for speed at low and high altitudes, time to height and other parameters. The type was also bought in vast numbers as a land-based fighter for air forces.

Production models
The initial carrier-based model was the **F-4B**, of which 649 were built (including 12 **F-4G** aircraft with revised navigation and systems and an advanced

Left: The Royal Navy's No. 892 Sqn operated its Phantom FG.Mk 1s from HMS Ark Royal. The type's main duty was air defence, with attack and close support as secondary roles.

VF-142 'Ghostriders' made four deployments to the Gulf of Tonkin with F-4Bs between 1964 and 1969, including three aboard USS Constellation.

datalink). This had a bulged nose to house the 0.81-m (32-in) diameter dish of the

McDonnell Douglas F-4B Phantom II
Type: two-seat carrier-based all-weather fighter
Powerplant: two 75.60-kN (17,000-lb) afterburning thrust General Electric J79-8B turbojets
Performance: maximum speed 'clean' at 14630 m (48,000 ft) 2390 km/h (1,485 mph); service ceiling 18900 m (62,000 ft); combat radius as an interceptor with tanks, over 1448 km (900 miles); ferry

range 3701 km (2,300 miles)
Weights: empty 12700 kg (28,000 lb); maximum take-off 24766 kg (54,600 lb)
Dimensions: wing span 11.71 m (38 ft 5 in); length 17.75 m (58 ft 3 in); height 4.95 m (16 ft 3 in); wing area 49.24 m² (530 sq ft)
Armament: four (or six) AIM-7 Sparrow III AAMs, up to four AIM-9 Sidewinder AAMs, and up to 7257 kg (16, 000 lb) of attack weapons

A pair of F-4Bs of the VMFA-513 'Flying Nightmares' demonstrates the Phantom's prodigious load-carrying ability, shortly after the type entered service with the squadron in 1963.

FAA service – No. 892 Sqn
Though primarily intended as a fleet defence interceptor, the Phantom FG.Mk 1 had a secondary attack and close air support role and was equipped to deliver a nuclear weapon if required. No. 892 was the only FAA front-line unit be equipped with the Phantom (from 1969 to 1978) and HMS Ark Royal the only carrier modified for Phantom operations.

AN/APQ-72 radar and a raised rear seat. It went to sea in August 1962 and became the standard all-weather fighter with the US Navy and US Marines, the latter service also buying 46 unarmed **F4H-1P** (**RF-4B**) multi-sensor reconnaissance aircraft. Service experience led to the **F-4J** of 1965, with the AWG-10 fire-control system, an extra tank, slotted tailplane, drooping ailerons, bigger wheels and brakes and (as a modification) ECM fin cap. This replaced the F-4B in the US Navy and US Marine Corps service, 522 being built, and many of the survivors being updated and fitted with slatted wings as the F-4S for service to 1992.

The Royal Navy bought 24 **F-4K** aircraft similar to the F-4J but with Rolls-Royce Spey engines, AN/AWG-11 radar in a hinged nose, double-extension nose leg and other changes, another 28 going to the RAF (service designation **Phantom FG.Mk 1**), which retired the last of its Phantom FG.Mk 1s in 1989. The RAF and many other air forces bought land-based versions.

The F-4 was the world's premier fighter of the 1960s and most of the 1970s. It saw extensive combat in Vietnam and has also been much used by Israel, Iran and other countries.

Some of the Phantoms ordered for the Royal Navy (above) passed directly to the RAF, while others were transferred in 1978. No. 43 Sqn 'Fighting Cocks' was the RAF's only Phantom-equipped interceptor squadron between 1969 and 1975, operating surplus FG.Mk 1s. This No. 43 Sqn aircraft (left) has intercepted a 'snooping' Soviet Tu-95 'Bear'.

Below: An F-4B of VF-21 'Freelancers' aboard USS Midway, releases a bomb on a medium-altitude bombing run. It was the US Navy's B-model Phantom that made the type's debut in Vietnam.

Naval Phantoms
Carrier and Marine Corps Phantoms

An important, but little known, role for the Phantom was the escort of reconnaissance aircraft, such as this RA-5C Vigilante. The naval Phantoms proved themselves as the masters of almost any task required of them time and again.

In service with the US Navy, US Marine Corps and Royal Navy, the Phantom has become one of the classic carrier aircraft of all time. Designed as a fleet interceptor, the aircraft also performed in the attack role with aplomb and served into 1992 with the USMC.

F-4J characteristics
Outwardly almost indistinguishable from the F-4B, the F-4J took advantage of an improved AN/ASW-21 datalink system, originally designed for the little-known US Navy F-4G. This provided an automated carrier-landing capability which included automatic approach power compensation.

Air-to-air load
On its 10 May mission, SHOWTIME 100 carried a full complement of AIM-9 Sidewinder heat-seeking missiles, but only two radar-guided AIM-7 Sparrows. Cunningham and Driscoll required just three Sidewinders to down the three MiGs they claimed that day.

F-4G Phantom II
Twelve production F-4G aircraft were produced from F-4B airframes on the production line. One other F-4B was converted to act as a prototype. With the F-4G, the USN tried to introduce an ocean-going system similar to the USAF's SAGE system. The F-4G was able to make hands-off, automatic carrier landings, as well as being datalinked to its ship and an E-2 Hawkeye control aircraft. The datalink allowed voice-free intercepts to be flown. The surviving F-4Gs were deconverted in 1966.

VF-213
Ten F-4Gs were passed to VF-96 for testing from early 1963. They were subsequently transferred to VF-213, which took them to war over Vietnam in USS *Kitty Hawk* from 19 October 1965. One of the aircraft was lost to AAA during the cruise.

Flying controls

To operate at optimum performance, the F-4J used an air data computer to monitor control input by the pilot, thus ensuring that the airframe was not overstressed. Three independent hydraulic systems activated the primary flight controls, and electrical power was supplied by an AC generator. The F-4J had an AN/APQ-13 radar and an AN/AJB-7 bombing system.

Versatile F-4J

The US Navy initially classed the Phantom as a 'fleet defence interceptor', able to defend the carrier battle group from air attack. But in Vietnam, this defensive role became secondary as the Phantom went on the offensive, hunting MiGs deep inside enemy airspace. It also carried large loads of bombs and rockets, becoming a truly 'multi-role' combat aircraft.

F-4J Phantom II

SHOWTIME 100 was the F-4J Phantom (Bureau of Aeronautics No. 155800) flown on 10 May 1972 by VF-96 pilots Lts Randall 'Duke' Cunningham and William P. 'Willie' Driscoll. In standard US Navy Gull Gray and White, with typical squadron markings for the time, this F-4J achieved glory, then fell to a SAM, all in a single action.

Flying powerhouse

The F-4J shipboard fighter was powered by two J79-GE-19 turbojets rated at 80-kN (17,900-lb) thrust with afterburning. As with previous Phantoms, in order to control airflow into the air intakes, a movable splitter plate separated the undisturbed airflow from the sluggish boundary layer close to the skin of the aircraft. The distinctive 'burner cans' at the exhaust of the F-4J were forged to contain the enormous heat produced by the engines.

Dark green camouflage

During the *Kitty Hawk* cruise, half of CVW-11's aircraft, including the F-4Gs, were finished in an experimental scheme with dark green upper surfaces. Other machines aboard *Constellation* and *Enterprise* also wore the scheme, whose results proved to be somewhat inconclusive in combat.

F-4B Phantom II

The Phantom began life as a Navy aircraft, and it was from carrier decks that it first went into action over South Vietnam in 1964. For the next 11 years the Phantom was the Navy's primary air-to-air fighter in the theatre (ably assisted by the Vought F-8), while sharing the burden of attack sorties. This particular aircraft, an F-4B, was that flown by Lieutenant Garry L. Weigand (pilot) and Lieutenant (Junior Grade) William C. Freckleton (RIO) on 6 March 1972, when the pair shot down a North Vietnamese MiG-17 (note the kill mark on the intake splitter plate). It is depicted launching for an attack mission with six Mk 82 low-drag general-purpose bombs in addition to a full load of Sparrows and two Sidewinders. At the time VF-111 'Sundowners' was on its first and only combat cruise with the F-4, having only transitioned to the Phantom from the F-8 Crusader in early 1971. Deployed aboard USS *Coral Sea* alongside VF-51, the 'Sundowners' were 'on the line' between 12 November 1971 and 17 July 1972, participating in the Freedom Train and early Linebacker campaigns. Weigand and Freckleton's MiG kill avenged a loss (to a SAM) sustained by the squadron in December. VF-111 returned to Vietnamese waters in 1973, and again in 1975.

The leading US Navy ace, with a total of five kills to his credit, Lt Randall H. Cunningham was often referred to by his callsign 'Duke'. Of the five kills he achieved during his tour in Vietnam, the final of his three successful engagements on 10 May 1972 is widely regarded as one of the most demanding and complex dogfights in history. His foe was an experienced North Vietnamese ace, who was ultimately downed with an AIM-9 Sidewinder after a series of vertical 'scissors' manoeuvres. Cunningham's Phantom was then hit by an SA-2 'Guideline' SAM, forcing Cunningham and his WSO to eject from their aircraft, only to be rescued by approaching US Navy helicopters. Here he relives his 10 May dogfight to an eager press audience. Cunningham was a graduate of the US Navy's Top Gun programme.

Weapons

The Phantom's basic air-to-air weaponry consisted of four AIM-7 Sparrows, carried in recesses along the sides of the underfuselage. AIM-9 Sidewinders or, occasionally, AIM-4 Falcons were carried on the inboard wing pylons. One centreline and four wing pylons were available for stores carriage, although at least one of these was usually occupied by a fuel tank on all but very short-range missions. The centreline and outer wing pylons were the standard positions for fuel tank carriage. Bombs were routinely carried on the inner wing pylons, using triple or multiple ejector racks, or on the centreline. A wide variety of ordnance was available, encompassing virtually every bomb, rocket and missile option available. Electronic countermeasures pods also became prevalent during the Vietnam War and beyond, often carried in one of the forward Sparrow recesses.

Infra-red sensor and RHAW

The prominent fairing under the radome of the F-4B housed the AAA-4 infra-red sensor. This required range data from the radar, but could then be used to passively track targets. It was the second such application of this technology outside the Soviet Union. Scabbed on to the underside of the IRST fairing was the forward antenna for the APR-30 RHAW (radar homing and warning) system, which was added part way through the F-4B's career to enhance its self-defence capability. Fore and aft antennas for this system were also fitted to the fin tip.

The first Phantom of them all, the YF4H-1 BuNo. 142259, is seen on its first flight on 27 May 1958. This photograph was taken from one of the two F-101 Voodoo chase aircraft that accompanied the flight.

Radar

The prototype F4H-1s were fitted with APQ-50 radar, as used in the Douglas F4D Skyray, but the developed APQ-72 was fitted to the first production aircraft. This initially retained the 61-cm (24-in) diameter reflector dish of the earlier radar, but did incorporate the APA-157 continuous-wave illuminator required to provide guidance for Sparrow missiles. From the 19th F4H-1, an 81-cm (32-in) antenna was fitted, dramatically altering the look of the Phantom while considerably increasing the radar's range. The larger antenna required a hydraulic drive. Other Phantom radars were the APQ-100 (updated APQ-72 with ground-mapping mode for the USAF's F-4C), APQ-109 (lightened APQ-100 for USAF's F-4D), APQ-120 (F-4E) and APG-59 (part of the AWG-10 system in the F-4J).

Undercarriage

Whether flown from land or ship, the Phantom employed a no-flare landing which was more akin to a controlled crash. Withstanding this considerable battering required an immensely strong undercarriage. That of the F-4 was designed to routinely handle sink rates of up to 22 ft (6.7 m) per second. The nose unit had twin self-centring wheels, and incorporated pneumatic oleo extension for catapult launches. For carrier launches the Phantom employed the old bridle system, which utilised a steel cable attached to hooks under the wing roots and then looped around the catapult shuttle. Secondary cables restrained the bridle, saving it for reuse. There was also a holdback bar which restrained the aircraft at full engine power for the cat' stroke. A frangible link with a set breaking strain shattered as the cat fired.

Powerplant

Apart from the Spey-powered British Phantoms, all F-4s were built with versions of the General Electric J79. Destined to become a classic fighter engine, the J79 was a single-spool turbojet (i.e. one turbine driving one compressor) but, by clever use of multiple variable-incidence stators, achieved a very high pressure ratio. Compared to contemporary engines, the J79 burned much less fuel to produce equivalent power levels. Considerably aiding engine performance was the design of the inlets. At the time of their development they (and those of the B-58 Hustler) were the only fully variable-incidence inlets in the world. Downstream from the vast splitter plate (which prevented the fuselage boundary layer air from entering the intake) were intake ramps which regulated the throat area of the intake, matching the airflow requirements to the speed of the aircraft. The thrustline of the engines was inclined downwards to provide a small lift force for good field/carrier performance. In the F-4B the engines were J79-GE-8s, which each developed 79.60 kN (17,000 lb) of thrust with afterburning.

Bent-wing bird

It was often joked that the Phantom's configuration came about as a result of someone treading on the blueprints, but the reality was more mundane. Having designed an immensely strong centre-section, the McDonnell engineers casually spliced on upturned outer panels at 12° dihedral to achieve the required configuration (5° dihedral as measured across the wing as a whole). This layout had hidden benefits when it came to designing the wing-folds, and also kept main undercarriage leg length (and therefore weight) down to a minimum. It did nothing for the looks of an aircraft which came to be known as the 'Double Ugly'. The wing had powerful leading-edge flaps, blown by engine bleed air, and a large single-section inboard trailing-edge flap (again 'blown'). The ailerons were located on the outer section of the flat wing section and, unusually, only deflected downwards. They were augmented for roll control by upper-surface spoilers.

North American A-5 (A3J) Vigilante Strike and recce aircraft

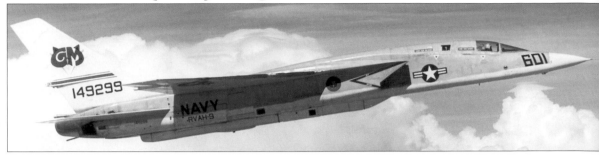

Though it never made the limelight, the **North American A3J** (**A-5** after 1962) **Vigilante** probably introduced more design innovations than any other aircraft in history, including fully variable inlets and nozzles; a one-piece moving fin; slab tailerons used for roll in conjunction with roll-control spoilers; variable-camber blown wings; complete inertial navigation with autopilot coupling; automatic bad-weather carrier approach; drogue-stabilised, rocket-augmented seats; and extensive titanium structure with gold coating in high-temperature areas. The first **YA3J-1** prototype was a tandem-seat, carrier-based bomber flown for the first in August 1958. Yet another advanced feature was the

large tunnel between the engines along the centreline. This housed two large fuel tanks and a nuclear weapon, all joined together and released as one unit over the target (the tanks then being empty and stabilising the fall of the bomb); the assembly was ejected to the rear by gas pressure.

By early 1962 the first combat unit, VAH-7, was operating from USS *Enterprise*, the original **A3J-1** designation becoming **A-5A**. North American delivered 57 A-5As, followed by six **A-5B** aircraft with a giant humped fuselage housing extra fuel, and with still further high-lift wing systems.

Recce Vigilante

By far the most important model was the **A3J-3P** (**RA-5C**) long-range, multi-sensor reconnaissance platform, which formed the airborne part of the US Navy's Integrated Operational Intelligence

The most important version of the Vigilante was the RA-5C. Its main sensor was an enormous SLAR mounted under the fuselage along with other cameras. RA-5s were usually escorted by F-4s over Vietnam to protect them from MiGs, a loaded F-4 requiring afterburner to 'keep with' a 'clean' RA-5C.

System with automatic real-time information processing on the carrier or at a shore base. The RA-5C replaced the bomb tunnel with extra fuel, and a giant SLAR (side-looking airborne radar) was housed in a fairing along the belly. An impressive array of cameras and Elint (electronic intelligence) sensors made up the most comprehensive reconnaissance system of its day.

Some 55 RA-5Cs were delivered, plus 53 converted from A3J-1s. RVAH-5 equipped with this fine aircraft in June 1964, operating from the USS *Ranger* in South East Asia. Not until 1980 did the RA-5C Vigilante begin to be replaced by F-14s carrying a pylon-mounted TARPS recce pallet.

SPECIFICATION	
North American RA-5C Vigilante **Type:** two-seat multi-sensor reconnaissance aircraft **Powerplant:** two 79.42-kN (17,860-lb) afterburning thrust General Electric J79-GE-10 turbojets **Performance:** maximum speed, 'clean' at high altitude 2229 km/h	(1,385 mph); range 4828 km (3,000 miles); operational ceiling 14750 m (48,400 ft) **Weights:** empty 17009 kg (37,498 lb); maximum take-off 29937 kg (66,000 lb) **Dimensions:** wing span 16.15 m (53 ft); length 23.32 m (76 ft 6 in); height 5.91 m (19 ft 5 in); wing area 70.05 m² (754 sq ft)

VAH-7 became the first unit to take the A-5A on an operational cruise, flying from USS Enterprise *during the Cuban Missile Crisis of 1962.*

Vought A-7 Corsair II Navy and Air Force attack aircraft

This highly successful subsonic attack aircraft originated from a US Navy requirement for an aircraft to replace the A-4 Skyhawk. On 19 March 1964 Vought was awarded a contract for three prototypes under the Navy designation **A-7**, the company reviving the name of its most famous wartime fighter in designating this new aircraft **Corsair II**. One of the requirements of the specification had been that the new aircraft should be based on an existing design, to keep costs low and to speed delivery, but while the A-7 was of basically similar

configuration to the F-8 Crusader it was, in fact, a completely new design with no large-scale commonality of structural assemblies.

Corsair prototype

The first prototype was flown on 27 September 1965, almost four weeks ahead of schedule, and initial deliveries to the US Navy began on 14 October 1966. Less than four months later, on 1 February 1967, VA-147 became the first squadron to be commissioned with the Corsair II.

Long before the first A-7 entered USN service in

December 1965, the USAF had decided to adopt a denavalised version of the aircraft to serve as a tactical fighter. The primary change was the selection of the Allison-built Rolls-Royce Spey to power it instead of the Pratt & Whitney TF30 turbofan of the Navy's A-7.

Corsair combat

US Navy Corsair IIs equipped 27 squadrons during the Vietnam War, flying more than 90,000 combat missions, and the type was also used by the USAF in that theatre, although to a far lesser extent. After being replaced on active-duty service by the A-10, the USAF's **A-7D** aircraft were issued to ANG units, where the type continued to have a productive career. In January 1981 the two-seat **A-7K** made its first flight, the 31 built being

SPECIFICATION	
Vought A-7E Corsair II **Type:** carrier-based attack bomber **Powerplant:** one 64.48-kN (14,500-lb) thrust Allison TF41-A-2 (derived from the Rolls-Royce Spey) turbofan **Performance:** maximum speed, clean, 1123 km/h (698 mph) at sea level; tactical radius with typical weapon load 1127 km (700 miles) **Weights:** empty 8841 kg	(19,490 lb); maximum take-off 19051 kg (42,000 lb) **Dimensions:** wing span 11.81 m (38 ft 9 in); length 14.06 m (46 ft 1½ in); height 4.9 m (16 ft ¾ in); wing area 34.84 m² (375 sq ft) **Armament:** one 20-mm M61A1 six-barrel cannon, plus up to 6804 kg (15,000 lb) of mixed stores carried externally

These Naval Air Warfare Center A-7Es are seen dropping inert 500-lb (227-kg) retarded bombs on a flight from their China Lake base.

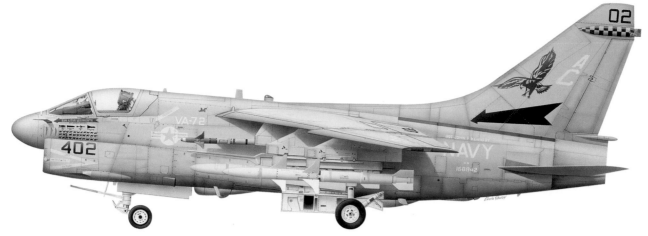

The US Navy's Corsair IIs saw combat for the last time during the 1991 Gulf War, when VA-46 joined VA-72 (illustrated) aboard USS John F. Kennedy.

issued only to Guard units.

In order to keep the A-7 viable in the 1990s, Vought began development of the **A-7F**, which involved a radical reworking of the ANG machines with afterburning

F100 turbofans, a lengthened fuselage and updated avionics. However, the programme was cancelled after two prototype conversions had flown, and the A-7 began a rapid withdrawal

from ANG service. The last was retired in 1993.

Exports of the Corsair were limited, sales to Pakistan and Switzerland having been thwarted. Portugal received two batches of aircraft from 1981 onwards, these being rebuilt Navy **A-7A** and **A-7B** aircraft. In service these were desig-

nated as the **A-7P**, the **TA-7P** being a two-seat derivative. The primary role of Portugal's Corsairs was maritime strike using AGM-65 Maverick missiles, but they also had a secondary air defence role. Greece purchased 60 **A-7H** and five **TA-7H** aircraft, based on the Navy's TF41-powered **A-7E**.

The fleet was bolstered by the transfer of 36 ex-US Navy aircraft, mostly A-7Es but also including a handful of **TA-7C** trainers. The final operator to receive the A-7 was the Royal Thai Navy, which received 14 ex-USN A-7Es and four ex-USN TA-7Cs in 1995.

Vought F-8 (F8U) Crusader Naval fighter

This 12F F-8E(FN) demonstrates the Aéronavale's preferred choice of MATRA R.550 Magic AAMs for its Crusaders. The French upgraded 17 F-8E(FN)s to F-8P (prolongé) standard, keeping them in service until 1999.

A 1952 US Navy requirement for a supersonic air-superiority fighter resulted in eight design submissions, and in May 1953 the Vought design was selected for prototype construction with a contract for two **XF8U-1** prototypes. The design's high-mounted foldable wing was of variable incidence, the increased angle of attack being used to keep the fuselage more nearly level during low-speed operations and thus enhance the pilot's view during, for example, landings aboard a carrier.

The first prototype flew for the first time on

25 March 1955 and deliveries of the **F8U-1** began in March 1957. The Crusader remained in production for eight years and its success in both Navy and Marine Corps hands during the Vietnam War enhanced its reputation.

Variants

The principal F-8 variants included the **F8U-1E** (**F-8B**) production version; **F8U-1P** (**RF-8A**) photo-recce version of the F8U-1; **F8U-2** (**F-8C**) production version with twin ventral fins and provision for four AIM-9s; **F8U-2N** (**F-8D**); **F8U-2NE** (**F-8E**) definitive

RF-8 Crusaders provided critical reconnaissance for over 20 years. VFP-62 traded its RF-8As (illustrated) for RF-8Gs in 1965.

production version; and the **F-8E(FN)** for the French navy. In addition, the Philippines received 35 of a total of 89 **F-8H** rebuilds from F-8D airframes.

Above: VF-124 was responsible for training many of the pilots who flew the Crusader in Vietnam. The unit was an early recipient of the all-weather F8U-2NE. Continuous improvements in the F-8's airframe and powerplant kept the aircraft viable well into the Vietnam conflict.

SPECIFICATION

Vought F-8E Crusader
Type: carrier-based fighter
Powerplant: one 80.05-kN (18,000-lb st) thrust Pratt & Whitney J57-P-20A turbojet
Performance: maximum speed approximately Mach 1.8, or 1802 km/h (1,120 mph) at 12190 m (40,000 ft); service ceiling 17680 m (58,000 ft); range 1609 km (1,000 miles)
Weight: maximum take-off 15422 kg (34,000 lb)

Dimensions: wing span 10.72 m (35 ft 2 in); length 16.61 m (54 ft 6 in); height 4.8 m (15 ft 9 in); wing area 32.52 m² (350 sq ft)
Armament: four 20-mm Colt-Browning cannon, two Sidewinder missiles and underfuselage rocket pack, or four Sidewinder missiles, plus underwing racks for two 2,000-lb (907-kg) bombs, or two Bullpup missiles, or 24 Zuni air-to-surface rockets

A bomb-laden Grumman A-6 Intruder launches from the forward catapult of USS Ranger. The A-6 was instrumental in improving the strike capabilities of the naval air wings, introducing greater range, load-carrying and adverse weather capability. VA-165 'Boomers' deployed twice in USS Ranger with its A-6As.

Vietnam Carrier Air Wing

The 'Tonkin Gulf Yacht Club'

Task Force 77, the US naval presence in the Gulf of Tonkin off northeast Vietnam, was centred around a constantly changing series of aircraft carriers. These eventually included 15 attack carriers, and four anti-submarine carriers – two of these latter operating in the attack role. To the sailors and airmen of Task Force 77, this conglomeration of ships and aircraft was known as the 'Tonkin Gulf Yacht Club'.

Camera installation

The RF-8G had four basic camera installations. Station 1 was in the bulged fairing under the fuselage, and housed the 'forward-fire' camera. Station 2 was actually the rear-most station, and initially mounted the trimetrogon cameras. These were later replaced in this station by vertical and oblique cameras, which also occupied Stations 3 and 4. Replacing the trimetrogon as a sensor was the panoramic camera, which was carried in a small angular fairing offset to starboard and provided horizon-to-horizon coverage.

F-4B sensors and weapons

The sensor package beneath the nose radome of the F-4B contained an AAA-4 IR sensor, beneath which later F-4Bs added an AN/APR-30 radar homing and warning receiver as seen here. Unlike the F-8 Crusader that it was beginning to replace, the F-4B had no internal gun, but it did offer compatibility with the semi-active radar-homing AIM-7 Sparrow. In theory this should have allowed BVR shots against enemy MiGs, but in practice strict rules of engagement usually disallowed a BVR launch.

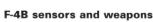

North American RA-5C Vigilante

Like their shipmates who flew the RF-8 Crusader, the RA-5C Vigilante crews suffered more than their fair share of losses. A generally more capable aircraft than the RF-8, the RA-5C was a complex machine with the ability to collect more than one type of reconnaissance data on a single sortie. Missions were usually flown with an F-4 escort, the scintillating performance of the 'Vigi' commonly obliging the missile- and drop tank-laden Phantoms to select minimum afterburner in order to keep the 'dry-running' RA-5C in sight.

Douglas A-1H Skyraider
VA-25 'Fist of the Fleet' made two A-1 deployments in USS *Coral Sea*, from 29 July 1966 to
23 February 1967 and 26 July 1967 to 6 April 1968. This latter cruise was with a mixed fleet of
A-1H/J aircraft, as was an earlier deployment aboard USS *Midway* in 1965. VA-25 returned to Vietnam
in February 1969 with A-7Bs. This aircraft has a typical Skyraider load of four-round 5-in (127-mm)
Zuni rocket pods, 2.75-in (70-mm) rocket pods and 250-lb (113-kg) Mk 81 Low-Drag General Purpose
(LDGP) bombs. In addition, a standard armament of four 20-mm cannon was also fitted.

Colours and markings
Throughout the Vietnam War, the majority of
US Navy aircraft were finished in a standard
Gull Gray over White scheme. Colourful unit
markings were the norm, as demonstrated by
these four machines, all of which are also in
the standard colour scheme. The large letters
on the fin of each aircraft denote the carrier air
wing to which the machine was assigned.

Vought RF-8G Crusader
Detachments of VFP-63 made seven deployments in USS
Oriskany with RF-8A and RF-8G (above) photo-
reconnaissance variants of the F-8 Crusader fighter. The
photo-Crusader's job was an extremely dangerous one,
the unarmed aircraft having to fly carefully planned
camera runs so that their fans of five cameras could record
material for the Photographic Intelligence Mates aboard
ship to analyse. All missions were hot, but especially the
post-strike bomb damage assesment sorties, since enemy
troops were always prepared for the solo recce bird which
invariably followed a strike. RF-8 losses were high,
but were kept to a minimum by extensive
training, careful mission planning and the use
of fighter escorts. No RF-8s fell to MiGs, all
those lost being destroyed by AAA or
SAMs.

McDonnell Douglas F-4B Phantom II
Although it had primarily been designed as a fleet defence fighter, the F-4
soon began taking on air-to-ground roles, delivering large ordnance loads
with considerable accuracy. VF-142 'Ghostriders' undertook four cruises
with the F-4B (above) between 5 May 1964 and 31 January 1969, before
returning with the F-4J on 11 August 1969. Three of the
F-4B cruises were in USS *Constellation*, the 10 December 1965 to
25 August 1966 deployment being based aboard USS *Ranger*.

F-8E Crusader

VF-191 'Satan's Kittens' flew this F-8E towards the end of its 1965/66 Vietnam combat cruise. It was assigned to the squadron's commanding officer, Commander Billy Phillips, and wears the 'double nuts' Modex as the CAG-bird. Other CAG markings include the legend 'Attack Carrier Air Wing Nineteen' on the fuselage under the wing, and the large tail diamond is faceted with red, yellow, blue and orange to signify the squadrons within the wing. VF-191 received its first F8U-1 in June 1960, going to sea with the Crusader aboard *Bon Homme Richard* in 1961. In 1963 the squadron upgraded to the F-8E. A total of eight cruises was made in the war zone, always partnered by the 'Red Lightnings' of VF-194. The first two cruises were in *Bon Homme Richard* (28 January 1964 to 21 November 1964 and 21 April 1965 to 13 January 1966). During the second of these cruises three F-8s were lost to AAA and one to a SAM. After a period back at Miramar, VF-191 and VF-194 transferred to *Ticonderoga* for a combat cruise (15 October 1966 to 29 May 1967) during which one F-8E was lost to AAA. The next cruise (27 December 1967 to 17 August 1968) was also aboard 'Tico', and was highlighted by the MiG-kill of LCdr John Nichols on 9 July. Upon their return from the war zone, both squadrons upgraded to the F-8J in preparation for more combat cruises in the theatre.

Eight S-2 Tracker squadrons made 13 deployments to the Tonkin Gulf During the Vietnam War. They generally flew sea surveillance and naval gunfire spotting missions, in addition to their usual ASW role. These aircraft are S-2Es from VS-33, which served all its cruise in USS Bennington.

Avionics
The F-8E featured the AN/AWG-4 fire control system, with the AN/APQ-94 radar, the AAS-15 infra-red search and track system allowing passive detection of targets. Data from the radar were displayed on a rectangular screen in the top centre of the instrument panel, and had varying range displays. The system could also cue the AIM-9 Sidewinder missiles. Navigation/ communication equipment included the APA-52 radio set/TACAN, APN-22 radar altimeter, APA-98 coder group, A/NAS Q/17B integrated system (controlling ARC-27A UHF transceiver, APX-6B IFF transponder and ARA-25 UHF direction finder), AES-6 autopilot and MA-1 gyro-stabilised magnetically-slaved compass. Fuse control was handled by the AWW-1 system.

Sidewinder missile
Three versions of the AIM-9 were used by the Crusader. The initial variant was the AIM-9B, as seen on this aircraft. This had a long tubular nose housing the IR seeker and a range of about 2 km (1.2 miles). The warhead was 4.5 kg (10 lb) of high explosive with blast fragmentation, and the launch weight was 76 kg (167 lb). The AIM-9C was a rarely employed semi-active radar-guided version with a long tubular nose and a launch weight of 93 kg (205 lb). The last major model used by the F-8 was the AIM-9D, with a refined seeker head in a short, conical nose. This had a launch weight of 90 kg (198 lb), of which 9 kg (20 lb) was a new high-explosive continuous rod warhead. The effective range was increased over the B to about 3 km (2 miles). The Crusader's reliance on short-range IR missiles and its four internal Colt-Browning 20-mm Mk 12 cannon made it seem poorly equipped for the air-to-air role by comparison with the F-4, but in fact the Crusader was probably more suited to the type of rigorously controlled, close-in fighting typical of the Vietnam War. The Crusader fought to the end of the war, especially from the smaller carriers which were unable to accommodate the larger, heavier F-4.

Early in the war A-3 Skywarriors performed bombing missions, even on targets in the heavily defended Hanoi area. However, as more advanced attack aircraft entered service, many A-3s were converted into tankers. These KA-3Bs provided inflight-refuelling for the returning strike aircraft. Other variants such as the EA-3B provided electronic intelligence. This KA-3B was based aboard USS America.

Powerplant

All Crusaders were powered by Pratt & Whitney's excellent J57 turbojet. Originally dubbed 'Turbo Wasp', this engine ushered in a new era of jet design, using a two-spool configuration. The nine-stage low-pressure compressor was attached to the inner of the two concentric shafts, driven by a two-stage turbine, while the seven-stage high-pressure compressor was driven via the outer shaft by a single-stage turbine. In between the turbines and compressor was the combustion chamber with eight interconnected flame tubes, with six fuel nozzles each. The Dash 20 as installed in the F-8E was 6.85 m (22 ft 5½ in) long and 1.03 m (3 ft 4½ in) in diameter. The engine developed 41.12 kN (9,150 lb) thrust at normal rating and 48.15 kN (10,700 lb) at military rating. It was mounted at two main points: the front mounting was on the main wing rear spar/engine-mounting bulkhead, the rear mounting was on the double frame rear fuselage break, the latter allowing the entire tail and rear fuselage to be removed for access to the engine. The afterburner incorporated a divergent/convergent variable nozzle which was enclosed completely within the outer skin of the airframe. This part of the rear fuselage was usually unpainted, but did not form part of the engine assembly. The hotter running temperatures of the Dash 16 and subsequent J57 variants required extra cooling for the afterburner area, resulting in the addition of cooling air scoops.

Raising wing

The Crusader's characteristic variable-incidence wing fulfiled two principal functions: it provided extra lift during take-off and allowed the aircraft to land with the fuselage (as opposed to the wing) at a low incidence, with beneficial effects on pilot visibility and undercarriage size/weight. During landing the wing flew at an incidence of 12.5°, while the fuselage was at an incidence of 5.5°. When boundary layer control was introduced on the F-8E(FN) and F-8J, the wing incidence was reduced to 5° (from 7°). The wing was actuated by a single hydraulic strut on the forward starboard position. This unit did not seem strong enough to handle the huge loads placed on it, and the actuator only weighed around 13.6 kg (30 lb). When retracted it was 0.86 m (34 in) long, and it extended 0.44 m (17½ in). Working at a hydraulic pressure of 20685 kPa (3,000 lb/in²), the strut was designed to exert a force of 7.56 kN (1,700 lb) for lowering the wing after take-off and 24 kN (5,400 lb) for raising the wing, the latter function obviously being aided greatly by the forces of gravity and aerodynamics.

Wing pylons

Another important feature of the F-8E was the introduction of heavy wing pylons, allowing the carriage of bombloads. Various bomb racks were used to attach a variety of weapons. The main ejector rack was the Aero 7A-1 four-hook unit which could mount the 2,000-lb (907-kg) Mk 84 bomb or the AGM-12 Bullpup missile directly. For multiple bomb carriage a number of racks was available. The A/A37B-1 multiple bomb rack assembly and A/A37B-6 multiple ejector rack (MER) were used for up to six bombs of 250-lb (113-kg) weight, four in the 500-lb (227-kg) class or two in the 1,000-lb (454-kg) class. The A/A37B-5 triple ejector rack (TER) was useful for the carriage of rocket pods (usually four-round LAU-10 Zuni launchers) or for cluster bombs.

USS Enterprise (CVAN-65) carries a load of CH-53 helicopters on its bow to help in the final evacuation of Saigon. Also aboard are two squadrons of Grumman F-14 Tomcats, which were entering a combat zone for the first time. Taking Enterprise as an example, a more typical carrier air wing might include two squadrons of F-4s (or F-14s), two of A-4s, one of A-6s, a detachment each of KA-3B tankers and EKA-3B jammer/tankers, a squadron of RA-5Cs, one of E-2A Hawkeyes and a detachment of UH-2 Seasprite helicopters.

Dassault Rafale M/N Next-generation naval fighter

Rafale M1, the first navalised production aircraft, maintains 80 per cent structural and systems commonality with the single-seat Rafale C. The initial software standard permits air defence missions against multiple targets, and in 2002 added IR-guided MICA AAMs, and a datalink for communication with the E-2C.

The ACX, later Rafale A, demonstrator flew several hundred test sorties, including touch-and-go deck-landings on the French carrier *Clemenceau*. As such, it proved the basic suitability of the new fighter design for carrier operations, paving the way for the **Rafale M** dedicated multi-role naval fighter.

Naval Rafale

Originally known as the **ACM (Avion de Combat Marine)**, the first Rafale M prototype made its initial flight on 12 December 1991. The main changes differentiating the Rafale M from its land-based counterparts weigh some 750 kg (1,653 lb) and include major reinforcement of the Messier-Bugatti landing gear (whose nosewheel unit also became the first in France to require attachment of a take-off catapult bar) plus provision of a 'jump-strut' for automatic unstick rotation.

Other changes include 13 rather than 14 hardpoints, and a maximum take-off weight reduced by 2000 kg (4,409 lb) to 19500 kg (42,989 lb). The Aéronavale's initial requirement for 86 single-seat Rafale Ms is unlikely to be satisfied.

Budget cuts have forced the total buy down to 60 aircraft. In addition, having studied aircraft performance during the 1991 Gulf War and the conflict over Kosovo, the Aéronavale has decided that it requires a mix of Rafale M and two-seat **Rafale N** aircraft. In May 2001, Flottille 12F was formed with four Rafale Ms. These early aircraft are equipped to **Standard F1**, optimised for the air-to-air role, and certain some systems of the definitive aircraft.

Later standards include **Standard F2**, for delivery from 2004, with improved air-to-surface capability. This will include Scalp, a jam-resistant passive optronic surveillance and imaging system with a laser rangefinder or an Optronique Secteur Frontale IR search-and-track system mounted forward of the cockpit and supplementing the radar for passive multi-target identification and tracking, and the MIDS datalink. The definitive multi-role **Standard F3**, with improved radar able to undertake simultaneous air search and terrain following should be in service by 2010. Rafale N is due to fly for the first time in 2005, for delivery in 2007.

The second naval prototype, M02, is shown here launching from FNS Foch with a typical air-to-air load of MICA and Magic 2 missiles.

In the closing stages of Operation Enduring Freedom during 2002, Rafales flew operationally from *Charles de Gaulle*, but saw no combat. Rafale M procurement continued with an order for a further 13 machines in early 2003, at which time the final M/N mix had not yet been announced.

SPECIFICATION

Dassault Rafale M
Type: single-seat carrierborne multi-role warplane
Powerplant: two SNECMA M88-2 turbofan engines each rated at 75 kN (16,861 lb st) with afterburning
Performance: maximum speed 2125 km/h (1,321 mph) 'clean' at 11000 m (36,090 ft); maximum climb rate at sea level 18290 m (60,000 ft) per minute; service ceiling 16765 m (55,000 ft); combat radius on a low-level penetration mission with 12 250-kg (551-lb) bombs, four MICA AAMs and three

drop tanks 1055 km (655 miles)
Weights: empty equipped 9800 kg (21,605 lb); normal take-off 16500 kg (36,376 lb)
Dimensions: wing span 10.9 m (35 ft 9 in) with tip-mounted AAMs; length 15.3 m (50 ft 2¼ in); height 5.34 m (17 ft 6¼ in); wing area 46 m² (495.16 sq ft)
Armament: one 30-mm GIAT/DEFA M791 fixed forward-firing cannon in the starboard side of the forward fuselage, plus up to 6000 kg (13,228 lb) of disposable stores

During Operation Enduring Freedom, the Aéronavale's first Rafale Ms took the opportunity for a little 'cross-deck' practice. Here John C. Stennis experiences a Rafale fly-by on 14 March 2002.

Dassault Super Etendard

Multi-role and attack carrierborne fighter

The Super Etendard was developed from the 1950s-vintage Etendard IV. A new nav/attack system was installed, but the thirsty SNECMA Atar engine was retained. Despite the aircraft's increased weight, the Super Etendard's new wing does give improved handling.

A French naval requirement of the early 1970s for 100 new carrierborne strike/attack fighters (for which procurement of the navalised SEPECAT Jaguar M was originally planned) eventually resulted in a 1973 contract to Dassault-Breguet for 60 examples of a development of its current Etendard IV warplane. The upgraded **Super Etendard** (super standard) was planned with the powerplant of one 49.03-kN (11,023-lb st) SNECMA Atar 8K-50 turbojet and some 90 per cent airframe commonality with the Etendard IV. A new wing leading-edge profile and redesigned flaps ensured a mainly unchanged carrier deck performance despite the Super Etendard's heavier operating weights.

Greater capability

To widen its anti-ship attack and air-to-air capabilities, the Super Etendard also featured a new ETNA nav/attack system and an Agave monopulse search and fire-control radar, an SKN602 INS, Crouzet 66 air data computer (and associated Crouzet 97 navigation display and armament system), and a HUD. A retractable inflight-refuelling probe was fitted forward of the cockpit.

Three Etendard IVM airframes were converted as prototypes, flying from 29 October 1974. Production of 71 Super Etendards was then undertaken, the first of them flying on 24 November 1977. The new type began to replace Etendard IVs and some Vought F-8E(FN) Crusader interceptors from June 1978.

Falklands hero

By the time the Falklands War started in April 1982, the Argentine navy (the sole Super Etendard export customer) had received the first five of 14 aircraft on order to equip its air arm's 2ª Escuadrilla, together with five Aérospatiale AM39 Exocet anti-ship missiles. These aircraft made their operational debut on 4 May 1982, sinking HMS *Sheffield* off the Falklands, followed on 25 May by the destruction of the supply ship *Atlantic Conveyor*. The squadron suffered no wartime losses. In October 1983, the Iraqi air force leased five Super Etendards and bought a substantial number of AM39 missiles for use against Iranian tankers in the Iran/Iraq war, scoring many successes. One of the aircraft was lost to an accident, however.

In service the Super Etendard has proved to be a useful type. This pair is taking fuel from a US Navy KA-6D Intruder. Note that the Super Etendards have the post-1984 camouflage scheme.

A mid-1980s upgrade programme was planned to extend the long-range and anti-ship attack capabilities of the Aéronavale's surviving force of nearly 60 Super Etendards (some 53 of which had already been modified to launch the ASMP stand-off nuclear missile). The main changes were: modernisation of the avionics, a revised cockpit with new instrumentation and HOTAS controls, and the new Anemone radar – incorporating track-while-scan, air-to-surface ranging, ground mapping and search functions. New systems included a wide-angle HUD

with TV or IR imaging, Sherloc RWR and a VCN65 ECM display together with the Barem jammer pod, a more modern INS, a weapons and air data computer with more processing capacity, and provision for night-vision goggles. Airframe changes, combined with on-going systems upgrades, will help to extend the Super Etendard's service life to about 2011.

The prototype of the upgraded **Super Etendard**

Modernisé first flew on 5 October 1990, Dassault modifying two more for operational development.

Following disbandment of Flottille 14F in July 1991, pending its eventual re-equipment as the Aéronavale's first Rafale M unit, its Super Etendards were used to replace the last 11 Etendard IVP reconnaissance aircraft equipping Escadrille 59S at Hyères. The Super Etendards were used for the operational conversion of French naval pilots after deck-landing training in Aérospatiale Zéphyr aircraft at the same base. Flottilles 11F and 17F comprise the Aéronavale's remaining front-line Super Etendard squadrons in mid 2003, flying Modernisé aircraft, and will operate the machines until they are replaced by Rafale Ms.

The Super Etendard gained fame during the Falklands campaign when Argentinian Super Etendards sank two British ships with Exocet missiles.

Sukhoi Su-27K (Su-33) 'Flanker-D' Naval Su-27

'Red 64' was assigned to the 1st Squadron of the Severomorsk Regiment, AV-MF, and was one of those aircraft deployed aboard Admiral Kuznetsov *for its first operational cruise in 1996.*

Development of a navalised, shipborne version of the Su-27 was launched in the early 1980s at the same time as the Soviet carrier programme. The aircraft was seen as a single-role fleet air defence aircraft, which would form one element in a mixed air wing alongside a new AWACS platform and the MiG-29K multi-role strike fighter. As such, the **Su-27K 'Flanker-D'** was developed from the basic Su-27, not the multi-role Su-27M.

Several Su-27s tested different aspects of the intended Su-27K production configuration, including canards for approach handling tests and an arrester hook. Three Su-27 prototypes and an early Su-27UB were used for early take-off trials from a dummy carrier deck. The first 'deck' take-off was made from the dummy deck at Saki on 28 August 1982. The dummy deck was subsequently rebuilt to incorporate a ski-ramp identical to that fitted to the first Soviet carrier, *Tbilisi*, and intended to reduce the take-off run.

Su-27K prototypes

The three modified Su-27s were followed by a batch of **T10K** (Su-27K) prototypes, each of which differed slightly from the others. The first Su-27K prototype made its maiden flight on 17 August 1987. All of the T10Ks featured twin nose-wheels, wing and tailplane folding, and double-slotted trailing-edge flaps.

The Su-27K prototypes were also all fitted with abbreviated 'tail stings' and square-section arrester hooks; none had brake 'chutes. Later prototypes also had an extra pair of inboard underwing weapons pylons, raising the total number to 12, including the wingtip stations.

Carrier landing trials began on 1 November 1989, when Victor Pugachev landed the second Su-27K aboard *Tbilisi*, becoming the first Russian pilot to land a conventional aircraft aboard the carrier. The second prototype was the first full-standard Su-27K.

Russian naval pilots began carrier operations on 26 September 1991. Service trials were highly successful and led to State Acceptance Trials, which were successfully passed in 1994.

Carrier fleet?

Had the Soviet Union's ambitious plan to build four aircraft-carriers reached fruition, perhaps as many as 72 production Su-27Ks would have been required simply for their air wings. However, the end of the Cold War led to a massive down-scaling of the USSR's carrier programme. With the *Admiral Kuznetsov* (formerly *Tbilisi*, and before that *Brezhnev*) the only carrier left for service with the Russian navy, both the AEW aircraft and MiG-29K programmes were abandoned.

If only one fixed-wing type was to be procured for the new carrier, logic would have dictated that it should be the multi-role MiG-29K. However, the political influence of Sukhoi's chief designer, Mikhail Simonov, was such that the Sukhoi was selected for production and service, and the Russian navy was forced to accept the aircraft's (and thus the carrier's) more limited role.

The Su-27K does enjoy some significant advantages over the MiG-29K, primarily exceptional range performance. Before entering service, the production Su-27K was redesignated **Su-33** by the OKB, but the aircraft remains a navalised version of the basic IA-PVO interceptor, with the same basic 'Slot Back' radar and with only a very limited ground-attack capability. It is uncertain whether the AV-MF regularly uses the Su-33 designation.

First cruise

Kuznetsov's first truly operational deployment took place in early 1996, when it spent two months in the Mediterranean. The ship's

Service introduction of the Su-27K made it eligible for a separate ASCC/NATO reporting name suffix, and the aircraft is now understood to have been known as 'Flanker-D'. The reporting name saw little use, however, since the aircraft's correct designation (and the OKB's Su-33 designation) became widely known and used.

complement included the Su-27K-equipped 1st Squadron of the Severomorsk Regiment. Although 24 Su-27Ks have been built, *Kuznetsov's* complement for this first cruise included just seven production Su-27K aircraft.

Since that first cruise, which revealed a number of operational deficiencies in the ship/aircraft combination, Russian defence spending has been further cut. Only a handful of cruises has therefore occurred, but Su-27K pilots have trained in inflight-refuelling with Il-78 tankers, and live weapons training with AAMs has been accomplished.

With the advent of the two-seat **Su-27KUB**, the Russian navy potentially has a formidable new asset. Originally considered to be a naval Su-32FN/Su-34 derivative by the West, the aircraft combines a two-seat side-by-side cockpit with a conical nose profile. Designed as a trainer, the Su-27KUB also has great potential as an ECM, reconnaissance or AEW platform. However, even if funding allows, it is likely to be many years before such developments could take effect.

An Su-27K runs up to full power on Admiral Kuznetsov. *Early in the Russian carrier programme, it was decided that the development of a steam catapult would not be possible within the timescale set for the first of the new carriers, and that they would be fitted with ski ramps instead. The Su-27K makes unassisted take-offs, using a combination of restrainers and take-off ramps.*

Mikoyan MiG-29K A carrierborne 'Fulcrum'

Wearing calibration markings enabling it to be accurately tracked during carrier trials work, the first MiG-29K is illustrated here in its standard MiG-29 camouflage finish.

The **MiG-29K** project was launched to provide a multi-role strike fighter to complement the Su-27K interceptor on the carriers intended to enter Soviet navy service during the 1990s. However, in the event only the Su-27K was procured for service.

Trials with the hooked **MiG-29KVP** proved that the MiG-29 could be operated safely from a ski-jump, and that arrested landings were possible at operationally useful weights. However, it was decided that the ideal carrierborne MiG-29 would require both additional wing area and additional thrust. Further, improved high-lift devices might produce a useful reduction in approach speed, without unacceptably raising the angle of attack on touch-down.

Since a new variant of the MiG-29 would be required, Mikoyan adapted it from the new multi-role MiG-29M, with its lightweight airframe, multi-mode/multi-role radar and PGM capability.

Uprated engines

There was a degree of cross-fertilisation between the MiG-29M and the MiG-29K, with the uprated RD-33K engines developed for the carrier aircraft eventually being adopted for the -29M, too. The new engine gave 92.17 kN (20,725 lb st) thrust for a limited period, useful on launch and in the event of a missed approach

or go-around. It also had FADEC (full-authority digital engine control) and was made of advanced materials.

New wing

The quintessence of the MiG-29K lay in its new wing, designed with power-folding at roughly one-third span. The wing was fitted with broader-chord double-slotted trailing-edge flaps, and featured the extended-span ailerons of the MiG-29M, though they were modified to droop (as flaperons) at low speed. The tip was moved further outboard, and increased in chord and depth, housing new ECM systems. The leading edge was of reduced sweep-back, giving only slightly greater chord at the root. The leading-edge flaps were redesigned.

In addition to the new wing, the MiG-29K introduced a new, strengthened, long-stroke undercarriage, and had a tailhook. The MiG-29K prototypes also introduced a neat, fully-retractable inflight-refuelling probe below the forward edge of the port side of the cockpit windscreen.

Production MiG-29Ks would have had a fully automatic carrier landing system, in addition to the Uzel beacon homing system. The prototypes used a system derived from that fitted to the Yak-38. This was sufficient to guarantee that the aircraft would touch down

The first MiG-29K, Bort '311', is seen during trials aboard Tbilisi. These included landing aboard with R-73 and R-77 missiles, the main air-to-air weapons of the type. The aircraft bore the brunt of the carrier trials, carrying photo-calibration marks on the nose. The extended and bulged wingtips housed electronic warfare equipment.

within a 6-m (20-ft) circle on the deck, within tight airspeed and vertical speed limits – not quite enough to guarantee getting a wire, and not quite enough to guarantee being on the deck centreline point.

Carrier trials

Commonality with the MiG-29M meant that only two prototypes of the MiG-29K would be required, to prove the carrier-specific items. The first prototype was flown on 23 June 1988, and was subsequently used for extensive trials aboard Tbilisi from 1 November 1989. The second prototype was used mainly for sys-

tems trials, and made only six carrier landings.

The end of the Cold War and the break-up of the USSR led to the abandonment of Tbilisi's planned sister ships. Tbilisi itself became Admiral Kuznetsov, while the procurement of two separate fighter aircraft types for its air wing seemed unmanageably extravagant, and it became obvious that a competition

was emerging between the Su-27K and MiG-29K.

The Su-27K emerged victorious from this competition, but all was not lost for the MiG-29K. In 2000, India purchased the carrier Admiral Gorshkov from Russia. Requiring a multi-role fighter to equip the carrier, the country has ordered 46 MiG-29Ks, for delivery after 2003.

While the first MiG-29K was finished in a standard light-grey scheme, the second aircraft, Bort '312', sported this slate-grey paint. Additional markings were MiG and MAPO (Moscow Aircraft Production Organisation) badges, and the St Andrew's Cross ensign of the Russian navy. The aircraft was still active in 1998.

British Aerospace Sea Harrier FRS.Mk 1

STOVL naval fighter

The FRS designation reflected the Sea Harrier's triple capability as a fleet defence fighter, reconnaissance platform and strike/attack aircraft. This Sea Harrier FRS.Mk 1 carries the markings of the squadron commander of No. 801 Sqn, FAA. After the Falklands War, twin AIM-9 rails were added to the Sea Harrier's outer pylons.

The **BAe Sea Harrier** was developed from the RAF's Harrier close support and reconnaissance warplane, the world's first and, at that time, only operational short take-off and vertical landing (STOVL) aircraft. The Sea Harrier fortuitously filled the gap left by the phase-out of the Fleet Air Arm's Phantoms and the 1979 decommissioning of HMS *Ark Royal*, the last conventional aircraft carrier in service with the Royal Navy. The advent of the Sea Harrier happily coincided with the introduction of a new generation of 20,000-ton light carriers intended primarily for the anti-submarine role. These three ships were intended to embark only helicopters, and

the Sea Harrier was instrumental in retaining some fixed-wing strike capability when the FAA was otherwise destined to become an all-helicopter force. Concurrent with the RN's receipt of HMS *Invincible*, dubbed a 'through-deck cruiser' rather than an aircraft carrier to get it past UK Treasury scrutiny, the Sea Harrier became one of the most important types ever procured by the FAA. The 1982 Falklands War then proved the prudency of the decision to adopt the Sea Harrier.

Harrier at sea

Although a Harrier, in its original P.1127 form, had landed on *Ark Royal* as early as 8 February 1963, the

Royal Navy initially had little interest in the programme. Naval interest gradually increased, however, spurred by the knowledge that no other fixed-wing aircraft could be ordered, and in May 1975 an initial order for 24 **Sea Harrier FRS.Mk 1** single-seat warplanes and one **Harrier T.Mk 4A** two-seat trainer was placed, followed by a further order for 10 more Sea Harrier FRS.Mk 1s in May 1978.

The main differences between the RAF's Harrier GR.Mk 3 and the Sea Harrier FRS.Mk 1 were the latter's front fuselage contours, with a painted radome covering a Ferranti Blue Fox radar. The cockpit was raised by 0.25 m (10 in) and the canopy was revised to give

the pilot better fields of vision. An improved Pegasus Mk 104 turbofan was fitted. An autopilot was added, as was a revised nav/attack system and a new HUD. Magnesium was deleted from all airframe areas likely to be exposed to corrosion from salt water.

Into service, into war

Embarking aboard HMS *Hermes* in June 1981, No. 800 Sqn was joined by No. 801 Sqn. Both units were subsequently deployed as part of the RN's fixed-wing air assets during the Falklands conflict, in which the Sea Harrier served with distinction. Particularly significant during the war was the supply from the USA of AIM-9L Sidewinder short-range

AAMs. Scoring 22 confirmed victories, the Sea Harrier force lost six aircraft, all of them to causes other than aerial combat.

Contributing greatly to the weapons load with which Sea Harriers were launched was the 'ski jump', a ramp fitted to carrier bows. Following the South Atlantic operation, 14 Sea Harrier FRS.Mk 1s were ordered as attrition replacements and, in 1984, nine more single-seaters as well as three **Harrier T.Mk 4(N)** trainers were added.

In 1979, the Indian navy ordered the first of its 23 **Sea Harrier FRS.Mk 51** and six **Harrier T.Mk 60** machines, to become the only export operator. The survivors remained in service in late 2002.

SPECIFICATION	
BAe Sea Harrier FRS.Mk 1 **Type:** single-seat carrierborne STOVL fighter, reconnaissance and strike/attack warplane **Powerplant:** one Rolls-Royce Pegasus Mk 104 vectored-thrust turbofan engine rated at 96 kN (21,500 lb st) **Performance:** maximum speed more than 1185 km/h (736 mph) at low altitude; initial climb rate about 15240 m (50,000 ft) per minute; service ceiling 15545 m (51,000 ft);	radius 750 km (460 miles) on a hi-hi-hi interception mission **Weights:** empty 6374 kg (14,052 lb); maximum take-off 11884 kg (26,200 lb) **Dimensions:** wing span 7.7 m (25 ft 3 in); length 14.5 m (47 ft 7 in); height 3.71 m (12 ft 2 in); wing area 18.68 m² (202.10 sq ft) **Armament:** up to a maximum of 3629 kg (8,000 lb) or normal 2268 kg (5,000 lb) of disposable stores for STO or VTO respectively

BAe's Sea Harrier entered FAA service with colourful markings applied over its Extra Dark Sea Grey/white colour scheme. The aircraft were repainted in more sombre tones on their way to the South Atlantic.

British Aerospace Sea Harrier FA.Mk 2 Upgraded 'Shar'

In refining the Sea Harrier as a more capable interceptor while retaining its reconnaissance and strike/attack capability, BAe made some significant changes to the airframe. The company received a contract in January 1985 for the project definition phase of the programme, which included two conversions of the Sea Harrier FRS.Mk 1 to the standard that was known as the **Sea Harrier FRS.Mk 2** up to May 1994, when it was changed to **Sea Harrier F/A.Mk 2** and then to **FA.Mk 2** in 1995.

In 1984 it had been reported that the Ministry of Defence planned to award a contract to BAe and Ferranti to cover a mid-life update of the entire Sea Harrier fleet, but these plans were substantially revised in 1985 to cover an upgrade of 30 airframes with Blue Vixen radar, an improved RWR, JTIDS and provision for the AIM-120 AMRAAM. The original BAe proposal also covered the installation of wing-tip Sidewinder rails. These additions, along with several aerodynamic refinements, were eventually cut

from the project, but a kinked wing leading edge and wing fence remained.

The FA.Mk 2 greatly improves the capabilities of the basic Sea Harrier, or 'Shar'. Nevertheless, the type is due for retirement in the period 2004-06.

A revised radome was needed to house the Blue Vixen radar, giving the Sea Harrier FA.Mk 2's nose a more elongated look than that of its predecessor.

The first of two prototype conversions flew on 19 September 1988. Despite the addition of an extra equipment bay and a recontoured nose to house the Blue Vixen radar, the Sea Harrier FA.Mk 2 is actually shorter overall due to the elimination of the nose-mounted pitot tube of the earlier variant.

Additional stores

No increase in wing span was found to be necessary to carry additional stores, including a pair of 190-Imp gal (864-litre) drop tanks plus AIM-120s (or ALARM anti-radar missiles) on each of the outer pylons, although ferry tips are available to increase span to 9.04 m (29 ft 8 in). The cockpit of the Sea Harrier FA.Mk 2 introduced new multi-function CRT displays and HOTAS controls to reduce pilot workload, and the type is powered by the Pegasus Mk 106 turbofan, a navalised version of the Mk 105 fitted to the AV-8B, with no magnesium in its construction.

On 7 December 1988 a contract was awarded for the conversion of 31 Sea Harrier FRS.Mk 1s to the Mk 2 standard. On 6 March 1990 the MoD revealed its intent to order at least 10 new-build Sea Harrier FRS.Mk 2s to augment the conversions, attrition having reduced the RN's Sea Harrier fleet to 39 aircraft. In January 1994 this intent was confirmed as an order for 18 Sea Harrier FRS.Mk 2s and an additional eight conversions, for a total of 57 Sea Harrier FA.Mk 2s.

In order to enhance pilot conversion training, a new two-seat **Harrier T.Mk 8** trainer was created, the four such aircraft supplementing the three surviving Harrier T.Mk 4Ns from 1996. Essentially a reconfigured T.Mk 4N, the Harrier T.Mk 8 duplicates the Sea Harrier FA.Mk 2's systems except for the radar.

McDonnell Douglas/BAe Harrier II CAS aircraft

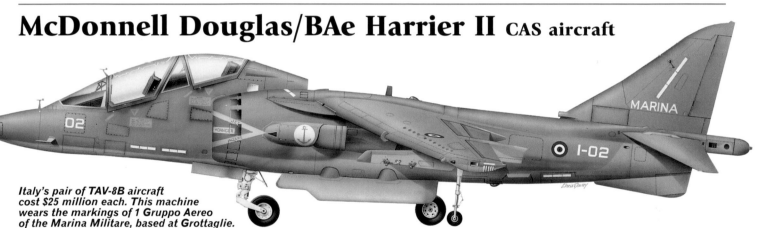

Italy's pair of TAV-8B aircraft cost $25 million each. This machine wears the markings of 1 Gruppo Aereo of the Marina Militare, based at Grottaglie.

With the AV-8A Harrier already in service, the USMC eventually backed the development of the advanced **AV-8B Harrier II**, which was intended to carry a larger warload and to provide better range/endurance characteristics.

The new design was based around a larger wing of supercritical section, and was also schemed with more carbon fibre in other airframe areas and a completely revised cockpit, with HOTAS controls and a higher seating position for the pilot. First flown on 9 November 1978, fitted to an AV-8A (which became the first of two YAV-8B service test aircraft), the new wing had six hardpoints.

Into production

The USMC took delivery of the first production aircraft during 1983, later aircraft introducing more powerful engines. A total of 286 aircraft was built, including six attrition replacements ordered after Desert Storm. Several two-seat **TAV-8B** aircraft were also built.

From the 167th airframe, all USMC AV-8Bs were provided with a night-attack capability with the installation of a FLIR, an improved HUD, an HDD and a colour moving map. The terms **Night Attack Harrier II** or **Night Attack AV-8B** are sometimes applied unofficially to these aircraft. The 205th AV-8B off the production line was the first fully equipped **AV-8B Harrier II Plus**. It made its maiden flight on 22 September 1992. Equipped with the APG-65 radar, the Harrier II Plus has a revised FLIR fairing, but is otherwise externally identical to late AV-8Bs. APG-65 gives compatibility with AIM-7 and AIM-120 AAMs. It also allows the use of the AGM-84 Harpoon AShM. The last 24 USMC aircraft were built as II Pluses, while many more were converted.

Spain and Italy have also purchased the AV-8B. With the commissioning of the carrier *Principe de Asturias* in 1989, the Spanish navy embarked 12 **EAV-8B** (**VA.2 Matador II**) aircraft. It also ordered 13 (later reduced to eight) Harrier II Pluses in November 1992 and the surviving EAV-8Bs are being upgraded to this standard. A two-seat **TAV-8B** was ordered in March 1992.

In May 1989, Italy ordered two TAV-8Bs from the USMC. Its first batch of three ex-USMC Harrier II Plus aircraft was ordered in July 1991, followed by a further 13 in November 1992.

As fitted to the Harrier II Plus, the APG-65 radar uses an antenna cropped by 5 cm (2 in) to fit the AV-8B's fuselage cross-section.

Boeing F/A-18 A/B/C/D Hornet
Carrier attack fighter

The US Navy's VFA-8 swopped its A-7 Corsair attack jets for F/A-18Cs in July 1987. The unit further upgraded to the night-attack F/A-18C, as shown here, in 1992

F404 turbofan
Hornets built after 1992 used the uprated F404-GE-402 EPE (Enhanced Performance Engine) as standard.

Radar
Once described as 'the world's best fighter radar', the Hornet's original APG-65 has been replaced in USN service by the APG-73.

Mk 83 AIR (Air Inflatable Retard) bombs fall away from a US Marine Corps F/A-18D. The use of IR-decoy flares acts as a defence against IR-homing SAMs

SPECIFICATION

Boeing F/A-18C Hornet
Type: single-seat carrierborne and land-based fighter and strike/attack warplane
Powerplant: two General Electric F404-GE-402 turbofan engines each rated at 78.73 kN (17,700 lb st) with afterburning
Performance: maximum speed more than 1915 km/h (1,190 mph) or Mach 1.80 at high altitude; initial climb rate 13715 m (45,000 ft) per minute, combat ceiling about 15740 m (50,000 ft), radius more than 740 km (460 miles) on a fighter mission or

1065 km (662 miles) for an attack mission
Weights: empty 10810 kg (23,832 lb); maximum take-off 15234 kg (33,585 lb) for a fighter mission or 21888 kg (48,753 lb) for an attack mission
Dimensions: wing span 11.43 m (37 ft 6 in) without tip-mounted missiles; length 17.07 m (56 ft) height 4.66 m (15 ft 3½ in); wing area 37.16 m2 (400 sq ft)
Armament: one internal 20-mm M61A1 Vulcan six-barrel cannon, plus up to 7031 kg (15,500 lb) of ordnance

The world's premier naval fighter originated as a derivative of the **Northrop YF-17** that was pitted successfully against the General Dynamics YF-16 in the USN's Air Combat Fighter programme of 1976. The first of 11 trials Hornets made its maiden flight on 18 November 1978.

Production of the initial **F/A-18A Hornet** single-seater eventually totalled 371 aircraft, the first US Navy squadron receiving its aircraft in 1983. Two

examples of the **TF-18A**, later redesignated F/A-18B, featured in the original contract. Procurement of the **F/A-18B** for the USN and USMC ended with the 40th example, and this version has never been employed by front-line forces.

The F/A-18 offers much greater weapons delivery accuracy than its predecessors, and is a genuinely multi-role aircraft, with remarkable dogfighting ability. The F/A-18 made its combat debut during the El

Dorado Canyon action against Libya in April 1986 and was heavily committed to action during Operation Desert Storm in 1991. The F/A-18A was superseded by the **F/A-18C**, which remained the principal single-seat production model up to 1999, some 347 having been ordered for US service.

The first F/A-18C made its maiden flight on 3 September 1986. This

introduced compatibility with the AIM-120 AMRAAM and the IIR version of the AGM-65 Maverick missile, as well as improved avionics – which from 1994 included the improved APG-73 variant of the Hornet's original APG-65 radar – and a new NACES ejection seat.

Night attack
After 137 baseline F/A-18Cs had been delivered, production switched to a night attack version with equipment including GEC Cat's Eye pilot's night vision goggles compatibility, an AAR-50 TINS (Thermal Imaging Navigation System) pod, Kaiser AVQ-28 raster HUD, externally carried AAS-38 FLIR (Forward-Looking Infra-Red) targeting pod, and colour multi-function displays. The first 'night-attack' Hornet was delivered on 1 November 1989. In addition, some 31 baseline two-seat **F/A-18D** trainers were built before 109 exam-

ples of the F/A-18D counterpart to the night-attack F/A-18C were produced. The night-attack version of the F/A-18D replaced the Grumman A-6 Intruder with the USMC's all-weather attack squadrons. Originally dubbed **F/A-18D+**, the aircraft features 'uncoupled' cockpits, usually with no control column in the rear cockpit but two sidestick weapons controllers. Marine Corps F/A-18Ds served with distinction during combat operations including Desert Storm in 1991 and Allied Force in 1999.

Export sales
The Hornet's versatility has led to substantial export sales. Canada was the first foreign customer, taking delivery of 98 single-seat **CF-188A** and 40 two-seat **CF-188B** aircraft, while Australia followed with an order for 57 **AF-18A** and 18 **ATF-18A** trainers. Spain purchased 60 **EF-18A** and 12 **EF-18B** machines (local designation **C.15** and **CE.15** respectively) and later acquired 24 former US Navy F/A-18As from late 1995. Kuwait received 32 **KAF-18C** warplanes and eight **KAF-18D** machines, while Switzerland took 26 F/A-18Cs and eight F/A-18Ds. Finland procured a fleet of 57 F/A-18Cs and seven F/A-18Ds, while Malaysia is unique in buying only the F/A-18D, of which eight were ordered.

Canada's much-depleted CF-188 fleet is involved in anti-narcotics work, as well as the air defence of Canada.

Setting out on an Enduring Freedom mission, this F/A-18C carries a pair of JDAM (Joint Direct Attack Munition) weapons with Mk 84 warheads. Note the use of four drop tanks – the Hornet has always been plagued by lack of range and has relied heavily on RAF tanker support for Enduring Freedom strikes.

Boeing F/A-18E/F Super Hornet

VFA-122 'Fighting Eagles'
VFA-122 brought the Super Hornet into US Navy fleet service on 15 January 1999.

Boeing is supplying the Super Hornet to replace the US Navy's F-14 Tomcats, many of its Hornets and, perhaps, the EA-6B.

Weapons
This aircraft is equipped with a typical SEAD warload of AGM-88 HARMs, AGM-154 JSOWs (Joint Stand-Off Weapons dispensers) and AIM-9s.

The first of McDonnell Douglas's (Boeing from 1997) Hornet upgrade concepts to reach fruition is the **F/A-18E Super Hornet**. The first F/A-18E made its maiden flight in November 1995 and the first aircraft was formally accepted into service with VFA-122 on 15 January 1999.

New avionics
The avionics upgrade is centred on the Raytheon APG-73 radar as already fitted to late versions of the F/A-18C. The IDECM (integrated defensive electronic counter-measures) system has three major elements: an ALR-67(V)3 RWR, ALQ-214 radio-frequency countermeasures system and ALE-55 fibre-optic towed decoy system; the last two are still under development, so the F/A-18E is initially being operated with the ALE-50 towed decoy system. The cockpit of the F/A-18E is similar to that of the F/A-18C with the exception of a larger flat-panel display in place of the current three HDDs (head-down displays).

A bigger bug
The enlarged airframe incorporates measures to reduce radar cross section and includes a fuselage lengthened by 0.86 m (2 ft 10 in), an enlarged wing characterised by a thicker section and two more hardpoints, enlarged LERXes, and horizontal and vertical tail surfaces. The Super Hornet also has a structure extensively redesigned to reduce weight and cost without sacrifice of strength. The Super Hornet also features a new quadruplex digital 'fly-by-wire' control system without the Hornet's mechanical back-up system.
The **F/A-18F Super**

Boeing has flown an F/A-18F in a configuration representing that which may be adopted by the Growler. This includes ALQ-99 jamming pods as carried by the EA-6B; the original concept of developing an all-new system for the EA-18 seems to have been abandoned.

Hornet is the two-seat development of the F/A-18E, with the rear cockpit equipped with the same displays as the front cockpit and otherwise configured for alternative combat or training roles. The USN had originally planned to procure 1,000 Super Hornets, but in 1997 the total was reduced to 548. Any delay in the service debut of the F-35 to a time later than 2008-10, however, will see the number of Super Hornets rise to 748. An F/A-18F electronic combat variant has been proposed as a replacement for the Grumman EA-6B Prowler. This will be capable of active jamming as well as lethal SEAD and is known in service as the **EA-18 Growler**.

An F/A-18F (upper) and F/A-18C cavort during testing. The Super Hornet is most easily distinguished from the Hornet by means of its square intakes and enlarged LERXes (Leading Edge Root Extensions).

SPECIFICATION

Boeing F/A-18E Super Hornet
Type: single-seat carrierborne and land-based multi-role fighter, attack and maritime air superiority warplane
Powerplant: two General Electric F414-GE-400 turbofan engines each rated at 97.86 kN (22,000 lb st) with afterburning
Performance: maximum speed more than 1915 km/h (1,190 mph) or Mach 1.80 at high altitude; service ceiling about 15240 m (50,000 ft); radius 1095 km (681 miles) on a hi-hi-hi interdiction mission with four 454-kg (1,000-lb) bombs, two AIM-9 Sidewinder AAMs and two drop tanks; 1901 km (560 miles) on a hi-lo-hi interdiction mission with the same stores, or 278 km (173 miles) on a 135-minute maritime air superiority mission with six AAMs and three drop tanks
Weights: empty 13864 kg (30,564 lb); maximum take-off 29937 kg (66,000 lb)
Dimensions: wing span 13.62 m (44 ft 8½ in) including tip-mounted AAMs; length 18.31 m (60 ft 1¼ in); height 4.88 m (16 ft); wing area 46.45 m² (500 sq ft)
Armament: one 20-mm M61A2 Vulcan rotary six-barrel cannon with 570 rounds, plus up to 8051 kg (17,750 lb) of disposable stores, including the 10/20-kiloton B57 and 100/500-kiloton B61 freefall nuclear weapons, AIM-120 AMRAAM, AIM 7 Sparrow and AIM-9 Sidewinder AAMs, AGM-88 HARM, AGM-65 Maverick ASM, AGM-84 Harpoon anti-ship missile, AGM-62 Walleye optronically-guided glide bomb, Paveway LGBs, Mk 80 series bombs, Rockeye and CBU-series cluster bombs, BLU-series napalm bombs and LAU-series multiple launchers for 2.75-in (70-mm) air-to-surface unguided rockets

Boeing F/A-18E Hornet

In keeping with the present trend towards two-seat combat aircraft, the F/A-18F is likely to take on a considerable operational tasking. The type is also likely to be the subject of much development and modification work in the future.

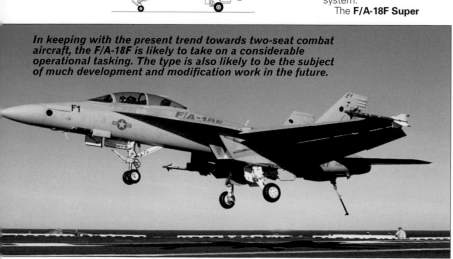

Boeing F/A-18 Hornet

Multi-role 21st-century fleet fighter

Designed as a multi-role fighter to ultimately replace the A-4 Skyhawk, A-7 Corsair II and F-4 Phantom II in US Navy service, the F/A-18 is one of the world's most important – and most impressive – warplanes. Although always outshone by the F-16 in terms of sales won, the Hornet has also achieved considerable export success with air forces worldwide.

F/A-18D Hornet

Cutaway key

1 Glass-fibre radome, hinged to starboard
2 Planar radar array radar scanner
3 Scanner tracking mechanism
4 Cannon port and gun gas purging intakes
5 Radar module withdrawal rails
6 Hughes AN/APG-73 radar equipment module
7 Formation lighting strip
8 Forward radar warning antennas
9 UHF/IFF antenna
10 Pitot head, port and starboard
11 Incidence transmitter
12 Canopy emergency release
13 Ammunition drum, 570 rounds
14 M61A1 Vulcan 20-mm rotary cannon
15 Retractable inflight-refuelling probe
16 Single piece wrap-around windscreen
17 Pilot's Kaiser AN/AVQ-28 raster HUD
18 Instrument panel with multi-function colour CRT displays
19 Control column
20 Rudder pedals
21 Ammunition loading chute
22 Ground power socket
23 Nose undercarriage wheel bay
24 Catapult strop link
25 Twin nosewheels, forward-retracting
26 Retractable boarding ladder
27 Nosewheel hydraulic jack
28 Nosewheel leg-mounted deck signalling and taxi lights
29 Forward avionics equipment bays, port and starboard
30 Engine throttle levers
31 Pilot's Martin-Baker SJU-6/A ejection seat
32 Rear cockpit rudder pedals (dual flight control system interchangeable with radar and weapons controllers)
33 Rear instrument console with multi-function CRT displays
34 Single-piece upward-opening cockpit canopy
35 AWW-7/9 datalink pod for Walleye missile, fuselage centreline pylon-mounted
36 AGM-62 Walleye II ER/DL air-to-surface missile, starboard outboard pylon only
37 Naval flight officer's helmet with GEC-Marconi Avionics Cats Eyes night-vision goggles
38 Naval flight officer's SJU-5/A ejection seat
39 Sidestick radar and weapons controllers, replacing dual flight-control system
40 Liquid oxygen converter
41 Ventral radar warning antenna
42 Rear avionics equipment bays, port and starboard
43 Cockpit rear pressure bulkhead
44 Canopy actuator
45 Starboard navigation light
46 Tailfin aerodynamic load-alleviating strake
47 Upper radar warning antennas
48 Forward fuselage bag-type fuel cell
49 Radar/avionics equipment liquid cooling units
50 Fuselage centreline pylon
51 Boundary layer splitter plate
52 Port navigation light
53 Fixed-geometry engine air intake
54 Cooling air spill louvres
55 Cabin air conditioning system equipment
56 Leading-edge flap drive motor
57 Boundary layer spill duct
58 Air conditioning system heat exchanger exhaust
59 Centre fuselage fuel cells
60 Wing panel root attachment joints
61 Central Garrett GTC36-200 auxiliary power unit (APU)
62 Airframe-mounted engine accessory equipment gearbox, port and starboard
63 Engine bleed air ducting to conditioning system
64 Fuel tank bay access panels
65 Upper UHF/IFF/datalink antenna
66 Starboard wingroot joint

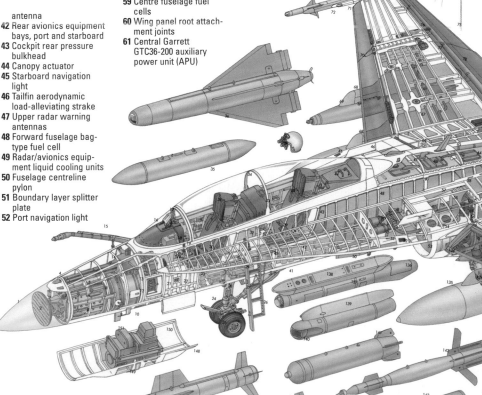

Above: In Australian service, the F/A-18A represents the primary element in the Royal Australian Air Force's fighter fleet. The F/A-18s have been upgraded and fly alongside an upgraded F-111 fleet. Advanced weapons for the Hornets include ASRAAM and laser-guided bombs.

Left: Having entered front-line US Navy service in 1985, the Hornet has remained at the top of the naval fighter tree for almost two decades. With the introduction of the F/A-18E (illustrated) and two-seat F/A-18F Super Hornet, the type regains its position as the world's premier carrierborne warplane.

SPECIFICATION

F/A-18C Hornet

Dimensions

Length: 17.07 m (56 ft)
Height: 4.66 m (15 ft 3½ in)
Wing span: 11.43 m (37 ft 6 in)
Wing span with tip-mounted AAMs: 12.31 m (40 ft 4¾ in)
Wing span with wings folded: 8.38 m (27 ft 6 in)
Wing area: 37.16 m² (400 sq ft)
Wheel track: 3.11 m (10 ft 2½ in)
Wheelbase: 5.42 m (17ft 9½ in)

Powerplant

Two General Electric F404-GE-402 turbofans each rated at 78.73 kN (17,700 lb st) with afterburning

Weights

Empty: 10455 kg (23,050 lb)
Take-off: 16652 kg (36,710 lb) for a fighter mission or 23541 kg (51,900 lb) on an attack mission
Maximum take-off: about 25401 kg (56,000 lb)

Fuel and load

Internal fuel: 4926 kg (10,860 lb)
External fuel: up to 3053 kg (6,732 lb) in three 330-US gal (1250-litre) drop tanks
Maximum ordnance load: 7031 kg (15,500 lb) on nine external stores stations

Performance

Maximum level speed 'clean' at high altitude: more than 1915 km/h (1,190 mph)
Maximum rate of climb at sea level: 13715 m (45,000 ft) per minute
Combat ceiling: about 15240 m (50,000 ft)
Take-off run at maximum take-off weight: less than 427 m (1,400 ft)
Approach speed: 248 km/h (154 mph)
Acceleration from 850 km/h (530 mph) to 1705 km/h (1060 mph) at 10670 m (35,000 ft): under two minutes

Range

Ferry range with drop tanks: more

than 3336 km (2,073 miles)
Combat radius: more than 740 km (460 miles) on a fighter mission, or 1065 km (662 miles) on an attack mission, or 537 km (340 miles) on a hi-lo-hi interdiction mission

Armament

Gun: M61A1 Vulcan 20-mm cannon with 570 rounds
Air-to-air missiles: AIM-120 AMRAAM; AIM-7 Sparrow; AIM-9 Sidewinder
Precision-guided munitions: AGM-65 Maverick; AGM-84 Harpoon; AGM-84E SLAM; AGM-88 HARM; AGM-62 Walleye EO- (Electro-Optic) guided bomb; AGM-123 Skipper; AGM-154 JSOW; GBU-10/12/16 laser-guided bombs; GBU-30/31/32 JDAM
Unguided munitions: B57 and B61 tactical nuclear bombs; Mk 80 series general-purpose bombs; Mk 7 dispenser (including Mk 20 Rockeye II, CBU-59, CBU-72 FAE, CBU-78 Gator mine dispenser); LAU-97 Zuni FFAR pods

Radar

Hughes AN/APG-65 or AN/APG-73
Effective radar range: more than 185 km (115 miles)

F/A-18B/D Hornet

Type: Two-seat, multi-role, attack fighter and trainer generally similar to the F/A-18A/C Hornet except

Weights

Normal take-off: 15234 kg (33,585 lb) on a fighter mission
Maximum take-off for an attack mission: 21319 kg (47,000 lb)

Fuel and load

Internal fuel reduced by less than six per cent to accommodate second seat

Range

Ferry range with internal and external fuel: 3520 km (2,187 miles)
Combat radius: 1020 km (634 miles)

---

73 AIM-9L Sidewinder air-to-air missile
74 Outer wing panel, folded position
75 Drooping aileron
76 Aileron hydraulic actuator
77 Wing-fold hydraulic rotary actuator
78 Drooping flap vane
79 Starboard slotted flap, operates as flaperon at low speeds
80 Flap hydraulic actuator
81 Hydraulic reservoirs
82 Reinforced fin-root attachment joint
83 Multi-spar fin structure
84 Fuel jettison pipe
85 Graphite/epoxy tail unit skin panels with glass-fibre tip fairings
86 Tail position light
87 AN/ALR-67 receiving antenna
88 AN/ALQ-165 low-band transmitting antenna
89 Fuel jettison
90 Starboard all-moving tailplane
91 Starboard rudder
92 Radar warning system

67 Starboard wing integral fuel tank
68 Stores pylons
69 Mk 83 1,000-lb (454-kg) LDGP bomb
70 Leading-edge flap
71 Starboard secondary navigation light
72 Wing tip missile launch rail

power amplifier
93 Rudder hydraulic actuator
94 Airbrake panel, open
95 Airbrake hydraulic jack
96 Fin formation lighting strip
97 Fuel venting air intake
98 Anti-collision beacon, port and starboard
99 Port rudder
100 Port AN/ALQ-165 antenna
101 AN/ALQ-67 receiving antenna
102 AN/ALQ-165 high-band transmitting antenna
103 Variable-area afterburner nozzles
104 Nozzle actuators
105 Afterburner duct
106 Port all-moving tailplane
107 Tailplane bonded honeycomb core structure
108 Deck arrester hook
109 Tailplane pivot mounting
110 Tailplane hydraulic actuator
111 Full-authority digital engine control (FADEC) unit
112 General Electric F404-GE-400 afterburning turbofan engine
113 Rear fuselage formation lighting strip
114 Engine fuel control units

115 Fuselage side mounted AIM-7 Sparrow air-to-air missile
116 Port slotted flap
117 Control surface bonded honeycomb core structure
118 Wing-fold rotary hydraulic actuator and hinge joint
119 Port aileron hydraulic actuator
120 Port drooping aileron
121 Wing-tip AIM-9L Sidewinder air-to-air missile
122 Port leading-edge flap
123 Mk 82SE Snakeye 500-lb (227-kg) retarded bomb
124 Mk 82 500-lb (227-kg) LDGP bombs
125 Twin stores carrier
126 Port wing stores pylons
127 Pylon mounting hardpoints
128 Multi-spar wing panel structure
129 Port wing integral fuel tank
130 Leading-edge flap-shaft driven rotary actuator
131 Port mainwheel
132 Levered suspension main undercarriage leg strut
133 Shock absorber strut
134 Ventral AN/ALE-39 chaff/flare launcher
135 330-US gal (1250-litre)

external fuel tank
136 Strike camera housing
137 AN/ASQ-173 laser spot tracker/strike camera (LST/SCAM) pod
138 Fuselage starboard side LST/SCAM pylon adaptor
139 Port side FLIR pod adaptor
140 AN/AAS-38 forward-looking infra-red (FLIR) pod
141 CBU-89/89B Gator sub-munition dispenser
142 GBU-12 D/B Paveway II 500-lb (227-kg) LGB
143 LAU-10A Zuni four-round rocket launcher
144 5-in (127-mm) FFAR
145 AGM-88 HARM anti-radar missile
146 AGM-65A Maverick air-to-ground anti-armour missile
147 AGM-84 SLAM air-to-surface missile
148 Advanced tactical airborne reconnaissance system (ATARS) unit, interchangeable with gun pack/ammunition magazine (F/A-18D(RC))
149 Sensor viewing apertures
150 Infra-red linescanner
151 Low- and/or medium-altitude electro-optical scanner

Mike Badrocke

VFA-115 was the US Navy's first front-line F/A-18E squadron. The Super Hornet will replace many of the older F/A-18C aircraft in service and will completely oust the F-14 Tomcat. Assuming that the EA-18G programme comes to fruition, it will also take over the Prowler's role and it also has a useful capability as an inflight refuelling tanker, allowing it to take over some of the missions of the Lockheed Viking.

Radar and cannon

The F/A-18A, two-seat B and early-production C-model aircraft were fitted with a Hughes AN/APG-65 multi-mode radar set; later F/A-18C, D, E and F-model machines have the more capable APG-73, which boasts faster processing and a larger memory. Also mounted in the nose of the aircraft is a General Electric M61A1 Vulcan 20-mm rotary cannon with 570 rounds of ammunition. Another weapon that dates from the 1950s, the Vulcan has a 6,000 round per minute rate of fire and has equipped numerous US combat types.

F/A-18A Hornet

This VMFA-314 F/A-18A was based aboard USS *Coral Sea* during attacks on Libyan SAM sites during Operations El Dorado Canyon and Prairie Fire in 1986. These operations marked the combat debut of both the Hornet and the AGM-88 HARM missile, one of which is seen being launched by this aircraft. For the duration of their cruise as part of CVW-13 aboard *Coral Sea*, VMFA-314's aircraft wore the 'AK' tailcodes of the Air Wing, rather than their own 'VW' codes.

Wing tip launch rail and FLIR pods

The wing tip launch rail is usually used to carry an AIM-9M Sidewinder heating-seeking air-to-air missile (AAM) as illustrated here. Like the AIM-7 Sparrow, the AIM-9 was developed, originally for the US Navy, in the early 1950s. The most widely-used and most successful AAM in the world, this short-range missile is still in production. It will eventually be replaced on the F/A-18C/D and F/A-18E/F by the AIM-9X. The F/A-18's wing tip rails may also be used for AIM-120 AMRAAMs, although these are generally carried on the underwing or fuselage shoulder hardpoints. Although AMRAAM is part of the Hornet's regular inventory, the older AIM-7M also remains in service. Another typical wing tip store is an Air Combat Manoeuvring Instrumentation (ACMI) pod, used when training on suitably-equipped ranges. Useful night/all-weather capability is available with the AN/AAS-38 NITE Hawk forward-looking infra-red (FLIR) pod, AAS-38A NITE Hawk FLIR-LTD/R (which adds a laser designating and ranging capability) or AAS-38B (with laser spot tracker). One of these occupies the port shoulder Sparrow/AMRAAM station when carried. The FLIR provides real-time thermal imagery on a TV-type display in the cockpit for target detection and tracking. Linked to the aircraft's computer, it can provide accurate line-of-sight angles and rates of angle change. The two-seat F/A-18D Night Attack Hornet, employed by USMC all-weather attack units, can also use an AN/AAR-50 navigation/FLIR pod for low-level night flying, on the starboard station.

Powerplant

For the initial versions of the F/A-18, General Electric developed the F404 afterburning low-bypass turbofan, rated at 71.2 or 78.3 kN (16,000 lb or 17,700 lb) thrust, with afterburning, depending on the variant. Derived from the YJ101 engine in the YF-17, the powerplant has proved reliable and fuel-efficient. Fuel is fed from four main tanks in the aircraft's spine, which hold 5300 litres (1,400 US gal) in total. External fuel may be carried in 330-US gal (1249-litre) drop tanks on wing pylons. For the redesigned F/A-18E/F, a more powerful F404 derivative has been developed. The F414-GE-400, producing 97.9 kN (22,000 lb st) with a new afterburner, is closely related to the F412 turbofan intended for the ill-fated A-12 Avenger II.

Fly-by-wire controls

Digital fly-by-wire controls manipulate the outboard ailerons and differential tailerons for roll control (aided by drooping flaperons at low speed), twin rudders for yaw and tailerons for pitch. For take-off and landing, the rudders are automatically toed-in to provide a nose-up pitch moment. Trailing- and leading-edge flaps are automatically programmed for optimum performance for both low-speed lift and high-speed manoeuvring. Advanced materials are used extensively in the Hornet's structure. For example, the all-moving horizontal tailplanes are constructed from a carbon-graphite epoxy over a light alloy honeycomb core with titanium alloy root fittings.

In mid 2003, work was continuing on the EA-18G Growler. This aircraft is based on the F/A-18F and adds podded and internal equipment suitable for the jamming missions currently undertaken by the hard-pressed US Navy/US Marine Corps EA-6B Prowler fleet.

Grumman F-14 Tomcat Swing-wing naval fighter

From May 1995, VF-2 re-equipped with F-14D Tomcats. This aircraft is depicted with a typical air-to-air load of four under-fuselage Phoenix long-range AAMs, and two each of the Sparrow and Sidewinder short-range missiles.

Designed as a successor to the F-4 Phantom II in the fleet air defence role for the US Navy, the **Grumman F-14 Tomcat** was originally conceived to engage and destroy targets at extreme range, before they could pose a threat to the carrier battle group. The **F-14A Tomcat** remains a formidable warplane, even though the original F-14A has been in service for almost 30 years. Production of the F-14A for the US Navy eventually totalled 556 examples, while 80 broadly similar machines were purchased by Iran before the downfall of the Shah. Of the latter, only 79 were actually delivered (one being diverted to the USN). The F-14 continues to be the Navy's primary air defence aircraft although with the introduction of the F/A-18E/F Super Hornet into service from late 1999, the days of the F-14 have been increasingly numbered.

Weapons system

The key to the F-14's effectiveness lies in its advanced avionics suite, the Hughes AWG-9 fire control system representing the most capable long-range interceptor radar in service, with the ability to detect, track and engage targets at ranges in excess of 160 km (100 miles). Early aircraft also had an infra-red search and track (IRST) system, replacing this during production (and by retrofit) with a long-range video camera known as TCS. The armament options allow the aircraft to engage targets over a huge range from

close up to extreme BVR (beyond visual range).

The AIM-54 Phoenix remains the longest-ranged air-to-air missile in Western service at the beginning of the 21st century and in tests it has demonstrated the ability to detect and kill targets at unparalleled distances. In the medium-range arena, Tomcat employs the AIM-7 Sparrow, not having been upgraded for compatibility with the AIM-120 AMRAAM. For short-range, close-in engagements, the F-14 carries the well-proven AIM-9 Sidewinder. Finally, there is a single M61A1 Vulcan 20-mm Gatling-type rotary

cannon in the lower port fuselage with 675 rounds of ammunition.

Tomcat development

Development was initiated in the late 1960s, following the cancellation of the ill-fated F-111B naval fighter, which initially left the Navy in the unenviable position of having no new fighter in prospect. Grumman had already invested a considerable amount of effort in the navalised F-111B, and used this experience in designing a new variable-geometry fighter (the **G-303**) which was duly selected by the Navy in January 1969.

Carrying a quartet of Mk 83 freefall bombs on its underfuselage stations, this F-14A is about to fly a practice strike. The aircraft hails from VF-211 'Checkmates', a unit based aboard USS John C. Stennis between January and July 2002 for the Tomcat's last cruise aboard the vessel.

Grumman's use of a variable-geometry wing allowed excellent high-speed performance to be combined with docile low-speed handling characteristics for operations around the carrier, and a high degree of agility. A dozen **YF-14A** development aircraft were ordered, with the first making its maiden flight on 21 December 1970.

The programme made

reasonably swift progress, culminating in deliveries to the Navy from October 1972, with the first operational cruise in 1974. Production continued into the 1980s and a total of 26 front-line and four second-line squadrons was eventually equipped with the F-14A Tomcat.

Although generally successful, the F-14 has suffered many difficulties

VX-9 'Vampires' is a test unit involved in developing all aspects of the F-14's air-to-air role. This F-14D has been finished in the black scheme traditionally worn by VX-4 aircraft and continued when VX-4 and VX-5 were combined into VX-9. The aircraft was photographed in 2002 during Operation Cope Snapper.

since entering fleet service.
Many were engine-related,
the TF30 turbofan proving
something of an Achilles
heel. Fan blade losses
caused several crashes
before improved quality control and steel containment
cases alleviated the worst
consequences of engine failure. In addition, the engine
was prone to compressor
stall, especially during air
combat manoeuvring train-
ing, and the aircraft's vicious
departure characteristics
(especially with one engine
out) resulted in many further
losses. Many problems
were solved when the
revised TF30-P-414A version
of the powerplant was
adopted as standard.

Other missions

In addition to fleet air
defence tasks, F-14As are
also used for reconnais-
sance missions, using the
Tactical Air Reconnaissance
Pod System (TARPS), and it
is usual for three TARPS-
capable aircraft to be
assigned to each carrier air
wing. New digital TARPS
pods have replaced the original wet-film units. More
recently, the F-14A has also
acquired a secondary air-to-
ground role, capitalising on a
modest attack capability that
was built in from the outset,
but never utilised. The **F-14A
'Bombcat'** initially carried
only conventional 'iron'
bombs, but has now had the
LANTIRN pod integrated for
use with laser-guided
bombs.

*Engine problems have plagued the
F-14 throughout its career. Later
TF30 models solved the worst of
these problems, but re-engining
with the F110 has transformed the
Tomcat's performance.*

Continuing problems with
the TF30 engine of the F-14A
were a key factor in the
development of re-engined
and upgraded variants of the
Tomcat. One of the original
prototype airframes was fitted with two F401-PW-400s
and employed for an abbreviated test programme as

the **F-14B** as early as 1973-
74. Technical problems and
financial difficulties forced
the abandonment of the programme, and the aircraft
was placed into storage,
re-emerging as the **F-14B
Super Tomcat** with
F101DFE (Derivative Fighter
Engine) turbofans. This
engine was developed into
the General Electric
F110-GE-400 turbofan, which
was selected to power
improved production Tomcat
variants. It was decided to
produce two distinct new
Tomcats, one designated **F-
14A+** (primarily by
conversion of existing
F-14As) with the new
engine, and another, designated **F-14D**, with the new
engine and improved digital
avionics. The F-14A+ was
originally regarded as an
interim type, all examples of
which would eventually be
converted to full F-14D
Tomcat standard.

'Bs' and 'Ds'

Subsequently, the F-14A+
was formally redesignated
as the **F-14B**, 38 new-build
examples being joined by 32
F-14A rebuilds in equipping
half-a-dozen deployable
squadrons starting in 1988.
These incorporated some
avionics changes, including a
modernised fire control system, new radios, upgraded
RWRs (radar warning
receivers), and various cockpit changes. F-14Bs were
the first re-engined Tomcats

*These F-14s were
photographed late in
2001 on the USS
Enterprise. Note the
over-sweep position of
the wings.*

to enter fleet service.
Two modified F-14As flew
as F-14D prototypes and the
first F-14D to be built as
such made its maiden flight
on 9 February 1990. The
F-14D also added digital
avionics, with digital radar
processing and displays
(adding these to standard
AWG-9 hardware under the
redesignation APG-71), and
a side-by-side undernose
TCS/IRST sensor pod. Other
improvements introduced by
the F-14D include OBOGS
(on-board oxygen-generating
system), NACES (Naval
Aircrew Common Escape
System) ejection seats, and
AN/ALR-67 radar warning
receiver equipment. Like the
F-14A, the F-14D has a full
ground attack capability.
However, a subsequent US
Department of Defense
decision to cease funding

the F-14D effectively halted
the Navy's drive to upgrade
its force of Tomcats. In consequence, the service has
received only 37 new-build F-
14Ds, while plans to
upgrade approximately 400
existing F-14As to a similar
standard were cancelled.
F-14D deliveries to the
Navy began in 1990, when
training squadron VF-124
accepted its first F-14D at
Miramar. The type has been
used in Operation Southern
Watch over Iraq, including an
unsuccessful Phoenix shot
against a pair of MiG-23s.
The F-14 performed well on
attack missions during
Operation Enduring
Freedom. The F-14 is slowly
being retired; the last F-14D
is due to leave the fleet in
2008.

SPECIFICATION	
Grumman F-14A Tomcat **Type:** two-seat carrierborne fleet air defence fighter and interceptor, with ground attack capability **Powerplant:** two Pratt & Whitney TF30-P-412A/414A turbofans each rated at 92.97 kN (20,900 lb st) with afterburning **Performance:** maximum level speed 'clean' at high altitude 2485 km/h (1,544 mph); maximum rate of climb at sea level more than 9145 m (30,000 ft) per minute; service ceiling more than 15240 m (50,000 ft); radius on a combat air patrol with six AIM-7 Sparrows and four AIM-9 Sidewinders 1233 km (766 miles) **Weights:** empty 18191 kg (40,104 lb) with -414A engines; maximum take-off 32098 kg (70,764 lb) with six Phoenix **Dimensions:** wing span 19.54 m	(64 ft 1½ in) spread, 11.65 m (38 ft 2½ in) swept and 10.15 m (33 ft 3½ in) overswept; length 19.1 m (62 ft 8 in); height 4.88 m (16 ft); wing area 52.49 m² (565 sq ft) **Armament:** standard armament consists of an internal M61A1 Vulcan 20-mm six-barrelled cannon and an AIM-9M Sidewinder on the shoulder launch rail of each wing glove pylon. The main launch rail of each glove pylon can accommodate either an AIM-7M Sparrow or an AIM-54C Phoenix. Four further AIM-7M or AIM-54C missiles can be carried under the fuselage between the engine trunks. 1011-litre (267-US gal) fuel tanks can be carried under the intakes, while 1,000-lb (454-kg) Mk 83 or 2,000-lb (907-kg) Mk 84 GP bombs or other free-fall weaponry can also be carried

F-14A Tomcat

This F-14A of VF-111 'Sundowners' is shown as it appeared while deployed aboard the USS *Carl Vinson* (CVN-70), with the US Navy Pacific Fleet around 1985. The Tomcat wears a low-visibility overall light grey camouflage scheme. On the nose are suitably toned-down unit 'sharkmouth' markings, which are also repeated on the external fuel tanks.

Above: On 24 July 2003 a VX-23 Hornet made the first arrested landing aboard CVN-76, USS Ronald Reagan, the US Navy's latest carrier. The ship became operational during 2004.

Vulcan cannon
The Tomcat carries the standard US fighter gun: the General Electric M61A-1 Vulcan. This 20-mm rotary cannon has six barrels and is capable of firing at 4,000 or 6,000 rounds per minute. The gun is mounted on the left side in the lower forward fuselage and is fed by a 675-round magazine drum.

AIM-7 Sparrow air-to-air missile
Raytheon AIM-7 Sparrow missiles are the F-14's primary medium-range (beyond-visual-range) weapons. Carried originally in AIM-7F but now in improved AIM-7M form, the missile is guided by a semi-active radar homing head which tracks the fighter's own radar signals reflected from the target. This has the disadvantage of requiring constant illumination of the target by the Tomcat's radar, thus greatly increasing the risk of a return shot.

Left: By 2007, the Tomcat will have all but disappeared from the US Navy's front-line, with the Super Hornet replacing it alongside the F/A-18C/D Hornet. This VF-211 F-14A Tomcat has launched from the angle of USS Enterprise's deck, while the F/A-18Cs wait to launch from one of the ship's bow catapults. The raised blast deflector behind the lead Hornet prevents its exhaust efflux from damaging the aircraft behind, a particularly important consideration if afterburner is selected.

Countermeasures equipment
Comprehensive protection from enemy weapons systems comes from both mechanical and electronic countermeasures (ECM). Passive warning of hostile radars is provided by AN/APR-45 receivers, which activate the AN/ALQ-126 deception jamming system. The internal radar warning receiver has two aft-facing aerials on the tips of the tailplanes. The AN/ALR-45(V) usually fitted, is a digital threat warning receiver. Transmitters for the deception jamming system are mounted on the fin-tips and in an undernose fairing, which is scabbed on underneath the TCS in aircraft so-configured. Another ECM transmitter aerial which operates on different wavebands from the fin-tip emitters is housed in the tailcone. Mechanical countermeasures are located beneath the rear fuselage in the form of AN/ALE-39 chaff/flare dispensers.

AIM-9 Sidewinder air-to-air missile

The AIM-9 Sidewinder is used for short-range engagements during close-in air combat. The missile's infra-red seeking head locks on to the heat emitted by the target aircraft, primarily the very hot engine exhausts, but also the heat caused by skin friction, such as that along the leading edges of the wings and fins. The missile is carried on the side launch rail of a 'cranked' wing pylon which is attached to the 'glove' portion of each wing. The main attachment carries a single Sparrow or Phoenix missile, or a Sidewinder when fitted with a suitable launch rail.

Flight controls

To enable the F-14 to maintain safe controllable flight at low speeds, its wing is fitted with full-span leading-edge slats and trailing-edge flaps which are extended to increase lift for take-off or landing. The flaps have three sections, the inboard sections being usable only when the wing is fully swept forward. All surfaces are fully deployed when the F-14 is approaching the carrier, giving it an ungainly appearance and thus its nickname 'Turkey'. The wingtip section incorporates flush-mounted navigation lights (red to port and green to starboard) and low-voltage formation strips.

With the Military Sealift Command replenishment ship USNS Supply alongside, USS George Washington continues flight operations early in December 2003. As well as the array of aircraft on its flight deck, 'GW' has just launched an F-14B Tomcat. With the F110 engine, the F-14B/D Tomcat finally left the engine problems which plagued the F-14A behind it. In addition, some launches can be made in military power – without the use of afterburner – with an attendant boost in endurance.

Northrop Grumman E-2 Hawkeye Carrier- and land-based

AEW&C aircraft

This E-2C Hawkeye is from the US Navy's VAW-126 'Seahawks', and is illustrated as it appeared when operating from USS Kennedy during the late 1990s.

Since entering service in 1964, the **E-2 Hawkeye** has protected US Navy carrier battle groups and acted as an airborne controller for their aircraft. One of very few types designed specifically for the AEW role, it was first flown in prototype form as long ago as October 1960. As a consequence of its ability to operate from aircraft carriers, the basic **Hawkeye** is extremely compact. A total of 59 production **E-2A** machines was delivered from January 1964; 51 were updated to **E-2B** standard, before production switched to the improved **E-2C**.

E-2C Hawkeye

The first E-2C flew on 23 September 1972 and Grumman had built 139 for the US Navy when the line closed in 1994. However, low-rate production began again in 2000.

External changes to the E-2 have been minor but its systems have been progressively updated. The E-2C was initially equipped with APS-125 search radar, but this was replaced by the AN/APS-139 in **Group I** aircraft from 1988 and the AN/APS-145 in the latest **Group II E-2C**. The latter radar allows a low-flying, fighter-sized aircraft to be detected at up to 407 km (253 miles) away with the E-2C flying at its operational altitude. A passive detection system gives warning of hostile emitters at ranges up to twice the radar detection range. After almost 30 years in service, the E-2C is still an evolving design, and Northrop Grumman developed the even more capable **E-2C Group II Plus** or **Hawkeye 2000**; the last of 21 such new-build machines is scheduled for completion during 2003. Subsequent to Hawkeye 2000, Northrop Grumman has begun development of the **Advanced Hawkeye**. This features all new systems and should reach initial operational capability with the USN in 2011. The Navy plans to buy 75 of the aircraft.

E-2Cs have been exported to Eygpt, France, Israel, Japan, Singapore and Taiwan. Many customers are upgrading their E-2s to Hawkeye 2000 standards.

SPECIFICATION

Northrop Grumman E-2C Hawkeye (Group I configuration onwards)
Type: carrierborne AEW aircraft
Powerplant: two Allison T56-A-427 turboprops each rated at 3803 kW (5,100 ehp)
Performance: maximum level speed 626 km/h (389 mph); maximum cruising speed at optimum altitude 602 km/h (374 mph); maximum rate of climb at sea level over 767 m (2,515 ft) per minute; service ceiling 11275 m (37,000 ft); unrefuelled time on station at 320 km (200 miles) from base 4 hours 24 minutes; endurance with maximum fuel 6 hours 15 minutes
Weights: empty 18363 kg (40,484 lb); maximum take-off 24687 kg (54,426 lb)
Dimensions: wing span 24.56 m (80 ft 7 in); folded width 8.94 m (29 ft 4 in); rotodome diameter 7.32 m (24 ft); length 17.54 m (57 ft 6¾ in); height 5.58 m (18 ft 3¾ in); wing area 65.03 m² (700 sq ft)

Hawkeye 2000 (illustrated) represented a major increase in the capabilities of the E-2 design. Advanced Hawkeye will look very similar.

Lockheed Martin F-35B and F-35C Future tactical fighters

On 26 October 2001, the US government announced that Lockheed Martin had won the JSF (Joint Strike Fighter) competition in the face of stiff opposition from Boeing. The JSF requirement was set out to provide a largely common air frame to fulfil three distinct niches: a CTOL aircraft for the USAF, a carrier-capable aircraft for the US Navy and a STOVL machine for the USMC.

X-35 in detail

Lockheed Martin's **X-35** demonstrators will form the basis of the operational **F-35** fighters, with the first F-35 flight planned for 2005 and the **F-35C** due to enter US Navy service around 2012. F-35C will have a longer-span wing than the other initial variants, with provision for folding. The aircraft will also be fitted with an arrester hook and strengthened landing gear, these and other modifications making it heavier than the CTOL F-35A. All F-35s will primarily carry their armament internally, in bays along the fuselage sides. Stealth was a major consideration in the design and the aircraft has

Pictured in the hover, the X-35B demonstrates the large doors in its upper fuselage. These open to feed air to the lift fan.

been carefully shaped to avoid producing large radar-reflecting surfaces. Apertures, doors and other panels generally have serrated edges, similar to those seen on the F-117.

UK involvement

From an early stage, the UK has been a full partner in the JSF programme. Like the USMC, the UK has opted for the STOVL **F-35B**. All of the F-35 models will initially be powered by the Pratt & Whitney F135 turbofan, delivering around 178 kN (40,000 lb) of thrust with afterburning and exhausting through a vectoring nozzle. On the F-35B, a lift fan, developed by Rolls-Royce and mounted horizontally in the forward fuselage, is

X-35C is immediately recognisable as a naval fighter demonstrator, thanks to the prominent arrester hook mounted beneath its rear fuselage.

driven by the main engine via a gearbox to provide the major part of the thrust

needed in vertical manoeuvres. The UK will base its F-35Bs on two new BAE

Systems/Thales aircraft carriers which are due to enter service in 2012 and 2015.

Export orders for F-35C are unlikely, but F-35B may find a market.

Lockheed S-3 Viking Multi-role naval aircraft

The **S-3B Viking** carries out the US Navy's carrier-based sea control mission. The S-3 was originally designed in the early 1970s with a sophisticated ASW sensor suite. The initial **S-3A** variant was replaced in the early 1990s by the S-3B. This incorporates anti-surface warfare upgrades such as the APS-137 inverse synthetic aperture radar and AGM-84 AShM capability. With the demise of the Soviet Union and the increasing dominance of littoral warfare, there has been decreased emphasis on the Viking's ASW role and more emphasis on anti-surface warfare and land-attack missions. Each carrier air wing includes one sea control

With its home base at Oceana, Virginia, this S-3A is seen as deployed onboard the nuclear carrier USS Nimitz with VS-24, air wing CV-8. Many S-3As were refitted with new weapons systems, including provision for Harpoon missiles, and redesignated as S-3B machines.

(VS) squadron equipped with S-3Bs. VS squadrons perform ASW, anti-shipping,

mine-laying, surveillance and tanking missions for the carrier battle group. This latter

mission is accomplished thanks to the D-704 'buddy-buddy' refuelling store, which incorporates a retractable hose for compatibility with the Navy's probe-equipped combat aircraft. Several upgrades have been applied to the Viking, including the addition of GPS, Carrier Aircraft Inertial Navigation System II, new tactical displays, computer memory, SATCOM equipment and improved radios. Several S-3Bs have been involved in anti-drug trafficking duties, using camera systems, FLIR and hand-held sensors. The S-3B is planned for replacement from 2015 by a variant of the Common Support Aircraft,

but may be retired on an accelerated schedule.

Shadow

Sixteen S-3A airframes were converted to **ES-3A Shadow** standard during the early 1990s, with a variety of electronic surveillance and intercept equipment to locate and identify hostile emitters and communications stations. In mid-1998, the Navy made the decision to withdraw the ES-3A from service without replacement. The aircraft's mission avionics suite, becoming obsolescent in the age of interconnectivity in the 'electronic battlefield', was deemed as too expensive to upgrade.

As a force multiplier, the S-3B Viking is a crucial US Navy asset. It is ultimately likely to lose its inflight-refuelling role to the F/A-18E/F.

As a multi-role support type, the Viking continues to have an important front-line role. This Hornet was receiving fuel during an Iraqi Freedom mission.

SPECIFICATION	
Lockheed S-3A Viking	(26,650 lb); maximum take-off
Type: four-crew carrierborne ASW warplane	23832 kg (52,540 lb)
Powerplant: two General Electric TF34-GE-2 turbofan engines each rated at 41.26 kN (9,275 lb st)	**Dimensions:** wing span 20.93 m (68 ft 8 in); length 16.26 m (53 ft 4 in); height 6.63 m (22 ft 9 in); wing area 55.56 m² (598 sq ft)
Performance: maximum speed 814 km/h (506 mph) at sea level; initial climb rate more than 1280 m (4,200 ft) per minute; service ceiling more than 10670 m (35,000 ft); radius 853 km (530 miles) with typical weapons load and a loiter of 4 hours 30 minutes	**Armament:** up to 3175 kg (7,000 lb) of disposable stores, including B57 or Mk 80-series bombs, Mk 53 mines, Mk 54 depth bombs, Mk 46 or Mk 53 Barracuda torpedoes, six Mk 20 Mod 2 Rockeye cluster bombs or LAU-10A/A, LAU-61/A, LAU-68/A or LAU-69/A rocket launchers
Weights: empty 12088 kg	

Aérospatiale Dauphin, HH-65A Dolphin and Eurocopter Panther Multi-role naval helicopters

Left: The SA 365 Dauphin is employed by French naval aviation units for shipboard duties, including small ships ASW/utility work, as well as land-based SAR. This is an example from Flotille 23S, a former ship-based 'Pédro' unit.

Below: This AS 565SB has the type's maximum load of four AS.15TT anti-ship missiles, as well as anti-ship radar with its antenna in a radome beneath the helicopter's nose.

The first version of the **Aérospatiale Dauphin** developed for naval warfare was based on the twin-engined **Dauphin 2** and built for the US Coast Guard. This **SA 366G** or **HH-65A Dolphin** was built for the SAR role. Subsequently, Aérospatiale developed the versatile **AS 365F** from the the AS 365N, intended primarily for the anti-ship role.

Three SA 365Fs were acquired by the Aéronavale for plane-guard duties. The helicopters now service the nuclear-powered aircraft carrier Charles de Gaulle.

The type is also available in SAR configuration, as well as with a more advanced ASW capability.

Eurocopter Panther
The first order for the type was placed by Saudi Arabia, which received 24 examples in two subvariants now designated in the **Eurocopter AS 565 Panther** military series as the **AS 565SC**

(four for the SAR role, later redesignated **AS 565MB**) and the **AS 565SA** (20 anti-ship helicopters, later redesignated **AS 565SB**). Other small export orders were received, Israel designating its AS 565SAs **Atalef**, or bat.

Eurocopter offers two naval variants of the AS 565: the unarmed **AS 565MA** (replaced from 1997 by the **AS 565MB**) for the SAR and sea surveillance roles, and the **AS 565SB** for the ASW as well as anti-ship roles.

SPECIFICATION

Eurocopter AS 565SA Panther
Type: two-seat light naval utility helicopter optimised for the anti-ship and anti-submarine roles
Powerplant: two Turboméca Arriel 1M1 turboshaft engines each rated at 558 kW (749 shp)
Performance: maximum cruising speed 274 km/h (170 mph) at sea level; initial climb rate 420 m (1,378 ft) per minute; service ceiling 4575 m (15,010 ft); hovering ceiling 2600 m (8,530 ft) in ground effect and 1860 m (6,100 ft) out of ground effect; radius 250 km (155 miles) with four AShMs
Weights: empty 2240 kg (4,938 lb);

maximum take-off 4250 kg (9,370 lb)
Dimensions: main rotor diameter 11.94 m (39 ft 2 in); length 13.68 m (44 ft 10¾ in) with rotor turning; height 3.98 m (13 ft ¾ in); main rotor disc area 111.97 m² (1,205.26 sq ft)
Armament: up to 600 kg (1,323 lb) of disposable stores, generally comprising four AS.15TT light anti-ship missiles or two Mk 46 lightweight ASW torpedoes
Payload: up to 10 passengers or 1700 kg (3,748 lb) of freight in the cabin, or 1600 kg (3,527 lb) of freight carried as a slung load

---

Aérospatiale SA 321 Super Frélon SAR and transport helo

To meet a French armed services requirement for a medium transport helicopter, Sud-Aviation flew the prototype **SE.3200 Frélon** (hornet) on 10 June 1959. Powered by three Turmo IIIB turboshafts, the SE.3200 had large external fuel tanks that left the interior clear for a maximum 28 troops, and a swing-tail fuselage to simplify cargo loading. However, development was terminated in favour of a larger and more capable helicopter designed in conjunction with Sikorsky and Fiat. What was to become Western

Europe's largest production helicopter emerged with a rotor system of Sikorsky design, and with a watertight hull suitable for amphibious operation. Two military prototypes of the Super Frélon were built, the **SA 3210-01** troop transport, and the **SA 3210-02** maritime version for the Aéronavale on 28 May 1963.

France's SA 321 Super Frelons are retained in service for SAR and heavylift transport, for which their long-range capability proves useful.

Four pre-production aircraft were built under the new designation **SA 321 Super Frélon**. These were followed in October 1965 by production **SA 321G** ASW helicopters for the Aéronavale. Apart from ship-based ASW missions, the SA 321G also carried out sanitisation patrols in support of 'Rédoutable'-class ballistic missile submarines. Some were modified with nose-mounted targeting radar for Exocet AShMs. Five **SA 321Ga** freighters, originally used in support of the Pacific nuclear test cen-

Delivery of 16 SA 321Ja Super Frélons to the Chinese navy took place between 1975 and 1977 and was expanded with licence-built Changhe Z-8s.

tre, were transferred to assault support duties. In 2004, the surviving Aéronavale Super Frélons are assigned to transport duties including commando transport, VertRep and SAR.

Exports

Six radar-equipped **SA 321GM** helicopters were delivered to Libya in 1980-81. The SA 321G was also modified for air force and army service. Designated

SA 321H, a total of 16 was delivered from 1977 to the Iraqi air force with radar and Exocets. These aircraft were used in the Iran-Iraq conflict and the 1991 Gulf War, in which at least one example was destroyed.

The **SA 321Ja** was a higher weight version of the commercial **SA 321J**, of which the People's Republic of China navy received 16 aircraft fitted with targeting radar. Non-amphibious mili-

tary export versions included 12 **SA 321K** transports for Israel, 16 similar **SA 321L** transports for South Africa and eight **SA 321M** SAR/transports for Libya.

When French production ended in 1983 a total of 99

Super Frélons had been built, but production continued in China under licence-agreement as the **Changhe Z-8**. Eight Israeli aircraft were re-engined with T58 engines and later sold to Argentina.

SPECIFICATION	
Aérospatiale SA 321G Super Frélon	1020 km (633 miles) with a 3500-kg (7,716-lb) payload
Type: medium SAR and transport helicopter	**Weights:** empty 6863 kg (15,130 lb); maximum take-off 13000 kg (28,660 lb)
Powerplant: three Turboméca Turmo IIIC7 turboshafts each rated at 1201 kW (1,610 shp)	**Dimensions:** main rotor diameter 18.9 m (62 ft); length overall, rotors turning 23.03 m (75 ft 6½ in); height overall 6.76 m (22 ft 2¼ in); main rotor disc area 12.57 m² (135.27 sq ft)
Performance: maximum cruising speed at sea level 248 km/h (154 mph); maximum rate of climb at sea level 300 m (984 ft) per minute; service ceiling 3100 m (10,170 ft); hovering ceiling 1950 m (6,400 ft) in ground effect; range	**Payload:** maximum payload 5000 kg (11,023 lb)

Westland Lynx Multi-role naval helicopter

Germany's Lynx Mk 88 fleet is being upgraded to the Mk 88A 'Super Lynx' standard shown.

SPECIFICATION	
Westland Lynx HAS.Mk 2	maximum take-off 4763 kg (10,500 lb)
Type: twin-engined naval helicopter	**Dimensions:** main rotor diameter 12.8m (42 ft); fuselage length 11.92 m (39 ft 1¼ in); height 3.48 m (11 ft 5 in); main rotor disc area 128.71 m² (1,385.44 sq ft)
Powerplant: two Rolls-Royce Gem 42-1 turboshafts each rated at 846 kW (1,135 shp)	**Armament:** pylons for two Mk 44, Mk 46 or Sting Ray torpedoes, two Mk 11 depth charges or four Sea Skua AShMs, plus one FN HMP 0.5-in (12.7-mm) machine-gun for self protection. An ALQ-167 ECM pod can also be carried
Performance: maximum continuous cruising speed at optimum altitude 232 km/h (144 mph); maximum rate of climb at sea level 661 m (2,170 ft) per minute; combat radius 178 km (111 miles) on a SAR mission with 11 survivors	
Weights: empty 2740 kg (6,040 lb);	

The first Lynx prototype flew on 21 March 1971, and the Royal Navy's **Lynx HAS.Mk 2** was the first production variant to fly, in February 1976. It was equipped for a wide range of shipboard missions including ASW, SAR, ASV, recce, troop transport, fire support, communication and fleet liaison, and VertRep.

The basic Lynx has one of the world's most advanced flight control systems and comprehensive navaids, systems which served it well during over 3,000 hours of combat operations off the Falklands in 1982. During this campaign the Sea Skua AShM was also brought into action for the first time.

The RN received the first of 23 upgraded **Lynx HAS.Mk 3** aircraft in March 1982, and converted its HAS.Mk 2s to this standard. Among the improved systems were Gem 41-1 engines. The **Lynx HAS.Mk 3ICE** designation covers a few downgraded aircraft for utility work on the

Antarctic patrol vessel HMS *Endurance*. Subsequently, seven HAS.Mk 3s were procured with secure speech facility and other upgrades as **HAS.Mk 3S** machines. Eighteen aircraft were upgraded to **Lynx HAS.Mk 3GM (Gulf Mod)** standard with improved cooling, and carried IR jammers and ALQ-167 ECM pods during Desert Storm. The final RN version added a central tactical system and a flotation bag (**Lynx HAS.Mk 3CTS**). The definitive upgraded aircraft is the

Lynx HMA.Mk 8, or export **Super Lynx**.

Super Lynx

Most of the RN's Lynx, plus the survivors of 26 French navy **Lynx HAS.Mk 2(FN)** helicopters, received new high-efficiency composite British Experimental Rotor Programme (BERP) main rotor blades.

The definitive Mk 8 has BERP blades and a reverse-direction tail rotor to improve yaw control at higher take-off weights. Other changes include a nose-mounted Sea Owl passive identification thermal imager turret, MAD, INS and GPS systems, Orange Crop ESM and a Yellow Veil jamming pod.

Many Mk 8 features are incorporated in the export Super Lynx, which has found several buyers for new or upgraded machines.

France's HAS.Mk 2(FN) machines (illustrated) have been upgraded to Mk 4(FN) standard, but will be retired from 2004/05.

EH Industries EH 101/Merlin ASW helicopter

This pre-production Merlin HM.Mk 1 was initially used for trials with the Type 23 frigate HMS Norfolk. It then moved onto sonobuoy drop trials and was fitted with full Merlin avionics.

The **EH 101** has its roots in the Westland WG.34 design that was adopted in late 1978 to meet the UK's Naval Staff Requirement 6646 for a replacement for the Westland Sea King. Work on the WG.34 was cancelled before a prototype had been completed, however, opening the way for revision of the design to meet Italian navy as well as Royal Navy requirements. European Helicopter Industries Ltd was given a formal go-ahead to develop the new aircraft in 1984.

The EH 101 is a three-engined helicopter with a five-bladed main rotor. Much use is made of composites throughout, although the fuselage itself is mainly of aluminium alloy. Systems and equipment vary with role and customer. For the Royal Navy, which calls its initial variant of the EH 101 the **Merlin HM.Mk 1**, IBM is the prime contractor in association with Westland and provides equipment as well as overall management and integration. Armament on the Merlin comprises four Marconi Sting Ray torpedoes, and there are also two sonobuoy dispensers.

Merlin HM.Mk 1

The initial Royal Navy requirement for 50 Merlins to operate from Type 23-class frigates, 'Invincible'-class aircraft carriers, ships of the Royal Fleet Auxiliary and other ships or land bases has been reduced to 44, with delivery starting late in 1998 rather than in 1996, as hoped. These British helicopters are each powered by RTM 322 turboshafts, whereas the Italian helicopters (16 on order, out of a requirement for 36) each have the alternative powerplant of three 1278-kW (1,714-shp) General Electric T700-GE-T6A turboshafts, assembled in Italy. Earlier CT7 commercial variants of the General Electric engine were used to power the prototypes, the first of which was a Westland-built machine that achieved its maiden flight on 9 October 1987. A similar Agusta-built basic model flew in Italy on 26 November 1987. Next to fly in Italy, on 26 April 1989, was a prototype of the Italian ASW version, followed in the UK by a basic ASW version on 15 June and then the definitive Merlin prototype on 24 October of that year.

The second prototype was lost in an accident on 21 January 1993, resulting in a suspension of all flight-testing until 24 June that year. The RTM 322 engines were first flown in the fourth prototype during July 1993, and subsequently fitted to the fifth prototype.

Canada ordered 35 of the naval version as the **CH-148**.

Merlin HM.Mk 1 equipment includes GEC Ferranti Blue Kestrel 360° search radar, GEC Avionics AQS-903 processing and display system, Racal Orange Reaper ESM and Ferranti/Thomson-CSF dipping sonar.

Merlin HM.Mk 1 options include the Exocet, Harpoon, Sea Eagle and Marte Mk 2 AShMs, as well as the Stingray torpedo (as here).

Petrel, to meet its New Shipborne Aircraft requirement for a Sea King replacement. Assembled and fitted out by IMP Group Ltd in Canada, these EH 101s were to have been powered by 1432-kW (1,920-shp) CT7-6A1 turboshaft engines. The deal was hard-fought, subject to constant scrutiny and not unimportant to the chances of the EH 101's long-term success. Deliveries were scheduled to begin early in 1998, although an increasingly bitter argument over the costs versus acquisition of less complex aircraft saw the EH 101 become a campaign issue in the Canadian elections of 1993. The pro-EH 101 Conservative government was ousted in favour of a Liberal administration which, true to its election pledge, cancelled the entire programme. Then, in January 1998, the Canadian government placed a new order for 15 examples of the revised AW320 **Cormorant** version for the SAR role, for delivery between 2000 and 2003.

Further development of the EH 101 could result in variants including an airborne early warning version of the type, which might be required by both the Italian navy and the Royal Navy.

SPECIFICATION

EH Industries Merlin HM.Mk 1

Type: one/two-crew shipborne and land-based anti-submarine and utility helicopter

Powerplant: three Rolls-Royce/Turboméca RTM 322-01 turboshaft engines each rated at 1724 kW (2,312 shp)

Performance: cruising speed 278 km (173 mph) at optimum altitude; hovering ceiling 3810 m (12,500 ft) in ground effect; range 1056 km (656 miles)

Weights: empty 10500 kg (23,149 lb); maximum take-off 14600 kg (32,188 lb)

Dimensions: main rotor diameter 18.59 m (61 ft); length 22.81 m (74 ft 10 in) with the rotors turning; height 6.65 m (21 ft 10 in) with the rotors turning; main rotor disc area 271.51 m² (2,922.60 sq ft)

Armament: up to 960 kg (2,116 lb) of disposable stores carried on the lower sides of the fuselage, and generally comprising four homing torpedoes

Payload: up to 45 troops, or up to 16 litters plus a medical team, or up to 3660 kg (12,000 lb) of freight carried internally or as a slung load

NH Industries NH90 ASW/ASV helicopter

In 1985 five European nations signed a memorandum of understanding covering a 'NATO helicopter for the '90s', or **NH 90**. The UK dropped out of the programme in 1987, leaving France, Germany, Italy and the Netherlands in the project by means of NH Industries, established in 1992 to control the programme.

Two initial versions were planned, the **NH 90 NFH** (**NATO Frigate Helicopter**) for the autonomous ASW

and anti-surface vessel roles with ASW torpedoes or AShMs and 360° search radar under the cabin as key elements in a fully integrated mission system, and the NH 90 TTH.

The NH 90 has a four-bladed main rotor and its powerplant of two turboshaft engines is installed to the rear of the main rotor and gearbox. The landing gear is fully retractable and the flightdeck is laid out for operation by a crew of two.

NH 90 NFH

NH 90 NFH is being developed under Agusta leadership, and its advanced mission suite includes radar, dipping sonar, FLIR, MAD, an ESM system and an ECM system, with weapons carried on two lateral hardpoints. Power is provided either by two RTM 322-01/9s or two General Electric T700-T6Es.

Development of the NH 90 was suspended in May 1994 but then resumed in July of the same year

after a short but rigorous effort to reduce cost escalation, and the first of five flying and one ground-test prototypes was the French-assembled PT 1 that first took to the air on 18 December 1995 with RTM 322 engines. The PT 2 second prototype was also assembled in France and first flew on 19 March 1997 as the initial machine with a fly-by-wire control system (initially analogue but later the definitive digital type). The third, fourth and fifth prototypes were assembled in France, Germany and Italy, respectively.

The overall helicopter totals required were trimmed from the original 726 to 647 in July 1996 and then to 642 in 1998 and the

number of naval helicopters now likely to be acquired includes 27 for the Aéronavale (which may also acquire 27 TTH aircraft to replace its Super Frélons), 38 for Germany, 56 for Italy, and 20 for the Netherlands. NH Industries has also secured export orders from Norway, while Sweden hopes for large export sales. There have been considerable delays in the signature of the production contract for the NH 90, which was originally scheduled for 1997 but finally took place in March 2000, when an initial 244 helicopters were ordered for the armed forces of the four partner nations. The first NH 90s will enter service in the period 2004-2007.

NH90 NFH is scheduled to enter French service in 2004-05, Italian service in 2005, German service in 2007 and operational Dutch service from 2007.

SPECIFICATION	
NH Industries NH 90 NFH **Type:** three/four-crew shipborne ASW/surface ship helicopter **Powerplant:** two RTM 322-01/9 turboshaft engines each rated at 1566 kW (2,100 shp) or two General Electric/Alfa Romeo T700-T6E turboshaft engines each rated at 1521 kW (2,040 shp) **Performance:** (estimated) maximum cruising speed 291 km/h (181 mph); initial climb rate 660 m (2,165 ft) per minute; hovering ceiling 3300 m (10,820 ft) in ground effect, or 2600 m (8,540 ft) out of	ground effect; radius 90 km (56 miles) for a loiter of 3 hours 18 minutes **Weights:** empty 6428 kg (14,171 lb); maximum take-off 10000 kg (22,046 lb) **Dimensions:** main rotor diameter 16.30 m (53 ft 5½ in); length 19.56 m (64 ft 2 in) with the rotors turning; height 5.44 m (17 ft 10 in) with the rotors turning; main rotor disc area 208.67 m² (2,246.18 sq ft) **Armament:** up to 1400 kg (3,086 lb) of disposable stores carried on two lateral hardpoints

Westland Wasp Multi-role naval helicopter

Though its development can be traced back to the **Saro P.531**, first flown in 1958, the **Westland Wasp HAS.Mk 1** emerged in October 1962 as a highly specialised machine for flying missions from small ships, such as frigates and destroyers with limited deck pad area. The missions were ASW and general utility, but the Wasp was not sufficiently powerful to carry a full kit of

ASW sensors as well as weapons, and thus in this role relied on the sensors of its parent vessel and other friendly naval forces. In the ASV role the Wasp was autonomous, and though it had no radar, it could steer the AS12 wire-guided missile under visual conditions over ranges up to 8 km (5 miles). Other duties included SAR, liaison, VIP ferrying, casevac,

ice reconnaissance and photography/ survey. The stalky quadricycle landing gear had wheels that castored so that, while the machine could be rotated on deck, it could not roll in any direction even in a rough sea. Sprag (locking) brakes were fitted to arrest all movement. Provision was made for various hauldown systems such as Beartrap to facilitate alighting on small

pads in severe weather.

Wasp service

Deliveries to the Royal Navy began in 1963, and a few were flown in Operation Corporate in the South Atlantic right at the end of their active lives when most had been replaced in RN service by the Lynx. Wasp HAS.Mk 1s operated from eight ships in that campaign,

The Westland Wasp took a long time to see action. In service with the Royal Navy for nearly 20 years, Wasps were very active during the Falklands War, just in the twilight of their careers.

all assigned to No. 829 Squadron, FAA. Most were used in reconnaissance and utility missions, though several operated in the casevac role. Three, two from HMS *Endurance* and one from the frigate HMS *Plymouth*, engaged the Argentine submarine *Santa Fe* and holed its conning tower with AS12s which passed clean through before exploding. Other Wasps served with the Australian, Brazilian, New Zealand and South African navies. In late 2003 the Wasp remained a front-line type with Indonesia and Malaysia, although the later was retiring its aircraft in favour of Fennecs.

SPECIFICATION	
Westland Wasp HAS.Mk 1 **Type:** light multi-role ship-based helicopter **Powerplant:** one 529-kW (710-shp) Rolls-Royce Nimbus 503 turboshaft **Performance:** maximum speed with weapons 193 km/h (120 mph); cruising speed 177 km/h (110 mph); range 435 km (270 miles)	**Weights:** empty 1566 kg (3,452 lb); maximum take-off 2495 kg (5,500 lb) **Dimensions:** main rotor diameter 9.83 m (32 ft 3 in); length overall 12.29 m (40 ft 4 in); height 3.56 m (11 ft 8 in); main rotor disc area 75.90 m² (816.86 sq ft) **Armament:** two Mk 44 AS torpedoes or two AS12 AShMs

Mil Mi-14 'Haze' Naval helicopter family

Illustrated as it appeared in Soviet service during the 1980s, this Mi-14PL shows the type's standard configuration. Early PLs had undercarriage doors, but these were soon deleted. Note the search radar radome beneath the forward fuselage.

In order to produce a replacement for the large numbers of Mi-4 'Hounds' in Soviet naval service, a version of the Mi-8 'Hip' with a boat-like hull was developed as the **Mi-14 'Haze'**. The prototype of the series, designated **V-14**, flew for the first time in 1973, to be followed by the initial production **Mi-14PL 'Haze-A'** ASW helicopter.

Improvements incorporated during production included more powerful engines and the switching of the tail rotor from the starboard to the port side for increased controllability.

New variants

The latest 'Haze-A' aircraft have revised equipment which includes a repositioned MAD system and are designated **Mi-14PLM**.

From 1983, trials were carried out with the **Mi-14BT 'Haze-B'** minesweeper. The helicopter has various airframe changes for its role and as primary equipment uses a towed mine sled. Although Mi-14BTs have been used on international mine-clearing operations, few were built. Russian forces prefer to use surface minesweepers, while some of the six BTs delivered to East Germany passed to the Luftwaffe as SAR helicopters, before emerging as civilian water bombers.

The final production 'Haze' variant was the **Mi-14PS 'Haze-C'** SAR helicopter. Built primarily for the AV-MF, 'Haze-C' was also exported to Poland.

A few non-standard Mi-14 versions and designations have also appeared. **Mi-14PL 'Strike'** was a variant proposed for attack missions with AS-7 'Kerry' ASMS. **Mi-14PW** is the Polish designation for the

The Mi-14BT lacks a towed MAD 'bird', the aft fuselage instead housing mine countermeasures towing equipment. Only 25-30 examples were built, including a pair for Bulgaria's Naval Air Arm (illustrated).

Mi-14PL, while the **Mi-14PX** is one Polish Mi-14PL stripped of ASW gear and used for SAR training. Other Mi-14s have been converted for civilian use.

SPECIFICATION

Mil Mi-14PL 'Haze-A'
Type: ASW helicopter
Powerplant: two Klimov (Isotov) TV3-117A turboshafts each rated at 1268 kW (1,700 shp) in early helicopters; or two TV3-117MT turboshafts each rated at 1434 kW (1,923 shp) in late helicopters
Performance: maximum level speed 'clean' at optimum altitude 230 km/h (143 mph); maximum cruising speed at optimum altitude 215 km/h (133 mph); initial rate of climb 468 m (1,535 ft) per minute; service ceiling 4000 m (13,123 ft);
range 925 km (575 miles) with standard fuel
Weights: empty 8902 kg (19,625 lb); maximum take-off 14000 kg (30,864 lb)
Dimensions: rotor diameter, each 21.29 m (69 ft 10¼ in); length overall, rotors turning 25.32 m (83 ft 1 in); height 6.93 m (22 ft 9 in); main rotor disc area 356 m² (3,832.08 sq ft)
Armament: one AT-1 or APR-2 torpedo, or one 'Skat' nuclear depth bomb, or eight depth charges

The boat hull of the 'Haze' allows operations in Sea States 3-4, or for planing at up to 60 km/h (37 mph). Note the sponson-mounted flotation bags and tail float of this Russian navy Mi-14PS.

Kamov Ka-25 'Hormone' Naval helicopter family

Designed to meet a 1957 Soviet navy requirement for a new shipborne ASW helicopter, the first member of the Ka-20/25 family was the **Ka-20 'Harp'**, which initially flew during 1960. The production **Ka-25BSh 'Hormone-A'** was of near identical size and appearance, but was fitted with operational equipment and uprated GTD-3F turboshaft engines (from 1973 these were replaced by GTD-3BMs). It entered service in 1967.

Although the lower part of the fuselage is sealed and watertight, the Ka-25 is not intended for amphibious operations, and flotation bags are often fitted to the undercarriage for use in the event of an emergency landing on the water. The cabin is adequate for the job, but is not tall enough to allow the crew to stand upright. Progressive additions of new equipment have made the interior more cluttered.

Primary sensors for the ASW mission are the

I/J-band radar (ASCC/NATO 'Big Bulge'), OKA-2 dipping sonar, a downward-looking 'Tie Rod' electro-optical sensor in the tailboom and a MAD sensor, either in a recess in the rear part of the cabin or in a fairing sometimes fitted below the central of the three tailfins. A box-like sonobuoy launcher can also be scabbed on to the starboard side of the rear fuselage. Dye-markers or smoke floats can also be carried externally. Comprehensive avionics,

SPECIFICATION

Kamov Ka-25BSh 'Hormone-A'
Type: ASW helicopter
Powerplant: two OMKB 'Mars' (Glushenkov) GTD-3F turboshafts each rated at 671 kW (898 shp) in early helicopters, or two GTD-3BM turboshafts each rated at 738 kW (900 shp) in late helicopters
Performance: maximum level speed 'clean' at optimum altitude 209 km/h (130 mph); normal cruising speed at optimum altitude 193 km/h (120 mph); service ceiling 3350 m (10,990 ft);
range 400 km (249 miles) with standard fuel
Weights: empty 4765 kg (10,505 lb); maximum take-off 7500 kg (16,534 lb)
Dimensions: rotor diameter, each 15.74 m (52 ft 7¾ in); fuselage length 9.75 m (32 ft); overall 5.37 m (17 ft 7½ in); main rotor disc area 389.15 m² (4,188.93 sq ft)
Armament: provision for torpedoes, conventional or nuclear depth charges and other stores up to a maximum of 1900 kg (4,190 lb)

defensive and navigation systems are also fitted as standard.

Armament is not normally carried, although the helicopter can be fitted with a long 'coffin-like' weapons bay which runs along the belly from the radome back to the tailboom, and small bombs or depth charges can be carried on tiny pylons just aft of the nosewheels. The under-fuselage bay can carry a variety of weapons, including nuclear depth charges.

When wire-guided torpedoes are carried, a wire reel is mounted on the port side of the forward fuselage.

It has been estimated that some 260 of the 450 or so Ka-25s produced were 'Hormone-As', but only a handful remains in Russian and Ukrainian service, mostly fulfiling secondary roles. Small numbers of Ka-25BShs were exported to India, Syria, Vietnam and former Yugoslavia, and most of these aircraft remained in use in mid-2003.

'Hormone' variants

The second Ka-25 variant identified in the West was given the NATO reporting name **'Hormone-B'**, and is designated **Ka-25K**. This variant is externally identifiable by its bulbous (instead of flat-bottomed) undernose radome and small datalink radome under the rear fuselage. Ka-25K was used for acquiring targets and providing mid-course missile guidance, for ship- and submarine-launched missiles.

On the 'Hormone-B' only, the four undercarriage units are retractable and can be lifted out of the scanning pattern of the radar.

The final version of the military Ka-25 is the **Ka-25PS 'Hormone-C'**. A dedicated SAR and transport helicopter, the Ka-25PS can carry a practical load of freight or up to 12 passengers, making it a useful ship-to-ship or ship-to-shore transport and vertrep platform. A quadruple Yagi antenna ('Home Guard') fitted to many aircraft is reportedly used for homing on to the personal locator beacons carried by aircrew. Most Ka-25PSs also have searchlights, and a 300-kg (660-lb) capacity rescue winch. Ka-25PS has largely been replaced by Ka-27.

Kamov Ka-27, Ka-29, and Ka-31 'Helix'
Naval helicopter family

Ka-29TB is a formidable assault and attack helicopter. It mounts a sizeable weapons load on braced fuselage outriggers.

Work on the **Ka-27** family began in 1969. The Ka-27 retains Kamov's well-proven contra-rotating co-axial rotor configuration, and has dimensions similar to those of the Ka-25.

With more than double the power of the Ka-25, the Ka-27 is a considerably heavier helicopter with a larger fuselage, but nevertheless offers increased performance with much-improved avionics and more modern flight-control system.

The first production variant was the **Ka-27PL 'Helix-A'** basic ASW version, which entered service in 1982. The Ka-27PL's fuselage is sealed over its lower portions for buoyancy, while extra flotation equipment can be fitted in boxes on the lower part of the centre fuselage. Ka-27 is extremely stable and easy to fly, and automatic height hold, automatic transition to and from the hover and autohover are possible in all weather conditions. Ka-27PL has all the usual ASW and ESM equipment, including dipping sonar and sonobuoys as well as Osminog (octopus) search radar.

SAR and planeguard

The main SAR and planeguard Ka-27 variant is the radar-equipped **Ka-27PS 'Helix-D'**. This usually carries external fuel tanks and flotation gear, and has a hydraulically-operated, 300-kg (661-lb) capacity rescue winch.

Ka-28 'Helix-A' is the export version of the Ka-27PL ordered by China, India, Vietnam and Yugoslavia and with a revised avionics suite.

Assault and transport

The **Ka-29TB (Transportno Boyevoya)** is a dedicated assault transport derivative of the Ka-27/32 family, intended especially for the support of Russian navy amphibious operations and featuring a substantially changed airframe. The first example was seen by Western eyes on the assault ship *Ivan Rogov* in 1987, the type having entered service in 1985, and the **Ka-29TB** was initially assumed to be the Ka-27B, resulting in the allocation of the NATO reporting designation **'Helix-B'**. Many of the new variants went unnoticed, and the Ka-29TB was initially thought to be a minimum-change version of the basic Ka-27PL without radar. In fact the Ka-29TB features an entirely new, much widened forward fuselage, with a flight deck seating three members of the crew side-by-side, one of these crew members acting as a gunner to aim the various types of air-to-surface unguided rocket carried on the four hardpoints of the helicopter's pair of strut-braced lateral pylons, and the trainable machine-gun hidden behind an articulated door on the starboard side of the nose. In addition, the two-piece curved windscreen of the Ka-27 has given way to a five-piece unit.

An air data boom projects from the port side of the nose, which also carries an EO sensor to starboard and a missile guidance/illuminating and TFR pod to port.

The basic Ka-29TB served as the basis for the **Ka-31**, which was originally known as the **Ka-29RLD (Radiolokatsyonnogo Dozora**, or radar picket helicopter). This AEW type first flew in 1988, and was first seen during carrier trials aboard *Kuznetsov*. All four landing gear units are retractable, making space for the movement of the E-801E Oko (eye) surveillance radar's antenna, which is a large rectangular planar array that rests flat under the fuselage when inactive.

SPECIFICATION

Kamov Ka-27PL 'Helix-A'
Type: three-crew shipborne anti-submarine and utility helicopter
Powerplant: two Klimov (Isotov) TV3-117V turboshaft engines each rated at 1633 kW (2,190 shp)
Performance: maximum speed 250 km/h (155 mph) at optimum altitude; cruising speed 230 km/h (143 mph) at optimum altitude; service ceiling 5000 m (16,404 ft); hovering ceiling 3500 m (11,483 ft) out of ground effect; range 800 km (497 miles) with auxiliary fuel
Weights: empty 6100 kg

(13,448 lb); maximum take-off 12600 kg (27,778 lb)
Dimensions: rotor diameter, each 15.9 m (52 ft 2 in); length, excluding rotors 11.27 m (37 ft 11¾ in); height to top of rotor head 5.45 m (17 ft 10½ in); rotor disc area, each 198.5 m² (2,136.6 sq ft)
Armament: up to 200 kg (441 lb) of disposable stores, generally comprising four APR-2E homing torpedoes or four groups of S3V guided anti-submarine bombs
Payload: up to 5000 kg (11,023 lb) of freight

Boeing Vertol H-46 Sea Knight Assault and transport helo

Shortly after the formation of the Vertol Aircraft Corporation in March 1956, the company initiated a design study for a twin-turbine commercial transport helicopter and in the event, the US armed forces showed an interest in the type's procurement.

Early Army interest

Allocated the designation **Vertol Model 107**, a prototype was flown for the first time on 22 April 1958. The first of the armed forces wishing to evaluate the new helicopter was the US Army which, in July 1958, ordered 10 slightly modified aircraft under the designation **YHC-1A**. The first of these

flew for the first time on 27 August 1959. By that time the US Army had come to favour a larger and more powerful helicopter, which Vertol had developed from the Model 107, and reduced its order to only three YCH-1A (later **YCH-46C**) machines. The company subsequently equipped the third of these with 783-kW (1,050-shp) T58-GE-6 turboshafts and rotors of increased diameter, and, with a commercial interior, this aircraft first flew as the **Model 107-II** on 25 October 1960. By that time Vertol had become a division of the Boeing company.

When the USMC showed an interest in this helicopter,

one was modified as the **Model 107M** with two T58-GE-8s and this was successful in winning a contract for the **HRB-1** (changed to **CH-46A** in 1962) production model, which was named **Sea Knight**. Since then, Sea Knights have been used extensively by the USMC and the USN. The former uses them for troop transport, the latter mainly in the vertical replenishment role.

Production variants

The first of 160 CH-46As entered full USMC service early in 1965. Since then, a number of versions has been built, these including 266 examples of the **CH-46D** for the USMC to a

standard generally similar to that of the CH-46A except for its 1044-kW (1,400-shp) T58-GE-10 engines; 174 examples of the **CH-46F** for the USMC to a standard generally similar to that of the CH-46D but with additional avionics; 14 examples of the **UH-46A**, similar to the CH-46A, for the USN; and 10 examples of the **UH-46D** for the USN to a standard virtually identical to that of the CH-46D. The USMC updated 273 of its older Sea Knights to the **CH-46E** standard with 1394-kW (1,870-shp) T58-GE-16 turboshafts and other improvements including structural strengthening and glassfibre rotor blades.

Foreign service

Six utility helicopters, almost identical to the CH-46A, were delivered to the RCAF in 1963 under the designation **CH-113 Labrador**, and 12 similar aircraft were built

for the Canadian Army during 1964-65, these being designated **CH-113A Voyageur**. In the Canadian Armed Forces' SARCUP (Search And Rescue Capability Upgrade Project), Boeing of Canada was later contracted to modify six CH-113s and five CH-13As to an improved SAR standard by mid-1984. In 1962-63 Boeing Vertol supplied Model 107-II helicopters to the Swedish air force for SAR, and to the Swedish navy for ASW and minesweeping duties; both of these versions received the local designation **Hkp 4A**.

In 1965 Kawasaki in Japan acquired the worldwide sales rights for the Model 107-II, and built the type up to about 1990 in several versions with the basic designation **Kawasaki-Vertol KV 107-II**. The type is now being retired from Japanese service.

Photographed in June 2003, this US Navy CH-46D is seen replenishing USS Sacramento from USS Carl Vinson in the Philippine Sea. The CH-46 is now long overdue for replacement.

SPECIFICATION	
Boeing Vertol CH-46A Sea Knight **Type:** two/three-crew twin-rotor transport helicopter **Powerplant:** two General Electric T58-GE-8B turboshaft engines each rated at 932 kW (1,250 shp) **Performance:** maximum speed 249 km/h (155 mph) at sea level; cruising speed 243 km/h (151 mph) at 1525 m (5,000 ft); initial climb rate 439 m (1,440 ft) per minute; service ceiling 4265 m (14,000 ft); hovering ceiling 2765 m (9,070 ft) in ground effect and 1707 m (5,600 ft) out of ground effect;	range 426 km (265 miles) with maximum internal payload **Weights:** empty 5627 kg (12,406 lb); maximum take-off 9707 kg (21,400 lb) **Dimensions:** rotor diameter, each 15.24 m (50 ft); length overall, rotors turning 25.4 m (83 ft 4 in); height 5.09 m (16 ft 8½ in); rotor disc area, total 364.82 m² (3,926.99 sq ft) **Payload:** up to 25 troops, or 1814 kg (4,000 lb) of freight carried internally or 2871 kg (6,330 lb) of freight carried externally

Bell Boeing V-22 Osprey Tiltrotor assault transport

In the early 1980s Bell Helicopter Textron and Boeing Vertol began collaboration to develop a larger derivative of

the XV-15 tilt-rotor demonstrator for the Joint Services Advanced Vertical Lift Aircraft programme. Combining the

vertical lift capabilities of a helicopter with the fast-cruise forward flight efficiencies of a fixed-wing turboprop, the

resulting **V-22 Osprey** was awarded full-scale development in 1985. The engines, mounted in wingtip nacelles,

can be swivelled through 97.5° and drive three-bladed proprotors through interconnected drive shafts. For

SPECIFICATION	
Bell Boeing MV-22A Osprey **Type:** three/four-crew land-based and shipborne multi-mission tilt-rotor transport **Powerplant:** two Allison T406-AD-400 turboshaft engines each rated at 4586 kW (6,150 shp) **Performance:** (estimated) maximum cruising speed 185 km/h (115 mph) at sea level in helicopter mode and 582 km/h (361 mph) at optimum altitude in aircraft mode; initial climb rate 707 m (2,320 ft) per minute; service ceiling 7925 m (26,000 ft); hovering ceiling 4330 m (14,200 ft) out-of-ground effect; range 935 km (592 miles) in amphibious assault role **Weights:** (estimated) empty 15032 kg (33,140 lb); maximum take-off 21546 kg (47,500 lb) for	VTO and 27443 kg (60,500 lb) for STO **Dimensions:** width overall 25.55 m (83 ft 10 in); wing span 14.02 m (46 ft) excluding nacelles; proprotor diameter, each 11.58 m (38 ft); length 17.47 m (57 ft 4 in) excluding probe; height 6.63 m (21 ft 9 in) with nacelles vertical; wing area 35.49 m² (382 sq ft); proprotor disc area, total 210.72 m² (2,268.23 sq ft) **Armament:** probably one or two 0.5-in (12.7-mm) trainable multi-barrel rotary machine-guns **Payload:** up to 24 troops, or 12 litters plus medical attendants or 9072 kg (20,000 lb) of freight carried internally, or 6804 kg (15,000 lb) of freight carried externally

On 29 May 2002, Osprey flight testing was resumed after being halted in December 2000 owing to safety concerns. A USMC test aircraft is illustrated.

Right: Aircraft number 10, one of the Engineering and Manufacturing Development (EMD) MV-22 Ospreys, performs shipboard tests onboard the amphibious assault ship USS Saipan during early 1999.

shipboard stowage, the main-planes pivot centrally to rotate along the fuselage top, the proprotor blades folding in parallel. Initial requirements called for 913 Ospreys, comprising 522 **MV-22A** assault aircraft for the USMC and US Army; 80 USAF CV-22As; and 50 USN **HV-22A** aircraft for combat SAR, special ops and fleet logistic support. The USN also foresaw a need for **SV-22A** ASW machines. Flight tests started on 19 March 1989, but a series of accidents, financial and

political reviews, and allegations of malpractice have resulted in a much revised programme.

Osprey status

During mid 2003, the Osprey programme was due to realise 360 **MV-22B** machines for the USMC and 48 **HV-22B** tiltrotors for the USN. The first production Ospreys were delivered in 1999 and the type should become operational with the USMC in 2004.

Kaman SH-2 Seasprite Multi-role naval helicopter

ASW was just one of the tasks assigned to US Navy Seasprites, like this SH-2F.

The **H-2 Seasprite** was conceived in response to a 1956 USN requirement for a high-speed, all-weather, long-range SAR, liaison and utility helicopter. The first of four **YHU2K-1** (from 1962 **YUH-2A**) service test prototypes made its maiden flight on 2 July 1959, and the type entered production as the **HU2K-1 (UH-2A)**. Later variants were progressively improved and updated, gaining a second engine (for a greater safety margin for ship-based operations), dual mainwheels and a four-bladed tail rotor. Manufacture stopped after the delivery of the last **UH-2B**. The helicopter was first used in the ASW role in October 1970, when the USN selected the **SH-2D** as an interim **LAMPS I (Light Airborne Multi-Purpose System Mk I)** platform.

LAMPS I

The SH-2D introduced an undernose Litton LN-66 search radar radome, an ASQ-81 MAD on the starboard fuselage pylon and a removable sonobuoy rack in the port side of the fuselage. Twenty were produced

as conversions from **HH-2D** armed-SAR standard, entering service in 1972.

Deliveries of the definitive **SH-2F**, which also bore the LAMPS I designation, began in May 1973. The primary role of the SH-2F was the generation of a major extension of the protected area provided by the outer defensive screen of a carrier battle group. It introduced T58-GE-8F engines, an improved main rotor, and strengthened landing gear including a tailwheel relocated farther forward. The SH-2F also featured an improved Marconi

LN-66HP surface search radar, ASQ-81(V)2 towed MAD bird and a tactical navigation and communications system. Some 88 machines were converted from earlier variants, and 16 SH-2Ds were also modified.

New production

The Seasprite was reinstated in production during 1981, when the USN placed an order for the first of an eventual 60 new-build SH-2Fs. From 1987 some 16 SH-2Fs received a package of modifications to allow them to operate in the

Persian Gulf. During the 1991 Gulf War, the SH-2F tested the ML-30 Magic Lantern laser sub-surface mine detector.

Continued development of the Seasprite resulted in the appearance of the **SH-2G Super Seasprite**. The prototype **YSH-2G** first flew on 2 April 1985, as an SH-2F conversion with T700 engines. The new type entered service in 1991, but the end of the Cold War reduced the USN's requirement to 23 machines and the Seasprite has left US Navy service. Kaman has

sold rebuilt surplus SH-2Fs to Egypt, which received **SH-2G(E)** helicopters from October 1997. In June 1997 the Royal Australian Navy and Royal New Zealand Navy ordered a total of 15 SH-2Gs rebuilt to an improved standard from SH-2F airframes. The rebuilt **SH-2G(NZ)** helicopters for New Zealand entered service in 2001, while the **SH-2G(A)** machines for Australia were delayed by avionics problems and became operational in 2004.

SPECIFICATION

Kaman SH-2G Super Seasprite
Type: three-crew shipborne ASW, missile defence, SAR and utility helicopter
Powerplant: two General Electric T700-GE-401/401C turboshaft engines each rated at 1285 kW (1,723 shp)
Performance: maximum speed 256 km/h (159 mph) at sea level; cruising speed 222 km/h (138 mph) at optimum altitude; initial climb rate 762 m (2,500 ft) per minute; service ceiling 7285 m (23,900 ft); hovering ceiling 6340 m (20,800 ft) in ground effect and 5485 m (18,000 ft) out of ground effect; radius 65 km (40 miles) for a patrol of 2 hours 10 minutes with one torpedo

Weights: empty 3483 kg (7,680 lb); maximum take-off 6123 kg (13,500 lb)
Dimensions: main rotor diameter 13.51 m (44 ft 4 in); length overall 16.08 m (52 ft 9 in) with rotors turning; height 4.58 m (15 ft ½ in) with rotors turning; main rotor disc area 143.41 m² (1,543.66 sq ft)
Armament: provision for two 0.3-in (7.62-mm) M60 trainable lateral-firing machine-guns on optional pintle mounts in the cabin doors, plus up to 726 kg (1,600 lb) of disposable stores
Payload: (with sonobuoy system removed) provision for up to four passengers, or two litters, or 1814 kg (4,000 lb) of freight carried as a slung load

Australia and New Zealand (illustrated) bought their Seasprites to equip their new 'Anzac'-class multi-role frigates. Australia may purchase further SH-2G(A)s.

Sikorsky S-61/H-3 Sea King ASW and multi-role helicopter

One of the most important helicopter families yet developed, and once a mainstay of the Western world's shipborne anti-submarine forces, the **Sikorsky SH-3 Sea King** series began life as the **HSS-2** anti-submarine helicopter for the US Navy. The prototype of this helicopter first flew on 11 March 1959, and the aircraft, which has the company designation **Sikorsky S-61**, was the first which could carry all the sensors and weapons needed for ASW missions without external help (though the US Navy policy developed to regard the aircraft as an extension of the ASW surface vessel from which it operates, so that helicopter-carried sensors detect the hostile submarine before the warship is called in for the kill).

Sea King features

New features included an amphibious boat hull with retractable tailwheel landing gear, twin turboshaft engines (for power, lightness, reliability and single-engine flight capability) above the cabin and an unobstructed tactical compartment for two sonar operators whose sensors included a dipping sonobuoy lowered through a keel hatch. Above the extensive avionic systems was an attitude-hold autopilot and a

The US Navy produced its 150-strong SH-3H (illustrated) fleet by converting earlier SH-3A, SH-3D and SH-3G aircraft.

sonar coupler which maintained exact height and station in conjunction with a radar altimeter and Doppler radar. Over 1,100 **H-3** type helicopters were built, the ASW models being SH-3s in four basic models.

ASW variants

The **SH-3A** was the original model with 933-kW (1,260-shp) T58-GE-8B turboshafts, the **SH-3D** is the upgraded version; the **SH-3G** is the utility version; and the **SH-3H** is the multi-role model fitted with dipping sonar and MAD gear for ASW and search radar for the detection of incoming anti-ship missiles. Single examples of the SH-3D and SH-3G, plus 50 SH-3Hs remained in US Navy service in mid-2003.

Licence-production

Agusta has built the Sea King under licence in Italy as the **AS-61/ASH-3**, some variants being equipped with Marte anti-ship missiles. Mitsubishi built 55 Sea Kings in three versions, all retaining the original HSS-2 designation, for the JMSDF. By far the most important

overseas manufacturer, however, has been Westland in the UK. Westland-built aircraft are powered by Rolls-Royce H.1400 Gnome-series engines and have much UK-sourced equipment. The initial **Sea King HAS.Mk 1** made its first flight on 7 May 1969 and was little more than a re-engined SH-3D. Subsequent ASW variants for the Royal Navy have included the **HAS.Mk 2**, **HAS.Mk 5** and **HAS.Mk 6**. To fill the massive gap that became apparent in the RN's airborne AEW coverage during the Falklands War, the **Sea King AEW.Mk 2A** was produced by conversion from HAS.Mk 2 standard. Later,

Italy will replace its ASH-3D (illustrated) and ASH-3H helicopters with the EH 101. The Sea Kings are flown from the Italian navy's larger vessels and the aircraft-carrier Garibaldi.

HAS.Mk 5 aircraft were converted to **AEW.Mk 5** and **AEW.Mk 7** standard. **Sea King HAR.Mk 3** and **Mk 3A** SAR helicopters have been built for the RAF and many Westland Sea Kings, including the **Sea King International**, have been built for export.

Sikorsky exported its Sea

Kings to many countries, including Canada, where the aircraft is designated **CH-124**. Specialised US SH-3 variants included the **RH-3** minesweeper, while the **VH-3** executive transport remains in service.

US Navy squadron HC-2 remained a Sea King operator in 2003. Its UH-3H utility helicopters were produced by conversion from SH-3H standard.

SPECIFICATION

Sikorsky SH-3D Sea King
Type: ASW helicopter
Powerplant: two 1044-kW (1,400-shp) General Electric T58-10 turboshafts
Performance: maximum speed 267 km/h (166 mph); range with maximum fuel and 10 per cent reserves 1005 km (625 miles)
Weights: empty 5382 kg (11,865 lb); maximum take-off

9752 kg (21,500 lb)
Dimensions: main rotor diameter 18.9 m (62 ft); fuselage length 16.69 m (54 ft 9 in); height 5.13 m (16 ft 10 in); main rotor disc area 280.5 m² (3,019.10 sq ft)
Armament: external hardpoints for a total of 381 kg (840 lb) of weapons, normally comprising two Mk 46 torpedoes

Sikorsky S-70/H-60 Seahawk ASW and multi-role helicopter

A derivative of the US Army's UH-60 Black Hawk, the **Sikorsky SH-60B Seahawk** (originally produced under the company designation **S-70L**, later **S-70B**) won the US Navy's LAMPS (Light Airborne Multi-Purpose System) III competition in September 1977. A complex and extremely expensive machine, the SH-60B was

designed for two main missions: ASW and ASST (anti-ship surveillance and targeting). The ASST mission involved the aerial detection

Mitsubishi has built SH-60Js (illustrated) and UH-60Js for the JMSDF. In 2003 SH-60Js were still being funded and a KAI upgrade programme is underway.

of incoming sea-skimming AShMs, and the provision of radar-derived data for similar weapons launched from US warships. Secondary missions included SAR, medevac and vertrep (vertical replenishment). The basic airframe differs from that of the UH-60 in being marinised, with a sealed tailboom, having its tailwheel moved and inflatable bags for emergency buoyancy fitted, and having an electrically-folding main rotor and pneumatically-folding tail (including upward-hinged tailplanes). Other modifications are greater fuel capacity and the removal of cockpit armour for the pilot and co-pilot. The type is also fitted with haul-down equipment to facilitate recovery

SPECIFICATION

Sikorsky SH-60B Seahawk
Type: multi-role shipboard helicopter
Powerplant: (aircraft delivered from 1988) two 1417-kW (1,900-shp) General Electric T700-GE-401C turboshafts
Performance: dash speed at 1525 m (5,000 ft) 234 km/h (145 mph); operational radius 92.5 km (57.5 miles) for a 3-hour loiter

Weights: (for the ASW mission) empty 6191 kg (13,648 lb); mission take-off 9182 kg (20,244 lb)
Dimensions: main rotor diameter 16.36 m (53 ft 8 in); fuselage length 15.26 m (50 ft ¾ in); height overall, rotors turning 5.18 m (17 ft); main rotor disc area 210.05 m² (2,262.03 sq ft)
Armament: normally two Mk 46 torpedoes, or Penguin AShMs

onto small platforms on pitching and rolling ships in heavy seas. Under the nose is the large APS-124 radar and on the left side of the fuselage is a large vertical panel with tubes for launching sonobuoys.

On the right of the rear

fuselage is a pylon for a towed MAD 'bird'. The first prototype flew on 12 December 1979 and a total of 181 was built for the USN.

Subsequent variants for US Navy service have included the **SH-60F Ocean Hawk**, equipped with dipping sonar for inner-zone ASW cover around aircraft-carriers; the **HH-60H Rescue Hawk** for ship-borne SAR, plane guard and special forces missions and the **MH-60R** multi-mission helicopter. The latter were to be produced by conversion from SH-60B/F/HH-60H helicopters, but 243 new-build helicopters will now be bought for delivery from 2005. They will join 237

The many roles now tackled by the SH-60 family are shown here by an HH-60H taking off for a plane guard sortie.

Easily identified by the two windows in its portside cabin door, this HH-60H is shown performing a vertrep mission.

MH-60S utility aircraft which combine much of the UH-60's airframe with SH-60 systems and began replacing Boeing-Vertol CH-46 Sea Knights in February 2002. Other, non-navy, versions

include the US Coast Guard's **HH-60J Jayhawk**, while naval variants have been widely exported and built under licence in Australia and Japan.

Sikorsky S-80/MH-53 Sea Dragon Mine-sweeping helicopter

An MH-53E from HM-14 'Vanguards' prepares for take-off. The aircraft was deployed to Bahrain in support of Operation Enduring Freedom.

Though the original Sikorsky S-65 production models, have only two engines, the **S-80**/H-53E has three engines each of 3266 kW (4,380 shp) and is the most powerful helicopter ever built outside Russia. Of the early versions, the CH-53A and more powerful CH-53D were transports for the US Marines Corps. All CH-53As were delivered with provisions for towed mine-sweeping equipment, but the US Navy decided that a dedicated mine-countermeasures version would need more power and additional modifications. Accordingly, 15 CH-53As were transferred to the US Navy as **RH-53A** mine-sweeping machines with 2927-kW (3,925-shp) T64-GE-413 turboshafts, and equipment for towing the EDO Mk 105 hydrofoil anti-mine sled.

Still more power

The RH-53As were used to explore the possibilities of these new mine-sweeping techniques, which had previ-

ously been tried only with machines of inadequate power, pending the arrival of 30 **RH-53D Sea Dragon** purpose-built machines. Equipped with drop tanks and, later, inflight-refuelling probes, the RH-53Ds were soon re-engined with 3266-kW (4,380-shp) T64-GE-415 turboshafts. The aircraft were delivered to the US Navy from the summer of 1973 and about 19 remained in US Navy service in early 2003, but were being replaced by MH-53Es. Six RH-53Ds were delivered to the Imperial Iranian Navy.

The CH-53E was developed to meet a 1973 demand for an upgraded heavy-lift transport for the US Navy and US Marine Corps. From it was developed the **MH-53E Sea Dragon**. This definitive MCM (mine countermeasures) version has enormously enlarged side sponsons for an extra 3785 litres (833 Imp gal) of fuel, for extended sweeping missions with the engines at sustained high power. The first prototype MH-53E made its initial flight on 23 December 1981 and

around 44 remained in service in 2003. The **MH-53J** has

been sold to the JMSDF.

SPECIFICATION

Sikorsky MH-53E Sea Dragon
Type: shipboard minesweeping helicopter
Powerplant: three 3266-kW (4,380-shp) General Electric T64-GE-416 turboshafts
Performance: maximum speed 315 km/h (196 mph); cruising speed at sea level 278 km/h (173 mph); maximum self-ferry range 2074 km (1,289 miles)
Weights: empty 16482 kg (36,336 lb); maximum take-off with

internal payload 31640 kg (69,750 lb); maximum take-off with external payload 33340 kg (73,500 lb)
Dimensions: main rotor diameter 24.08 m (79 ft); length overall, rotors turning 30.19 m (99 ft ½ in); height to top of main rotor head 5.32 m (17 ft 5½ in); main rotor disc area 455.38 m² (4,901.7 sq ft)
Armament: provision for window-mounted 0.5-in (12.7-mm) or 0.3-in (7.62-mm) guns

Left: The 'Wasp' class of LHD, represented by USS Iwo Jima, is the US Navy's most versatile amphibious assault ship, capable of carrying a typical complement of 30 helicopters and six to eight AV-8B Harriers.

Below: The Cobra provides the USMC with close/offensive air support, armed escort, forward air control and reconnaissance. A normal load of six AH-1Ws are carried aboard each LHA or LHD vessel.

US amphibious assault
Marine Corps in action

The end of the Cold War, and the amphibious operations in the Gulf bought the amphibious operation back into sharp focus. Amphibious forces can rapidly deploy to a war-torn state, and are ideally suited to the complex nature of modern warfare.

The first major amphibious operation by the US Marines since the Korean War occurred in 1991 during Operation Desert Storm. A huge armada of ships and a massive force of amphibious troops was assembled off the coast of Kuwait. Forty-three amphibious ships, two command ships and 18,000 US Marines prepared to land on the beaches of Kuwait to assist the eviction of the Iraqis.

The Marines' show of force was designed as a grand deception, intended to convince Iraq that the Coalition would attack from the sea. However, the beaches were well defended. Any operation would have been costly despite the superior technology and tactics at the Marine's disposal.

The threat posed by the Marines caused Saddam

Hussein to divert several divisions of troops away from the Saudi border to defend Kuwait's coastline, reducing the strength of the troops who were supposed to stop the Coalition land attack.

Amphibious Squadrons

The core of American amphibious capability is the Amphibious Squadron, or PHIBRON. Eight are currently operational with the US Navy. A PHIBRON normally consists of a large Amphibious Assault Ship (LHD or LHA), an Amphibious Transport Dock (LPD) and a Dock Landing Ship (LSD). It includes a Fleet Surgical Team, a Fleet Information Warfare Center detachment, a Naval Beach Group detachment, a Search and Rescue detachment, an Explosive Ordinance Disposal detachment, a Tactical Air

Replacing the M60A1 in USMC service, the M1A2 Abrams, seen offloading from an LCAC, is specially prepared for the amphibious assault role, with deep water fording equipment and additional tie-down points for stowage onboard ship or air-cushion vehicle.

Control Squadron (TACRON), and a Naval Special Warfare Task Unit.

In the past, getting Marines ashore required the use of specialist landing craft and amphibious assault craft. These are slow and relatively short-ranged, and require the launching ships to stand in relatively close to the shore – within the range of defences. The first means of giving the

amphibious force a stand-off capability was the helicopter, but while this can deliver troops inland rapidly, it cannot carry heavy equipment.

AFVs and artillery are now landed by fast air-cushioned landing craft, or LCACS. All modern US Navy amphibious ships are designed to operate with such craft, enabling an amphibious force to launch attacks from over the horizon, while still landing troops faster than would have been possible from much shorter ranges with old-style landing craft. The new generation of amphibious assault vehicle (AAV) will also be much faster on water, to match the performance of the LCACs.

Marines units

The main purpose of the PHIBRON is to provide the platform from which the Marines conduct operations. The unit in the Marines specifically groomed for the task of fighting amphibious battles is the Marine Expeditionary Unit or MEU.

A MEU is normally built around a reinforced battalion, a composite aircraft squadron, and a MEU Service Support group totalling about 2,000 personnel in all. Commanded by a colonel, the MEU is employed to fulfil routine forward deployments with fleets in the Mediterranean, the Western Pacific, and periodically, the Atlantic and Indian Oceans.

The MEU's very existence is vital because with the decline of American bases abroad, it is possible that the only US forces available to respond to worldwide crisis quickly will be the Marines. The MEU is an expeditionary intervention force with the ability to rapidly organise for combat operations in virtually any environment. There are always three MEUs forward deployed.

Each MEU is embarked on Navy ships as part of the Amphibious Ready Group (ARG) which is, in turn, a member of a carrier task force. Travelling with the Navy, each MEU is capable of reaching 75 per cent of the littoral waters of the world within five days. MEUs are constantly forward-deployed

ALLIED FORCE:
MEU IN ACTION

An AV-8B from HMM-266 lands on board USS *Nassau* following a strike mission over Kosovo. Embarked aboard the 'Tarawa'-class LHA USS *Nassau*, HMM-266 launched the amphibious battle group's first strikes in support of NATO Operation Allied Force. The unit was part of the 26th MEU(SOC), which comprised 2,400 troops deployed aboard *Nassau* on station in the Adriatic, and supported by one 'Austin'-class LPD (USS *Nashville*) and the 'Anchorage'-class LSD USS *Pensacola*. The MEU later supported the NATO relief operation in Albania.

to designated 'hot' regions and are able to execute contingency missions within those regions with just six hours notice. Each MEU deploys for six months and can operate ashore for 15 days without replenishment.

The Ground Combat Element of the MEU is based on an infantry battalion, which becomes a Battalion Landing Team with the addition of tanks, artillery, engineers, amphibious vehicles, light armoured vehicles, and other combat support assets. Typically it includes 2200 troops, four MBTs, 13 AAVs and six howitzers.

Aviation component

The Aviation Combat Element is a composite squadron of both fixed- and rotary-wing aircraft with 22 helicopters, including CH-46 Sea Knights, CH-53s, AH-1 gunships, and up to eight AV-8B Harrier IIs.

The Marine Expeditionary Units are the smallest and most visible examples of the Marine-Air Ground Task Force (MAGTF) Concept.

The largest is the Marine Expeditionary Forces (MEFs) Commanded by a 3-Star General Officer, a MEF consists of one or more full Marine Aircraft Wings, one or more Force Service Support

LAVs are among the vehicles transportable from ship to shore aboard an LCAC such as this one carried aboard the LHD USS Bonhomme Richard, seen on deployment in support of Operation Enduring Freedom.

Groups and one or more complete Infantry Divisions. An MEF can account for anything between 20,000 to 90,000 Marines, averaging around 40,000 men and women.

In between are the Marine Expeditionary Brigades (MEBs), which are organised to respond to a full range of crises, from forcible entry to humanitarian assistance. The USMC has three numbered MEBs. A MEB deploys on 15 amphibious ships of which five are large deck ships such as LHA or LHD ships and has the capacity to sustain operations for 30 days. Rapid deployment continues to be important. In 1999, during Allied Force, the USMC deployed from the Aegean Sea to Kosovo in under four days.

A US Navy Landing Craft Utility (LCU) approaches the well deck of the USS Nassau. The floodable docking well of the 'Tarawa'-class vessel is capable of accommodating four LCU 1610 type landing craft, which in turn can carry two M1A1 MBTs or 350 troops.

Amphibious warfare

21st century assault

In the immediate post-war years, amphibious forces were somewhat neglected by western navies. Most were equipped with vessels little different from those that were used in Normandy and the Pacific.

The end of the Cold War has brought about a major revolution in military affairs. Whereas before the superpowers had concentrated on developing weapons able to play their parts in an all-out nuclear exchange, the end of the 20th century has seen the rise in importance of worldwide power projection and intervention, and vessels dedicated to amphibious operations have become increasingly important.

Amphibious warfare is littoral in nature, in that it takes place in coastal waters, across the shore and immediately inland. Littoral areas are home to three-quarters of world's population, and 80 per cent of the world's capital cities are located on or near coasts.

Counter-terrorism

The end of the Cold War has seen a widespread breakdown of order, with trouble caused by rival ethnic and religious groups being predominant. One new element are the 'non-state' terrorist organisations, many of whom are believed to be pursuing

Above: Based on the design of the 'Invincible' class, the helicopter carrier HMS Ocean will serve alongside the new LPDs Albion and Bulwark, providing the UK with a significant amphibious capability.

Left: The MV-22 Osprey is as fast as a conventional fixed-wing turboprop, but thanks to its tilting rotors can take off and land vertically. It is intended to replace US Navy medium helicopters.

Top: The 'Wasp' class large amphibious assault ship is a one-ship landing force. Able to operate rotorcraft and V/STOL jets, it has a docking well for LCAC hovercraft and AAV7 amphibious vehicles. USS Iwo Jima (LHD-7) commissioned in June 2001.

'FOUDRE' CLASS LSD: FLEXIBLE PAYLOADS

The French 'Foudre' class of LSD is typical of modern multi-purpose assault ships. Designed to carry up to 467 troops and a load of 1,880 tons, the well dock can accommodate either landing craft (typically one LCT and four LCMs) or, with the use of moveable decks, it can provide vehicle parking space: VAB armoured personnel carriers and P4 light vehicles are seen embarked. The flight deck can support up to four AS 532 Cougar medium transport helicopters.

or acquiring weapons of mass destruction.

The viability, planning, and conduct of amphibious operations is dependent on a number of key factors including geography, distance, allies and enemy capabilities.

Since the end of World War II the US has been involved in more than 200 military operations of all sizes. However, the closure of bases overseas has eliminated much of the United States' continuous military presence, and has made the need for an offensive amphibious capability even more important.

The likely types of conflict will determine the nature of future amphibious operations. Many experts felt that the days of large-scale, conventional operations seen in World War II were over, but the 1991 Gulf War proved otherwise. However, most modern amphibious operations have arisen out of regional crises – Grenada, the Falklands, Somalia and Afghanistan are typical.

Operational needs

There is little chance of achieving operational surprise, given current intelligence capabilities and the instant nature of modern news gathering and broadcasting. However, modern technology provides more options for landing. Invasions no longer need a beach, at least in the initial assault phase. The range of modern aircraft may offer deployment alternatives such as vertical envelopment which improves the chances of avoiding enemy resistance at the shoreline

In any case, a direct assault against a fortified beach, World War II-style, may no longer be feasible given the capabilities and widespread deployment of sophisticated modern guided weaponry.

The US Navy has tackled the problem by improving its 'over-the-horizon' capability. The use of Landing Craft, Air Cushion (LCAC) hovercraft enables an amphibious force to deliver heavy equipment at great speed, while standing well out to sea. A new generation of amphibious assault vehicles is in development, which will allow troops to be delivered to the beach and beyond at much greater speed than is currently possible with the existing AAV7.

The Bell-Boeing MV-22 Osprey will add further capability. The tiltrotor design combines the vertical flight capabilities of a helicopter with the speed and range of a fixed-wing turboprop aircraft and permits aerial refuelling and also world-wide self-deployment.

Strategic option

While peacekeeping or peace enforcement missions in places as diverse as Somalia, Liberia and the Balkans prove that crisis-response operations remain the most likely missions for amphibious forces, the planned amphibious landings against Iraq during Operation Desert Storm showed that large-scale amphibious assaults are still considered a viable military strategic option.

Expeditionary warfare will be the foundation for most peacetime military operations in the 21st century. As a result, amphibious forces must be ready to mount operations from the sea.

Developed in conjunction with the Dutch 'Rotterdam' class of LPD, the Galicia is one of two dock landing ships built for the Spanish navy. It can transport and land a Marine battalion of 600 men and carries a complement of six AB 212 or four SH-3H helicopters.

'Jeanne d'Arc' class Helicopter carrier

Commissioned in 1964, the Jeanne d'Arc is equipped to act as an amphibious command ship to transport a battalion of marines, or to operate up to eight Super Frelon and Lynx helicopters. During training cruises, the vessel is more likely to embark French army Cougar or Gazelle helicopters. By April 1997, Jeanne d'Arc had conducted 33 training cruises and was docked for extensive repairs to its propulsion machinery. This was the vessel's third major refit, following upgrades in 1989 and 1990 in order to extend service life into the 21st century.

The French navy's helicopter carrier, Jeanne d'Arc. Used as a training ship in peacetime, the vessel can be rapidly converted in wartime to a commando ship, ASW helicopter carrier or troop transport.

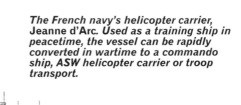

SPECIFICATION

Jeanne d'Arc
Commissioned: 1 July 1964
Displacement: 10,000 tons standard and 13,270 tons full load
Dimensions: length 182 m (597 ft 1 in); beam 24 m (78 ft 8½ in); draught 7.5 m (24 ft 7 in)
Propulsion: two geared steam turbines delivering 29828 kW (40,000 shp) to two shafts
Speed: 26.5 kts
Complement: 455 (33 officers) plus 13 instructors and 158 cadets
Troops: 700 (commando carrier)
Cargo: three Dauphin helicopters,
war inventory includes up to eight Super Frelon and Lynx; four LCVPs
Armament: two single 100-mm (3.9-in) DP guns, two triple MM 38 Exocet surface-to-surface missile launcher-containers, four 12.7-mm (0.5-in) machine-guns
Electronics: one DRBV 22D air search radar, one DRBV 51 air/surface search radar, one DRBN 34A navigation radar, three DRBC 32A fire-control radars, one SRN-6 TACAN, one SQS-503 sonar, DUBV 24C active hull sonar, two Syllex ECM rocket launchers

The single vessel of the **'Jeanne d'Arc' class** was laid down at Brest Naval Dockyard in 1960, launched in 1961 and commissioned in 1964. Although used in peacetime as a training ship for 158 officer cadets, **Jeanne d'Arc (R 97)** can be rapidly converted for wartime use as an amphibious assault, anti-submarine war-

fare or troop transport vessel. The helicopter platform is 62 m (203 ft 5 in) wide and is connected to the hangar deck by a 12218-kg (26,935-lb) capacity elevator located at the after end of the flight deck. The deck is capable of flying-on two Super Frelon heavy-lift helicopters and can accommodate a further four parked. The hangar, with

some internal modifications, can accommodate a further eight helicopters. At the aft end extensive machine, inspection and maintenance workshops are sited with weapon handling rooms and magazines for the armaments carried by the helicopters. In the commando carrier or troop transport role the ship has

facilities for a 700-man infantry battalion with light equipment in its fully air-conditioned interior.

A modular type action information and operations room is fitted, together with a separate helicopter control bridge and a combined command and control centre for amphibious warfare operations. A SENIT-2 combat data system was to be installed,

but was cancelled as a cost-saving measure. On each side of the funnel two LCVPs are normally carried.

In the future, *Jeanne d'Arc* may lose its two 100-mm (3.9-in) guns from the quarter-deck. The vessel's service life may be extended to 2010, in order that it can be replaced by a dedicated training ship, rather than a 'Mistral'-class LND as is planned for 2006.

'Iwo Jima' class Amphibious Assault Ships Helicopter (LPH)

The 'Iwo Jima'-class LPHs were the world's first ship class designed and constructed specifically to operate helicopters. Each LPH could carry a Marine battalion landing team with all its equipment, a reinforced helicopter squadron, and supporting personnel.

Ever since 1955, when the former escort carrier *Thetis Bay* was converted to a helicopter assault ship, the United States Navy has maintained a vertical airlift capability for the US Marine Corps. The ships of the **'Iwo Jima' class** were built to an improved World War II escort carrier design with accommodation for a US Marine infantry battalion landing team fore and aft of the cen-

trally located box hangar. These vessels were the first in any navy to be designed specifically to carry and operate helicopters, and as such no catapult or arrester gear was fitted. The flight deck was able to operate or recover up to seven CH-46 Sea Knight or four CH-53 Sea Stallions simultaneously. The hangar deck, with a 6.1-m (20-ft) height clearance could accommodate 19 CH-46s or

11 CH-53s. The normal air group was a mixture of 24 CH-46, CH-53, AH-1 and UH-1 helicopters. On **LPH-2**, **LPH-3**, **LPH-11** and **LPH-12** two foldable 22727-kg (50,100-lb) capacity deck-edge lifts were carried, whilst on **LPH-7**, **LPH-9** and **LPH-10** the lifts were reduced to 20000-kg (44,090-lb) capacity. Because (with the exception of LPH-12 which had two LCVPs on davits) they did not

carry landing craft the ships were limited in the size of equipment they could carry for the embarked US Marines. Two small elevators carried palletised cargo from the cargo holds to the flight deck, whilst a small parking area for light vehicles and towed artillery pieces was also provided.

During 1972-74 LPH-9 operated as an interim sea control ship carrying AV-8A

Harriers and SH-3 Sea King ASW helicopters. When converted back to an LPH it retained the Air Surface Classification and Analysis Centre (ASCAC) that was fitted for the experimental role. Several other LPHs also operated as minesweeping headquarters boats, embarking US Navy RH-53 helicopter minesweeping units. These vessels cleared North Vietnamese ports in 1973 and

USS **Inchon**, the sole surviving 'Iwo Jima'-class ship, now serves in the mine warfare role and embarks eight **MH-53E** Sea Dragons, having undergone conversion to become a Mine Countermeasures Command, Control and Support Ship (MCS) by 1996.

the Suez Canal in 1974. All helicopter operations were controlled from a dedicated command and control centre located in the flight deck island. All except LPH-10 carried the same satellite communications equipment as the LCCs, and they had the same 300-bed hospital unit as the LHAs. Four ships served with the Atlantic fleets and three with the Pacific fleets. LPH-12 was subsequently permanently converted for the mine warfare role as **MCS-12**, whilst the remaining five vessels in the class were decommissioned between 1993-97.

'Raleigh' and 'Austin' classes Amphibious Transport Docks (LPD)

The LPD is a further development of the dock landing ship (LSD) with an increased troop and vehicle capacity at the expense of a reduction in the dock well size. The LPD essentially combines the troop-carrying of the APA with part of the cargo-carrying AKA, and the vehicle and landing craft capabilities of the LSD designs in one hull. Of the three-ship **'Raleigh' class** one was converted to the Command Middle East Force flagship. This ship, **USS La Salle**, now serves as flagship in the Mediterranean. The 'Raleigh'-class ships have a stern docking well 51.2 m (168 ft) long and 15.2 m (50 ft) wide that can accommodate one LCU and three LCM6s, or four LCM8s, or 20 AAV7 amphibious vehicles. In addition two LCM6s or four LCPLs are carried on the heli-

copter deck and lifted overboard by crane. The helicopter deck covers the landing craft well, but there are no onboard hangar or maintenance facilities. Up to six CH-46 helicopters can be operated for short times from the deck. An overhead monorail stores transfer system is used to load the landing craft in the well deck from the forward cargo holds. Ramps connect the vehicle decks, docking well and flight deck, which can also be used to park additional vehicles if required. Side ports in the hull provide a roll-on/roll-off capability when docks are available.

The later **'Austin'-class** ships are enlarged versions of the 'Raleigh' class. The docking well is the same size, but a 12-m (39.4-ft) extension has been inserted just forward of

the well to increase the vehicle- and cargo-carrying capacities. A fixed flight deck is located above the well with two landing spots. All except **LPD-4** are fitted with a variable 17.7 m (58 ft) to 19.5 m (64 ft) long, 5.8 m (19 ft) to 7.3 m (24 ft) wide hangar that can be extended to about 24.4 m (80 ft) long if required. Up to six CH-46s can be operated, although the hangar can accommodate only one utility helicopter. The AAV7 capacity is increased to 28 with alternative loads of one LCU and three LCM6s or nine LCM6s or four LCM8s. **LPD-7** to **LPD-13** are fitted with amphibious squadron flagship duties with an additional superstructure deck. Both classes have satellite communications systems of the type fitted to the LCCs. Five 'Austin'-class ships serve

with the Atlantic fleets, whilst six 'Raleigh'-class ships serve in the Pacific fleets. **Coronado** (**LPD-11**) was converted to become a command ship in 1980, as a temporary replacement for *La Salle*, and is now based at San Diego and has served as a Joint Force Command Ship since 1997. **LPD-1** and **LPD-2** decommissioned in 1991-92.

Above: Similar to but larger than the 'Fearless' class, USS Shreveport, can, like several of its sisters, act as an amphibious squadron flagship. Two additional Mk 38 25-mm guns can be carried for self-defence.

Left: An SH-60B from HSL-41 'Seahawks' shadows USS Denver during operations in the Pacific. Six 'Austin'-class vessels can now operate the Pioneer UAV.

Below: The 'Austin'-class LPD USS Dubuque. From 1986 onwards this class, together with the 'Iwo Jima'-class LPHs, underwent a service life extension programme.

'Cabildo', 'Thomaston' and 'Anchorage' classes LSD

The LSD (Landing Ships Dock) is a World War II design for carrying landing craft and heavy vehicles such as tanks. There are no **'Cabildo' class** LSDs still in service with the US Navy, but one remains in service with Taiwan as **Chung Cheng** (and was fitted with a Sea Chaparral SAM system in 1992). Single vessels of the class were also operated by Greece and Spain. The 9,375-ton full load 'Cabildo' class can carry three LCUs or 18 LCM6s or 32 LVTP-5/7 amphibious carriers in its 103 m (338 ft) long, 13.3 m (43 ft 8½ in) wide well deck. The class can also carry 1,347 tons of cargo, and 100 2½-ton trucks or 27 M48 MBTs or 11 helicopters as well. Troop accommodation is limited to 137 overnight or 500 for

short day runs. The crew numbers 18 officers and 283 enlisted men. Maximum speed is 15.4 kts and the original armament was a variable number of 40-mm AA guns. A helicopter platform is fitted over the well deck although no hangar or maintenance facilities are carried.

The **'Thomaston' class** was the first post-war LSD design, and stemmed from Korean War experiences. The docking well is 119.2 m (391 ft) long and 14.6 m (48 ft) wide, and can accommodate three LCUs or 19 LCM6s or nine LCM8s or 48 AAV7s. A vehicle-parking area forward of the dock can accommodate a further 30 AAV7s if required. The ship carries two LCVPs and two LCPLs in davits, but no palletised cargo is carried. The

'Thomaston'-class ships were replaced by the new 'Whidbey Island' class.

The **'Anchorage' class** is similar to the 'Thomaston' class, but the ships have a tripod mast to distinguish them. A removable helicopter landing platform is fitted over the major part of the docking well; the size of which was increased to 131.1 m (430 ft) long by 15.2 m (50 ft) wide to accommodate three LCUs or 21 LCM6s or eight LCM8s or 50 AAV7s. The vessels also carry one or two LCM6s stowed on deck and one LCPL and one LCVP on davits. Troop capacity is also increased.

Three 'Anchorage'-class vessels (**USS Anchorage**, **USS Portland** and **USS Mount Vernon**) remained in service with the US Navy in

The 'Anchorage'-class LSD USS Mount Vernon and the 'Oliver Hazard Perry'-class guided missile frigate USS Sides steam together off the coast of Japan. Mount Vernon was the first West Coast ship to operate the LCAC air cushion assault craft.

2003, two with the Pacific Fleet and one with the Atlantic Fleet. One further vessel was sold to Taiwan in

2000 and serves as **Shiu Hai**. A second such vessel may be acquired by Taiwan in the future.

Above: The 'Anchorage'-class LSD USS Portland is viewed from the LHA USS Saipan in the Atlantic Ocean during Operation Enduring Freedom in 2003.

Left: Lead ship of its class, USS Anchorage is seen off the Australian coast during a routine deployment to the Western Pacific. These ships can accommodate three LCUs or LCACs or up to 48 AAV7 amphibians.

SPECIFICATION	
'Thomaston' and 'Anchorage' classes **Names:** *Thomaston* (LSD-28), *Plymouth Rock* (LSD-29), *Fort Snelling* (LSD-30), *Point Defiance* (LSD-31), *Spiegel Grove* (LSD-32), *Alamo* (LSD-33), *Hermitage* (LSD-34) and *Monticello* (LSD-35); *Anchorage* (LSD-36), *Portland* (LSD-37), *Pensacola* (LSD-38), *Mount Vernon* (LSD-39), *Fort Fisher* (LSD-40) **Commissioned:** 1954 to 1972 **Displacement:** LSD-28/31 and LSD-35 11,270 tons full load; LSD-32/34 12,150 tons full load; LSD-36/40 13,700 tons full load **Dimensions:** (LSD-28 to LSD-35) length 155.5 m (510 ft), beam 25.6 m (84 ft); draught 5.8 m (19 ft); (LSD-36 to LSD-40) length 168.6 m (553 ft 4 in); beam 25.6 m (84 ft); draught 6 m (20 ft) **Propulsion:** two geared steam turbines delivering 17896.8 kW (24,000 shp) to two shafts **Speed:** 22.5 kts maximum and	20 kts sustained **Complement:** LSD-28/35 331-341 (18 officers plus 313-323 enlisted men) and LSD-36/40 341-345 (18 officers plus 323-328 enlisted men) **Troops:** LSD-28/35 340, and LSD-36/40 376 **Cargo:** LSD-28/35 total 975-m² (10,500-sq ft) vehicle parking area, LSD-36/40 1115-m² (12,000-sq ft) vehicle parking area; three LCUs or 19 LCM6s or LCM8s or 48 AAV7s; 85 m³ (3,000 cu ft) ammunition; 4540 litres (1,200 US gal) of AVGAS or MOGAS; 147650 litres (39,000 US gal) of diesel fuel **Armament:** three twin Mk 33 3-in (76-mm) AA guns (replaced by two 20-mm Mk 16 Phalanx CIWS and two 25-mm Mk 38 Bushmaster guns) **Electronics:** one SPS-10 surface search radar, one SPS-6 (or SPS-40 in LSD-36/40) air search radar, one Mk 36 SRBOC system with associated ESM equipment

The 'Thomaston'-class LHD USS Hermitage. This class was very similar to the later and marginally larger 'Anchorage'-class LSD. Two 'Thomaston'-class vessels, Ceará and Rio de Janeiro, continued to be operated by the Brazilian navy in 2003.

'Fearless' class Amphibious Transport Dock

The two British **'Fearless'-class** LPDs, HMS *Fearless* and HMS *Intrepid*, were formerly under the command of Flag Officer Third Flotilla (FOF3) which was concerned with the larger warships of the Royal Navy and the naval air elements. The infamous 1981 Defence Review forecast the disposal of *Intrepid* (**L 11**) in 1982 and of *Fearless* (**L 10**) in 1984, but sanity finally prevailed within the Ministry of Defence in February 1982, and it was decided that both ships would continue in service, their worth later being proved during the Falkland Islands war, since without them there could not have been an assault landing to recapture the islands.

Assault capacity
The 'Fearless'-class ships were tasked to provide amphibious assault lift capabilities using an onboard naval assault group/brigade headquarters unit with a fully equipped assault operations room from which the force commanders could mount and control all the air, sea and land force assets required for the operation. The ships also carried an amphibious detachment that consisted of an assault squadron subdivided into a landing craft (LC) squadron with four LCUs (ex-LCM9s) and four LCVPs, an amphibious beach unit (ABU) with its own Land Rover and a Centurion Beach Armoured Recovery Vehicle (BARV) to attend to stranded vehicles and landing craft, and a vehicle deck party (VDP) for marshalling vehicles for embarkation on the landing craft. The LCU could carry either one Chieftain or two Centurion MBTs, or four 4-ton trucks or eight Land Rovers and trailers, or 100 tons of cargo, or 250 troops as its payload. The LCVP carried either 35

HMS Fearless *signals HMS* Antrim *prior to the San Carlos landings. The run of the Falkland Sound was made at night, with the first troops landing at San Carlos at 04.00 hours on 21 May 1982.*

troops or two Land Rovers.
A 50.29-m (165-ft) by 22.86-m (75-ft) flight deck was built over the well deck and was capable of operating most NATO helicopter types or, if required, Sea Harrier V/STOL fighter aircraft. Three vehicle decks were provided, in the form of one for tracked vehicles such as tanks or self-propelled guns, one for wheeled trucks, and a halfdeck that was reserved for Land Rover vehicles and trailers.

The overload troop capacity was sufficient for a light infantry battalion or Royal Marine Commando with an attached artillery battery. Further light vehicle stowage space could be obtained by using the helicopter flight deck. The vessels could also act as training ships, in which 150 midshipmen and naval cadets could be embarked for nine-week courses.

A Wessex HU.Mk 5 commando assault helicopter departs HMS Fearless. *Note the single LCU in the well deck, one of four that could be accommodated. Each LCU could carry one or two MBTs or up to 250 troops.*

Left: HMS Fearless *was subject to a re-fit in 1990, receiving two Vulcan Phalanx CIWS and new decoy launchers. Both vessels were retired during 1999-2002.*

SPECIFICATION

HMS *Fearless* (L 10) and *Intrepid* (L 11)
Commissioned: L 10 25 November 1965 and L 11 11 March 1967
Displacement: 12,210 tons full load
Dimensions: length 158.5 m (520 ft); beam 24.4 m (80 ft); draught 6.2 m (20 ft 6 in)
Propulsion: two geared steam turbines delivering 22,000 shp to two shafts
Speed: 21 kts
Complement: 617 (37 officers, 500 ratings and 80 Royal Marines)
Troops: 330 normal, 500 overload and 670 maximum
Cargo: maximum 20 MBTs, one BARV, 45 4-ton trucks with 50 tons of stores, or up to 2,100 tons of

stores; four LCUs and four LCVPs; five Wessex HU.Mk 5 or four Sea King HC.Mk 4 plus three Gazelle or Lynx helicopters
Armament: two GWS 20 quadruple Sea Cat SAM launchers, two twin Oerlikon 30-mm DP guns (L 11), two Oerlikon 20-mm AA guns, variable numbers of 0.3-in (7.62-mm) GPMGs and Blowpipe man-portable SAM launchers; L 10 later received two 20-mm Mk 15 Vulcan Phalanx guns
Electronics: one Type 978 navigation radar, one Type 994 air and surface search radar, one SCOT satellite communications system, one ESM system with Knebworth/Corvus chaff launchers, one CAAIS operations room command and control system

Falklands assault
Amphibious task force

*The amphibious assault ship **HMS** Fearless and the V/STOL carrier **HMS** Hermes complete the transfers of assault units immediately prior to the British assault on the Falkland Islands.*

The Falklands campaign involved the largest British landing since World War II, and demonstrated that amphibious forces still have a vital role to play in modern warfare. At the time, the UK's amphibious power projection capability lay primarily with the two vessels of the 'Fearless' class. These amphibious transport docks (LPDs) also had the command and communication facilities needed for the control of all sea, land and air forces involved in a brigade-level landing operation. Without the participation of HMS *Fearless* and HMS *Intrepid*, the Falkland Islands operations would probably not have been possible.

HMS *Fearless*

1 Navigation radar
2 Air search radar
3 Main mast structure
4 Fore funnel (behind main mast)
5 Chute
6 Radar control room
7 Operations room
8 Main bridge
9 40-mm Bofors gun
10 Bridge house
11 Fore mast structure
12 Life rafts
13 Quadruple launcher for Seacat SAMs
14 Anchor
15 Troop deck/stores (1)
16 Troop deck/stores (2)
17 Troop deck/stores (3)
18 Light lorries deck
19 Tank deck
20 Landing craft davit
21 Landing craft (LCVP type), capacity 36 troops or two Land Rovers with crew
22 Pulley system for raising ramp, upper and lower
23 Mobile ramp for moving AFVs from one deck to another
24 Ship's launch
25 Alvis Scorpion light reconnaissance vehicle
26 Fixed loading ramp, ship to landing craft
27 Retractable ladder companionway
28 Overhanging walkway
29 Landing craft LCM(9) type, capacity two tanks or 100 tons of vehicles or other cargo
30 Fixed ramp, vehicle access deck to deck
31 Five-blade propeller with a diameter of 3.8 m (12 ft 6 in)
32 Rudder
33 Stern well gate
34 Small crane (starboard)
35 Large crane (port) for handling cargo and landing craft
36 Aft ensign staff
37 Flight platform
38 Westland Wessex HU.Mk 5 (commando assault duties)
39 Life rafts
40 Forward crane for handling deck cargo
41 Aft funnel
42 Radio whip antenna

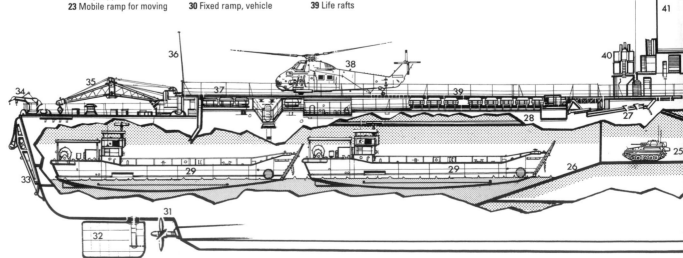

FALKLAND ISLANDS TASK FORCE

Falkland Islands Task Force (part)

Royal Navy & Royal Fleet Auxiliary

Aircraft carriers
Hermes and *Invincible*

Destroyers & frigates
'Type 82' class: *Bristol*
'County' class: *Antrim* and *Glamorgan*
'Type 42' class: *Cardiff, Coventry, Exeter, Glasgow* and *Sheffield*
'Type 22' class: *Active, Alacrity, Ambuscade, Antelope, Ardent, Arrow* and *Avenger*
'Leander (Exocet)' class: *Argonaut, Penelope* and *Minerva*
'Leander (Broad-beam Converted)' class: *Andromeda*
'Rothesay' class: *Plymouth* & *Yarmouth*

Ice-patrol ship
Endurance

Submarines
'Swiftsure' class: *Spartan* and *Splendid*
'Churchill' and 'Valiant' classes:
Conqueror, Valiant and *Courageous*
'Oberon' and 'Porpoise' class: *Onyx*

Landing Platforms Dock
Fearless and *Intrepid*

Landing Ships Logistic
Sir Bedivere, Sir Galahad, Sir Geraint, Sir Lancelot, Sir Percivale and *Sir Tristram*

Army & Royal Marines

3rd Commando Brigade
29 Commando Regiment, RA
59 Independent Commando Squadron, RE
40 Commando, RM
42 Commando, RM
45 Commando, RM
2nd Battalion, The Parachute Regiment
3rd Battalion, The Parachute Regiment
Commando Logistics Regiment, RM
3 Commando Brigade HQ and Signals Squadron, RM
3 Commando Brigade Air Squadron

5th Infantry Brigade
2nd Battalion, The Scots Guards
1st Battalion, The Welsh Guards
1st/7th Duke of Edinburgh's Own Gurkha Rifles
97 Battery, RA
656 Squadron, Army Air Corps

Above: Only after the lodgement area at San Carlos had been seized and consolidated were larger transports, which were STUFT (Ships Taken Up From Trade) brought in toward the beach-head. The unloading of the ships could be performed effectively only by intermediaries such as landing craft, and here the nature of 'ro-ro' ('roll-on/roll-off') ferries proved very useful.

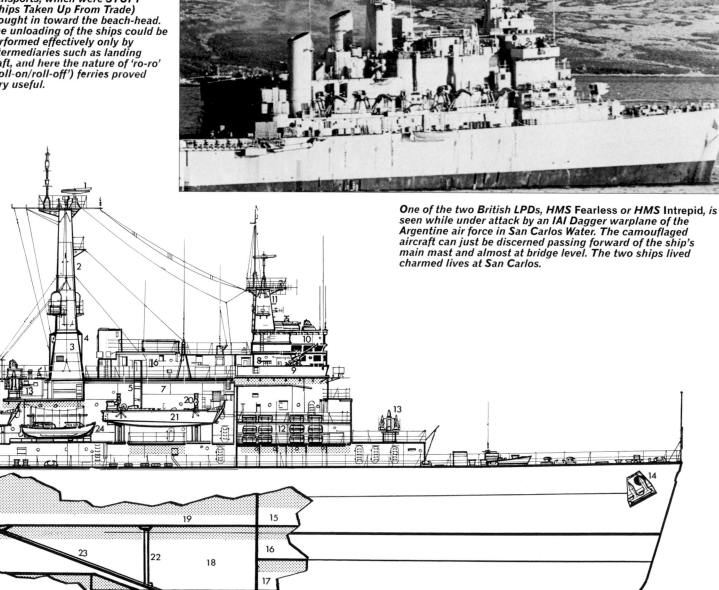

One of the two British LPDs, HMS Fearless or HMS Intrepid, is seen while under attack by an IAI Dagger warplane of the Argentine air force in San Carlos Water. The camouflaged aircraft can just be discerned passing forward of the ship's main mast and almost at bridge level. The two ships lived charmed lives at San Carlos.

HMS *Fearless*

Deleted from British service in 2002, HMS *Fearless* was built by Harland & Wolff in Belfast for launching in December 1963 and commissioning in November 1965. Like its sister ship, HMS *Intrepid* built by John Brown on Clydebank at much the same time, the *Fearless* was in effect an updated version of the dock landing ship created in World War II, and was essentially a scaled-down version of the 'Raleigh' class building for the US Navy. Carrying a normal load of some 15 tanks and 27 other vehicles as well as 400 or, under austere conditions, 700 troops, the ship was only lightly armed even for self-defence purposes, but offered adequate command and control capabilities. By the mid-1980s the ships' steam propulsion machinery had become costly and difficult to maintain, but both were available in 1982 for the recapture of the Falklands.

As well as their own guns and short-range SAMs, the British assault ships could rely on the weapons of escorting destroyers and frigates, and also on the Blowpipe shoulder-launched SAMs of troops once these had got ashore.

Helicopter capability

Above the docking well in her stern, HMS *Fearless* had a platform able to handle rotary-wing aircraft (either five Westland Wessex or four Westland Sea King helicopters) for the movement of men and, more importantly perhaps, weapons and equipment between the ship and the shore.

Docking well

In the stern HMS *Fearless* had a floodable docking well carrying four LCM(9) medium landing craft each able to carry two main battle tanks, or four other vehicles, or 100 tons of equipment or supplies. The ship also carried four LVCP light landing craft in davits, each of these being able to move 35 men or one half-ton motor vehicle.

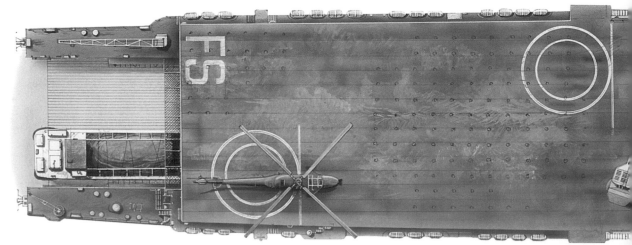

Propulsion

HMS *Fearless* was moved through the water by two propellers driven by the 16405 kW (22,000 shp) delivered by a pair of English Electric geared turbines powered by the steam from two Babcock & Wilcox oil-fired boilers.

On 21 May 1982 the Argentine air force made a determined effort to cripple the British naval forces operating in San Carlos Water for the amphibious landings on East Falkland. The British assault ships HMS Fearless and Intrepid were clearly primary targets, but both of them escaped essentially unhurt. This is the Fearless under attack from IAI Dagger warplanes of the Argentine air force's Grupo 6 de Caza.

Electronics

The electronic sensors carried by HMS *Fearless* were limited to one Type 994 air/surface search radar and one Type 978 navigation radar, and defence was aided by a pair of Knebworth Corvus countermeasures launchers. The ship was equipped with the CAAIS (Computer-Assisted Action Information System) and was also fitted out as a naval assault group/brigade headquarters with an assault operations room allowing the combined naval and military staffs to mount and control an amphibious assault.

Defensive armament

HMS *Fearless* was designed to operate under the cover of carrierborne if not land-based aircraft against air attack, and of other ships of the task forces in the event of a surface or submarine threat. This was the primary reason for the ship's wholly indifferent electronic and armament fits. The armament was intended solely for last-ditch protection against air attack, and comprised two 40-mm Bofors guns (originally L/60 but finally L/70 weapons), and four quadruple launchers for Seacat short-range surface-to-air missiles in the GWS20 optically controlled system that was later upgraded to the GWS22 standard with tracking radar for continued operability at night and in adverse weather conditions.

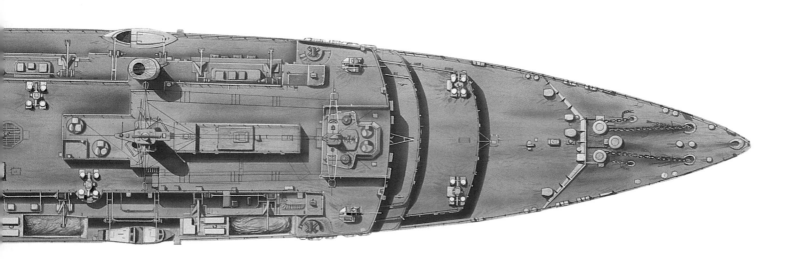

'Ouragan' class Landing Ship Dock (TCD/LSD)

The **'Ouragan' class** of dock landing ship is used both for amphibious warfare and logistic transport by the French navy. They are fitted with a well dock some 120 m (393 ft 8½ in) in length that has a stern gate measuring 14 m (45 ft 11 in) by 5.5 m (18 ft). The well dock can accommodate two 670-ton full load EDIC LCTs (carrying 11 light tanks, or 11 trucks or five LVTs) or 18 LCM6s (carrying 30 tons of cargo or vehicles). Above the well deck is a 36-m (79.4-ft) long six-section removable helicopter deck capable of operating one SA 321G Super Frelon heavy-lift helicopter or three SA 319B Alouette III utility helicopters. If required, a 90-m (295-ft 4-in) long temporary deck can also be fitted to stow cargo or vehicles, but its use reduces the number of landing craft carried as half the well deck is taken up. If used with this extra deck as a logistic transport then the total cargo capacity of the vessel becomes some 1,500 tons. This can comprise either 18 Super Frelon or 80 Alouette III helicopters, or 120 AMX-10s or 84 light amphibious vehicles or 340 light utility vehicles or 12 50-ton barges. A typical load may comprise one 380-ton CDIC LCT, four 56-ton CTMs, 10 AMX-10RC armoured cars

and 21 further vehicles or a total of 150 to 170 vehicles (without landing craft). There is a permanent helicopter deck for up to four Super Frelons or 10 Alouette IIIs located next to the starboard bridge area. Two 35-ton capacity cranes handle the heavy equipment carried. Each of the two ships also has command and control facilities to operate as amphibious force flagships. They also carry an extensive range of repair and maintenance workshops to support the units embarked. Troop accommodation is provided for 349 men under normal conditions, although 470 can be carried for short distances. Three LCVPs are carried as deck cargo.

Nuclear test role

The **FN** *Orage* (**L 9022**) was allotted to the French Pacific nuclear experimental centre as the logistic transport to and from France. It was also employed as the centre's floating headquarters, employing a modular facility within the well deck area. In 1993, both vessels received two twin Simbad launchers for Mistral SAMs and new search radars.

Both the *Orage* and **Ouragan** (**L 9021**) have had service life extensions and are due to be replaced in 2005/6 when the two new

Used for both amphibious warfare and as a logistic transport, **Ouragan** *is capable of deploying and supporting half a battalion of marines (349 troops). In addition, a typical helicopter load comprises three or four Super Frelon or 10 Alouette III, although the former is today rarely carried, and the Super Puma or Cougar (for CSAR operations) are more likely to be deployed.*

20,000-ton 'Mistral'-class LHDs are due to be commissioned into service.

Below: The **Orage** *has an enclosed flag bridge; it has served as a floating headquarters for France's nuclear test mission in the South Pacific.*

SPECIFICATION	
Names: *Ouragan* (L 9021) and *Orage* (L 9022)	**Troops:** 349 (14 officers plus 335 enlisted men) normal, 470 overload
Commissioned: L9021 1 June 1965; L9022 1 April 1968	**Cargo:** 1,500 tons as logistic transport; two LCTs, or up to 8 CTMs or 18 LCM6s; plus 3 LCVP
Displacement: 5,800 tons light; 8,500 tons full load	**Armament:** two Matra Simbad twin launchers for Mistral SAMs, four single 40-mm Bofors guns (two later replaced by Breda/Mauser 30-mm guns)
Dimensions: length 149 m (488 ft 10 in); beam 23 m (75 ft 6 in); draught 5.4 m (17 ft 8½ in)	
Propulsion: two diesels delivering 6413 kW (8,600 shp) to two shafts	**Electronics:** one DRBN 32 navigation radar, one DRBV 51A air/surface search radar, one SQS-17 sonar (L 9021)
Speed: 17 kts	
Complement: 211 (10 officers plus 201 enlisted men)	

'Foudre' class Landing Ship Dock (TCD/LSD)

For many years the French navy's amphibious capability was based on two LSDs dating back to the 1960s, *Ouragan* and *Orage*. Unlike the British defence establishment, the French recognised the limitations of its ageing LSDs and ordered a new TCD (Transport de Chalands de Débarquement)/LSD in 1984. The **FN** *Foudre* (**L 9011**) was laid down at Brest in 1986, launched in 1988 and commissioned in 1990. A sistership was authorised in 1994: the **Siroco** (**L 9012**) was laid down that year, launched in 1996 and commissioned in 1998.

The **'Foudre' class** are designed to carry a mecha-

Foudre *has a 1450-m² (15,608 cu ft) flight deck, with two landing spots, one of which is fitted with a landing grid and a helicopter landing system.*

nised battalion of France's Rapid Action Force (FAN), the model for the new professional army that replaces the conscript force of the 20th century. The vessels can also act as logistics support ships. A typical load for these vessels consists of one CDIC (Chaland de Débarquement d'Infanterie et de Chars) – a 380-ton LCT of which the French built a pair to operate with the 'Foudre' class; four CTMs (Chalands de Transport de Matériel) – 56-ton LCMs; ten AMX-10RC armoured cars, and up to 50 other vehicles. Without the landing craft embarked, the 'Foudre' class can carry up to 200 vehicles. The well dock measures 122 by 14 m (400 ft 4 in by 45 ft 11 in) and can accept a 400-ton ship. Cranes of 52-ton (*Foudre*) or 38-ton (*Siroco*) capacity assist in handling heavy equipment.

In terms of personnel, the 'Foudre' class can accommodate 467 troops (plus 1,880 tons load) or as many as 1,600 troops for an emergency situation. With 700 personnel embarked, the 'Foudre'-class LSD has an endurance of 30 days.

Both vessels carry comprehensive command and control facilities and medical

provision includes two operating theatres and 47 beds. *Siroco* is designed to accommodate a modular field hospital.

Helicopter operations
There are two landing spots on the 1450-m² (15,608 cu ft) flight deck plus one on the removable rolling cover above the well deck. They can operate a pair of Super Frelons or four AS 332F Super Puma helicopters. The landing deck on *Siroco* is extended aft as far as the lift, in order to give an increased area of 1740 m² (18,730 cu ft).

Foudre has been sched-

uled to receive the same anti-aircraft gun armament as the *Siroco* since the late 1990s but the work has yet to take place. Air defence against close-in threats and sea-skimming missiles is handled by a pair of Matra Simbad lightweight twin launchers for Mistral IR-homing missiles; these are located on either side of the bridge. Without the three Breda/Mauser 30-mm guns as fitted to *Siroco*, *Foudre* relies on a single 40-mm Bofors gun forward of the bridge, and two GIAT 20F2 20-mm guns; both ships are also armed with two 12.7-mm (0.5-mm) machine-

guns. In 1997, a Sagem optronic fire-control system was fitted to both vessels. A Dassault Electronique ESM/ECM system is also

due to be fitted. The two ships are based at Toulon and assigned to the FAN; *Siroco* was deployed to East Timor for operations in 1999.

Twin Simbad launchers for the Mistral IR-homing SAM provide the 'Foudre' class with air defence out to a range of 4 km (2.5 miles).

'San Giorgio' class Amphibious Transport Dock (LPD)

Capable of operating three SH-3D Sea King or EH 101 Merlin or five AB 212 helicopters from a carrier-type flight deck, the **'San Giorgio' class** LPDs each carry a battalion of Italian infantry. ITS *San Giorgio* (**L 9892**) and *San Marco* (**L 9893**) have bow doors for amphibious landings but *San Giusto* (**L 9894**) does not. All three can ship two LCMs in the stern docking well. The *San Giorgio* and *San Marco* were laid down in 1985 and 1986 respectively while the slightly larger *San Giusto* was not ordered until 1991. The first two ships were launched in 1987 and commissioned in 1987 and 1988. The *San Giusto*, launched in 1993 (late due to industrial unrest) and finally commissioned in 1994, is some 300 tons heavier as a result of a

longer island and increased accommodation. *San Marco* was funded by the Italian Ministry of Civil Protection and, although run by the Italian navy, is specially fitted for disaster relief operations.

Modernisation
From 1999, the ships' original 20-mm guns were replaced by 25-mm Breda Oerlikon weapons, while the *San Giorgio* has had its 76-mm (3-in) gun removed, and its LCVP installation relocated from davits to a port side sponson. The vessel has also had its flight deck lengthened to allow simultaneous operations of two EH 101s and two AB 212s. The bow doors are also being removed, and similar modifications are to be undertaken for the *San Marco*.

Four landing spots are

San Marco, with medium trucks carried on the deck. The stern docking well, which can accept two LCMs, measures 20.5 by 7 m (67 ft 3 in by 23 ft). The 'San Giorgio'-class LPDs are based at Brindisi and are assigned to the Third Naval Division.

provided, and a 30-ton lift and two 40-ton travelling cranes are used for transporting the 64.6-ton LCMs.

A typical load would include a battalion of 400 personnel, plus 30-36 APCs or 30 medium tanks. A total of

two (on davits) or three (on port side sponson) LCVPs can be carried.

San Giorgio and San Marco are seen at dock, with SH-3D and AB 212 helicopters embarked. Note the port side sponsons for LCVP carriage.

'Oosumi' class Amphibious transport dock/landing ship tank

The so-called LPD/LSTs of the Japanese **'Oosumi' class** look remarkably like aircraft carriers, the first to fly the rising sun naval emblem since 1945. With their stern docking wells and flight deck, the ships strongly resemble scaled-down US-type LHAs rather than the tank landing ships they purport to be. If this sounds like anachronistic paranoia, Japan's ability to maintain secrecy over its naval projects was an enduring feature of the first half of the 20th century.

The **Oosumi** was approved in 1990 but not laid down until December 1995 in Mitsui's Tamano yard. Those of the initial drawings that were released showed a ship half the size of the one actually completed and resembling the Italian 'San Giorgio' class. Launched in 1996 and commissioned in 1998, it was followed by the **Shimokita** from the same yard, and a third unit, the **Kunisaki** is currently under construction at Hitachi's Maizuru yard, with a fourth

unit planned.

Designed for the movement of a full battalion of marines together with a tank company, the 'Oosumi' class accords fully

with the recent Japanese power-projection operations into the Indian Ocean as well as around the Pacific. Each ship's defensive armament is limited to a pair of

Phalanx CIWS systems with a six-barrel rotary cannon, but the ships operate within a naval task force whose other ships provide primary protection.

SPECIFICATION

'Osumi' class	**Armament:** two Phalanx CIWS
Displacement: 8,900 tons standard	**Electronics:** OPS-14C air search, OPS-28D surface search, and OPS-20 navigation radars
Dimensions: length 178 m (584 ft); beam 25.8 m (84 ft 8 in); draught 6 m (19 ft 8 in)	**Military lift:** 330 troops, 10 Type 90 tanks or 1,400 tons of cargo, and two LCACs
Propulsion: two Mitsui diesels delivering 20580 kW (27,600 shp) to two shafts	**Aircraft:** platform for two CH-47J Chinook helicopters
Performance: speed 22 kts	**Complement:** 135

*The **Shimokita** is the second of a planned four 'Oosumi'-class ships, which combine LPD and LST capabilities in a single hull with a stern docking well.*

'Rotterdam' & 'Galicia' classes Amphibious transport dock

This collaborative venture between Dutch and Spanish shipbuilders is known to the Dutch navy as the **'Rotterdam' class** and by the Spanish navy as the **'Galicia' class**. The **Rotterdam** and **Galicia** were both laid down in 1996, and were commis-

sioned in 1997 and 1998 respectively. The **Castilla** was laid down in 1997 and commissioned in 2000. It is planned that a second Dutch ship, the **Johan de Witt**, should enter service in 2007.

The ships of the class are designed to carry a battalion

of marines and all its associated combat and support vehicles. Carrying a large docking well in the stern, the ships can operate their landing craft and helicopters in varying degrees of bad weather conditions. They carry extensive medical facilities including a treatment

room, operating theatre and medical laboratory, and have already been used to help out during humanitarian emergencies. In addition to land forces and their kit, the ships are designed to carry additional naval ordnance (including up to 30 torpedoes) in their magazines to

support a task force operating at some distance from home ports.

The defensive armament differs between the Spanish and Dutch ships, each carrying indigenous CIWS mountings in the form of the Meroka and Goalkeeper, in addition to 20-mm cannon.

*The **Rotterdam** was built at the Royal Schelde yard at Vlissingen, and provides capabilities for the delivery of a full battalion of marines with all necessary kit.*

SPECIFICATION

'Rotterdam'/'Galicia' class	11125 km (6,910 miles) at 12 kts
Displacement: 12,750 tons standard; 16,750 tons ('Rotterdam') or 13,815 ('Galicia') full load	**Armament:** ('Rotterdam') two 30-mm Goalkeeper CIWS and four 20-mm cannon, and ('Galicia') two 20-mm Meroka CIWS
Dimensions: length 166 m (544 ft 7 in) ('Rotterdam') and 160 m (524 ft 11 in) ('Galicia'); beam 25 m (82 ft); draught 5.9 m (19 ft 4 in)	**Electronics:** DA-08 air/surface and Scout surface search radars
Propulsion: four diesel generators delivering current to two electric motors delivering 12170 kW (16,320 shp) to two shafts	**Military lift:** 611 troops, 33 tanks or 170 APCs, and 6 LCVPs or 4 LCUs or LCMs
Performance: speed 19 kts; range	**Aircraft:** six NH 90 or four EH 101 helicopters
	Complement: 113

*The 'Rotterdam' and 'Galicia' classes provide a large area over the stern for the operation of helicopters above the dock from which landing craft operate. The **Johan de Witt** has a stronger helicopter deck than the **Rotterdam** on a hull that is longer and wider.*

'Ivan Rogov' class Amphibious transport dock

Given the designation *bol'shoy desantnyy korabl'* (BDK, or large landing craft) by the Soviets, the **Ivan Rogov** was launched in 1976 at the Kaliningrad shipyard. The vessel entered service in 1978 as the largest amphibious warfare ship built by the Soviets. A second unit, the **Aleksandr Nikolayev**, was laid down in 1979 and completed in 1983, and the third unit, laid down in 1985 and completed in 1990, is the **Mitrofan Moskalenko**. A fourth unit was not completed, and the first two were decommissioned in 1996 and 1997, one of them for possible overhaul and sale to Indonesia.

The ship can carry a reinforced Naval Infantry battalion landing team with all its APCs and other vehicles plus 10 PT-76 light amphibious tanks. An alternative load is a Naval Infantry tank battalion. The vessels were unique in Soviet amphibious ship design as they had both a well dock and a helicopter flight deck and hangar. This allowed the ship to perform not only the traditional role of over-the-beach

assault by use of bow doors and ramp, but also the stand-off assault role using a mixture of helicopters, landing craft, air-cushion vehicles (ACVs) and amphibious vehicles.

Accessibility

The bow doors and internal ramp position provide access to a vehicle parking deck located in the lower forward part of the ship. Further vehicles can be accommodated in the midships area of the upper deck, access to this being by hydraulically operated ramps that lead from the bow doors and the docking well. The vehicle deck itself leads directly into the floodable well which is some 79 m (259 ft 2 in) long with a stern door some 13 m (42 ft 8 in) across. The well can accom-

modate either two pre-loaded 'Lebed'-class ACVs and a 145-ton full load 'Ondatra'-class LCM, or three 'Gus'-class troop-carrying ACVs.

Two helicopter landing spots are provided, one forward and one aft above the well dock, each with its own flight control station. Both spots have access to the massive block superstructure, in which a hangar could accommodate five Kamov Ka-25 'Hormone-C' utility helicopters, later replaced by four Ka-29 helicopters.

Accommodation for the embarked Naval Infantry is located within the superstructure block, which also includes vehicle and helicopter workshops. To starboard, immediately in front of the block, is a tall deck house on

top of which is mounted a 122-mm (4.8-in) rocket-launcher system with two 20-round packs of launcher tubes, one to each side of a pedestal mounting that trains them in azimuth and elevation. The rockets are used to provide a saturation shore bombardment capability for the assault units. A twin 76.2-mm (3-in) DP gun turret is located on the forecastle, and a pop-up two-rail launcher bin units for SA-N-4 SAMs and

four 30-mm CIWS mountings are mounted on top of the main superstructure block to provide an air-defence capability. Extensive command, control and surveillance equipment is fitted for amphibious force flagship duties.

The two Pacific Fleet units have paid off, leaving only the *Mitrofan Moskalenko* in service with the Northern Fleet from the base at Severomorsk.

SPECIFICATION

'Ivan Rogov' class
Displacement: 8,260 tons standard; 14,060 tons full load
Dimensions: length 157.5 m (516 ft 9 in); beam 24.5 m (80 ft 6 in); draught 6.5 m (21 ft 4 in)
Propulsion: two gas turbines delivering 29820 kW (39,995 shp) to two shafts
Performance: speed 19 kts; range 13900 km (8,635 miles) at 14 kts
Armament: one twin launcher for 20 SA-N-4 'Gecko' SAMs, one twin 76.2-mm (3-in) DP gun, four 30-mm ADG-630 CIWS mountings, two SA-N-5 quadruple launchers, and two 122-mm (4.8-in) rocket launchers
Electronics: one 'Top Plate-A' 3D

radar, two 'Don Kay' or 'Palm Frond' navigation radars, two 'Squeeze Box' optronic directors, one 'Owl Screech' 76.2-mm gun fire-control radar, one 'Pop Group' SA-N-4 missile fire-control radar, two 'Bass Tilt' CIWS fire-control radars, one 'Salt Pole-B' IFF system, three 'Bell Shroud' ESM systems, two 'Bell Squat' ECM systems, 20 decoy launchers, and one 'Mouse Tail' VDS
Military lift: 522 troops, typically 20 MBTs or an equivalent volume of APCs and trucks, 2,500 tons of freight, and three ACVs or six LCMs
Aircraft: four Ka-29 'Helix' helicopters
Complement: 239

'Albion' class LPD

The Royal Navy's two assault ships, HMS *Fearless* and HMS *Intrepid*, laid down in 1962, were due for deletion in 1981 as part of the Conservative government's decision to end the Royal Marines' amphibious capability. This ruling played a major role in the Argentine decision of the following year to invade the Falklands Islands. The two ships were reprieved and played a vital role in the liberation of the islands. It was another 10 years before a decision was taken to authorise replacements for what were, by the 1991 Gulf War, very elderly ships. Even then, the two **'Albion'-class** LPDs were not laid down until 1998 and 2000 respectively, by which time the *Intrepid* had been cannibalised to keep the *Fearless*

operational. Even then, the fire in the ship's engine room during November 2000 as the *Fearless* was operating off Sierra Leone, riven by civil war, demonstrated the dangers in relying on a 40-year old ship. Keeping it in service was estimated to require another £2 million, so the *Fearless* was paid off in March 2002.

The £429 million replacement programme was accelerated after the events of 11 September 2001, and the requirement was altered to demand the capability for the mounting of more than one amphibious operation at a time. HMS *Albion* was launched in March 2001, but its in-service date of March 2002 slipped by a year. HMS **Bulwark** was launched in November 2001, but workers

on it were transferred to accelerate the completion of the *Albion*.

Much larger and more capable LPDs than the ships they are replacing, the 'Albion'-class units are part of a wider modernisation of the British amphibious capability. They will serve alongside the new helicopter carrier HMS *Ocean* and the four 'Bay'-class landing ships (logistic) planned to replace the 'Sir Bedivere'-class LSLs. The extensive command and control systems aboard the 'Albion' class represent a great leap forward for the Royal Navy and Marines.

One feature worthy of note is the diesel-electric propulsion system, the first to be used by a British surface warship. This requires only two-thirds the engineering complement of the older LPDs and, in overall terms, automation and new technology have reduced the manning requirement from

550 to 325. The four new LCU Mk 10 'ro-ro' landing craft operated by each 'Albion'

The two 'Albion'-class assault ships were built by BAE Systems (formerly Vickers) at Barrow-in-Furness, and were somewhat delayed by lack of skilled workers.

are capable of carrying a Challenger 2 MBT.

HMS Albion and HMS Bulwark are Royal Navy ships that provide the Royal Marines with a quantum leap forward in their amphibious assault capabilities.

SPECIFICATION

'Albion' class
Displacement: 19,560 tons full load; 21,500 tons docked down
Dimensions: length 176 m (577 ft 5 in); beam 29.9 m (98 ft 1 in); draught 6.7 m (22 ft)
Propulsion: diesel generators powering two electric motors driving two shafts
Performance: speed 20 kts; range 14825 km (9,210 miles) at 14 kts
Armament: two 30-mm Goalkeeper CIWS mountings and

two twin 20-mm AA guns
Electronics: one Type 996 air/surface-search, one surface search and two navigation radars, ADAWS 2000 combat data system, UAT-1/4 ESM system and eight Sea Gnat decoy launchers
Military lift: 305 or overload 710 troops, six Challenger 2 tanks or 30 APCs, four LCUs and four LCVPs
Aircraft: two/three medium helicopters
Complement: 325

'Tarawa' class Amphibious assault

Light helicopters

Typically a 'Tarawa'-class vessel will carry a pair of UH-1 utility helicopters and four to six Sea Cobra attack helicopters. Today the UH-1N is principally used in the special forces insertion role from LHD and LHA ships, and is due to be replaced by the improved UH-1Y with four-bladed main rotor. The Hellfire-capable AH-1W Super Cobra entered service in 1996 and it is in turn due for replacement by the AH-1Z, which has substantial commonality with the UH-1Y, including sharing the T700 engine and transmission. The UH-1Y and AH-1Z are scheduled for initial operational capability (IOC) in 2004 and 2006, respectively.

Fixed-wing aircraft

The AV-8B provides the Marines with an organic close air support (CAS) capacity. In its latest Harrier II Plus guise, the AV-8B offers enhanced anti-air and surface strike capabilities, using AIM-120 AMRAAM and AGM-84 Harpoon missiles, respectively. In the past, the OV-10 Bronco observation aircraft has also been deployed aboard 'Tarawa'-class LHAs. A usual combination of aircraft allows for the support of six AV-8Bs.

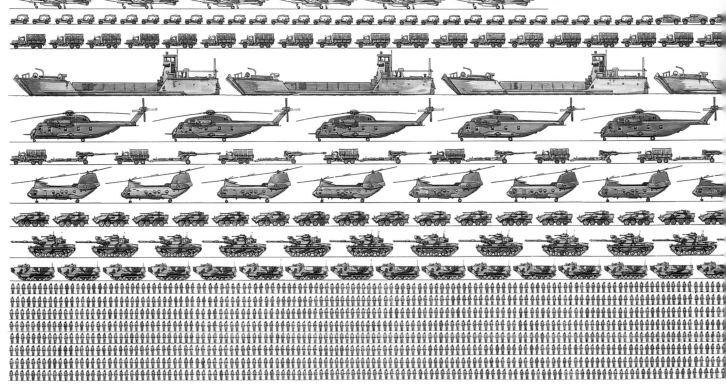

Above: A US Navy LCAC (Landing Craft Air Cushion) of Assault Craft Unit Five delivers troops and cargo to the USS Peleliu during an amphibious exercise off the coast of Southern California.

Right: Mainstay of the USMC's heavylift capability, a CH-53E Super Stallion lands on the deck of the USS Nassau off the coast of Nova Scotia. In service with five active duty units, the three-engined CH-53E variant is capable of externally lifting any USMC tactical jet or an LAV.

The main function of an assault ship is to get troops ashore in the shortest possible time, with assault troops riding into battle within amphibious assault vehicles. Here an AAV7A1 Amphibious Assault Vehicle from the USS Nassau advances onto the beach during a mock invasion of Newfoundland. In the post Cold War era, such realistic training exercises improve the skills that may be called upon during a NATO-led peacekeeping support operation. The AAV is the heart of the Marine assault, 'Tarawa'-class vessels carrying up to 40 examples.

Light vehicles

These include Jeeps and its replacement, the ¾-ton HMMWV 'Hummer'. The latter is the standard vehicle in its class throughout all four US services, and two examples can be carried underslung by the CH-53.

Medium trucks

These will mostly consist of 2½-ton vehicles. Trucks and AFVs are accomodated within the ship's large garage.

Landing craft

The four utility landing craft (LCUs) can land either two to three MBTs (depending on size), cargo or troops.

Medium-/heavy-lift

Both the medium-lift CH-53D Sea Stallion (with capacity for 37 troops or six tons of cargo) and the heavy-lift CH-53E Super Stallion (55 troops, 16 tons), can be carried, and both are capable of carrying an underslung howitzer or HAWK missile.

Artillery

The 155-mm (6-in) M198 towed medium howitzer has a range of over 20 km (12 miles) and can be lifted by the CH-53.

Troop transport

Twelve CH-46Es can move 300 troops or equivalent cargo at a time, although a more normal load is 12-18 troops each. Sea Knights generally deploy as part of the Marine Expeditionary Unit (MEU) Air Combat Element (ACE) in 12-ship squadrons.

Light Armored Vehicles

More mobile than tracked armour, the 8x8 LAV can be used for reconnaissance.

Tanks

A company of M60A1 MBTs (illustrated) could be carried, although these have now been replaced by the M1A1. USMC examples are equipped with a Deep Water Fording Kit, allowing the tank to ford to a depth of almost 2 m (6 ft 7 in) and are LCAC-compatible.

Amphibious Assault Vehicles

The AAV7A1 is fully amphibious, propelled by tracks or waterjets, and can carry 25 troops. Once ashore it can provide troops with light fire support.

Troops

A Reinforced Marine Battalion comprises somewhere between 1,700 and 1,900 men and women.

'GATOR NAVY': US AMPHIBIOUS ASSAULT

The five 'Tarawa'-class vessels form an important component of the US Navy's assault fleet, or 'Gator Navy'. Although these ships are now ageing, to date only a single additional 'Wasp'-class ship has been ordered to replace the USS Tarawa. The latter may replace the USS Inchon in the specialist mine warfare role. Nocturnal operations are illustrated aboard the USS Nassau during the Combined Joint Task Force Exercise '96, with a CH-46 preparing for a night launch (below right) and a USMC LAV (Light Armored Vehicle) backing onto a US Navy landing craft in prior to amphibious operations from the ship's well deck (right). The 'Tarawa' class have also been active in military campaigns. Pictured below is an AV-8B taxiing aboard the USS Tarawa in the Persian Gulf in support of Operation Southern Watch, enforcing the No-Fly Zone over southern Iraq in December 1998.

USS *Tarawa*

The 'Tarawa'-class general-purpose assault ships (LHAs) were the largest amphibious warfare vessels built, before the arrival of the 'Wasp'-class LHA, which was itself derived from the 'Tarawa' design. The slab-sided configuration of the 'Tarawa' maximises internal capacity, allowing the storage of heavy artillery and vehicles. The 'Tarawa' class was designed to expand the potential for heliborne assault, providing landing spots for 12 CH-46 or nine CH-53 helicopters compared to landing spots for seven CH-46s or four CH-53s for its forerunner, the 'Iwo Jima'-class helicopter carrier (LPH). Unlike the 'Iwo Jima' class, the 'Tarawas' could be called upon to give fire support to the beachhead, being equipped with three (later two) 5-in (127-mm) Mk 45 guns on the starboard side, although these were deleted in 1997-98. Autonomous assault operations can be directed from the ships' capable command and control centre.

A US Navy LCAC of Assault Craft Unit Five (ACU-5) launched from the USS Tarawa offloads Marines from Battalion Landing Team 2/3 on Kauai, Hawaii, during a beach assault training exercise in July 2002. An H-3H helicopter from the Pacific Missile Range facility hovers overhead and serves as a safety observer. Operated by a crew of five, the LCAC can transport 24 troops, a single MBT or 60-75 tons of cargo.

Landing craft

Tarawa can operate four LCU utility landing craft out of the docking well. Each of these versatile 375-ton steel-hulled craft can carry two M1 MBTs or up to 350 troops. An alternative load comprises two LCU and two 111-ton LCM 8 vessels. The LCM 8 mechanised landing craft, seen here leaving the docking well, can carry a load of 54 tons or 200 troops, or as seen here, a single MBT. Another possible load comprises 17 64-ton LCM 6 mechanised landing craft. These can be carried on the deck, and launched by crane. Used in diminishing numbers for utility duties, the LCM 6 can accomodate 34 tons of cargo or 80 troops. A further option is up to four LCPL personnel landing craft. Two of these 11-ton vessels may be seen astern of the island. The LCPL can carry up to 17 troops and is normally used as a control craft aboard the 'Tarawa' ships as well as the 'Austin'-class amphibious transport docks (four examples carried), 'Whidbey Island' and 'Harpers Ferry' dock landing ships (two) and 'Newport'-class tank landing ships (two).

Hangar

The USS *Tarawa*'s hangar deck is immediately above the docking well. It is 82 m (268 ft) long by 24 m (78 ft) wide, and can hold a total of 26 CH-46 or 19 CH-53 helicopters. It is served by an 18-ton capacity side lift to port and by a 36-ton capacity centreline lift at the stern, immediately above the entrance to the docking well. The 'Tarawa'-class LHAs are also due to operate RQ-8A Fire Scout vertical take-off UAVs in due course.

Flight deck

Although *Tarawa* looks like an aircraft carrier, it has neither catapults nor arrester gear, so it cannot handle most conventional take-off and landing (CTOL) aircraft. Vertical take-off machines are a different matter, however and, *Tarawa* can handle 10 helicopter or Harrier movements simultaneously. The helicopters seen on deck in this illustration are USMC CH-46 Sea Knights, of which a total of 30 can be shipped by *Tarawa*. Each can carry a payload of 1089-1996 kg (2,400-4,400 lb) cargo or 12-18 troops.

Docking well

The well deck is the same size as the hangar deck immediately above. In action, the stern of the ship is 'flooded down' and the rear doors are opened, to allow assault craft to swim out of the mother ship. When not in operation, the rear doors are closed and the well deck is pumped dry. The US Navy's 'Wasp'-class amphibious assault ships have modified docking wells optimised for the operation of LCAC air-cushion landing craft. 'Wasp'-class vessels can accomodate three LCACs comapred to the single example carried by the 'Tarawa' class.

Left: Over 500 sailors and Marines aboard the USS Belleau Wood mark the one-year anniversary of the September 2001 terrorist attacks on the US. At the time the vessel was deployed as the lead element of a three-ship Amphibious Readiness Group in support of Operation Enduring Freedom.

Command and control

Like all major warships, the USS *Tarawa* has an extensive electronics fit. The Combat Information Center is located in the island, behind the bridge. Lit by radar screens and electronic displays, it is from here that the ship is controlled in battle. *Tarawa* is also fitted with an Integrated Tactical Amphibious Warfare Data System, which is used to control the entire amphibious force. The 'Tarawa'-class ships are multi-role vessels, equally able to act as auxilliary 'sea control' aircraft carriers, to command a fleet, or to make up the heart of a major amphibious assault task force.

Hospital

Amphibious assaults on defended shores are risky and casualties can be heavy. Each 'Tarawa'-class assault vessel has a 300-bed hospital with operating theatres, X-ray facilities, an isolation ward, laboratories, a pharmacy and a dental surgery.

Island

Most of *Tarawa*'s island is taken up by the uptakes from the vessel's steam turbines. However, it provides a convenient location for the ship's radar systems, which include search radars, gun fire-control systems, missile fire-control systems, navigation antennas and communications gear. Astern of the island is a crane able to handle 64-ton LCM 6 landing craft.

Close-in defence

When built, Tarawa was fitted with two eight-tube Mk 25 Sea Sparrow missile launchers, one in front of the bridge and one on a sponson at the stern. By 1991, these had been replaced by a pair of Phalanx Close-In Weapons Systems (CIWS), the radar-guided 20-mm cannon system designed to destroy incoming missiles at very close range. The Vulcan Phalanx Mk 15 has an effective range of 1.5 km (0.93 miles) and the Block 1 version has a rate of fire of 4,500 rounds per minute. In 1993-95, Rolling Airframe Missile (RAM) systems were fitted to all ships in the class, one Mk 49 launcher being mounted above the bridge offset to port, the other on the starboard side at the aft end of the flight deck. Each launcher is provided with 21 RAM rounds, which have a range of 9.6 km (5.97 miles) and operate in concert with the Mk 23 D-band target acquisition radar (TAS).

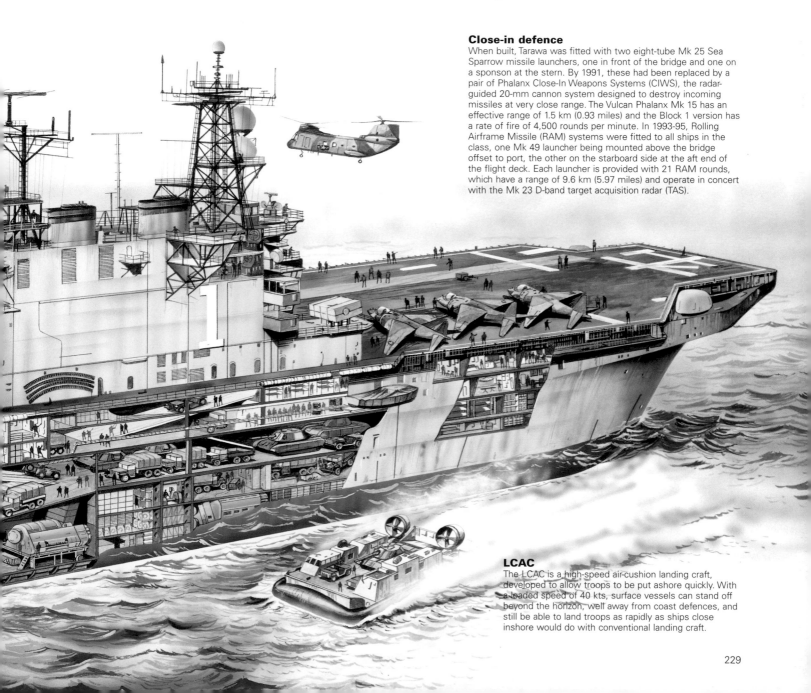

LCAC

The LCAC is a high-speed air-cushion landing craft, developed to allow troops to be put ashore quickly. With a loaded speed of 40 kts, surface vessels can stand off beyond the horizon, well away from coast defences, and still be able to land troops as rapidly as ships close inshore would do with conventional landing craft.

'Whidbey Island' and 'Harpers Ferry' class Landing ships

Based on the 'Anchorage' class, the **'Whidbey Island' class** were conceived as replacements for the 'Thomaston'-class LSDs. The first 'Whidbey Island' vessel was laid down in 1981. In 1988 the class was enlarged from 8 to 12 units, the last four forming a sub-class (the **'Harpers Ferry'-class LSD-CV**s or Landing Ship Dock-Cargo Variant ships) with an enhanced cargo capacity. The **LSD 41** (Landing Ship Dock-41) programme replaced the eight ageing LSD 28-class ships which reached the end of their service lives during the 1980s.

Enter the hovercraft

The 'Whidbey Island' class were designed from the outset to operate LCAC (Landing Craft Air Cushion) hovercraft. These carry a 60-ton payload and travel at speeds in excess of 40 kts in calm conditions, enabling amphibious assaults to be made over greater distances and against a wide variety of beaches. The well deck

measures 134.1 m (440 ft) by 15.2 m (50 ft). It can accommodate four hovercraft, which is more than any other amphibious assault vessel.

The most obvious visual differences between the sub-classes are that the LSD-CVs have only one crane and that the forward Phalanx CIWS is mounted atop the bridge on LSD 41-48 but below and forward of the superstructure on the 'Harpers Ferry' class.

Ship self defence

USS *Whidbey Island* trialled the QRCC (Quick Reaction Combat Capability) system from June 1993. The combination of RIM-116A missiles, Phalanx CIWS and AN/SLQ-32 EW system was accorded a higher priority after the Iraqi Exocet attack against the USS *Stark* on 17 May 1987. Now designated the SSDS (Ship Self Defense System) it has been installed on all 'Whidbey Island'-class ships.

The 'Whidbey Island'-class ships are intended to land a

As well as having generous freight space, the 'Whidbey Island'-class LSDs also feature a potent self defence weapons system. This is LSD 44, the USS Gunston Hill.

battalion of US Marines via four LCAC hovercraft, 21 LCMs (Landing Craft Medium) or three LCUs (Landing Craft Utilities). Alternatively, the troops can be landed in 64 AAV7A1 amphibious tracked armoured personnel carriers. The LSD-CV cargo variants deploy fewer landing craft: two hovercraft, nine LCMs or one

LCU. In addition to the anti-aircraft and anti-missile guns and missiles carried for active defence, extensive passive measures are available. A powerful ESM suite is complemented by chaff rockets capable of 'seducing' incoming missiles and AN/SLQ-49 chaff buoys that are effective for several hours in moderate sea conditions, producing a

radar signature greater than that of the ship. The Nixie decoy system has a similar effect on torpedoes.

The first two units cost over $300 million. The last four averaged $150 million per ship. 1996 figures quoted the annual operating cost of one of these vessels at around $20 million.

A 'Whidbey Island'-class LSD disgorges an LCAC hovercraft from the well deck at the rear of the vessel. Stores can be seen stacked on the helo deck, which is normally used by CH-53 helicopters.

SPECIFICATION	
'Whidbey Island' class **Displacement:** 15,726 tons full load (LSD 41-48); 16,740 tons (LSD 49-52) **Dimensions:** length 185.8 m (609 ft 6 in); beam 25.6 m (84 ft); draught 6.3 m (20 ft 6 in) **Propulsion:** four diesel engines delivering 24608 kW (33,000 shp) to two shafts **Speed:** 22 kts **Range:** 8,000 nm (14816 km; 9,206 miles) at 18 kts (33 km/h; 20 mph) **Complement:** 22 officers and 391 enlisted personnel **Troops:** 402 but surge capacity is 627 **Cargo:** 141.6 m³ (5,000 cu ft) available for general cargo plus 1161 m² (12,500 sq ft) for vehicles (including four pre-loaded	hovercraft in the well deck); LSD 49-52 have 1914 m³ (67,600 cu ft) space for cargo plus 1877 m² (20,200 sq ft) for motor transport but only two or three hovercraft **Armament:** two General Dynamics 20-mm six-barrelled Vulcan Phalanx Mk 15 guns; two 25-mm Mk 38 guns; eight or more 0.5-in (12.7-mm) machine-guns **Countermeasures:** four Loral Hycor SRBOC six-barrelled Mk 36 launchers, AN/SLQ-25 Nixie acoustic torpedo decoy, AN/SLQ-49 chaff buoys, AN/SLQ-32 radar warning/jammer/deception system **Electronics:** AN/SPS-67 surface search radar, AN/SPS-49 air search radar, AN/SPS-64 navigation radar **Aircraft:** two CH-53 Sea Stallions (platform only)

'Wasp' class Amphibious assault ship

The **'Wasp'-class** ships are the largest amphibious assault vessels in the world, providing the US Navy with an unrivalled ability to attack hostile shores around the world. They are the first ships specifically designed to operate both the AV-8B Harrier II and a complement of LCAC hovercraft. The last three of the class to be completed have cost an average of $750 million each. The US plans for a 12-strong ARG (Amphibious Ready Group) to be deployed by 2010, when the

first 'Tarawa'-class vessel will be 35-years-old.

The 'Wasp' class is a follow-on from the 'Tarawa' class and its ships share the same basic hull and engineering plant. However, the bridge is two decks lower than the LHAs (Landing Helicopter Amphibious) and the command, control and communications centres are inside the hull where they less easy to disable. To facilitate landing and recovery operations, the ships can ballast some 15,000 tons of sea water for trimming.

The USS Wasp (LHD 1) *alongside the underway replenishment (UNREP) vessel USNS* Supply *during a deployment in support of Operation Enduring Freedom.* Wasp's *airwing includes AV-8B and CH-53 aircraft.*

SPECIFICATION

'Wasp' class
Displacement: 41,150 tons
Dimensions: length 253.2 m (844 ft); beam 31.8 m (106 ft); draught 8.1 m (32 ft)
Propulsion: two geared steam turbines delivering 33849 kW (70,000 shp) to two shafts
Speed: 22 kts
Range: 9,500 nm (17594 km; 10,933 miles) at 18 kts (33 km/h; 20 mph)
Complement: 1,208 personnel
Troops: 1,894
Cargo: 2860 m³ (101,000 cu ft) for general stores plus 1858 m² (20,000 sq ft) for vehicles
Aircraft: number deployed depends on mission but can include AV-8B, AH-1W, CH-46, CH-53 and UH-1N
Armament: two Raytheon GMLS Mk 29 octuple SAM launchers for

Sea Sparrow semi-active radar homing missiles, two GDC Mk 49 RAM launchers for RIM-116A infra-red/radiation homing missiles, three General Dynamics 20-mm six-barrelled Vulcan Phalanx Mk 15 guns (only two on LHD 5-7), four 25-mm Mk 38 guns (three on LHD 5-7) and four 0.5-in (12.7-mm) machine-guns
Countermeasures: four or six Loral Hycor SRBOC 6-barrelled Mk 36 launchers, AN/SLQ-25 Nixie acoustic torpedo decoy, Sea Gnat missile decoy, AN/SLQ-49 chaff buoys, AN/SLQ-32 radar warning/jammer/deception system
Electronics: one AN/SPS-52 or AN/SPS-48 (later vessels) air search radar, one AN/SPS-49 air search radar, one SPS-67 surface search radar, navigation and fire control radars, AN/URN 25 TACAN

In addition to deploying a powerful air component, the 'Wasp'-class vessels can operate three LCAC hovercraft (pictured) or 12 LCM landing craft.

Capable of embarking a 2,000-strong MEU (Marine Expeditionary Unit), the 'Wasp' class can land its troops on the beach using its own landing craft, or deliver them inland via helicopters (a manoeuvre known as 'vertical envelopment'). Each 'Wasp' class can accommodate up to three LCACs or twelve LCMs in the 81 m x 15.2 m (267 x 50 ft) well deck. In total, 61 AAVs (Amphibious Assault Vehicles – the AAV7A1) can be shipped aboard, 40 stowed in the well deck and 21 in the upper vehicle storage area.

The flight deck has nine landing spots for helicopters and up to 42 CH-46 Sea Knights can be operated; the class can also deploy AH-1 SeaCobra attack helicopters or other transports such as the CH-53E Super Stallion, UH-1N Twin Huey or the multi-purpose SH-60B Seahawk. The 'Wasp' class can operate six to eight AV-8B Harrier IIs in the combat role, but can support up to 20. There are two aircraft elevators, one amidships on the port side, the other to starboard, abaft the 'island'. When the ships pass through the Panama Canal these lifts have to be folded inboard.

Air wing
The composition of the air group depends on the mission. The 'Wasp' class can function as aircraft carriers, operating 20 AV-8Bs in the sea control role, plus six ASW helicopters. For amphibious assault, a typical group consists of six AV-8Bs, four AH-1W attack helicopters, 12 CH-46 Sea Knights, nine CH-53 Sea Stallions or Super Stallions and four UH-1N Twin Hueys. Alternatively, it can also operate 42 CH-46s.

The 'Wasp'-class ships are designed to carry a balanced force of combat vehicles, including five M1 Abrams main battle tanks, 25 AAV7A1 armoured personnel carriers, eight M198 155-mm self-propelled guns, 68 lorries and a dozen or so other support vehicles. They can transport and land ashore all manner of equipment and vehicles. Monorail trains moving at up to 183 m (600 ft) per minute deliver cargo from the storage areas to the well deck, which opens to the sea through gates in the stern.

Each ship also features a 600-bed hospital with six operating theatres, so reducing an amphibious task force's dependence on medical facilities ashore.

The 'Wasp' class has been replacing the older LHAs since the mid-1990s. USS *Bataan* was built by pre-outfitting and modular construction techniques. Subassemblies were brought together to produce five hull and superstructure modules. These modules were then joined together on land. The result of this construction technique was that the ship was three-quarters complete on launch. *Bataan* is the first amphibious assault ship designed from the outset to accommodate female personnel, both in the crew and Marine contingent. Full accommodation for up to 450 female officers, enlisted personnel and troops is provided on the vessel.

'San Antonio' class Amphibious transport docks

The 12 ships of the **LPD 17** or **'San Antonio' (Landing Platform Dock) class** will eventually replace three classes of amphibious assault vessel: LPD 4s, LSD 36s and LSTs, as well as the LKA (already retired in 2002) – a total of 41 vessels in all. This will not only modernise an increasingly elderly amphibious assault fleet but deliver significant savings in life-cycle costs and personnel numbers. However, costs of the first three vessels are substantially over-budget: the LPD 17 class will cost more than $800 million against an estimate of $617 million. This is despite numerous cost-saving measures including the decision to adopt a commercial surface search radar

(AN/SPS-73). The design process exploited virtual reality computer programmes, enabling many internal layouts to be tested without prototypes being built. Input from over 2,500 serving personnel is intended to produce a vessel truly designed for the men and women who will live onboard.

Mobility triad
Approved in 1993, construction of the LPD 17 was delayed by legal disputes over the award of contracts but the first of the class, **San Antonio**, is due to join the fleet by 2003.

The US Marine Corps has developed the concept of the 'mobility triad' and the LPD 17 class is the first assault ship designed from the outset to accommodate all three modes of transport: the MV-22 Osprey tiltrotor aircraft, the LCAC hovercraft and the AAV amphibious APC. It is thus capable of landing troops some 173 nm (320 km; 200 miles) inland, making 'littoral operations' far greater in scope than ever previously imagined. Two LCAC hovercraft or one LCU are embarked along with 14 AAVs. The well deck and stern layout are similar to that of the 'Wasp' class but the superstructure is angled to reduce radar signature. A 24-bed hospital is included with two operating theatres and a casualty overflow capacity of 100 persons. Defensive weapons systems will include the SSDS which will be fitted as construction of the vessels is completed.

The LPD 17 class ships deploy up to four CH-46 Sea Knight helicopters simultaneously or two MV-22 Ospreys. Four MV-22s can be spotted on deck and one more in the hanger. Alternatively the hanger can accommodate one CH-53E, two CH-46s or two UH-1s. With double the vehicle storage space of the old LPD 4 class, the LPD 17 class is also designed for maximum survivability, the combination of reduced radar profile and advanced computer systems to coordinate defensive weaponry is intended to allow the ship to operate alone if required, although it would normally be part of an amphibious ready group. *San Antonio* is the first US warship to be equipped with a fibre-optic Shipboard Wide Area Network (SWAN) that connects all ship systems, sensors and weapons, providing integrated real-time data to its combat command centre.

On 7 September 2002, about one year after the attack on the World Trade Center, Secretary of the Navy, Gordon England, announced that the fifth ship of the class would be named *New York*.

The LPD 17-class vessels have been designed with low-observable characteristics. An MV-22 Osprey can be seen on the flight deck in this artist's impression.

SPECIFICATION

San Antonio class
Displacement: 25,300 tons full load
Dimensions: length 208.4 m (684 ft); beam 31.9 m (105 ft), draught 7 m (23 ft)
Propulsion: four diesels delivering 29828 kW (40,000 shp) to two shafts
Speed: 22 kts
Range: unknown
Complement: 32 officers and 465 enlisted personnel
Troops: 699 (surge capacity 800)
Cargo: 708 m³ (25,000 cu ft) cargo space below decks plus 2323 m² (25,000 sq ft) deck space for vehicles
Armament: Mk 41 VLS (Vertical Launch System) for two octuple

Sea Sparrow systems and 64 missiles, two GDC Mk 31 RAM launchers, two Bushmaster Mk 46 30-mm close-in guns, two Mk 26 0.5-in (12.7-mm) machine guns
Countermeasures: four Mk 36 SRBOC launchers, Nulka rocket-launched hovering decoy system, AN/SLQ-25 Nixie acoustic homing torpedo decoy, AN/SLQ-32A radar warning/jamming/deception system
Electronics: AN/SPS-48 air-search radar, AN/SPS-73 surface-search radar, AN/SPQ-9 fire-control radar, navigation radars and sonar
Aircraft: two CH-53 Sea Stallions/Super Stallions or four CH-46 Sea Knights or two MV-22 Ospreys or four UH-1N Twin Hueys

'Mistral' class Amphibious assault ship

Ordered from the Brest yard of the state-owned Direction des Construction Navales, in conjunction with the commercial yard Chantiers de l'Atlantique, late in 2000 for completion in 2004-05 and 2005-06 respectively, the *Mistral* and *Tonnere* of the new **'Mistral' class** are amphibious assault ships classified by the French navy as NTCD (*Nouvelles Transports de Chalands de Debarquement*). The two ships are to serve as pre-positioned command platforms and landing docks within the context of national and multi-national amphibious operations, and will also be able to undertake non-combatant evacuation and humanitarian relief.

The two 'Mistral'-class ships are successors to the *Ouragan* and *Orage* which entered service in 1965 and 1968 respectively, and as such to complement the *Foudre* and *Siroco* that entered service in 1990 and 1998 respectively.

To keep cost under control, the ships were laid down in 2002 and 2002 for construction to civil rather than naval standards, the forward sections and accommodation modules being built at St Nazaire by Chantiers de l'Atlantique, and the middle and aft sections (operations and payload) by DCN, which will combine its own sections with those delivered from St Nazaire. The ships will be outfitted as flagships for joint task force operations, and will include satellite communications as well as national and NATO data-link systems, the object being close co-operation with British, Dutch, Italian and Spanish vessels.

The 'Mistral'-class design is of the 'through-deck' type with two lifts (one astern and the other abaft the island) connecting the hangar deck with the flight deck, which will have spots for six helicopters. The stern dock will be compatible with US LCAC (air-cushion landing craft) as well as a new class of LCM (Landing Craft Mechanised).

Each of the ships will have a complete 63-bed hospital, and will have provision for further facilities erected from containerised field hospital units.

Due to replace the two 'Ouragan'-class LSDs (landing ships dock) from 2005 and 2006, the pair of 'Mistral'-class LHDs (landing ships helicopter and dock) will transform the French navy's amphibious capabilities.

SPECIFICATION

'Mistral' class
Displacement: 20,670 tons full load
Dimensions: length 199 m (652 ft 11 in); beam 32 m (105 ft); draught 8 m (26 ft 3 in)
Propulsion: four diesel generators delivering 15210 kW (20,400 hp) to two podded propulsor units trainable though 360° and to one bow thruster
Performance: speed 19 kts; endurance 20400 km (12,675 miles) at 15 kts

Armament: two sextuple launchers for Mistral short-range SAMs, two 30-mm cannon and four 0.5-in (12.7-mm) machine-guns
Electronics: one MRR 3D air/surface search radar, two Racal navigation radars, two optronic directors, and one SIC 21 command support system
Aircraft: up to 16 NH 90 or Cougar helicopters
Lift: 450 troops and 60 AFVs or 230 vehicles
Complement: 160

'Endurance' class Landing platform dock/landing ship tank

In the early 1990s the Republic of Singapore decided to press ahead with the creation of a modern amphibious assault capability, and in September 1994 ordered from the Banoi yard of Singapore Technologies Marine four **'Endurance'-class** vessels named **Endurance, Resolution, Persistence** and **Endeavour**. Laid down in 1997-98 and launched in 1998-2000 for completion between March 2000 and April 2001, these four units are combined LPD (landing platform dock) and LST (tank landing ship) vessels. Based at Changi, the ships constitute the Singapore navy's 191st Squadron.

The design is of a US roll-on/roll-off (drive-through) type with stern and bow ramps, the former a virtually full-width unit and the latter installed behind opening bow sec-

The lead unit of a four-ship class, the **Endurance** *is a comparatively small but nonetheless capable* **LPD/LST** *type, and well suited to short- and medium-range operations in Far Eastern waters.*

tions. Internally there is a single intermediate deck with vehicle movement between decks made possible by three hydraulic ramps.

The docking well is located in the after part of the design with the large helicopter deck above it. The docking well can accommodate four LCUs (Landing Craft Utility), and further ship-to-shore movement is facilitated by the carriage in davits on four LCVPs (Landing Craft Vehicle and Personnel). The design has hangar accommodation, immediately forward of the helicopter deck, for two Super Puma medium-lift helicopters. On

Evident in any view from astern of an 'Endurance'-class LPD/LST is the large rear ramp that closes over the docking well below the helicopter operating deck.

each side of the helicopter hangar door is a 25-ton capacity crane.

Self protection is entrusted to a pair of twin launchers for Mistral short-range SAMs (one launcher on each beam above and between the LCVP davits), and one 76.2-mm (3-in) Otobreda Super Compact gun forward of the bridge. The IAI Barak vertical-launch SAM system may be retrofitted in due course.

A striking feature of the 'Endurance' class, here epitomised by the Resolution, is the hull's great freeboard.

'Ocean' class Landing platform helicopter

The result of a programme launched in 1987 and then allowed to lapse until 1993, when an order was placed with Vickers Shipbuilding of Barrow-in-Furness as prime contractor to complete a hull built by Kvaerner at Govan on the River Clyde, HMS *Ocean* is an LPH (Landing Platform Helicopter). The ship was laid down in May 1994, launched in October 1995, sailed to Barrow under her own power in November 1996, and was commissioned in September 1998.

Providing the Royal Navy with a modern helicopter lift and assault capability, the *Ocean* is based on the design of the 'Invincible'-class light carrier with a

completely revised superstructure and propulsion. As such, the ship can embark, support and operate a squadron of helicopters (assault transport or attack) and a complete Royal Marine commando with all its vehicles, weapons, ammunition and other equipment. The ship is also large enough to carry up to 20 BAE Systems Harrier STOVL warplanes, but does not embark the stores and other equipment necessary to support these fixed-wing warplanes.

The helicopter deck is large and strong enough to support six Boeing Chinook twin-rotor helicopters, and is marked with six landing and parking spots. The twin

20-mm cannon mountings, designed for last-ditch defence against aircraft and small craft, are often not shipped, and may be replaced by single 20-mm cannon.

Right: HMS Ocean is based on a modified version of the design for the 'Invincible'-class carrier but, of course, has no need for the carrier's 'ski-jump' bow.

Below: HMS Ocean's ability to defend itself against anti-ship missiles is vested primarily in the Phalanx CIWS mountings installed over the bow and on each quarter.

Eurocopter AS 565 Panther Multi-role utility helicopter

The SA 360 Dauphin single-engined helicopter was developed into the twin-engined **Aérospatiale SA 365C Dauphin 2** that first flew in prototype form on 24 January 1975.

Following on its development of the SA 361H military prototype of SA 360, Aérospatiale produced a dedicated military version of the SA 365. The first step in this direction was the **AS 365M** prototype that first flew on 29 February 1984 with the ability to carry up to 12 troops or an armament of up to eight HOT anti-tank missiles or 44 68-mm (2.68-in) SNEB air-to-surface unguided rockets. Further development resulted in the April 1986 appearance of the **AS 365K** prototype, which was named **Panther**.

Panther variants

The name was retained for the subsequent military developments, which are now listed in the **Eurocopter AS 565** series. Other features of the Panther include greater use of composite materials, a longer fuselage fitted with armoured seats, cable-cutters for safer low-altitude flying, a strengthened cabin floor and landing gear, sliding rather than hinged doors, crash-resistant fuel tanks, IR-reducing exhausts, and the use of composite materials and special paints to reduce electromagnetic and thermal signatures.

The Panther has been offered in two basic forms for the land warfare and naval roles. The land-warfare form has been offered in three subvariants as the **AS 565AA** (from 1997 **AS 565AB**) armed model, the **AS 565CA** anti-tank model and the **AS 565UA** (from 1997 **AS 565UB**) unarmed utility model. The AS 565AA/AB has two lateral outriggers, each carrying a single hardpoint for the

carriage of two multiple launchers for air-to-surface unguided rockets, or two NC 20M621 pods, each carrying one 20-mm GIAT M621 cannon with 180 rounds, or four two-round

This HM-1 demonstrates the efficiency of the air intake filters protecting its Arriel engines during operations from a rough landing site.

packs of MATRA Mistral short-range AAMs. The AS 565CA carries two four-tube launchers for HOT ATMs aimed via a Viviane day/night sight. The AS 565UA is designed to carry eight or 10 assault troops, or alternatively freight in the form of an internal or slung payload. The only operator of the AS 565K series is Brazil, with 36 AS 565AAs operated under the local designation **HM-1**. The **AS 565 Panther 800**, first flown in June 1992, is a derivative of the AS 565 powered by two 986-kW (1,322-shp) LHTEC T800-LHT-800 turboshaft engines, and with an IBM suite of integrated avionics.

Although Eurocopter continues to market the Panther as a land-based military helicopter, few orders have been forthcoming. A Brazilian HM-1 is illustrated.

This Panther was photographed during trials of the Euromissile ATGW-3LR Trigat anti-tank missile. As well as the four-round Trigat launcher, the helicopter also mounts a mast-mounted sight.

Eurocopter AS 532 and EC 725 Cougar Medium helicopter

Logically, if unimaginatively, known as the **Super Puma** when first proposed in 1974, the **Aérospatiale AS 332** was devised as a successor to the SA 330 Puma. Retaining the Puma's overall appearance, but profiting from the introduction of more advanced features made possible by developments in glassfibre rotor technology, the Super Puma is most readily identifiable by its prominent ventral fin and nose radome. Aimed primarily at the civil market, the helicopter nevertheless incorporates features of value to military operators, including a gearbox operable for one hour without lubricant and rotors which remain safe for 40 hours after hits by 12.7-mm (0.5-in) small-arms fire.

Super Puma

First flown on 13 September 1978 with Makila engines, multi-purpose air inlets, a lightweight Starflex rotor head, uprated transmission, thermally de-iced main rotor blades, and wider-track main landing-gear units with single wheels, the Super Puma entered service in 1981 as the military **AS 332B** and civilian AS 332C. Both these initial variants retained the Puma's cabin, with accommodation for 12-15 fully-equipped troops. During the following year delivery began of the 'stretched' civil AS 332L and military **AS 332M**, with their fuselages lengthened by 0.76 m (2 ft 6 in).

In January 1990, the military variants were renamed **Cougar** (later **Cougar Mk I**), renumbered **AS 532** and accorded new variant suffixes: the **AS 532AC** and **AS 532UC** were the armed and unarmed short-fuselage helicopters, the **AS 532AL** and **AS 532UL** were the armed and unarmed long-fuselage helicopters, the **AS 532MC** was the unarmed naval SAR and surveillance helicopter, and the **AS 532SC** was the armed naval ASW/AShW helicopter. Both maritime models had previously been known by the designation **AS 332F**, there being no long-fuselage maritime model. Later examples of the Cougar Mk I have 1400-kW (1,877-shp) Makila 1A1 engines.

Cougar Mk II

On 6 February 1987 the development prototype of the **Cougar Mk II**, known in its civil form as the **AS 332L2 Super Puma Mk II**, made its first flight with the powerplant of two 1569-kW (2,104-shp) Makila 1A2 engines, Spheriflex main and tail rotor heads with elastomeric bearings, longer main rotor blades, larger lateral sponsons carrying additional fuel, life rafts, etc., and a further 'stretch' of the fuselage to provide accommodation for 28 passengers. The Mk II version of the Super Puma and Cougar entered service in 1992 and was to have been used as the platform for French army aviation's HORI-

ZON (Hélicoptère d'Observation Radar et d'Investigation sur ZONe) battlefield surveillance radar in the late 1990s. However, the combination of the Orchidée radar system and the Cougar Mk II proved prohibitively expensive and the combination was abandoned in 1990, only to be resurrected for the 1991 Gulf War. The experience gained from 24 missions with an SA 330-mounted Orphée radar led to the HORIZON concept being resurrected. Eurocopter received a development contract in October 1992 for two aircraft, combining the capabilities of Orchidée with the endurance of the AS 532UL. The first of four such **AS 532UL Cougar Horizon** helicopters was delivered in

At least four AS 532A2 Cougar MK II helicopters have been ordered by l'Armée de l'Air for use in the CSAR and special ops roles. The CSAR aircraft are named Cougar RESCO (Recherche et Sauvetage en Combat) in service and up to 14 are required.

April 1994. The French army has also replaced some of its original AS 330s with AS 532s, the first 22 aircraft being delivered to the Force d'Action Rapide by the end of 1991. In addition, in November 2002, the French air force ordered ten of the re-engined **EC 725 Cougar** for special ops/CSAR work. Due for certification in 2003, the EC 725 also features advanced avionics.

Weapons

While armament options for the army Cougar are restricted to gun and rocket pods, the naval AS 532SC

has provision for a pair of AM.39 Exocet AShMs or homing torpedoes. Operation from ship platforms is also possible, using hauldown gear to permit flying in rough seas. Large sponsons with inflatable floats are standard naval equipment, and are optional on other models. IPTN (Eurocopter) in Indonesia produces the AS 332C and AS 332L as the **NAS-332**. Other foreign service designations include Brazil (**CH-34**), Spain (**HD.21** for SAR and **HT.21** for VIP transport) and Sweden (**HKP 10**).

SPECIFICATION

Eurocopter France AS 532UC Cougar Mk I

Type: two/three-crew general-purpose tactical medium helicopter

Powerplant: two Turboméca Makila 1A1 turboshaft engines each rated at 1400 kW (1,877 shp)

Performance: maximum cruising speed 262 km/h (163 mph) at sea level; initial climb rate 420 m (1,378 ft) per minute; service ceiling 4100 m (13,450 ft); hovering ceiling 2700 m (8,860 ft) in ground effect and 1600 m (5,250 ft) out of ground

effect; range 618 km (384 miles) with standard fuel

Weights: empty 4330 kg (9,546 lb); maximum take-off 9350 kg (20,615 lb)

Dimensions: main rotor diameter 15.6 m (51 ft 2¼ in); length 18.7 m (61 ft 4¼ in) with the rotors turning; height 4.92 m (16 ft 1¾ in); main rotor disc area 191.13 m² (2,057.42 sq ft)

Payload: up to 21 troops or 4500 kg (9,921 lb) of freight carried as an internal or external load

Above: Along with UH-1s, AB 212s and Chinooks, Spanish Army Aviation operates AS 532 Super Pumas/Cougars in the crucial battlefield mobility role.

Left: The Icelandic Coast Guard operates a single AS 332L2 Super Puma from Reykjavik airport for search and rescue (SAR), air ambulance and fisheries patrol work.

EH Industries EH 101 Heavy multi-role assault helicopter

In the late 1970s, a forward-looking requirement for a new NATO naval helicopter to replace the Sea King was identified. A joint venture company formed by Agusta and Westland, as EH Industries, was formed to develop the new machine, which in the event emerged as the **EH 101**, in both a naval helicopter and an assault machine against an Italian requirement. This latter aircraft featured a rear loading ramp, this and other features making the helicopter sufficiently attractive to win a 1995 RAF order for a Wessex replacement.

RAF Merlin

Of the nine prototype aircraft, PP7 and PP9 were both built with ramps as military prototypes by Agusta.

The RAF settled on a need for 22 **Merlin HC.Mk 3** aircraft, with comprehensive mission equipment making them suitable for assault, CSAR, general transport and special forces infil/exfil work. Standard Merlin HC.Mk 3 equipment includes a FLIR system, an integrated defensive aids suite (consisting of laser-warning, radar-warning and IR decoy systems) and a rescue winch. An inflight-refuelling (IFR) probe can also be fitted, on the lower nose, offset to starboard. The first HC.Mk 3 completed its maiden flight on

No. 28 Sqn RAF is the world's only operator of the assault Merlin. However, the type seems well placed to fill the JASDF's requirement for a new CSAR helicopter to replace the H-60.

24 December 1998, with the first operational aircraft being received on 27 June 2000 and the helicopter's first operating unit, No. 28 Sqn, re-forming on the aircraft on 17 July 2001.

The introduction of the Merlin HC.Mk 3 into service has been a relatively slow process, but in the spring of 2003 No. 28 Sqn made its first operational deployment with the type, in support of UN operations in the Balkans region.

Above: Low-level operations in difficult terrain are the Merlin HC.Mk 3's forte. The last of the RAF's aircraft was completed in mid-2002.

SPECIFICATION

EH Industries Merlin HC.Mk 3
Type: heavy assault and transport helicopter
Powerplant: three Rolls-Royce/Turboméca RTM 322 turboshaft engines each rated at a maximum of 1724 kW (2,312 shp)
Performance: cruising speed 278 km (173 mph) at optimum altitude; endurance 5 hours
Weights: operating empty 10250 kg (22,597 lb); maximum take-off 14600 kg (32,188 lb)
Dimensions: main rotor diameter 18.59 m (61 ft); length 22.81 m (74 ft 10 in) with the rotors turning; height 6.65 m (21 ft 10 in) with the rotors turning; main rotor disc area 271.51 m² (2,922.5 sq ft)
Payload: up to 24 combat-equipped troops or 3120 kg (6,878 lb) of freight

EH 101 is also in consideration for a US order to replace the presidential VH-3D. Note that RAF Merlins do not have their IFR probes fitted.

NH Industries NH 90 Medium assault helicopter

In 1985 five European nations signed a memorandum of understanding covering a 'NATO helicopter for the '90s', or **NH 90**. The UK dropped out of the programme in 1987, leaving France, Germany, Italy and the Netherlands in the project by means of NH Industries, established in France during August 1992 to control a collaborative programme involving Eurocopter France (41.6 per cent with NFT [Norway] as a risk-sharing partner from 1994), Agusta (28.2 per cent), Eurocopter Deutschland (23.7 per cent) and Fokker (6.5 per cent).

Stated requirements were 220 helicopters for France, 214 for Italy, 272 for Germany and 20 for the Netherlands, and it was anticipated that a first flight in 1995 would pave the way for deliveries from 1999. The two initial versions are the NH 90 NFH (NATO Frigate Helicopter) and the **NH 90 TTH (Tactical Transport Helicopter)** for assault transport, rescue, electronic warfare and VIP transport duties. The TTH variant is being developed under Eurocopter Deutschland leadership, with a cabin for 20 troops or one 2000-kg (4,409-lb) vehicle. It can carry area-suppression and self-defence weapons. A FLIR is standard to provide a night and adverse-weather nap-of-the-Earth flight capability, and both models are controlled via a quadruplex fly-by-wire control system.

Export success

Two engine types are available to increase the NH 90's export potential. The first of five flying and one ground-test prototypes was the French-built PT1 that first flew on 18 December 1995 with RTM 322 engines.

By the autumn of 2003, NH Industries had received initial orders for 60 TTH helicopters from Italy for its army, plus 10 for its navy; 50 for the German army and 30 for the Luftwaffe (of which as many as 23 may

be used for CSAR). In addition, Portugal has committed to 10 TTH aircraft; Sweden to 13 specially-equipped dual-role assault/SAR **TTT/SAR** aircraft for delivery from

2005-2009; and Finland to 20 TTH helicopters for assault and SAR and for delivery in the period 2004-2008. On 29 August 2003, Greece ordered 16 TTHs and four TTH special forces

helicopters for its army, with another 12 TTH and two special ops aircraft on option. If the options are

taken up, deliveries should commence in 2005 and be completed in 2010.

NH 90 has suffered a somewhat protracted development period, but in the autumn of 2003 was approaching operational service. A prototype machine is shown here.

Some of the nations to have committed to TTH will also fly their aircraft on SAR duties. Germany and Greece intend to use some aircraft for CSAR and special ops work, respectively.

SPECIFICATION	
NH Industries NH 90 TTH	30 minutes
Type: two-crew medium tactical transport helicopter	**Weights:** empty 5400 kg (11,905 lb); maximum take-off 10000 kg (22,046 lb)
Powerplant: two RTM 322-01/9 turboshaft engines each rated at 1566 kW (2,100 shp) or two General Electric/Alfa Romeo T700-T6E turboshaft engines each rated at 1521 kW (2,040 shp)	**Dimensions:** main rotor diameter 16.3 m (53 ft 5½ in); length 19.56 m (64 ft 2 in) with the rotors turning; height 5.44 m (17 ft 10 in) with the rotors turning; main rotor disc area 208.67 m² (2,246.18 sq ft)
Performance: (estimated) maximum speed 300 km/h (186 mph); endurance 4 hours	**Payload:** up to 20 equipped troops or 4600 kg (10,141 lb) of freight

Left: NH90 has been performing better in terms of sales when compared to Europe's other modern assault helicopter, the EH 101, but it is a lighter, less capable and therefore cheaper machine.

Atlas Oryx/IAR 330L Puma Foreign Puma developments

South Africa was a major customer for the French-built Aérospatiale Puma and began to add improvements and upgrades to the aircraft early in its career. Atlas soon built considerable experience and expertise with the type, and in order to circumvent UN sanctions, manufactured frequently required items such as tyres, transparencies, acrylic floor panels, gearboxes, engine hot sections, and rotor blades. It also manufactured newly-designed components optimised for SAAF use, including fuel tanks and armoured seats.

XTP-1 Beta

The first major upgrade programme resulted in the **XTP-1 Beta**, which featured extended engine intake filters, denoting installation of the Super Puma's Makila turboshafts, and a tail unit similar to that fitted to the AS 532 Cougar. These modifications were later

disclosed to be intended for retrofit across the Puma fleet, whereas the other modifications, which gave the aircraft its XTP- (**Experimental Test Platform**) designation, were not. These modifications included a long air data probe projecting from the port side of the cockpit, and stub wings mounted on the cabin sides, which apparently required the cabin doors to be 'sealed shut'. The wings each carried two articulated weapons pylons and a 20-mm GA1 cannon was installed in a ventral turret and was aimed by helmet-mounted sight.

Originally the XTP-1 was expected to form the basis of a gunship conversion of the Puma, but in fact it was a systems and weapons testbed, marking a further step towards the indigenous Rooivalk. The aircraft was later used as the basis of a low-cost alternative to the Rooivalk, and several stub-

winged, cannon-armed Pumas entered operational evaluation during mid-1990. These had wingtip launch rails for the IR-homing Darter or Viper AAM, and a laser designator for the Swift anti-tank missile. Atlas offered offered various gunship configurations, but none seems to have entered regular service.

Oryx

The XTP-1's tail and engine modifications, together with a new Super Puma-style nose radome, formed the basis of the **Oryx**, originally known as **Gemsbok**, upgrade. The Oryx cockpit is also configured for single pilot operations. Pumas converted to this standard were delivered from 1988, entering full service in 1994. Some confusion exists concerning their exact status and some sources suggest that Atlas, later Denel, built most, if not all, of the aircraft from new.

Romanian production

Under licence agreements with Aérospatiale, IAR in Romania established a production line for the SA 330L Puma in 1977. Exports have reportedly included some for the SAAF, but the majority of IAR production was for the Romanian air force, and included an armed variant

The licence-built IAR 330 is the mainstay of the Romanian air force's rotary-wing fleet. Note that this aircraft is fitted with the larger sponsons.

developed locally. This carries two 20-mm cannon cheek pods on the lower front fuselage sides and with steel tube mountings on each side of the main cabin (behind the entry doors) capable of carrying four rocket pods and AT-3 'Sagger' anti-armour missiles. Alternatively, machine-gun pods or bombs can be carried. In addition, pintle mountings are fitted for one machine-gun in each cabin doorway.

The **IAR 330L Puma** is powered by Turbomecanica (Romania) Turmo IVC turboshafts of 1175 kW (1,575 shp) each, but IAR has also produced the **Puma**

2000, featuring more powerful engines and a range of advanced equipment as standard or optional fit. The standard Puma 2000 has hands on collective and stick (HOCAS) controls, helmet-mounted sights, EFIS and MIL STD 1553 technology. The aircraft has an NVG compatible cockpit. Options include TV/FLIR for the surveillance role, a laser designator for target acquisition and a wide range of weapons for anti-armour or infantry fire support missions. Israel's Ellbit is the primary avionics contractor and the aircraft has been entered Romanian service as the **IAR/Elbit IAR 330 SOCAT**.

SPECIFICATION	
Atlas Oryx	**Dimensions:** main rotor diameter
Type: twin-engined medium-assault helicopter	15 m (149 ft 2½ in); length overall rotors turning 18.15 m (59 ft 6½ in)
Powerplant: two Turboméca Makila 1A1 each rated at 1400 kW (1,877 shp) for take-off and 1184 kW (1,588 shp) for continuous running	and fuselage 14.06 m (46 ft 1½ in); height overall 5.14 m (16 ft 10½ in) and to top of rotor head 4.38 m (14 ft 4½ in); main rotor disc area 176.71 m² (1,902.2 sq ft)

Mil Mi-26 'Halo' Heavylift helicopter

The **Mi-26 'Halo'** was designed as a replacement for Mil's Mi-6 but was intended to offer between 50 and 100 per cent greater capability. The type was initially schemed under the designation **Mi-6M** with a hold broadly equivalent to that of the C-130 Hercules, the Mi-26 being the world's most powerful helicopter. The first of several prototype and pre-production helicopters made the type's maiden flight on 14 December 1977, and squadron-strength military evaluation began in 1983, with full service entry following in 1985.

The helicopter's powerplant comprises two D-136

turboshaft engines, which are more than twice as powerful as the engines installed in the Mi-6, and the combination of its high power and advanced eight-bladed main rotor allows the Mi-26 to lift almost twice the payload of the Mi-6.

In addition to its crew of four and provision on the flightdeck for an optional fifth person, the Mi-26 can carry four passengers in a compartment to the rear of the flightdeck and also up to 80 fully equipped troops or 60 litters plus four or five attendants in the hold, to which passenger access is provided by one starboard-side and two port-side

airstair doors. The hold can also be used for the accommodation of freight, loaded and unloaded by means of the power-operated rear ramp/door, which comprises a bottom-hinged lower ramp and two side-hinged upper clamshell doors.

Standard form

In overall configuration the helicopter is basically standard, with a pod-and-boom fuselage, fixed tricycle landing gear with twin wheels on each unit, and a dynamic system based on the side-by-side pair of turboshaft engines driving eight-bladed main and five-bladed tail rotors each based on tita-

nium heads carrying the rotor blades. The Mi-26's equipment includes an integrated flight and navigation system, weather radar and, on the military variants, provision for IR jammers and suppressors, and IR decoy dispensers.

The basic version is the **Mi-26**, which is the standard military transport model. By the end of the 20th century some 300 aircraft of the 'Halo' family had been deliv-

ered, with production continuing at a low rate, and included in this total are a number of other variants. The **Mi-26A** is an improved transport with the PNK-90 integrated flight and navigation system allowing automatic approach and descent to a critical decision point. The **Mi-26T** is the basic civil transport generally similar to the Mi-26, but also available as the **Mi-26TS** certificated to Western stan-

SPECIFICATION	
Mil Mi-26 'Halo-A'	with standard fuel
Type: four/five-crew heavy transport helicopter	**Weights:** empty 28200 kg (62,170 lb); maximum take-off 56000 kg (123,457 lb)
Powerplant: two ZMDB 'Progress' (Lotarev) D-136 turboshaft engines each rated at 8500 kW (11,240 shp)	**Dimensions:** main rotor diameter 32 m (105 ft 9 in); length 40.03 m (131 ft 3¾ in) with the rotors turning; height overall 8.15 m (26 ft 8¼ in) to top of rotor head; main rotor disc area 804.25 m² (8,657.13 sq ft)
Performance: maximum level speed at optimum altitude 295 km/h (183 mph); normal cruising speed at optimum altitude 255 km/h (158 mph); service ceiling 4600 m (15,090 ft); hovering ceiling 1800 m (5,905 ft) out of ground effect; range 800 km (497 miles)	**Payload:** up to 20000 kg (44,092 lb) of freight carried internally or externally

The hold of the Mi-26 is 12.00 m (39 ft 4¼ in) long with the ramp raised, increasing to 15.00 m (49 ft 2½ in) with the ramp lowered. The Indian air force had around 15 of these giant helicopters in service during 2003.

dards. Further variants include the **Mi-26MS** aeromedical variant outfitted as a high-quality flying hospital including an operating theatre and the **Mi-26NEF-M**, the ASW helicopter with search radar in a faired radome under the nose and a MAD system

whose towed sensor can be streamed from the ramp. The **Mi-26P** is a more comfortable passenger transport. The **Mi-26PK** is the flying crane model with an external operator's gondola on the side of the fuselage. The **Mi-26PP** is apparently a radio relay version. The

Mi-26TM is the alternative flying crane model with a shallower operator's gondola under the fuselage or under the rear loading ramp. The **Mi-26TP** is a firefighting model. The **Mi-26TZ** is the tanker model with the ability to deliver 14050 litres (3,088 Imp gal) of fuel and

1040 litres (228 Imp gal) of lubricant discharged by means of four hoses. The **Mi-26M** is an upgraded version of the basic transport under development with a number of improvements including 10700-kW (14,350-shp) D-127s driving improved rotors with blades

of all-glassfibre construction. Finally, the **Mi-27** is thought to be an airborne command post development.

The Mi-26 has been sold to operators in some 20 countries, but the only military users outside the CIS are India, Mexico and Peru.

Westland Commando and Sea King HC.Mk 4
Sea King assault versions

A land-based transport version of the Sea King was first projected in 1972, and it was soon named **Commando**. Egypt placed the first order for the type, which emerged in **Commando Mk 1** form as something of an interim type. It was, in reality, not a Commando as such, but a basic troop-carrying version of the initial Sea King HAS.Mk 1, with increased fuel capacity. The first Commando flew initially on 12 September 1973, and the aircraft were delivered from 29 January 1974.

Commando Mk 2

With strongest Commando sales prospects in the Middle and Far East, it became clear that the helicopter's performance would have to be maximised to cope with 'hot-and-high' conditions. Accordingly, Westland combined the airframe of the Commando

with the H.1400-1 engines and six-bladed tail rotor of the Sea King HAS.Mk 2 to produce the **Commando Mk 2**. Weight was saved by fitting non-folding main rotor blades and a simplified fixed undercarriage, and by removing the sponsons. Removal of the sponsons also improved the aircraft's ability to carry weapons, by clearing the stub wing and providing an optional wingtip hardpoint outboard of the undercarriage. The new version retained the stretched cabin and increased-capacity fuel tankage. The first Commando Mk 2 first flew on 16 January 1975 and was bought by Egypt.

Qatar placed an order for three **Commando Mk 2A** helicopters in 1974, these being generally identical to the Egyptian machines. Two more aircraft were delivered to Egypt specially fitted out for the VIP transport role. These have an extra pair of

cabin windows on the starboard side and a single additional window to port and are designated as **Commando Mk 2B** aircraft. Qatar also ordered a VIP version, designated as the **Commando Mk 2C** and little different to the Mk 2B.

The **Commando Mk 2E** is a somewhat different machine, being a dedicated autonomous EW platform, equipped with the Italian Selenia/Elettronica IHS-6 integrated ESM/ECM system. Four were built for Egypt following a 1978 order. The first Mk 2E made its maiden flight on 1 September 1978.

Commando Mk 3

Despite their Commando designation, the final Qatari aircraft are externally almost indistinguishable from Sea Kings, since they have undercarriage sponsons and a dorsal radome, as well as a folding tail rotor pylon. Like

The Sea King HC.Mk 4 has seen the most action among Royal Navy Sea King variants and NAVSTAR GPS was added for Operation Granby, along with various defences. Door guns are routinely fitted.

SPECIFICATION	
Westland Commando Mk 2 **Type:** twin-engined medium-assault helicopter **Powerplant:** two Rolls-Royce Gnome H.1400-1T turboshaft engines each rated at 1238 kW (1,660 shp) for take-off and 1092 kW (1,465 shp) for continuous running **Performance:** never exceed speed 226 km/h (140 mph) at sea level; maximum climb rate 619 m (2,030 ft) per minute at sea level; range 396 km (246 miles) with	maximum payload **Weights:** operating empty 5620 kg (12,390 lb); maximum take-off 9752 kg (21,500 lb) **Dimensions:** main rotor diameter 18.9 m (62 ft); length overall, rotors turning 22.15 m (72 ft 8 in); height overall 5.13 m (16 ft 10 in) with rotors turning; main rotor disc area 280.47 m² (3,019.07 sq ft) **Payload:** 28 fully equipped troops, or up to 3629 kg (8,000 lb) of freight

the Commando 2 series, the aircraft retains a single extra window at the rear of the stretched cabin, on the port side. This is of 'bubble' type for improved all-round visibility. The **Commando Mk 3** was intended to perform utility duties and also to operate in the ASV role. The aircraft appear to carry Exocet as standard, but can carry a range of other weapons. The first Commando Mk 3 flew on 14 June 1982.

Sea King HC.Mk 4

It was not until 1978 that the Royal Navy asked Westland to study a Commando variant to replace its assault-transport

Egypt's Commando Mk 2 was the first of the full-spec Commando models.

Wessex HU.Mk 5s. The RN aircraft (designated **Sea King HC.Mk 4**) were based on the Sea King HAS.Mk 2 and retain folding main rotors and tail rotor pylons. The aircraft have the same extended cabin as other Commandos and SAR Sea Kings as well as the standard Commando Mk 2 undercarriage.

The first Sea King HC.Mk 4 flew for the first time on 26 September 1979. Some 42 Sea King HC.Mk 4s were built. The first batch of 10 aircraft was available for use in the Falklands, along with some of the second-batch aircraft.

Interestingly, the Sea King HC.Mk 4 has proved to be a popular test and trials platform and two specially prepared **Sea King Mk 4X** aircraft are used for trials.

Westland Lynx Army variants

The first **WG.13 Lynx** prototype made its maiden flight on 21 March 1971. The aircraft was one of five prototypes which were utilised for development flying. The prototypes had an early-style rotor head, cabin doors with three windows, Rolls-Royce BS.360 turboshafts and the first three aircraft had a characteristic short-nose configuration. Later, it was civil registered and re-engined with a pair of Pratt & Whitney PT6B-34 turboshafts. These prototypes led to a surprisingly diverse range of army-dedicated Lynx versions.

Lynx AH.Mk 1

Planned as replacement for the Sycamore and Wessex, the Lynx entered service initially as the unarmed **Lynx AH.Mk 1** battlefield utility helicopter in 1978. Inevitably, the spectacular performance and agility of the Lynx led some to call for its adaptation for anti-tank duties. A TOW missile installation was quickly designed, with clusters of four missiles on each side of the cabin, and with an M65 gyro-stabilised sight roof-mounted above the left side of the cockpit. The Lynx also had a spacious cabin which could be used to accommodate up to eight 'reloads' or Milan missile teams, making it a much more potent anti-tank asset than the earlier Scout. Following trials, some 60 Lynx AH.Mk 1s were retrofitted with TOW from 1981; the missile has since been upgraded to Improved TOW (ITOW) standard with an enhanced warhead.

The Qatar Police became the only export customer for the Army/Battlefield Lynx when it purchased three **Lynx HC.Mk 28** helicopters. These aircraft were broadly similar to the AH.Mk 1,

albeit with sand filters over the engine intakes.

Lynx AH.Mk 5

The **Lynx AH.Mk 5** was planned as an interim helicopter, primarily to test and evaluate features planned for the definitive second-generation Army Air Corps Lynx – the **Lynx AH.Mk 7** – and was powered by the Gem 41-1 engine. In addition to the small batch of AH.Mk 5s for AAC evaluation and trials, three dedicated test/trials Mk 5s were ordered for the RAE/MoD. After trials, one of the aircraft was adopted by the Empire Test Pilots School.

Lynx AH.Mk 7

The second-generation AH.Mk 7 differs from the AH.Mk 1 in a number of ways. The larger tail rotor rotates in the opposite direction and the aircraft has provision for massive engine exhaust suppressors. The Gem 42 powerplant drives British Experimental Rotor Programme (BERP) rotor blades which are now standard on all AH.Mk 7s and the aircraft has a higher all-up weight, along with airframe strengthening and a redesigned tailcone. Improved survivability is a key part of the AH.Mk 7 and, in addition to the IR suppressors, an ALQ-144 IRCM jammer is fitted under the root of the tailboom and the crew are provided with armoured seats. The AH.Mk 7 can also be fitted with a door-mounted general-purpose machine-gun (GPMG). GPMGs were regularly used on deployment in Bosnia and Northern Ireland; it is believed that a 0.5-in (12.7-mm) gun can also be fitted. Other new equipment includes a Brightstar IR landing light, NVG-compatible external lights and a Sky Guardian 2000 RWR. A total of 107

AH.Mk 1s was converted to AH.Mk 7 standard.

AAC Lynxes deployed during Operation Granby were fitted with new sand filters on their engine intakes, IR suppressors and Sky Guardian 200-13 RWRs. The aircraft were camouflaged in two-tone sand and stone, and received white recognition stripes: three around the boom, three beneath the fuselage and one around the nose.

The Lynx's roles in Northern Ireland have long included surveillance, and the type has used Heli-Tele to record demonstrations and incidents. At least one Lynx had its capability enhanced by the fitting of new 'Chancellor' equipment. This consisted of

Above: This Lynx AH.Mk 7 was photographed during a UN mission over Bosnia. Note the IRCM 'lantern' beneath the fuselage/tail boom joint.

Top: The Lynx AH.Mk 9 has no TOW provision, but can carry IR-suppressors, as demonstrated by this aircraft. Note the wheeled undercarriage.

a digital video camera and FLIR and a downlink carried on a 'Chancellor' ball on an angled, articulated arm on the port side of the cabin.

Lynx AH.Mk 9

When a contract was placed for a batch of new utility Lynxes to support the British Army's 24 Airmobile Brigade, the decision was taken to fit these aircraft with an extremely 'crash-

worthy' wheeled undercarriage, like that developed for the **Lynx 3** demonstrator. By allowing rolling take-offs, the new undercarriage permits higher weights and an uprated gearbox allows 1373-kW (1,840-shp) of power to be delivered from the Gem 42s. The AAC ordered 16 new **Lynx AH.Mk 9** helicopters and a further eight were converted from Mk 7s.

SPECIFICATION	
Westland Lynx AH.Mk 7 **Type:** anti-tank and utility helicopter **Powerplant:** (from 1987) two Rolls-Royce Gem Gem 42-1 turboshafts each rated at 846 kW (1,135 shp) **Performance:** maximum continuous cruising speed 259 km/h (161 mph); standard range 630 km (392 miles) **Weights:** empty 2578 kg (5,683 lb); maximum take-off 4876 kg (10,750 lb)	**Dimensions:** main rotor diameter 12.8 m (40 ft); length overall, rotors turning 15.16 m (49 ft 9 in); height overall, rotors stationary 3.66 m (12 ft); main rotor disc area 128.71 m² (1,385.44 sq ft) **Armament:** about 549 kg (1,210 lb) of ordnance, including one or two 20-mm cannon, 0.3-in (7.62-mm) Miniguns or rocket projectile pods; six AS11s, two Stinger or eight HOT, Hellfire, TOW or ITOW air-to-surface missiles

Above: The 'Chancellor' aircraft also featured a fairing or strengthening strap, running along the bottom of its cabin door, and non-standard blade antennas below the nose and under the tailboom.

Right: This Lynx AH.Mk 1 was engaged in trials with the TOW missile. TOW later entered service on the Lynx in four-round launchers.

Bell Model 212/Model 412/UH-1N Iroquois Later Hueys

As the realisation grew in the US that the Huey needed more power, a separate initiative was being forged between Bell Helicopter, the Canadian government and Pratt & Whitney Canada. Their plan was to fit the single-engined UH-1H with two PT6T-3 Turbo Twin-Pac engines. This would increase all-round performance and give the aircraft twin-engined safety and reliability. On 1 May 1968, Bell announced that a CAF order for 50 aircraft had launched the new project, which became the **Model 212**.

'Twin Huey'

Once the **'Twin Huey'** had received its go-ahead, the US began to take a closer interest in the aircraft. The US Navy, US Marines and USAF quickly became customers. The Model 212 was allocated the new designation **UH-1N**. Canadian deliveries began in May 1971, as the **CUH-1N**, though these helicopters were later redesignated **CH-135 Twin Huey**. In Vietnam the US aircraft were used for special missions tasks, and the Marines and Navy were particularly appreciative of the UH-1N's much-improved over-water safety characteristics. The Marines and the Navy used their UH-1Ns intensively as assault transports – a role which is still paramount for the UH-1N in service with the Corps in 2003. These veteran UH-1Ns are being modernised and upgraded to **UH-1Y** standard.

The Model 212 was sold widely to forces which needed its heavier-lift capabilities, most of which were already UH-1 operators.

Italy's Hueys

Agusta-built Model 212s are known as **AB 212** machines. Agusta also developed a

Some USMC UH-1Ns have a Navigational Thermal Imaging System (NTIS) mounted under the cockpit, as on this aircraft. NTIS greatly enhances the helicopter's ability to operate at night.

range of special missions versions of the AB 212. The most widely-sold version was the shore-/ship-based anti-submarine variant, the **AB 212ASW**. For its primary ASW role, the aircraft is fitted with a dipping sonar and an operator's station in the main cabin. A pair of lightweight torpedoes can be carried, and the same basic aircraft can also be equipped for anti-surface warfare missions. For this role a search radar is mounted above the forward cabin. Typical armament is a pair of OTO-Melara Sea Killer AShMs, although a version delivered to Turkey can be armed with the BAe Sea Skua. Agusta has also developed Elint and Comint versions of the AB 212, chiefly for the Italian army.

Four-bladed successor

By the late 1970s, Bell was looking to squeeze yet more performance out of the Model 212/UH-1N design, with customers increasingly looking for more speed and better range. To offer these improvements, while making minimum changes to the basic airframe, Bell introduced the **Model 412**. The standard Pratt & Whitney Canada PT6T-3B engines gave way to a pair of uprated PT6T-3B-1s and onboard fuel capacity was increased. The major change came through the addition of an entirely new four-bladed main rotor system which uses Bell's elastometric bearings/hub technology, with all-composite blades.

The first Model 412, actually a modified Model 212,

made its maiden flight in August 1979. Agusta also undertook licence production of the Model 412, as the **AB 412**, often competing with and beating Bell in winning European orders. In Indonesia, IPTN built 100 **NBell 412** helicopters, most of them for the military.

Major orders for the Model 412 have come from Canada, for the **CH-148 Griffon**, Norway for **Model**

Among the features suiting the Bell 412 to an assault role are its self-sealing fuel tanks and high-impact skids. These Zimbabwean machines are two of the seven operated by the air force. The total includes two machines configured for VIP transport.

412SP helicopters, which are named **Arapaho** locally and the UK. The British aircraft are designated **Griffin HT.Mk 1** in service and are leased from civil operators

for combined helicopter training. Italy has the AB 412 in military service as the **Grifone**. Its roles include transport and SAR.

SPECIFICATION

Bell UH-1N Iroquois
Type: medium-lift and utility helicopter
Powerplant: one 1342-kW (1,800-shp) Pratt & Whitney Canada T400-CP-400 turboshaft flat rated to 842 kW (1,130 shp) for continuous running
Performance: maximum cruising speed at sea level 230 km/h (142 mph); range 420 km (261 miles)

Weights: empty 2787 kg (6,143 lb); maximum take-off 5080 kg (11,200 lb)
Dimensions: main rotor diameter 14.69 m (48 ft 2¼ in); length overall, rotors turning 17.46 m (57 ft 3¼ in); height to top of rotor head 3.91 m (12 ft 10 in); main rotor disc area 173.9 m² (1,871.91 sq ft)
Payload: maximum external load 2268 kg (5,000 lb); maximum internal load 1814 kg (4,000 lb)

Left: Designated HKP 11 locally, the Swedish army's AB 412s fly transport and casevac missions, the latter in remote areas of northern Sweden.

Right: British use of the Huey includes three Bell 212s flown in the utility and communications roles with the Army, and the Bell 412 Griffin HT.Mk 1s at RAF Shawbury. The HT.Mk 1s of No. 66(R) Sqn/Defence Helicopter Flying School are used for the training of RAF personnel for multi-engined operations. Two Griffins are usually detached to the Search and Rescue Training Unit (illustrated) at Valley, and are equipped with a winch installation and flotation bags.

Bell Boeing V-22 Osprey Multi-role tiltrotor aircraft

The Osprey programme has not been a happy one. The aircraft's pioneering configuration and advanced technologies might be expected to produce problems, but accidents, not all of them directly related to problems with the aircraft, as well as political wrangling and irregularities in the running of the programme have all conspired to cause delay after delay. Nevertheless, it seems certain that Osprey will mature into a capable machine. The second aircraft is shown here.

Bell and Boeing Vertol joined forces in the early 1980s to use the XV-15 as the basis of a machine to satisfy the Joint Services Advanced Vertical Lift Aircraft (formerly JVX) programme. Combining the vertical lift capabilities of a helicopter with the fast-cruise efficiencies of a fixed-wing turboprop aircraft, the resulting machine was given the military designation **Bell Boeing V-22 Osprey**. It was designed around two Allison turboshafts in nacelles at the tips of the slightly forward-swept wing, and driving three-bladed proprotors which could be swivelled through a total of 97.5°.

A 1985 US Navy contract specified the manufacture of six prototypes as well as several static test airframes, composite materials accounting for some 59 per cent of the Osprey's airframe weight.

Initial joint service requirements were for 913 V-22s, comprising 552 **MV-22A** assault machines as CH-46 replacements for the USMC; 231 similar machines for the

US Army; 80 **CV-22A** machines for the USAF in the role of long-range transport of special forces personnel; and 50 **HV-22A** machines for the USN's combat SAR, special warfare and fleet logistic support roles, with a 20,000-lb (9072-kg) payload. The USN also foresaw an additional need for up to 300 more V-22 aircraft optimised for the ASW role.

Osprey in trouble?

Bell flew the first machine on 19 March 1989 and on 14 September 1989 this V-22 achieved the first transition from helicopter to wing-borne flight. The remaining prototypes had all flown by mid-1991, except for the sixth, which was not completed. The fifth machine was badly damaged in a non-fatal incident on its first flight, but the programme suffered a more serious setback on 21 July 1992 when the fourth machine crashed, killing all seven persons on board.

Flight-testing resumed in June 1993. In mid-1992 the

For shipboard stowage the wing of the V-22 was designed with a central pivot so that it could be turned through 90° into alignment with the top of the fuselage, the blades of the proprotors also folding in parallel.

USMC Osprey requirement was finally settled at 425 as replacements for the CH-53 as well as the CH-46. The requirement was also thrown open to several competing helicopters through the USMC's Medium-Lift Replacement (MLR) helicop-

ter programme, but the overall superiority of the V-22 was recognised in August 1993. The USAF has also confirmed its committment to the CV-22A.

However, following further crashes, the last of which occurred in December 2000, and allegations of irregularities in the running

Osprey Number 3 hints at the underslung load-carrying capabilities of the type. The ability to move heavy underslung loads in helicopter mode adds considerably to the versatility of the aircraft, further emphasising its unique nature.

of the programme, the Osprey was grounded for almost 18 months. Critical ship compatibility trials, aimed for May 2003, seem likely to decide the project's future. Should production go ahead, the first USMC operator – VMM-264 – should receive its first MV-22A around 2005.

SPECIFICATION

Bell Boeing MV-22A Osprey
Type: three-/four-crew land-based and shipborne multi-mission tilt-rotor transport
Powerplant: two Allison T406-AD-400 turboshaft engines each rated at 4586 kW (6,150 shp)
Performance: (estimated) maximum cruising speed 185 km/h (115 mph) at sea level in helicopter mode and 582 km/h (361 mph) at optimum altitude in aircraft mode; initial climb rate 707 m (2,320 ft) per minute; service ceiling 7925 m (26,000 ft); hovering ceiling 4330 m (14,200 ft) out-of-ground effect; range 935 km (592 miles) in amphibious assault role and 3892 km (2,418 miles) in ferry mode after STO
Weights: (estimated) empty 15032 kg (33,140 lb); maximum

take-off 21546 kg (47,500 lb) for VTO and 27443 kg (60,500 lb) for STO
Dimensions: width overall 25.55 m (83 ft 10 in); wing span 14.02 m (46 ft) excluding nacelles; proprotor diameter, each 11.58 m (38 ft); length 17.47 m (57 ft 4 in) excluding probe; height 6.63 m (21 ft 9 in) with nacelles vertical; wing area 35.49 m² (382 sq ft); proprotor disc area, total 210.72 m² (2,268.23 sq ft)
Armament: probably one or two 0.5-in (12.7-mm) trainable multi-barrel rotary machine-guns
Payload: up to 24 troops, or 12 litters plus medical attendants or 9072 kg (20,000 lb) of freight carried internally, or 6804 kg (15,000 lb) of freight carried externally

Boeing Helicopters H-47 Chinook
Medium-lift and assault helicopter

CH-47C Chinooks in service with the Italian army were licence-built in Italy by Elicotteri Meridionali. Surviving aircraft are used as heavy transports and in operations with Italian paratroops.

Following the evaluation of submissions by five US manufacturers, in March 1959 the US Army selected the **Boeing Vertol Model 114** to settle its requirements for a battlefield mobility helicopter. The aircraft was expected to be equipped for all-weather operations, lift a load of 4,000 lb (1814 kg) internally or 16,000 lb (7258 kg) externally, carry a maximum of 40 fully-equipped troops, have straight-in rear loading, be suitable for the casualty evacuation role, and be able to airlift any component of the Martin Marietta Pershing SSM system. A contract for five **YHC-1B** pre-production examples was placed in June 1959, these soon being redesigned as the **YCH-47A Chinook**.

A bigger CH-46

The Model 114 was, in effect, a larger and more powerful version of the same company's CH-46, with fixed quadricycle landing gear, and a fuselage fitted with pods on each lower side to supplement the buoyancy of the sealed lower fuselage for water operations. The first YHC-1B made its initial flight on 21 September 1961, with deliveries of the 354 production **CH-47A** helicopters beginning in August 1962.

A number of versions has

followed, the first of these being the **CH-47B**, of which 108 were delivered with 2125-kW (2,850-shp) T55-L-7C engines, redesigned rotor blades and other refinements. The second improved model was the **CH-47C (Model 234)**, of which 270 were delivered with more power, a strengthened transmission system, and increased fuel capacity. Nine aircraft similar to the CH-47C were built for the Canadian Armed Forces under the designation **CH-147**, for delivery from September 1974.

Southeast Asia

During the Vietnam War, four **ACH-47A** aircraft were built, similar to the CH-47A but equipped with armour and heavily armed. Three of these were evaluated in Vietnam, but no further examples were built.

Chinooks operating in Southeast Asia proved themselves invaluable, not only for the transport of troops and supplies as well as for casualty evacuation, but also for the recovery of disabled aircraft and the airlift of refugees. Chinooks are still considered a vital component of the US Army, and 472 surviving CH-47A, B and C helicopters were later modernised. The first of the modernised **CH-47D** prototypes first flew on

26 February 1982 with more powerful 3356-kW (4,500-shp) T55-L-712 turboshafts driving a higher-rated transmission and many other changes.

RAF Chinooks

Under the designation **Chinook HC.Mk 1**, the RAF ordered 33 helicopters based on the export CH-47C. These have British avionics and equipment, as well as a number of special provisions. The first was handed over in August 1980, and the number for British service was later increased to 41, of which the survivors were subsequently upgraded to **Chinook HC.Mk 1A** standard. Some 32 of the helicopters were later modernised to **Chinook HC.Mk 2** (basically CH-47D) standard, with T55-L-712F engines. Another 17 were later ordered, eight to HC.Mk 2 standard and

After some powerplant problems, the Chinook HC.Mk 2 is now fully committed to operations. This example was flying over Sierra Leone.

the others to **Chinook HC.Mk 3** standard similar to the **MH-47E** US special operations Chinook. The HC.Mk 3s have since been returned to the US.

Since 1970 Chinooks have been built in Italy by Elicotteri Meridionali for European and Middle East customers. However, production by Boeing Helicopters of new military Chinooks is now limited to the **Model 414**, which is the **CH-47SD International**

Chinook export version. Among Chinook export customers, Japan has received Kawasaki-built **CH-47J Chinook** helicopters.

In 2004, Boeing is scheduled to deliver the first of at least 300 CH-47Ds upgraded to a new **CH-47F** standard for service into 2030. In addition, further MH-47Es are to be built, and these and surviving **MH-47D** helicopters are likely to be brought up to a common standard.

Still the mainstay of US Army medium-lift helicopter operations, the CH-47D Chinook will be upgraded to improved CH-47F configuration.

SPECIFICATION	
Boeing Vertol CH-47C Chinook **Type:** two/three-crew twin-rotor medium transport helicopter **Powerplant:** two Avco Lycoming T55-L-11A turboshaft engines each rated at 2796 kW (3,750 shp) **Performance:** maximum speed 286 km/h (178 mph) at sea level; cruising speed 257 km/h (160 mph) at optimum altitude; service ceiling 3290 m (10,800 ft); radius 185 km (115 miles) with maximum internal payload	**Weights:** empty 9736 kg (21,464 lb); maximum take-off 17463 kg (38,500 lb) **Dimensions:** rotor diameter, each 18.29 m (60 ft); length overall, rotors turning 30.18 m (99 ft); height 5.68 m (18 ft 11 in); rotor disc area, total 523.34 m² (5,654.86 sq ft) **Payload:** up to 55 troops, or 24 litters or freight carried internally or externally

H-47 Chinook

Boeing Helicopters' workhorse

Having entered service as early as 1962, the Chinook represents a design that is over 40 years old. However, in its latest versions – with upgraded powerplants and avionics – it remains the world's premier medium- and heavy-lift military helicopter.

CH-47D Chinook

Cutaway key
1 Pitot tubes
2 Forward lighting
3 Nose compartment access hatch
4 Vibration absorber
5 IFF aerial
6 Windscreen panels
7 Windscreen wipers
8 Instrument panel shroud
9 Rudder pedals
10 Yaw sensing ports
11 Downward vision window
12 Pilot's footboards
13 Collective pitch control
14 Cyclic pitch control column
15 Co-pilot's seat
16 Centre instrument console
17 Pilot's seat
18 Glideslope indicator
19 Forward transmission housing fairing
20 Cockpit overhead window
21 Doorway from main cabin
22 Cockpit emergency exit doors
23 Sliding side window panel
24 Cockpit bulkhead
25 Vibration absorber
26 Cockpit door release handle
27 Radio and electronics racks
28 Sloping bulkhead
29 Stick boost actuators

30 Stability augmentation system actuators
31 Forward transmission mounting structure
32 Windscreen washer

The CH-47JA has radar, AAQ-16 FLIR and long-range tanks to increase greatly the operational capability of the type in JGSDF service. The Japanese aircraft are licence built by Kawasaki.

33 Rotor control hydraulic jack
34 Forward transmission gearbox
35 Rotor head fairing
36 Forward rotor head mechanism
37 Pitch change control levers

38 Blade drag dampers
39 Glassfibre rotor blades
40 Titanium leading-edge capping with de-icers
41 Rescue hoist/winch

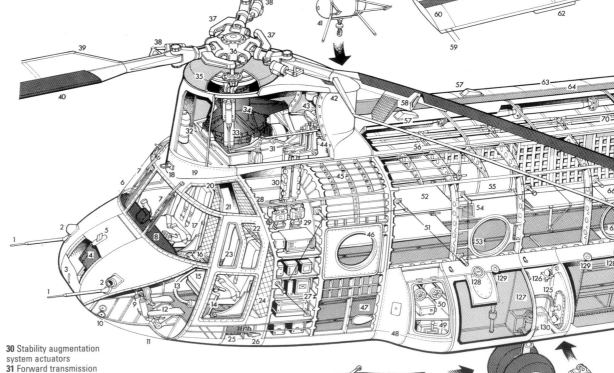

SPECIFICATION

CH-47D Chinook

Dimensions

Length overall, rotors turning: 30.14 m (98 ft 10¾ in)
Fuselage: 15.54 m (51 ft)
Height to top of rear rotor head: 5.77 m (18 ft 11 in)
Wheel track: 3.2 m (10 ft 6 in)
Wheel base: 6.86 m (22 ft 6 in)
Rotor diameter: 18.29 m (60 ft)
Rotor disc area: 525.34 m² (5,654.86 sq ft)

Powerplant

Two Textron Lycoming T55-L-712 turboshafts each rated at 2796 kW (3,750 shp) for take-off and 2237 kW (3,000 shp) for continuous running, or two Textron Lycoming T55-L-712 SSB turboshafts each rated at 3264 kW (4,378 shp) for take-off and 2339 kW (3,137 shp) for continuous running, in both cases driving a transmission rated at 5593 kW (7,500 shp) on two engines and 3430 kW (4,600 shp) on one engine

Weights

Empty: 10151 kg (22,379 lb)
Normal take-off: 20866 kg (46,000 lb)
Maximum take-off: 22679 kg (50,000 lb)

Fuel and load

Internal fuel: 3899 litres (1,030 US gal)
Maximum payload: 10341 kg (22,798 lb)
Ferry range: 2026 km (1,259 miles)
Operational radius with maximum internal and maximum external payloads respectively: Between 185 and 56 km (115 and 35 miles)

Performance

Maximum level speed at sea level: 298 km/h (185 mph)
Maximum cruising speed at optimum altitude: 256 km/h (159 mph)
Maximum rate of climb at sea level: 669 m (2,195 ft) per minute
Service ceiling: 6735 m (22,100 ft)
Hovering ceiling: 3215 m (10,550 ft)

A Dutch CH-47D repositions a tactical vehicle during manoeuvres. Equipped with an EFIS cockpit, nose radar and T55-L-714 engines, the Dutch Chinooks are among the most advanced in service. The first seven were converted from ex-Canadian CH-147s.

42 Forward transmission aft fairing
43 Hydraulic system modules
44 Control levers
45 Front fuselage frame and stringer construction
46 Emergency exit window, main entry door on starboard side
47 Forward end of cargo floor
48 Fuel tank fuselage side fairing
49 Battery
50 Electrical system equipment bay
51 Aerial cable
52 Stretcher rack (up to 24 stretchers)
53 Cabin window panel
54 Cabin heater duct outlet
55 Troop seats stowed against cabin wall
56 Cabin roof transmission and control run tunnel
57 Formation-keeping lights
58 Rotor blade cross section
59 Static dischargers
60 Blade balance and tracking weights pocket
61 Leading-edge anti-erosion strip
62 Fixed tab
63 Fuselage skin plating
64 Maintenance walkway
65 Transmission tunnel access doors
66 Troop seating (up to 44 troops)
67 Cargo hook access hatch
68 VOR aerial
69 Cabin lining panels
70 Control runs
71 Main transmission shaft
72 Shaft couplings
73 Centre fuselage construction
74 Centre aisle seating (optional)
75 Main cargo floor, 40.78-m³ (1,440-cu ft) cargo volume
76 Ramp-down 'dam' for waterborne operations
77 Ramp hydraulic jack
78 Engine bevel drive gearbox
79 Transmission combining gearbox
80 Rotor brake
81 Transmission oil tank
82 Oil cooler
83 Engine drive shaft fairing
84 Engine screen
85 Starboard engine nacelle
86 Cooling air grilles
87 Tail rotor pylon construction
88 Hydraulic equipment
89 Access door
90 Maintenance step
91 Tail rotor drive shaft
92 Tail rotor bearing mounting
93 Rotor head fairing
94 Tail rotor head mechanism
95 Main rotor blades, glass-fibre construction
96 Rotor control hydraulic jack
97 Vibration absorber
98 Pylon aft fairing construction
99 Rear lighting
100 Solar T62T-2B auxiliary power unit
101 APU-driven generators
102 Maintenance walkways
103 Engine exhaust duct
104 Textron Lycoming T55-L-712 turboshaft engine
105 Detachable engine cowlings
106 Aft fuselage frame and stringer construction
107 Rear cargo doorway
108 Ramp extensions
109 Cargo ramp, lowered
110 Ramp ventral strake
111 Fuselage side fairing aft extension
112 Ramp control lever
113 Ramp hydraulic jack
114 Rear landing gear shock absorber
115 Landing gear leg strut
116 Single rear wheels
117 Rear wheel optional ski fitting
118 Maintenance steps
119 Rear fuel tank
120 Fuel tank interconnections
121 Ventral strake
122 Main fuel tank; total system capacity 3899 litres (1,030 US gal)
123 Floor beam construction
124 Fuel tank attachment joint
125 Fuel system piping
126 Fire extinguishers
127 Forward fuel tank
128 Fuel filler caps
129 Fuel capacity transmitters
130 Front landing-gear mounting
131 Twin forward wheels
132 Forward wheels optional ski-fitting
133 Triple cargo hook system; forward and rear hooks 9072-kg (20,000-lb) capacity
134 Main cargo hook, 12701-kg (28,000-lb) capacity

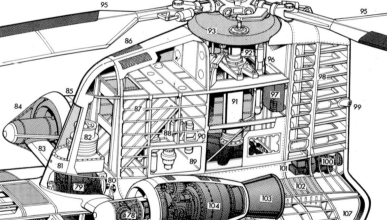

Chinook HC.Mk 1

The Royal Air Force has been operating the Boeing Helicopters Chinook for over 25 years, during which time the helicopter has become the premier workhorse of the Support Helicopter Force. The Chinook's serviceability, lift and multi-mission capabilities continue to match or exceed planned requirements. As new global strategic and tactical missions and operational priorities change, with the emphasis turning to more mobile and flexible force structures, the RAF Chinook's versatility and mission flexibility continue to expand. This HC.Mk 1 wears the colours of No. 7 Sqn, based at RAF Odiham, Hants – like all RAF HC.Mk 1s, it has since been upgraded to HC.Mk 2 standard.

Cockpit

The Chinook's cockpit is spacious and modern, with side-by-side seating for the captain (to starboard) and co-pilot (to port) and with a folding jump seat in the cockpit entrance. Like all RAF and Army Air Corps tactical helicopters, the Chinook HC.Mk 1 was fitted with Decca TANS, a useful precision navigation computer. Only a handful of RAF Chinook HC.Mk 1s had NVG-compatible cockpits. One of these was 'Bravo November' which, in the Falklands War, escaped the destruction of the *Atlantic Conveyor* and performed invaluable heavy-lift duties across the war zone.

Italy's Elicotteri Meridionali, part of the Agusta group, acquired rights to manufacture the CH-47C Chinook in 1968 in collaboration with SIAI-Marchetti. The biggest customers for the Agusta CH-47C were the Italian army (as illustrated) which took 35 (plus two Boeing-built aircraft) and Iran, which acquired 38 assembled from Boeing kits, and 30 wholly-built by Agusta.

Main landing gear

The Chinook is fitted with non-retractable quadricycle-type landing gear with twin-wheel forward units. All the undercarriage units have oleo-pneumatic shock absorbers, and the forward units are fitted with single-disc hydraulic brakes. There is provision for detachable wheel skis. The mainwheel tyres are inflated to 6.07 bar (88 lb/sq in).

With its huge lifting power (far greater than that of any other US Army helicopter) and two extra hooks, the CH-47D has vastly increased the mobility of the US Army. Here, aircraft are seen carrying the army's standard 2½-ton truck. The Chinook played a major part in the Gulf War, US Army CH-47Ds being heavily involved in General Schwarzkopf's famous 'left hook' encircling manoeuvre around Kuwait. The aircraft stood up well to the rigours of operations in extremely dusty conditions, as they did during Operations Enduring Freedom and Iraqi Freedom.

RAF Chinooks at war

Since the Chinook entered service with the RAF, it has been involved in a number of conflicts. In 1982 four Chinooks were shipped to the Falklands during the war with Argentina to provide heavy-lift support. However, three were destroyed when the *Atlantic Conveyor*, the ship on which they were travelling, was hit by an Exocet missile. Meanwhile, Chinooks were heavily engaged in supporting British troops in West Germany, ready to block a potential Soviet advance. RAF Chinooks operated in two roles during Desert Storm: regular army support and Special Forces duties. For the latter, several aircraft received hastily applied 'experimental night camouflage', SATCOMs (satellite communications) and door guns. Chinooks were then used in the Kurdish humanitarian effort, distributing food and supplies. Over Bosnia, six RAF HC.Mk 2s supported the UK's 24 Airmobile Brigade and were given a series of upgrades including armour-plating and defensive avionics. Two Chinooks of No. 7 Sqn were painted white and undertook UN humanitarian missions in the Krajina region. In June 1999, eight Chinooks formed the main transport element of NATO's opening insertion into Kosovo. The aircraft airlifted elements of the UK's 5 Airborne Division into key positions, including the vital Kacanik gorge, which secured the main route from Macedonia to the capital, Pristina. Most recently, the Chinook HC.Mk 2 has been active over Afghanistan and during Operation Iraqi Freedom.

AIR FORCE

EQ

ZA 718

Chris Davey

Sikorsky UH-60 Black Hawk Modern helicopter family

Australia's S-70A-9 Black Hawks originally served with the RAAF, but in 1990, all were transferred to the army.

A medevac interior kit is available as standard for the UH-60L and the winch-equipped UH-60Q (as here). Note that this aircraft also has auxiliary tanks on its ESSS wings.

As early as 1965, the US Army began considering a helicopter to replace its Bell UH-1 fleet. Commitments to the war in Vietnam delayed the issuing of the subsequent UTTAS (utility tactical transport aircraft system) requirement until 1972. Sikorsky responded with the YUH-60A version of its S-70 design, the aircraft first flying on 17 October 1974.

Beating Boeing

In December 1976, it was announced that Sikorsky had won a production order for its new helicopter, beating the rival Boeing Vertol YUH-61. The first production UH-60A Black Hawk flew for the first time on 17 October 1978, with service entry in June 1979.

Compared to the UH-1H, the UH-60A offered similar troop capacity, but with greater performance and much improved crashworthiness. The Black Hawk was made even more versatile with the addition of optional External Stores Support System (ESSS) wings and pylons, which enabled the carriage of drop tanks, external weapons and even additional loads, including motorcycles. Its impressive survivability was improved with the Hover Infra-Red Suppressor Subsystem (HIRSS), wire-strike protection equipment and comprehensive defensive avionics. However, the addition of extra equipment increased empty weight, decreasing payload and performance, especially under hot-and-high conditions.

More power

Accordingly, the UH-60L was developed with 1447-kW (1,940-shp) T700-GE-701C turboshafts. This became the standard production model in 1989 and is likely to remain in production until 2007. At this point, it is planned to intro-duce the UH-60M, a machine which rectifies all the shortcomings of the earlier models, to produce a true 21st century assault helicopter. Late in 2002, more than 1,550 UH-60s were in US Army service, around one third of them being UH-60Ls and the remainder various standards of UH-60A. Many of these aircraft are now to be upgraded to UH-60M standard, with the first due for completion in 2003.

Variants and exports

Such is the versatility of the basic UH-60 airframe that a plethora of variants for both US service and export have been produced. Perhaps the most important of these are the various HH-60 and MH-60 rescue and special forces helicopters. The complex development of these advanced machines has resulted in MH-60K special forces infil/exfil helicopters being in Army service and HH-60G/MH-60G aircraft flying with the USAF. Other variants include the EH-60 communications/jamming helicopter, the UH-60Q medevac machine and the VH-60 VIP transports.

The Black Hawk has been widely exported, usually under the S-70 company designation and to a standard similar to UH-60L.

SPECIFICATION

Sikorsky MH-60G Pave Hawk
Type: all-weather special forces and CSAR helicopter
Powerplant: two General Electric T700-GE-700 turboshafts each rated at 1210 kW (1,622 shp)
Performance: maximum level speed 296 km/h (184 mph) 'clean' at sea level; maximum vertical rate of climb at sea level more than 137 m (450 ft) per minute; service ceiling 5790 m (19,000 ft);

operational radius about 964 km (599 miles) with two 450-US gal (1703-litre) drop tanks
Weights: maximum take-off 9979 kg (22,000 lb); maximum payload 3629 kg (8,000 lb)
Dimensions: main rotor diameter 16.36 m (53 ft 8 in); length overall, rotors turning 19.76 m (64 ft 10 in); height overall, rotors turning 5.13 m (16 ft 10 in); main rotor disc area 210.05 m² (2,262.03 sq ft)

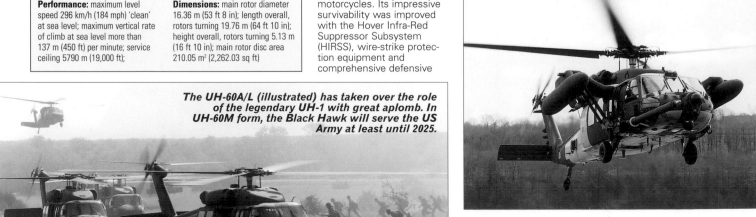

The UH-60A/L (illustrated) has taken over the role of the legendary UH-1 with great aplomb. In UH-60M form, the Black Hawk will serve the US Army at least until 2025.

Above: Basically similar to the USAF's HH-60G/MH-60G aircraft, the first production example of the US Army's MH-60K is seen here.

Sikorsky CH/MH-53 Heavylift and special forces helicopters

These images illustrate well some of the differences between the CH-53E and original H-53 airframes. Note the upper fuselage exhaust nozzle on the CH-53E above, and the vertical tail fin of the CH-53G at right.

Answering a US Marine Corps requirement to replace its Sikorsky CH-37 heavylift helicopters, the prototype **S-65** was first flown on 14 October 1964, entering service in September 1965. The initial **CH-53A** version has passed out of US service, the last being retired in July 1993.

Powered by two T64 engines mounted either side of the upper fuselage, driving the transmission proven by the CH-54 Tarhe, the CH-53 has a large box-like cabin with a rear loading ramp and forward side doors. The main undercarriage retracts into sponsons on the fuselage sides. Known as the **Sea Stallion**, the CH-53A became the USMC's principal heavylift helicopter, a position the CH-53 has held ever since.

The second major variant of the first-generation Stallions was the **CH-53D**, of which 124 were built with

uprated engines and other improvements. The type remains in USMC service, as do two **VH-53D** VIP-configured helicopters.

Other operators

A small number of ex-USMC CH-53As was transferred to the USAF as **TH-53A** trainers for the **MH-53** fleet. The USAF also purchased **HH-53B** and **HH-53C** rescue platforms, which introduced a refuelling probe and external fuel tanks. The similar **CH-53C** lacked the probe, and was used for training and support duties. Survivors of the CH/HH fleet were upgraded to **MH-53J Pave Low III** standard in the 1980s, progressing through a number of variants to the ultimate **MH-53M Pave Low IV**, which will remain in service with AFSOC until at least 2012.

Exports of the early H-53 models were made to Austria (**S-65Ö**), Israel

(**S-65C-3**; the majority of which have been upgraded to **Yas'ur 2000** (Albatros 2000) standard) and West Germany (**CH-53G**).

Requiring a helicopter with even greater lifting

capabilities that the CH-53D, the USMC also purchased the **CH-53E Super Stallion**. This impressive machine adds a third T-64 engine to the basic H-53 airframe, along with a seven-bladed

main rotor, canted tail fin and strut-braced, gull tailplane.

Like the first-generation Stallion, the CH-53E has spawned naval minesweeper variants which have won export orders, but the basic CH-53E was not exported. Upgrading of the CH-53E is now likely, following delays in the Osprey programme and placing the type back into production has been mooted.

Left: Slated for retirement when the CV-22 Osprey enters service, the MH-53 remains a potent and capable special forces and CSAR platform. The aircraft has FLIR and terrain-following radar.

SPECIFICATION	
Sikorsky CH-53E Super Stallion **Type:** heavylift helicopter **Powerplant:** three General Electric T64-GE-416 turboshafts each rated at 2756 kW (3,696 shp) for continuous running **Performance:** maximum level speed 315 km/h (196 mph) 'clean' at sea level; maximum rate of climb at sea level 762 m (2,500 ft) per minute with an 11340-kg (25,000-lb) payload; service ceiling 5640 m (18,500 ft); hovering ceiling 3520 m (11,500 ft); radius with a	9072-kg (20,000-lb) external payload 925 km (575 miles) **Weights:** empty 15072 kg (33,228 lb); maximum take-off 33340 kg (73,500 lb) with an external load; maximum external payload over a 92.5-km (57.5-mile) radius 14515 kg (32,000 lb) **Dimensions:** main rotor diameter 24.08 m (79 ft); length overall, rotors turning 30.19 m (99 ft ½ in); height overall 8.97 m (29 ft 5 in); main rotor disc area 455.38 m² (4,901.7 sq ft)

Israel's Yas'urs were originally similar to the HH-53C. They have since been upgraded to CH-53D-2000 standard. Israel also later purchased the two S-65Os from Austria.

AIRCRAFT CARRIERS

Index